A WORLD ATLAS OF MILITARY HISTORY

Volume One - to 1500

A WORLD ATLAS

by ARTHUR BANKS

with an Introduction
by Lord Chalfont

OF MILITARY HISTORY

VOLUME ONE
TO 1500

SEELEY SERVICE & CO
London 1973

First Published in Great Britain 1973 by
SEELEY SERVICE & CO LTD
196 Shaftesbury Avenue
London WC2H 8JL

ISBN 0 85422 078 X

Printed in Great Britain by
Hollen Street Press Ltd
at Slough, Bucks.

CONTENTS

PREFACE

For twenty years I have been fighting to impress upon publishers, authors and cartographical draughtsmen the need and value of clear maps in text-books. I became an historical cartographer largely because so many of the maps I saw in books and atlases were difficult to understand. Maps are visual aids: they do not supersede text-books. What are required are simple, clear drawings that one can assimilate with ease.

The greatest drawback to historical maps is that historians are not usually good draughtsmen and cartographers are not usually well-read in history. Furthermore, there is an important difference between a *cartographer* (who can devise and plan a map) and a *cartographical draughtsman* who can only draw the final result from a cartographer's draft. And whereas authors obviously want as many maps as possible in their books, publishers try to keep these to a minimum for economic reasons.

This atlas is an attempt to produce a book of clear and simple maps printed in black and grey with a 'story' line attached. One cannot satisfy everyone's requirements within 154 pages and I can only hope that it proves useful and informative to the reader. In this opening volume I have included 'general' maps in addition to 'war' maps since one cannot readily grasp military campaigns in early times unless one has a background map to assist one.

ARTHUR BANKS
Oxshott
June, 1972

ACKNOWLEDGEMENTS

During the preparation of this volume I consulted some six hundred reference works, examined innumerable maps and general atlases and had the good fortune to be advised on various items by friends, colleagues and associates.

I should like to thank Dr R. A. Banks (my brother) for his expert suggestions on the Vikings and Alfred the Great maps in particular, and for his inspection of the various story panels.

Mr I. Baxter of the India Records Office supplied details on the maps dealing with India and Asia, and Mr Lim and Mr Freeberne of the School of African and Oriental Studies meticulously checked my spellings in the Chinese, Indian and Asian maps and proffered detailed advice on Far Eastern geography and history in general.

Mr A. Henderson checked my ancient and classical sections with diligence and vigour, and suggested much information to assist my work throughout. Mr R. B. Welsh, my friend since childhood, nobly read extensive notes I supplied, and researched much material for me, notably on Egypt, India, China and Asia. General Sir James Marshall-Cornwall supplied details on guns, rocketry and gunpowder items.

I must also thank Mr I. Rudd, Miss J. Gibbs and Mr J. Watkins for their assistance with the cartographical draughtsmanship on certain maps.

The Chief Librarian and Staff of the Study and Information Department of the Surrey County Library Headquarters and the Branch Library at Leatherhead, Surrey went to great lengths to assist me in my research. To them also I proffer my thanks.

Before the maps were printed Mr Alan Palmer and his wife Veronica gave them a detailed scrutiny for which I am indebted.

INTRODUCTION

BY LORD CHALFONT

I am particularly pleased to have been invited to write the introduction to this and to the later volumes in this series. The project is one of immense interest and value.

Arthur Banks' technique, which seems to me altogether admirable, is especially suited to the extremely challenging task of explaining in clear and easily understood terms campaigns, strategies and developments in military history which are often regarded as complicated and difficult to understand.

War is one of the most profoundly important manifestations of the human condition. From the first tentative experiments in the organisation of society disputes have been resolved, insults avenged and goods and territory seized or defended by violence, by force of arms, by war. It has been condemned as an obscenity; justified by theological scholars as the last resort against intolerable tyranny; and even, from time to time, glorified as the status symbol of the sovereign nation state. To the civilized mind it is astonishing that men are capable of inflicting upon each other the appalling cruelty and suffering of war; but so far no-one has been able to devise any other way of settling international quarrels or achieving political aims against determined opposition. There have been attempts to bring about disarmament by international agreement; to achieve peaceful settlement of disputes by arbitration; and to impose order on chaos by the establishment of such ambitious institutions as the League of Nations and its successor, the United Nations. None of them has succeeded. Organised violence remains the ultimate sanction in international affairs; it is still considered legitimate for a government in the pursuit of its foreign policy to indulge in the killing or maiming of thousands of human beings, and the destruction of their homes, their crops and their possessions. And it is arguable that the situation will remain unchanged so long as the nation state remains the basic unit of the structure of world society.

The phenomenon of war permeates every aspect of human behaviour. Its vocabulary fills our everyday language with vivid metaphors—the war on want, the battle for survival, the population explosion. It has inspired unforgettable music, immortal painting and some of our greatest literature. It has produced men of greatness and compassion; and others of indescribable evil. Napoleon called it "a simple art, consisting entirely of execution". For Erasmus it was the one human activity which "it is encumbent on every man, by every lawful means, to avoid, to deprecate, to oppose". But perhaps the most perceptive, if possibly the most cynical reflection was that of Thomas Hardy—"My argument is that War makes rattling good history; but Peace is poor reading."

The history of war, then, is at least as old as the recorded history of man. Most military historians divide it into periods roughly corresponding with the principal developments in the technology of war. The primitive, or ancient period of warfare is generally regarded as beginning in about 5,000 BC, when the Sumerians, who lived in the fertile lands between the Tigris and the Euphrates, became the targets of attack by the desert and mountain tribes. One of the earliest Sumerian sculptures shows soldiers carrying spears and shields; and on the ivory handle of a flint-bladed knife, found at Gebel el-Arak in Egypt and dated about 3,000 BC, there is a carving depicting soldiers fighting on a beach. Historic, or medieval warfare dates roughly from AD 500 to 1500, and modern warfare from then on.

Until about 3,000 BC it is probable that war was mainly a highly formalised method of avenging insults between one tribe and another—it was only rarely a matter of economic gain or political conquest. It was the transition from man's hunting and collecting period to that of primitive agriculture which almost certainly brought with it the military organisation designed to further political and economic aims. The ability of some tribes to till fertile lands and to establish reserves of food—the beginnings of organised society—aroused the envy of others, who sought by violence to acquire what they had been unable to provide for themselves. As the nomadic life gave way to the development of permanent communities and villages, the phenomenon later to be described as the "territorial imperative" began to emerge in a recognizable form, and success in war began to confer a hierarchical title to pleasant living space and productive lands. The development of primitive military technology was at first a matter almost entirely of the manufacture of new weapons—swords, shields, spears and bows and arrows. The first significant innovation was the introduction of the horse and the impact of cavalry on military tactics, a development which enabled the Hyksos, a warlike Indo-European people, probably nomads, to conquer Egypt in 1750 BC and to occupy the country for a century and a half.

Much of our knowledge of early military history is indeed identified with Ancient Egypt and its Asiatic Empire, although China and India too provide essential evidence of the various stages in the development of warfare. The Egyptians created one of the greatest and most enduring civilisations in history. It lasted 3000 years and passed through three great eras—the Old and Middle Kingdoms, from 2700 to 1500 BC, when the Egyptians consolidated and improved their occupation of the valley of the River Nile; and the New Kingdom, or Empire, when they occupied lands outside the boundaries of present day Egypt. This period, between 1560 and 1085 BC, represents the summit of Egyptian military power. It opened with the expulsion of the Hyksos ('the desert charioteers') by the Pharaoh Amosis (or Ahmose) I, who also reorganised northern Nubia (originally occupied by Sesostris II about 1850 BC). The successor of Ahmose, Thutmosis (or Thutmose) I, carried on the expansion of Egypt both to the south, beyond the fourth and fifth cataracts of the Nile, and north-eastwards through Palestine and Syria to the banks of the Euphrates. This was, in effect, the cradle of military history.

For almost five hundred years the Egyptians maintained a regular army to secure its great new Empire. Although the basic arm was infantry, much use was made now of the horse-drawn chariot, a weapon adapted from the Hyksos; and the pikes and spears of the Old and Middle Kingdoms were augmented by bows, swords, battle-axes and daggers. At this time also there began to appear the first signs of cohesive military organisation. A quartermaster corps was formed to take care of logistical supplies, and as the Empire developed the traditional skirmishing and head-on pitched battles gave way to more sophisticated tactical methods. The technique of the battle square emerged and the two-man chariots were used as a primitive cavalry, either in massed charges or individually in support of infantry operations.

After 1085 BC the Egyptian Empire began to decline as the power of the military caste grew and the generals began to set themselves up, together with the priests, as the feudal overlords of independent regions. Eventually Egypt collapsed under the invasion of the Assyrians, a cruel and warlike people under whose dominion there were further developments in organisation and tactics. Larger chariots, each drawn by two horses and driven by three men, made their appearance. The foot soldiers were organised into heavy and light infantry, and a corps of engineers was established. Some of the first signs of total war began to emerge, with the massacre of prisoners, mass deportations and the plundering and pillaging of enemy towns and villages. The Assyrians in their turn were expelled with the aid of Greek mercenaries, but in 525 BC Egypt was once again invaded and occupied, this time by the Persians under King Cambyses. The Persians made comparatively little impact on the science of war and the only interesting military innovations of this period were the introduction of the elephant and the development of flexible tactical doctrines which allowed for operations both by large massed formations and by small detachments of troops. Meanwhile the size of armies had grown substantially. Whereas in the early Sumerian period the typical city state had perhaps 1000 foot soldiers, some estimates put the strength of Darius's Persian Army at the Battle of Arbela, against Alexander the Great, in 331 BC, at a million foot soldiers and 40,000 horsemen. The most conservative estimate suggests that the strength was certainly not less than 300,000. In 332 BC the conquest of Egypt by Alexander brought to an end the long supremacy of the Egyptian Empire. The centre of power had moved decisively to Greece.

The Greek civilisation, later to become the Greco-Roman, had already, in the fifth century BC, entered a period of almost continuous warfare which was to last nearly four hundred years. Before the Greco-Persian wars, military operations in the Greek peninsula had been primitive affairs; the early Minoan civilization on the island of Crete had been conquered by the Achaeans in 1600 BC and for the next eight hundred years the Greek mainland and islands were subjected to a series of invasions from the north—the Dorians, Ionians and eventually the Aeolians. There then arose the city states of Classic Greece, dominated by Athens and Sparta. It was the liberal, civilised Athens which rose first to pre-eminance, principally through its leading part in the wars with Persia. At the beginning of the fifth century Darius sent his army to invade Greece and was defeated in 490 by the Athenians at Marathon. Ten years later the Persians returned in greater numbers under Xerxes, but were again defeated. This time the Persians came within striking distance of Athens, and attempts to halt them in a naval battle off Artemisium and a land battle at Thermopylae were unsuccessful, in spite of a heroic Greek stand at Thermopylae under a Spartan—Leonidas. The way to Athens was now open, but an Athenian-Spartan coalition inflicted a heavy defeat on the Persians at Plataea in 479 BC. Thirty years later, in 449 BC, the Persians finally admitted defeat and abandoned the Aegean to the Greeks.

As has so often been the case throughout history, the disappearance of the external threat meant the beginning of internal struggles in Greece. The Peloponnesian War of 431-404 BC led to the defeat of Athens by Sparta and the establishment of over half a century of Spartan hegemony. This was followed by a brief period of Theban predominance, during which there emerged a tactical development of some significance—the device employed by Epaminondas of Thebes in his battle with the Spartans at Leuctra in 371 BC. The Spartan commander, King Cleumbrotus, formed his Army of 1,000 cavalrymen and 10,000 *hoplites* in traditional phalanx formation, with his élite troops, as usual, on the right flank. Instead of doing the same, Epaminondas concentrated his numerically inferior force in great strength on his *left* flank, in a striking phalanx, four times as deep as the enemy immediately to their front. They smashed into the Spartan ranks like a battering ram—the first recorded example of a commander exerting irresistible force at a chosen point of attack.

A little later in the fourth century BC Macedonia began to emerge as a significant military power, and in 338 BC Philip II of Macedonia defeated the Greeks, who had succeeded in forming a coalition of their warring city states in an attempt to meet this new threat at Chaeronea. It was a battle in which his son, Alexander, played a decisive part when he massacred the 'Sacred Band' (a battalion of élite Theban troops) on the right flank of the Greek United Armies, and then wheeled behind the Greek lines in a classic cavalry manoeuvre.

With the makeshift coalition of Greek city states crushed, Alexander, who had succeeded Philip in 336 BC, proclaimed Greek unity and required each of the City States to provide troops for his Asian campaigns. There followed, over a period of twelve years, one of the greatest military campaigns in history, as Alexander the Great set out to punish the Persians for their earlier invasions of Greece and to create an Empire extending over most of the known world. He defeated the Persians in three great battles at Granicus (334 BC), Issus (333 BC) and Arbela (331 BC), and swept on to the frontiers of India where, on the River Hydaspes (now the Jhelum River) a tributary of the Indus, he fought one of his most brilliant battles against the Indians in 326 BC. This was, however, the last of his great victories. Three years later he died, at the age of 32, in Babylon, and his Empire gradually disintegrated.

Technically the art and science of war had advanced considerably during this period. The main weapon of the Greek city states was the thrusting spear carried by the *hoplites* or heavy infantrymen, who were formed in compact masses of up to 5,000—the phalanx—which formed the centre of the basic battle formation, with cavalry and light infantry on the flanks and the *psiloi*—special skirmishing forces—out in front. The Athenian armies also had well organised auxiliary services, including a medical corps of a rudimentary kind. Their tactics were fairly simple, often involving no more than a head-on confrontation between phalanxes.

When Alexander the Great succeeded his father, however, his impact on the military art was dramatic. Tactically he refined the rudimentary but original ideas of Epaminondas of Thebes, developing a system in which the individual phalanx did not advance 'in line'—that is to say in a straight battle front—but roughly in the shape of a V pointing at the enemy. This created a dent in the opposing line and enabled the *hoplites* to pin down the opposing infantry, allowing the cavalry to sweep in on the flanks. The cavalry thus became the decisive arm in battle instead of being used principally as a protection for the infantry. At the same time new engines of war began to make their appearance, the siege tower, the catapult or *ballista*, and the *testudo*, a battering ram under a protective covering of shields. The artillery began to emerge as an organised arm. But the principal factor in the military developments of the era was Alexander the Great himself—one of the greatest generals in history. He showed an extraordinary and precocious skill in combining and manoeuvring forces of all arms; his mastery of tactics was complete and he was able to adapt his method to any form of warfare with which he was confronted, from guerilla warfare to the investing of fortified villages. He was a strategist of remarkable skill and imagination; yet he did not hesitate to lead his own cavalry on the battlefield. Although his basic instincts were aggressive, he never moved on to a new phase in a campaign without first consolidating his gains. In the course of the great twelve year campaign which took him to the borders of India, he never outran his lines of communication or his administrative support. He brought a new dimension to the military art.

Alexander's vision of an Empire encompassing the known world was, however, achieved not by the Greeks, but by the Romans, who had become the masters of Italy in 275 BC after four centuries of war—principally against the Etruscans in the North and the Greek colonists in the south. There followed the period of the Punic Wars, in which Rome and Carthage fought for the control of the Mediterranean. When the First Punic War began in 264 BC, Carthage dominated the north coast of Africa, the south coast of Spain and most of the Mediterranean islands, including part of Sicily. After destroying the Carthaginian fleet at Mylae in Sicily in 260, the Romans landed in Africa but were defeated at Tunis in 255 by Xanthippus. The Second Punic War, which lasted from 218-201 BC, began when Hannibal, crossing the Pyrenees from Spain, defeated the Romans at the River Trebia, Lake Trasimene and Cannae; but after the defeat of Hannibal's brother, Hasdrubal, at the Metaurus River in 207 BC, the Romans sent Scipio to Africa. Hannibal, having returned to Carthage in 203, was defeated by Scipio at the Battle of Zama and Carthage was reduced to the status of a trading port. The defeat of Carthage was finally completed in the Third Punic War (149-146 BC) and by 100 BC the Roman Empire had been extended to cover Spain, Cisalpine Gaul, Illyria, Macedonia, Greece, Tripolitania, and Proconsular Africa.

The principal contribution of the Romans to military organisation and tactics was the legion. It consisted of 4,000 to 6,000 men in three ranks, the first of *hastati*, the second of *principes* and the third of *triarii*. Each rank was divided into 10 *maniples*, each of 120 to 160 men, organised into two *centuries* of 60-80. In the third rank of *triarii* this was varied—each maniple consisting of only one century. Each legion had horsemen in support on the flanks, and *velites* for skirmishing in front. The main advantage over the phalanx was tactical flexibility. With each maniple operating on a 20 yard front, with a similar distance between maniples, it was possible to adapt quickly to uneven terrain or to change formation and pass units rapidly through each other's positions as the tactical situation required. This flexibility was reflected in the equipment of the legion, the *hastati* in the front rank carrying shields, swords and javelins; the *principes* and *triarii* carrying pikes instead of javelins; and the *velites* carrying light javelins or *iacula*. The Romans also developed siege engines, mobile bridging equipment, catapults designed to fire huge arrows and bolts, and the technique of the fortified camp. Administrative arrangements became relatively elaborate and signalling and communications systems were comparatively highly organised.

It was upon this military basis that the great campaigns of Julius Caesar, Pompey, Augustus and Mark Antony were fought. From 61 to 51 BC Caesar's Gallic Wars extended the Roman Empire through Spain and Gaul as far as Britain. He then returned to Rome and a period of civil war followed, in which he defeated his rival Pompey. Caesar's successor Octavian (later the Emperor Augustus) defeated *his* main rival Mark Antony and then began a series of campaigns in Germany and Central Europe from 15 BC to 10 AD.

The reign of Augustus was the beginning of the end of the military power of Rome. He reduced the professional army to just over 300,000 men and disarmed the free civilians. For the next four hundred years the Roman Army underwent fundamental changes. The size of the legion was progressively reduced and large numbers of barbarians were enlisted to protect the Empire from external attack. When, in the third century, the Gothic frontier invasion began, the Army was reorganised into the Palatine Army—a campaign force of shock troops, and *limitani* or border troops. Meanwhile two factors had combined to consolidate the superior status of the cavalry; the need for a high degree of mobility in an Army used mainly for dealing with border raids, and the generally low calibre of the infantry which required them to be massed together for the purpose of improving their morale, thus allowing horsemen to predominate as the offensive arm. There were corresponding changes in arms, and by the 4th century the bow and the sling were beginning to rival the sword and the javelin. At the same time a vast complex of defensive works (the *limes*) had been built up by Rome in Europe, Africa and the Middle East.

There were persistent attacks on this, notably by the Goths and Visigoths in the 2nd, 3rd and 4th centuries; by the Vandals over the same period; and finally by the Huns under Attila, in the 5th century. At the same time the Angles, Picts and Jutes had invaded Britain and the Herulians had established a kingdom in Italy, only to be defeated by the Ostrogoths under Theodoric. Under these repeated assaults the Roman Empire, for all practical purposes, disintegrated. It was split up into barbarian kingdoms ruled by *foederati*, the leaders of Roman auxiliary troops raised from the barbarian peoples.

In 481, as the Roman Empire withered away, Europe came under the Merovingian dynasty; the Frankish King, Clovis, extended his rule through most of Gaul and he and his successors expanded their Empire gradually until in 771 Charlemagne inherited the Frankish Kingdom from his father Pepin III, and rapidly pushed south and east into Italy, Bavaria and Carinthia, south-west into Spain and north-east to the River Elbe. In 800 Charlemagne was crowned Emperor by the Pope in Rome, but in 843 the Treaty of Verdun divided the Empire into three kingdoms. The Carolingian Army was surprisingly small—6,000 to 10,000 men, of whom more than half were mounted troops. Heavy chariots carried supplies in convoys. It was a cumbersome, unimpressive Army, but Charlemagne commanded it in person and his intelligence and boundless energy enabled him to make the best of his limited resources.

When the Carolingian Empire came to its end the feudal system began its period of domination in European history and warfare moved into its historic or medieval phase of development. For more than two hundred years the Vikings from Scandinavia ranged over most of England, Ireland and Northern France. They were a fierce, well-disciplined fighting force, who landed in their shallow-draft long ships, seized horses and weapons from their enemies and used them in marauding cavalry tactics. Their most effective series of campaigns were those against Britain throughout the 9th century.

Meanwhile there began that great period of history, lasting from the end of the Carolingian Empire to the Italian Renaissance in the 15th century, which saw the birth of modern Europe. In the military sense it was not at first a period of dramatic change. The basic fighting unit was the knight, or armoured horseman. The manufacture of armour was raised almost to the level of an art; and there were impressive developments in the techniques of fortification and siege warfare; but tactics remained basically simple. A typical battle would begin with the cavalry formed up within a wall of infantry, which at a given signal would open, allowing the cavalry to charge upon the enemy. The infantry were generally either pikemen or bowmen, armed with either the crossbow or the longbow—the latter enthusiastically adopted by the English armies fighting against the Welsh and the Scots in the 13th century. It was a weapon which was later to have a decisive effect at the Battle of Crécy on August 26th, 1346, the first great English victory over the French in the Hundred Years' War.

Meanwhile William the Conqueror had invaded Britain in 1066 and transformed the structure of English society; and from 1096 to 1192 the Crusades had taken armies from Western Europe on three great expeditions to the Middle East. A number of military lessons emerged from the Crusades—including the importance of sea-power and the value of being able to manoeuvre rapidly with mixed forces of infantry and cavalry. But possibly the most important lesson affected the construction of fortifications and defence systems. The Middle Ages was the great era of fortification, although it was not until the end of the twelfth century that true castles and fortified cities began to replace the feudal residence with its rudimentary protective wall. With the development of strongly fortified areas, siege machinery began to play an increasingly important role. Explosives were still unknown, but it was possible to hurl huge projectiles, at first with giant catapults mounted on towers and later with the *trebuchet*, a counter-weighted sling. The arts of sapping and mining were refined and an early example of 'artificial moonlight' appeared when the trees surrounding medieval fortresses were soaked in oil and set alight to illuminate the surrounding countryside and so discourage night attacks.

While these developments in military science and technology were taking place in Europe, there had been a remarkable century of conquest by the Arabs from 632-732. Within this period they had conquered territory from the Syrian border in the east, across Egypt and North Africa, and north through Spain to the Pyrenees. This extraordinary interlude, however, had little impact on the development of warfare. The campaigns were fought by tribes using camel-borne cavalry and infantry armed with bows and arrows. The Bedouin techniques of surprise attack and rapid movement were fully exploited. Battles usually began with a volley from the archers followed by a cavalry charge with sabre and lance. Even against the comparatively unsophisticated feudal militia their success was predictably short-lived.

The Middle Ages, in spite of the apparent pre-occupation with invasion and counter-invasion, was in fact a period characterised by certain obvious limitations on the scope and scale of warfare. As the Roman Empire gave way to Christendom, the moral authority of the Church increased, and with it the inhibitions against organised violence. Even the great battles of medieval history were trivial affairs by modern standards (at Poitiers and Agincourt, for example, fewer than 30,000 men were engaged) and even long bitter campaigns could be conducted without great hardship to the general population or serious disruption of society. It was not until the 14th and 15th centuries that this situation began to change, leading to the vastly different all pervading experience of modern war. The crucial period of transition was the Hundred Years' War from 1337 to 1453. While it raged in France, the Anglo-Scottish conflict which had begun in 1297 ended when the Scots were defeated at Homildon Hill in 1402; and Owain Glyndwr's brief but brave attempt to achieve independence for Wales finally failed in 1412. Meanwhile, in Europe, Switzerland had emerged as a substantial military power, with a special reputation for effective infantry, highly disciplined and meticulously trained. Military organisation during this period was totally transformed and for the first time there appeared the 'regular Army'—a paid Army owing allegiance to the Crown and not to a feudal lord. Tactically the infantry became once again the Queen of Battles, ending a thousand years of cavalry predominance; gunpowder artillery appeared to change irrevocably the nature of war.

The great battles of the Hundred Years' War were at Crécy (1346), Poitiers (1356) and Agincourt (1415)—all decisive victories for the English. In 1429, however, the French resurgence began with Joan of Arc, and by 1453 the English had been driven from France, their only territorial gain after over a century of war being the port of Calais. This was the end of the Hundred Years' War and, by common consent of most historians, the end of the Middle Ages. The Wars of the Roses, between York and Lancaster, ravaged England for another thirty years, but in general Medieval Europe began to give way to the modern Europe of the nation state—a crucial development in political, economic and military history.

It is, however, not only in Europe, North Africa and the Middle East that military history has its origins—China was at one time the most militarily advanced country in the ancient world. The dates of the early Chinese dynasties and the development of their armies are the subject not of history but of legend. It is likely that in the first two dynasties, the Hsia and the Shang (or Yin), the warrior class became predominant. Certainly the third dynasty, the Chou, who defeated the Shang and moved into Anyang, the Shang capital, in about 1028 BC, were basically a military hierarchy. In about 770 BC they established their capital at Loyang, and there followed a period of internal struggle in China. The country split into a series of loose confederations and until 221 BC there was almost continuous civil war, with enormous walls being built after 450 BC to protect the border states from attacks by the Asiatic Huns. In 221 BC one of the fiercest of the warring leaders—Cheng, who at the age of 22 had come to power in the state of Ch'in—succeeded in reuniting China and, as Shih Huang Ti (First Emperor), founded the fourth (Ch'in) dynasty. Under his rule the sections of wall built under the Chou dynasty were linked together to form the Great Wall of China, and the country was divided into 36 regions. In spite of his efforts, however, China again split into kingdoms at the beginning of the third century BC and it was not until 206 BC that the country was reunited again under Wu Ti, who founded the Han Dynasty, which was to last for four centuries (Western Han 206 BC-24 AD and Eastern Han 25-221 AD). Although he was a soldier, Wu Ti established a civil administration; under his rule, however, there was almost continuous fighting against the

Huns, and the military hierarchy achieved great power and prestige. The Chinese cavalry was improved by a systematic horse-breeding policy and iron weapons were widely used. The Huns were not only driven out of the regions of northern China which they had occupied while China was still in a state of internal disorder; they were also driven west from the borders of China in a series of military campaigns between 128 and 36 BC.

In 221 AD, however, the Han dynasty fell, and yet another period of unrest followed. The period of the Three Kingdoms (San Huo) saw renewed attacks by barbarians from the north and under the Western Tsin Dynasty (265-317) the Huns invaded North China and established a Hun Dynasty. There followed a period of division and conflict, with North and South China under separate dynasties for nearly two centuries. It was not until the end of the Sixth century that the Sui dynasty was founded by Yang Chien (also called Wen Ti) who made a determined attempt to reunite China. He had the Great Wall of China extended and repaired and the country began to enjoy a period of comparative tranquility, under which Chinese civilisation began to flower. The barbarians on the frontiers, however, remained a serious threat, and under the T'ang Dynasty (618-907) the Emperor Li Yuan (also called T'ae Tsu) defeated the Turks with an Army which came to be feared and respected all over Asia. It was towards the end of the T'ang dynasty that gunpowder made its first recorded appearance.

In the tenth century there was yet another internal struggle in China, which culminated in the seizure of power in 960 by a general, Chao K'uang-yin (also called Sung T'ai Tsu) who founded the Sung Dynasty. Chao was a great military leader, but like his predecessor Wu Ti, he insisted on the army being subordinated to the civil authority. The Army, however, continued to develop and it soon reached a strength of one million men—mostly volunteers. Arms and equipment, however, were still rudimentary, the cross-bow being still the basic weapon of the Chinese soldier. Gunpowder was now being used for making bombs launched by catapult and China was centuries ahead of Europe in its siege techniques.

Chao K'uang-yin's successors in the Sung dynasty, however, lacked his military talents and in about 1260 after a period of progressive degeneration in the army, the great Mongol invasion of China began.

The Mongol Army was almost exclusively an Army of horsemen, drawn from a barbarian, patriarchal community living on the Eurasian Steppes. Their military organisation and tactics were simple and effective, and military skills were highly regarded in the Mongol tribes. The cavalrymen were mounted on small, tough horses; they wore leather breast-plates, carried leather shields and were armed with bows and arrows, javelins and lances. They were expert archers and ruthless, savage soldiers. Their tactics were based on the exploitation of surprise and mobility, using small numbers of infantry only to pin down an enemy and set the scene for their cavalry attacks. These were terrifying affairs, carried out at first in total silence, messages being sent by flags; in the final charge they terrorised the enemy with battle cries. This implacable, highly disciplined, military hierarchy produced two of the greatest but most terrifying warriors in History—Genghis Khan and Tamerlane. It was Genghis Khan who, in a sustained military campaign between 1219 and 1225 penetrated into Turkestan, Iran and Afghanistan; and reached the banks of the Indus, Azerbaijan, the Caucasus and South Russia. Under his command no method of waging war was too frightful—civilians, men, women and children, were used as a living screen for his attacks; cities were ruthlessly sacked and mutilation, rape and desecration were systematically used as instruments of terror.

When he died in 1227, Genghis Khan's successors were marginally less barbaric and notably less bellicose, and it was not until the middle of the 14th century that the Mongol military tradition was revived under Tamerlane (Timur i leng or Timur the lame), who between 1380 and 1395 overran Khurasan and Eastern Persia, Iraq, Azerbaijan, Armenia, Mesopotamia and Georgia. During his campaigns he proved to be an apt disciple of Genghis Khan, destroying cities, murdering whole populations and building towns out of the skulls of beheaded prisoners. Like Genghis Khan, he organised his soldiers meticulously; his tactics were imaginative and well-planned, and his disciple draconian and rigid.

The Mongol invasion of China reached its peak in 1279, with the establishment of the Yuan dynasty, and ended nearly a century later with the establishment of the Ming dynasty. In the East, as in the West, the scene was set for a new era in military history.

A WORLD ATLAS OF MILITARY HISTORY

Volume One - to 1485

FOUR EARLY VERSIONS OF THE WORLD

1 As visualised by Hecataeus c. 500 B.C.

Hecataeus of Miletus was a much-travelled Greek historian and geographer who thought the world was round. His works have perish

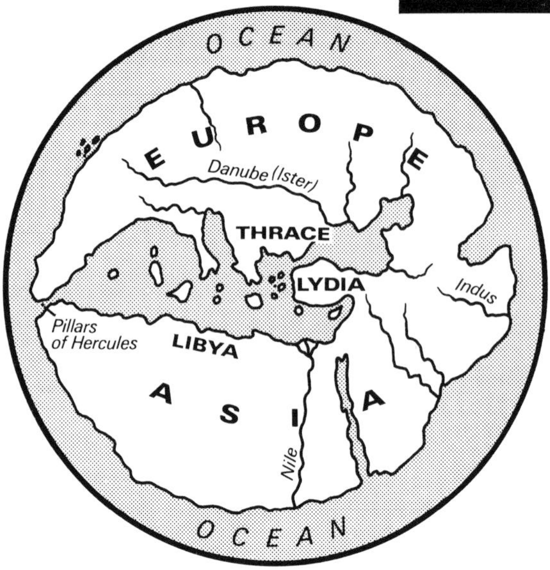

2 As visualised by Herodotus c. 450 B.C.

Herodotus, born in Halicarnassus in 484 B.C. was a much-travelled Greek historian who wrote a detailed account of the ancient world

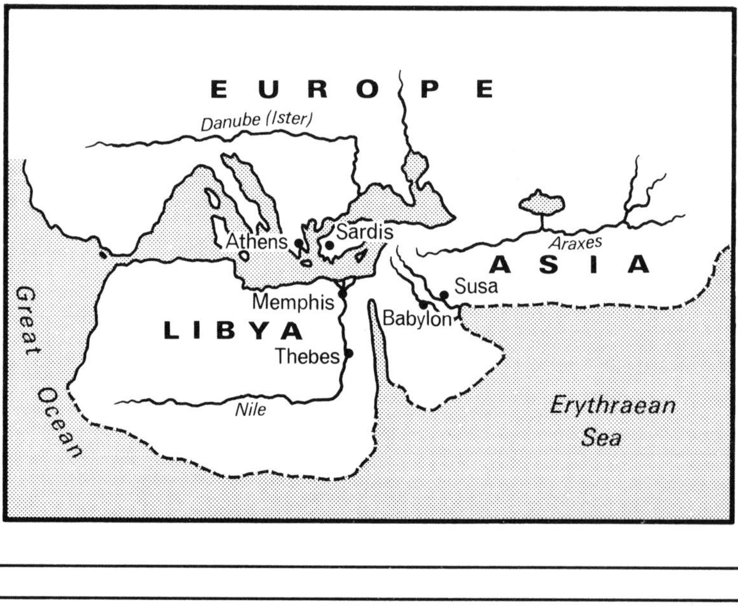

❸ As visualised by Eratosthenes c.200 B.C.

Eratosthenes, born at Cyrene in 276 B.C., was a scholar of geography, history, astronomy, philosophy, and geometry, and chief librarian at Alexandria. Most of his works have perished.

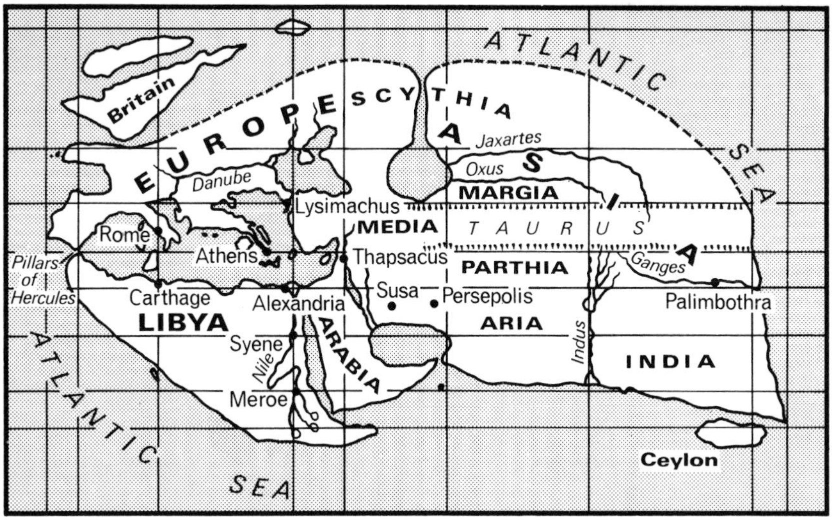

❹ As visualised by Ptolemy c. A.D. 150

Ptolemy (Ptolemaeus, Claudius) was a geographer, astronomer, and mathematician.

IDENTIFIABLE TRENDS IN EARLY MILITARY HISTORY

NOTE: 'EARLY' HISTORY IS MUCH-DISPUTED BY SCHOLARS

❶ The Fertile Riverine Areas

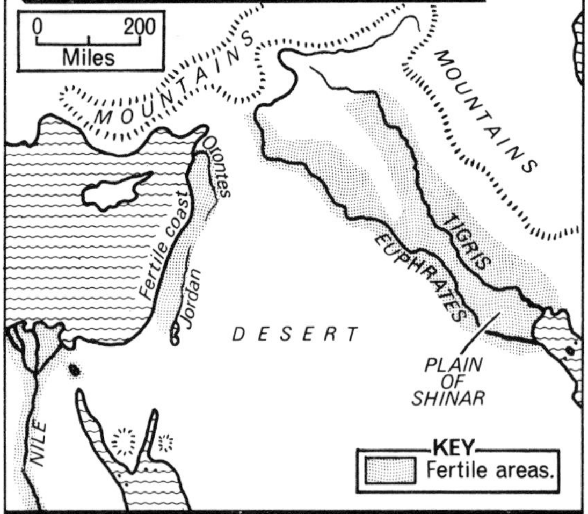

Early wars (in the sense of organized struggles) appear to have occurred in the area now known loosely as the Middle East and came about due to geography. In about 5000 B.C., people known as Sumerians occupied the area called the Plain of Shinar, and this fertile region became the envy of surrounding desert and mountain tribes.

❷ Early Wars and Invasions

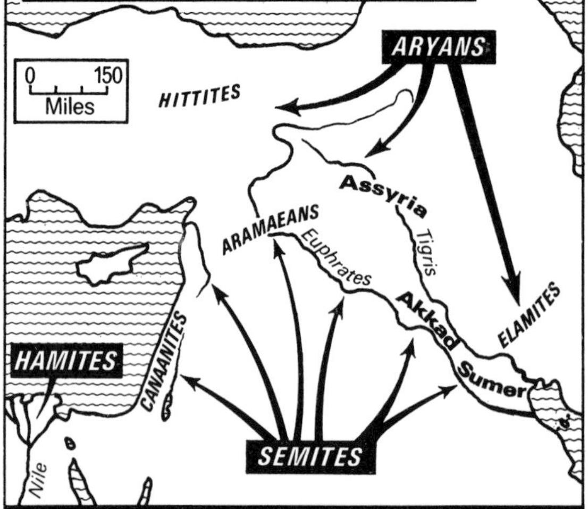

There were three main tribal groupings: Hamites, Semites, and Aryans (or Indo-Europeans). About 3000 B.C., Semitic tribes invaded Akkad-Sumer, and Aryans attacked Assyria. A long struggle ensued, and at one time (c.2320 B.C.), the tribes appear to have occupied the complete area between the rivers Tigris and Euphrates (under Sargon of Akkad).

❸ The Middle East c.2300-1500 B.C.

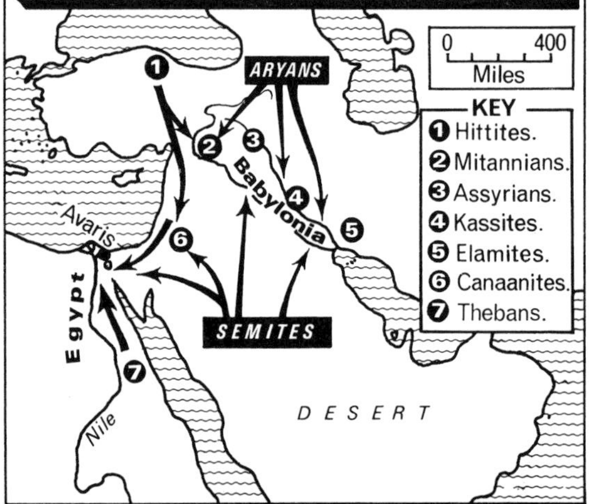

By c.2300 B.C., the main groups had split up into smaller tribes. Fierce struggles continued for the 'land of the two rivers', now known as Babylonia. Raids on the Nile delta were made by desert horsemen (Hyksos) who set up a base at Avaris. They were opposed by the Thebans. An Aryan group from the Black Sea (Hittites) expanded southwards.

❹ The Middle East c.1500-1000 B.C.

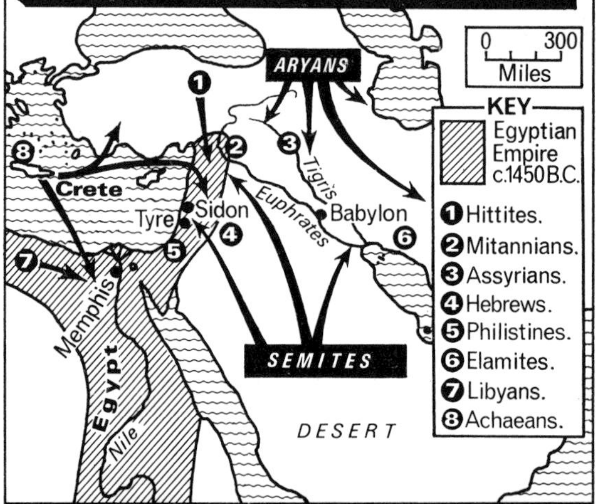

The Egyptian peoples eventually expelled the Hyksos, and despite attacks from similar border groups, established a great empire. The Phoenicians, a sea-faring people, settled at Tyre and Sidon. The Achaean peoples of Aryan stock advanced southwards from Greece, occupied Minoan Crete, and then expanded eastward into the Middle East.

5 India before c.600 B.C.

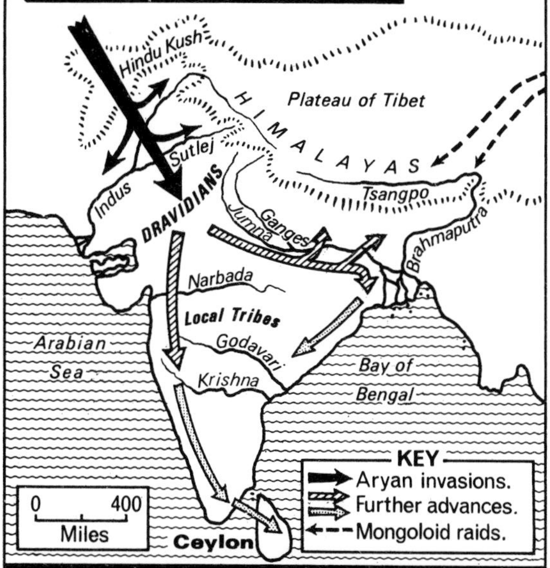

c.2000 B.C., migrations from Asia into India occurred in a pattern similar to the Middle East. Aryan tribal groups advanced over the Hindu Kush to the riverine areas of the Indus and Ganges, and later moved south, even to Ceylon. Infrequent Mongoloid invasions from the north-east were hindered by the Himalayas and Tibetan plateaux.

6 China before c.600 B.C.

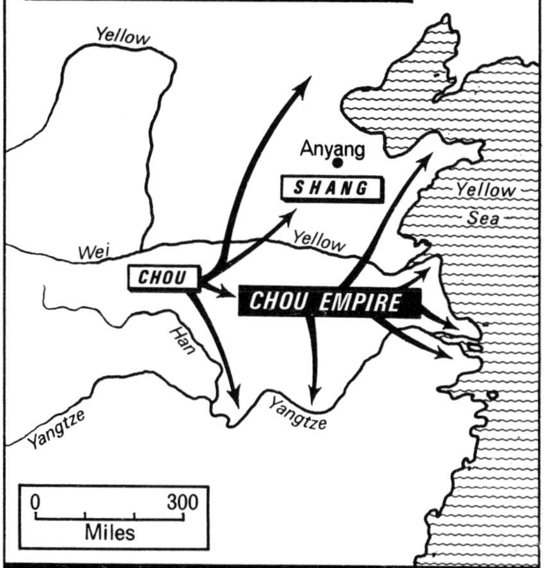

c.1766 B.C., the Shang dynastic empire was created in the region of Anyang, its capital. After c.1130 the semi-barbaric Chou from the Wei area moved eastwards, defeated the Shang, and later formed a great empire from the Yangtze to present-day Manchuria. From 800-600 B.C. there were constant feuds between autonomous war-lords.

7 Italy before c.600 B.C.

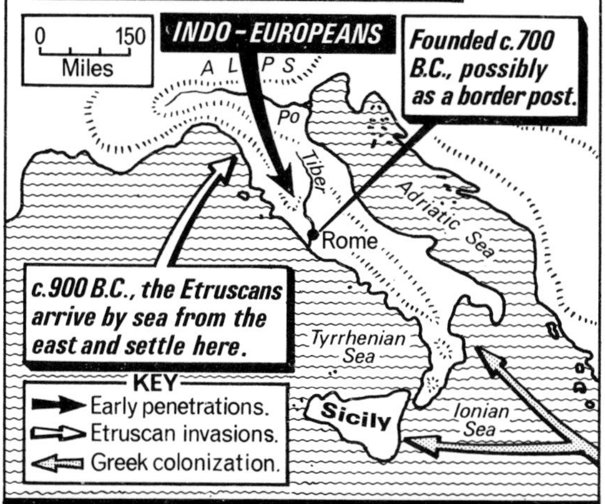

c.2000 B.C., Indo-European tribes migrated across the Alps and pressed southwards bringing the Bronze Age to Italy and Sicily. c.900 B.C., Etruscans (of different racial origin), arrived by sea and infiltrated north-west Italy. From 750-600 B.C., there were frequent wars between the two groups. Meanwhile, Greeks were colonizing Sicily and southern Italy.

8 Greece before c.600 B.C.

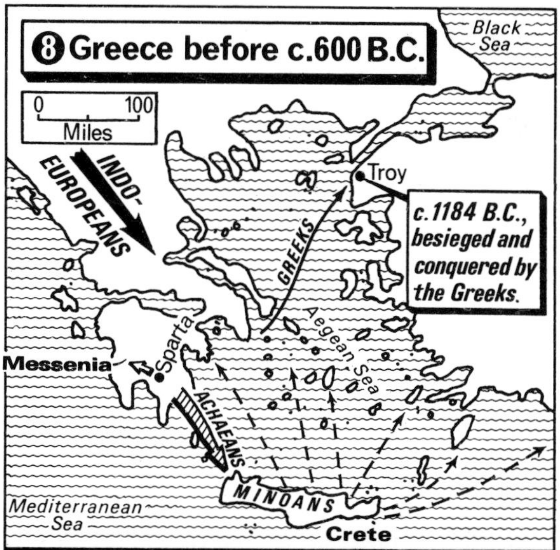

c.1400 B.C., Indo-European people from Achaea in southern Greece (which had been invaded by the Dorians) conquered the highly civilized Minoans of Crete, whose culture had spread over most of the Aegean. From c.1000 B.C., Sparta became militarily dominant and won two wars against the Messenians (c.700-680 B.C., and c.640-620 B.C.).

5

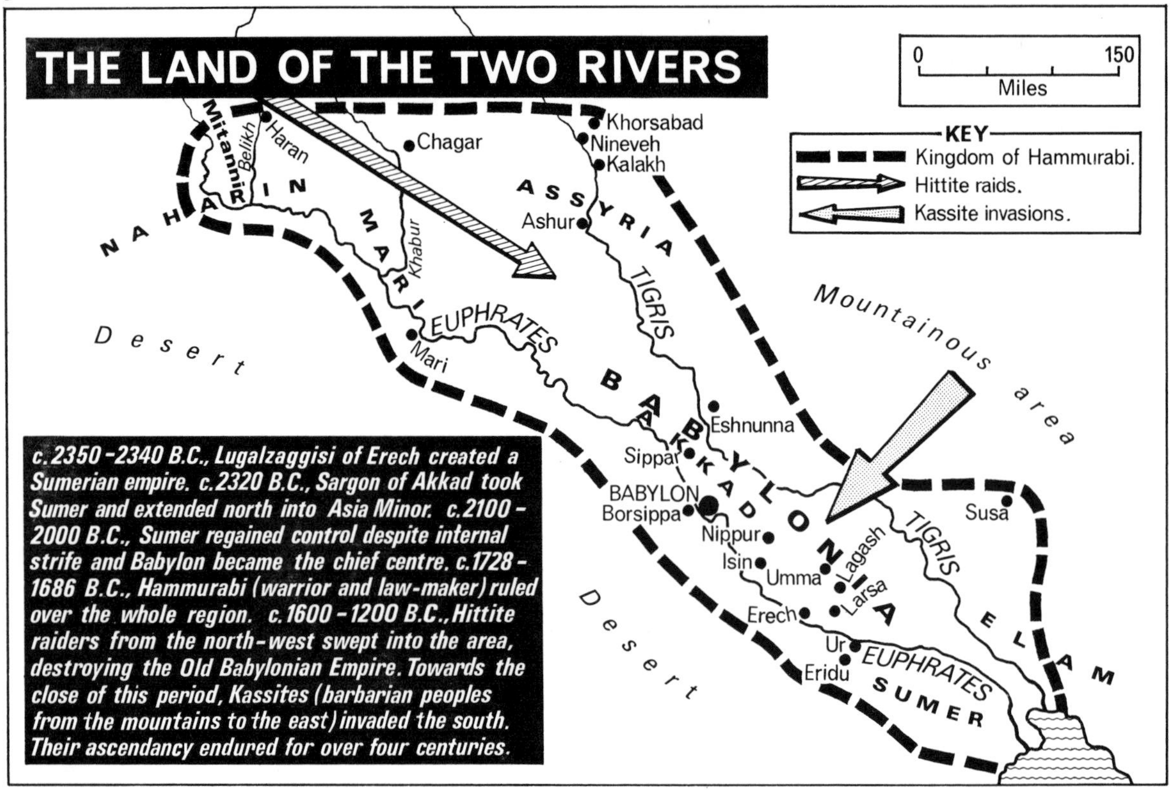
THE LAND OF THE TWO RIVERS
0 150
Miles
KEY
Kingdom of Hammurabi.
Hittite raids.
Kassite invasions.
c.2350–2340 B.C., Lugalzaggisi of Erech created a Sumerian empire. c.2320 B.C., Sargon of Akkad took Sumer and extended north into Asia Minor. c.2100–2000 B.C., Sumer regained control despite internal strife and Babylon became the chief centre. c.1728–1686 B.C., Hammurabi (warrior and law-maker) ruled over the whole region. c.1600–1200 B.C., Hittite raiders from the north-west swept into the area, destroying the Old Babylonian Empire. Towards the close of this period, Kassites (barbarian peoples from the mountains to the east) invaded the south. Their ascendancy endured for over four centuries.
Mitanni
Belikh
Haran
NAHARIN
Chagar
MARI
Khabur
Khorsabad
Nineveh
Kalakh
ASSYRIA
Ashur
TIGRIS
Mountainous area
Desert
EUPHRATES
Mari
BABYLONIA
AKKAD
Eshnunna
Sippar
BABYLON
Borsippa
Nippur
Isin
Umma
Lagash
Larsa
Erech
Ur
Eridu
EUPHRATES
SUMER
TIGRIS
Susa
ELAM
Desert

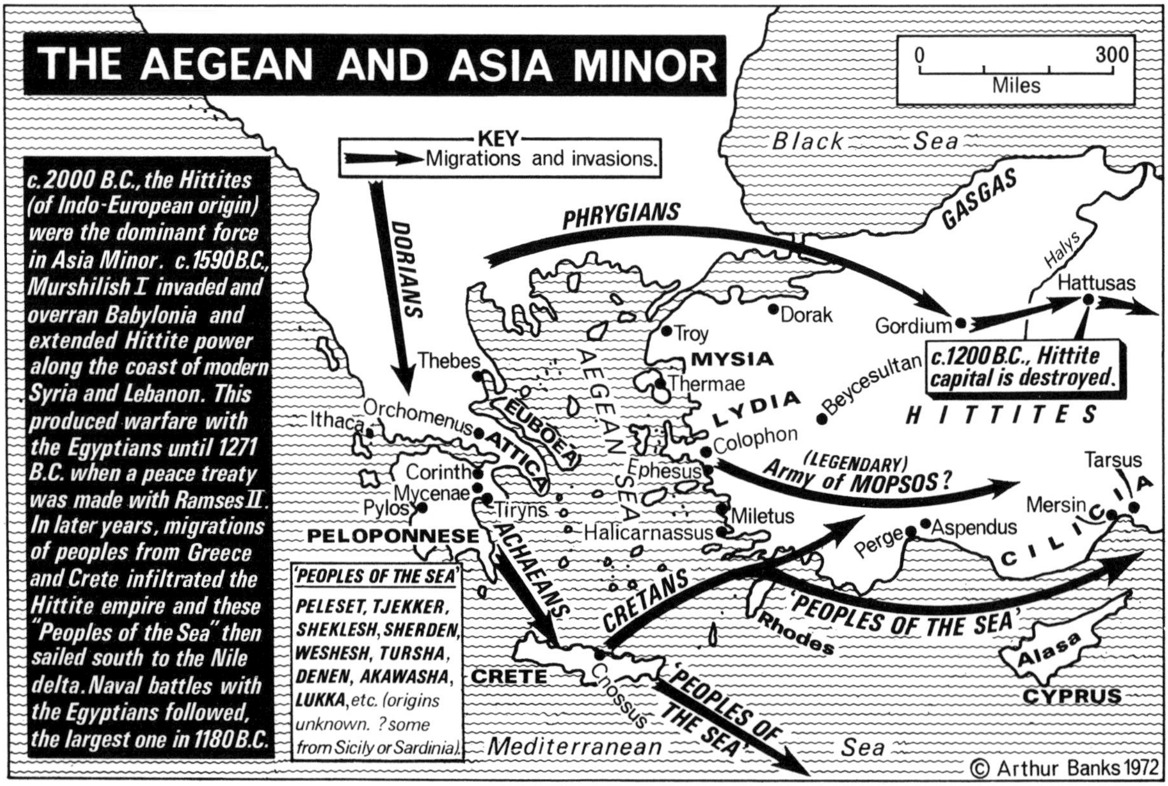
THE AEGEAN AND ASIA MINOR
0 300
Miles
KEY
Migrations and invasions.
c.2000 B.C., the Hittites (of Indo-European origin) were the dominant force in Asia Minor. c.1590 B.C., Murshilish I invaded and overran Babylonia and extended Hittite power along the coast of modern Syria and Lebanon. This produced warfare with the Egyptians until 1271 B.C. when a peace treaty was made with Ramses II. In later years, migrations of peoples from Greece and Crete infiltrated the Hittite empire and these "Peoples of the Sea" then sailed south to the Nile delta. Naval battles with the Egyptians followed, the largest one in 1180 B.C.
Black Sea
GASGAS
PHRYGIANS
DORIANS
Halys
Hattusas
Dorak
Gordium
Troy
MYSIA
Thermae
c.1200 B.C., Hittite capital is destroyed.
Thebes
AEGEAN SEA
LYDIA
Beycesultan
HITTITES
Ithaca
Orchomenus
EUBOEA
ATTICA
Colophon
Ephesus
(LEGENDARY) Army of MOPSOS?
Tarsus
Corinth
Mycenae
Pylos
Tiryns
Miletus
Mersin
CILICIA
PELOPONNESE
Halicarnassus
Perge
Aspendus
ACHAEANS
'PEOPLES OF THE SEA'
PELESET, TJEKKER, SHEKLESH, SHERDEN, WESHESH, TURSHA, DENEN, AKAWASHA, LUKKA, etc. (origins unknown. ?some from Sicily or Sardinia).
CRETANS
Rhodes
'PEOPLES OF THE SEA'
Alasa
CRETE
Cnossus
'PEOPLES OF THE SEA'
CYPRUS
Mediterranean Sea
© Arthur Banks 1972

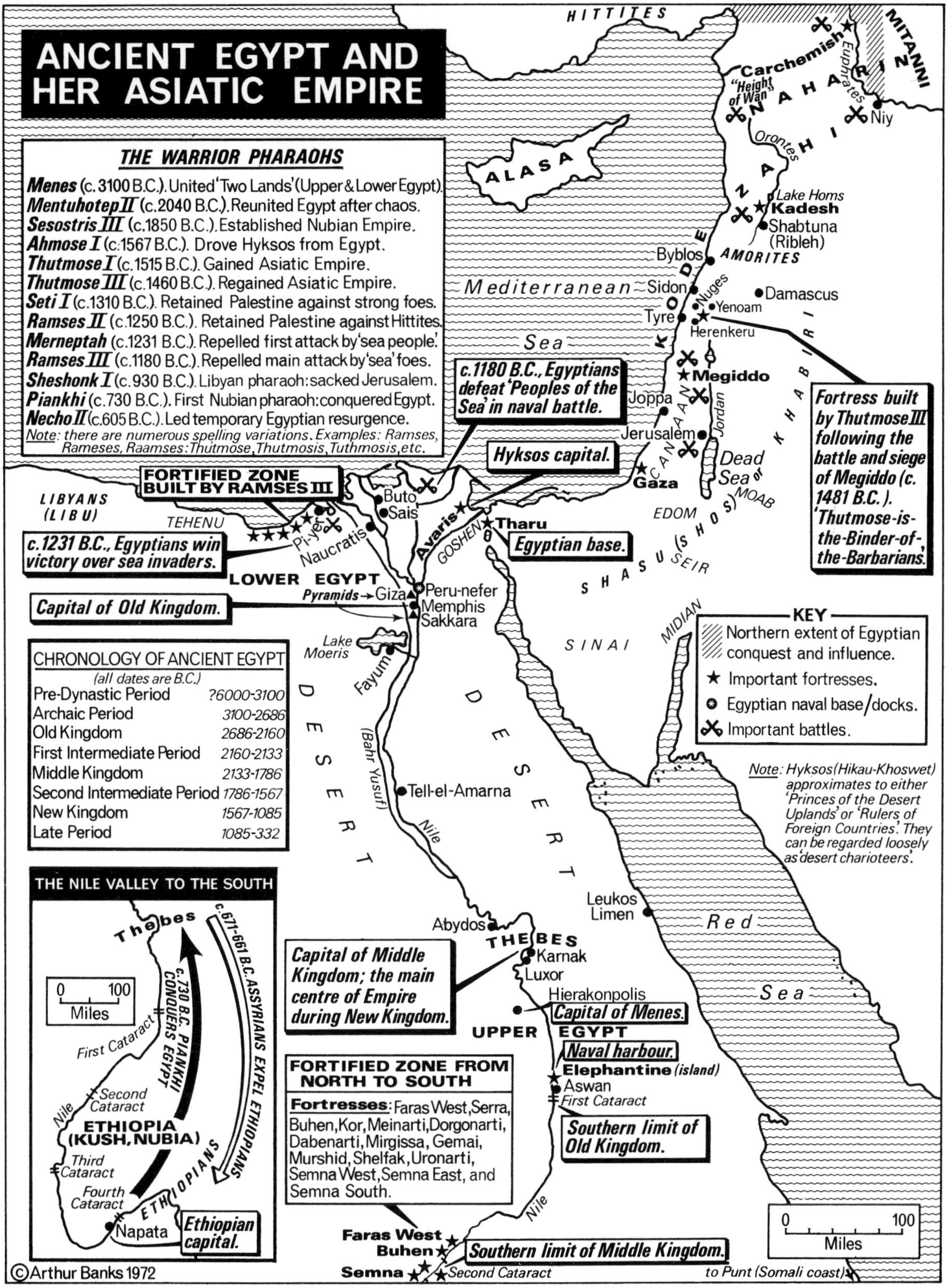
ANCIENT EGYPT AND HER ASIATIC EMPIRE
THE WARRIOR PHARAOHS
Menes (c.3100 B.C.). United 'Two Lands' (Upper & Lower Egypt).
Mentuhotep II (c.2040 B.C.). Reunited Egypt after chaos.
Sesostris III (c.1850 B.C.). Established Nubian Empire.
Ahmose I (c.1567 B.C.). Drove Hyksos from Egypt.
Thutmose I (c.1515 B.C.). Gained Asiatic Empire.
Thutmose III (c.1460 B.C.). Regained Asiatic Empire.
Seti I (c.1310 B.C.). Retained Palestine against strong foes.
Ramses II (c.1250 B.C.). Retained Palestine against Hittites.
Merneptah (c.1231 B.C.). Repelled first attack by 'sea people'.
Ramses III (c.1180 B.C.). Repelled main attack by 'sea' foes.
Sheshonk I (c.930 B.C.). Libyan pharaoh: sacked Jerusalem.
Piankhi (c.730 B.C.). First Nubian pharaoh: conquered Egypt.
Necho II (c.605 B.C.). Led temporary Egyptian resurgence.
Note: there are numerous spelling variations. Examples: Ramses, Rameses, Raamses: Thutmose, Thutmosis, Tuthmosis, etc.
CHRONOLOGY OF ANCIENT EGYPT
(all dates are B.C.)
Pre-Dynastic Period ?6000-3100
Archaic Period 3100-2686
Old Kingdom 2686-2160
First Intermediate Period 2160-2133
Middle Kingdom 2133-1786
Second Intermediate Period 1786-1567
New Kingdom 1567-1085
Late Period 1085-332
THE NILE VALLEY TO THE SOUTH
0 100 Miles
Thebes
c.730 B.C. PIANKHI CONQUERS EGYPT
c.671-661 B.C. ASSYRIANS EXPEL ETHIOPIANS
First Cataract
Second Cataract
Nile
ETHIOPIA (KUSH, NUBIA)
Third Cataract
Fourth Cataract
ETHIOPIANS
Napata
Ethiopian capital.
©Arthur Banks 1972
HITTITES
MITANNI
Carchemish
"Height of Wan"
Euphrates
NAHARINNI
Niy
Orontes
ALASA
ZAHI
Lake Homs
Kadesh
Shabtuna (Ribleh)
Byblos
AMORITES
Mediterranean
Sidon
Nuges
Damascus
Yenoam
Tyre
Herenkeru
Sea
KODE
Megiddo
Joppa
CANAAN
Jordan
Jerusalem
Dead Sea
Gaza
MOAB
EDOM
KHABIRI or
SHASU (SHOS)
SEIR
c.1180 B.C., Egyptians defeat 'Peoples of the Sea' in naval battle.
Hyksos capital.
Fortress built by Thutmose III following the battle and siege of Megiddo (c. 1481 B.C.). 'Thutmose-is-the-Binder-of-the-Barbarians'.
FORTIFIED ZONE BUILT BY RAMSES III
LIBYANS (LIBU)
TEHENU
Pi-yer
c.1231 B.C., Egyptians win victory over sea invaders.
Buto
Sais
Naucratis
Avaris
GOSHEN
Tharu
Egyptian base.
LOWER EGYPT
Pyramids
Giza
Peru-nefer
Memphis
Sakkara
Capital of Old Kingdom.
Lake Moeris
Fayum
SINAI
MIDIAN
KEY
Northern extent of Egyptian conquest and influence.
Important fortresses.
Egyptian naval base/docks.
Important battles.
Note: Hyksos (Hikau-Khoswet) approximates to either 'Princes of the Desert Uplands' or 'Rulers of Foreign Countries'. They can be regarded loosely as 'desert charioteers'.
DESERT
(Bahr Yusuf)
Tell-el-Amarna
Nile
DESERT
Leukos Limen
Red
Abydos
THEBES
Karnak
Luxor
Capital of Middle Kingdom; the main centre of Empire during New Kingdom.
Hierakonpolis
Capital of Menes.
Sea
UPPER EGYPT
Naval harbour.
Elephantine (island)
Aswan
First Cataract
FORTIFIED ZONE FROM NORTH TO SOUTH
Fortresses: Faras West, Serra, Buhen, Kor, Meinarti, Dorgonarti, Dabenarti, Mirgissa, Gemai, Murshid, Shelfak, Uronarti, Semna West, Semna East, and Semna South.
Southern limit of Old Kingdom.
Nile
0 100 Miles
Faras West
Buhen
Semna
Second Cataract
Southern limit of Middle Kingdom.
to Punt (Somali coast)

THE BATTLE AND SIEGE OF MEGIDDO 1481 B.C.

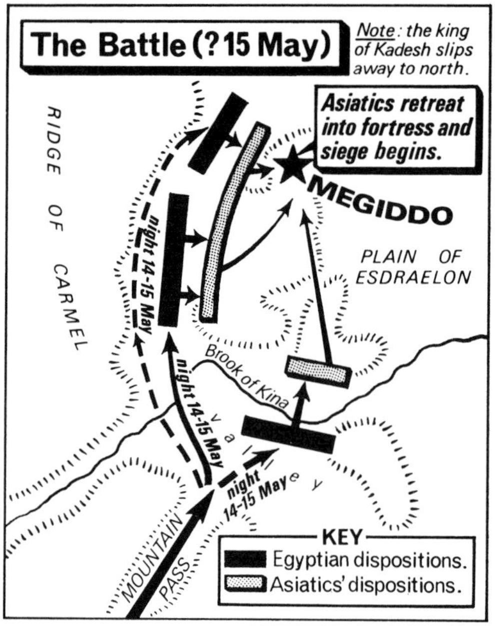
The Battle (?15 May)
Note: the king of Kadesh slips away to north.
Asiatics retreat into fortress and siege begins.
MEGIDDO
PLAIN OF ESDRAELON
RIDGE OF CARMEL
night 14-15 May
night 14-15 May
night 14-15 May
Brook of Kina
valley
MOUNTAIN PASS
KEY
Egyptian dispositions.
Asiatics' dispositions.

Egyptian Pre-Battle Strategy
0 3 Miles
RIDGE OF CARMEL
Zefti Road
MEGIDDO
Morning of battle, Asiatics redeploy in great haste west and south of fort.
Aruna
Pass
Taanach
ASIATICS' FIRST POSITION
Egyptians (?20,000) advance in file over narrow mountain pass.
to Damascus
Asiatics expect the Egyptians to attack from this direction.
from Yehem
Damascus Road

In May 1481 B.C., the king of Kadesh led a revolt of the Egyptian Empire's Asiatic city kings against the pharoah, Thutmose III. The Egyptian army marched to Megiddo, defeated the insurgents in battle, and besieged the fortress. After a campaign to secure the northern regions, Thutmose III returned to Thebes in October.

THE BATTLE OF KADESH 1288 B.C.

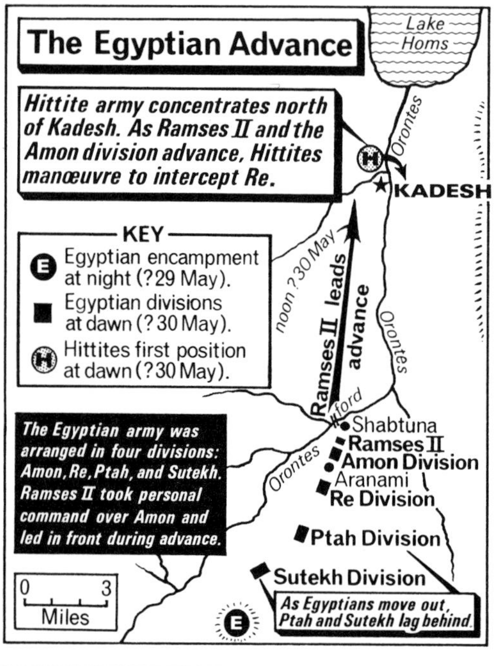
The Egyptian Advance
Lake Homs
Hittite army concentrates north of Kadesh. As Ramses II and the Amon division advance, Hittites manœuvre to intercept Re.
KADESH
Orontes
KEY
Egyptian encampment at night (?29 May).
Egyptian divisions at dawn (?30 May).
Hittites first position at dawn (?30 May).
noon ?30 May
Ramses II leads advance
Orontes
ford
Shabtuna
Ramses II
Amon Division
Aranami
Re Division
Ptah Division
Sutekh Division
Orontes
The Egyptian army was arranged in four divisions: Amon, Re, Ptah, and Sutekh. Ramses II took personal command over Amon and led in front during advance.
0 3 Miles
As Egyptians move out, Ptah and Sutekh lag behind.

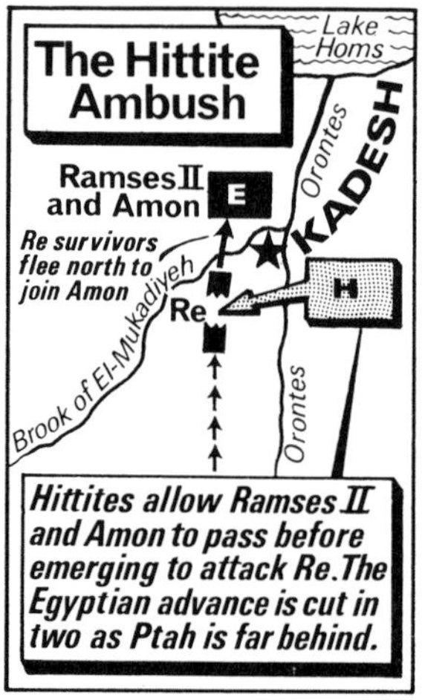
The Hittite Ambush
Lake Homs
Ramses II and Amon
Orontes
KADESH
Re survivors flee north to join Amon
Re
Brook of El-Mukadiyeh
Orontes
Hittites allow Ramses II and Amon to pass before emerging to attack Re. The Egyptian advance is cut in two as Ptah is far behind.

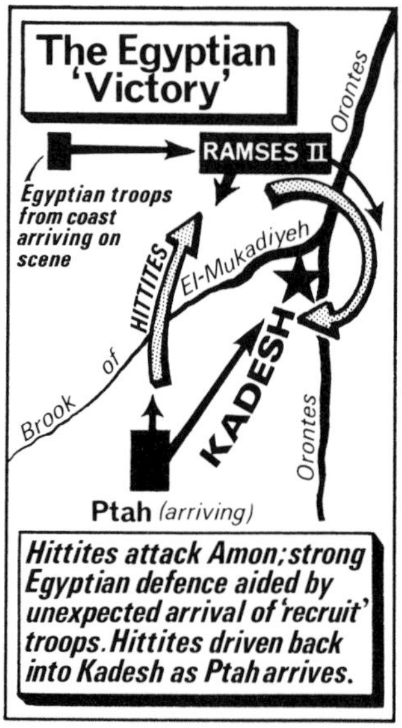
The Egyptian 'Victory'
Orontes
RAMSES II
Egyptian troops from coast arriving on scene
HITTITES
El-Mukadiyeh
Brook of
KADESH
Orontes
Ptah (arriving)
Hittites attack Amon; strong Egyptian defence aided by unexpected arrival of 'recruit' troops. Hittites driven back into Kadesh as Ptah arrives.

By 1288 B.C., the Hittites under Metella had swept southwards and made Kadesh their base. Ramses II led his army to engage them and a battle ensued at Kadesh. Each army numbered about 20,000 and despite gaining an early tactical success, Metella was beaten. This battle is notable for the extensive use of chariots in warfare.

ANCIENT PALESTINE AND THE ISRAELITES

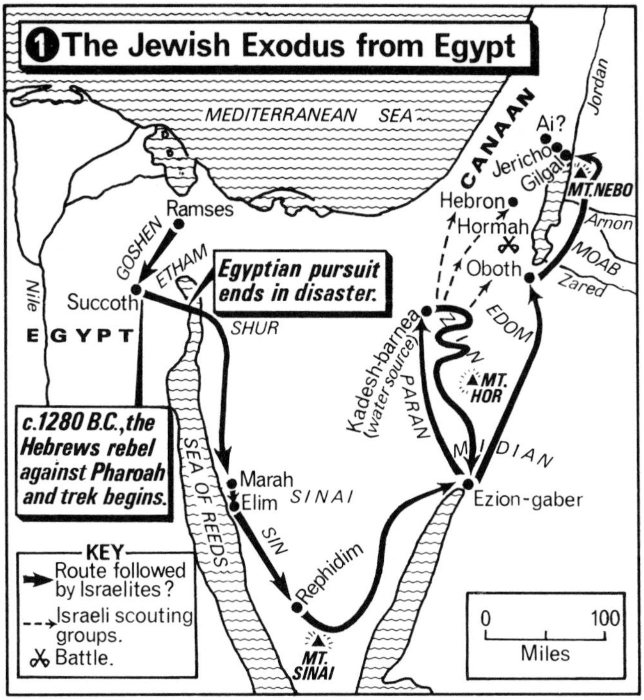
1 The Jewish Exodus from Egypt
MEDITERRANEAN SEA
CANAAN
Jordan
Ai?
Jericho
Gilgal
MT. NEBO
Hebron
Hormah
Arnon
MOAB
Oboth
Zared
EDOM
Ramses
GOSHEN
ETHAM
Egyptian pursuit ends in disaster.
Succoth
Nile
EGYPT
SHUR
Kadesh-barnea (water source)
PARAN
ZIN
MT. HOR
c.1280 B.C., the Hebrews rebel against Pharoah and trek begins.
SEA OF REEDS
Marah
Elim
SINAI
MIDIAN
Ezion-gaber
SIN
Rephidim
KEY
Route followed by Israelites?
Israeli scouting groups.
Battle.
MT. SINAI
0 100
Miles

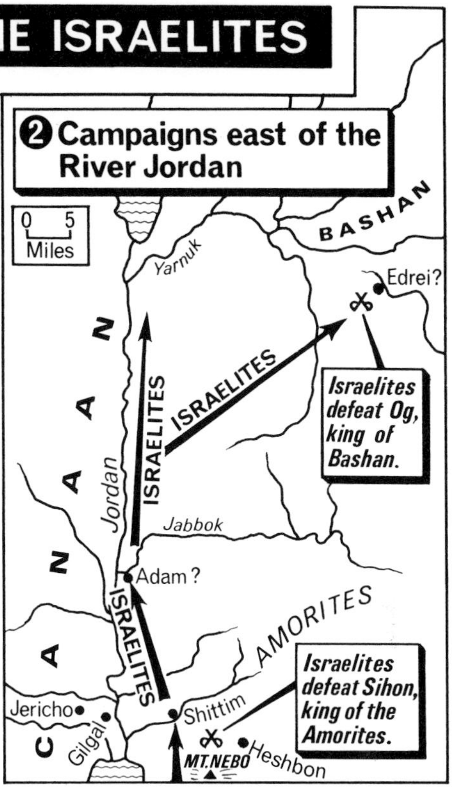
2 Campaigns east of the River Jordan
0 5
Miles
BASHAN
Yarmuk
Edrei?
ISRAELITES
ISRAELITES
Israelites defeat Og, king of Bashan.
CANAAN
Jordan
Jabbok
Adam ?
ISRAELITES
AMORITES
Israelites defeat Sihon, king of the Amorites.
Jericho
Gilgal
Shittim
MT. NEBO
Heshbon

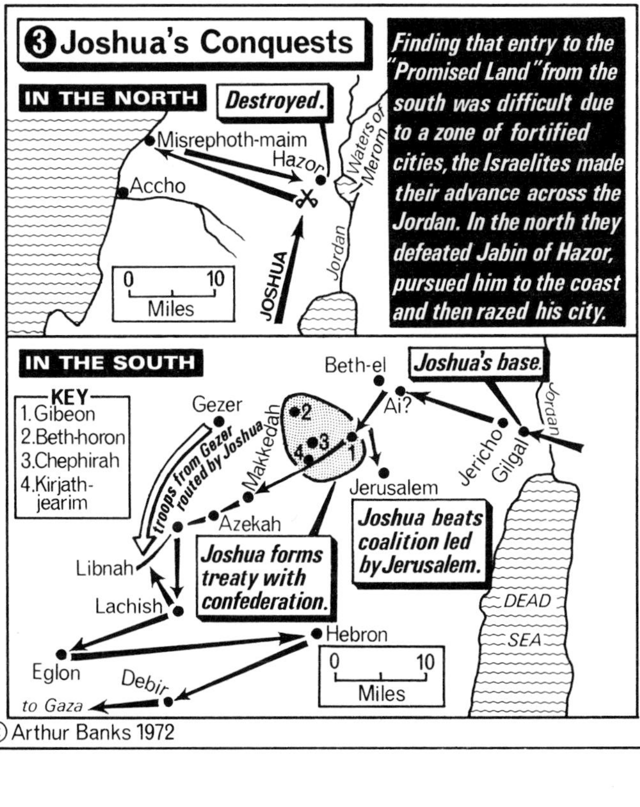
3 Joshua's Conquests
IN THE NORTH
Destroyed.
Finding that entry to the "Promised Land" from the south was difficult due to a zone of fortified cities, the Israelites made their advance across the Jordan. In the north they defeated Jabin of Hazor, pursued him to the coast and then razed his city.
Misrephoth-maim
Hazor
Waters of Merom
Accho
Jordan
JOSHUA
0 10
Miles
IN THE SOUTH
Beth-el
Joshua's base.
KEY
1. Gibeon
2. Beth-horon
3. Chephirah
4. Kirjath-jearim
Gezer
Ai?
Jordan
Makkedah
Jericho
Gilgal
troops from Gezer routed by Joshua
Jerusalem
Azekah
Joshua beats coalition led by Jerusalem.
Libnah
Joshua forms treaty with confederation.
Lachish
DEAD SEA
Hebron
Eglon
Debir
to Gaza
0 10
Miles

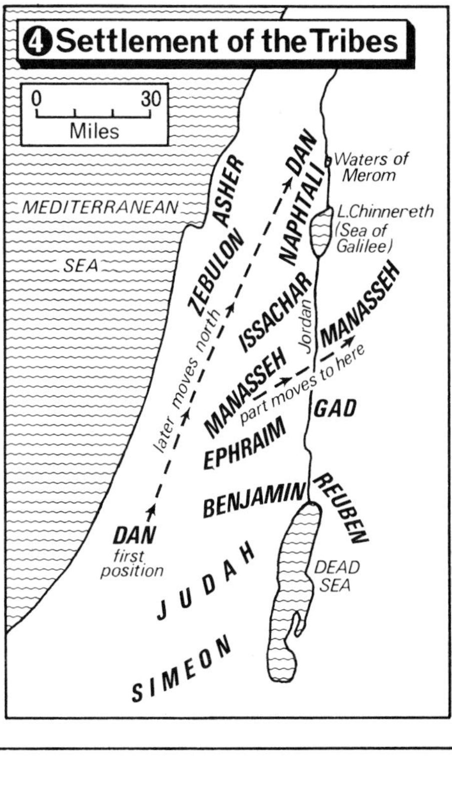
4 Settlement of the Tribes
0 30
Miles
MEDITERRANEAN SEA
ASHER
DAN
Waters of Merom
NAPHTALI
L. Chinnereth (Sea of Galilee)
ZEBULON
ISSACHAR
Jordan
MANASSEH
later moves north
MANASSEH
part moves to here
GAD
EPHRAIM
BENJAMIN
REUBEN
DAN first position
JUDAH
DEAD SEA
SIMEON

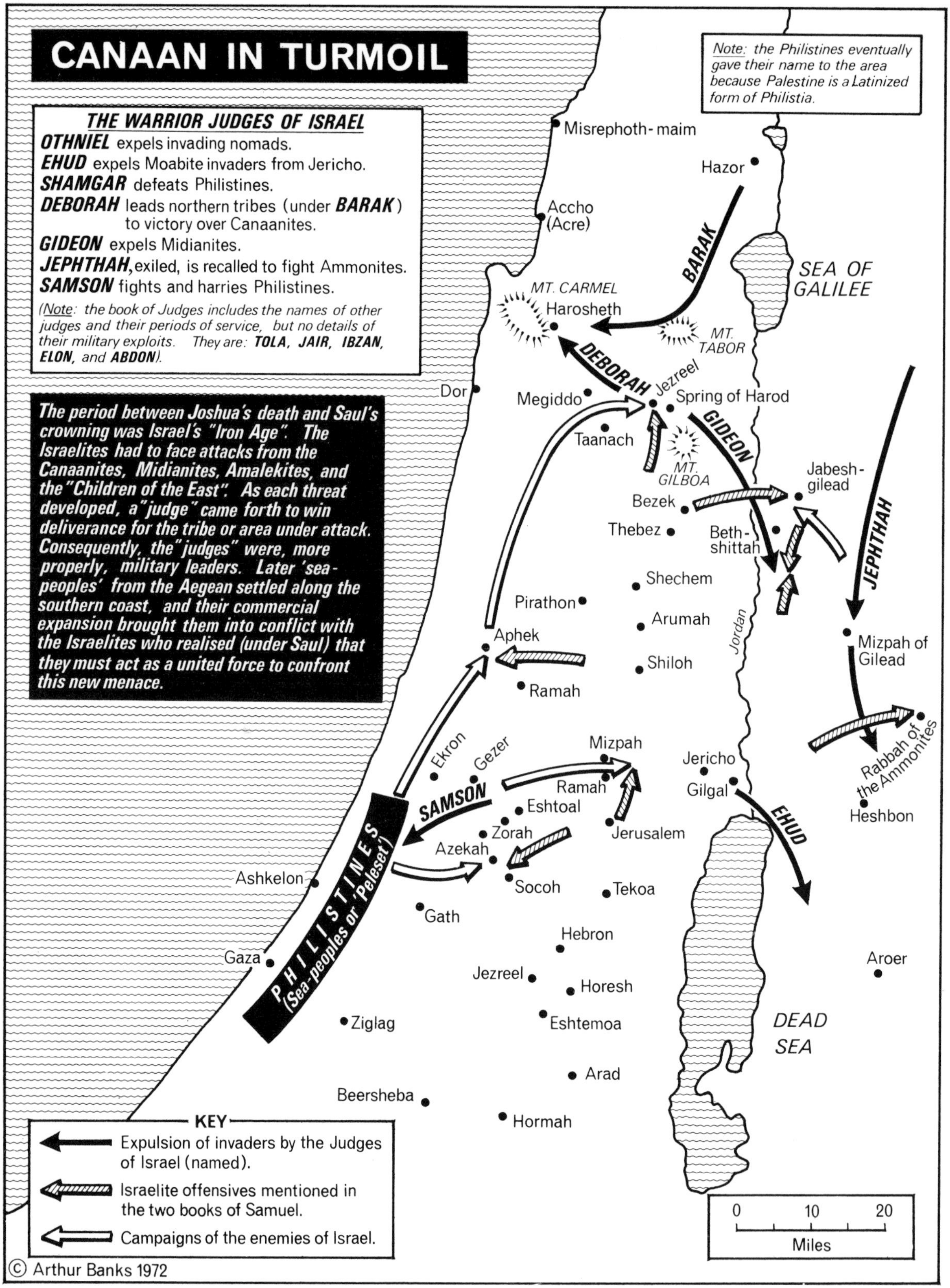
CANAAN IN TURMOIL
THE WARRIOR JUDGES OF ISRAEL
OTHNIEL expels invading nomads.
EHUD expels Moabite invaders from Jericho.
SHAMGAR defeats Philistines.
DEBORAH leads northern tribes (under BARAK) to victory over Canaanites.
GIDEON expels Midianites.
JEPHTHAH, exiled, is recalled to fight Ammonites.
SAMSON fights and harries Philistines.
(Note: the book of Judges includes the names of other judges and their periods of service, but no details of their military exploits. They are: TOLA, JAIR, IBZAN, ELON, and ABDON).
The period between Joshua's death and Saul's crowning was Israel's "Iron Age". The Israelites had to face attacks from the Canaanites, Midianites, Amalekites, and the "Children of the East". As each threat developed, a "judge" came forth to win deliverance for the tribe or area under attack. Consequently, the "judges" were, more properly, military leaders. Later 'sea-peoples' from the Aegean settled along the southern coast, and their commercial expansion brought them into conflict with the Israelites who realised (under Saul) that they must act as a united force to confront this new menace.
Note: the Philistines eventually gave their name to the area because Palestine is a Latinized form of Philistia.
Misrephoth-maim
Hazor
Accho
(Acre)
BARAK
SEA OF
GALILEE
MT. CARMEL
Harosheth
MT.
TABOR
DEBORAH
Dor
Megiddo
Jezreel
Spring of Harod
Taanach
GIDEON
MT.
GILBOA
Jabesh-
gilead
Bezek
Thebez
Beth-
shittah
JEPHTHAH
Shechem
Pirathon
Arumah
Jordan
Aphek
Mizpah of
Gilead
Shiloh
Ramah
Ekron
Gezer
Mizpah
Jericho
Rabbah of
the Ammonites
Ramah
Gilgal
SAMSON
Eshtoal
Heshbon
Zorah
Jerusalem
EHUD
Azekah
PHILISTINES
(Sea-peoples or 'Peleset')
Ashkelon
Socoh
Tekoa
Gath
Hebron
Gaza
Aroer
Jezreel
Horesh
Ziglag
Eshtemoa
DEAD
SEA
Arad
Beersheba
Hormah
KEY
Expulsion of invaders by the Judges of Israel (named).
Israelite offensives mentioned in the two books of Samuel.
Campaigns of the enemies of Israel.
0
10
20
Miles
© Arthur Banks 1972

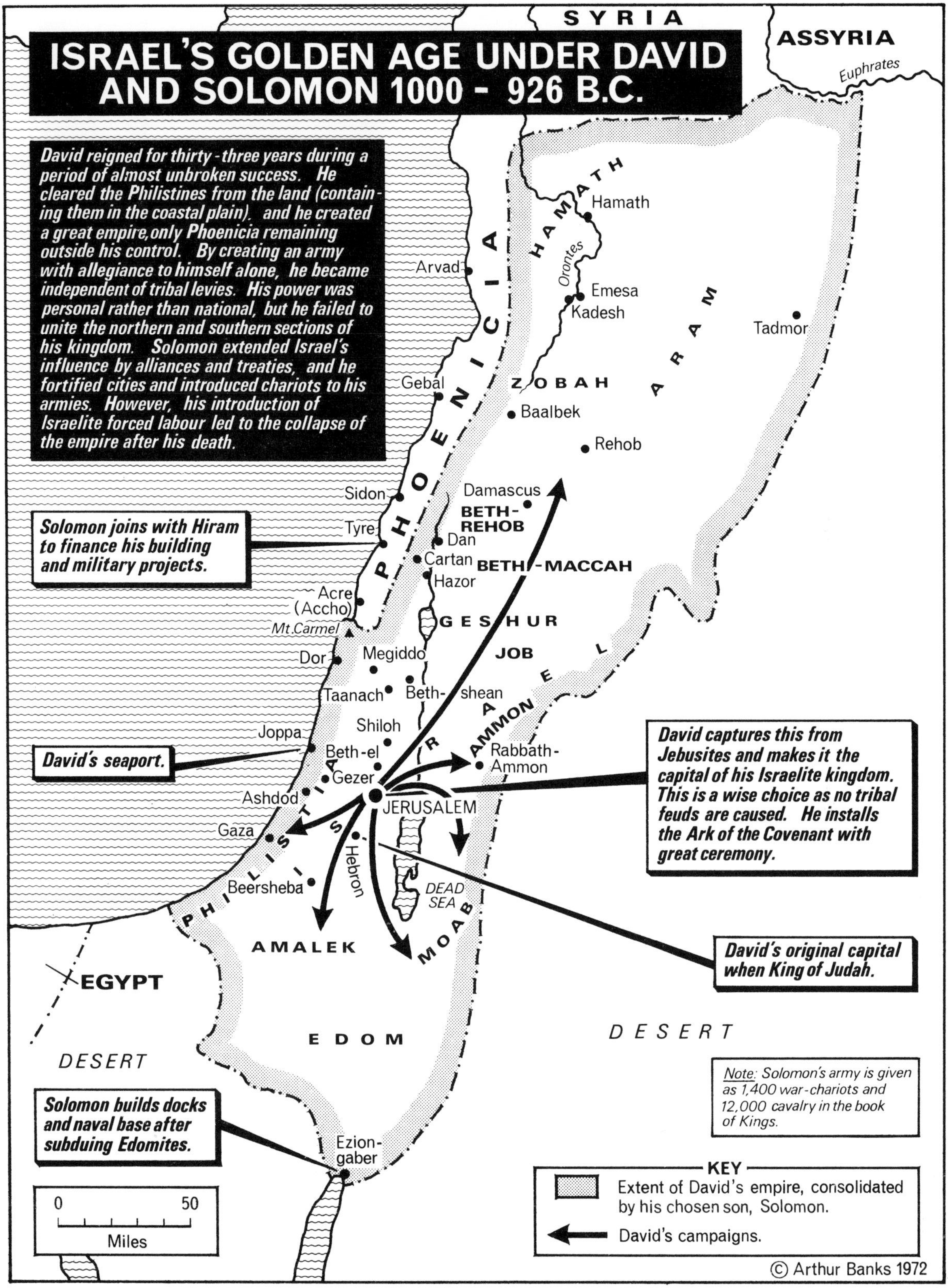
ISRAEL'S GOLDEN AGE UNDER DAVID AND SOLOMON 1000 - 926 B.C.
David reigned for thirty-three years during a period of almost unbroken success. He cleared the Philistines from the land (containing them in the coastal plain), and he created a great empire, only Phoenicia remaining outside his control. By creating an army with allegiance to himself alone, he became independent of tribal levies. His power was personal rather than national, but he failed to unite the northern and southern sections of his kingdom. Solomon extended Israel's influence by alliances and treaties, and he fortified cities and introduced chariots to his armies. However, his introduction of Israelite forced labour led to the collapse of the empire after his death.
Solomon joins with Hiram to finance his building and military projects.
David's seaport.
David captures this from Jebusites and makes it the capital of his Israelite kingdom. This is a wise choice as no tribal feuds are caused. He installs the Ark of the Covenant with great ceremony.
David's original capital when King of Judah.
Solomon builds docks and naval base after subduing Edomites.
Note: Solomon's army is given as 1,400 war-chariots and 12,000 cavalry in the book of Kings.
KEY
Extent of David's empire, consolidated by his chosen son, Solomon.
David's campaigns.
0
50
Miles
© Arthur Banks 1972
SYRIA
ASSYRIA
Euphrates
HAMATH
Hamath
Orontes
Emesa
Kadesh
Tadmor
ARAM
Arvad
PHOENICIA
ZOBAH
Gebal
Baalbek
Rehob
Sidon
Damascus
BETH-REHOB
Tyre
Dan
Cartan
BETH-MACCAH
Hazor
Acre (Accho)
Mt.Carmel
GESHUR
Dor
Megiddo
JOB
Taanach
Beth-shean
ISRAEL
AMMON
Shiloh
Joppa
Beth-el
Rabbath-Ammon
Gezer
Ashdod
JERUSALEM
Gaza
PHILISTIA
Hebron
Beersheba
DEAD SEA
MOAB
AMALEK
EGYPT
EDOM
DESERT
DESERT
Ezion-gaber

ANCIENT CHINA

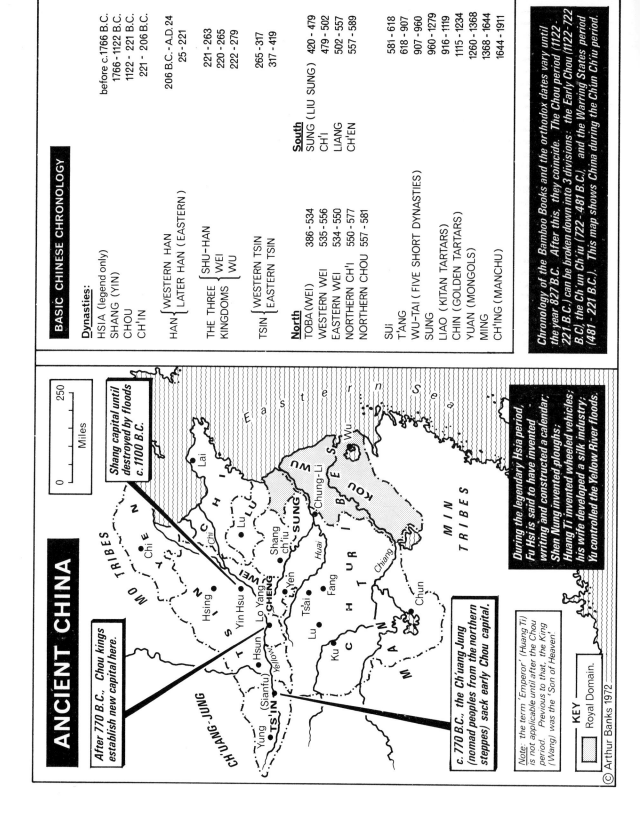

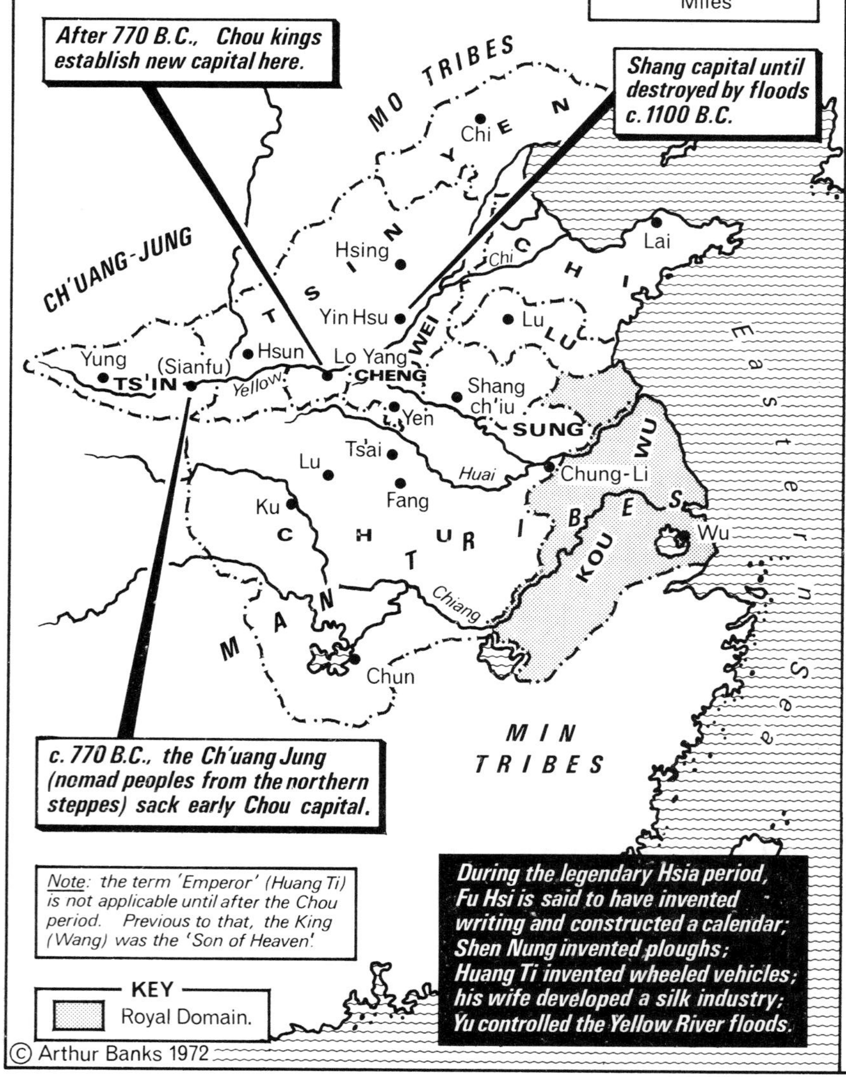
0 250
Miles
After 770 B.C., Chou kings establish new capital here.
Shang capital until destroyed by floods c. 1100 B.C.
MO TRIBES
CH'UANG-JUNG
Chi
Hsing
Yin Hsu
Lo Yang
CHENG
WEI
Chi
Lai
Lu
LU
Shang ch'iu
SUNG
Yen
Tsai
Lu
Fang
Huai
Chung-Li
WU
Wu
KOU
Ku
Yung
TS'IN
(Sianfu)
Hsun
Yellow
Chiang
Chun
MIN TRIBES
Eastern Sea
c. 770 B.C., the Ch'uang Jung (nomad peoples from the northern steppes) sack early Chou capital.
Note: the term 'Emperor' (Huang Ti) is not applicable until after the Chou period. Previous to that, the King (Wang) was the 'Son of Heaven'.
KEY
Royal Domain.
During the legendary Hsia period, Fu Hsi is said to have invented writing and constructed a calendar; Shen Nung invented ploughs; Huang Ti invented wheeled vehicles; his wife developed a silk industry; Yu controlled the Yellow River floods.

BASIC CHINESE CHRONOLOGY

Dynasties:

HSIA (legend only)		before c.1766 B.C.
SHANG (YIN)		1766 - 1122 B.C.
CHOU		1122 - 221 B.C.
CH'IN		221 - 206 B.C.
HAN	WESTERN HAN	206 B.C. - A.D. 24
	LATER HAN (EASTERN)	25 - 221
THE THREE KINGDOMS	SHU-HAN	221 - 263
	WEI	220 - 265
	WU	222 - 279
TSIN	WESTERN TSIN	265 - 317
	EASTERN TSIN	317 - 419

North		South	
TOBA (WEI)	386 - 534	SUNG (LIU SUNG)	420 - 479
WESTERN WEI	535 - 556	CH'I	479 - 502
EASTERN WEI	534 - 550	LIANG	502 - 557
NORTHERN CH'I	550 - 577	CH'EN	557 - 589
NORTHERN CHOU	557 - 581		

SUI	581 - 618
T'ANG	618 - 907
WU-TAI (FIVE SHORT DYNASTIES)	907 - 960
SUNG	960 - 1279
LIAO (KITAN TARTARS)	916 - 1119
CHIN (GOLDEN TARTARS)	1115 - 1234
YUAN (MONGOLS)	1260 - 1368
MING	1368 - 1644
CH'ING (MANCHU)	1644 - 1911

Chronology of the Bamboo Books and the orthodox dates vary until the year 827 B.C. After this, they coincide. The Chou period (1122 - 221 B.C.) can be broken down into 3 divisions: the Early Chou (1122-722 B.C), the Ch'un Ch'iu (722 - 481 B.C.), and the Warring States period (481 - 221 B.C.). This map shows China during the Ch'un Ch'iu period.

ANCIENT INDIA
IMPORTANT: SEE MAPS ON PAGE 42.
0 400
Miles
1 c.500 B.C.
Annexed to the Persian Empire under Darius.
Area populated by following clans in sixth century B.C: SAKIYAS, BULIS, KALAMAS, BHAGGAS, KOLIYAS, MORIYAS, MALLAS OF PAVA AND KUSINARA, VIDEHAS OF MITHILA, LICCHAVIS OF VESALI.
KAPISA
KAMBOJA
ACHAEMENID EMPIRE
GANDHARA
Indus
Jhelum
Chenab
Beas
Ravi
Sutlej
KURU
Ganges
Tsangpo
MATSYA
SURASENA
PANCHALA
KOSALA
MALLA
old course of Indus?
Brahmaputra
Jumna
Ganges
CHEDI
VATSA
KASI
ANSA
MAGADHA
Son
AVANTI
Narbada
Mahanadi
BHOJAS
VIDARBHA
MULAKA
ASMAKA
Godavari
DAKSHINAPATHA
KALINGA
ANDHRA
Krishna
KEY
MAGADHA etc. Main powers of northern India.
MALLA etc. Other powers or tribes.
Area linked with history of Persian Empire under Cyrus and Darius.
The bow was the primary weapon employed by foot-soldiers. Cavalry and chariots were employed by the early Hindu princes, and later (c. 500 B.C.) war-elephants were introduced. The first military commander of note was Chandragupta I (c. 350-297 B.C.) who was thought to have met Alexander the Great during his campaign in north-west India.
2 c.250 B.C.
This area ceded to Chandragupta Maurya by Seleucus Nikator.
KEY
Mauryan Empire.
Settlements, rock or pillar edicts.
1 Shahbazgarhi.
2 Mansera.
3 Topra.
4 Mirath.
5 Indraprastha.
6 Mathura.
7 Prayaga.
8 Sravasti.
9 Kapilavastu.
10 Rummindi.
11 Lalita Patan.
12 Rampurwa.
13 Lauriya Nandangarh.
14 Lauriya Araraj.
15 Sahasram.
16 Champa.
17 Tamralipti.
18 Rupnath.
19 Sanchi.
20 Sopara.
21 Tosali.
22 Jaugada.
23 Kopbal.
24 Siddapura.
25 Nellore.
PAROPANISADAI
Beas
Asoka's capital.
Pataliputra
MAGADHA
VANGA
AVANTI
SURASHTRA
PULINDAS
261 B.C.
PITINIKAS
RASHTRIKAS
KALINGA
ANDHRA
Maski
SATIYAPUTRA
KERALAPUTRA
CHOLAS
PANDYAS
TAMRAPARNI
Rock edict mentions Asoka.
1 326 B.C., Alexander at R. Beas.
2 323 B.C., Nanda (Magadha ruler) overthrown by Chandragupta.
3 323-297 B.C., Chandragupta expanded his domains.
4 305 B.C., Chandragupta obtained concessions from Seleucus Nikator.
5 297-274 B.C., Bindusara expanded empire to the south.
6 274-232 B.C., Asoka brought Mauryan Empire to its greatest power and extent.
MILITARY KEY
Asoka's campaign against Kalinga.

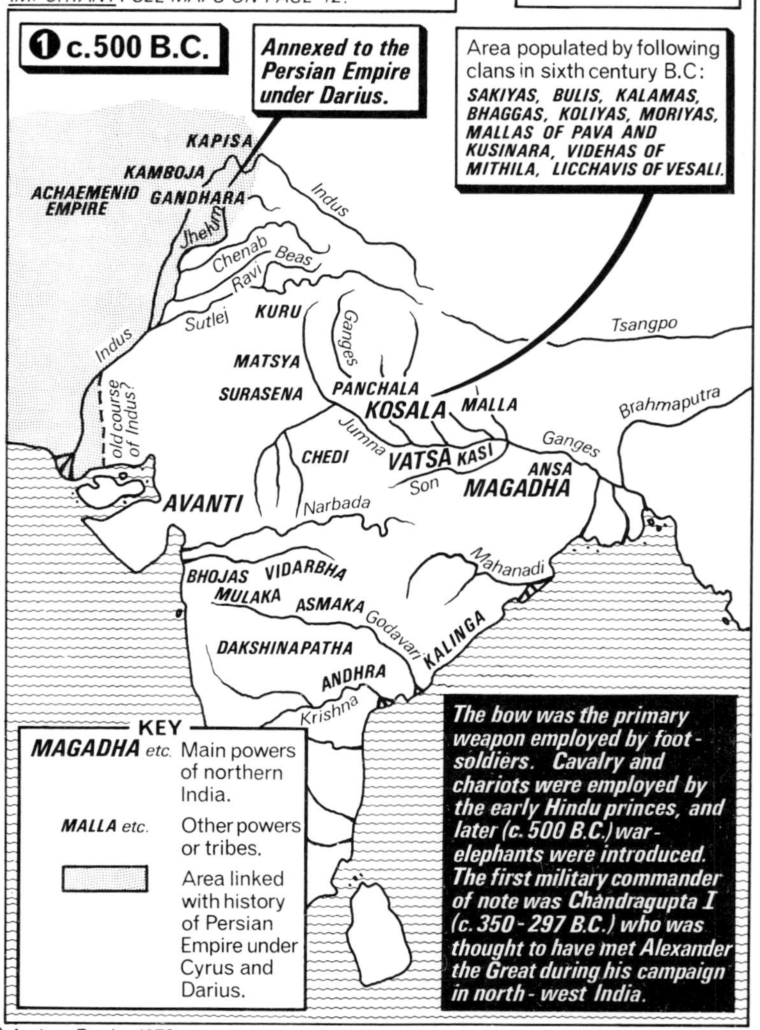

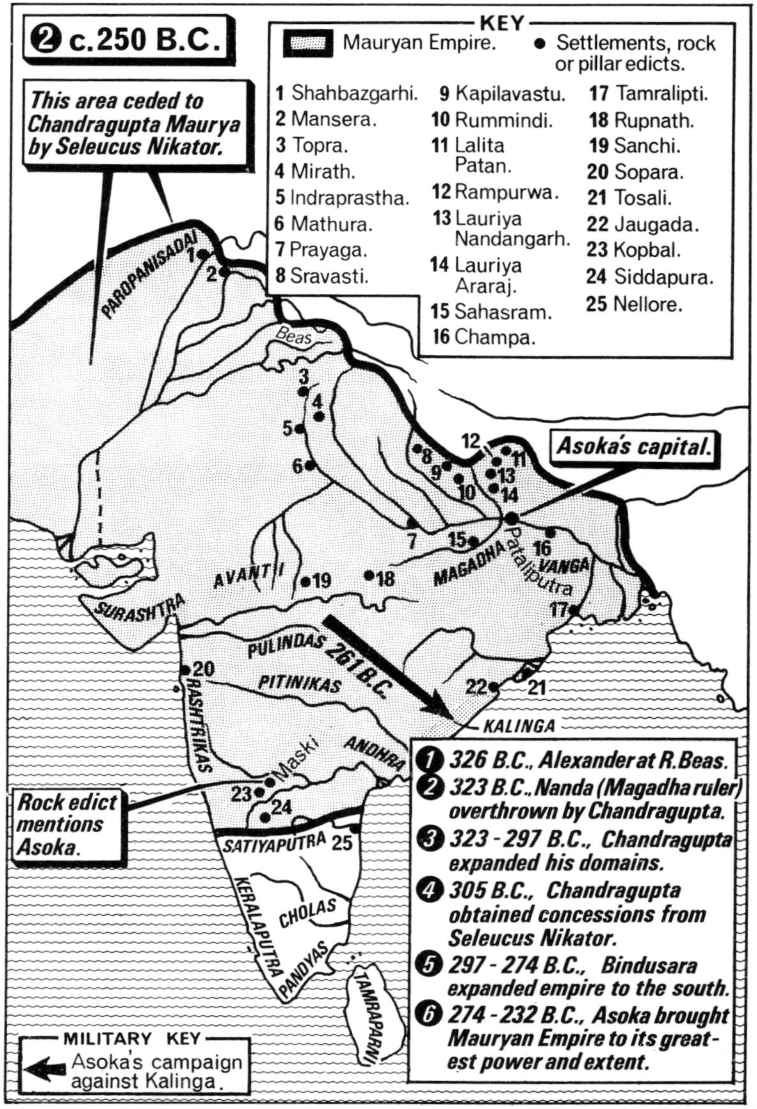

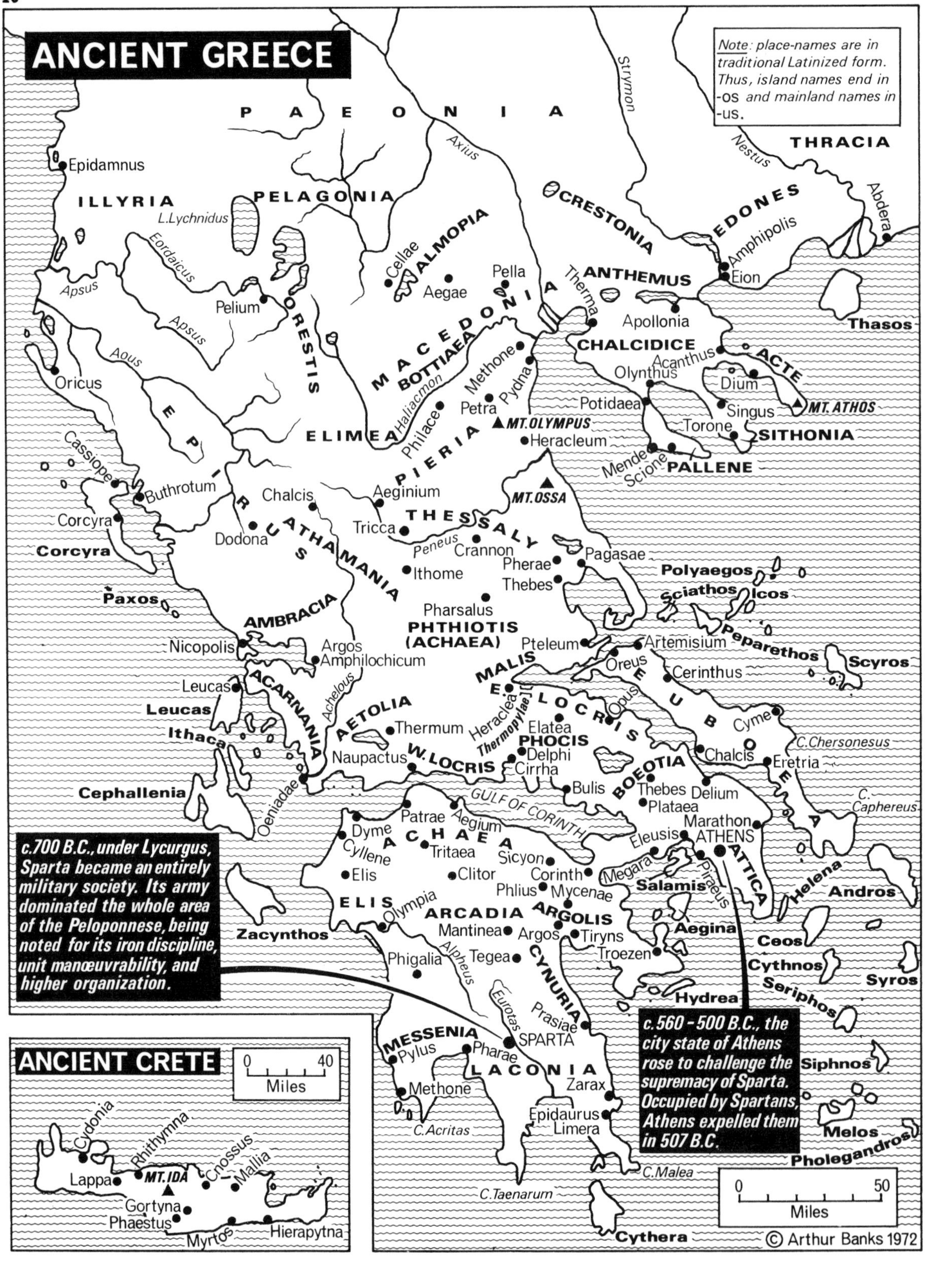
ANCIENT GREECE
Note: place-names are in traditional Latinized form. Thus, island names end in -os and mainland names in -us.
P A E O N I A
THRACIA
Strymon
Nestus
Axius
Epidamnus
ILLYRIA
L.Lychnidus
PELAGONIA
ALMOPIA
CRESTONIA
EDONES
Abdera
Amphipolis
Eion
Eordaicus
Apsus
Pelium
Cellae
Aegae
Pella
Therma
ANTHEMUS
Apollonia
Thasos
ORESTIS
MACEDONIA
BOTTIAEA
Methone
Pydna
CHALCIDICE
Acanthus
ACTE
Dium
Olynthus
Oricus
Aous
EPIRUS
Haliacmon
Petra
Potidaea
Singus
MT. ATHOS
MT. OLYMPUS
Torone
SITHONIA
ELIMEA
Philace
PIERIA
Heracleum
Mende
Scione
PALLENE
Cassiope
Buthrotum
Chalcis
Aeginium
MT. OSSA
Corcyra
Corcyra
Dodona
ATHAMANIA
Tricca
THESSALY
Peneus
Crannon
Pagasae
Pherae
Thebes
Polyaegos
Ithome
Sciathos
Icos
Paxos
Pharsalus
AMBRACIA
PHTHIOTIS (ACHAEA)
Pteleum
Artemisium
Peparethos
Scyros
Nicopolis
Argos Amphilochicum
MALIS
Oreus
Cerinthus
Leucas
Leucas
ACARNANIA
Achelous
E. LOCRIS
Opus
EUBOEA
Ithaca
AETOLIA
Thermum
Heraclea
Thermopylae
Elatea
Cyme
PHOCIS
C. Chersonesus
Naupactus
W. LOCRIS
Delphi
Cirrha
Chalcis
Eretria
Cephallenia
Oeniadae
Bulis
BOEOTIA
Thebes
Delium
Plataea
C. Caphereus
GULF OF CORINTH
Patrae
Aegium
Dyme
ACHAEA
Marathon
Eleusis
ATHENS
Cyllene
Tritaea
Sicyon
ATTICA
Elis
Clitor
Corinth
Megara
Helena
Andros
Phlius
Mycenae
Salamis
Piraeus
ELIS
Olympia
ARCADIA
ARGOLIS
Zacynthos
Mantinea
Argos
Tiryns
Aegina
Ceos
Phigalia
Alpheus
Tegea
CYNURIA
Troezen
Cythnos
Syros
Eurotas
Hydrea
Seriphos
Prasiae
MESSENIA
Pharae
SPARTA
Pylus
LACONIA
Siphnos
Methone
Zarax
Epidaurus Limera
Melos
C. Acritas
Pholegandros
C. Malea
C. Taenarum
0 50 Miles
Cythera
© Arthur Banks 1972
c.700 B.C., under Lycurgus, Sparta became an entirely military society. Its army dominated the whole area of the Peloponnese, being noted for its iron discipline, unit manœuvrability, and higher organization.
c.560 - 500 B.C., the city state of Athens rose to challenge the supremacy of Sparta. Occupied by Spartans, Athens expelled them in 507 B.C.
ANCIENT CRETE
0 40 Miles
Cydonia
Rhithymna
Cnossus
Mallia
Lappa
MT. IDA
Gortyna
Phaestus
Myrtos
Hierapytna

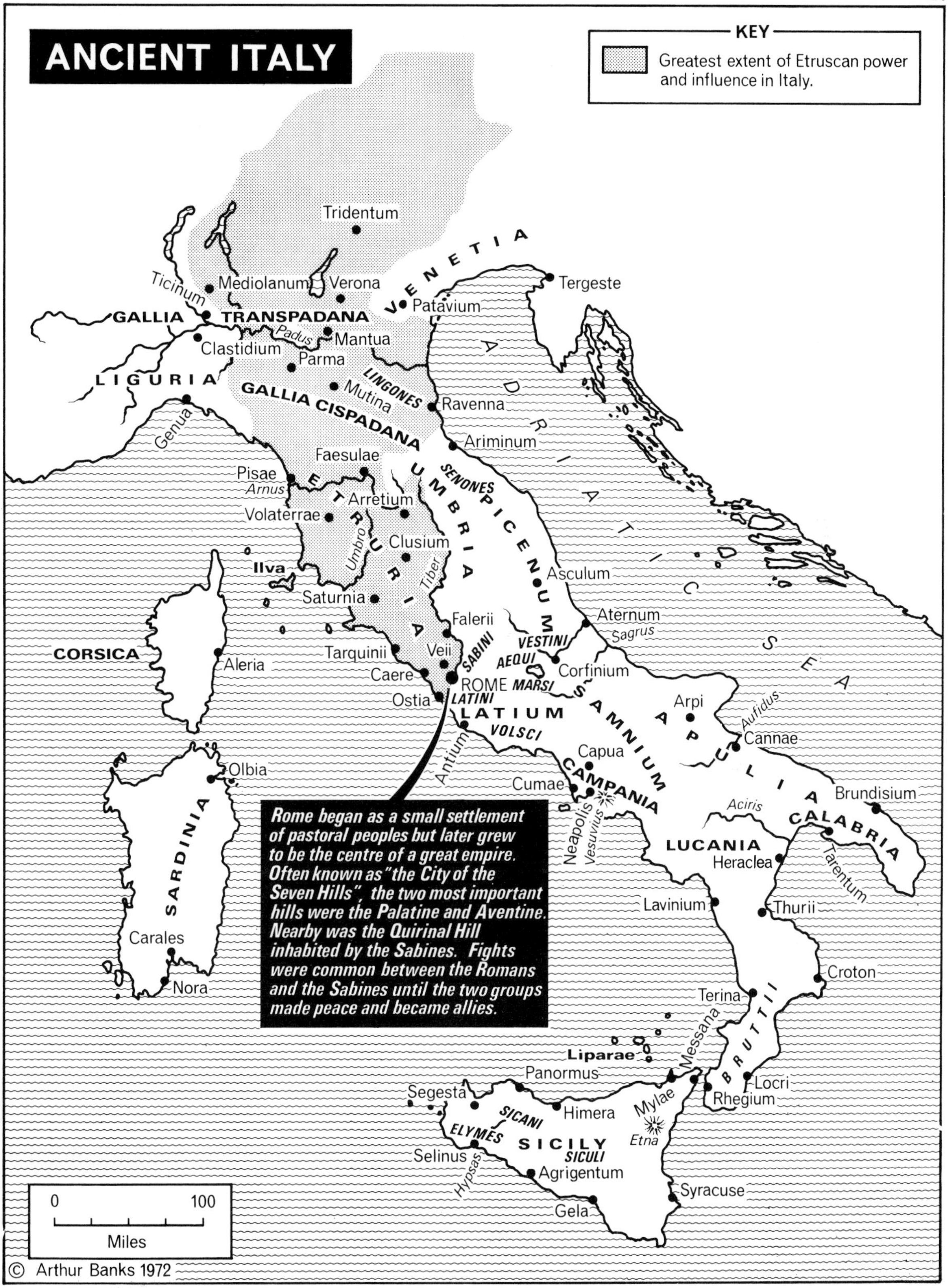
ANCIENT ITALY
KEY
Greatest extent of Etruscan power and influence in Italy.
Rome began as a small settlement of pastoral peoples but later grew to be the centre of a great empire. Often known as "the City of the Seven Hills", the two most important hills were the Palatine and Aventine. Nearby was the Quirinal Hill inhabited by the Sabines. Fights were common between the Romans and the Sabines until the two groups made peace and became allies.
Tridentum
VENETIA
Tergeste
Patavium
Verona
Mediolanum
Ticinum
GALLIA
TRANSPADANA
Padus
Mantua
Clastidium
Parma
LIGURIA
LINGONES
Mutina
GALLIA CISPADANA
Ravenna
Genua
Ariminum
Faesulae
Pisae
Arnus
ETRURIA
UMBRIA
SENONES
PICENUM
Arretium
Volaterrae
Umbro
Clusium
Tiber
Ilva
Asculum
Saturnia
ADRIATIC SEA
Aternum
Sagrus
Falerii
VESTINI
SABINI
CORSICA
Aleria
Tarquinii
Veii
AEQUI
Corfinium
Caere
ROME
MARSI
Ostia
LATINI
LATIUM
SAMNIUM
Arpi
APULIA
Aufidus
Cannae
VOLSCI
Antium
Capua
Olbia
CAMPANIA
Cumae
SARDINIA
Neapolis
Vesuvius
Brundisium
Aciris
CALABRIA
LUCANIA
Heraclea
Tarentum
Lavinium
Thurii
Carales
Nora
Croton
Terina
BRUTTII
Messana
Liparae
Panormus
Locri
Rhegium
Segesta
Mylae
SICANI
Himera
ELYMES
SICILY
SICULI
Etna
Selinus
Hypsas
Agrigentum
Syracuse
Gela
0
100
Miles
© Arthur Banks 1972

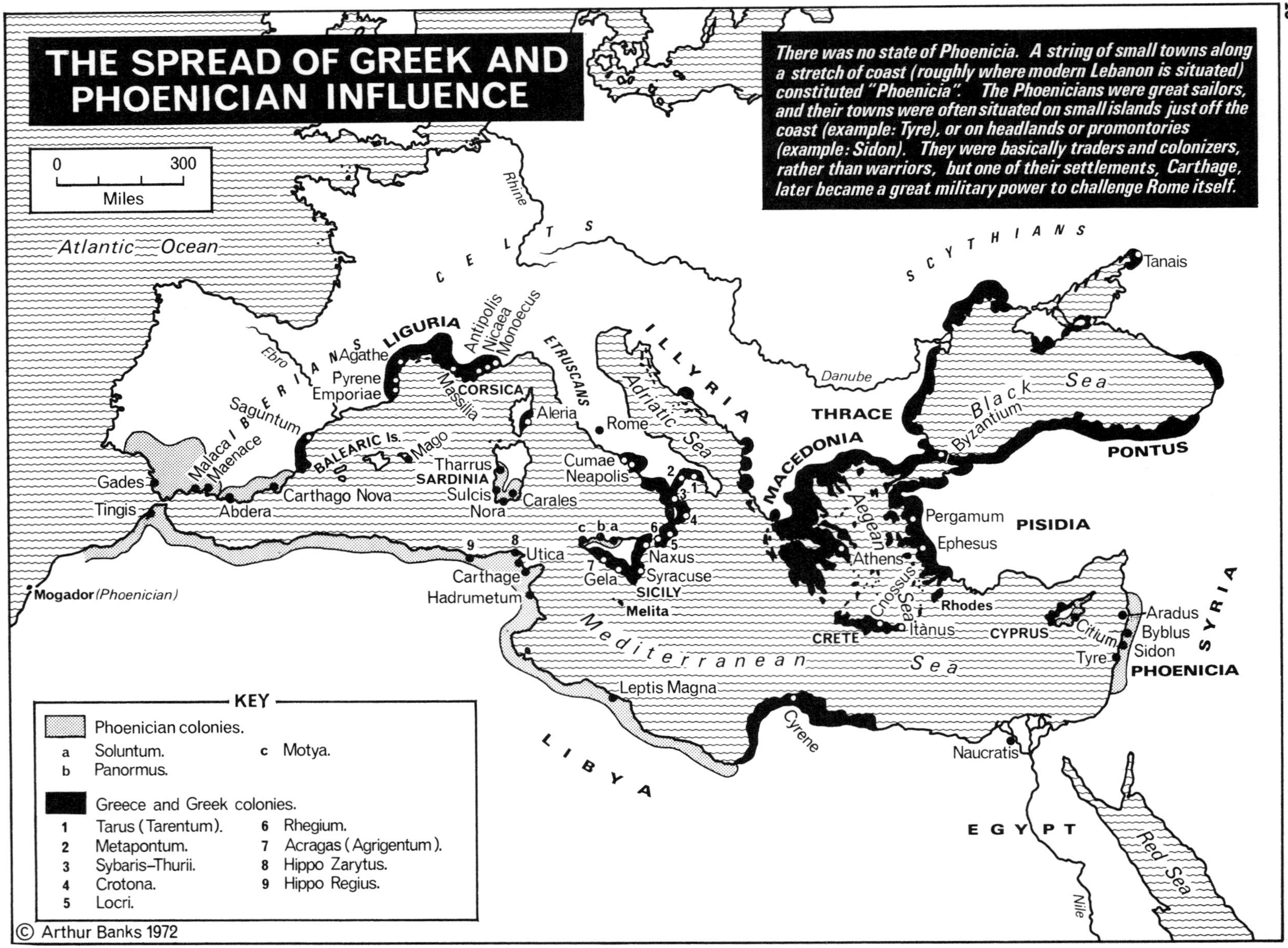
THE SPREAD OF GREEK AND PHOENICIAN INFLUENCE
There was no state of Phoenicia. A string of small towns along a stretch of coast (roughly where modern Lebanon is situated) constituted "Phoenicia". The Phoenicians were great sailors, and their towns were often situated on small islands just off the coast (example: Tyre), or on headlands or promontories (example: Sidon). They were basically traders and colonizers, rather than warriors, but one of their settlements, Carthage, later became a great military power to challenge Rome itself.
0 300
Miles
Atlantic Ocean
CELTS
SCYTHIANS
Rhine
Danube
Ebro
IBERIANS
Agathe
Pyrene
Emporiae
Saguntum
Malaca
Maenace
Gades
Tingis
Abdera
Carthago Nova
BALEARIC Is.
Mago
LIGURIA
Massilia
Antipolis
Nicaea
Monoecus
CORSICA
Aleria
ETRUSCANS
SARDINIA
Tharrus
Sulcis
Nora
Carales
Rome
Cumae
Neapolis
ILLYRIA
Adriatic Sea
THRACE
MACEDONIA
Black Sea
Byzantium
PONTUS
Tanais
Aegean Sea
Athens
Pergamum
Ephesus
PISIDIA
Rhodes
Cnossus
Itànus
CRETE
CYPRUS
Citium
Aradus
Byblus
Sidon
Tyre
SYRIA
PHOENICIA
SICILY
Naxus
Syracuse
Gela
Melita
Utica
Carthage
Hadrumetum
Mogador (Phoenician)
Mediterranean Sea
Leptis Magna
Cyrene
LIBYA
Naucratis
EGYPT
Nile
Red Sea
KEY
Phoenician colonies.
a Soluntum.
b Panormus.
c Motya.
Greece and Greek colonies.
1 Tarus (Tarentum).
2 Metapontum.
3 Sybaris–Thurii.
4 Crotona.
5 Locri.
6 Rhegium.
7 Acragas (Agrigentum).
8 Hippo Zarytus.
9 Hippo Regius.
© Arthur Banks 1972

THE ASSYRIAN SUPREMACY

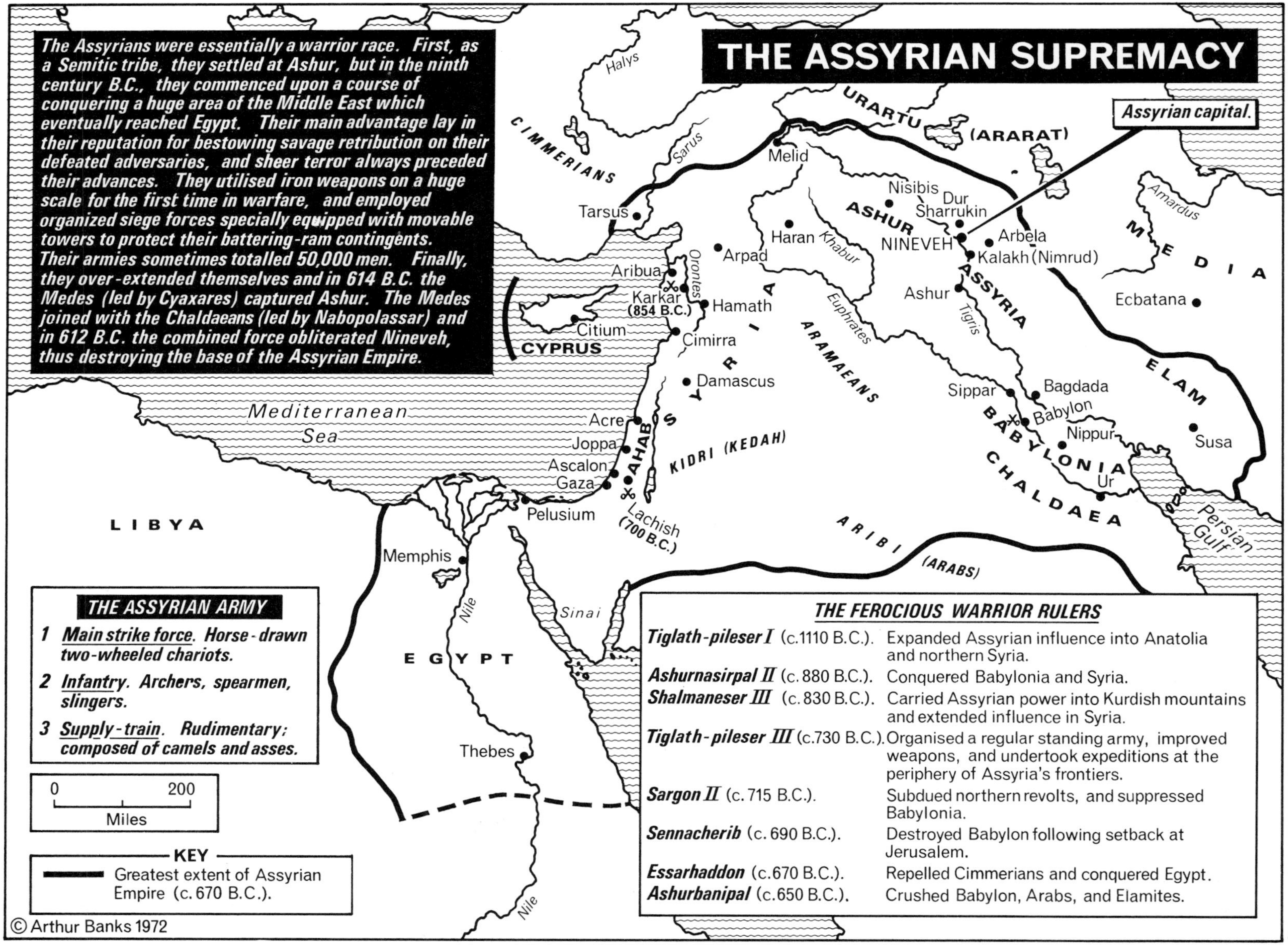

The Assyrians were essentially a warrior race. First, as a Semitic tribe, they settled at Ashur, but in the ninth century B.C., they commenced upon a course of conquering a huge area of the Middle East which eventually reached Egypt. Their main advantage lay in their reputation for bestowing savage retribution on their defeated adversaries, and sheer terror always preceded their advances. They utilised iron weapons on a huge scale for the first time in warfare, and employed organized siege forces specially equipped with movable towers to protect their battering-ram contingents. Their armies sometimes totalled 50,000 men. Finally, they over-extended themselves and in 614 B.C. the Medes (led by Cyaxares) captured Ashur. The Medes joined with the Chaldaeans (led by Nabopolassar) and in 612 B.C. the combined force obliterated Nineveh, thus destroying the base of the Assyrian Empire.

THE ASSYRIAN ARMY

1. ***Main strike force.*** *Horse-drawn two-wheeled chariots.*
2. ***Infantry.*** *Archers, spearmen, slingers.*
3. ***Supply-train.*** *Rudimentary; composed of camels and asses.*

THE FEROCIOUS WARRIOR RULERS

Tiglath-pileser I (c.1110 B.C.).	Expanded Assyrian influence into Anatolia and northern Syria.
Ashurnasirpal II (c. 880 B.C.).	Conquered Babylonia and Syria.
Shalmaneser III (c. 830 B.C.).	Carried Assyrian power into Kurdish mountains and extended influence in Syria.
Tiglath-pileser III (c.730 B.C.).	Organised a regular standing army, improved weapons, and undertook expeditions at the periphery of Assyria's frontiers.
Sargon II (c. 715 B.C.).	Subdued northern revolts, and suppressed Babylonia.
Sennacherib (c. 690 B.C.).	Destroyed Babylon following setback at Jerusalem.
Essarhaddon (c.670 B.C.).	Repelled Cimmerians and conquered Egypt.
Ashurbanipal (c.650 B.C.).	Crushed Babylon, Arabs, and Elamites.

THE EMPIRES OF CHALDAEA, MEDIA, AND LYDIA

CHALDAEANS

c.1500 - 700 B.C., a Semitic desert people infiltrated Babylonia. c.612 B.C., following the overthrow of Assyria, the Chaldaeans dominated all of previous Assyria west of the Tigris. c.612 B.C., Nabopolassar defeated the Egyptian pharaoh Necho II at Carchemish. c.600 B.C., Nebuchadnezzar conquered Syria, Palestine, and Phoenicia, but failed to take Tyre.

MEDIANS

c.800 - 625 B.C., descendants of Asiatic Scythians occupied present-day Persia (Iran). c.625 - 593 B.C., Cyaxares joined with Nabopolassar (of Chaldaea) to overthrow Assyria, and expanded his empire in the east, almost to the river Indus. A war with Lydia (c.600 - 580 B.C.) ended in the establishment of the river Halys as a frontier line.

LYDIANS

The kingdom of Phrygia was destroyed c.676 by the Cimmerians (migrating barbarians), who were driven south by the horse-archer Scythians. Lydia was a successor-state; it drove out the Cimmerians and destroyed Smyrna. c.678 - 648 B.C., Gyges founded the Lydian military dynasty. c.585 - 560 B.C., Lydia shared an uneasy balance of power with Chaldaea, Media, Egypt, and Persia. c.546 B.C., Cyrus (of Persia) defeated Croesus (of Lydia) at the Battle of Thymbra and captured Sardis.

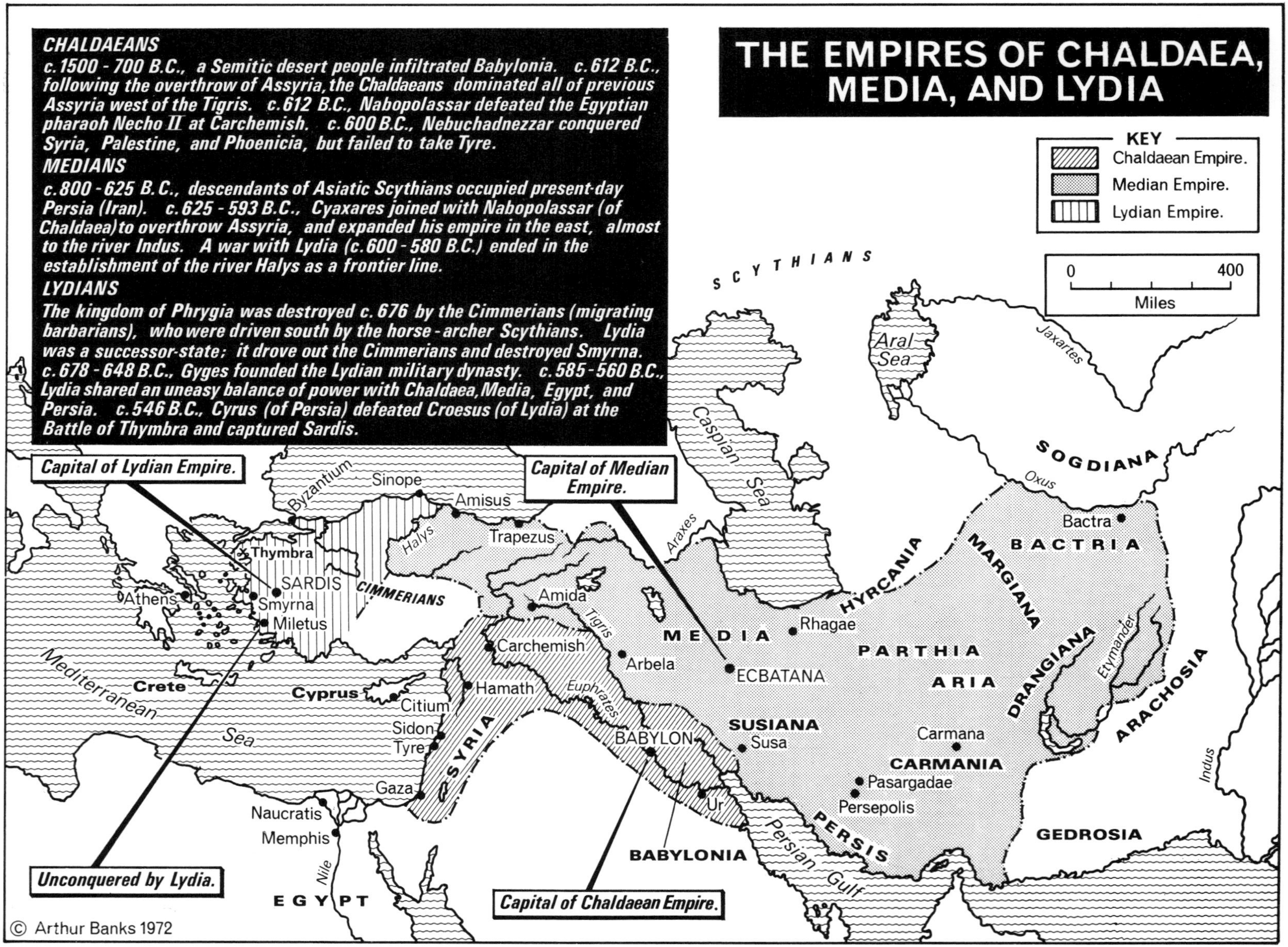

THE PERSIAN EMPIRE

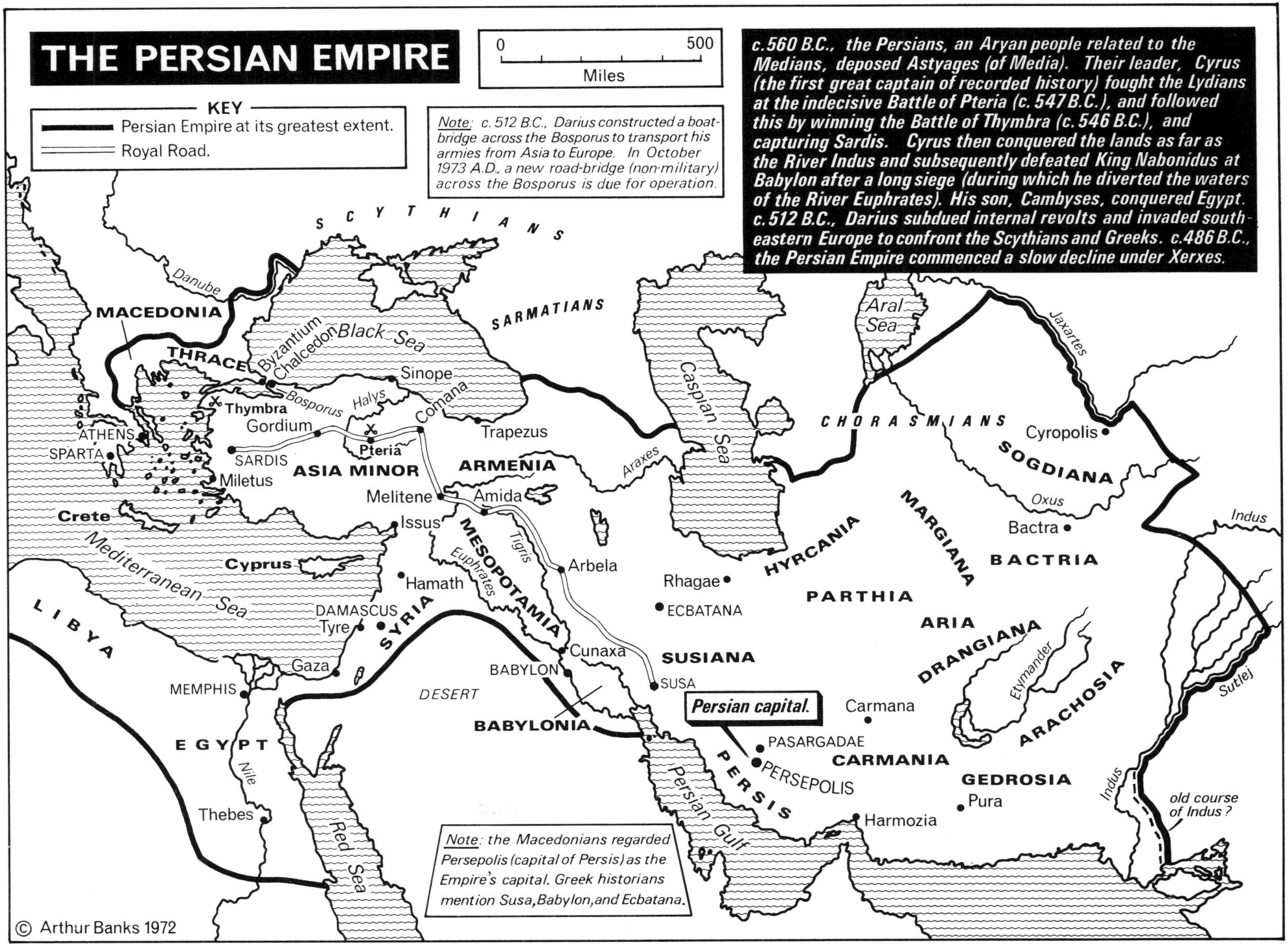

Note: c. 512 B.C., Darius constructed a boat-bridge across the Bosporus to transport his armies from Asia to Europe. In October 1973 A.D., a new road-bridge (non-military) across the Bosporus is due for operation.

c.560 B.C., the Persians, an Aryan people related to the Medians, deposed Astyages (of Media). Their leader, Cyrus (the first great captain of recorded history) fought the Lydians at the indecisive Battle of Pteria (c. 547 B.C.), and followed this by winning the Battle of Thymbra (c. 546 B.C.), and capturing Sardis. Cyrus then conquered the lands as far as the River Indus and subsequently defeated King Nabonidus at Babylon after a long siege (during which he diverted the waters of the River Euphrates). His son, Cambyses, conquered Egypt. c.512 B.C., Darius subdued internal revolts and invaded south-eastern Europe to confront the Scythians and Greeks. c.486 B.C., the Persian Empire commenced a slow decline under Xerxes.

Note: the Macedonians regarded Persepolis (capital of Persis) as the Empire's capital. Greek historians mention Susa, Babylon, and Ecbatana.

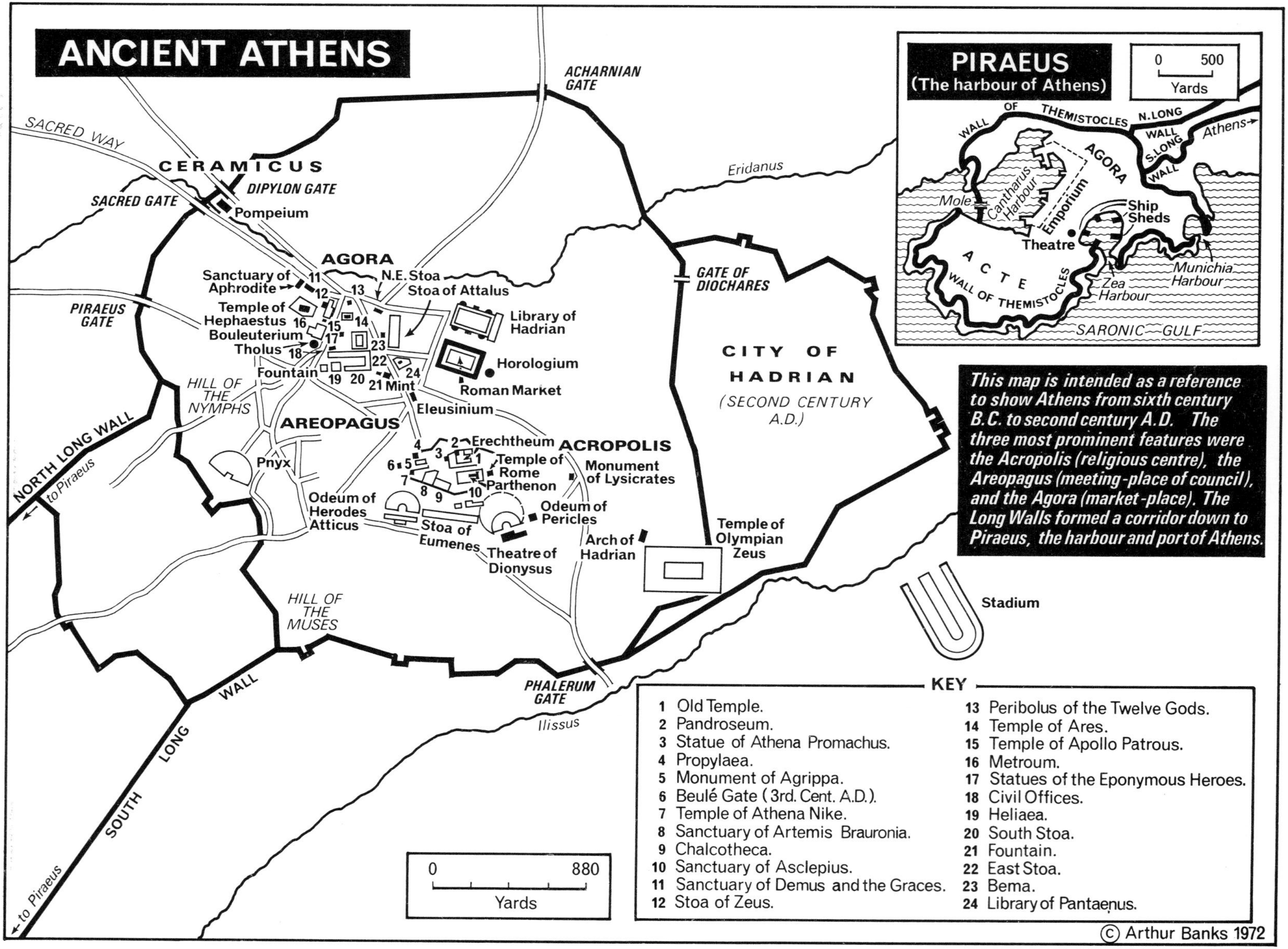
ANCIENT ATHENS
SACRED WAY
CERAMICUS
DIPYLON GATE
SACRED GATE
Pompeium
ACHARNIAN GATE
Eridanus
AGORA
Sanctuary of Aphrodite
N.E. Stoa
Stoa of Attalus
PIRAEUS GATE
Temple of Hephaestus
Bouleuterium
Tholus
Library of Hadrian
Horologium
Roman Market
Fountain
Mint
HILL OF THE NYMPHS
Eleusinium
AREOPAGUS
Erechtheum
ACROPOLIS
Temple of Rome
Parthenon
Monument of Lysicrates
Pnyx
Odeum of Herodes Atticus
Stoa of Eumenes
Theatre of Dionysus
Odeum of Pericles
Arch of Hadrian
NORTH LONG WALL
to Piraeus
GATE OF DIOCHARES
CITY OF HADRIAN
(SECOND CENTURY A.D.)
Temple of Olympian Zeus
Stadium
HILL OF THE MUSES
PHALERUM GATE
Ilissus
SOUTH LONG WALL
to Piraeus
0 880
Yards
PIRAEUS
(The harbour of Athens)
0 500
Yards
WALL OF THEMISTOCLES
N. LONG WALL
S. LONG WALL
Athens
AGORA
Mole
Cantharus Harbour
Emporium
Ship Sheds
Theatre
ACTE
WALL OF THEMISTOCLES
Zea Harbour
Munichia Harbour
SARONIC GULF
This map is intended as a reference to show Athens from sixth century B.C. to second century A.D. The three most prominent features were the Acropolis (religious centre), the Areopagus (meeting-place of council), and the Agora (market-place). The Long Walls formed a corridor down to Piraeus, the harbour and port of Athens.
KEY
1 Old Temple.
2 Pandroseum.
3 Statue of Athena Promachus.
4 Propylaea.
5 Monument of Agrippa.
6 Beulé Gate (3rd. Cent. A.D.).
7 Temple of Athena Nike.
8 Sanctuary of Artemis Brauronia.
9 Chalcotheca.
10 Sanctuary of Asclepius.
11 Sanctuary of Demus and the Graces.
12 Stoa of Zeus.
13 Peribolus of the Twelve Gods.
14 Temple of Ares.
15 Temple of Apollo Patrous.
16 Metroum.
17 Statues of the Eponymous Heroes.
18 Civil Offices.
19 Heliaea.
20 South Stoa.
21 Fountain.
22 East Stoa.
23 Bema.
24 Library of Pantaenus.
© Arthur Banks 1972

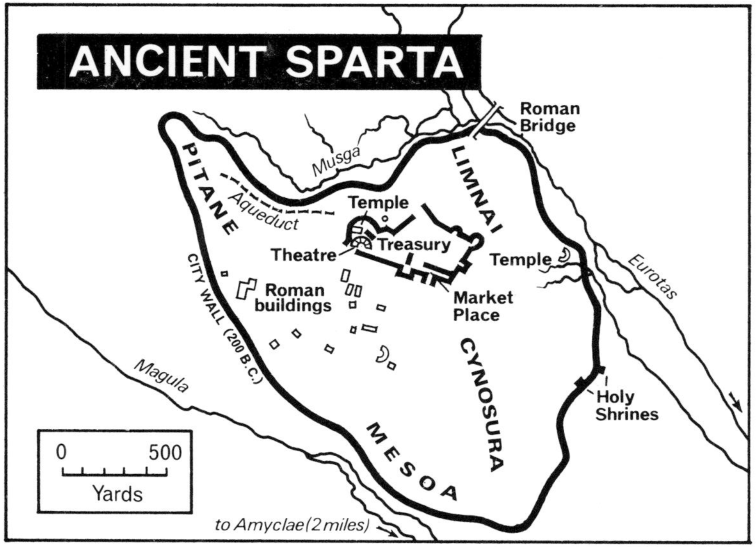
ANCIENT SPARTA
Roman Bridge
PITANE
LIMNAI
Musga
Aqueduct
Temple
Treasury
Theatre
Temple
Roman buildings
Market Place
CITY WALL (200 B.C.)
CYNOSURA
Eurotas
Magula
MESOA
Holy Shrines
0 500 Yards
to Amyclae (2 miles)

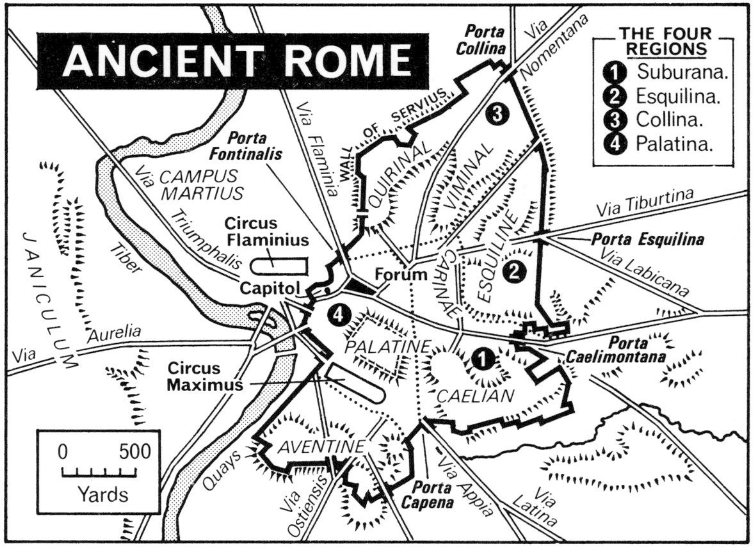
ANCIENT ROME
Porta Collina
Via Nomentana
THE FOUR REGIONS
1 Suburana.
2 Esquilina.
3 Collina.
4 Palatina.
WALL OF SERVIUS
Via Flaminia
Porta Fontinalis
Via CAMPUS MARTIUS
Triumphalis
QUIRINAL
VIMINAL
ESQUILINE
Circus Flaminius
Via Tiburtina
Porta Esquilina
Via Labicana
JANICULUM
Tiber
Capitol
Forum
CARINAE
Via Aurelia
PALATINE
Porta Caelimontana
Circus Maximus
CAELIAN
AVENTINE
Quays
Via Ostiensis
Porta Capena
Via Appia
Via Latina
0 500 Yards

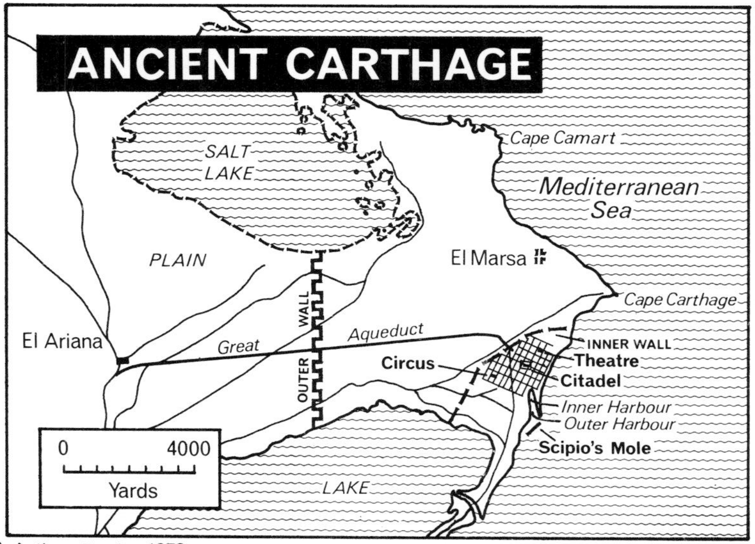
ANCIENT CARTHAGE
SALT LAKE
Cape Camart
Mediterranean Sea
PLAIN
El Marsa
OUTER WALL
Cape Carthage
El Ariana
Great Aqueduct
INNER WALL
Circus
Theatre
Citadel
Inner Harbour
Outer Harbour
Scipio's Mole
0 4000 Yards
LAKE

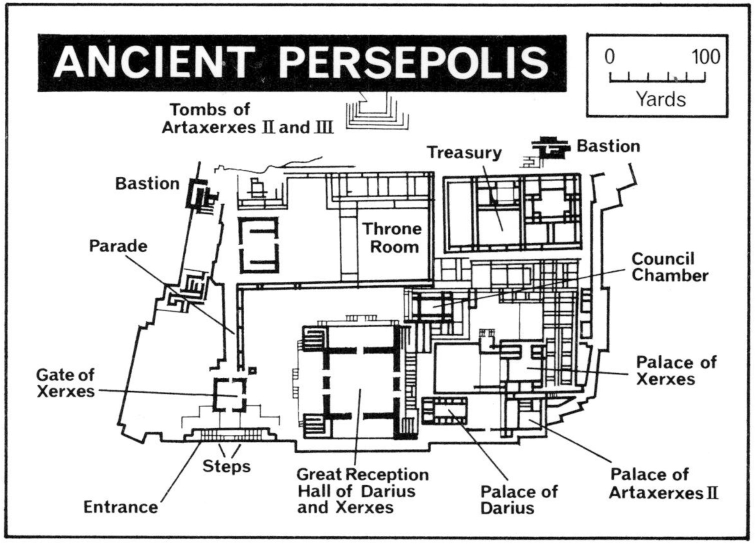
ANCIENT PERSEPOLIS
0 100 Yards
Tombs of Artaxerxes II and III
Treasury
Bastion
Bastion
Throne Room
Parade
Council Chamber
Gate of Xerxes
Palace of Xerxes
Steps
Great Reception Hall of Darius and Xerxes
Palace of Darius
Palace of Artaxerxes II
Entrance

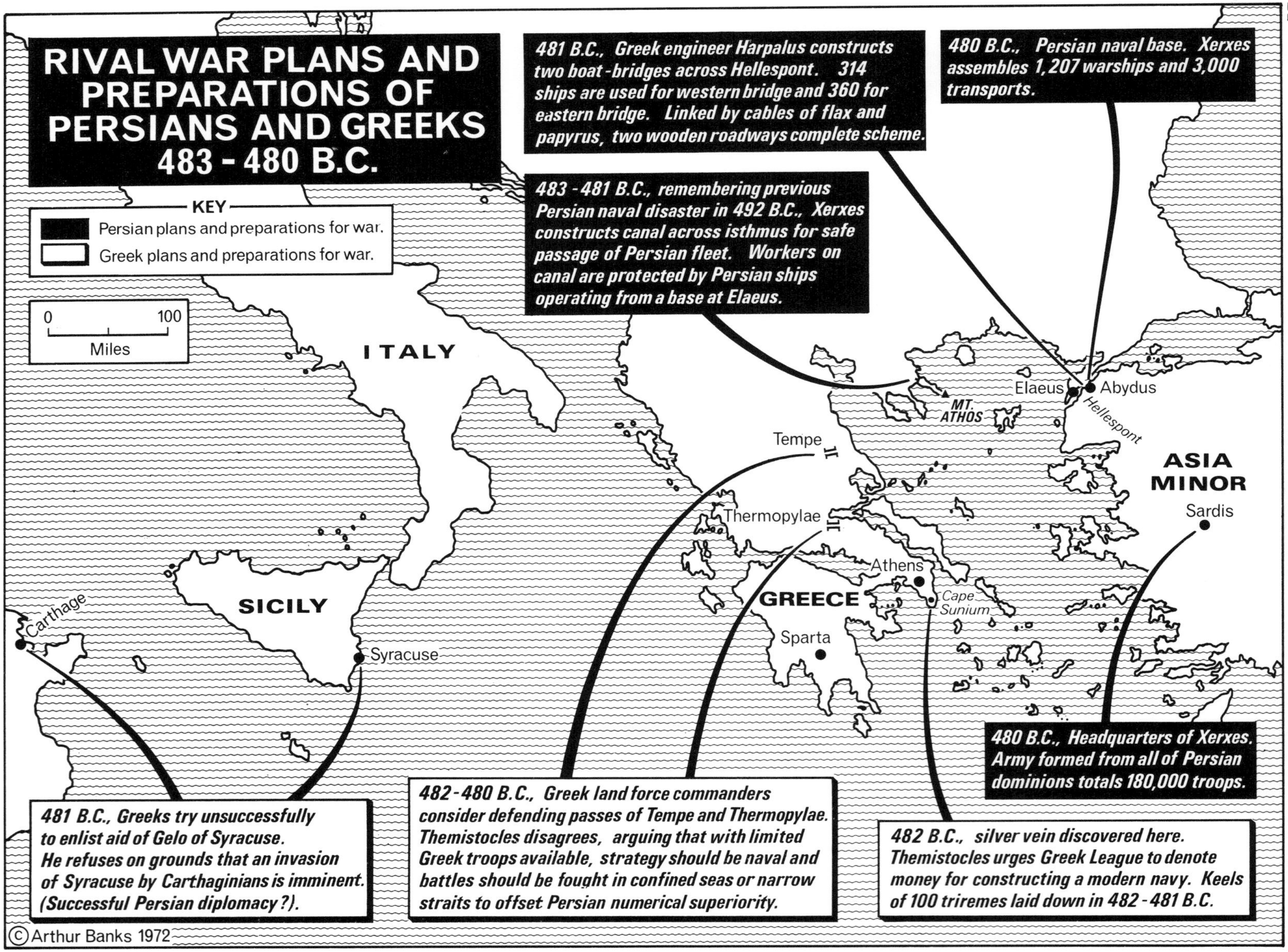
RIVAL WAR PLANS AND PREPARATIONS OF PERSIANS AND GREEKS 483 - 480 B.C.
KEY
Persian plans and preparations for war.
Greek plans and preparations for war.
0
100
Miles
481 B.C., Greek engineer Harpalus constructs two boat-bridges across Hellespont. 314 ships are used for western bridge and 360 for eastern bridge. Linked by cables of flax and papyrus, two wooden roadways complete scheme.
480 B.C., Persian naval base. Xerxes assembles 1,207 warships and 3,000 transports.
483 - 481 B.C., remembering previous Persian naval disaster in 492 B.C., Xerxes constructs canal across isthmus for safe passage of Persian fleet. Workers on canal are protected by Persian ships operating from a base at Elaeus.
ITALY
SICILY
GREECE
ASIA MINOR
Carthage
Syracuse
Tempe
Thermopylae
Athens
Sparta
Cape Sunium
MT. ATHOS
Elaeus
Abydus
Hellespont
Sardis
480 B.C., Headquarters of Xerxes. Army formed from all of Persian dominions totals 180,000 troops.
481 B.C., Greeks try unsuccessfully to enlist aid of Gelo of Syracuse. He refuses on grounds that an invasion of Syracuse by Carthaginians is imminent. (Successful Persian diplomacy?).
482 - 480 B.C., Greek land force commanders consider defending passes of Tempe and Thermopylae. Themistocles disagrees, arguing that with limited Greek troops available, strategy should be naval and battles should be fought in confined seas or narrow straits to offset Persian numerical superiority.
482 B.C., silver vein discovered here. Themistocles urges Greek League to denote money for constructing a modern navy. Keels of 100 triremes laid down in 482 - 481 B.C.
© Arthur Banks 1972

PERSIAN MILITARY AND NAVAL EXPEDITIONS AGAINST GREECE

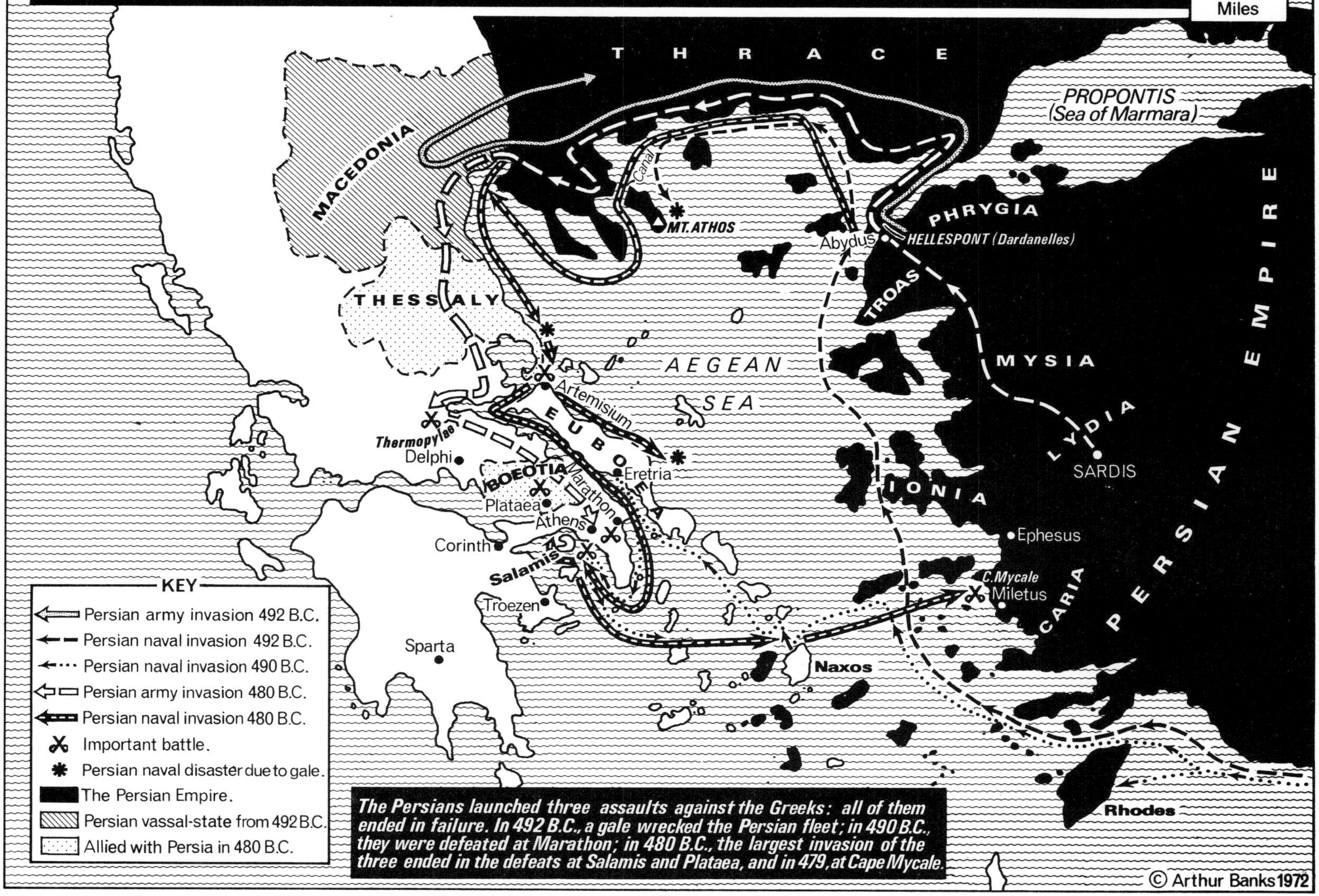
0 30
Miles
THRACE
PROPONTIS
(Sea of Marmara)
MACEDONIA
MT. ATHOS
Canal
PHRYGIA
Abydus
HELLESPONT (Dardanelles)
TROAS
THESSALY
AEGEAN
SEA
MYSIA
LYDIA
SARDIS
PERSIAN EMPIRE
Artemisium
EUBOEA
Eretria
Thermopylae
Delphi
BOEOTIA
Marathon
Plataea
Athens
Corinth
Salamis
Troezen
Sparta
IONIA
Ephesus
C. Mycale
Miletus
CARIA
Naxos
Rhodes
KEY
Persian army invasion 492 B.C.
Persian naval invasion 492 B.C.
Persian naval invasion 490 B.C.
Persian army invasion 480 B.C.
Persian naval invasion 480 B.C.
Important battle.
Persian naval disaster due to gale.
The Persian Empire.
Persian vassal-state from 492 B.C.
Allied with Persia in 480 B.C.
The Persians launched three assaults against the Greeks: all of them ended in failure. In 492 B.C., a gale wrecked the Persian fleet; in 490 B.C., they were defeated at Marathon; in 480 B.C., the largest invasion of the three ended in the defeats at Salamis and Plataea, and in 479, at Cape Mycale.

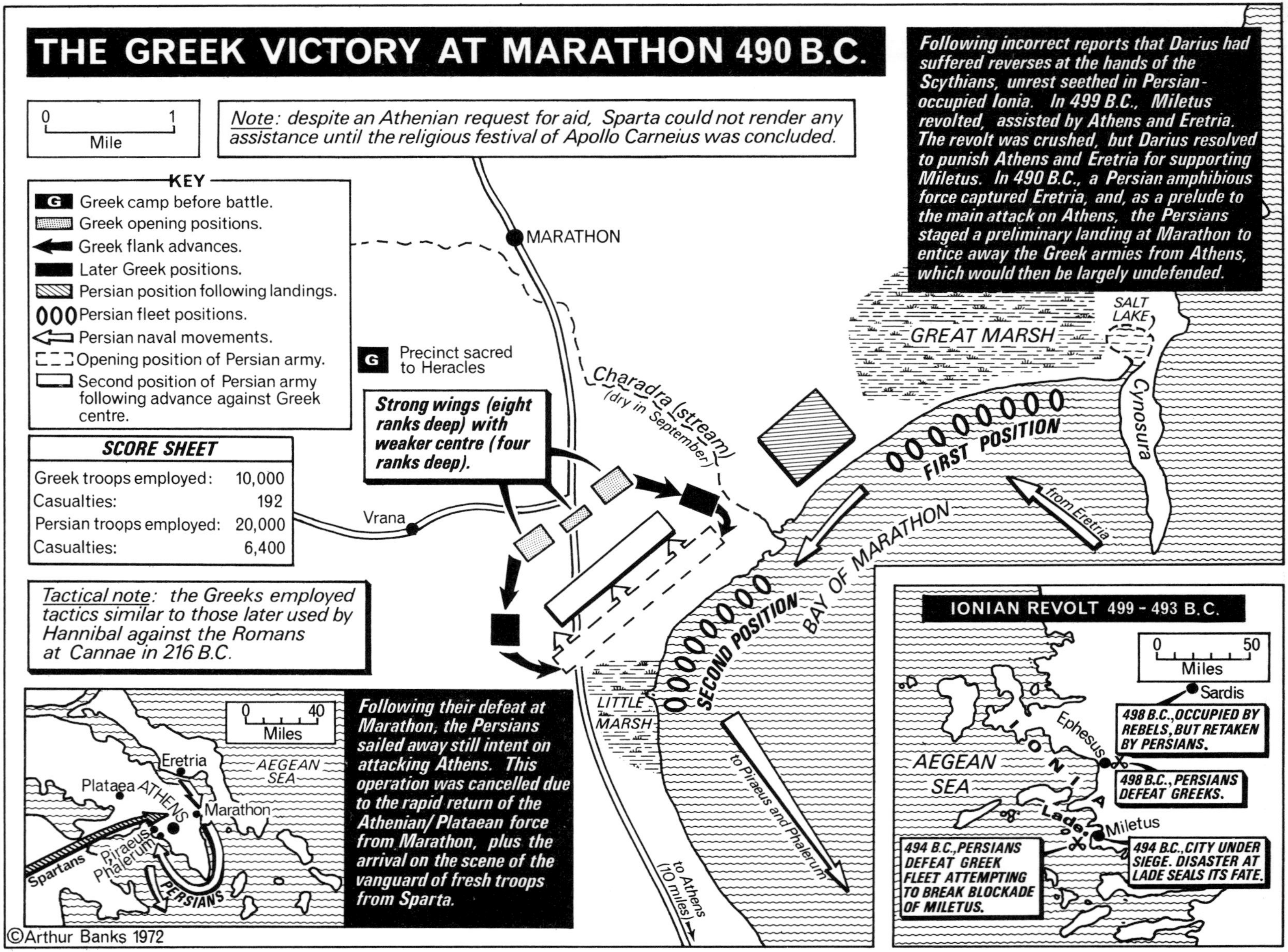
THE GREEK VICTORY AT MARATHON 490 B.C.
0 1 Mile
Note: despite an Athenian request for aid, Sparta could not render any assistance until the religious festival of Apollo Carneius was concluded.
KEY
G Greek camp before battle.
Greek opening positions.
Greek flank advances.
Later Greek positions.
Persian position following landings.
000 Persian fleet positions.
Persian naval movements.
Opening position of Persian army.
Second position of Persian army following advance against Greek centre.
SCORE SHEET
Greek troops employed: 10,000
Casualties: 192
Persian troops employed: 20,000
Casualties: 6,400
Tactical note: the Greeks employed tactics similar to those later used by Hannibal against the Romans at Cannae in 216 B.C.
MARATHON
G Precinct sacred to Heracles
Strong wings (eight ranks deep) with weaker centre (four ranks deep).
Vrana
Charadra (stream) (dry in September)
Following incorrect reports that Darius had suffered reverses at the hands of the Scythians, unrest seethed in Persian-occupied Ionia. In 499 B.C., Miletus revolted, assisted by Athens and Eretria. The revolt was crushed, but Darius resolved to punish Athens and Eretria for supporting Miletus. In 490 B.C., a Persian amphibious force captured Eretria, and, as a prelude to the main attack on Athens, the Persians staged a preliminary landing at Marathon to entice away the Greek armies from Athens, which would then be largely undefended.
SALT LAKE
GREAT MARSH
Cynosura
FIRST POSITION
from Eretria
BAY OF MARATHON
SECOND POSITION
LITTLE MARSH
to Piraeus and Phalerum
to Athens (10 miles)
0 40 Miles
Eretria
AEGEAN SEA
Plataea
ATHENS
Marathon
Spartans
Piraeus
Phalerum
PERSIANS
Following their defeat at Marathon, the Persians sailed away still intent on attacking Athens. This operation was cancelled due to the rapid return of the Athenian/Plataean force from Marathon, plus the arrival on the scene of the vanguard of fresh troops from Sparta.
IONIAN REVOLT 499 - 493 B.C.
0 50 Miles
Sardis
498 B.C., OCCUPIED BY REBELS, BUT RETAKEN BY PERSIANS.
Ephesus
IONIA
AEGEAN SEA
498 B.C., PERSIANS DEFEAT GREEKS.
Lade
Miletus
494 B.C., PERSIANS DEFEAT GREEK FLEET ATTEMPTING TO BREAK BLOCKADE OF MILETUS.
494 B.C., CITY UNDER SIEGE. DISASTER AT LADE SEALS ITS FATE.
©Arthur Banks 1972

GREEK EFFORTS TO STEM PERSIAN ADVANCE

In 480 B.C., Xerxes' expedition against Greece was within striking distance of Athens and the Isthmus of Corinth, and the Athenian-dominated Greek Congress decided to stage two simultaneous actions to the north to stem the Persian advance. The first, a naval battle fought off Artemisium, proved indecisive despite the occurrence of two storms which wrecked over 500 Persian warships. The second, a land battle at the narrow Pass of Thermopylae, ended in disaster despite an heroic stand by 7,000 Greek troops led by the Spartan, Leonidas. 20,000 Persians and 4,000 Greeks perished in the fight, the outcome of which was determined when 10,000 Persians outflanked the main Greek position by traversing a mountain track to attack Leonidas from the rear. The way to Athens was now unguarded and its citizens were hurriedly evacuated.

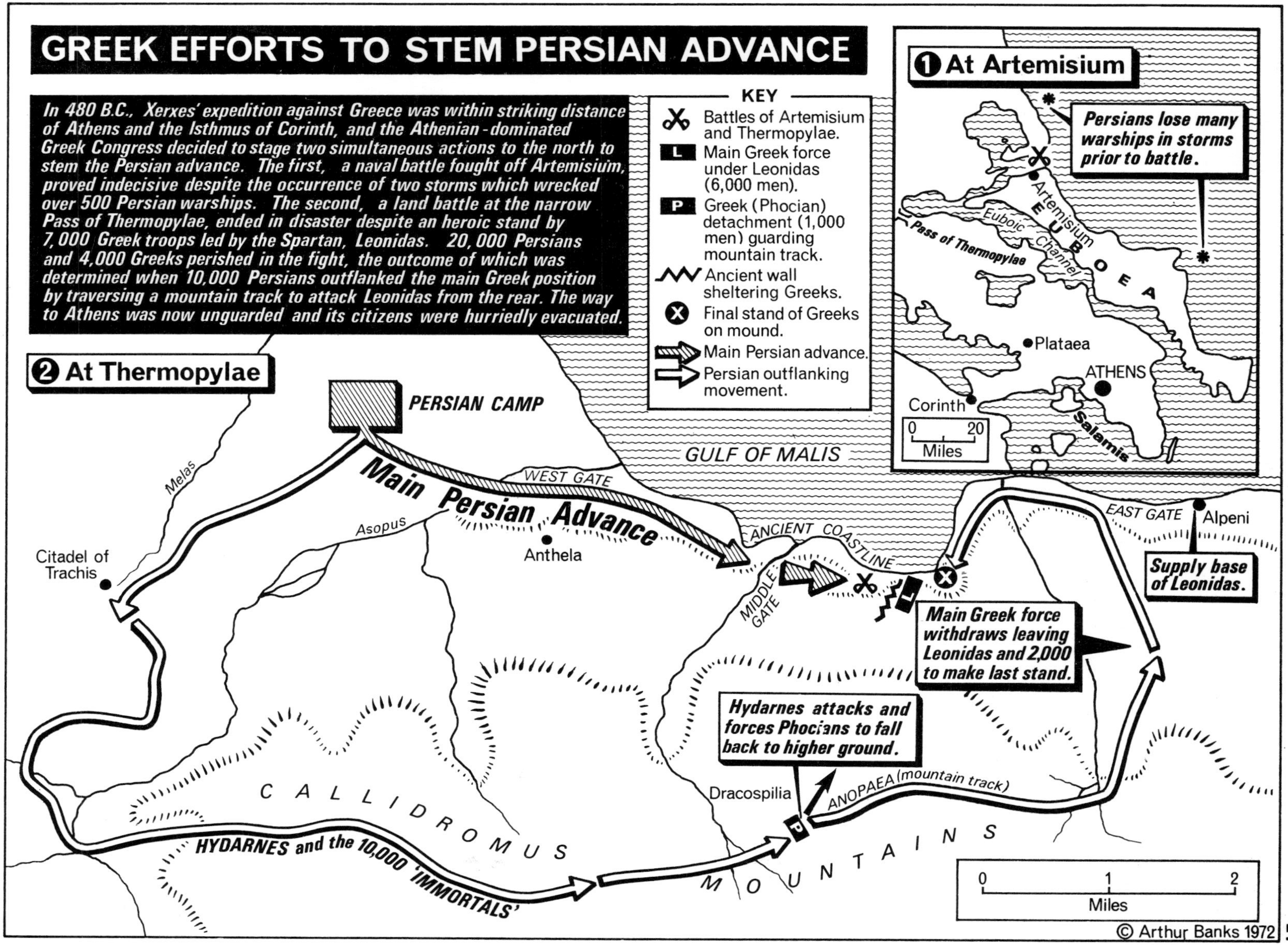

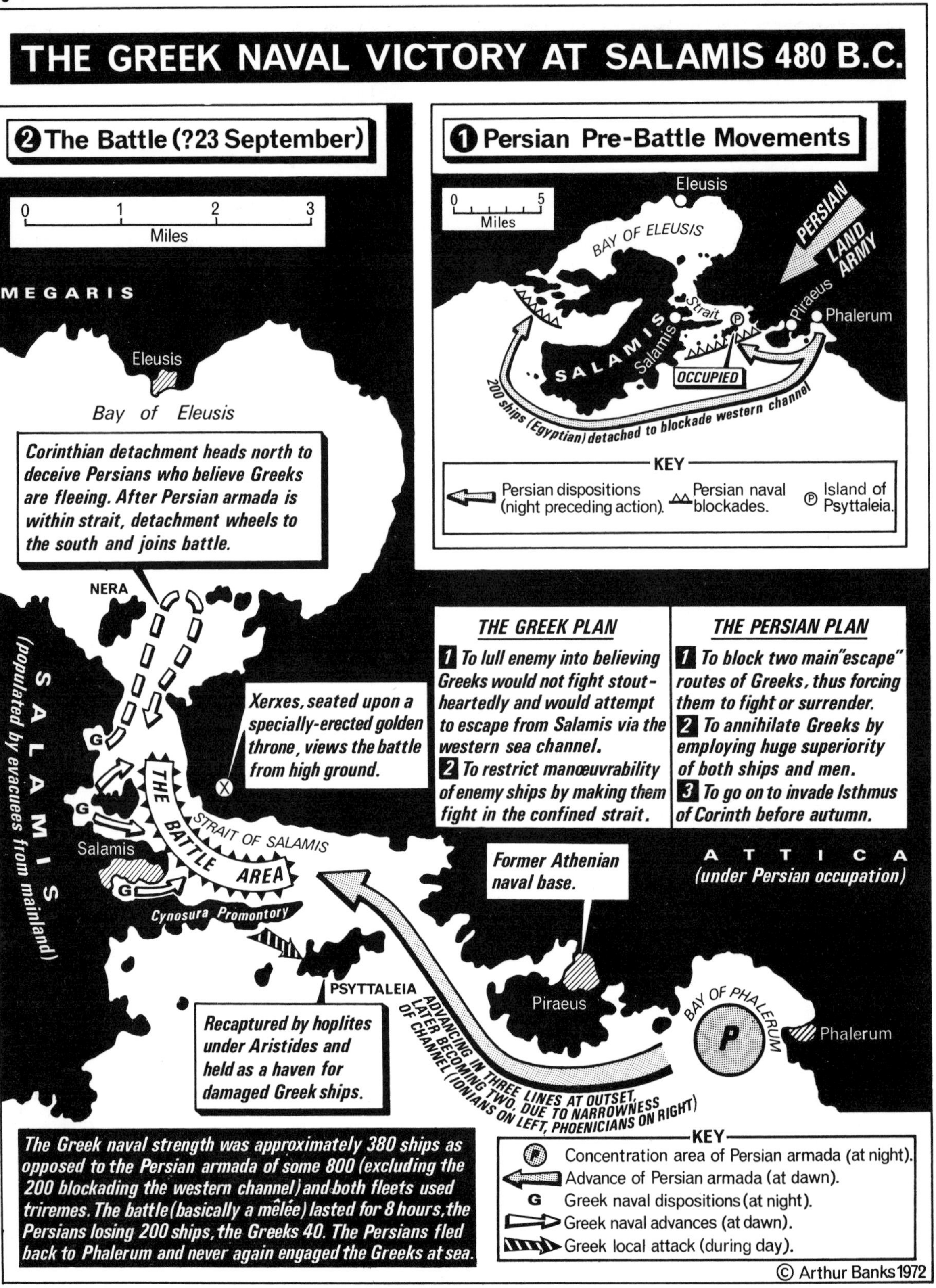
THE GREEK NAVAL VICTORY AT SALAMIS 480 B.C.
2 The Battle (?23 September)
0 1 2 3
Miles
MEGARIS
Eleusis
Bay of Eleusis
Corinthian detachment heads north to deceive Persians who believe Greeks are fleeing. After Persian armada is within strait, detachment wheels to the south and joins battle.
NERA
SALAMIS
(populated by evacuees from mainland)
G
G
Salamis
G
Xerxes, seated upon a specially-erected golden throne, views the battle from high ground.
THE BATTLE AREA
STRAIT OF SALAMIS
Cynosura Promontory
PSYTTALEIA
Recaptured by hoplites under Aristides and held as a haven for damaged Greek ships.
Former Athenian naval base.
Piraeus
ADVANCING IN THREE LINES AT OUTSET, LATER BECOMING TWO, DUE TO NARROWNESS OF CHANNEL (IONIANS ON LEFT, PHOENICIANS ON RIGHT)
BAY OF PHALERUM
P
Phalerum
ATTICA
(under Persian occupation)
1 Persian Pre-Battle Movements
0 5
Miles
Eleusis
BAY OF ELEUSIS
PERSIAN LAND ARMY
Strait
Piraeus
Phalerum
SALAMIS
Salamis
OCCUPIED
200 ships (Egyptian) detached to blockade western channel
KEY
Persian dispositions (night preceding action).
Persian naval blockades.
Ⓟ Island of Psyttaleia.
THE GREEK PLAN
1 To lull enemy into believing Greeks would not fight stout-heartedly and would attempt to escape from Salamis via the western sea channel.
2 To restrict manœuvrability of enemy ships by making them fight in the confined strait.
THE PERSIAN PLAN
1 To block two main "escape" routes of Greeks, thus forcing them to fight or surrender.
2 To annihilate Greeks by employing huge superiority of both ships and men.
3 To go on to invade Isthmus of Corinth before autumn.
The Greek naval strength was approximately 380 ships as opposed to the Persian armada of some 800 (excluding the 200 blockading the western channel) and both fleets used triremes. The battle (basically a mêlée) lasted for 8 hours, the Persians losing 200 ships, the Greeks 40. The Persians fled back to Phalerum and never again engaged the Greeks at sea.
KEY
Concentration area of Persian armada (at night).
Advance of Persian armada (at dawn).
G Greek naval dispositions (at night).
Greek naval advances (at dawn).
Greek local attack (during day).
© Arthur Banks 1972

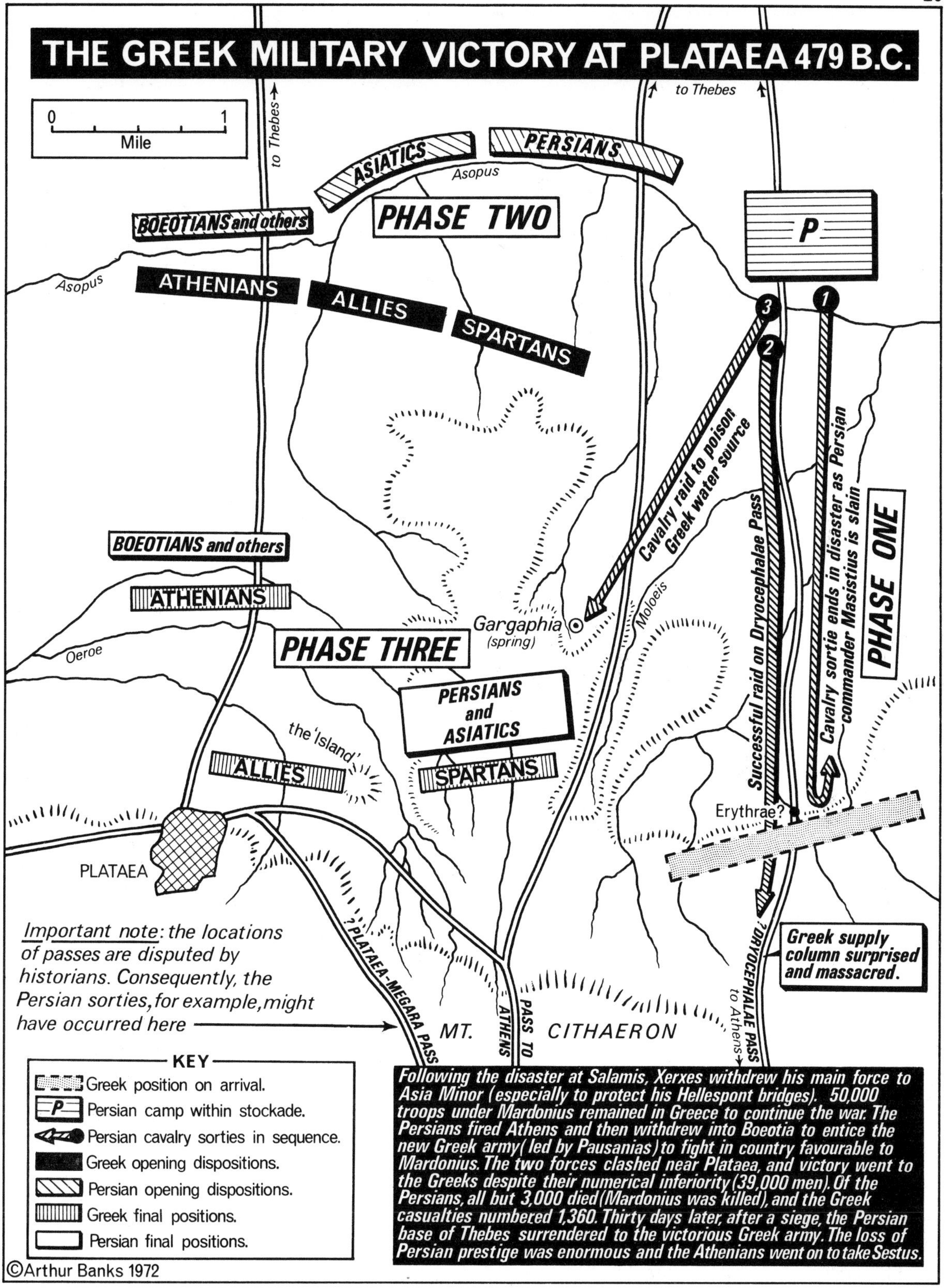
THE GREEK MILITARY VICTORY AT PLATAEA 479 B.C.
0 1
Mile
to Thebes
to Thebes
ASIATICS
PERSIANS
Asopus
PHASE TWO
P
BOEOTIANS and others
Asopus
ATHENIANS
ALLIES
SPARTANS
3
2
1
Cavalry raid to poison Greek water source
Successful raid on Dryocephalae Pass
Cavalry sortie ends in disaster as Persian commander Masistius is slain
PHASE ONE
BOEOTIANS and others
ATHENIANS
Oeroe
Gargaphia
(spring)
Moloeis
PHASE THREE
PERSIANS and ASIATICS
the 'Island'
ALLIES
SPARTANS
Erythrae?
PLATAEA
Greek supply column surprised and massacred.
Important note: the locations of passes are disputed by historians. Consequently, the Persian sorties, for example, might have occurred here
?PLATAEA-MEGARA PASS
MT. CITHAERON
PASS TO ATHENS
?DRYOCEPHALAE PASS
to Athens
KEY
Greek position on arrival.
Persian camp within stockade.
Persian cavalry sorties in sequence.
Greek opening dispositions.
Persian opening dispositions.
Greek final positions.
Persian final positions.
Following the disaster at Salamis, Xerxes withdrew his main force to Asia Minor (especially to protect his Hellespont bridges). 50,000 troops under Mardonius remained in Greece to continue the war. The Persians fired Athens and then withdrew into Boeotia to entice the new Greek army (led by Pausanias) to fight in country favourable to Mardonius. The two forces clashed near Plataea, and victory went to the Greeks despite their numerical inferiority (39,000 men). Of the Persians, all but 3,000 died (Mardonius was killed), and the Greek casualties numbered 1,360. Thirty days later, after a siege, the Persian base of Thebes surrendered to the victorious Greek army. The loss of Persian prestige was enormous and the Athenians went on to take Sestus.
©Arthur Banks 1972

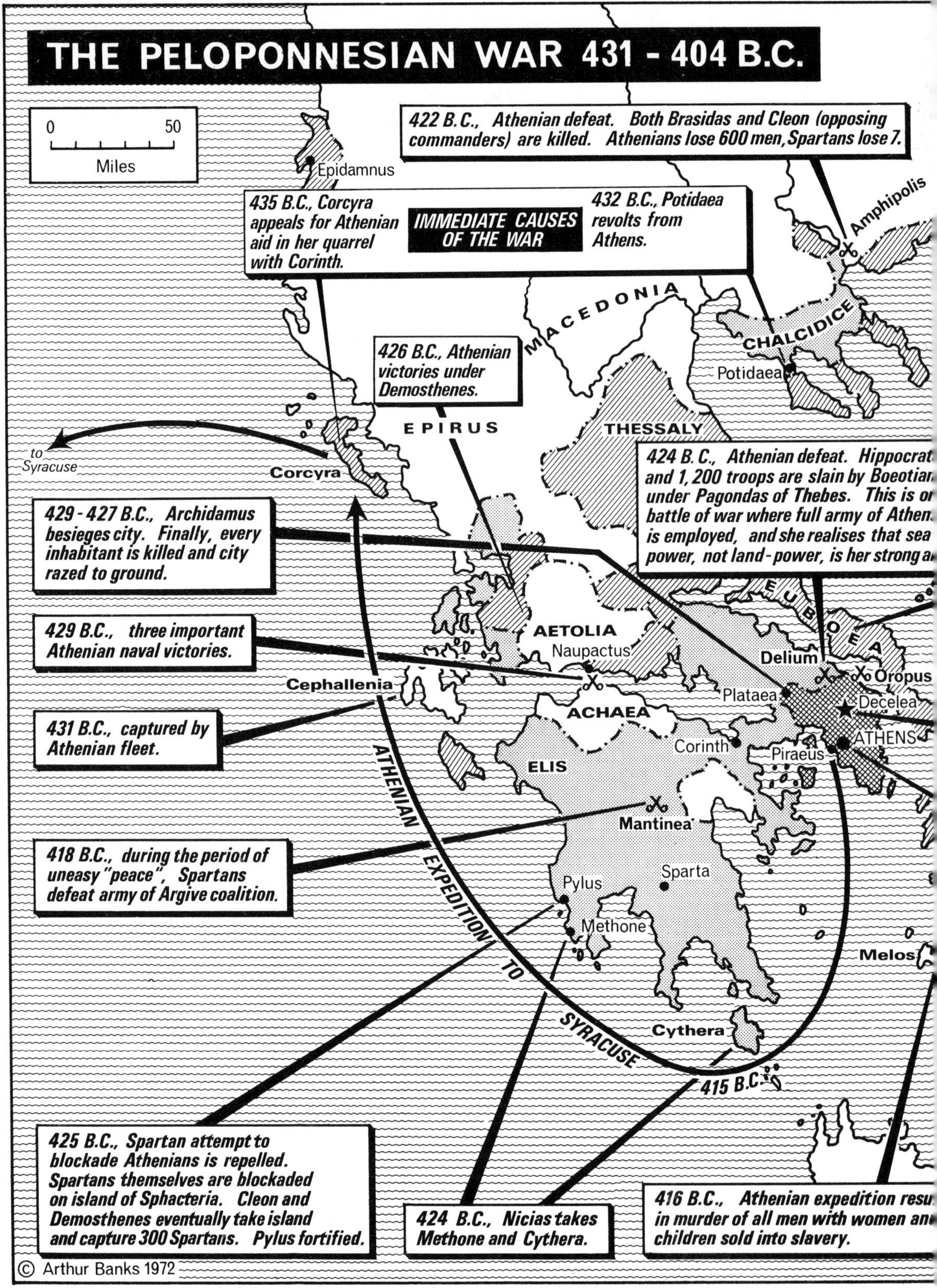
THE PELOPONNESIAN WAR 431 - 404 B.C.
0 50 Miles
422 B.C., Athenian defeat. Both Brasidas and Cleon (opposing commanders) are killed. Athenians lose 600 men, Spartans lose 7.
Epidamnus
435 B.C., Corcyra appeals for Athenian aid in her quarrel with Corinth.
IMMEDIATE CAUSES OF THE WAR
432 B.C., Potidaea revolts from Athens.
Amphipolis
MACEDONIA
CHALCIDICE
Potidaea
426 B.C., Athenian victories under Demosthenes.
EPIRUS
THESSALY
to Syracuse
Corcyra
424 B.C., Athenian defeat. Hippocrat
and 1,200 troops are slain by Boeotiar
under Pagondas of Thebes. This is o
battle of war where full army of Athen
is employed, and she realises that sea
power, not land-power, is her strong a
429 - 427 B.C., Archidamus besieges city. Finally, every inhabitant is killed and city razed to ground.
EUBOEA
AETOLIA
Naupactus
Delium
Oropus
429 B.C., three important Athenian naval victories.
Cephallenia
Plataea
Decelea
ACHAEA
ATHENS
431 B.C., captured by Athenian fleet.
Corinth
Piraeus
ELIS
Mantinea
ATHENIAN EXPEDITION TO SYRACUSE
418 B.C., during the period of uneasy "peace", Spartans defeat army of Argive coalition.
Sparta
Pylus
Methone
Melos
Cythera
415 B.C.
425 B.C., Spartan attempt to blockade Athenians is repelled. Spartans themselves are blockaded on island of Sphacteria. Cleon and Demosthenes eventually take island and capture 300 Spartans. Pylus fortified.
424 B.C., Nicias takes Methone and Cythera.
416 B.C., Athenian expedition resu
in murder of all men with women an
children sold into slavery.
© Arthur Banks 1972

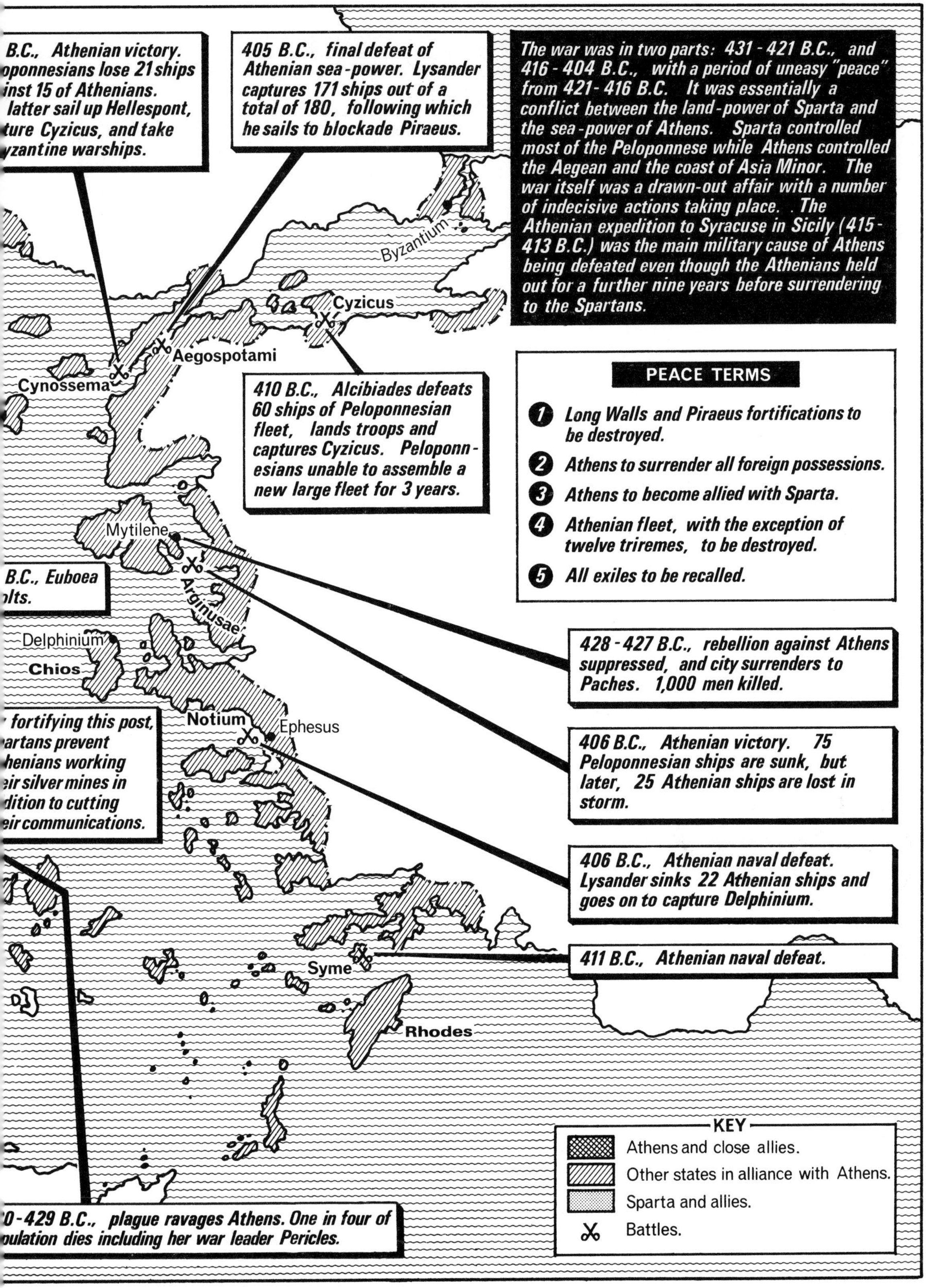
B.C., Athenian victory.
oponnesians lose 21 ships
inst 15 of Athenians.
latter sail up Hellespont,
ture Cyzicus, and take
yzantine warships.
405 B.C., final defeat of Athenian sea-power. Lysander captures 171 ships out of a total of 180, following which he sails to blockade Piraeus.
The war was in two parts: 431 - 421 B.C., and 416 - 404 B.C., with a period of uneasy "peace" from 421 - 416 B.C. It was essentially a conflict between the land-power of Sparta and the sea-power of Athens. Sparta controlled most of the Peloponnese while Athens controlled the Aegean and the coast of Asia Minor. The war itself was a drawn-out affair with a number of indecisive actions taking place. . The Athenian expedition to Syracuse in Sicily (415 - 413 B.C.) was the main military cause of Athens being defeated even though the Athenians held out for a further nine years before surrendering to the Spartans.
Byzantium
Cyzicus
Aegospotami
Cynossema
410 B.C., Alcibiades defeats 60 ships of Peloponnesian fleet, lands troops and captures Cyzicus. Peloponnesians unable to assemble a new large fleet for 3 years.
PEACE TERMS
1 Long Walls and Piraeus fortifications to be destroyed.
2 Athens to surrender all foreign possessions.
3 Athens to become allied with Sparta.
4 Athenian fleet, with the exception of twelve triremes, to be destroyed.
5 All exiles to be recalled.
Mytilene
B.C., Euboea
lts.
Arginusae
Delphinium
Chios
428 - 427 B.C., rebellion against Athens suppressed, and city surrenders to Paches. 1,000 men killed.
fortifying this post,
artans prevent
henians working
eir silver mines in
dition to cutting
eir communications.
Notium
Ephesus
406 B.C., Athenian victory. 75 Peloponnesian ships are sunk, but later, 25 Athenian ships are lost in storm.
406 B.C., Athenian naval defeat. Lysander sinks 22 Athenian ships and goes on to capture Delphinium.
411 B.C., Athenian naval defeat.
Syme
Rhodes
KEY
Athens and close allies.
Other states in alliance with Athens.
Sparta and allies.
Battles.
0 - 429 B.C., plague ravages Athens. One in four of
oulation dies including her war leader Pericles.

THE DISASTROUS SICILIAN EXPEDITION 415-413 B.C.

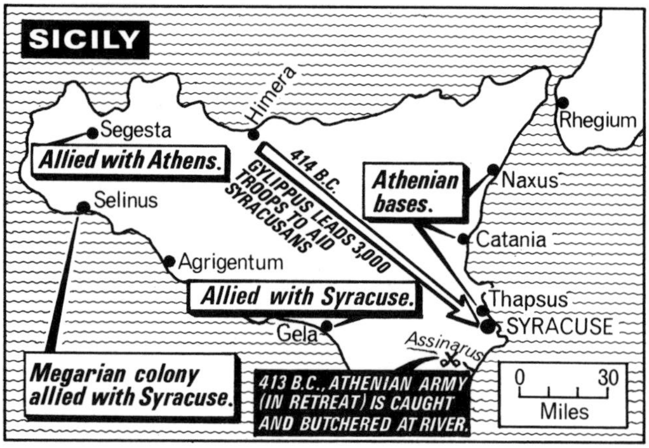
SICILY
Segesta
Allied with Athens.
Himera
414 B.C. GYLIPPUS LEADS 3,000 TROOPS TO AID SYRACUSANS
Selinus
Athenian bases.
Rhegium
Naxus
Catania
Agrigentum
Allied with Syracuse.
Thapsus
SYRACUSE
Gela
Assinarus
Megarian colony allied with Syracuse.
413 B.C., ATHENIAN ARMY (IN RETREAT) IS CAUGHT AND BUTCHERED AT RIVER.
0 30
Miles

GREECE
By fortifying Decelea, Sparta severed communications to Athens, forcing her to fight a war on two fronts.
Naupactus
Decelea
Athens
Corinth
Sparta
25 Corinthian triremes engage Athenian fleet to cover the departure of a force sent to relieve Syracuse.
0 50
Miles

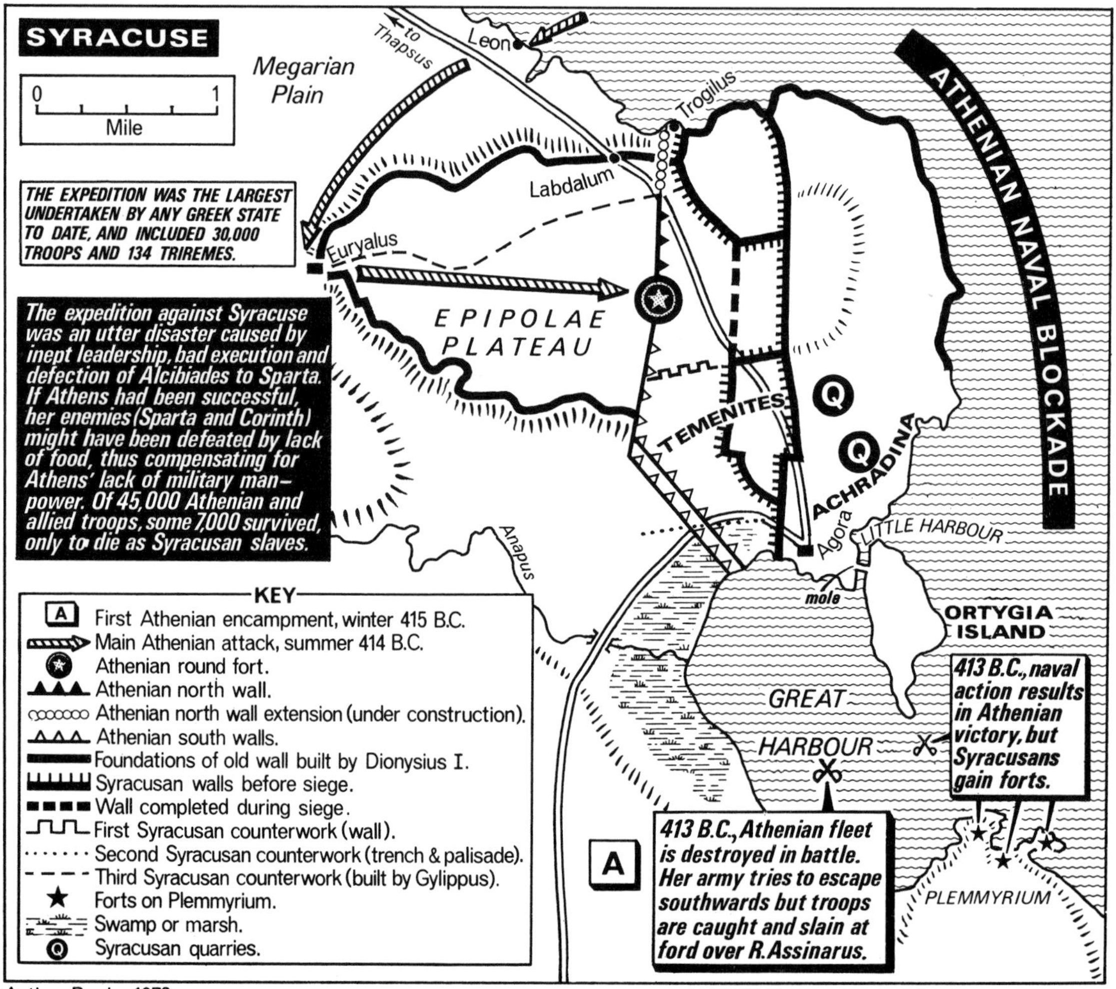
SYRACUSE
0 1
Mile
to Thapsus
Leon
Megarian Plain
Trogilus
ATHENIAN NAVAL BLOCKADE
Labdalum
THE EXPEDITION WAS THE LARGEST UNDERTAKEN BY ANY GREEK STATE TO DATE, AND INCLUDED 30,000 TROOPS AND 134 TRIREMES.
Euryalus
EPIPOLAE PLATEAU
The expedition against Syracuse was an utter disaster caused by inept leadership, bad execution and defection of Alcibiades to Sparta. If Athens had been successful, her enemies (Sparta and Corinth) might have been defeated by lack of food, thus compensating for Athens' lack of military man-power. Of 45,000 Athenian and allied troops, some 7,000 survived, only to die as Syracusan slaves.
TEMENITES
Q
Q
ACHRADINA
Agora
LITTLE HARBOUR
Anapus
mole
ORTYGIA ISLAND
KEY
A First Athenian encampment, winter 415 B.C.
Main Athenian attack, summer 414 B.C.
Athenian round fort.
Athenian north wall.
Athenian north wall extension (under construction).
Athenian south walls.
Foundations of old wall built by Dionysius I.
Syracusan walls before siege.
Wall completed during siege.
First Syracusan counterwork (wall).
Second Syracusan counterwork (trench & palisade).
Third Syracusan counterwork (built by Gylippus).
Forts on Plemmyrium.
Swamp or marsh.
Syracusan quarries.
GREAT HARBOUR
413 B.C., naval action results in Athenian victory, but Syracusans gain forts.
A
413 B.C., Athenian fleet is destroyed in battle. Her army tries to escape southwards but troops are caught and slain at ford over R. Assinarus.
PLEMMYRIUM

THE ASCENDANCY OF SPARTA 404-380 B.C.

To defeat Athens, Sparta had sold the Asiatic Greeks to Persia, thus restoring Persia's influence in the Greek world. Sparta's strength rested upon Persia, and thus her attempt to build her own empire failed. Also there was not in Sparta the spirit that had made Athens great.
CHALCIDICE
381 B.C., league of cities suppressed by Sparta.
PHRYGIA
396 B.C., overrun by Agesilaus who collects much booty.
Athenians under Thrasybulus hold out against rule of the 'Thirty' in Athens. 403 B.C., Spartan king Pausanias makes peace.
PERSIAN EMPIRE
394 B.C., Spartan Agesilaus wins victory.
Coronea
382 B.C., seized by Sparta.
Thebes
Phyle
Elis
Corinth
Athens
Mantinea
Argos
387 B.C., Artaxerxes of Persia makes 'King's Peace' settlement. States of Greece are independent but Asiatic Greeks left subject to Persia.
Destroyed by Sparta.
SPARTA
Successes won by Iphicrates and his peltasts (light-armed troops).
394 B.C., Persians (under Athenian Conon) crush Spartan navy.
Cnidus
0
50
Miles

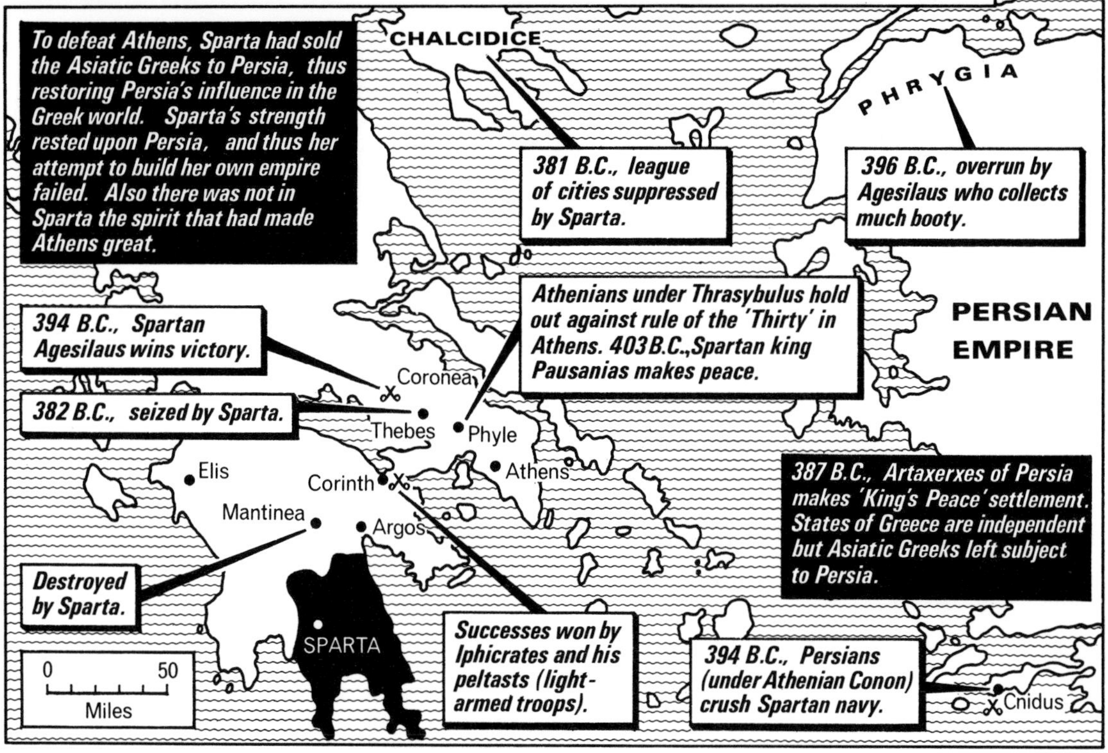

MARCH OF THE 'TEN THOUSAND' AGAINST PERSIA 401-400 B.C.

Sinope
KEY
Advance of the 'Ten Thousand'.
Retreat of the 'Ten Thousand'.
Byzantium
Perinthus
Chalcedon
Trapezus
Gymnias
City friendly to the expedition.
Erzerum
0
100
Miles
PERSIAN
Pergamum
Sardis
401 B.C.
Celaenae
Iconium
Tyana
Tarsus
Issus
Euphrates
Tigris
EMPIRE
Nineveh
Larissa
401 B.C.
Thapsacus
Erzi
400 B.C.
To oust his brother Artaxerxes from the Persian throne, Cyrus formed an army to invade Persia, among whom were 10,000 Spartan hoplites. The advance electrified Greece; never had a Greek army penetrated the very heart of the Persian Empire and escaped.
401 B.C., Cyrus is killed in battle and further advance of the expedition is abandoned.
Cunaxa

© Arthur Banks 1972

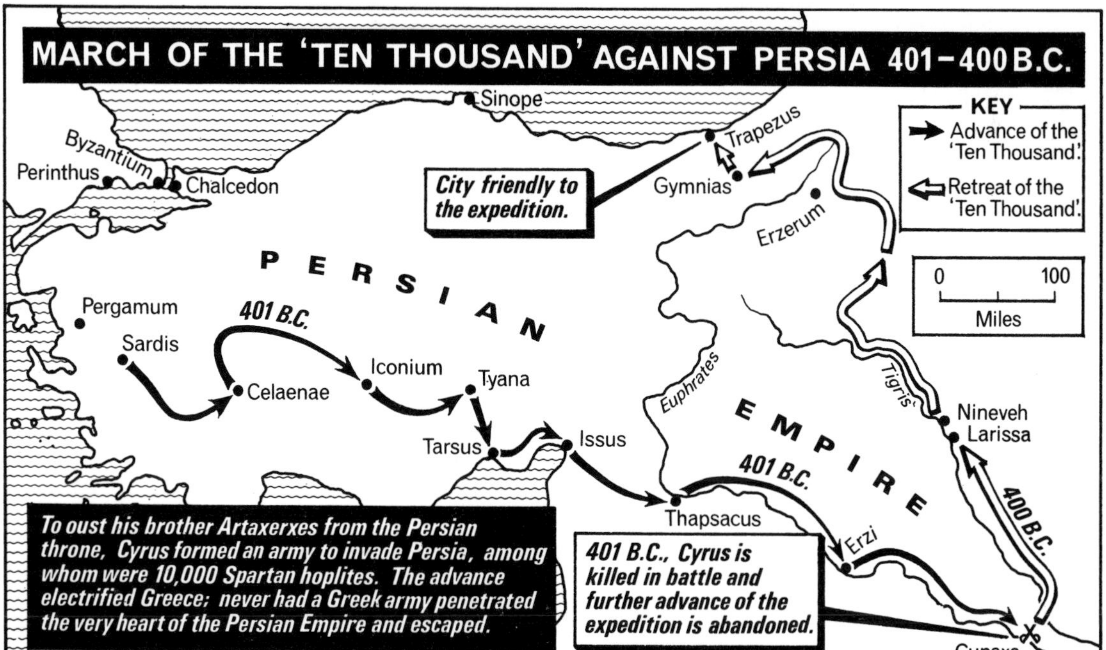

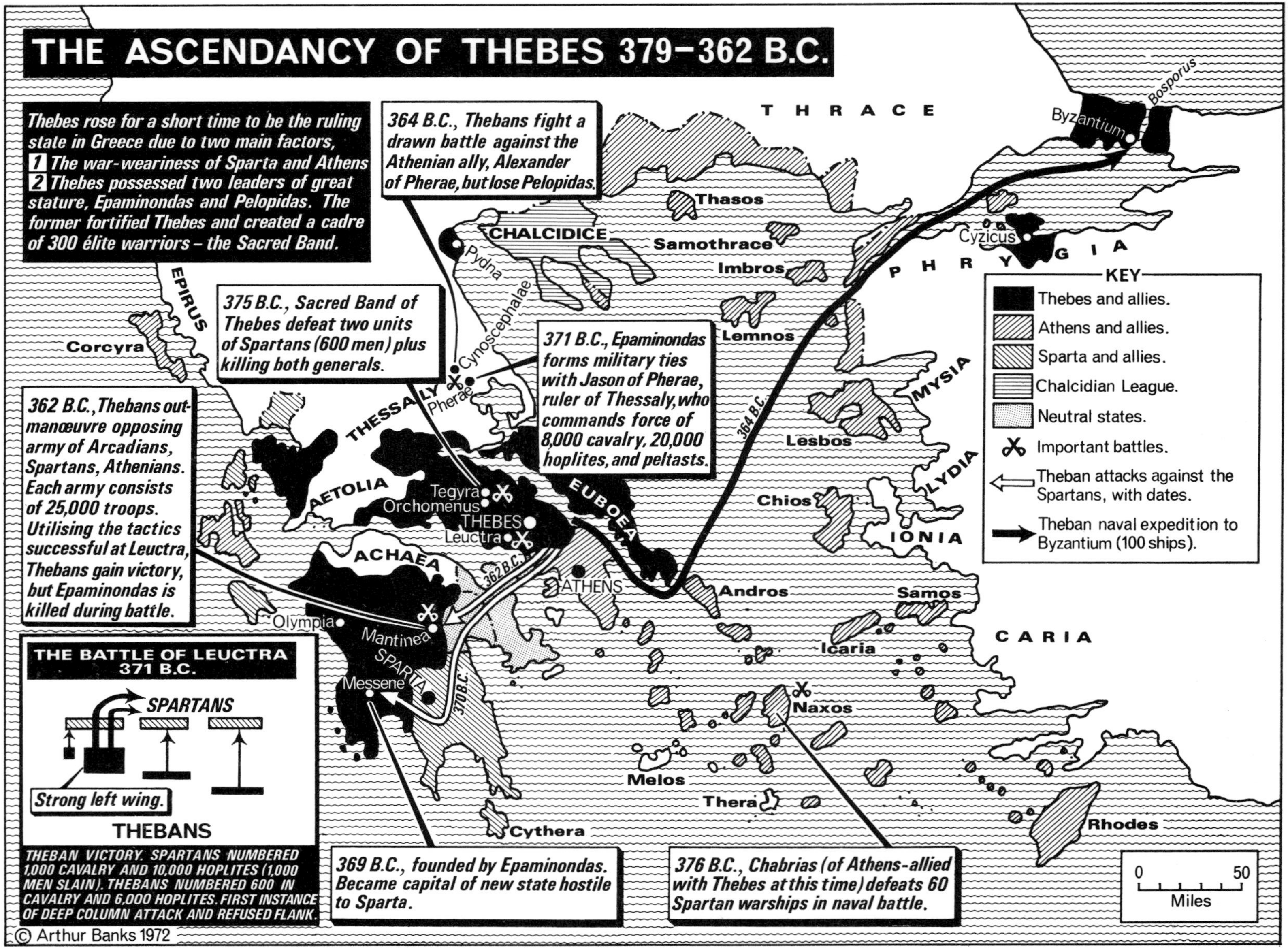
THE ASCENDANCY OF THEBES 379–362 B.C.
Thebes rose for a short time to be the ruling state in Greece due to two main factors, 1 The war-weariness of Sparta and Athens 2 Thebes possessed two leaders of great stature, Epaminondas and Pelopidas. The former fortified Thebes and created a cadre of 300 élite warriors – the Sacred Band.
364 B.C., Thebans fight a drawn battle against the Athenian ally, Alexander of Pherae, but lose Pelopidas.
375 B.C., Sacred Band of Thebes defeat two units of Spartans (600 men) plus killing both generals.
371 B.C., Epaminondas forms military ties with Jason of Pherae, ruler of Thessaly, who commands force of 8,000 cavalry, 20,000 hoplites, and peltasts.
362 B.C., Thebans outmanœuvre opposing army of Arcadians, Spartans, Athenians. Each army consists of 25,000 troops. Utilising the tactics successful at Leuctra, Thebans gain victory, but Epaminondas is killed during battle.
THE BATTLE OF LEUCTRA 371 B.C.
SPARTANS
Strong left wing.
THEBANS
THEBAN VICTORY. SPARTANS NUMBERED 1,000 CAVALRY AND 10,000 HOPLITES (1,000 MEN SLAIN). THEBANS NUMBERED 600 IN CAVALRY AND 6,000 HOPLITES. FIRST INSTANCE OF DEEP COLUMN ATTACK AND REFUSED FLANK.
369 B.C., founded by Epaminondas. Became capital of new state hostile to Sparta.
376 B.C., Chabrias (of Athens-allied with Thebes at this time) defeats 60 Spartan warships in naval battle.
KEY
Thebes and allies.
Athens and allies.
Sparta and allies.
Chalcidian League.
Neutral states.
Important battles.
Theban attacks against the Spartans, with dates.
Theban naval expedition to Byzantium (100 ships).
0 50
Miles
THRACE
PHRYGIA
MYSIA
LYDIA
IONIA
CARIA
Bosporus
Byzantium
Cyzicus
Thasos
Samothrace
Imbros
Lemnos
Lesbos
Chios
Samos
Icaria
Andros
Naxos
Melos
Thera
Rhodes
Cythera
CHALCIDICE
Pydna
Cynoscephalae
Pherae
THESSALY
EPIRUS
Corcyra
AETOLIA
Tegyra
Orchomenus
THEBES
Leuctra
EUBOEA
ATHENS
ACHAEA
Olympia
Mantinea
SPARTA
Messene
364 B.C.
362 B.C.
370 B.C.
© Arthur Banks 1972

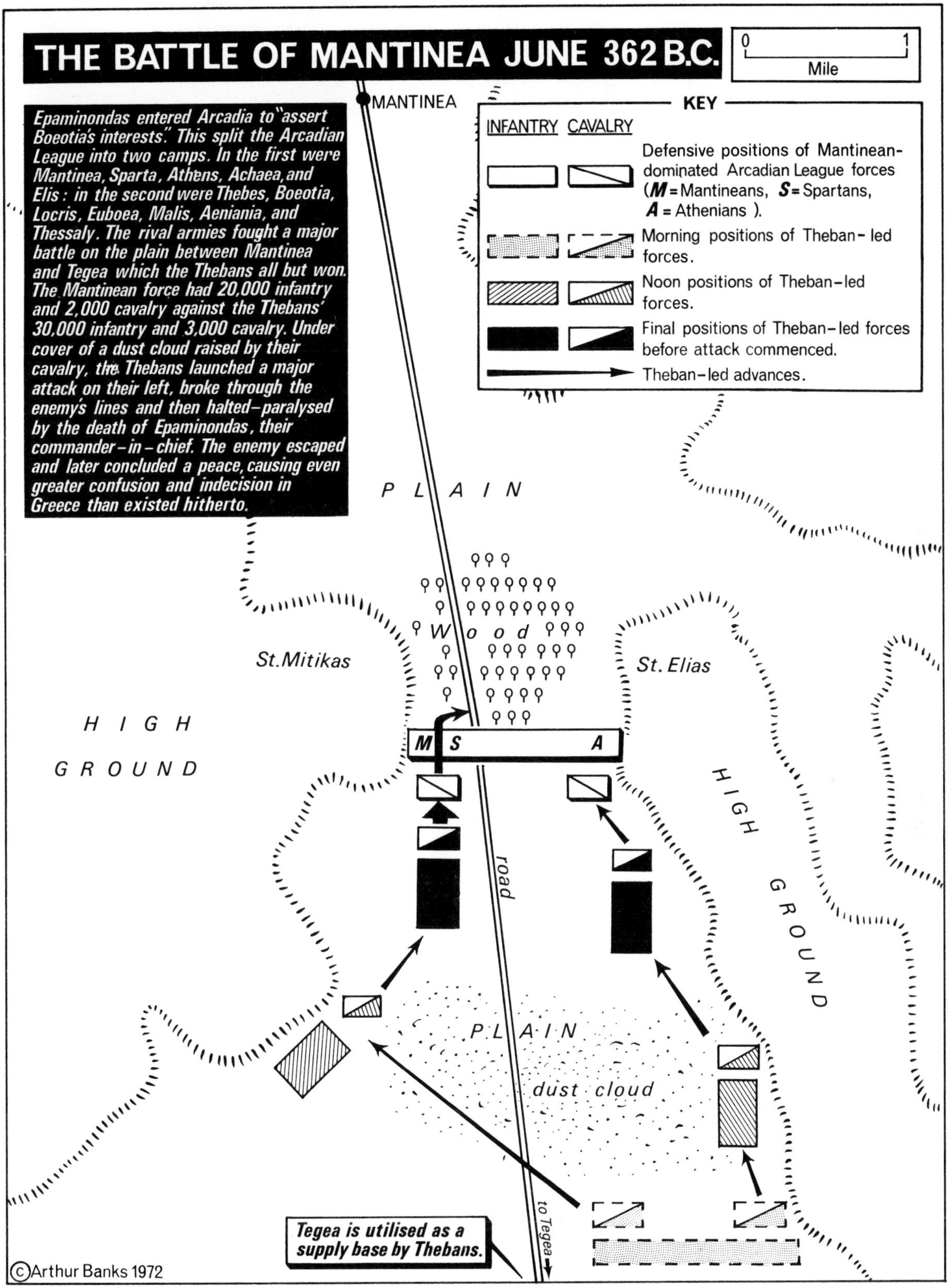
THE BATTLE OF MANTINEA JUNE 362 B.C.
0 1 Mile
Epaminondas entered Arcadia to "assert Boeotia's interests." This split the Arcadian League into two camps. In the first were Mantinea, Sparta, Athens, Achaea, and Elis: in the second were Thebes, Boeotia, Locris, Euboea, Malis, Aeniania, and Thessaly. The rival armies fought a major battle on the plain between Mantinea and Tegea which the Thebans all but won. The Mantinean force had 20,000 infantry and 2,000 cavalry against the Thebans' 30,000 infantry and 3,000 cavalry. Under cover of a dust cloud raised by their cavalry, the Thebans launched a major attack on their left, broke through the enemy's lines and then halted–paralysed by the death of Epaminondas, their commander-in-chief. The enemy escaped and later concluded a peace, causing even greater confusion and indecision in Greece than existed hitherto.
MANTINEA
KEY
INFANTRY CAVALRY
Defensive positions of Mantinean-dominated Arcadian League forces (M = Mantineans, S = Spartans, A = Athenians).
Morning positions of Theban-led forces.
Noon positions of Theban-led forces.
Final positions of Theban-led forces before attack commenced.
Theban-led advances.
PLAIN
Wood
St. Mitikas
St. Elias
HIGH GROUND
M S A
road
HIGH GROUND
PLAIN
dust cloud
to Tegea
Tegea is utilised as a supply base by Thebans.
©Arthur Banks 1972

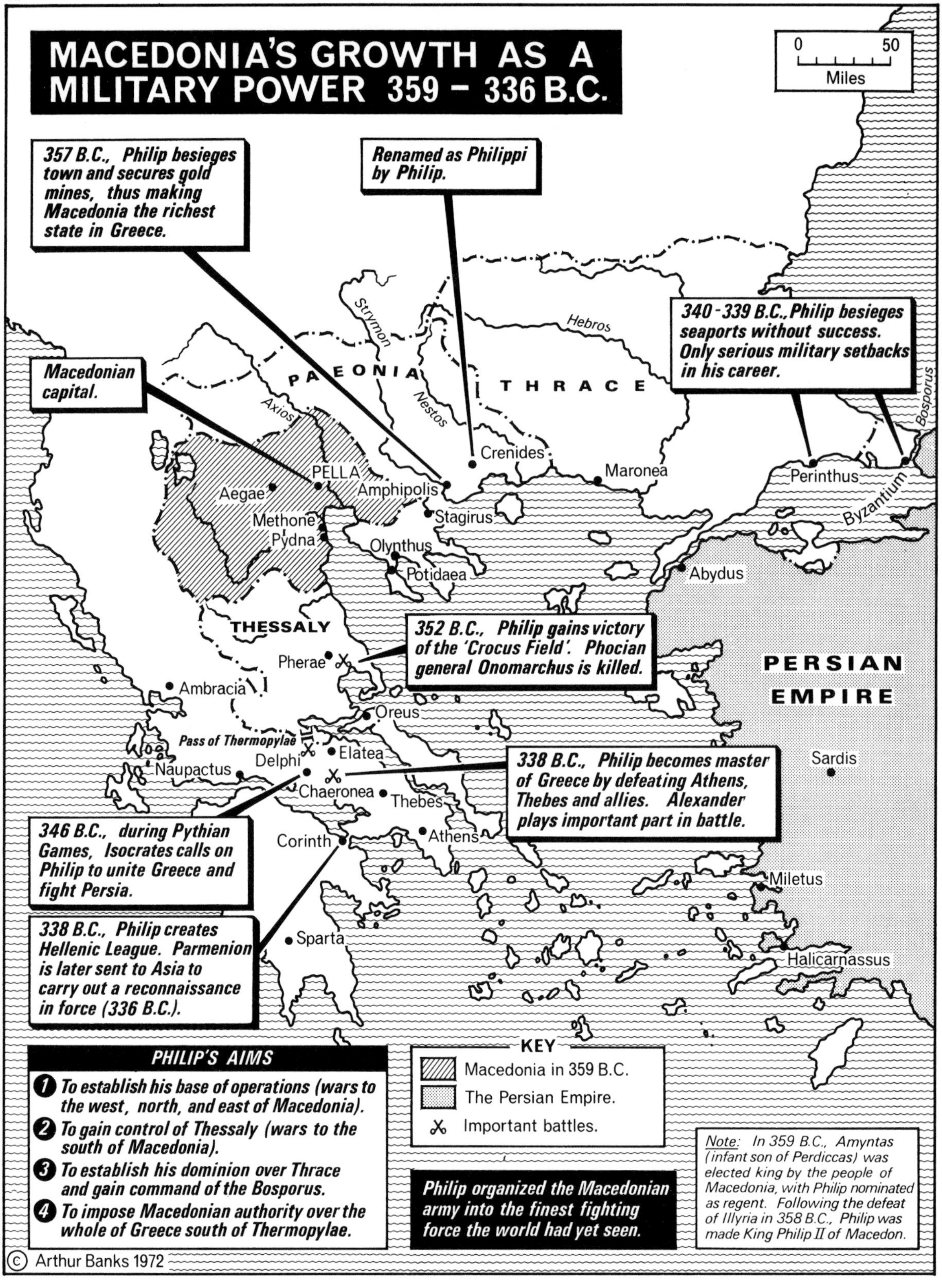
MACEDONIA'S GROWTH AS A MILITARY POWER 359 – 336 B.C.
0 50 Miles
357 B.C., Philip besieges town and secures gold mines, thus making Macedonia the richest state in Greece.
Renamed as Philippi by Philip.
340-339 B.C., Philip besieges seaports without success. Only serious military setbacks in his career.
Macedonian capital.
352 B.C., Philip gains victory of the 'Crocus Field'. Phocian general Onomarchus is killed.
338 B.C., Philip becomes master of Greece by defeating Athens, Thebes and allies. Alexander plays important part in battle.
346 B.C., during Pythian Games, Isocrates calls on Philip to unite Greece and fight Persia.
338 B.C., Philip creates Hellenic League. Parmenion is later sent to Asia to carry out a reconnaissance in force (336 B.C.).
Strymon
Hebros
Bosporus
PAEONIA
THRACE
Axios
Nestos
Crenides
Maronea
Perinthus
Byzantium
PELLA
Aegae
Amphipolis
Stagirus
Methone
Pydna
Olynthus
Potidaea
Abydus
THESSALY
Pherae
PERSIAN EMPIRE
Ambracia
Oreus
Pass of Thermopylae
Elatea
Delphi
Naupactus
Chaeronea
Thebes
Sardis
Corinth
Athens
Miletus
Sparta
Halicarnassus
PHILIP'S AIMS
1 To establish his base of operations (wars to the west, north, and east of Macedonia).
2 To gain control of Thessaly (wars to the south of Macedonia).
3 To establish his dominion over Thrace and gain command of the Bosporus.
4 To impose Macedonian authority over the whole of Greece south of Thermopylae.
KEY
Macedonia in 359 B.C.
The Persian Empire.
Important battles.
Philip organized the Macedonian army into the finest fighting force the world had yet seen.
Note: In 359 B.C., Amyntas (infant son of Perdiccas) was elected king by the people of Macedonia, with Philip nominated as regent. Following the defeat of Illyria in 358 B.C., Philip was made King Philip II of Macedon.
© Arthur Banks 1972

THE MACEDONIAN VICTORY AT CHAERONEA 338 B.C.

Realising that the Athenians were the weakest section of the enemy, Philip advanced his personal battalions, the 'Hypaspists.' The Greeks stood firm, whereupon Philip organized a 'step by step' orderly withdrawal, meanwhile advancing his phalanx and Alexander's cavalry. (Note: This "withdrawal" was notable for Macedonian discipline). Seeing Philip's apparent retreat, the whole Greek front (except the 'Sacred Band') advanced, veering to its left to concentrate on Philip. This manœuvre created a gap in the Greek lines into which Alexander's cavalry charged, first massacring the 'Sacred Band,' then turning right to attack the Greek rear. Philip ordered a general advance and the Greeks were trapped, their cavalry (in reserve) retreating in panic. This battle is not dissimilar in tactics to those of Leuctra in 371 B.C.

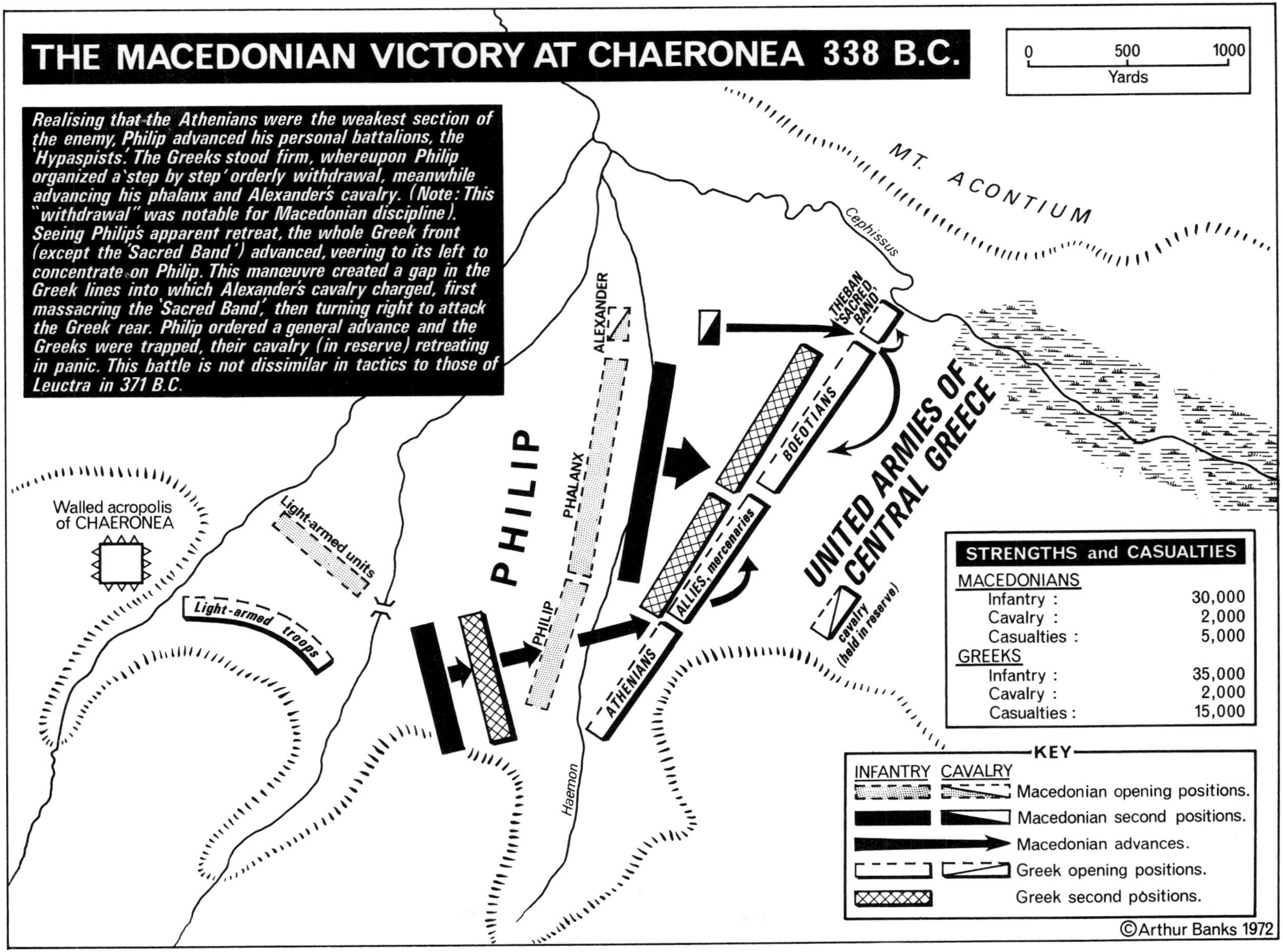

STRENGTHS and CASUALTIES

MACEDONIANS	
Infantry :	30,000
Cavalry :	2,000
Casualties :	5,000
GREEKS	
Infantry :	35,000
Cavalry :	2,000
Casualties :	15,000

THE CAMPAIGNS OF ALEXANDER THE GREAT 336–323 B.C.

ALEXANDER'S OBJECTIVES

1. *To secure his home base.*
2. *To establish a stable overseas base.*
3. *To gain command of the seas.*
4. *To defeat the Persians on land.*

ALEXANDER'S ARMY OF INVASION (Total: 40,000)

The aim of the invasion ideological: to avenge wr done to Hellas by Xerxe

INFANTRY	CAVALRY	MISCELLANEOUS
12,000 Macedonians. 7,000 Greek League hoplites. 6,000 Agrianian javelin-men, Thracians, Cretan archers. 5,000 mercenary hoplites.	2,000 Companions. 2,000 Thessalians. 1,000 Thracians, Paeonians, Greek allied horse, lancers.	5,000 artillerists, sappe surveyors, siege-engine transport-drivers, serva camp-followers, etc.

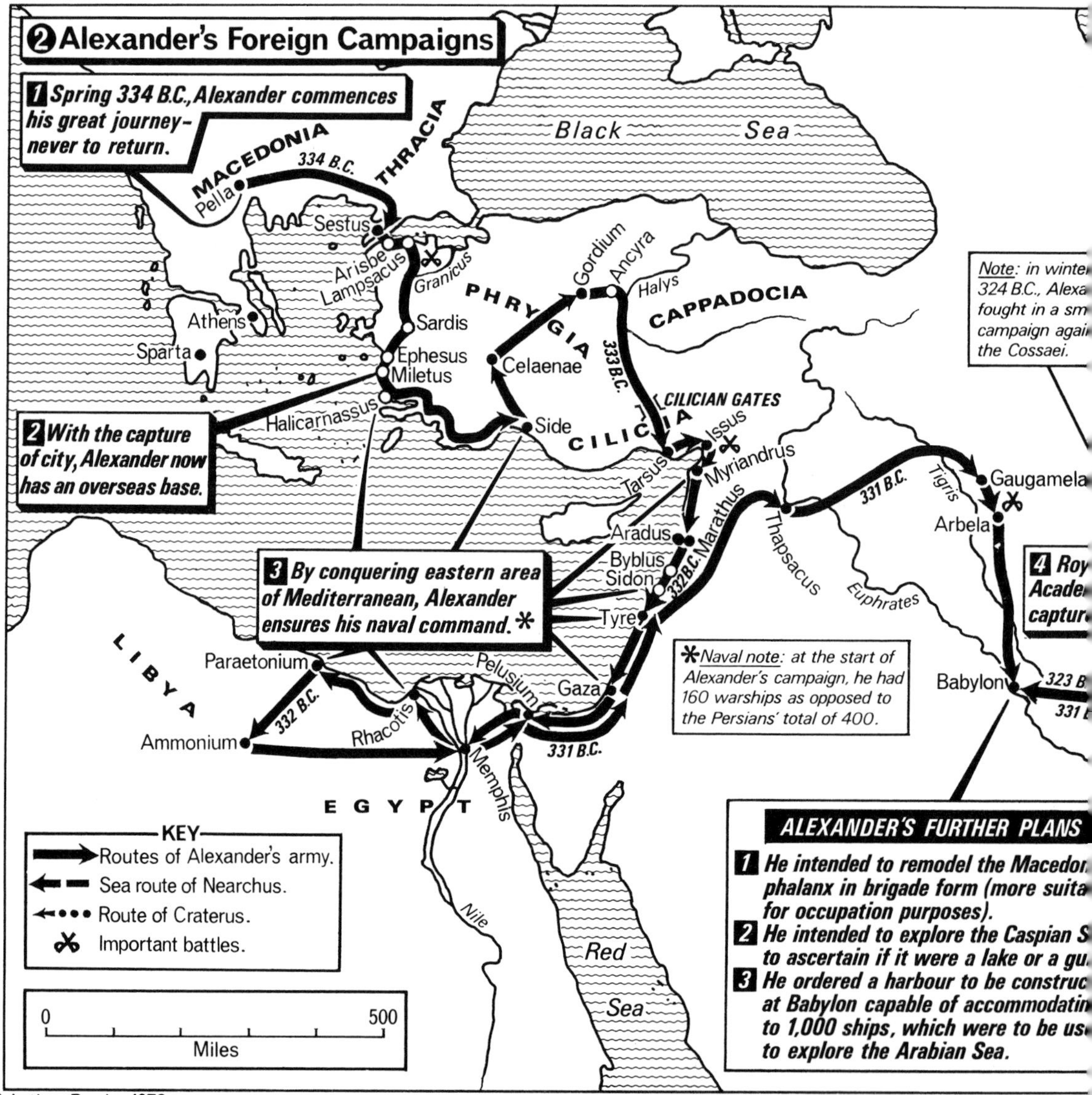

Securing the Home Base

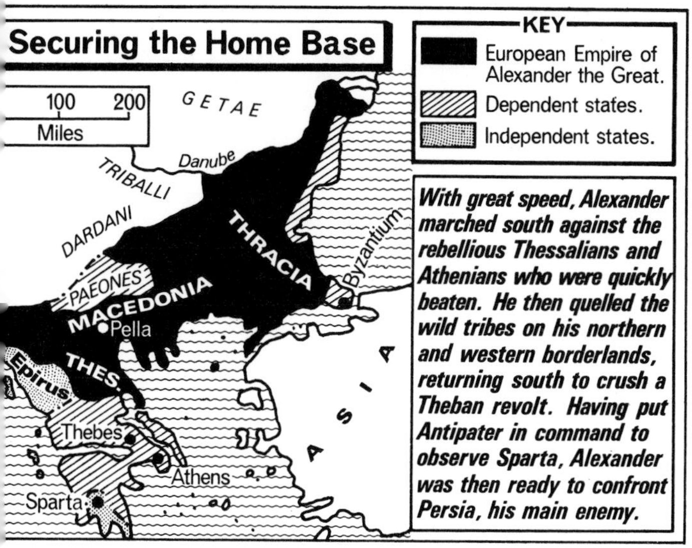

With great speed, Alexander marched south against the rebellious Thessalians and Athenians who were quickly beaten. He then quelled the wild tribes on his northern and western borderlands, returning south to crush a Theban revolt. Having put Antipater in command to observe Sparta, Alexander was then ready to confront Persia, his main enemy.

Alexander lived from 356 B.C. to 323 B.C. Son of Philip II of Macedonia (who was murdered in 336 B.C.), he became king at the early age of 19, and in the following twelve years created by conquest a large empire extending from Greece eastwards across Asia to the borders of India. After first establishing his authority in Greece in the early years of his reign between 336 B.C. and 334 B.C., he recruited and led an army against the Persian Empire, whose armies he defeated in a long series of battles and sieges. Following a number of small wars in the east, he returned to Babylon to consolidate his empire. There he died of malaria at the age of 33.
As well as being a great military captain, Alexander was a statesman, diplomat and explorer. He founded at least seventeen "Alexandrias" during his career.

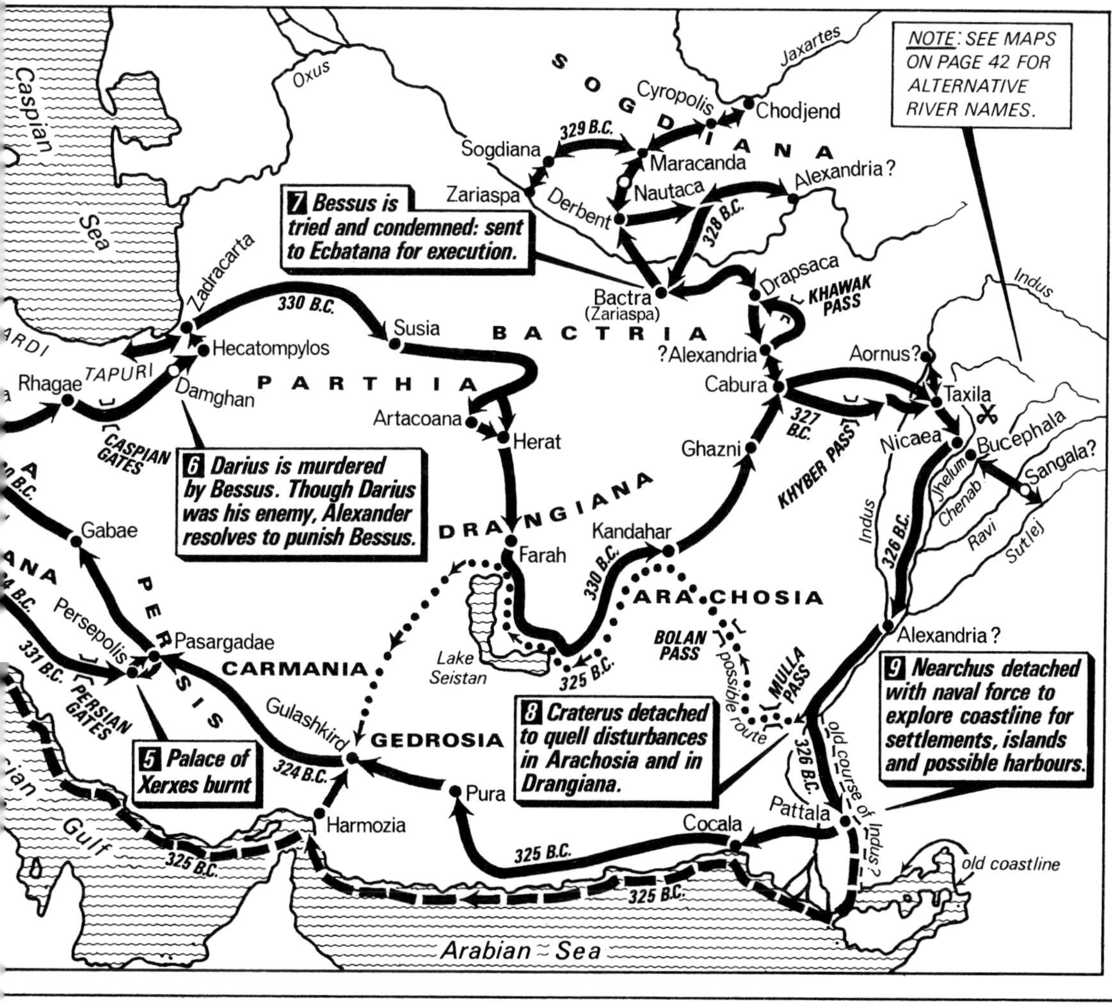

ALEXANDER'S GREAT BATTLES AND SIEGES

Army stren... and losses ... estimates o...

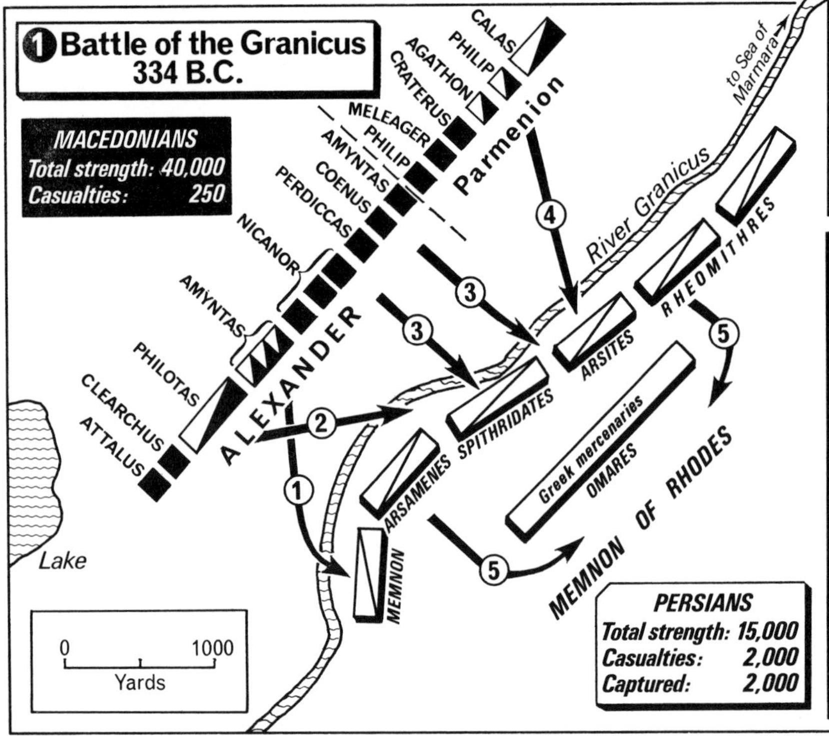

KEY

- Macedonian infantry.
- Macedonian cavalry.
- Main Macedonian attack numbered in sequen...
- Persian infantry.
- Persian cavalry.

Persian movements in this bat... have been omitted for clarity. They were mainly defensive, f... the Macedonians made the fir... attack. In early warfare it v... essential to kill or capture the... opposing commanders since pa... among their soldiers invariabl... followed. Thus the Persians w... intent on eliminating Alexand... but he survived. On the ot... hand, the Persians lost a num... of their own unit commanders... factor of some significance in... the battles to come. In view... the importance of the leaders... units are shown with the na... of their respective commande...

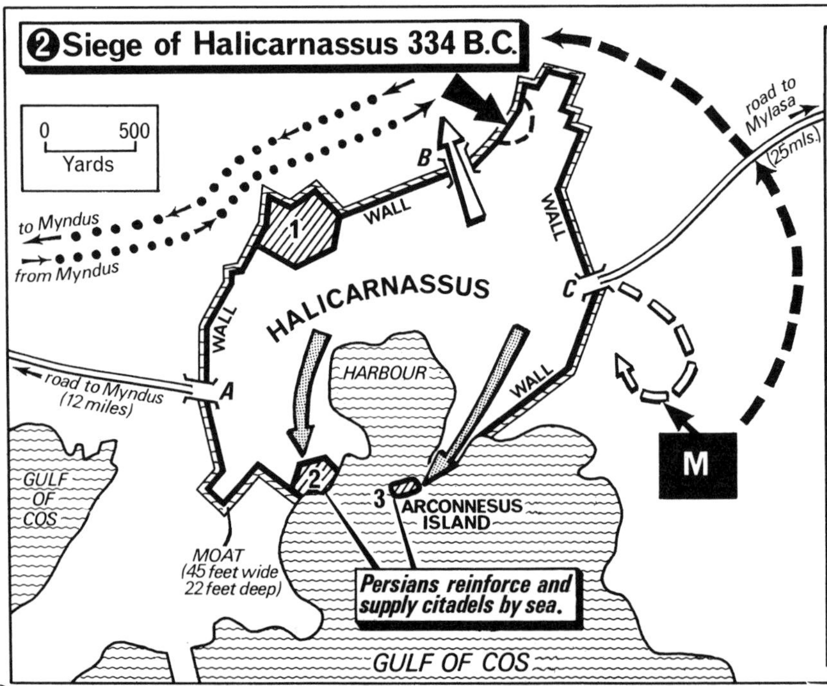

KEY

- Citadels of Halicarnass...
  - 1 Acropolis.
  - 2 Fortress of Salmacis.
  - 3 King's Castle.
- Gates of Halicarnassus
  - *A* Myndus Gate.
  - *B* Triple Gate.
  - *C* Mylasa Gate.
- M Macedonian encampme...
- Sortie by the garrison.
- Macedonian reconnaiss... of the walls.
- Alexander's abortive ma... to subdue Myndus.
- Main Macedonian attac...
- Garrison's abortive cou... attack.
- Garrison's attempt to fi... the breached wall.
- Garrison's retreat into ... citadels. Despite the ... Macedonian land block... citadels resisted for a ye...

Battle of Issus 333 B.C.

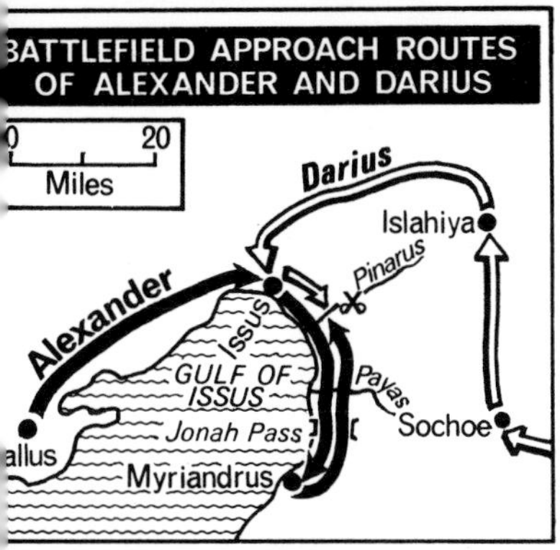

lexander marched from Issus en route r Myriandrus, just missing Darius who eached Issus twenty-four hours later. n his arrival at Myriandrus, Alexander as surprised to learn that Darius was dvancing behind him. Realising that his ne of retreat had been cut, Alexander esolved to surprise Darius in return by eversing his line of advance and resting is men, then launching a rapid attack n the weary Persians.

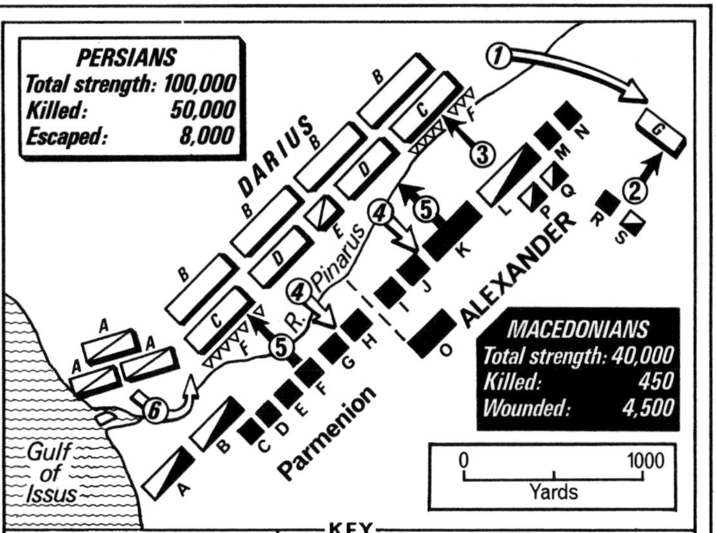

KEY

- Macedonian infantry.
- Macedonian cavalry.
- Macedonian thrusts.
- Persian infantry.
- Persian cavalry.
- Persian archers.
- Persian advances.

MACEDONIANS
- **A** Allied Greek cavalry.
- **B** Thessalian cavalry.
- **C** Thracian javelin-men.
- **D** Cretan archers.
- **E** Phalanx (Amyntas).
- **F** Phalanx (Ptolemy).
- **G** Phalanx (Meleager).
- **H** Phalanx (Craterus).
- **I** Phalanx (Perdiccas).
- **J** Phalanx (Coenus).
- **K** Hypaspists.
- **L** Companion cavalry.
- **M** Macedonian archers.
- **N** Agrianians.
- **O** Greek mercenaries.
- **P** Lancers.
- **Q** Paeonian light horsemen.
- **R** Agrianians.
- **S** Light horse squadron.

PERSIANS
- ***A*** Cavalry (Nabarzanes).
- ***B*** Asiatic levies.
- ***C*** Cardaces.
- ***D*** Greek mercenaries.
- ***E*** Bodyguard (Darius).
- ***F*** Archers.
- ***G*** Light troop detachment.

Siege of Tyre 332 B.C.

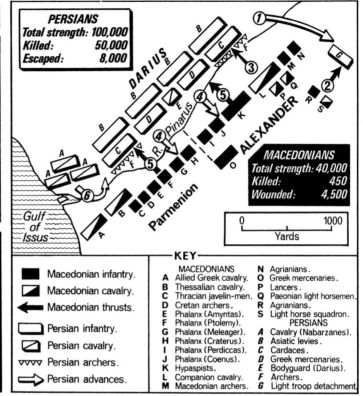

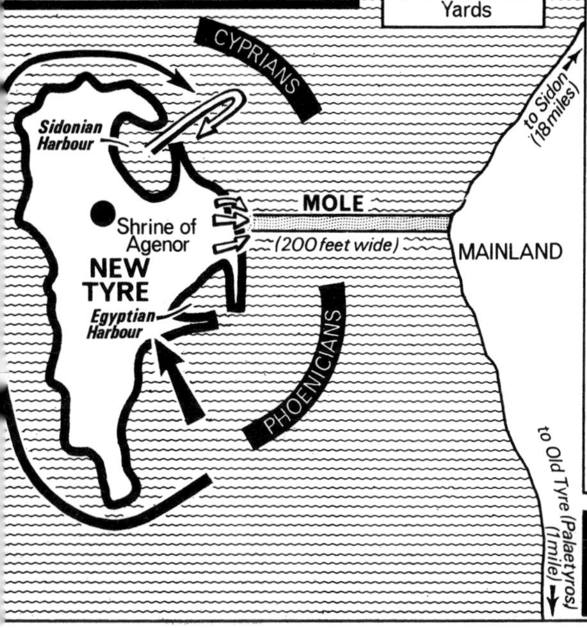

1 ***Alexander's first task is to construct a mole from the mainland to New Tyre. The work is hindered by Tyrian attacks, including a fire-ship's sortie.***

2 ***Alexander decides to blockade the two Tyrian harbours with two fleets.***

3 ***Tyrian navy sorties out from Sidonian Harbour, but despite initial success, it is thwarted by Alexander sailing round west coast of island to reinforce his Cyprian contingent.***

4 ***Alexander finally breaches city wall south of Egyptian Harbour and advances into city. Simultaneously his naval contingents storm the two harbours.***

5 ***Tyrians make final stand at Shrine of Agenor but are overwhelmed.***

The siege lasted for seven months. 8,000 Tyrians were killed and 30,000 sold into slavery. During the various assaults, 400 Macedonians were killed.

ALEXANDER'S BATTLES–continued

⑤ Battle of Arbela (Gaugamela) 331 B.C.

PERSIAN KEY

Cavalry — Infantry — Asiatic levies — o o o o o Chariots (total: 200) — ● ● ● ● ● Elephants (total: 15)

1 Sacesinians.	*10* Cappadocians.	*19* Carians.
2 Albanians.	*11* Armenians.	*20* Cadusians.
3 Hyrcanians.	*12* Mardians (archers).	*21* Susians.
4 Tapurians.	*13* Indians.	*22* Persians.
5 Sacians.	*14* Greeks (mercen's).	*23* Arachosians.
6 Parthians.	*15* Persians (horse).	*24* Dahaeians.
7 Medians.	*16* Persians (foot).	*25* Bactrians.
8 Mesopotamians.	*17* Persians (horse).	*26* Scythians.
9 Coelo-Syrians.	*18* Greeks (mercen's).	*27* Bactrians.

PRE-BATTLE DISPOSITIONS

MACEDONIAN KEY (arranged under commanders)

Cavalry — Infantry

1 Andromachus.	6 Clearchus.	11 Polyperchon.	16 Attalus.	21 Aretes.
2 Agathon.	7 Philip.	12 Meleager.	17 Briso.	22 Ariston.
3 Coeranus.	8 Erigyius.	13 Perdiccas.	18 Balacrus.	23 Attalus.
4 Sitalces.	9 Craterus.	14 Coenus.	19 Philotas.	24 Briso.
5 (mercenaries).	10 Simmias.	15 Nicanor.	20 Menidas.	25 Cleander.

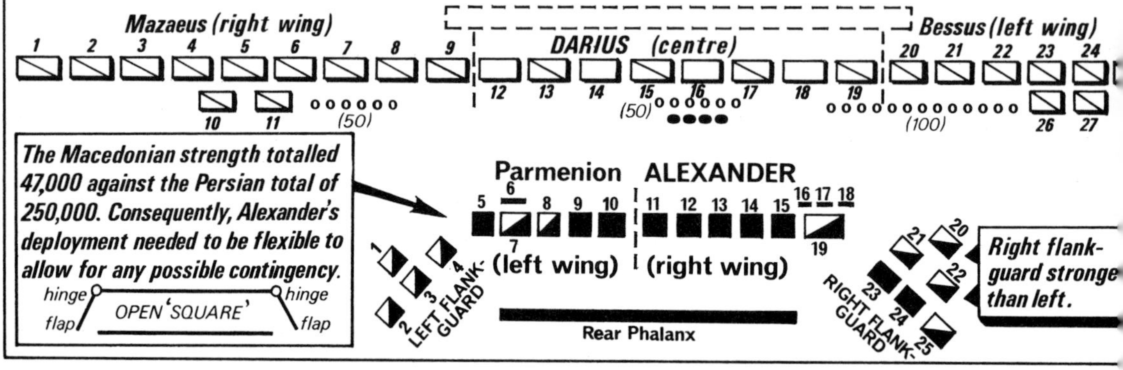

THE BATTLE–PHASE ONE

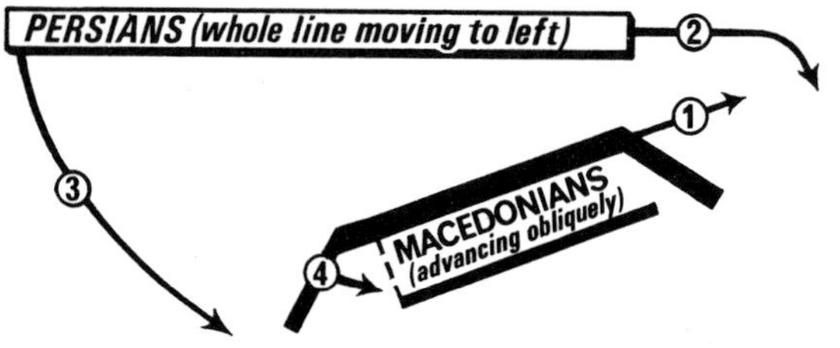

① *Without physical features (such as hills or rivers) upon which to position his flanks, Alexander moves in an oblique direction towards the Persian line (twice the length of his own) veering to the right.*

② *Persians commence moving to left to keep abreast of Alexander, their left-wing cavalry racing ahead to intercept Macedonian advance.*

③ *Persian right-wing cavalry moves forward to envelop Macedonians from rear.*

④ *Macedonian left flank-guard closes to main body to prevent Persian breakthrough.*

THE BATTLE–PHASE TWO

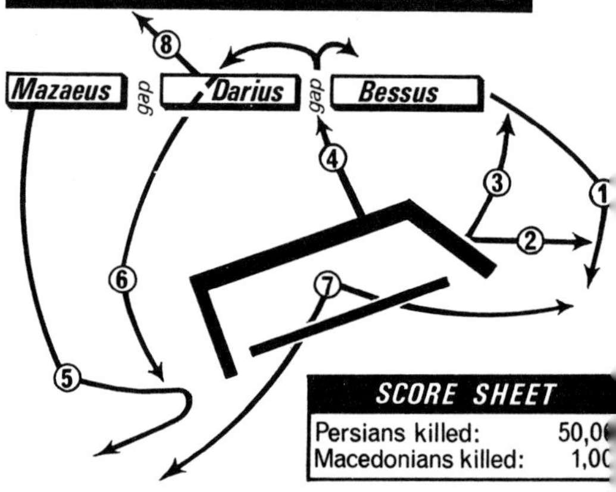

SCORE SHEET	
Persians killed:	50,0
Macedonians killed:	1,0

① *Rapidity of Persian cavalry advance creates gaps Persian main line.* ② *and* ③ *Macedonian right flan guard engages Persian cavalry.* ④ *Alexander advanc into gap between Bessus and Darius; fierce fighting mêlée-style ensues.* ⑤ *Persian right-wing nearly brea through, but* ⑥ *is intercepted by Alexander answering Parmenion's call for help.* ⑦ *Macedonians attack Persi cavalry in strength.* ⑧ *Darius flees.*

6 Battle of the Hydaspes* 326 B.C.

*Note: modern name is Jhelum.

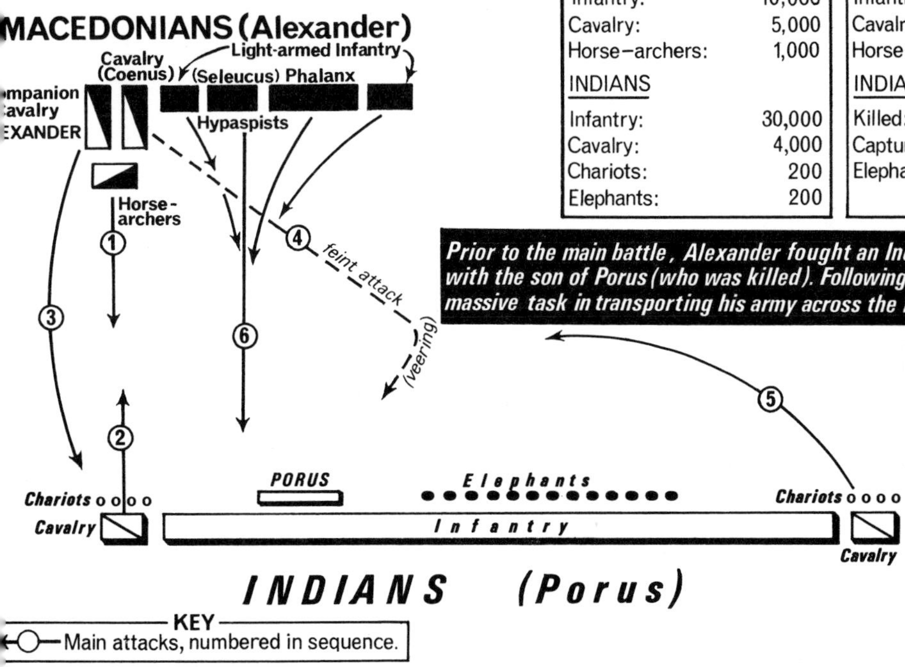

STRENGTHS	
MACEDONIANS	
Infantry:	10,000
Cavalry:	5,000
Horse–archers:	1,000
INDIANS	
Infantry:	30,000
Cavalry:	4,000
Chariots:	200
Elephants:	200

CASUALTIES	
MACEDONIANS (killed)	
Infantry:	700
Cavalry:	280
Horse–archers:	10
INDIANS	
Killed:	12,000
Captured:	9,000
Elephants captured:	80

Prior to the main battle, Alexander fought an Indian delaying-action with the son of Porus (who was killed). Following this, he undertook a massive task in transporting his army across the River Hydaspes.

ALEXANDER'S TACTICS

In his major battles, Alexander positioned himself on the right wing and opened his attack from that side. This avoided a 'centre' confrontation at the outset and compelled his foes to rearrange their dispositions.

ALEXANDER'S "ALEXANDRIAS"

Note: there is no evidence of an Alexandria at Kandahar.

Alexander founded at least seventeen "Alexandrias" and promised an eighteenth (Alexandria Troas) which was never built. Six are "certain," in that they are represented by modern towns. A further seven existed well down into Greek history. The remaining four were built but the precise location of Alexandria in Babylonia is unknown.

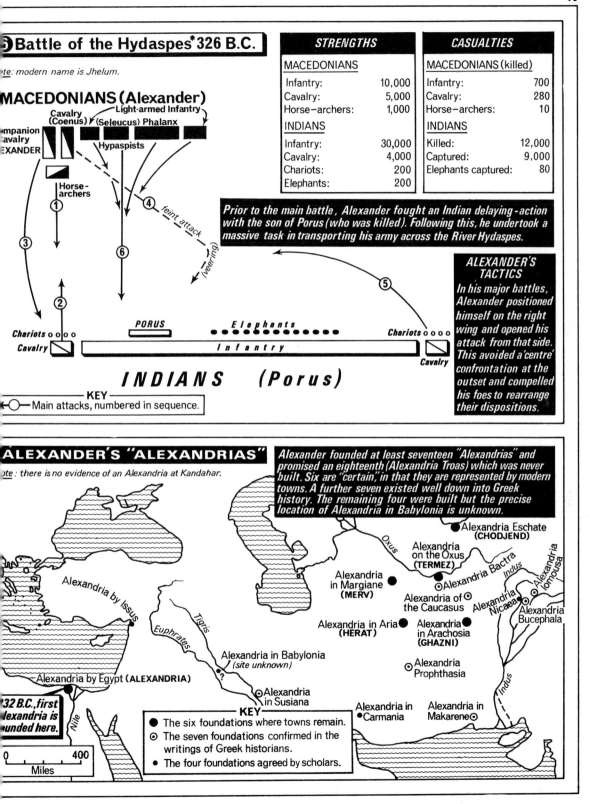

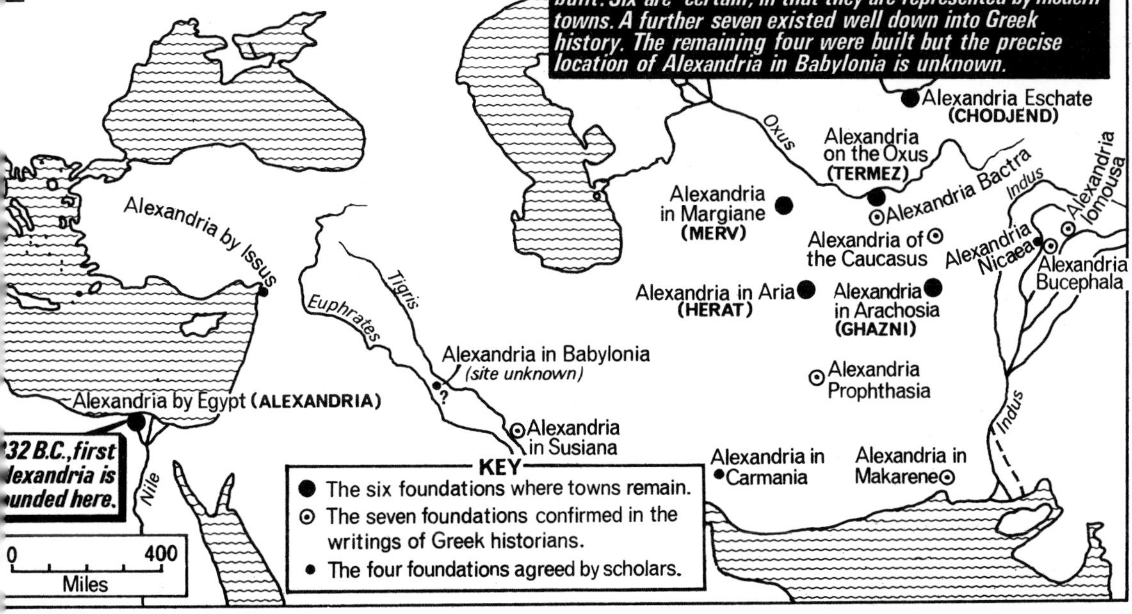

THE EFFECT ON WORLD HISTORY OF AN ARMY 'MUTINY' IN 326 B.C.

1 Alexander's Campaigns in North-West India

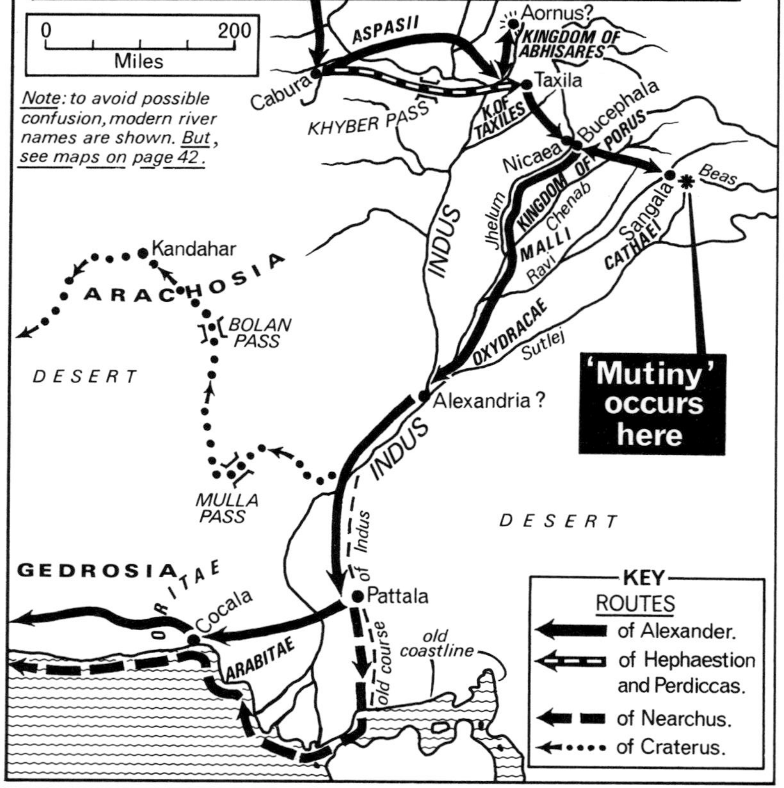

Following his victory over Porus at the river Hydaspes (Jhelum), Alexander built Nicaea and Bucephala, stormed Sangala (capital of the Cathaei), and then advanced to the river Hyphasis (Beas). At this point his army staged a "mutiny." Exhausted and homesick after eight years of campaigning, during which they had marched 17,000 miles, the troops refused to go on, and returned to Nicaea.

2 Two Rivers and Two Civilizations

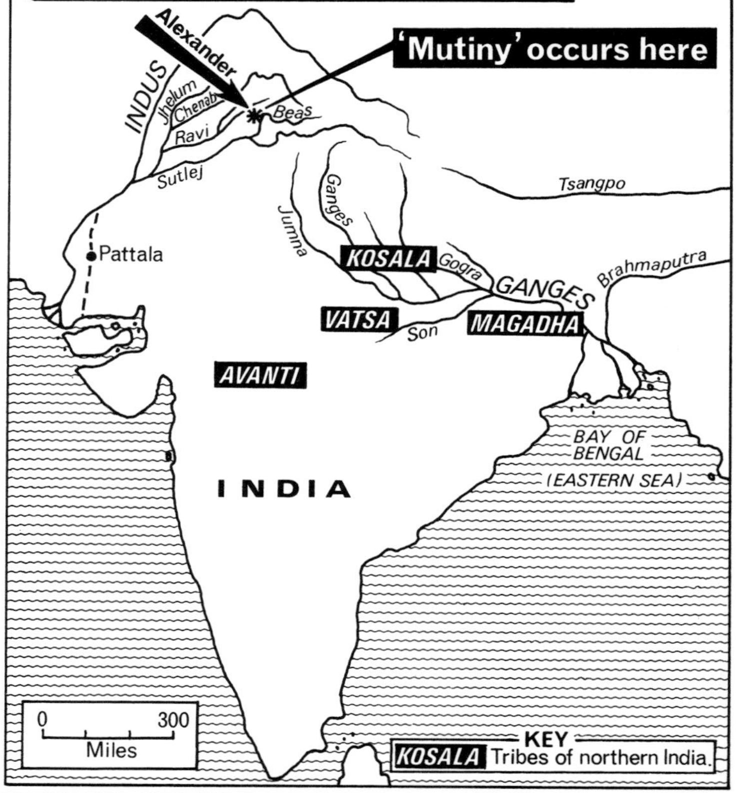

Alexander knew of the existence of the River Ganges and wished it to be the line of his eastern frontier. If the "mutiny" had not occurred, he could not have failed to collide with the tribes of northern India, consequently affecting future world events. Sandracottus (Chandragupta), India's first great military leader, was in Alexander's camp at this particular period.

PROBLEMS OF CHANGING NOMENCLATURE IN HISTORY: THE "LAND OF THE FIVE RIVERS"

1 Greek Historians' Versions of Indian Names

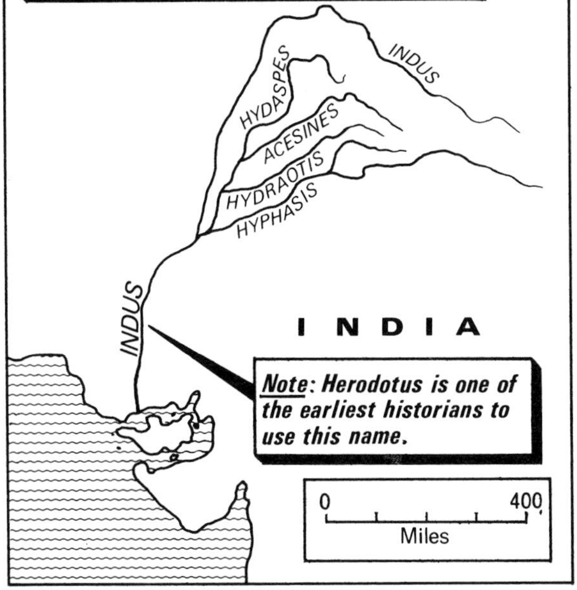

2 Ancient Indian Names

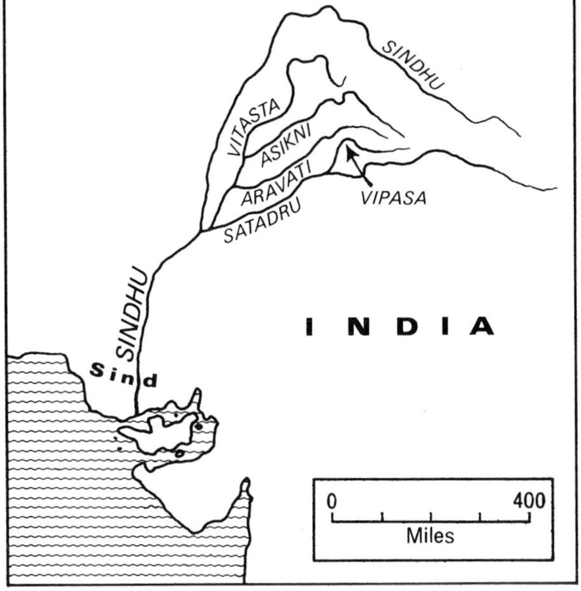

3 Names Current in Medieval and Modern History

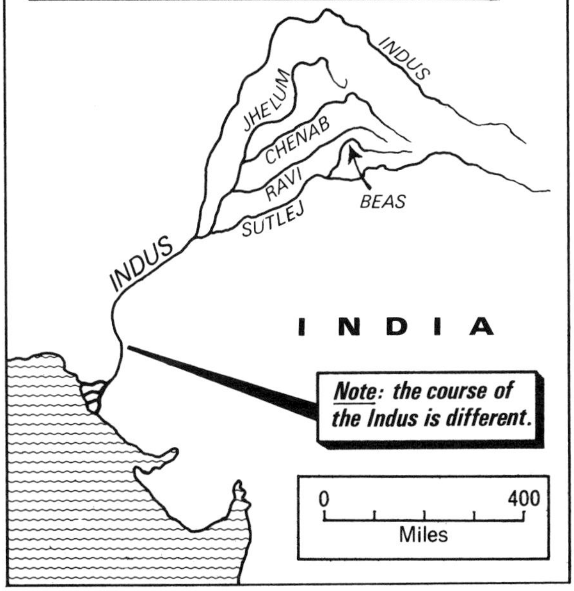

Just as one city may be famous in history under different names (for example, Byzantium - Constantinople - Istanbul), so other changes of name at different periods present a problem to historical cartographers.
The area of north-west India shown on these three sections illustrates this problem, and touches upon another: rivers may change their courses (for example, the Yellow River or Huang Ho in China), and coastlines alter at different periods of history. Often, as at Thermopylae, these changes affect the tactical characteristics of an area.
Side by side with changing nomenclature, goes the additional problem of transliteration (for example, Rheims - Reims).
The Indus (Sindhu in Sanskrit) is the origin of the name India, as well as of Sind.

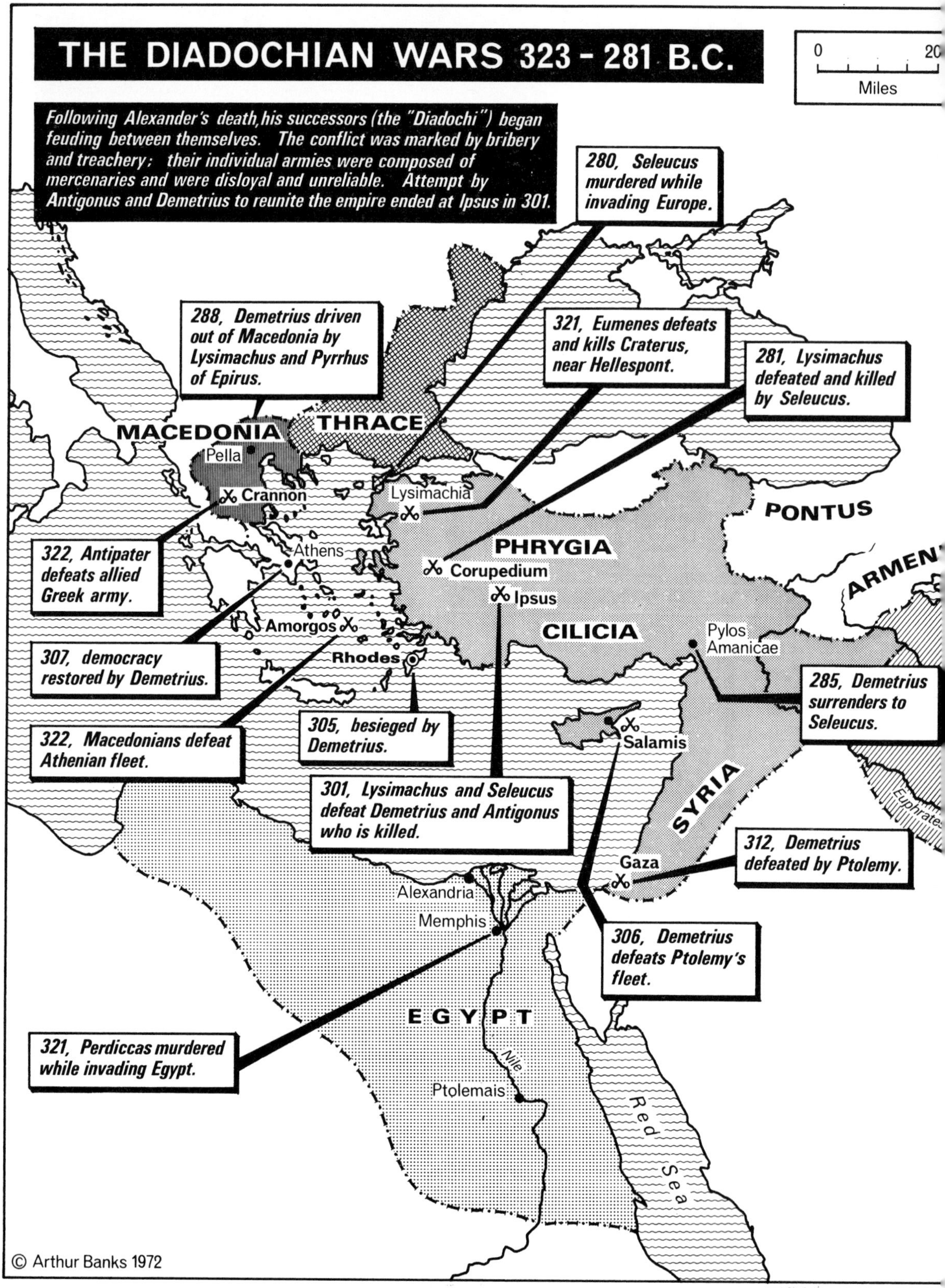
THE DIADOCHIAN WARS 323 - 281 B.C.
0 20
Miles
Following Alexander's death, his successors (the "Diadochi") began feuding between themselves. The conflict was marked by bribery and treachery; their individual armies were composed of mercenaries and were disloyal and unreliable. Attempt by Antigonus and Demetrius to reunite the empire ended at Ipsus in 301.
280, Seleucus murdered while invading Europe.
288, Demetrius driven out of Macedonia by Lysimachus and Pyrrhus of Epirus.
321, Eumenes defeats and kills Craterus, near Hellespont.
281, Lysimachus defeated and killed by Seleucus.
MACEDONIA
THRACE
Pella
Crannon
Lysimachia
PONTUS
PHRYGIA
Corupedium
Ipsus
ARMEN
322, Antipater defeats allied Greek army.
Athens
Amorgos
CILICIA
Pylos Amanicae
307, democracy restored by Demetrius.
Rhodes
285, Demetrius surrenders to Seleucus.
305, besieged by Demetrius.
Salamis
322, Macedonians defeat Athenian fleet.
SYRIA
Euphrates
301, Lysimachus and Seleucus defeat Demetrius and Antigonus who is killed.
312, Demetrius defeated by Ptolemy.
Gaza
Alexandria
Memphis
306, Demetrius defeats Ptolemy's fleet.
EGYPT
321, Perdiccas murdered while invading Egypt.
Nile
Ptolemais
Red Sea
© Arthur Banks 1972

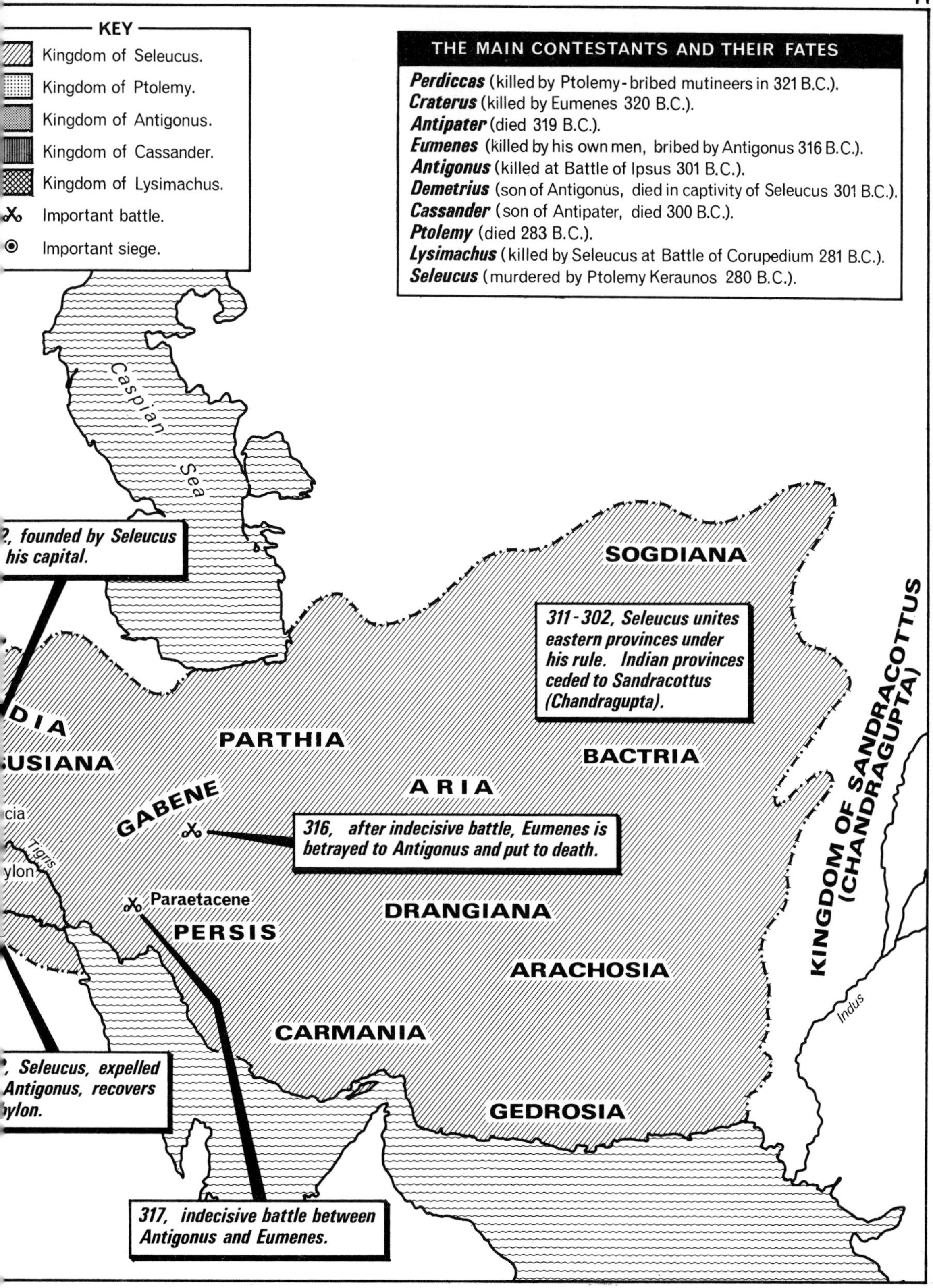
KEY
Kingdom of Seleucus.
Kingdom of Ptolemy.
Kingdom of Antigonus.
Kingdom of Cassander.
Kingdom of Lysimachus.
Important battle.
Important siege.
THE MAIN CONTESTANTS AND THEIR FATES
Perdiccas (killed by Ptolemy-bribed mutineers in 321 B.C.).
Craterus (killed by Eumenes 320 B.C.).
Antipater (died 319 B.C.).
Eumenes (killed by his own men, bribed by Antigonus 316 B.C.).
Antigonus (killed at Battle of Ipsus 301 B.C.).
Demetrius (son of Antigonus, died in captivity of Seleucus 301 B.C.).
Cassander (son of Antipater, died 300 B.C.).
Ptolemy (died 283 B.C.).
Lysimachus (killed by Seleucus at Battle of Corupedium 281 B.C.).
Seleucus (murdered by Ptolemy Keraunos 280 B.C.).
Caspian Sea
, founded by Seleucus
his capital.
SOGDIANA
311-302, Seleucus unites eastern provinces under his rule. Indian provinces ceded to Sandracottus (Chandragupta).
KINGDOM OF SANDRACOTTUS (CHANDRAGUPTA)
DIA
USIANA
PARTHIA
BACTRIA
ARIA
GABENE
cia
Tigris
ylon
316, after indecisive battle, Eumenes is betrayed to Antigonus and put to death.
Paraetacene
PERSIS
DRANGIANA
ARACHOSIA
Indus
CARMANIA
, Seleucus, expelled
Antigonus, recovers
ylon.
GEDROSIA
317, indecisive battle between Antigonus and Eumenes.

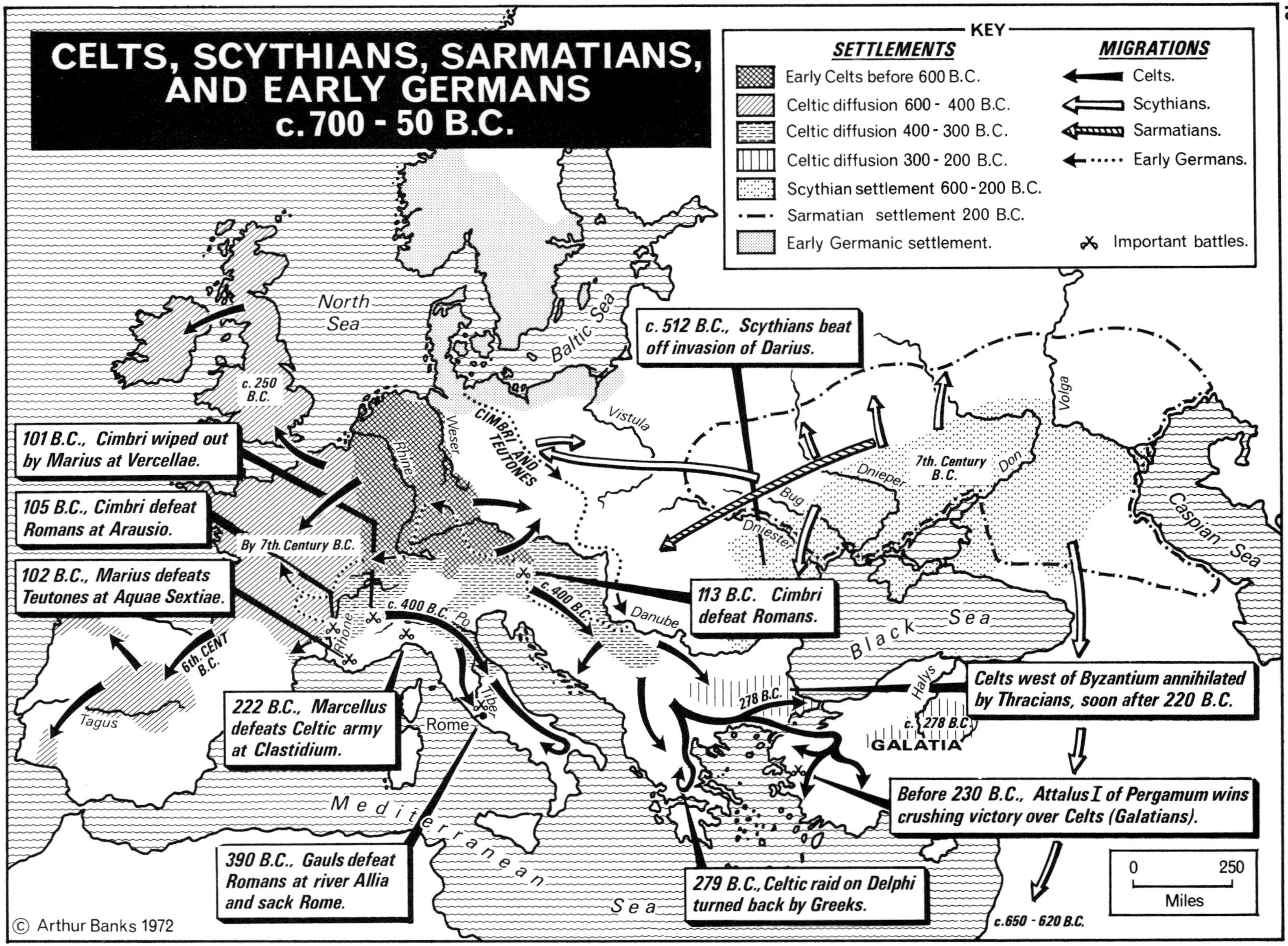
CELTS, SCYTHIANS, SARMATIANS, AND EARLY GERMANS c. 700 - 50 B.C.
KEY
SETTLEMENTS
Early Celts before 600 B.C.
Celtic diffusion 600 - 400 B.C.
Celtic diffusion 400 - 300 B.C.
Celtic diffusion 300 - 200 B.C.
Scythian settlement 600 - 200 B.C.
Sarmatian settlement 200 B.C.
Early Germanic settlement.
MIGRATIONS
Celts.
Scythians.
Sarmatians.
Early Germans.
Important battles.
North Sea
Baltic Sea
Vistula
Weser
Rhine
CIMBRI AND TEUTONES
c. 250 B.C.
By 7th. Century B.C.
c. 512 B.C., Scythians beat off invasion of Darius.
101 B.C., Cimbri wiped out by Marius at Vercellae.
105 B.C., Cimbri defeat Romans at Arausio.
102 B.C., Marius defeats Teutones at Aquae Sextiae.
113 B.C. Cimbri defeat Romans.
c. 400 B.C.
Po
Rhone
Danube
Dnieper
Bug
Dniester
Don
Volga
7th. Century B.C.
Caspian Sea
Black Sea
6th. CENT B.C.
Tagus
222 B.C., Marcellus defeats Celtic army at Clastidium.
Rome
Tiber
278 B.C.
Halys
c. 278 B.C.
GALATIA
Celts west of Byzantium annihilated by Thracians, soon after 220 B.C.
Before 230 B.C., Attalus I of Pergamum wins crushing victory over Celts (Galatians).
Mediterranean Sea
390 B.C., Gauls defeat Romans at river Allia and sack Rome.
279 B.C., Celtic raid on Delphi turned back by Greeks.
0 250 Miles
c. 650 - 620 B.C.

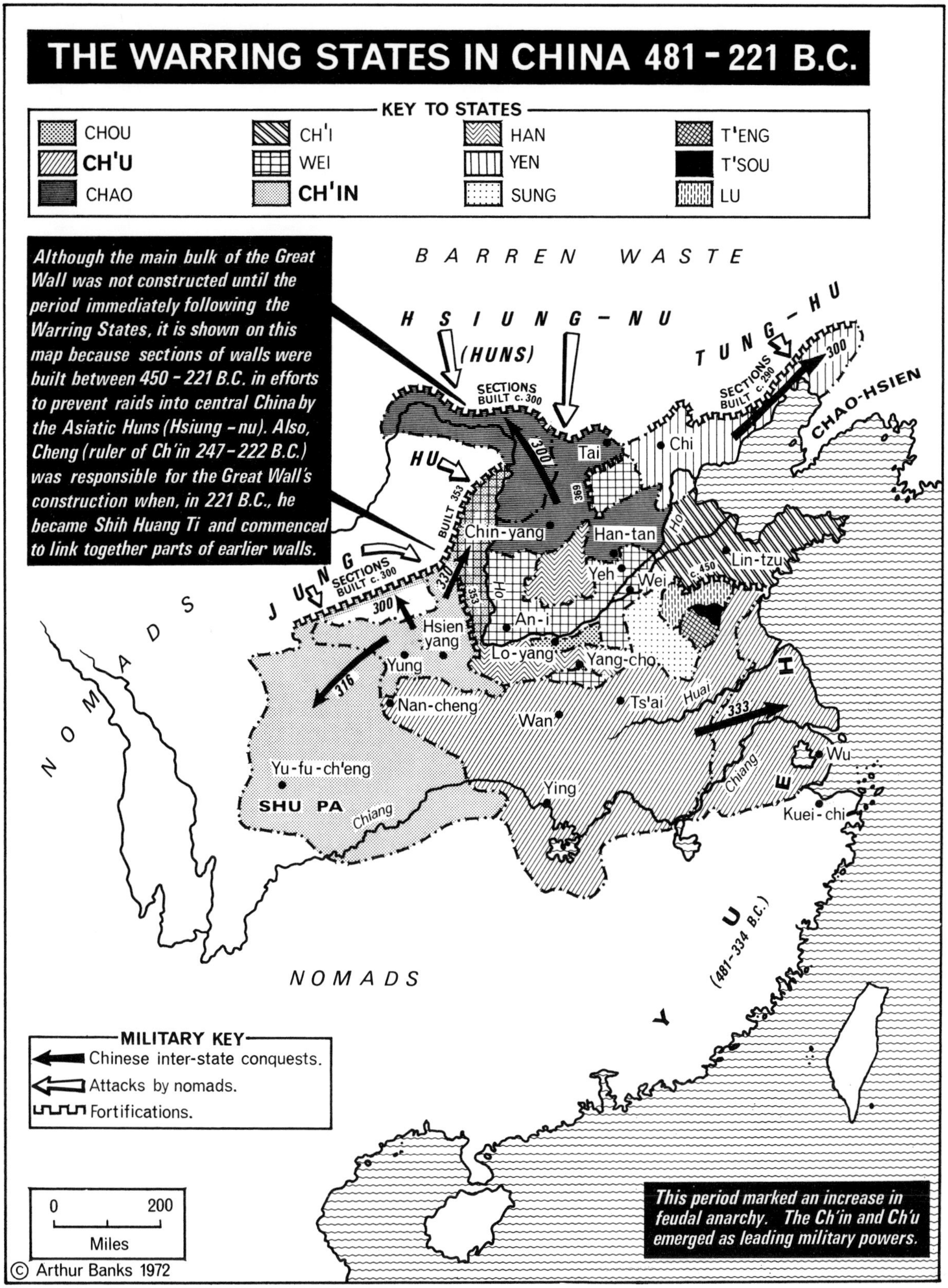
THE WARRING STATES IN CHINA 481 - 221 B.C.
KEY TO STATES
CHOU
CH'U
CHAO
CH'I
WEI
CH'IN
HAN
YEN
SUNG
T'ENG
T'SOU
LU
Although the main bulk of the Great Wall was not constructed until the period immediately following the Warring States, it is shown on this map because sections of walls were built between 450 - 221 B.C. in efforts to prevent raids into central China by the Asiatic Huns (Hsiung - nu). Also, Cheng (ruler of Ch'in 247 - 222 B.C.) was responsible for the Great Wall's construction when, in 221 B.C., he became Shih Huang Ti and commenced to link together parts of earlier walls.
BARREN WASTE
HSIUNG - NU
(HUNS)
TUNG - HU
SECTIONS BUILT c. 300
SECTIONS BUILT c. 290
CHAO-HSIEN
HU
BUILT 353
JUNG
SECTIONS BUILT c. 300
NOMADS
Tai
Chi
Chin-yang
Han-tan
Lin-tzu
Yeh
Wei
Ho
An-i
Hsien yang
Yung
Lo-yang
Yang-cho
Nan-cheng
Ts'ai
Huai
Wan
Wu
Yu-fu-ch'eng
SHU PA
Chiang
Ying
Kuei-chi
YUE
YU (481-334 B.C.)
NOMADS
300
369
353
330
316
450
333
MILITARY KEY
Chinese inter-state conquests.
Attacks by nomads.
Fortifications.
0 200
Miles
This period marked an increase in feudal anarchy. The Ch'in and Ch'u emerged as leading military powers.

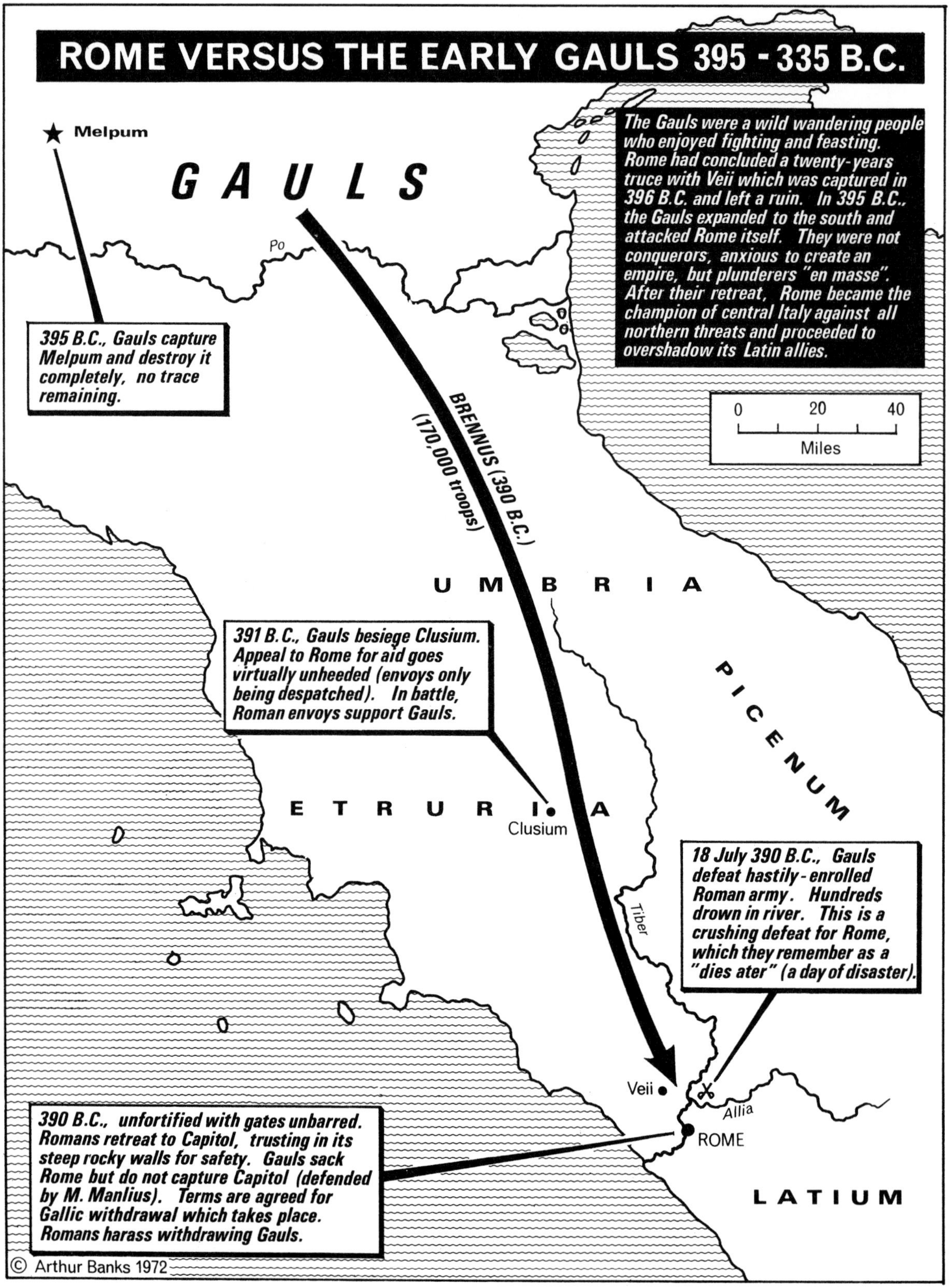
ROME VERSUS THE EARLY GAULS 395 - 335 B.C.
Melpum
GAULS
Po
The Gauls were a wild wandering people who enjoyed fighting and feasting. Rome had concluded a twenty-years truce with Veii which was captured in 396 B.C. and left a ruin. In 395 B.C., the Gauls expanded to the south and attacked Rome itself. They were not conquerors, anxious to create an empire, but plunderers "en masse". After their retreat, Rome became the champion of central Italy against all northern threats and proceeded to overshadow its Latin allies.
395 B.C., Gauls capture Melpum and destroy it completely, no trace remaining.
0 20 40
Miles
BRENNUS (390 B.C.)
(170,000 troops)
UMBRIA
391 B.C., Gauls besiege Clusium. Appeal to Rome for aid goes virtually unheeded (envoys only being despatched). In battle, Roman envoys support Gauls.
PICENUM
ETRURIA
Clusium
18 July 390 B.C., Gauls defeat hastily-enrolled Roman army. Hundreds drown in river. This is a crushing defeat for Rome, which they remember as a "dies ater" (a day of disaster).
Tiber
Veii
Allia
ROME
390 B.C., unfortified with gates unbarred. Romans retreat to Capitol, trusting in its steep rocky walls for safety. Gauls sack Rome but do not capture Capitol (defended by M. Manlius). Terms are agreed for Gallic withdrawal which takes place. Romans harass withdrawing Gauls.
LATIUM
© Arthur Banks 1972

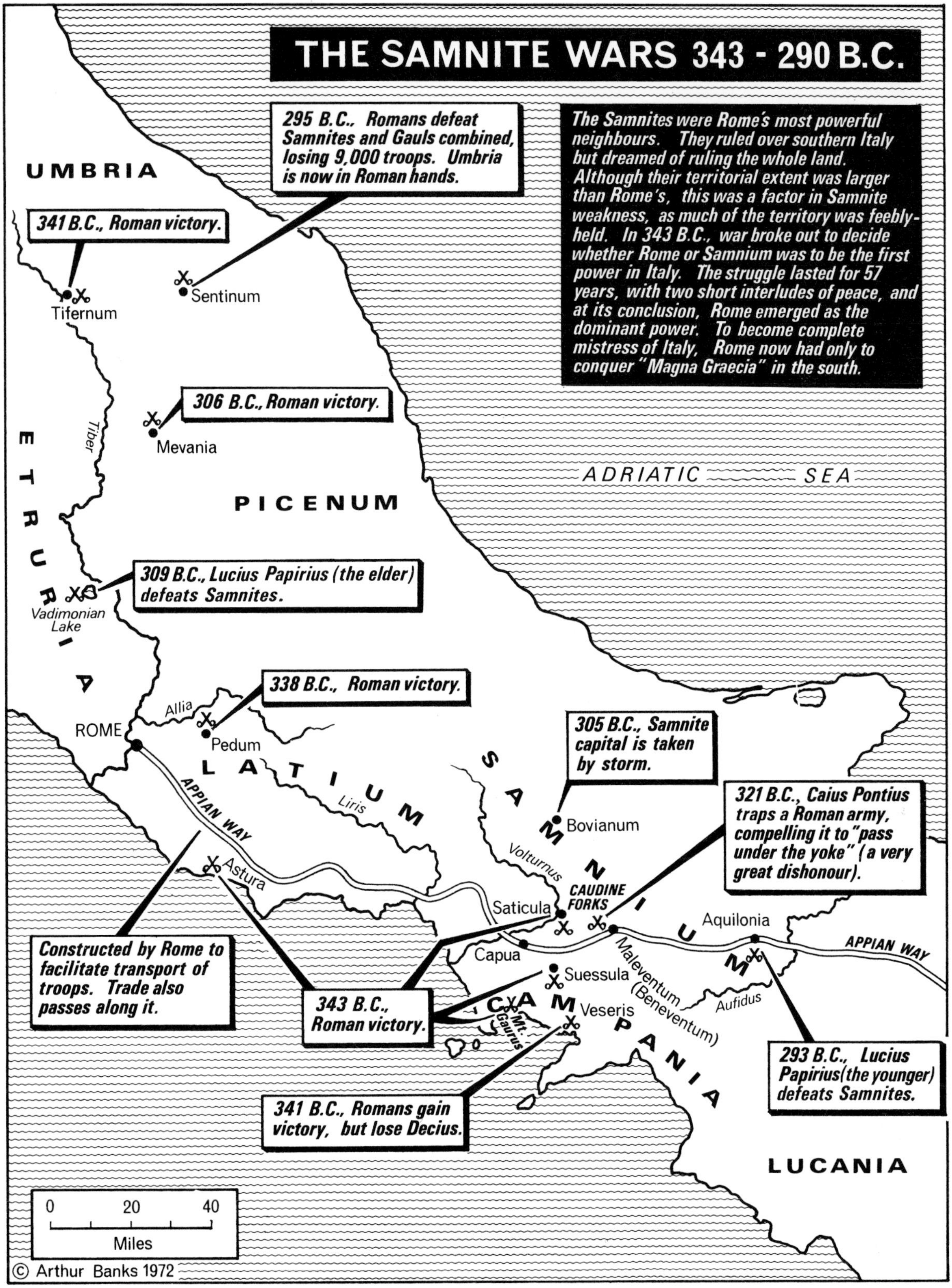
THE SAMNITE WARS 343 - 290 B.C.
The Samnites were Rome's most powerful neighbours. They ruled over southern Italy but dreamed of ruling the whole land. Although their territorial extent was larger than Rome's, this was a factor in Samnite weakness, as much of the territory was feebly-held. In 343 B.C., war broke out to decide whether Rome or Samnium was to be the first power in Italy. The struggle lasted for 57 years, with two short interludes of peace, and at its conclusion, Rome emerged as the dominant power. To become complete mistress of Italy, Rome now had only to conquer "Magna Graecia" in the south.
295 B.C., Romans defeat Samnites and Gauls combined, losing 9,000 troops. Umbria is now in Roman hands.
UMBRIA
341 B.C., Roman victory.
Tifernum
Sentinum
306 B.C., Roman victory.
Mevania
Tiber
ETRURIA
PICENUM
ADRIATIC SEA
309 B.C., Lucius Papirius (the elder) defeats Samnites.
Vadimonian Lake
338 B.C., Roman victory.
Allia
ROME
Pedum
LATIUM
Liris
APPIAN WAY
Astura
SAMNIUM
305 B.C., Samnite capital is taken by storm.
Bovianum
321 B.C., Caius Pontius traps a Roman army, compelling it to "pass under the yoke" (a very great dishonour).
Volturnus
CAUDINE FORKS
Saticula
Aquilonia
APPIAN WAY
Capua
Suessula
Maleventum (Beneventum)
Aufidus
Constructed by Rome to facilitate transport of troops. Trade also passes along it.
343 B.C., Roman victory.
CAMPANIA
Mt. Gaurus
Veseris
293 B.C., Lucius Papirius (the younger) defeats Samnites.
341 B.C., Romans gain victory, but lose Decius.
LUCANIA
0 20 40
Miles
© Arthur Banks 1972

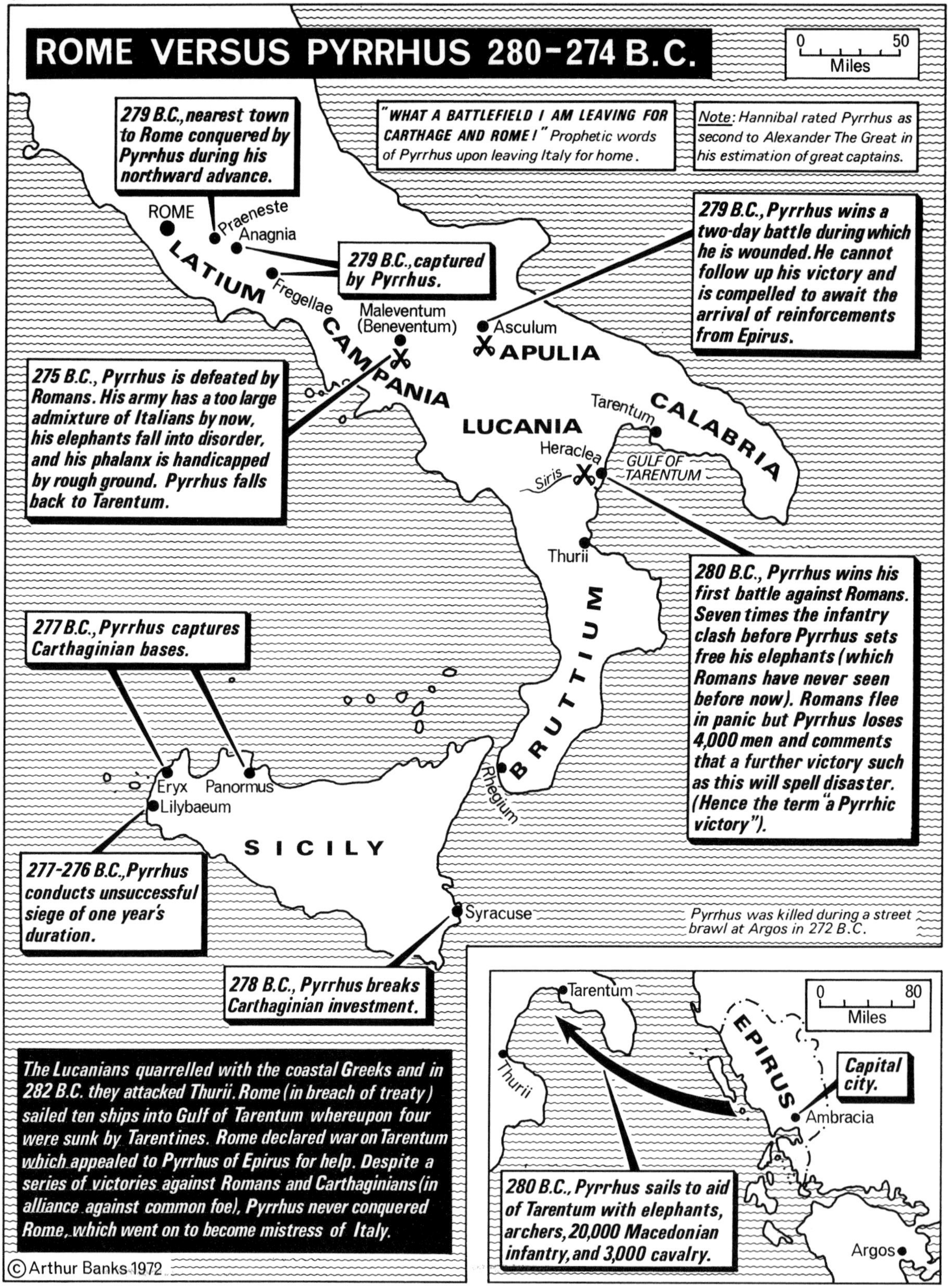
ROME VERSUS PYRRHUS 280-274 B.C.
0 50 Miles
279 B.C., nearest town to Rome conquered by Pyrrhus during his northward advance.
"WHAT A BATTLEFIELD I AM LEAVING FOR CARTHAGE AND ROME!" Prophetic words of Pyrrhus upon leaving Italy for home.
Note: Hannibal rated Pyrrhus as second to Alexander The Great in his estimation of great captains.
ROME
Praeneste
Anagnia
LATIUM
Fregellae
279 B.C., captured by Pyrrhus.
279 B.C., Pyrrhus wins a two-day battle during which he is wounded. He cannot follow up his victory and is compelled to await the arrival of reinforcements from Epirus.
Maleventum (Beneventum)
Asculum
APULIA
CAMPANIA
275 B.C., Pyrrhus is defeated by Romans. His army has a too large admixture of Italians by now, his elephants fall into disorder, and his phalanx is handicapped by rough ground. Pyrrhus falls back to Tarentum.
Tarentum
CALABRIA
LUCANIA
Heraclea
Siris
GULF OF TARENTUM
Thurii
BRUTTIUM
280 B.C., Pyrrhus wins his first battle against Romans. Seven times the infantry clash before Pyrrhus sets free his elephants (which Romans have never seen before now). Romans flee in panic but Pyrrhus loses 4,000 men and comments that a further victory such as this will spell disaster. (Hence the term "a Pyrrhic victory").
277 B.C., Pyrrhus captures Carthaginian bases.
Eryx
Panormus
Lilybaeum
Rhegium
SICILY
277-276 B.C., Pyrrhus conducts unsuccessful siege of one year's duration.
Syracuse
Pyrrhus was killed during a street brawl at Argos in 272 B.C.
278 B.C., Pyrrhus breaks Carthaginian investment.
The Lucanians quarrelled with the coastal Greeks and in 282 B.C. they attacked Thurii. Rome (in breach of treaty) sailed ten ships into Gulf of Tarentum whereupon four were sunk by Tarentines. Rome declared war on Tarentum which appealed to Pyrrhus of Epirus for help. Despite a series of victories against Romans and Carthaginians (in alliance against common foe), Pyrrhus never conquered Rome, which went on to become mistress of Italy.
Tarentum
Thurii
EPIRUS
0 80 Miles
Capital city.
Ambracia
280 B.C., Pyrrhus sails to aid of Tarentum with elephants, archers, 20,000 Macedonian infantry, and 3,000 cavalry.
Argos

CARTHAGINIAN POWER IN THE WESTERN MEDITERRANEAN

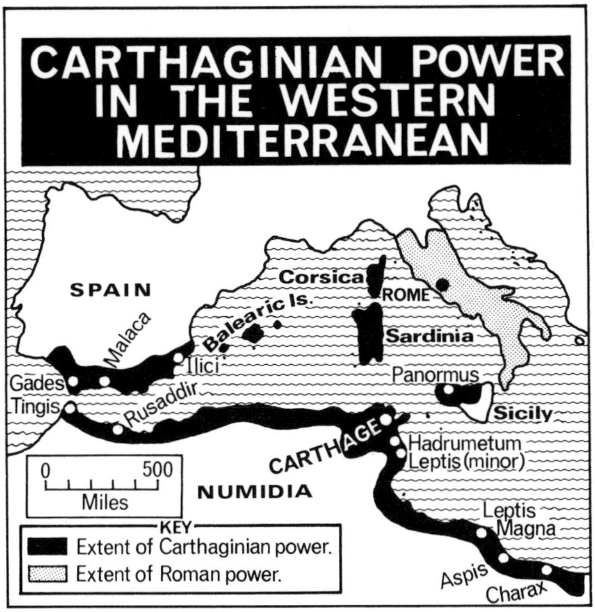

The forthcoming struggle between Rome and Carthage (the "Punic city") was to decide which power was to rule the world. In the event, Rome emerged victorious, with its subsequent influence on history. Two great commanders were involved: Hannibal (for Carthage) and Scipio (for Rome).

ROMAN ITALY

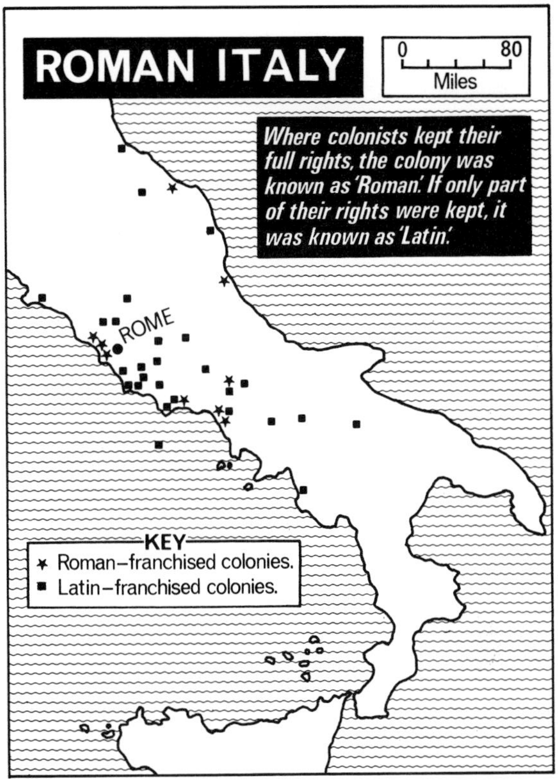

Where colonists kept their full rights, the colony was known as 'Roman.' If only part of their rights were kept, it was known as 'Latin.'

THE TWO GIANTS COMPARED

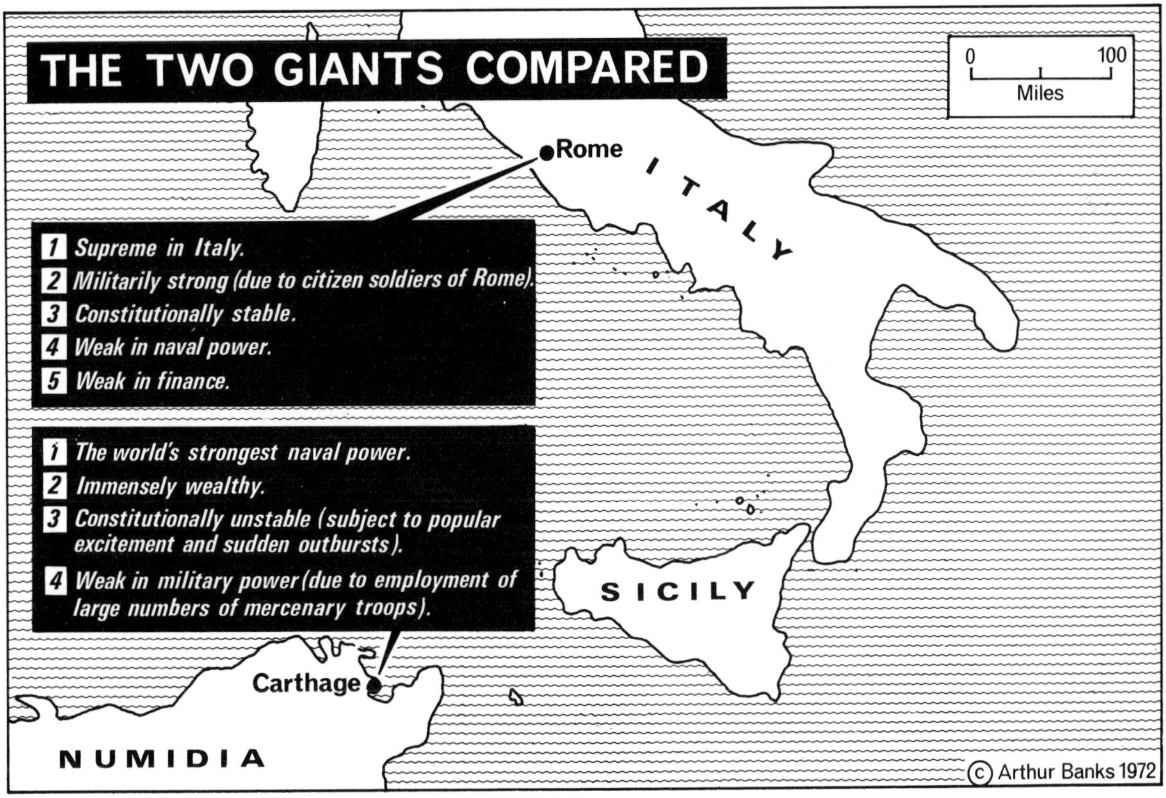

1 Supreme in Italy.
2 Militarily strong (due to citizen soldiers of Rome).
3 Constitutionally stable.
4 Weak in naval power.
5 Weak in finance.

1 The world's strongest naval power.
2 Immensely wealthy.
3 Constitutionally unstable (subject to popular excitement and sudden outbursts).
4 Weak in military power (due to employment of large numbers of mercenary troops).

THE FIRST PUNIC WAR 264 - 242 B.C.

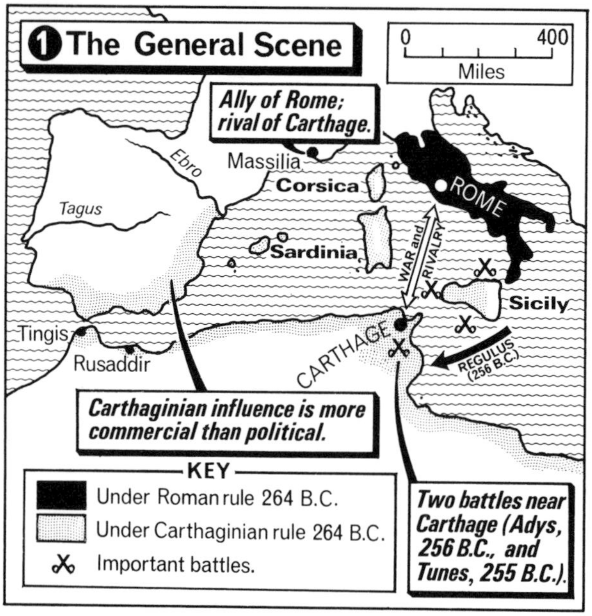

1 The General Scene
0 400 Miles
Ally of Rome; rival of Carthage.
Massilia
Ebro
Tagus
Corsica
Sardinia
ROME
WAR and RIVALRY
Sicily
Tingis
Rusaddir
CARTHAGE
REGULUS (256 B.C.)
Carthaginian influence is more commercial than political.
KEY
Under Roman rule 264 B.C.
Under Carthaginian rule 264 B.C.
Important battles.
Two battles near Carthage (Adys, 256 B.C., and Tunes, 255 B.C.).

CAUSES OF THE WAR

1. The Mamertines (Campanian mercenaries) seized Messana but were defeated by Hiero II of Syracuse at Mylae (270 B.C.), whereupon they appealed to Carthage for help.
2. Hanno arrived from Carthage and occupied citadel at Messana.
3. Romans ousted Hanno and made treaty with Hiero II.
4. Thus, the war was to decide whether Rome or Carthage was to be paramount in Sicily.

THE NAVAL WAR

1. The Carthaginians were supreme at the outset, so the Romans started a programme of naval construction.
2. Battles apart, the Romans unfortunately lost 700 ships and 200,000 troops in four sudden storms during war.
3. Roman tactics were to row their vessels next to the enemy crafts, secure them together with 'corvi' (crows), and fight a semi land-battle across the decks.

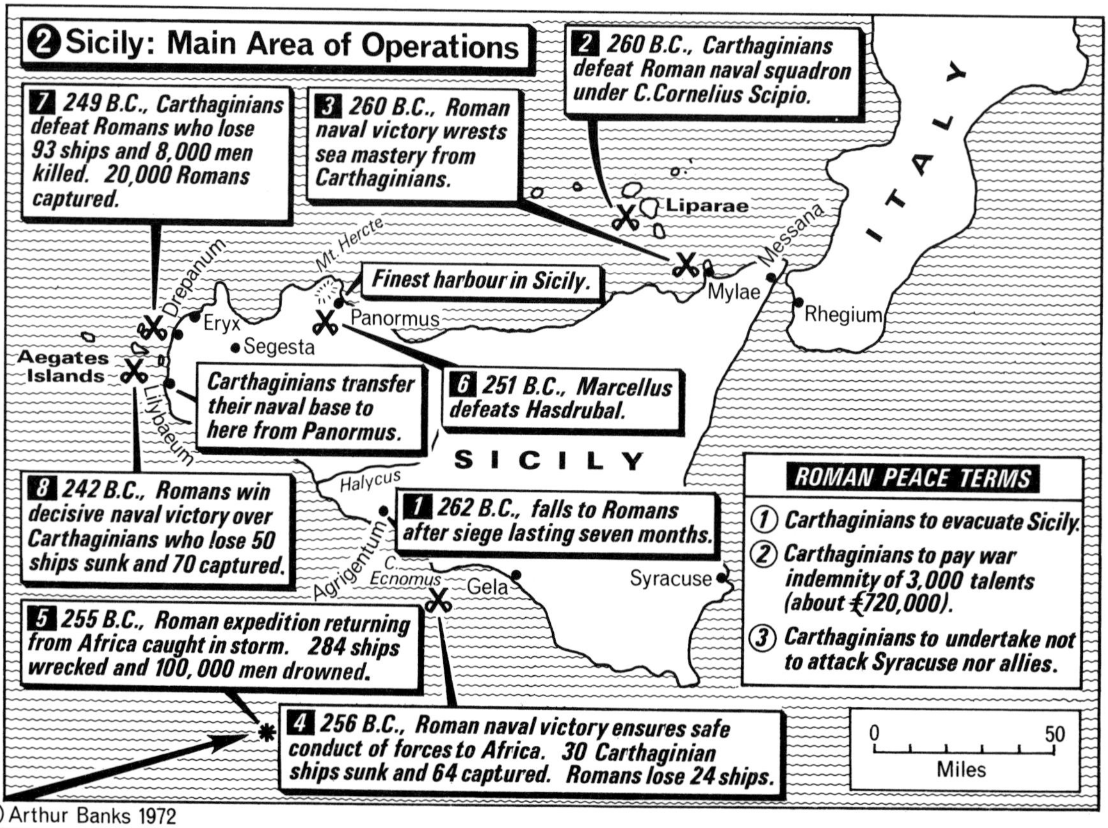

2 Sicily: Main Area of Operations
2 260 B.C., Carthaginians defeat Roman naval squadron under C.Cornelius Scipio.
7 249 B.C., Carthaginians defeat Romans who lose 93 ships and 8,000 men killed. 20,000 Romans captured.
3 260 B.C., Roman naval victory wrests sea mastery from Carthaginians.
ITALY
Liparae
Messana
Mylae
Rhegium
Mt. Hercte
Finest harbour in Sicily.
Drepanum
Eryx
Panormus
Segesta
Aegates Islands
Lilybaeum
Carthaginians transfer their naval base to here from Panormus.
6 251 B.C., Marcellus defeats Hasdrubal.
SICILY
Halycus
8 242 B.C., Romans win decisive naval victory over Carthaginians who lose 50 ships sunk and 70 captured.
1 262 B.C., falls to Romans after siege lasting seven months.
Agrigentum
C. Ecnomus
Gela
Syracuse
ROMAN PEACE TERMS
(1) Carthaginians to evacuate Sicily.
(2) Carthaginians to pay war indemnity of 3,000 talents (about £720,000).
(3) Carthaginians to undertake not to attack Syracuse nor allies.
5 255 B.C., Roman expedition returning from Africa caught in storm. 284 ships wrecked and 100,000 men drowned.
4 256 B.C., Roman naval victory ensures safe conduct of forces to Africa. 30 Carthaginian ships sunk and 64 captured. Romans lose 24 ships.
0 50 Miles

THE GENERAL SCENE BETWEEN FIRST AND SECOND PUNIC WARS

The First Punic War had been fought for possession of Sicily. the Second Punic War was to be for possession of Spain. Between the two main wars, a number of smaller wars and skirmishes occurred. In 229 B.C., the Greek states requested Roman aid in suppressing Illyrian piracy and this assistance was forthcoming. 225 - 222 B.C., a Gallic invasion of Italy forced the Romans to extend their existing military road (between Rome and Spoletium) to Ariminium and to fight a number of battles with the Boii. Meanwhile, as Rome prepared Sicily as a new base for possible operations against Spain and Africa, Hannibal had a fresh plan in mind — to invade Italy itself!

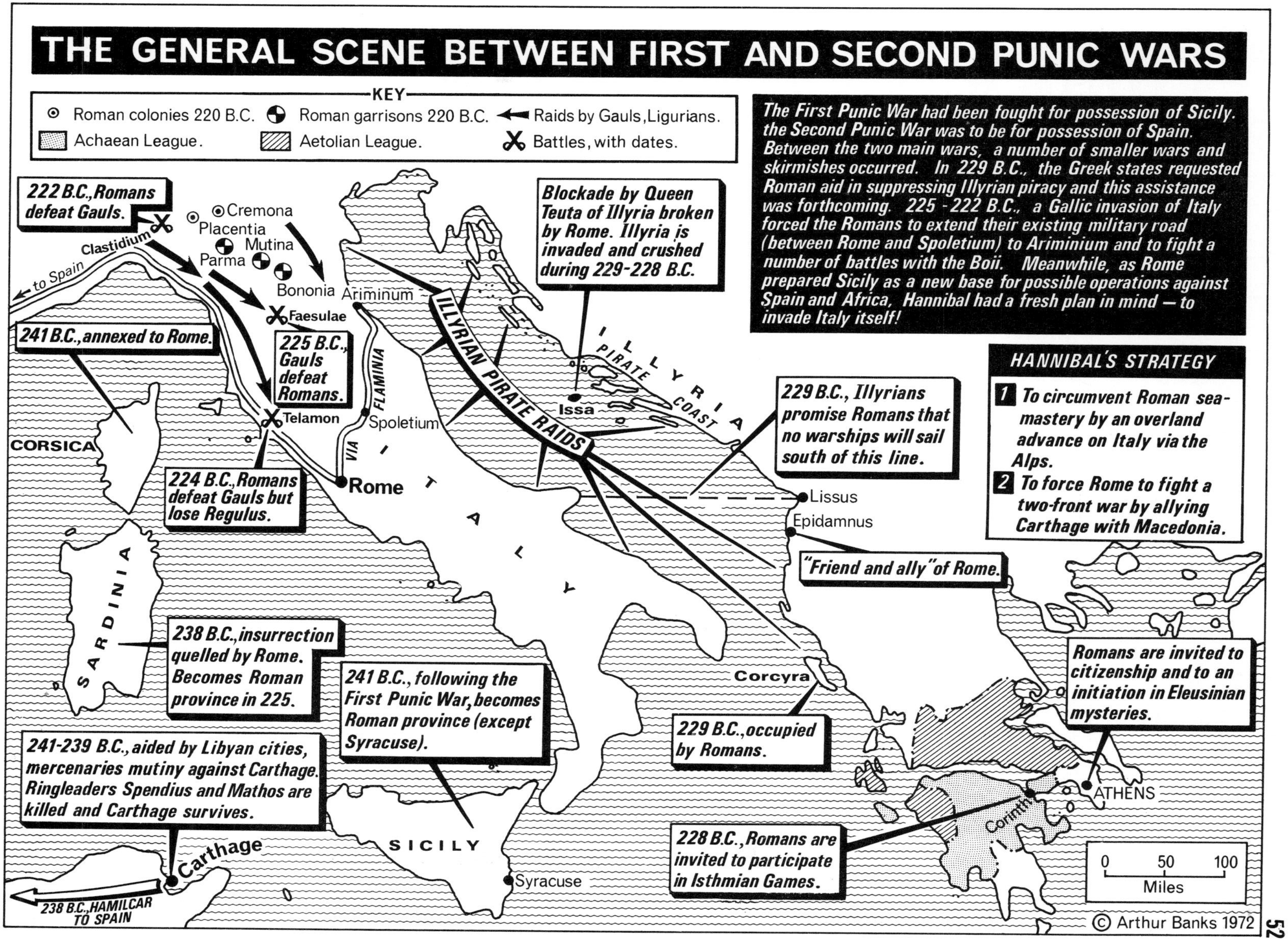

KEY
Roman colonies 220 B.C.
Roman garrisons 220 B.C.
Raids by Gauls, Ligurians.
Achaean League.
Aetolian League.
Battles, with dates.
HANNIBAL'S STRATEGY
1 To circumvent Roman sea-mastery by an overland advance on Italy via the Alps.
2 To force Rome to fight a two-front war by allying Carthage with Macedonia.
222 B.C., Romans defeat Gauls.
241 B.C., annexed to Rome.
225 B.C., Gauls defeat Romans.
224 B.C., Romans defeat Gauls but lose Regulus.
Blockade by Queen Teuta of Illyria broken by Rome. Illyria is invaded and crushed during 229-228 B.C.
229 B.C., Illyrians promise Romans that no warships will sail south of this line.
"Friend and ally" of Rome.
238 B.C., insurrection quelled by Rome. Becomes Roman province in 225.
241 B.C., following the First Punic War, becomes Roman province (except Syracuse).
229 B.C., occupied by Romans.
Romans are invited to citizenship and to an initiation in Eleusinian mysteries.
241-239 B.C., aided by Libyan cities, mercenaries mutiny against Carthage. Ringleaders Spendius and Mathos are killed and Carthage survives.
228 B.C., Romans are invited to participate in Isthmian Games.
238 B.C., HAMILCAR TO SPAIN
to Spain
Clastidium
Cremona
Placentia
Mutina
Parma
Bononia
Ariminum
Faesulae
Telamon
VIA FLAMINIA
Spoletium
Rome
CORSICA
SARDINIA
ITALY
SICILY
Syracuse
Carthage
ILLYRIAN PIRATE RAIDS
ILLYRIA
PIRATE COAST
Issa
Lissus
Epidamnus
Corcyra
Corinth
ATHENS
0 50 100
Miles
© Arthur Banks 1972

HANNIBAL AND THE SECOND PUNIC WAR 218-201 B.

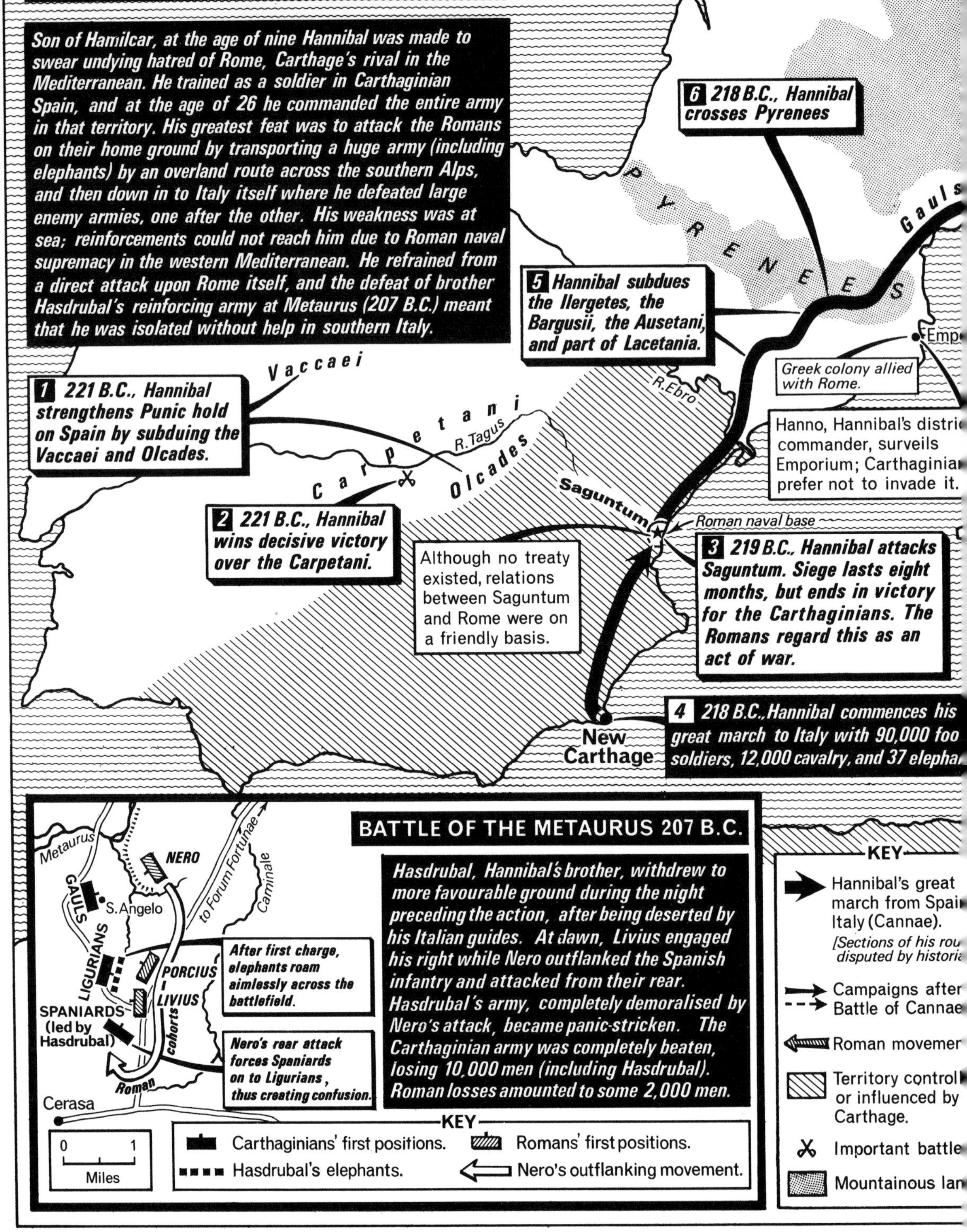
Son of Hamilcar, at the age of nine Hannibal was made to swear undying hatred of Rome, Carthage's rival in the Mediterranean. He trained as a soldier in Carthaginian Spain, and at the age of 26 he commanded the entire army in that territory. His greatest feat was to attack the Romans on their home ground by transporting a huge army (including elephants) by an overland route across the southern Alps, and then down in to Italy itself where he defeated large enemy armies, one after the other. His weakness was at sea; reinforcements could not reach him due to Roman naval supremacy in the western Mediterranean. He refrained from a direct attack upon Rome itself, and the defeat of brother Hasdrubal's reinforcing army at Metaurus (207 B.C.) meant that he was isolated without help in southern Italy.
6 218 B.C., Hannibal crosses Pyrenees
PYRENEES
Gauls
5 Hannibal subdues the Ilergetes, the Bargusii, the Ausetani, and part of Lacetania.
Empo
Greek colony allied with Rome.
Vaccaei
1 221 B.C., Hannibal strengthens Punic hold on Spain by subduing the Vaccaei and Olcades.
Carpetani
R. Tagus
R. Ebro
Olcades
Hanno, Hannibal's distri commander, surveils Emporium; Carthaginia prefer not to invade it.
Saguntum
Roman naval base
2 221 B.C., Hannibal wins decisive victory over the Carpetani.
Although no treaty existed, relations between Saguntum and Rome were on a friendly basis.
3 219 B.C., Hannibal attacks Saguntum. Siege lasts eight months, but ends in victory for the Carthaginians. The Romans regard this as an act of war.
4 218 B.C., Hannibal commences his great march to Italy with 90,000 foo soldiers, 12,000 cavalry, and 37 elepha
New Carthage
BATTLE OF THE METAURUS 207 B.C.
Metaurus
NERO
to Forum Fortunae
Caminale
GAULS
S. Angelo
LIGURIANS
PORCIUS
LIVIUS
cohorts
SPANIARDS (led by Hasdrubal)
Roman
Cerasa
After first charge, elephants roam aimlessly across the battlefield.
Nero's rear attack forces Spaniards on to Ligurians, thus creating confusion.
Hasdrubal, Hannibal's brother, withdrew to more favourable ground during the night preceding the action, after being deserted by his Italian guides. At dawn, Livius engaged his right while Nero outflanked the Spanish infantry and attacked from their rear. Hasdrubal's army, completely demoralised by Nero's attack, became panic-stricken. The Carthaginian army was completely beaten, losing 10,000 men (including Hasdrubal). Roman losses amounted to some 2,000 men.
0 1 Miles
KEY
Carthaginians' first positions.
Hasdrubal's elephants.
Romans' first positions.
Nero's outflanking movement.
KEY
Hannibal's great march from Spai Italy (Cannae).
[Sections of his rou disputed by historia
Campaigns after Battle of Cannae
Roman movemer
Territory control or influenced by Carthage.
Important battle
Mountainous lan

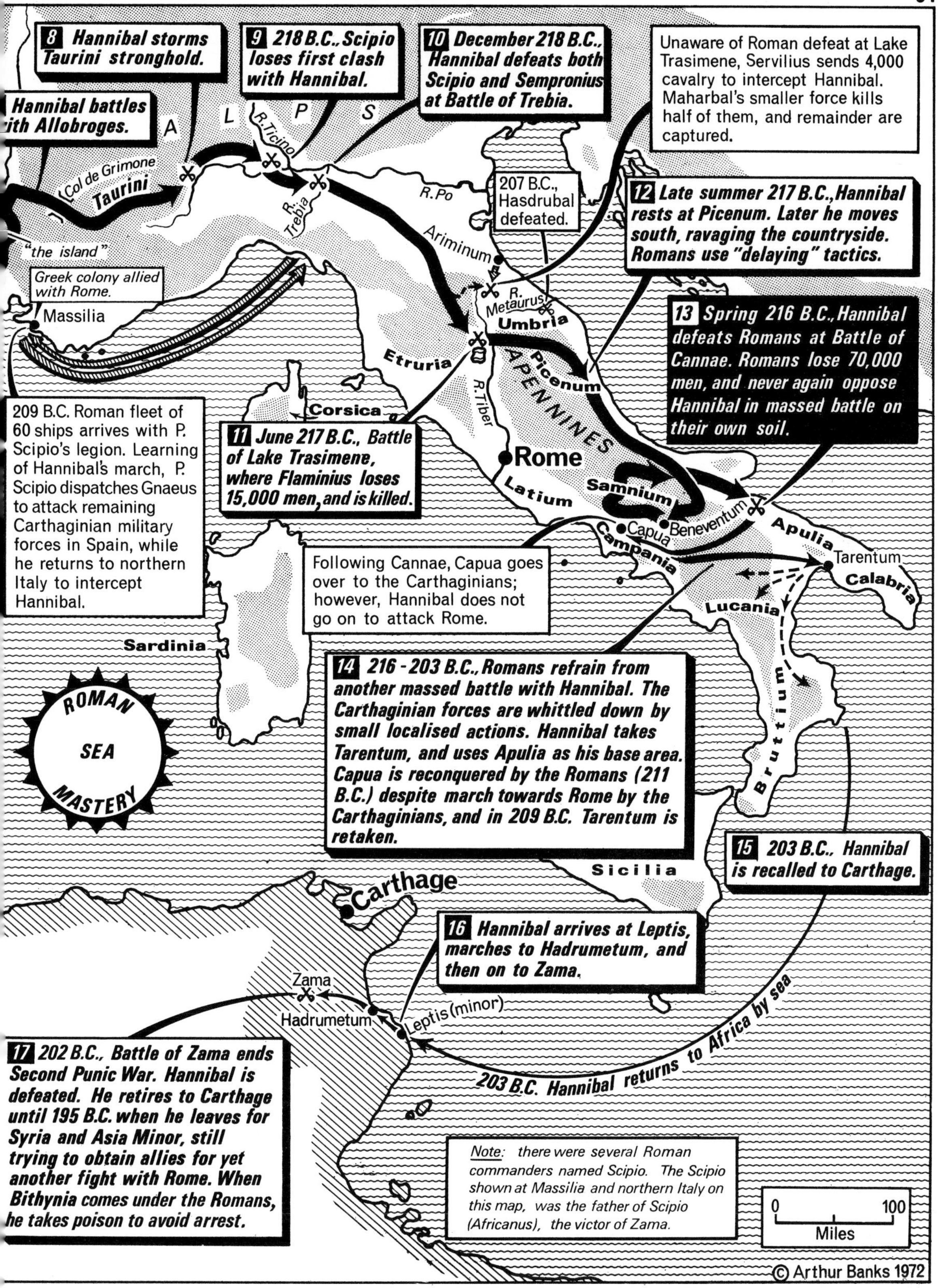

8 Hannibal storms Taurini stronghold.
9 218 B.C., Scipio loses first clash with Hannibal.
10 December 218 B.C., Hannibal defeats both Scipio and Sempronius at Battle of Trebia.
Unaware of Roman defeat at Lake Trasimene, Servilius sends 4,000 cavalry to intercept Hannibal. Maharbal's smaller force kills half of them, and remainder are captured.
Hannibal battles ith Allobroges.
A L P S
R. Ticino
Col de Grimone
Taurini
R. Trebia
R. Po
207 B.C., Hasdrubal defeated.
12 Late summer 217 B.C., Hannibal rests at Picenum. Later he moves south, ravaging the countryside. Romans use "delaying" tactics.
"the island"
Greek colony allied with Rome.
Massilia
Ariminum
R. Metaurus
Umbria
Etruria
Picenum
APENNINES
13 Spring 216 B.C., Hannibal defeats Romans at Battle of Cannae. Romans lose 70,000 men, and never again oppose Hannibal in massed battle on their own soil.
209 B.C. Roman fleet of 60 ships arrives with P. Scipio's legion. Learning of Hannibal's march, P. Scipio dispatches Gnaeus to attack remaining Carthaginian military forces in Spain, while he returns to northern Italy to intercept Hannibal.
Corsica
R. Tiber
11 June 217 B.C., Battle of Lake Trasimene, where Flaminius loses 15,000 men, and is killed.
Rome
Latium
Samnium
Beneventum
Capua
Campania
Apulia
Tarentum
Calabria
Lucania
Following Cannae, Capua goes over to the Carthaginians; however, Hannibal does not go on to attack Rome.
Sardinia
ROMAN SEA MASTERY
14 216 - 203 B.C., Romans refrain from another massed battle with Hannibal. The Carthaginian forces are whittled down by small localised actions. Hannibal takes Tarentum, and uses Apulia as his base area. Capua is reconquered by the Romans (211 B.C.) despite march towards Rome by the Carthaginians, and in 209 B.C. Tarentum is retaken.
Bruttium
15 203 B.C., Hannibal is recalled to Carthage.
Sicilia
Carthage
16 Hannibal arrives at Leptis, marches to Hadrumetum, and then on to Zama.
Zama
Hadrumetum
Leptis (minor)
203 B.C. Hannibal returns to Africa by sea
17 202 B.C., Battle of Zama ends Second Punic War. Hannibal is defeated. He retires to Carthage until 195 B.C. when he leaves for Syria and Asia Minor, still trying to obtain allies for yet another fight with Rome. When Bithynia comes under the Romans, he takes poison to avoid arrest.
Note: there were several Roman commanders named Scipio. The Scipio shown at Massilia and northern Italy on this map, was the father of Scipio (Africanus), the victor of Zama.
0 100 Miles

HANNIBAL'S GREAT BATTLES

0 1 2 3 4 5 6 7
Miles

❶ Trebia: December 218 B.C.

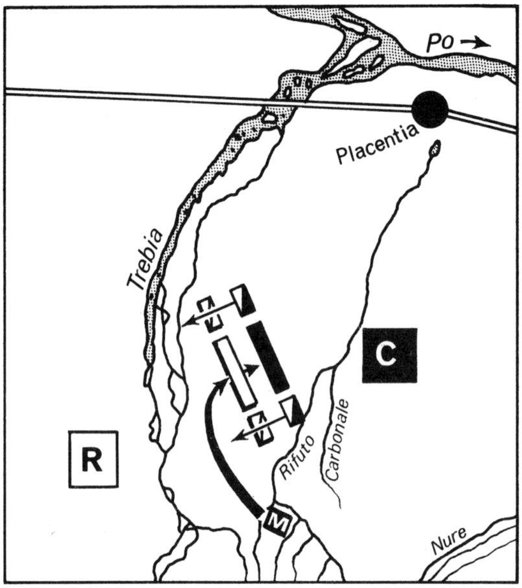

KEY

- C Carthaginian encampment.
- Carthaginian infantr
- Carthaginian cavalry.
- M Mago's detachment.
- R Roman encampment.
- Roman infantry.
- Roman cavalry.

RIVAL STRENGTHS

CARTHAGINIANS	ROMANS
28,000 infantry.	36,000 infantry.
10,000 cavalry.	4,000 cavalry.

Two Roman armies were concentrated near Placentia, under bo Scipio (father of Scipio 'Africanus') and Sempronius. Hannibal h 2,000 men (under his brother Mago) in a ravine to the south, and then attacked the Roman encampment. Feigning defea Hannibal retired across the Trebia hotly pursued by Semproni. Driving rain over the battlefield obscured the advance of Mag who attacked the Romans from their rear. Thus, the Roman forces were trapped between the two Carthaginian position and virtually annihilated. As a result of this victory, 60,000 previously "uncommitted" tribesmen (mainly Gauls) flocked to join Hannibal, swelling his ranks.

❷ Lake Trasimene: April 217 B.C.

In an ambush north of Lake Trasimer Hannibal surprised Flaminius (who h not adequately reconnoitred the wa ahead). 40,000 Romans were trapp in a four-mile defile and attacked fr three directions simultaneously. 15,000 Romans were killed (includin Flaminius and another 15,000 captur A 4,000-strong cavalry force sent o by Servilius was likewise annihilate

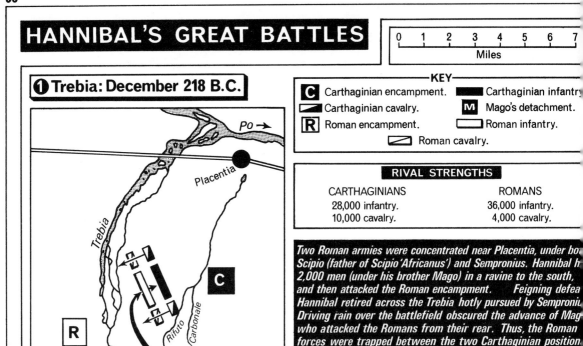

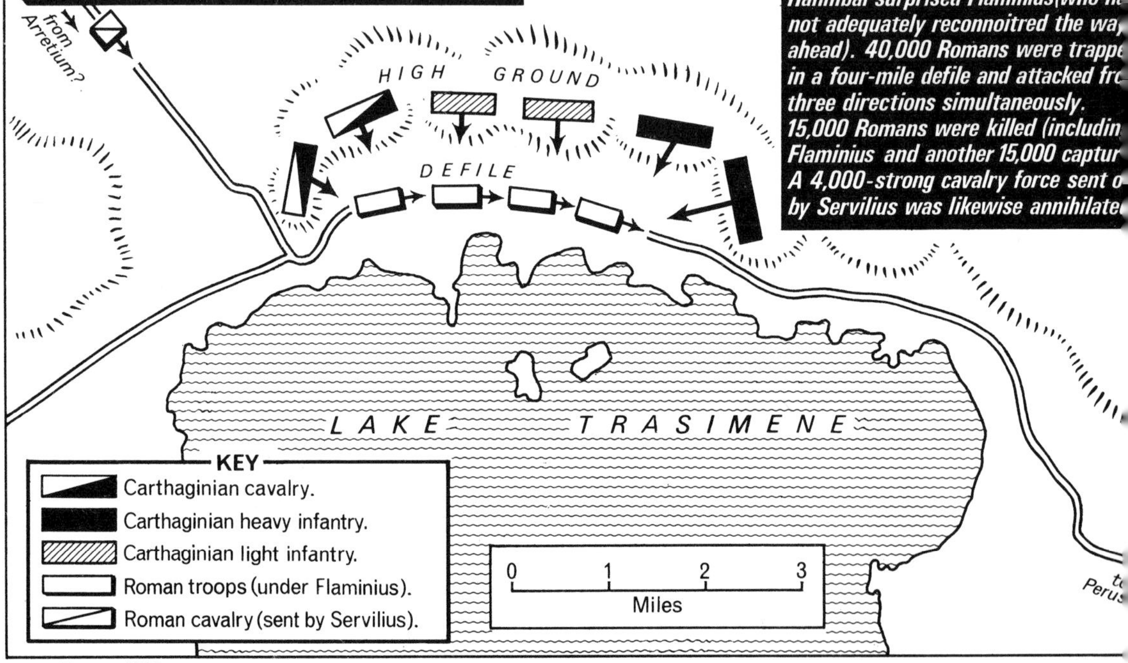

KEY

- Carthaginian cavalry.
- Carthaginian heavy infantry.
- Carthaginian light infantry.
- Roman troops (under Flaminius).
- Roman cavalry (sent by Servilius).

0 1 2 3
Miles

Cannae: 2 August 216 B.C. (Hannibal's greatest victory)

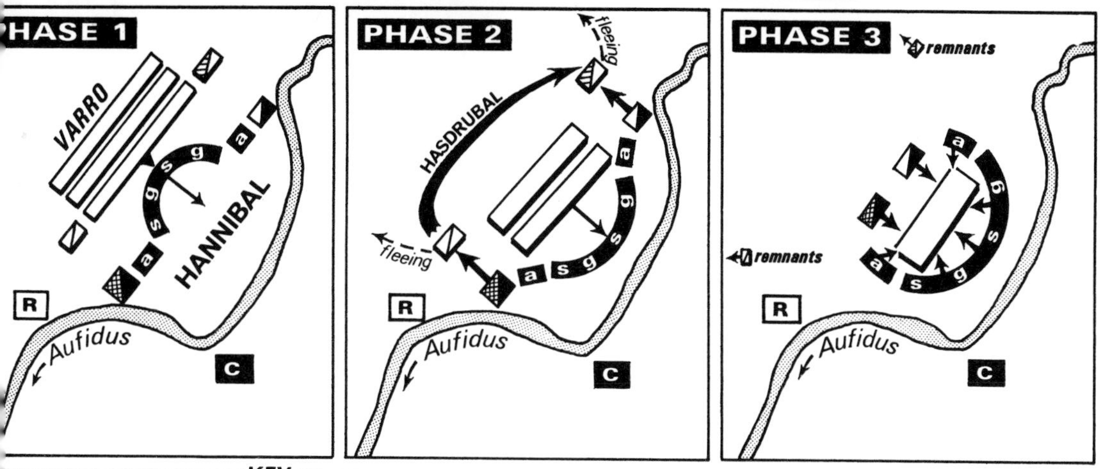

KEY

RTHAGINIANS
- Carthaginian encampment.
- Spanish and Gallic heavy cavalry.
- Numidian light cavalry.
- African infantry.
- Spanish and Gallic infantry.

ROMANS
- Roman encampment.
- Roman cavalry.
- Allied horsemen.
- Allied infantry.

Phase 1 *Hannibal's infantry was drawn up in convex formation with cavalry on the wings. As the Romans advanced, the centre was withdrawn to a concave line.* ***Phase 2*** *Hannibal's cavalry defeated the Roman cavalry.* ***Phase 3*** *Roman front and flanks were now engulfed and encirclement was completed by Hannibal's cavalry units. Of Roman army of 89,600, 70,000 were killed (according to Polybius). Carthaginian losses were only 5,700.*

Zama: 19 October 202 B.C. (Hannibal's defeat by Scipio)*

** Later known as 'Africanus' by the Romans. (Full name: PUBLIUS CORNELIUS SCIPIO AFRICANUS).*

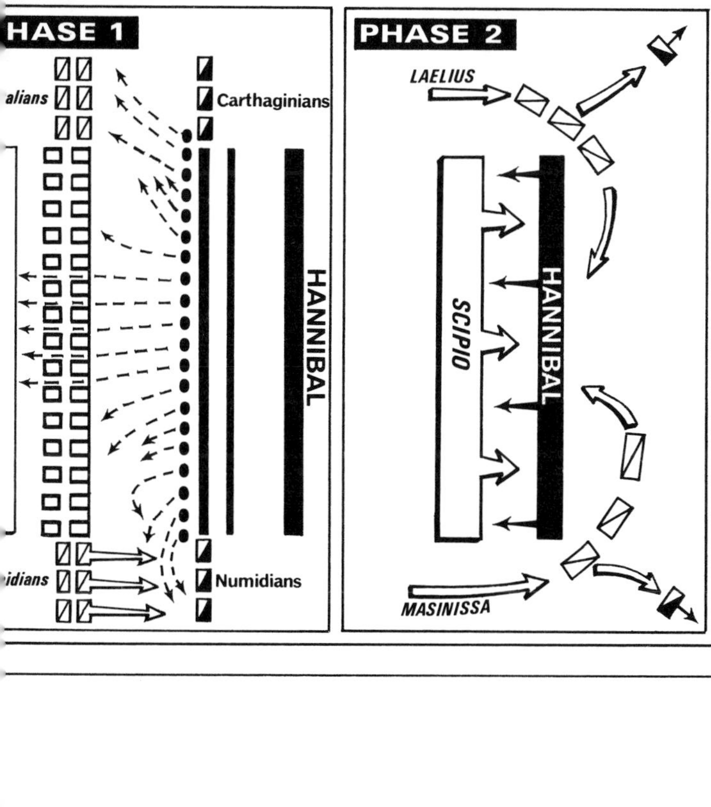

KEY

HANNIBAL
- Main Carthaginian force (Bruttians).
- Ligurian and Gallic infantry.
- Carthaginian and African infantry.
- Cavalry.
- 80 elephants (disposed in advance).
- Advances and retreats.

SCIPIO
- Main Roman force (triarii).
- First line of velites (hastati).
- Second line of velites (principes).
- Cavalry.
- Advances.

Phase 1 *Hannibal advanced his elephants; most were diverted by Roman horn blasts. Masinissa advanced his Numidian cavalry.* ***Phase 2*** *Scipio's infantry engaged Hannibal and initially the Carthaginians held firm. Cavalry attacks by Laelius and Masinissa on the rear ultimately proved decisive. Carthaginian losses were 20,000; Romans lost 1,500. Hannibal fled to Hadrumentum.*

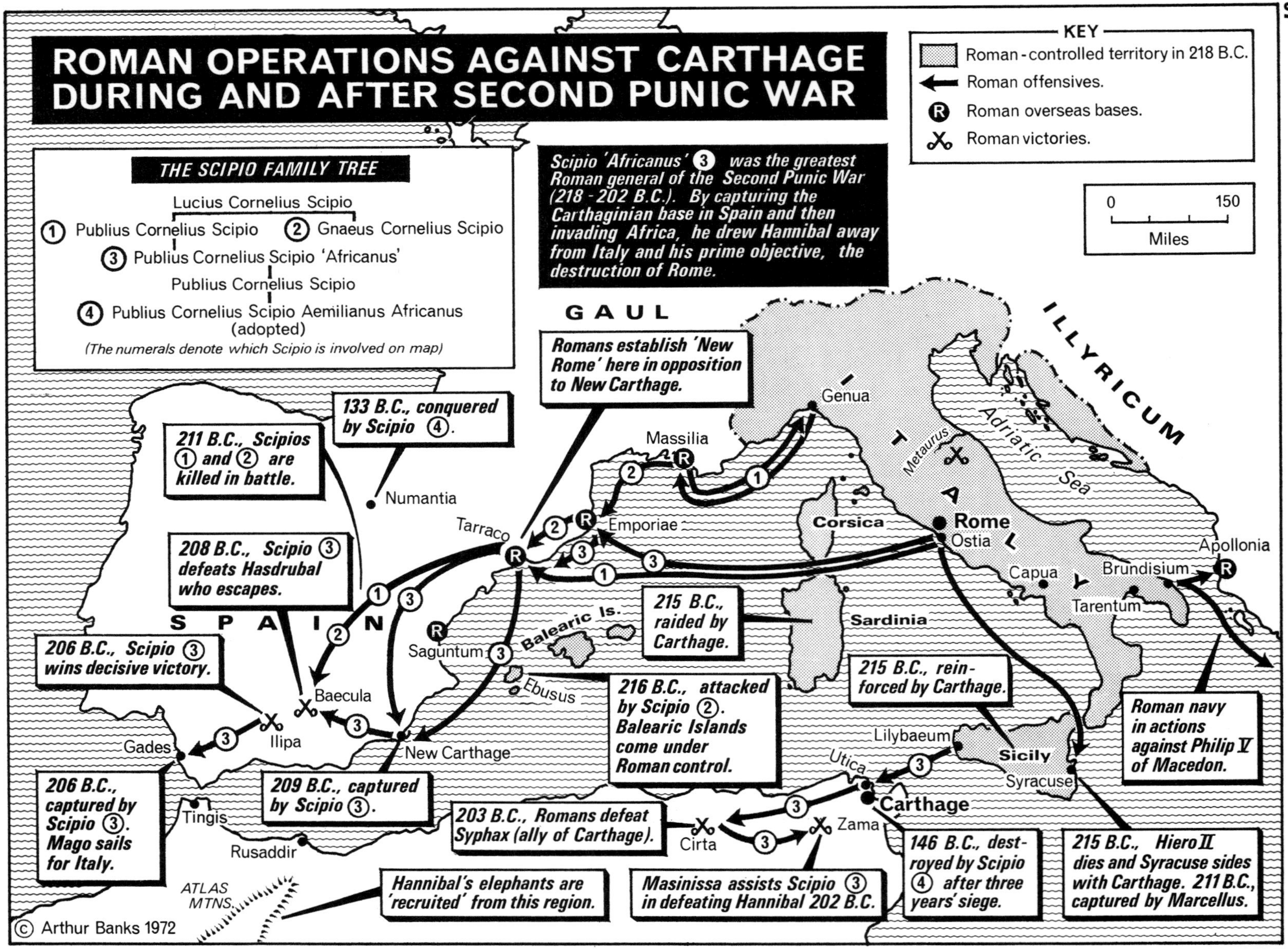
ROMAN OPERATIONS AGAINST CARTHAGE
DURING AND AFTER SECOND PUNIC WAR
KEY
Roman-controlled territory in 218 B.C.
Roman offensives.
Roman overseas bases.
Roman victories.
0 150
Miles
THE SCIPIO FAMILY TREE
Lucius Cornelius Scipio
(1) Publius Cornelius Scipio
(2) Gnaeus Cornelius Scipio
(3) Publius Cornelius Scipio 'Africanus'
Publius Cornelius Scipio
(4) Publius Cornelius Scipio Aemilianus Africanus (adopted)
(The numerals denote which Scipio is involved on map)
Scipio 'Africanus' (3) was the greatest Roman general of the Second Punic War (218 - 202 B.C.). By capturing the Carthaginian base in Spain and then invading Africa, he drew Hannibal away from Italy and his prime objective, the destruction of Rome.
GAUL
ILLYRICUM
ITALY
SPAIN
Romans establish 'New Rome' here in opposition to New Carthage.
133 B.C., conquered by Scipio (4).
211 B.C., Scipios (1) and (2) are killed in battle.
208 B.C., Scipio (3) defeats Hasdrubal who escapes.
206 B.C., Scipio (3) wins decisive victory.
206 B.C., captured by Scipio (3). Mago sails for Italy.
209 B.C., captured by Scipio (3).
215 B.C., raided by Carthage.
216 B.C., attacked by Scipio (2). Balearic Islands come under Roman control.
215 B.C., rein-forced by Carthage.
Roman navy in actions against Philip V of Macedon.
203 B.C., Romans defeat Syphax (ally of Carthage).
Hannibal's elephants are 'recruited' from this region.
Masinissa assists Scipio (3) in defeating Hannibal 202 B.C.
146 B.C., dest-royed by Scipio (4) after three years' siege.
215 B.C., Hiero II dies and Syracuse sides with Carthage. 211 B.C., captured by Marcellus.
Genua
Massilia
Emporiae
Tarraco
Numantia
Saguntum
Balearic Is.
Ebusus
Baecula
Ilipa
Gades
New Carthage
Tingis
Rusaddir
ATLAS MTNS.
Corsica
Sardinia
Metaurus
Adriatic Sea
Rome
Ostia
Capua
Brundisium
Tarentum
Apollonia
Sicily
Lilybaeum
Syracuse
Utica
Carthage
Zama
Cirta

ROMAN CONSULAR ARMY IN THE TIME OF HANNIBAL c. 220 B.C.

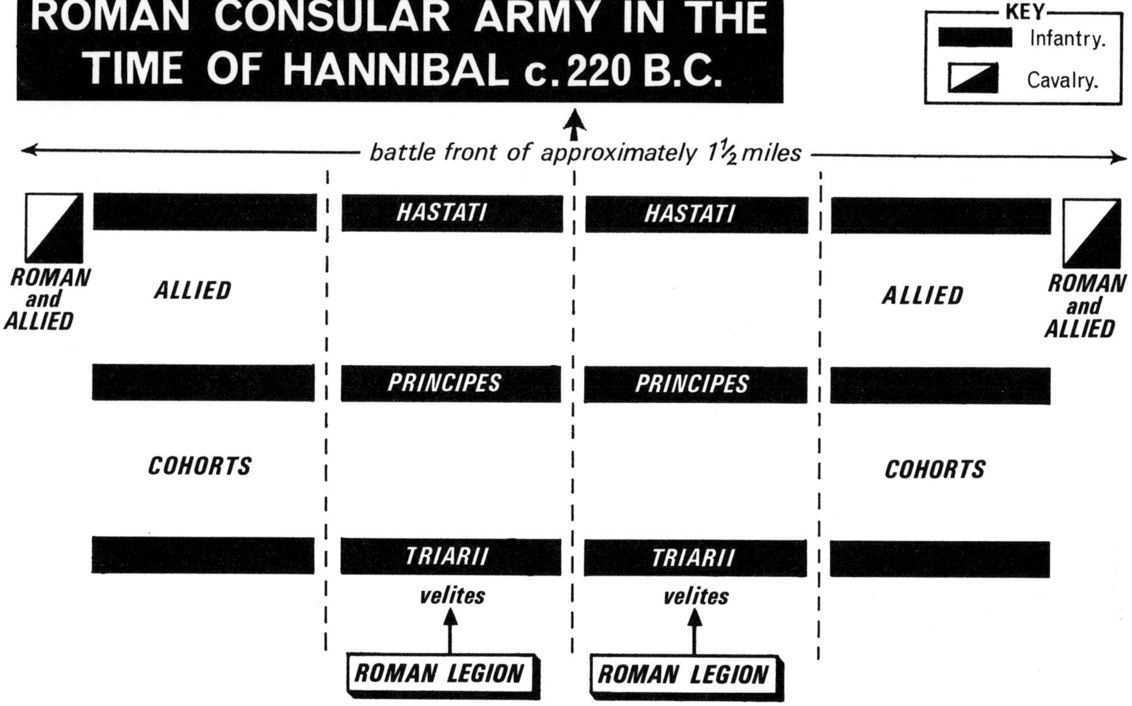

A consular army comprised some 17,500 men of Romans and "auxilia". A Roman** legion **contained some 3,000 heavy infantrymen arranged in three main classifications or groupings according to experience and age. The hastati (20-30 age range) were the front line troops; the principes (30-35 age range) were veterans and the backbone of the legion; the triarii were the oldest men. In addition, velites (young light infantry) and cavalry were utilised. Each legion contained ten** cohorts **of 300 heavy infantry and these were broken down in to** manipuli (maniples)**. In battle, the principes covered gaps in the ranks of the hastati and the triarii covered gaps in the ranks of the principes. The cavalry (total 600) was positioned on the wings and the velites, initially skirmishing in front, withdrew to take up a rear position.

ROMAN LEGION

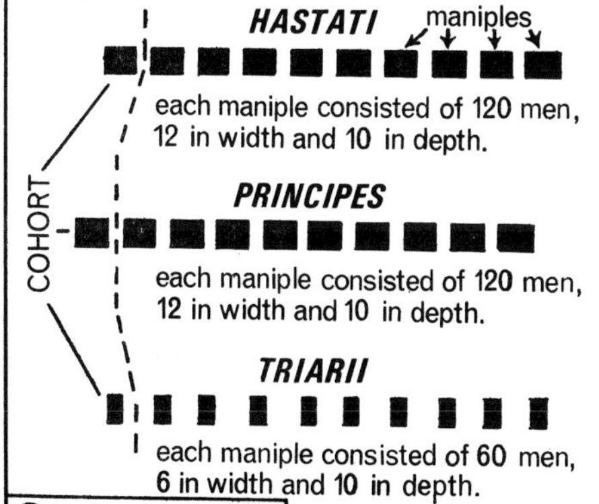

HASTATI
maniples
each maniple consisted of 120 men, 12 in width and 10 in depth.
COHORT
PRINCIPES
each maniple consisted of 120 men, 12 in width and 10 in depth.
TRIARII
each maniple consisted of 60 men, 6 in width and 10 in depth.

A ROMAN SOLDIER'S WEAPONS IN THE PUNIC WARS

HASTATI

Helmet (bronze) with purple and black 18 inch plume.
Bronze breastplate.
Greaves (leg-armour).
Shield (scutum) about 2½ by 4 feet: two layers of wood glued together, leather-covered and bound with iron. Iron boss (umbo) in centre, with handgrip inside.
Two javelins (pila) 4 feet long with 9 inch iron head (neck bent on impact to prevent use by enemy).
Sword (Spanish gladius) 2 foot blade, 2 inches wide, for cut and thrust work.

PRINCIPES and TRIARII

As hastati, but triarii carry pike (hasta) instead of two javelins.

VELITES (light missile troops)

(Probably operating in front, then withdrawing to rear. May have been administratively attached to triarii, who had only 600 men, as opposed to 1200 hastati and principes).
Helmet without crest.
Light circular shield (parma) 3 feet in diameter. Light javelins (iacula).

ROME TURNS EAST AFTER ZAMA

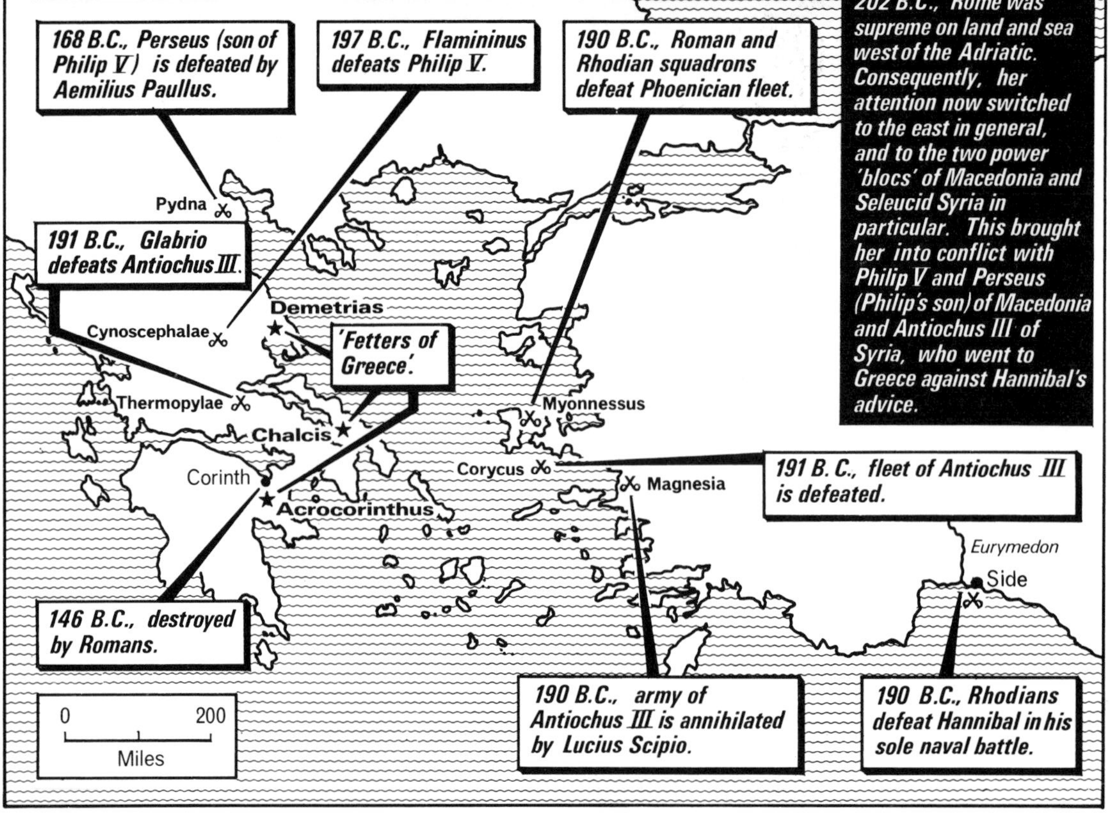
168 B.C., Perseus (son of Philip V) is defeated by Aemilius Paullus.
197 B.C., Flamininus defeats Philip V.
190 B.C., Roman and Rhodian squadrons defeat Phoenician fleet.
Pydna
191 B.C., Glabrio defeats Antiochus III.
Demetrias
Cynoscephalae
'Fetters of Greece'.
Thermopylae
Myonnessus
Chalcis
Corinth
Corycus
Magnesia
191 B.C., fleet of Antiochus III is defeated.
Acrocorinthus
Eurymedon
Side
146 B.C., destroyed by Romans.
0
200
Miles
190 B.C., army of Antiochus III is annihilated by Lucius Scipio.
190 B.C., Rhodians defeat Hannibal in his sole naval battle.

Following Scipio's victory over Hannibal at Zama in 202 B.C., Rome was supreme on land and sea west of the Adriatic. Consequently, her attention now switched to the east in general, and to the two power 'blocs' of Macedonia and Seleucid Syria in particular. This brought her into conflict with Philip V and Perseus (Philip's son) of Macedonia and Antiochus III of Syria, who went to Greece against Hannibal's advice.

THE BATTLE OF CYNOSCEPHALAE 197 B.C.

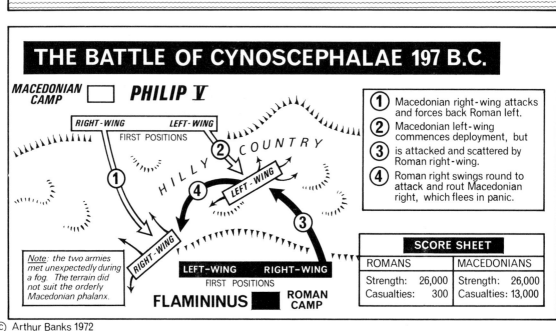

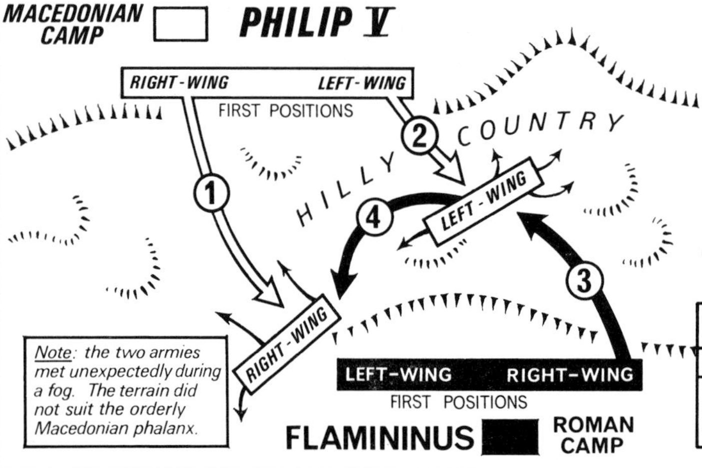
MACEDONIAN CAMP
PHILIP V
RIGHT-WING
LEFT-WING
FIRST POSITIONS
HILLY COUNTRY
1
2
3
4
LEFT-WING
RIGHT-WING
LEFT-WING
RIGHT-WING
FIRST POSITIONS
FLAMININUS
ROMAN CAMP

1. Macedonian right-wing attacks and forces back Roman left.
2. Macedonian left-wing commences deployment, but
3. is attacked and scattered by Roman right-wing.
4. Roman right swings round to attack and rout Macedonian right, which flees in panic.

Note: the two armies met unexpectedly during a fog. The terrain did not suit the orderly Macedonian phalanx.

SCORE SHEET

ROMANS		MACEDONIANS	
Strength:	26,000	Strength:	26,000
Casualties:	300	Casualties:	13,000

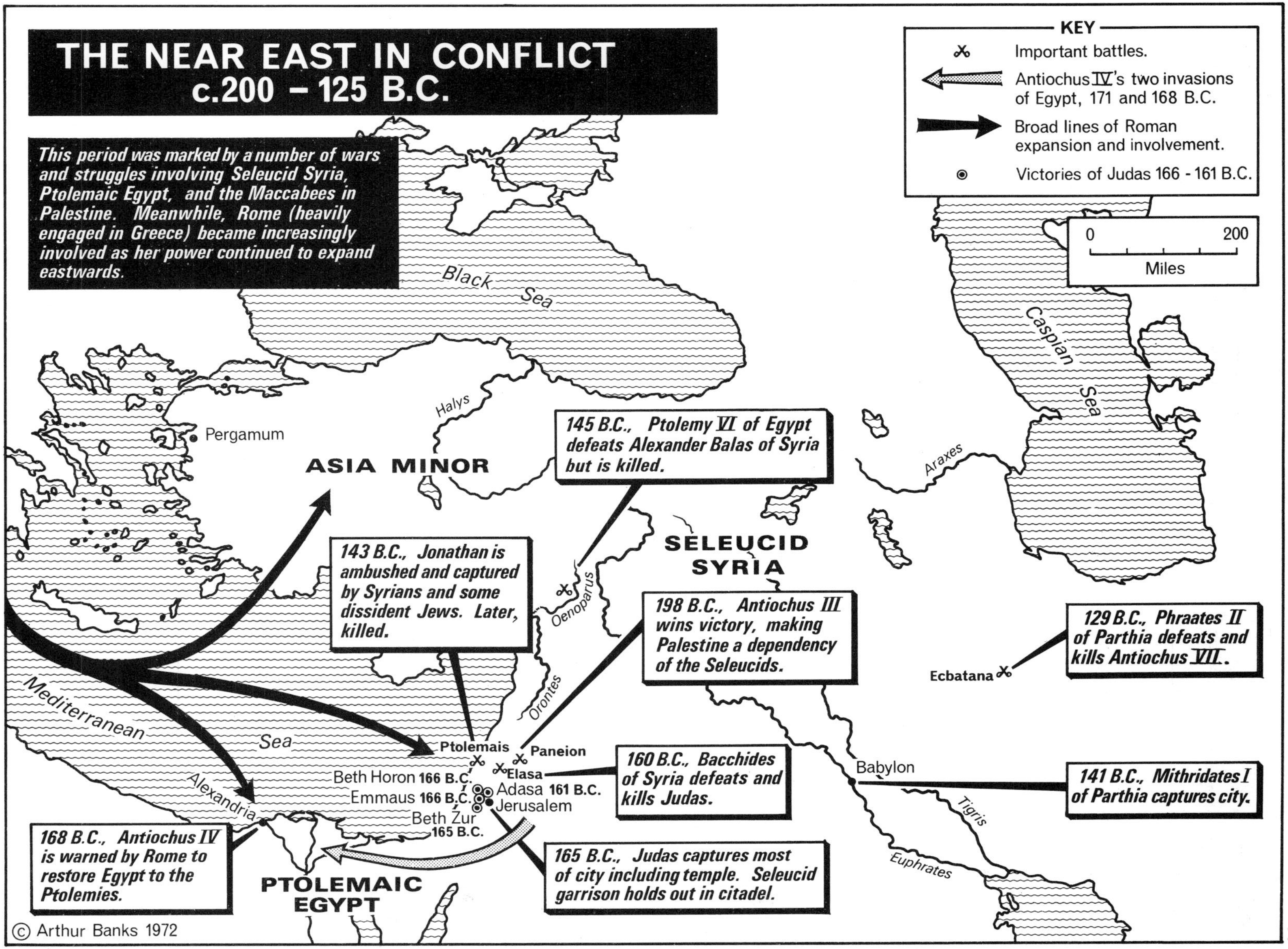
THE NEAR EAST IN CONFLICT
c.200 – 125 B.C.
This period was marked by a number of wars and struggles involving Seleucid Syria, Ptolemaic Egypt, and the Maccabees in Palestine. Meanwhile, Rome (heavily engaged in Greece) became increasingly involved as her power continued to expand eastwards.
KEY
Important battles.
Antiochus IV's two invasions of Egypt, 171 and 168 B.C.
Broad lines of Roman expansion and involvement.
Victories of Judas 166 - 161 B.C.
0
200
Miles
Black Sea
Caspian Sea
Mediterranean Sea
Halys
Pergamum
ASIA MINOR
Araxes
SELEUCID SYRIA
Oenoparus
Orontes
145 B.C., Ptolemy VI of Egypt defeats Alexander Balas of Syria but is killed.
143 B.C., Jonathan is ambushed and captured by Syrians and some dissident Jews. Later, killed.
198 B.C., Antiochus III wins victory, making Palestine a dependency of the Seleucids.
129 B.C., Phraates II of Parthia defeats and kills Antiochus VII.
Ecbatana
Ptolemais
Paneion
Elasa
Beth Horon 166 B.C.
Emmaus 166 B.C.
Adasa 161 B.C.
Jerusalem
Beth Zur
165 B.C.
Alexandria
160 B.C., Bacchides of Syria defeats and kills Judas.
Babylon
141 B.C., Mithridates I of Parthia captures city.
Tigris
Euphrates
168 B.C., Antiochus IV is warned by Rome to restore Egypt to the Ptolemies.
165 B.C., Judas captures most of city including temple. Seleucid garrison holds out in citadel.
PTOLEMAIC EGYPT
© Arthur Banks 1972

ROMAN EXPANSION IN THE NEAR EAST

❶ Following Battle of Magnesia 190 B.C.

0 300
Miles

KEY
- ❶ Rhodes.
- ❷ Bithynia.
- ❸ Paphlagonia.
- ❹ Pontus.
- ❺ Galatia.
- ❻ Cappadocia.
- ❼ Armenia.
- ❽ Syria.

KEY
- Kingdom of Pergamum (Eumenes II).
- Greek free states and dependencies.
- Achaean League (280–146 B.C.).
- Aetolian League (220–146 B.C.).

Peace treaty (188) between Rome and Antiochus III.

❷ Prior to Mithridatic Wars 89 B.C.

0 300
Miles

KEY
- ❶ Asia.
- ❷ Bithynia.
- ❸ Paphlagonia.
- ❹ Pontus.
- ❺ Galatia.
- ❻ Cappadocia.
- ❼ Greater Armenia.
- ❽ Commagene.
- ❾ Syria.
- ❿ Lycaonia.
- ⓫ Pisidia.
- ⓬ Lycia.
- ⓭ Achaea.
- ⓮ Epirus.
- ⓯ Macedonia.

KEY
- Roman provinces.
- Roman protectorates.
- Kingdom of Mithridates VI.
- Allied with Mithridates VI.

PARTHIAN EMPIRE

❸ Following Pompey's Settlement 62 B.C.

0 300
Miles

KEY
- ❶ Asia.
- ❷ Bithynia.
- ❸ Cilicia.
- ❹ Pontus.
- ❺ Galatia.
- ❻ Cappadocia.
- ❼ Greater Armenia.
- ❽ Syria.
- ❾ Lycaonia.
- ❿ Palestine.
- ⓫ Achaea.
- ⓬ Epirus.
- ⓭ Macedonia.
- ⓮ Sophene.
- ⓯ Commagene.
- ⓰ Lycia.

KEY
- Roman provinces.
- Roman protectorates.
- Parthian Empire.

PARTHIAN EMPIRE

Ctesiphon

Buffer states under Parthian control.

© Arthur Banks 1972

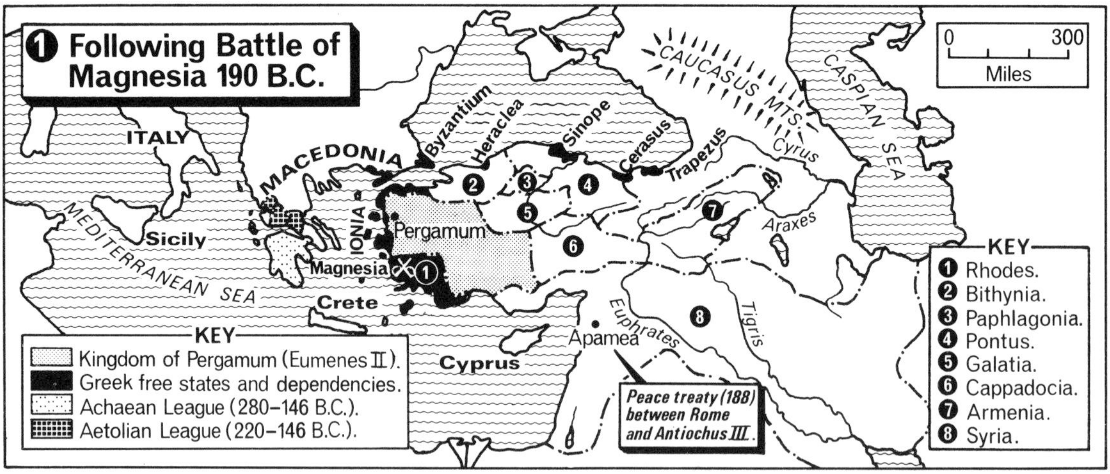

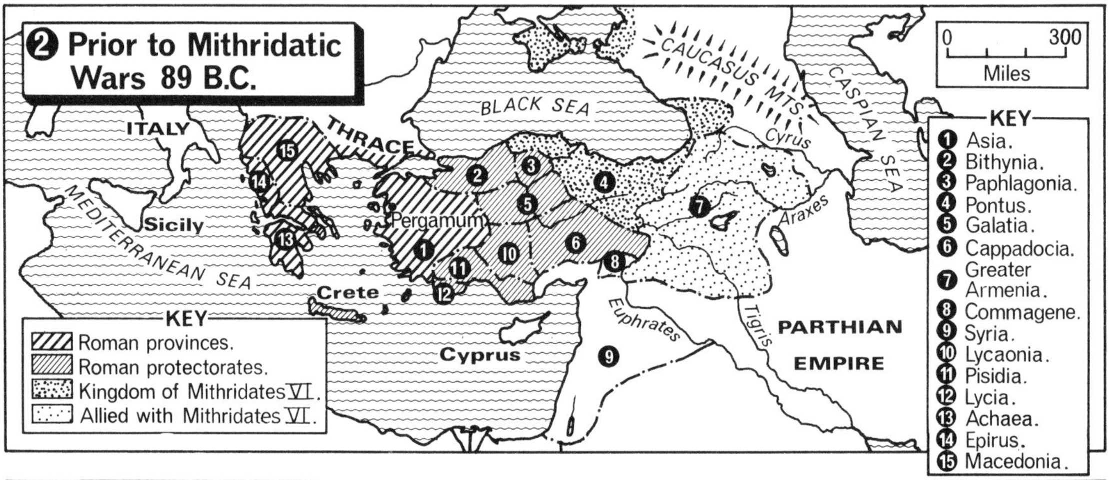

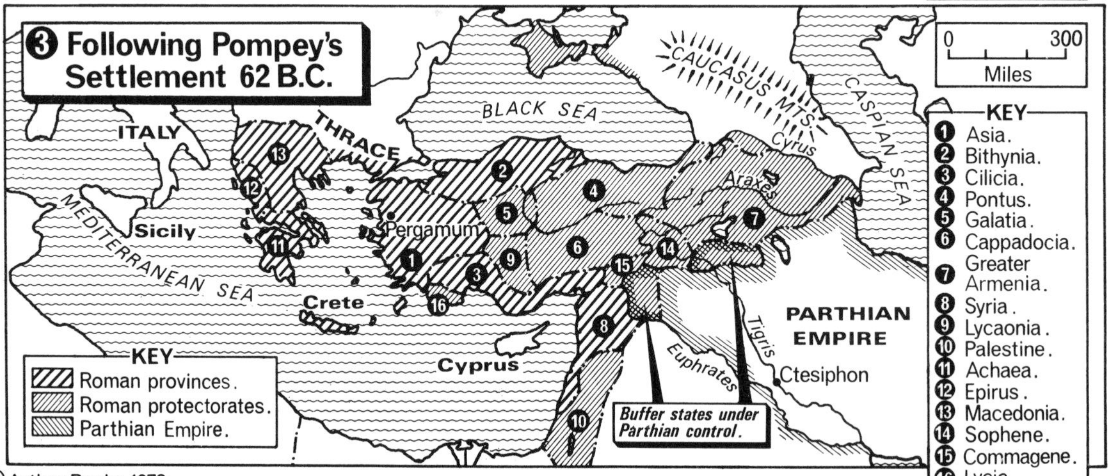

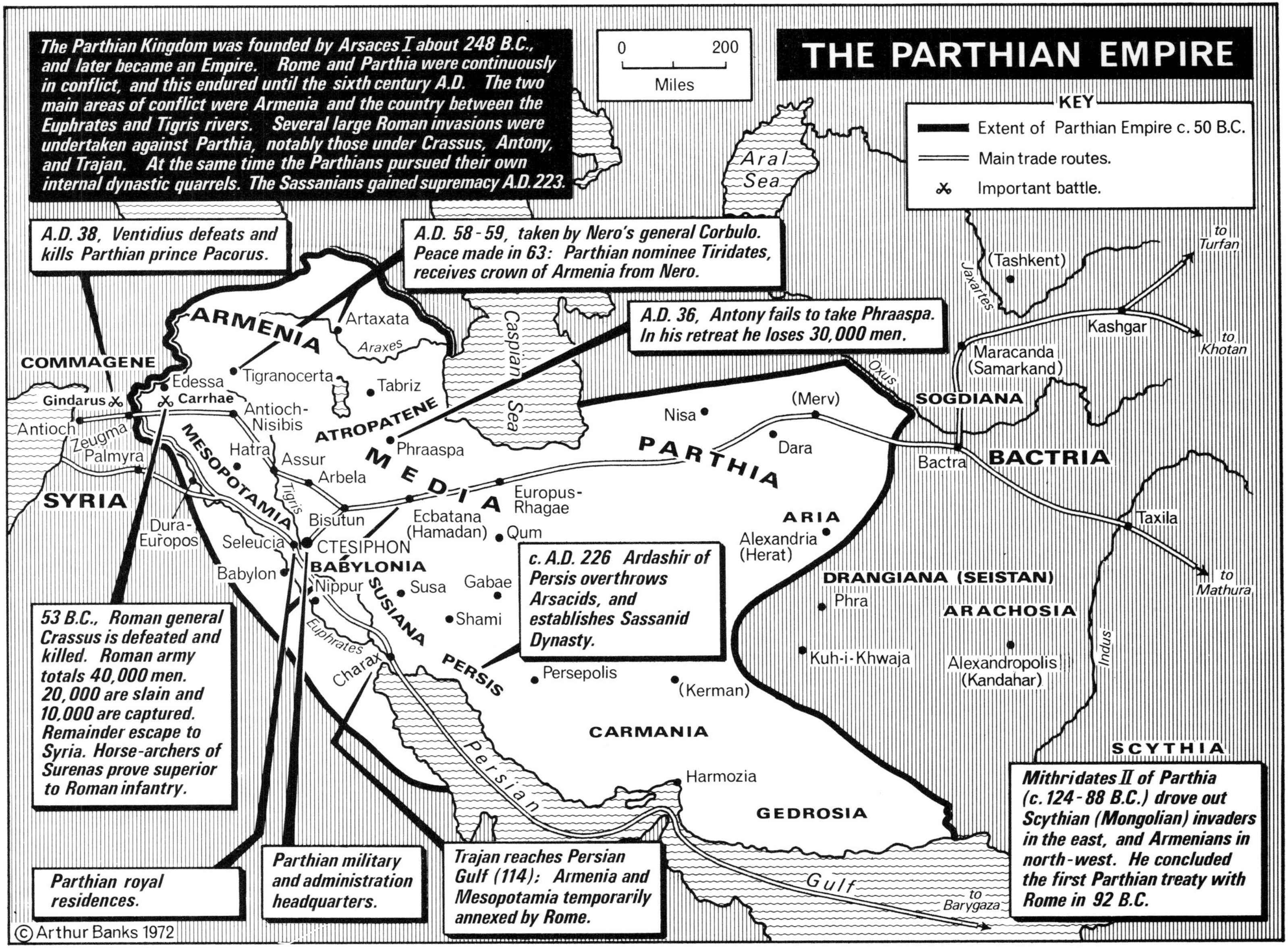
THE PARTHIAN EMPIRE
The Parthian Kingdom was founded by Arsaces I about 248 B.C., and later became an Empire. Rome and Parthia were continuously in conflict, and this endured until the sixth century A.D. The two main areas of conflict were Armenia and the country between the Euphrates and Tigris rivers. Several large Roman invasions were undertaken against Parthia, notably those under Crassus, Antony, and Trajan. At the same time the Parthians pursued their own internal dynastic quarrels. The Sassanians gained supremacy A.D. 223.
0 200 Miles
KEY
Extent of Parthian Empire c. 50 B.C.
Main trade routes.
Important battle.
A.D. 38, Ventidius defeats and kills Parthian prince Pacorus.
A.D. 58 - 59, taken by Nero's general Corbulo. Peace made in 63: Parthian nominee Tiridates, receives crown of Armenia from Nero.
A.D. 36, Antony fails to take Phraaspa. In his retreat he loses 30,000 men.
c. A.D. 226 Ardashir of Persis overthrows Arsacids, and establishes Sassanid Dynasty.
53 B.C., Roman general Crassus is defeated and killed. Roman army totals 40,000 men. 20,000 are slain and 10,000 are captured. Remainder escape to Syria. Horse-archers of Surenas prove superior to Roman infantry.
Parthian royal residences.
Parthian military and administration headquarters.
Trajan reaches Persian Gulf (114); Armenia and Mesopotamia temporarily annexed by Rome.
Mithridates II of Parthia (c. 124 - 88 B.C.) drove out Scythian (Mongolian) invaders in the east, and Armenians in north-west. He concluded the first Parthian treaty with Rome in 92 B.C.
Aral Sea
Caspian Sea
ARMENIA
COMMAGENE
SYRIA
MESOPOTAMIA
ATROPATENE
MEDIA
PARTHIA
BABYLONIA
SUSIANA
PERSIS
CARMANIA
GEDROSIA
ARIA
DRANGIANA (SEISTAN)
ARACHOSIA
BACTRIA
SOGDIANA
SCYTHIA
Artaxata
Araxes
Tigranocerta
Tabriz
Edessa
Carrhae
Gindarus
Antioch
Zeugma
Palmyra
Antioch-Nisibis
Hatra
Assur
Arbela
Tigris
Phraaspa
Bisutun
Ecbatana (Hamadan)
Europus-Rhagae
Qum
Dura-Europos
Seleucia
CTESIPHON
Babylon
Nippur
Susa
Gabae
Shami
Euphrates
Charax
Persepolis
(Kerman)
Persian Gulf
Harmozia
Nisa
(Merv)
Dara
Oxus
Alexandria (Herat)
Phra
Kuh-i-Khwaja
Alexandropolis (Kandahar)
Indus
Bactra
Taxila
Maracanda (Samarkand)
(Tashkent)
Jaxartes
Kashgar
to Turfan
to Khotan
to Mathura
to Barygaza
© Arthur Banks 1972

THE EXPANSION OF CH'IN POWER AND INFLUENCE

Cheng took the title of Shih Huang Ti, proclaiming himself Emperor of China. (The name China is derived from Ch'in). He built the Great Wall to prevent raids into China by northern nomads, and made military expeditions south of the Yangtze. His two main generals were Ming T'ien and Chao T'o.

The Great Wall of China (constructed from brick, stone, and earth), was 1,500 miles in length, with watchtowers every few hundred yards. Along the top ran a 12 feet-wide roadway, and at irregular intervals there were gatehouses. Moats protected vulnerable sections of the wall on its northern side.

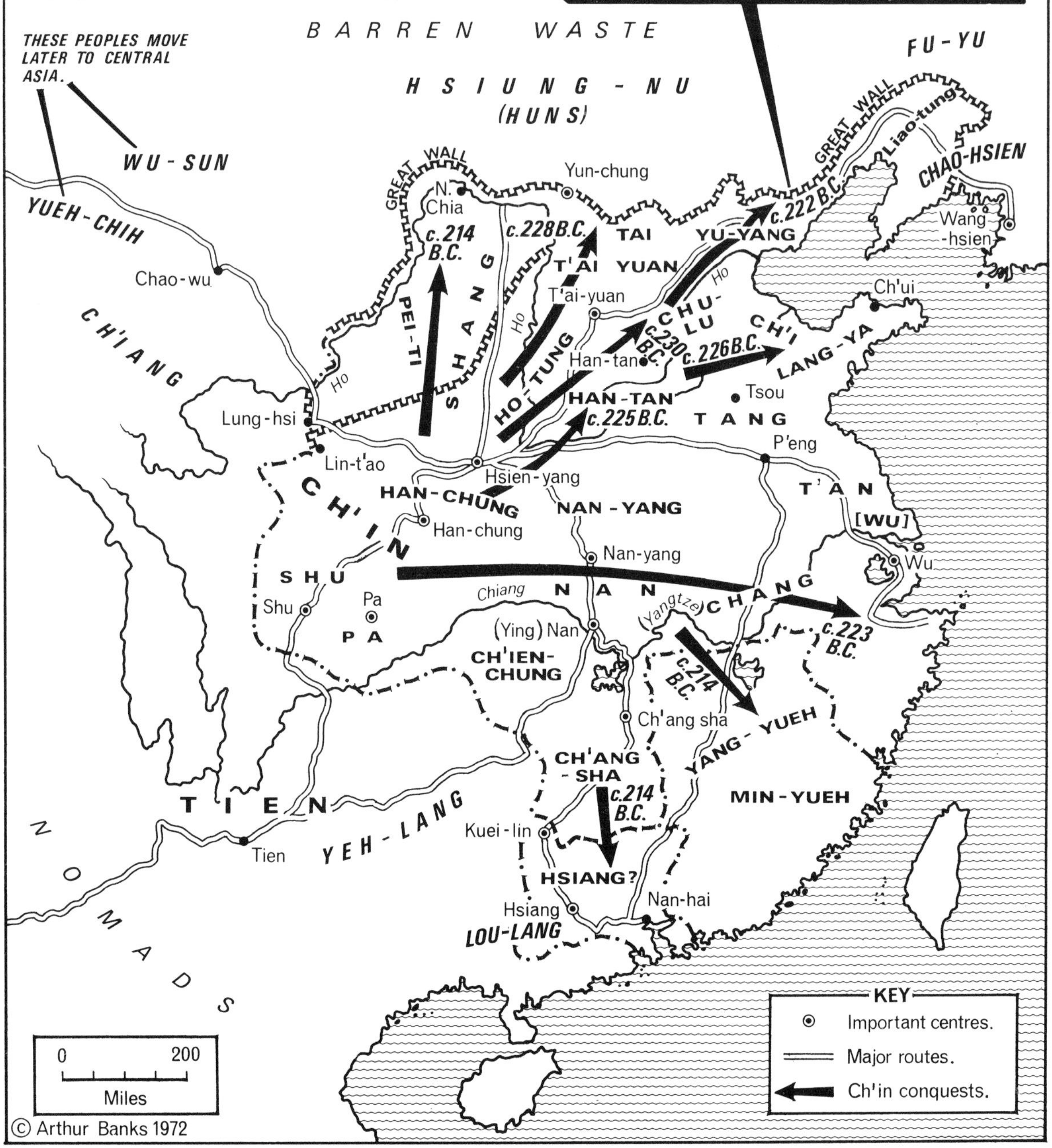

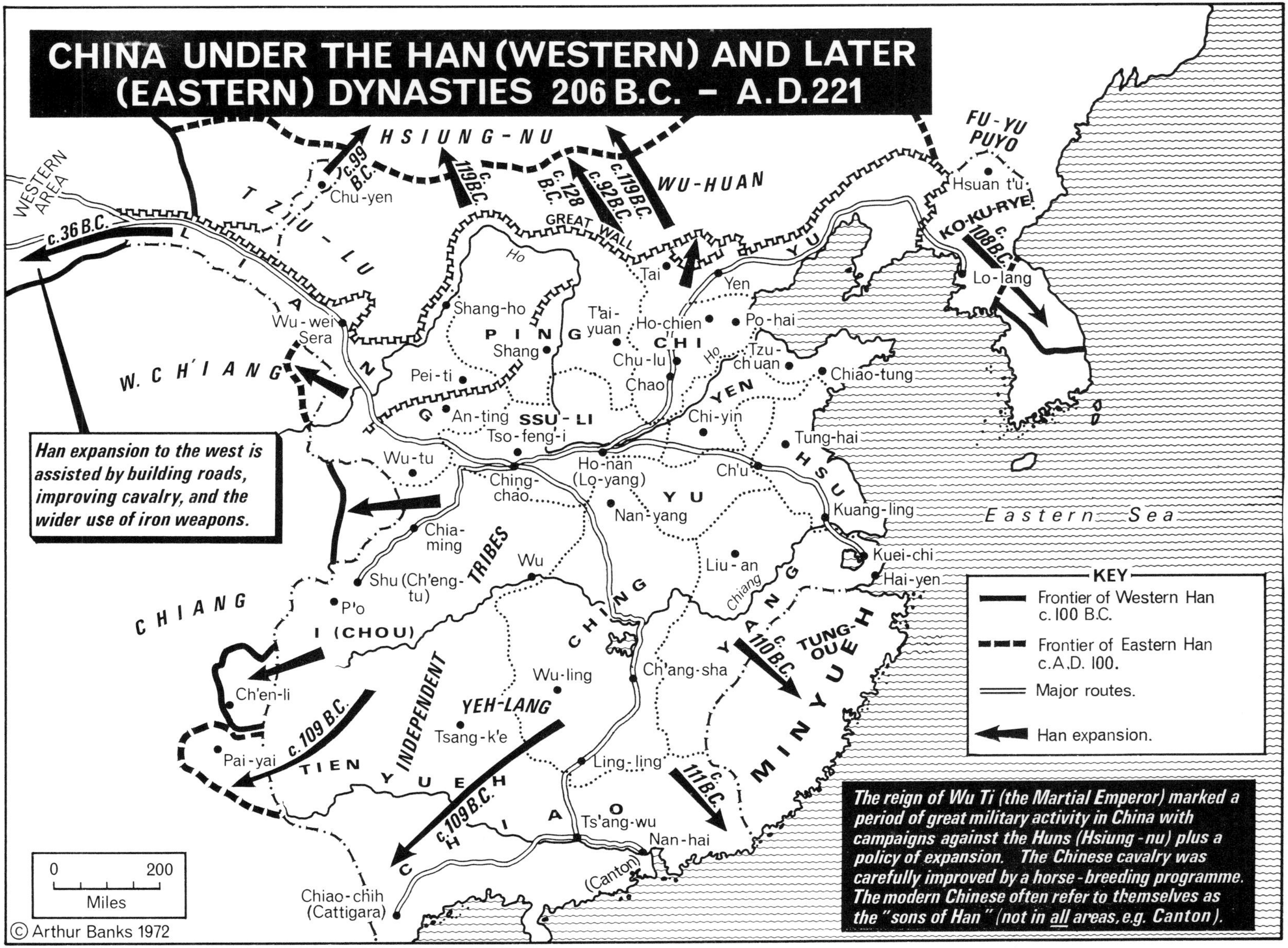
CHINA UNDER THE HAN (WESTERN) AND LATER (EASTERN) DYNASTIES 206 B.C. – A.D. 221
HSIUNG-NU
WU-HUAN
FU-YU PUYO
KO-KU-RYE
c. 108 B.C.
Hsuan t'u
Lo-lang
c. 99 B.C.
c. 119 B.C.
c. 128 B.C.
c. 92 B.C.
c. 119 B.C.
GREAT WALL
WESTERN AREA
c. 36 B.C.
TZU-LU
LIANG
Chu-yen
Wu-wei
Sera
W. CH'IANG
Ho
Shang-ho
PING
Shang
Pei-ti
An-ting
SSU-LI
Tso-feng-i
T'ai-yuan
Tai
Yen
YU
Ho-chien
Po-hai
CHI
Chu-lu
Chao
Tzu-ch'uan
Chiao-tung
YEN
Chi-yin
Tung-hai
HSU
Ho-nan (Lo-yang)
Ch'u
Kuang-ling
Eastern Sea
Kuei-chi
Hai-yen
Wu-tu
Ching-chao
YU
Nan-yang
Liu-an
Chiang
YANG
Chia-ming
TRIBES
Shu (Ch'eng-tu)
Wu
P'o
I (CHOU)
CHIANG
CHING
Ch'en-li
Wu-ling
YEH-LANG
Tsang-k'e
INDEPENDENT
TIEN YUEH
c. 109 B.C.
Pai-yai
c. 109 B.C.
Ch'ang-sha
c. 110 B.C.
TUNG-OUEH
MIN YUEH
Ling-ling
c. 111 B.C.
CHIAO
Ts'ang-wu
Nan-hai
(Canton)
Chiao-chih (Cattigara)
KEY
Frontier of Western Han c. 100 B.C.
Frontier of Eastern Han c. A.D. 100.
Major routes.
Han expansion.
Han expansion to the west is assisted by building roads, improving cavalry, and the wider use of iron weapons.
The reign of Wu Ti (the Martial Emperor) marked a period of great military activity in China with campaigns against the Huns (Hsiung-nu) plus a policy of expansion. The Chinese cavalry was carefully improved by a horse-breeding programme. The modern Chinese often refer to themselves as the "sons of Han" (not in all areas, e.g. Canton).
0 200
Miles
© Arthur Banks 1972

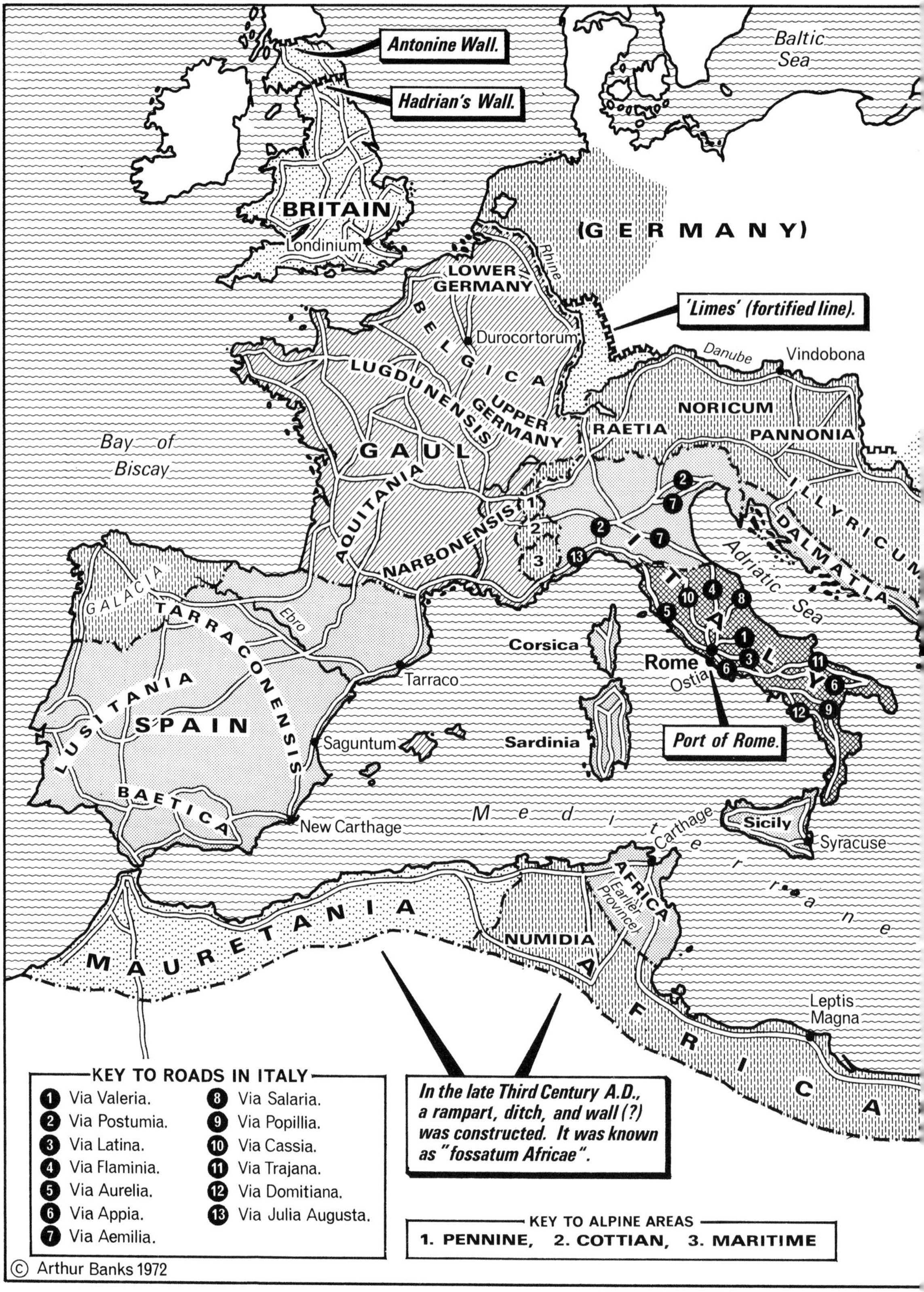
Antonine Wall.
Hadrian's Wall.
Baltic Sea
BRITAIN
Londinium
(GERMANY)
Rhine
LOWER GERMANY
'Limes' (fortified line).
BELGICA
Durocortorum
Danube
Vindobona
LUGDUNENSIS
UPPER GERMANY
NORICUM
RAETIA
PANNONIA
Bay of Biscay
GAUL
AQUITANIA
NARBONENSIS
ILLYRICUM
DALMATIA
Adriatic Sea
ITALY
GALACIA
TARRACONENSIS
Ebro
Corsica
Rome
Ostia
Tarraco
LUSITANIA
SPAIN
Saguntum
Sardinia
Port of Rome.
BAETICA
New Carthage
Mediterranean
Carthage
Sicily
Syracuse
AFRICA (Earlier Province)
MAURETANIA
NUMIDIA
AFRICA
Leptis Magna
KEY TO ROADS IN ITALY
1 Via Valeria.
2 Via Postumia.
3 Via Latina.
4 Via Flaminia.
5 Via Aurelia.
6 Via Appia.
7 Via Aemilia.
8 Via Salaria.
9 Via Popillia.
10 Via Cassia.
11 Via Trajana.
12 Via Domitiana.
13 Via Julia Augusta.
In the late Third Century A.D., a rampart, ditch, and wall (?) was constructed. It was known as "fossatum Africae".
KEY TO ALPINE AREAS
1. PENNINE, 2. COTTIAN, 3. MARITIME
© Arthur Banks 1972

STAGES IN THE DEVELOPMENT OF THE ROMAN EMPIRE

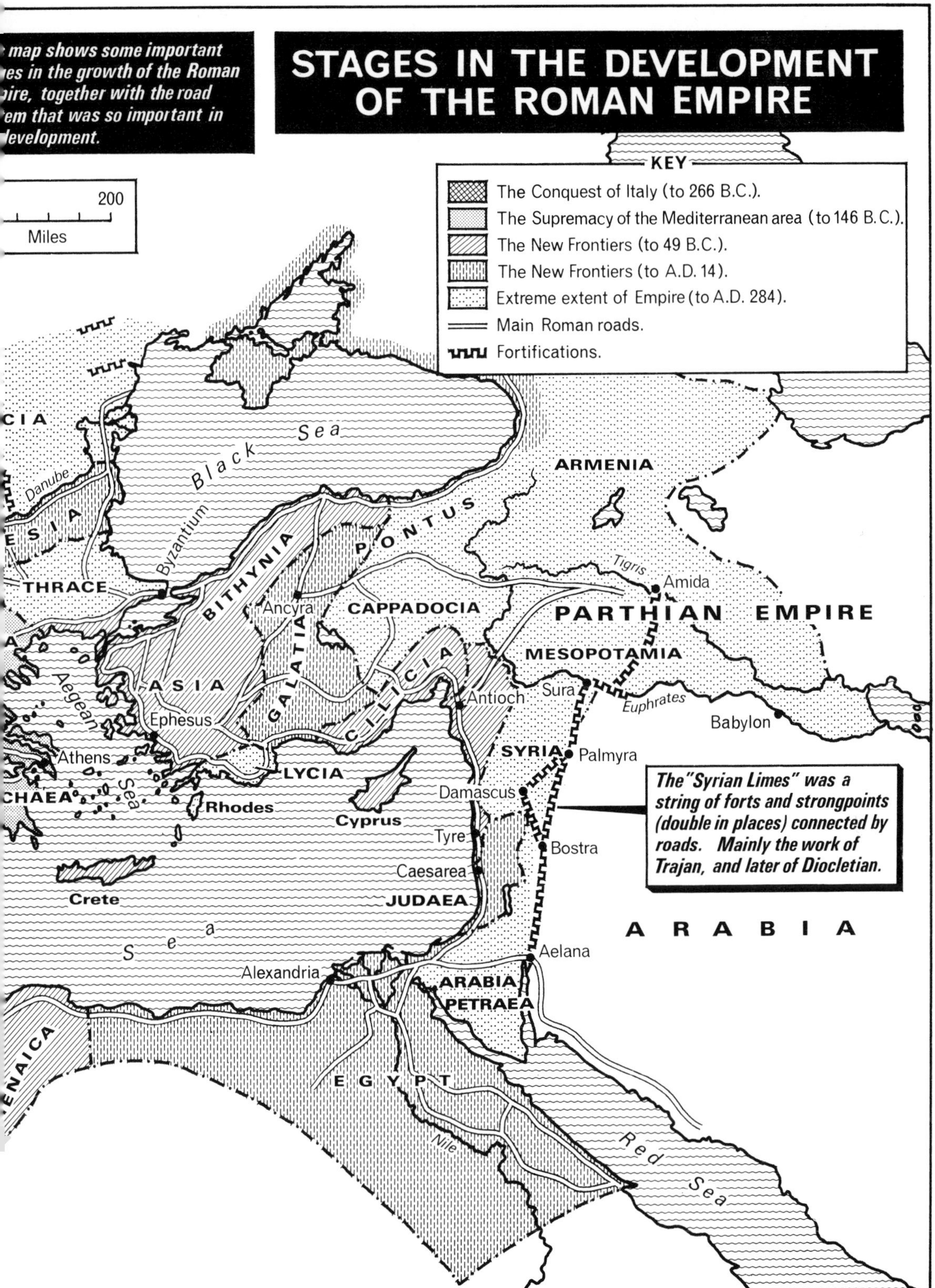
map shows some important
es in the growth of the Roman
pire, together with the road
em that was so important in
development.
200
Miles
KEY
The Conquest of Italy (to 266 B.C.).
The Supremacy of the Mediterranean area (to 146 B.C.).
The New Frontiers (to 49 B.C.).
The New Frontiers (to A.D. 14).
Extreme extent of Empire (to A.D. 284).
Main Roman roads.
Fortifications.
Black Sea
Danube
THRACE
Byzantium
BITHYNIA
PONTUS
ARMENIA
Ancyra
CAPPADOCIA
GALATIA
ASIA
CILICIA
Tigris
Amida
PARTHIAN EMPIRE
MESOPOTAMIA
Sura
Euphrates
Babylon
Antioch
Aegean Sea
Ephesus
Athens
LYCIA
Rhodes
SYRIA
Palmyra
Damascus
Cyprus
Tyre
Bostra
Caesarea
JUDAEA
Crete
Sea
Alexandria
Aelana
ARABIA
ARABIA PETRAEA
EGYPT
Nile
Red Sea
The "Syrian Limes" was a string of forts and strongpoints (double in places) connected by roads. Mainly the work of Trajan, and later of Diocletian.

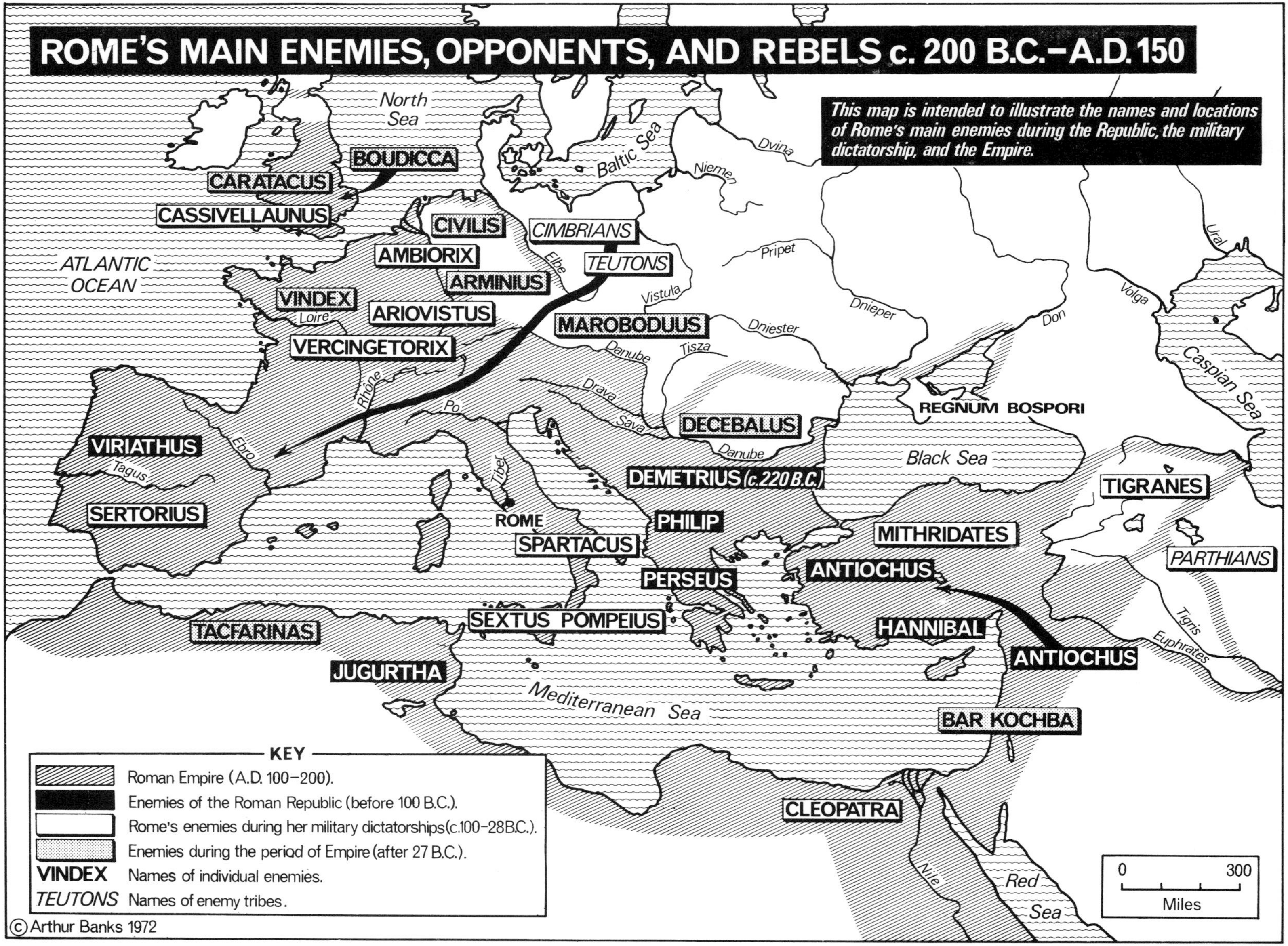
ROME'S MAIN ENEMIES, OPPONENTS, AND REBELS c. 200 B.C.–A.D. 150
This map is intended to illustrate the names and locations of Rome's main enemies during the Republic, the military dictatorship, and the Empire.
North Sea
Baltic Sea
ATLANTIC OCEAN
BOUDICCA
CARATACUS
CASSIVELLAUNUS
CIVILIS
CIMBRIANS
TEUTONS
AMBIORIX
ARMINIUS
VINDEX
ARIOVISTUS
VERCINGETORIX
MAROBODUUS
Loire
Rhône
Elbe
Vistula
Dvina
Niemen
Pripet
Dnieper
Dniester
Don
Volga
Ural
Caspian Sea
Danube
Tisza
Drava
Sava
Po
Tiber
Ebro
Tagus
VIRIATHUS
SERTORIUS
REGNUM BOSPORI
DECEBALUS
Black Sea
DEMETRIUS (c.220 B.C.)
ROME
PHILIP
SPARTACUS
TIGRANES
MITHRIDATES
PARTHIANS
ANTIOCHUS
PERSEUS
SEXTUS POMPEIUS
HANNIBAL
ANTIOCHUS
Tigris
Euphrates
TACFARINAS
JUGURTHA
Mediterranean Sea
BAR KOCHBA
CLEOPATRA
Nile
Red Sea
0
300
Miles
KEY
Roman Empire (A.D. 100–200).
Enemies of the Roman Republic (before 100 B.C.).
Rome's enemies during her military dictatorships (c.100–28 B.C.).
Enemies during the period of Empire (after 27 B.C.).
VINDEX Names of individual enemies.
TEUTONS Names of enemy tribes.
© Arthur Banks 1972

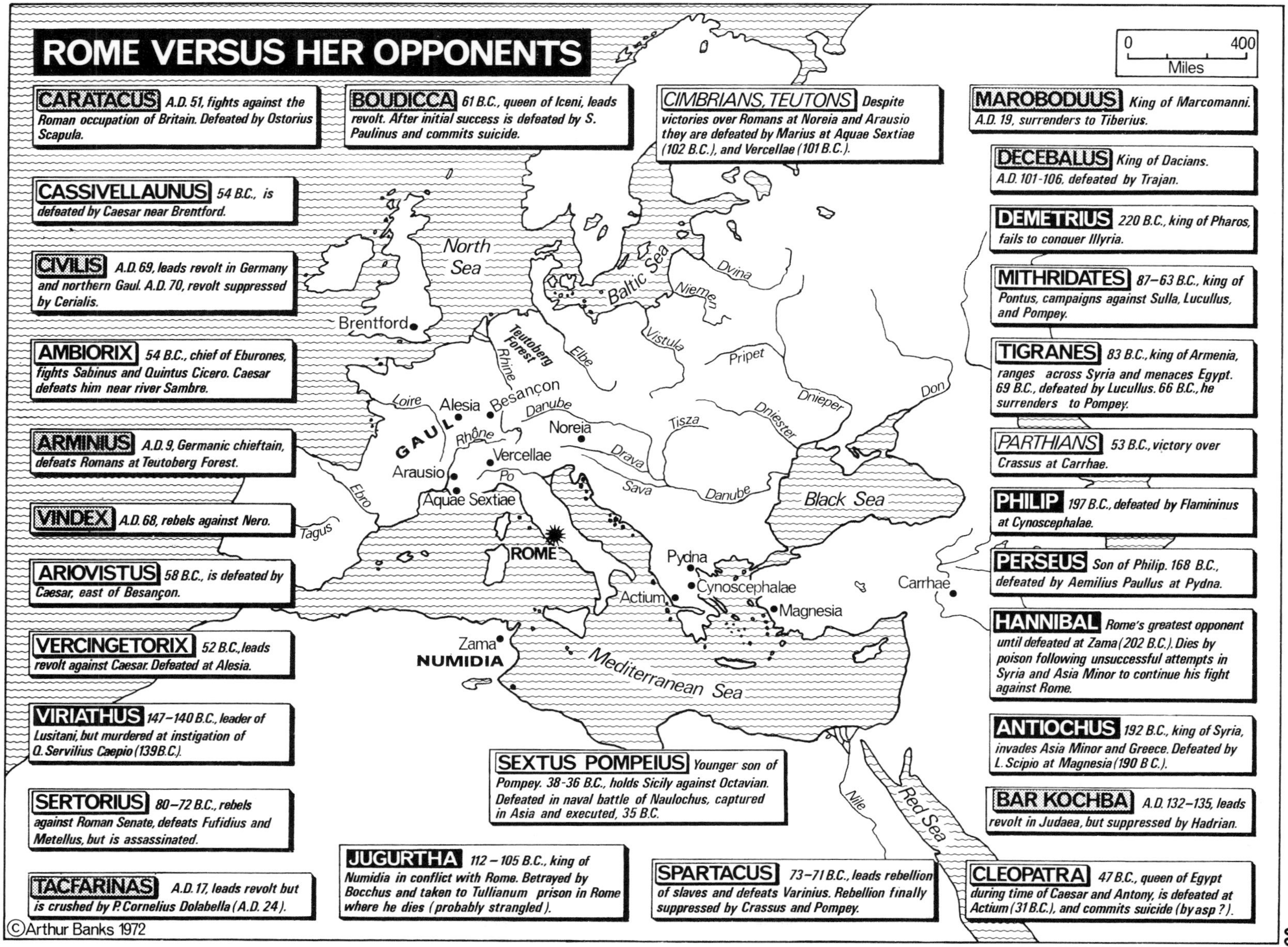
ROME VERSUS HER OPPONENTS
CARATACUS A.D. 51, fights against the Roman occupation of Britain. Defeated by Ostorius Scapula.
BOUDICCA 61 B.C., queen of Iceni, leads revolt. After initial success is defeated by S. Paulinus and commits suicide.
CIMBRIANS, TEUTONS Despite victories over Romans at Noreia and Arausio they are defeated by Marius at Aquae Sextiae (102 B.C.), and Vercellae (101 B.C.).
MAROBODUUS King of Marcomanni. A.D. 19, surrenders to Tiberius.
DECEBALUS King of Dacians. A.D. 101-106, defeated by Trajan.
DEMETRIUS 220 B.C., king of Pharos, fails to conquer Illyria.
MITHRIDATES 87–63 B.C., king of Pontus, campaigns against Sulla, Lucullus, and Pompey.
TIGRANES 83 B.C., king of Armenia, ranges across Syria and menaces Egypt. 69 B.C., defeated by Lucullus. 66 B.C., he surrenders to Pompey.
PARTHIANS 53 B.C., victory over Crassus at Carrhae.
PHILIP 197 B.C., defeated by Flamininus at Cynoscephalae.
PERSEUS Son of Philip. 168 B.C., defeated by Aemilius Paullus at Pydna.
HANNIBAL Rome's greatest opponent until defeated at Zama (202 B.C.). Dies by poison following unsuccessful attempts in Syria and Asia Minor to continue his fight against Rome.
ANTIOCHUS 192 B.C., king of Syria, invades Asia Minor and Greece. Defeated by L. Scipio at Magnesia (190 B.C.).
BAR KOCHBA A.D. 132–135, leads revolt in Judaea, but suppressed by Hadrian.
CLEOPATRA 47 B.C., queen of Egypt during time of Caesar and Antony, is defeated at Actium (31 B.C.), and commits suicide (by asp ?).
SPARTACUS 73–71 B.C., leads rebellion of slaves and defeats Varinius. Rebellion finally suppressed by Crassus and Pompey.
JUGURTHA 112 – 105 B.C., king of Numidia in conflict with Rome. Betrayed by Bocchus and taken to Tullianum prison in Rome where he dies (probably strangled).
SEXTUS POMPEIUS Younger son of Pompey. 38-36 B.C., holds Sicily against Octavian. Defeated in naval battle of Naulochus, captured in Asia and executed, 35 B.C.
CASSIVELLAUNUS 54 B.C., is defeated by Caesar near Brentford.
CIVILIS A.D. 69, leads revolt in Germany and northern Gaul. A.D. 70, revolt suppressed by Cerialis.
AMBIORIX 54 B.C., chief of Eburones, fights Sabinus and Quintus Cicero. Caesar defeats him near river Sambre.
ARMINIUS A.D. 9, Germanic chieftain, defeats Romans at Teutoberg Forest.
VINDEX A.D. 68, rebels against Nero.
ARIOVISTUS 58 B.C., is defeated by Caesar, east of Besançon.
VERCINGETORIX 52 B.C., leads revolt against Caesar. Defeated at Alesia.
VIRIATHUS 147–140 B.C., leader of Lusitani, but murdered at instigation of Q. Servilius Caepio (139 B.C.).
SERTORIUS 80–72 B.C., rebels against Roman Senate, defeats Fufidius and Metellus, but is assassinated.
TACFARINAS A.D. 17, leads revolt but is crushed by P. Cornelius Dolabella (A.D. 24).
0
400
Miles
North Sea
Baltic Sea
Brentford
Teutoberg Forest
Rhine
Elbe
Vistula
Nieme
Dvina
Pripet
Dnieper
Dniester
Don
Loire
Alesia
Besançon
Danube
Noreia
GAUL
Rhône
Vercellae
Arausio
Po
Aquae Sextiae
Ebro
Tagus
Tisza
Drava
Sava
Danube
Black Sea
ROME
Pydna
Cynoscephalae
Actium
Magnesia
Carrhae
Zama
NUMIDIA
Mediterranean Sea
Nile
Red Sea

THE HUNS AND HANS IN ASIA

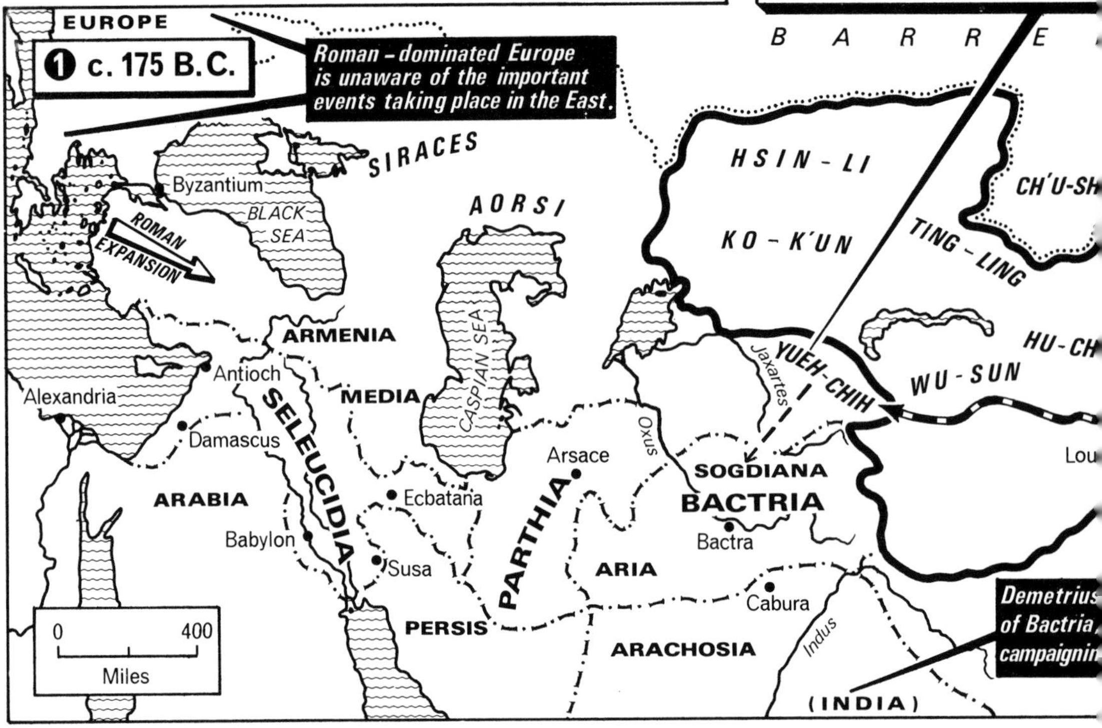
The Yueh-chih contact Bactria, the
Greek kingdom struggling for existe
B A R R E
1 c. 175 B.C.
EUROPE
Roman - dominated Europe
is unaware of the important
events taking place in the East.
SIRACES
Byzantium
BLACK SEA
ROMAN EXPANSION
AORSI
HSIN-LI
KO-K'UN
CH'U-SH
TING-LING
ARMENIA
CASPIAN SEA
YUEH-CHIH
Jaxartes
HU-CH
WU-SUN
Antioch
Alexandria
MEDIA
SELEUCIDIA
Damascus
Oxus
Arsace
SOGDIANA
Lou
ARABIA
Ecbatana
BACTRIA
PARTHIA
Bactra
Babylon
Susa
ARIA
Cabura
PERSIS
Demetrius
of Bactria,
campaignin
Indus
ARACHOSIA
0 400
Miles
(INDIA)

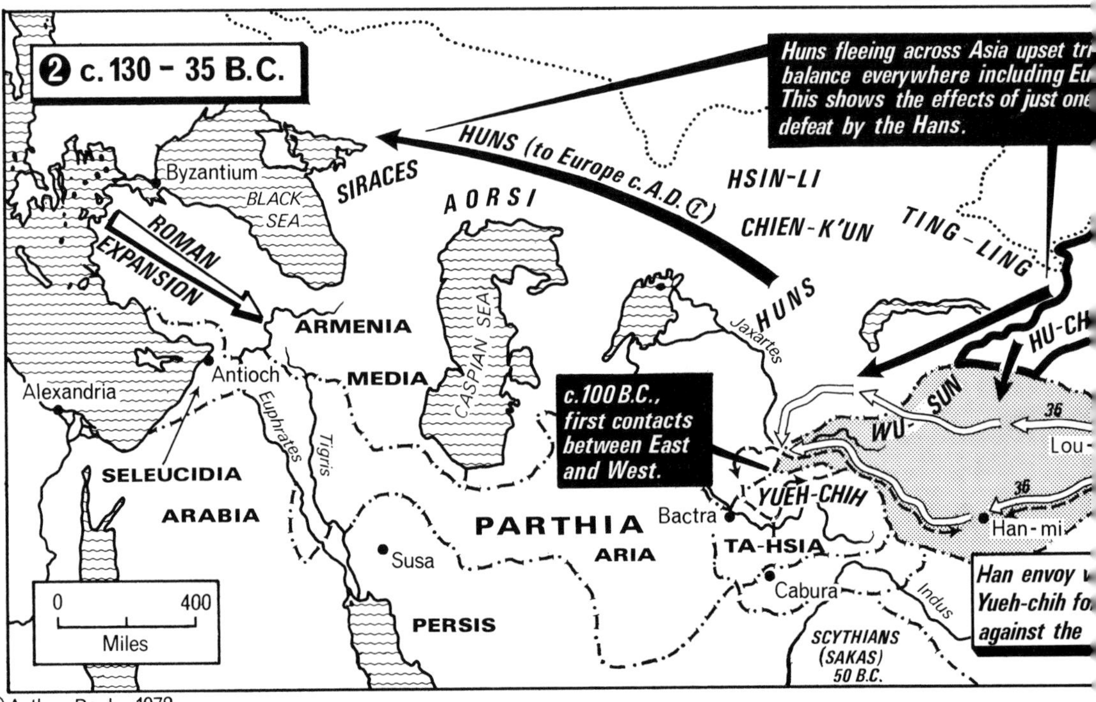
2 c. 130 - 35 B.C.
Huns fleeing across Asia upset tr
balance everywhere including Eu
This shows the effects of just one
defeat by the Hans.
HUNS (to Europe c. A.D. ①)
SIRACES
Byzantium
BLACK SEA
HSIN-LI
AORSI
CHIEN-K'UN
TING-LING
ROMAN EXPANSION
HUNS
CASPIAN SEA
ARMENIA
Jaxartes
HU-CH
Antioch
MEDIA
Alexandria
Euphrates
Tigris
c. 100 B.C.,
first contacts
between East
and West.
WU-SUN
36
Lou
SELEUCIDIA
ARABIA
YUEH-CHIH
36
PARTHIA
Bactra
Han-mi
TA-HSIA
Susa
ARIA
Han envoy
Yueh-chih fo
against the
0 400
Miles
Cabura
Indus
PERSIS
SCYTHIANS
(SAKAS)
50 B.C.

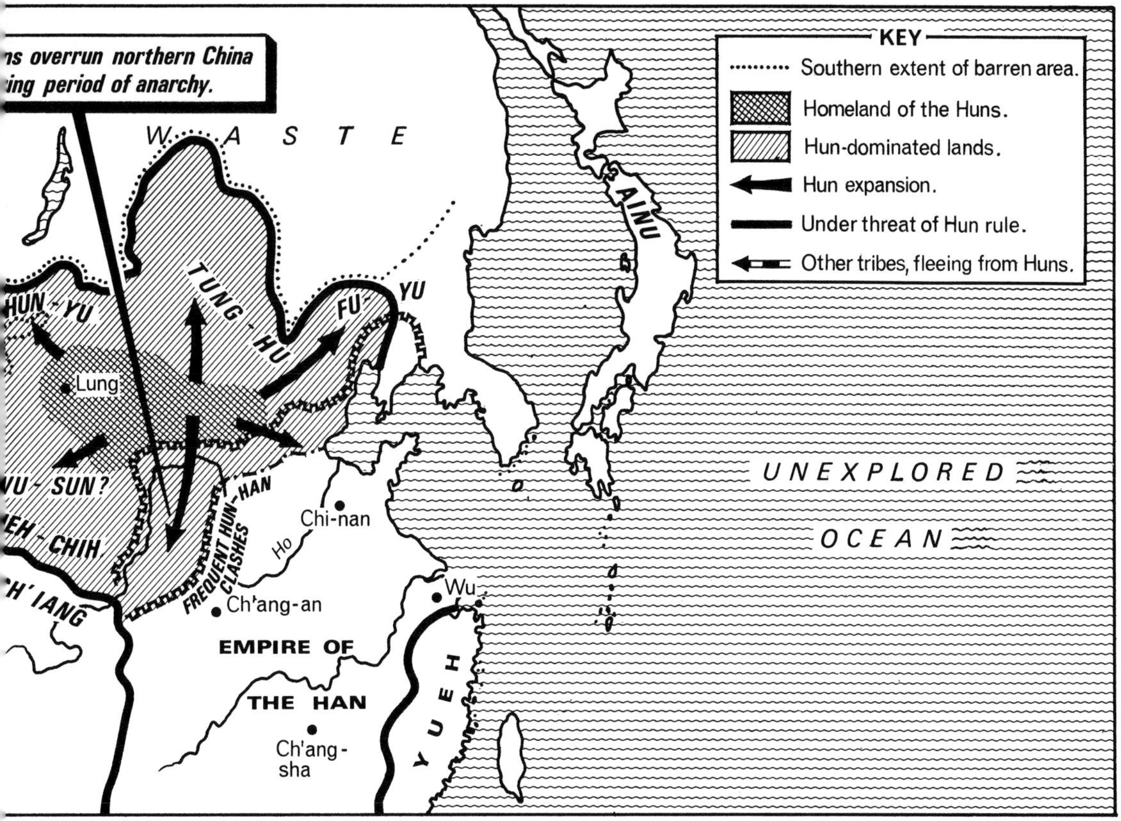
ns overrun northern China
ing period of anarchy.
KEY
Southern extent of barren area.
Homeland of the Huns.
Hun-dominated lands.
Hun expansion.
Under threat of Hun rule.
Other tribes, fleeing from Huns.
W A S T E
HUN-YU
TUNG-HU
FU-YU
AINU
Lung
WU-SUN?
EH-CHIH
FREQUENT HUN-HAN CLASHES
Chi-nan
Ho
Ch'ang-an
H'IANG
Wu
EMPIRE OF THE HAN
Ch'ang-sha
YUEH
UNEXPLORED
OCEAN

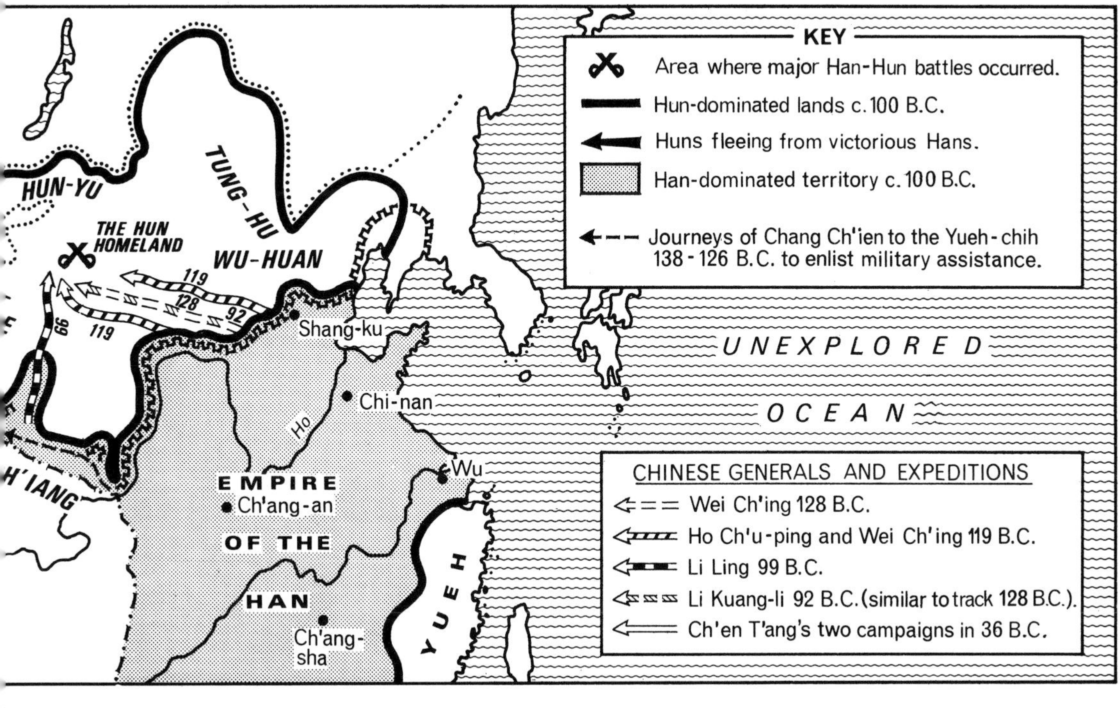
KEY
Area where major Han-Hun battles occurred.
Hun-dominated lands c.100 B.C.
Huns fleeing from victorious Hans.
Han-dominated territory c.100 B.C.
Journeys of Chang Ch'ien to the Yueh-chih 138-126 B.C. to enlist military assistance.
HUN-YU
TUNG-HU
THE HUN HOMELAND
WU-HUAN
119
128
92
99
119
Shang-ku
Chi-nan
Ho
UNEXPLORED
OCEAN
H'IANG
Wu
EMPIRE OF THE HAN
Ch'ang-an
Ch'ang-sha
YUEH
CHINESE GENERALS AND EXPEDITIONS
Wei Ch'ing 128 B.C.
Ho Ch'u-ping and Wei Ch'ing 119 B.C.
Li Ling 99 B.C.
Li Kuang-li 92 B.C. (similar to track 128 B.C.).
Ch'en T'ang's two campaigns in 36 B.C.

ROMAN DEFENCE SYSTEMS

Wall was built by Hadrian 122 - 128, nort of the Stanegate, the road which formed Trajan's frontier. It was 80 Roman miles long, 8-feet wide and at least 16-feet h with 15 forts, 80 milecastles, and interme turrets. Restored by Severus 200 - 205; Constantius c. 297, and again in 369.

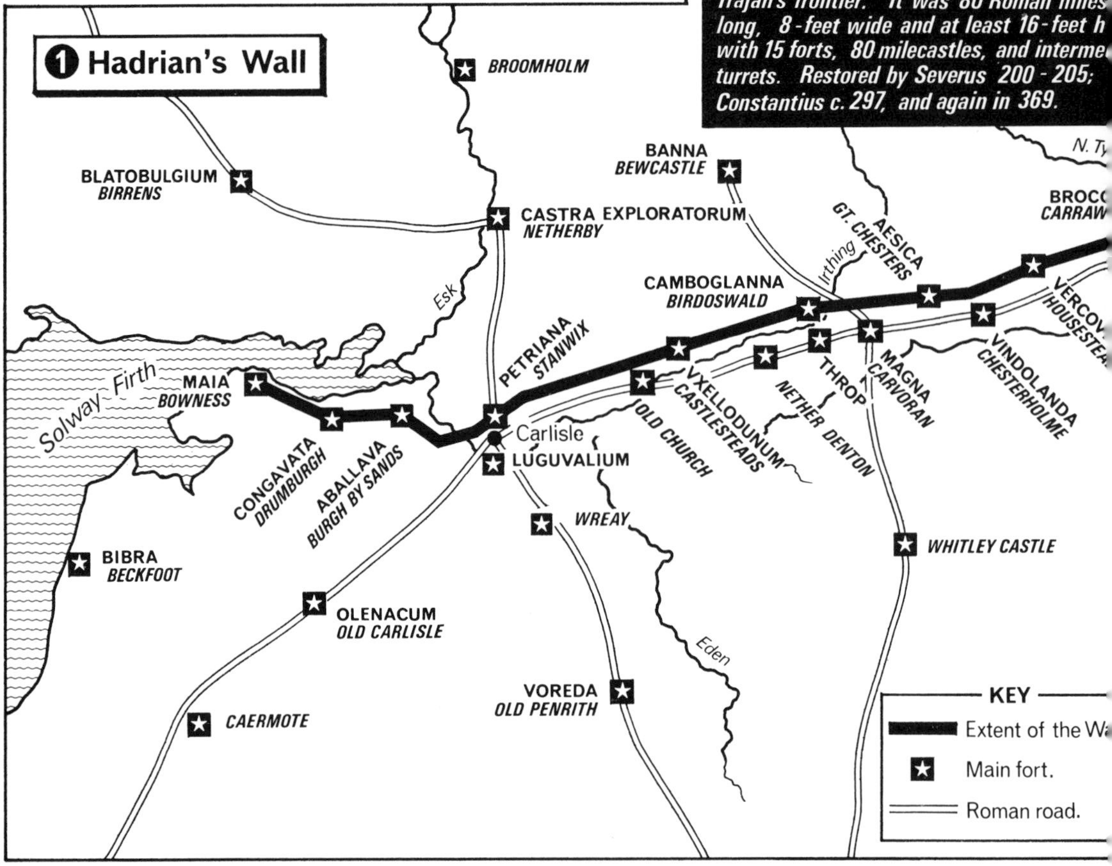

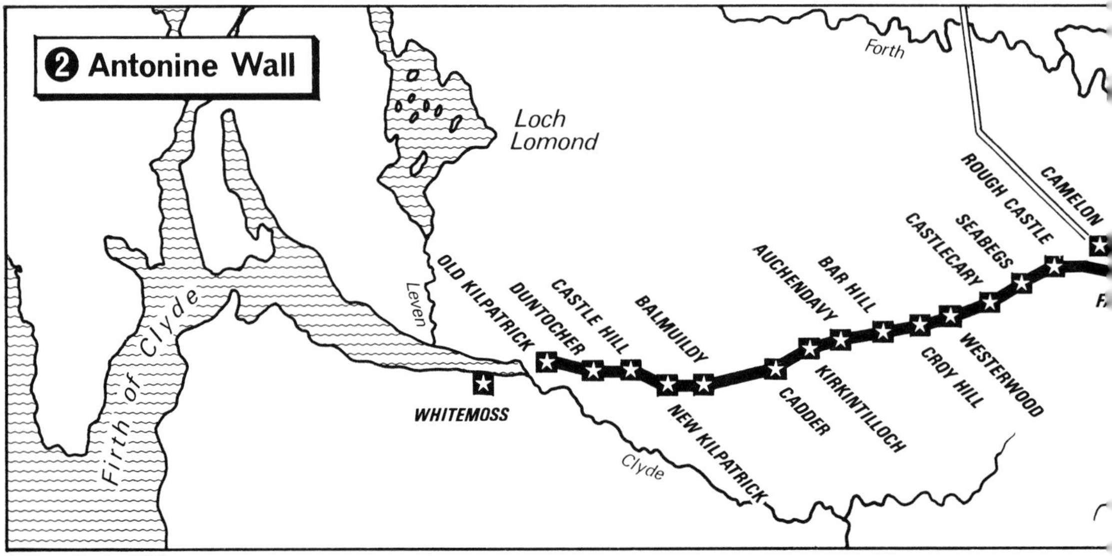

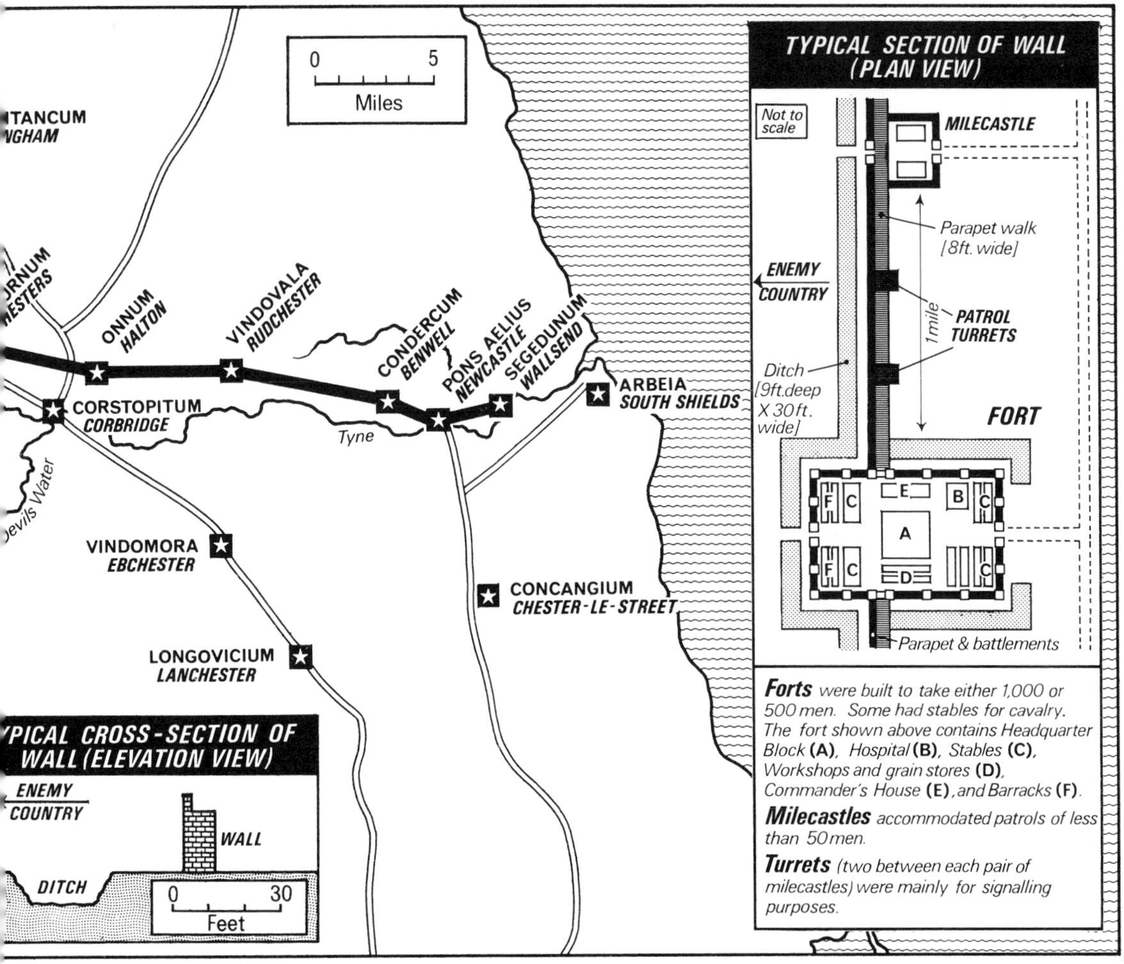

0 5 Miles
ITANCUM
NGHAM
RNUM
HESTERS
ONNUM
HALTON
VINDOVALA
RUDCHESTER
CONDERCUM
BENWELL
PONS AELIUS
NEWCASTLE
SEGEDUNUM
WALLSEND
ARBEIA
SOUTH SHIELDS
CORSTOPITUM
CORBRIDGE
Tyne
Devils Water
VINDOMORA
EBCHESTER
CONCANGIUM
CHESTER-LE-STREET
LONGOVICIUM
LANCHESTER
TYPICAL SECTION OF WALL (PLAN VIEW)
Not to scale
MILECASTLE
Parapet walk [8ft. wide]
ENEMY COUNTRY
1 mile
PATROL TURRETS
Ditch [9ft. deep X 30ft. wide]
FORT
A
B
C
D
E
F
Parapet & battlements
Forts were built to take either 1,000 or 500 men. Some had stables for cavalry. The fort shown above contains Headquarter Block (A), Hospital (B), Stables (C), Workshops and grain stores (D), Commander's House (E), and Barracks (F).
Milecastles accommodated patrols of less than 50 men.
Turrets (two between each pair of milecastles) were mainly for signalling purposes.
TYPICAL CROSS-SECTION OF WALL (ELEVATION VIEW)
ENEMY COUNTRY
WALL
DITCH
0 30 Feet

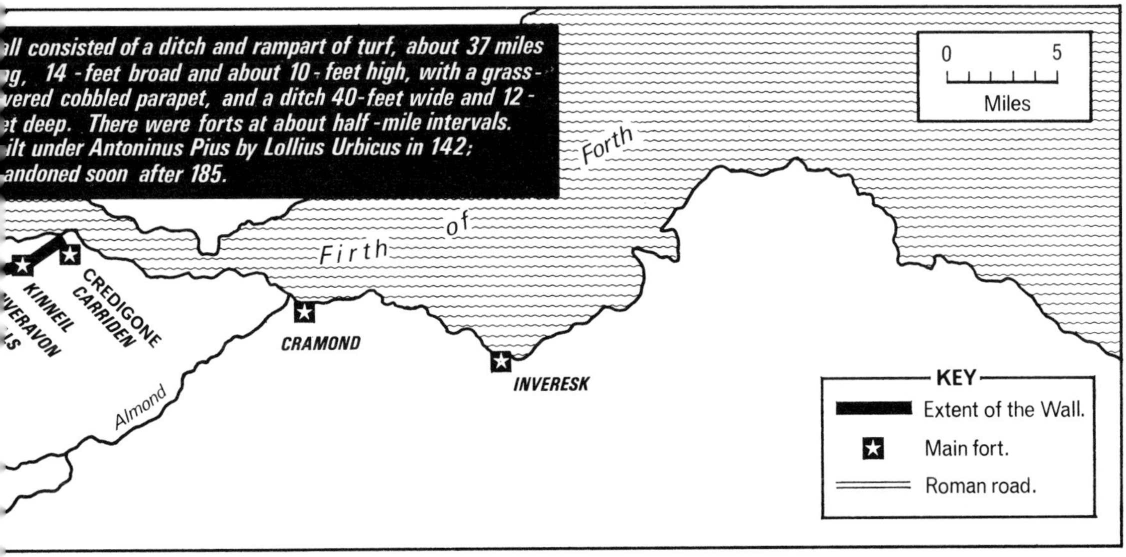

ll consisted of a ditch and rampart of turf, about 37 miles
g, 14-feet broad and about 10-feet high, with a grass-
vered cobbled parapet, and a ditch 40-feet wide and 12-
et deep. There were forts at about half-mile intervals.
ilt under Antoninus Pius by Lollius Urbicus in 142;
andoned soon after 185.
0 5 Miles
Firth of Forth
KINNEIL
VERAVON
CREDIGONE
CARRIDEN
CRAMOND
INVERESK
Almond
KEY
Extent of the Wall.
Main fort.
Roman road.

ROMAN DEFENCE SYSTEMS - continued

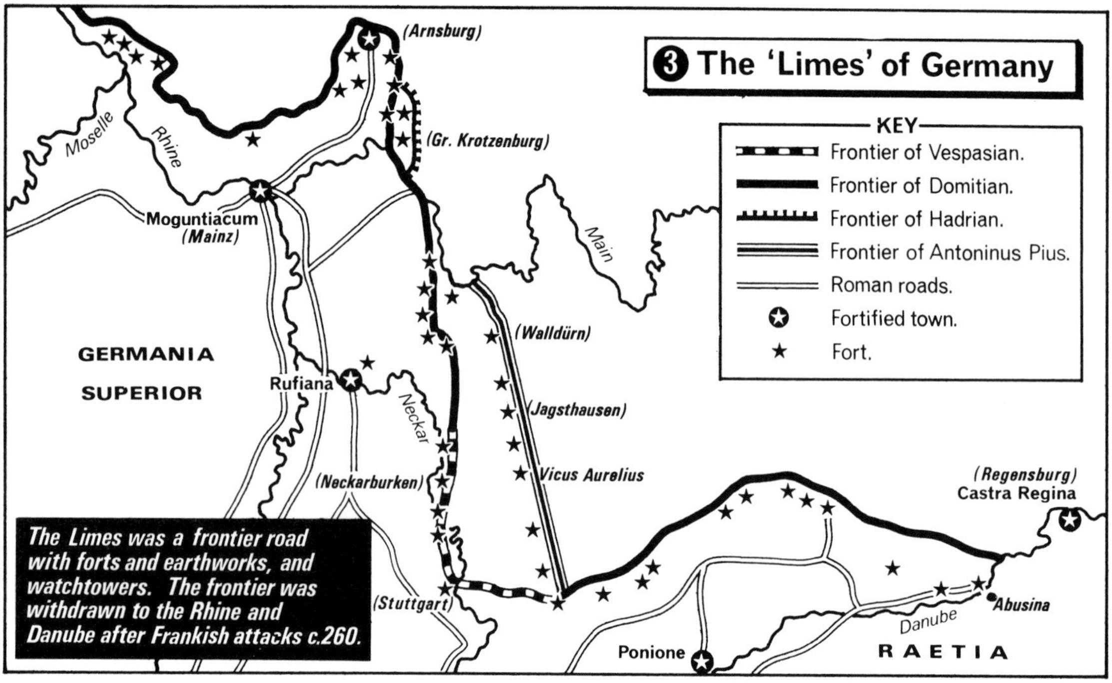

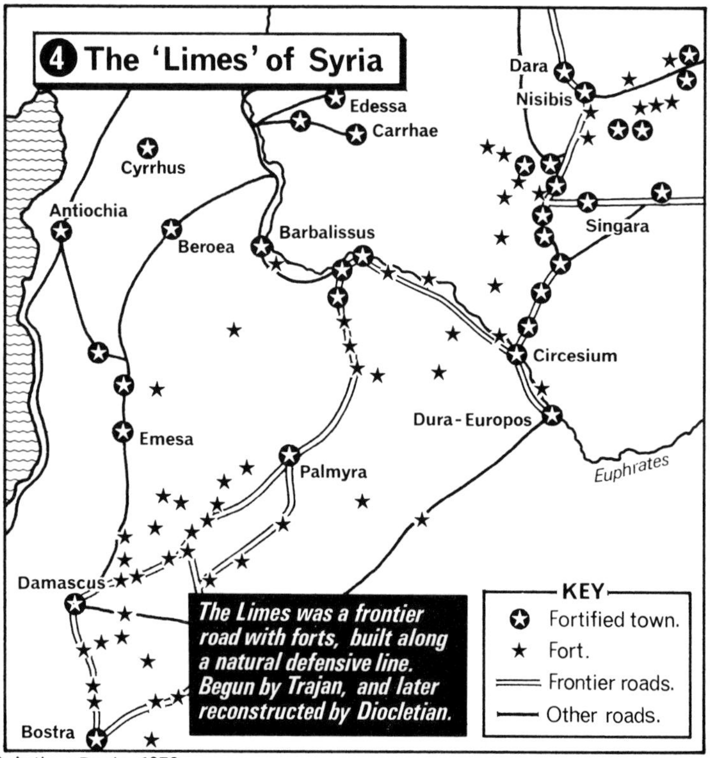

5 A Typical Roman Camp

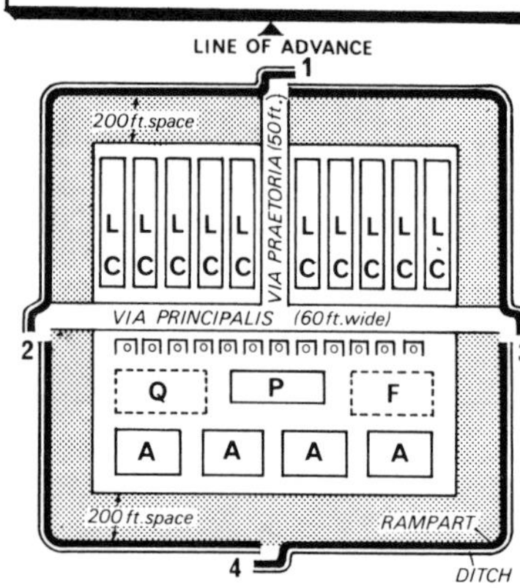

L Legionaries' lines, in 8-men leather tents.
C Centurions' tents, at end of men's lines.
P Praetorium: Commander's tent and HQ area.
Q Quaestorium: Quartermaster's area.
F Forum: Market-place or parade-ground.
A Lines of allied troops.
⌂ Tents of officers (legionary tribunes & allied praefecti).

Area required for one legion's camp: about 20 acres.

1 *PORTA PRAETORIA*
2 *PORTA PRINCIPALIS SINISTRA*
3 *PORTA PRINCIPALIS DEXTRA*
4 *PORTA DECUMANA*

6 Camp Entrances

To prevent direct enemy assaults on the gates of camps, the following methods of construction were used:

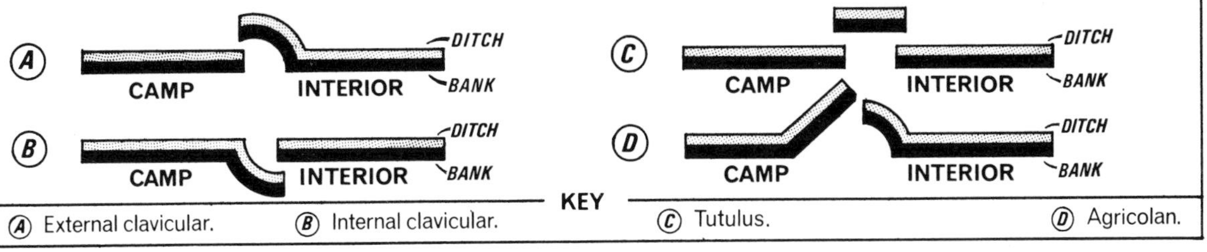

7 The 'Limes' of Africa

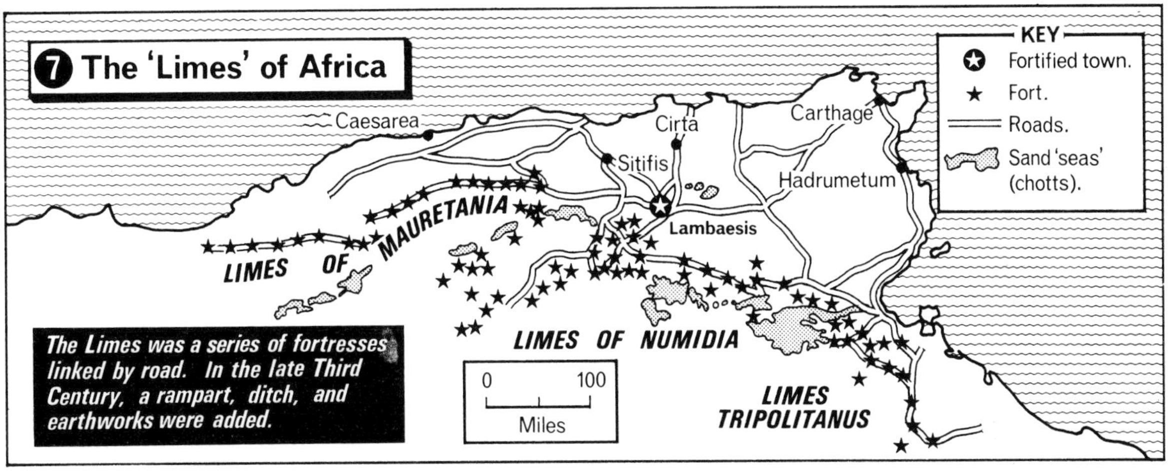

The Limes was a series of fortresses linked by road. In the late Third Century, a rampart, ditch, and earthworks were added.

8 The 'Limes' of Dacia and the Danube

In 80, Domitian constructed fortifications north of the Danube, and in 106, Trajan established a Limes in Dacia. In 271, Aurelian abandoned Dacia to the barbarians, and the frontier fell back to the river Danube.

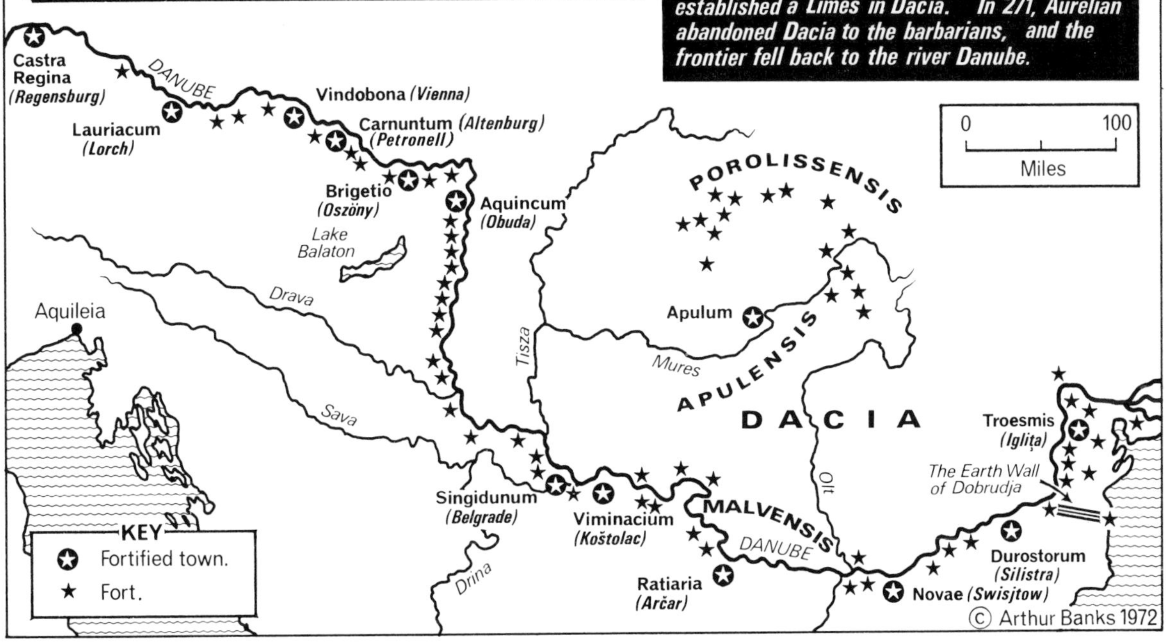

BASIC ORGANIZATION OF THE ROMAN LEGION

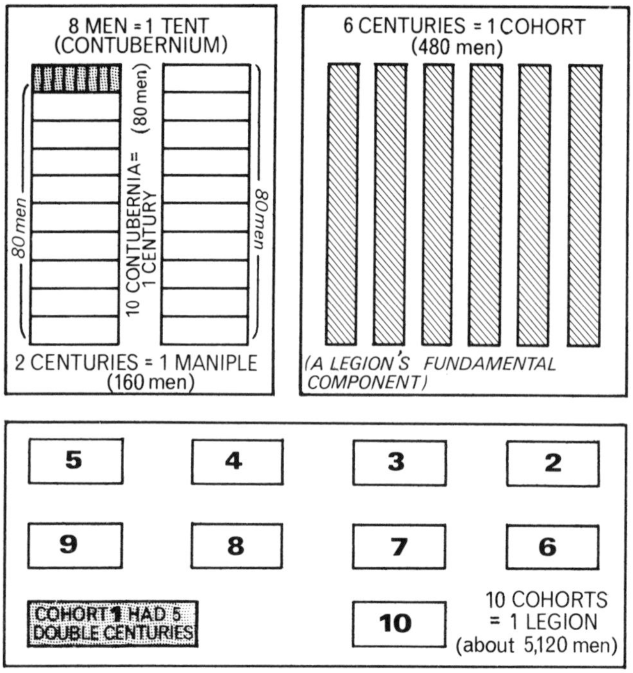

ROMAN LEGION IN BATTLE ORDER

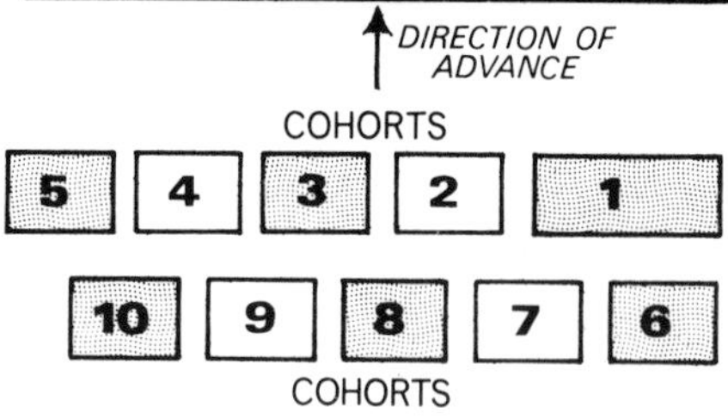

(*Note*: *strongest cohorts shown* [shaded box])

Allies (auxilia) stationed where required.

Cavalry often positioned on the wings.

Least experienced soldiers in cohorts **7** and **9**.
Cohort **1** could be a useful independent sub-unit.

(above arrangement according to Vegetius)

OFFICERS

1 Commander (legatus); 1 senior tribune;
1 Praefectus castrorum; 5 junior tribunes.
60 Centurions (senior one is primipilus).
120 horsemen per legion (scouts and despatch riders).

IMPORTANT ROMAN NAVAL BASES

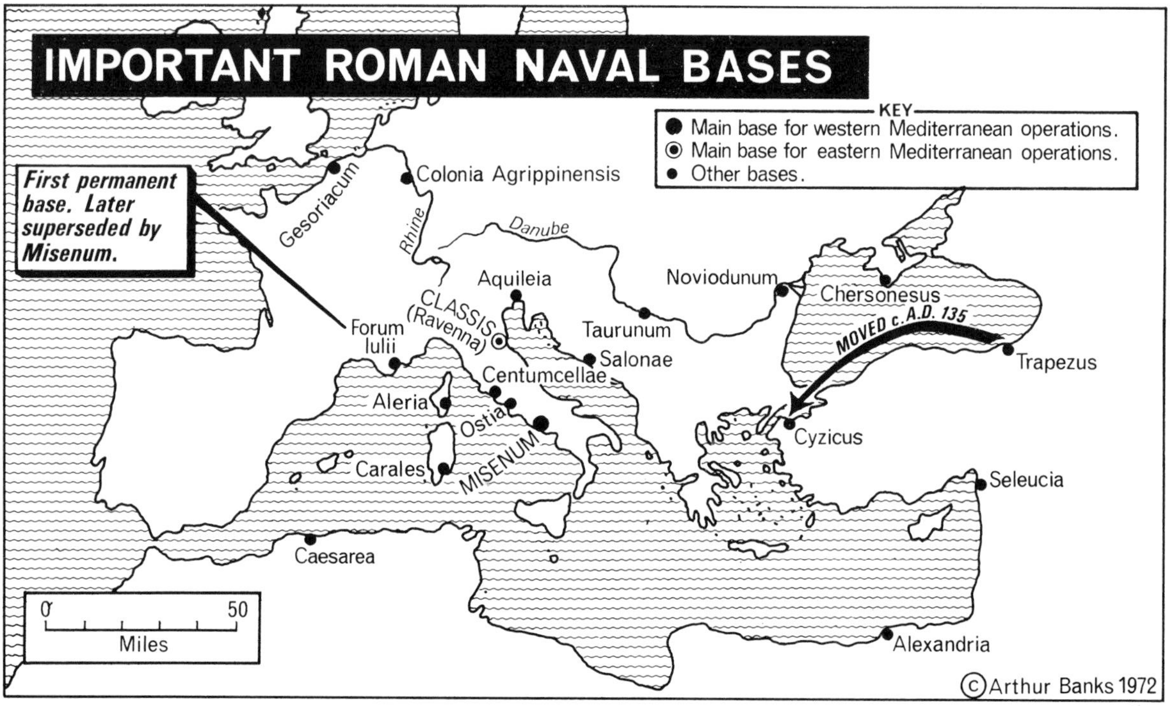

THE CAMPAIGNS OF JULIUS CAESAR 74–45 B.C.

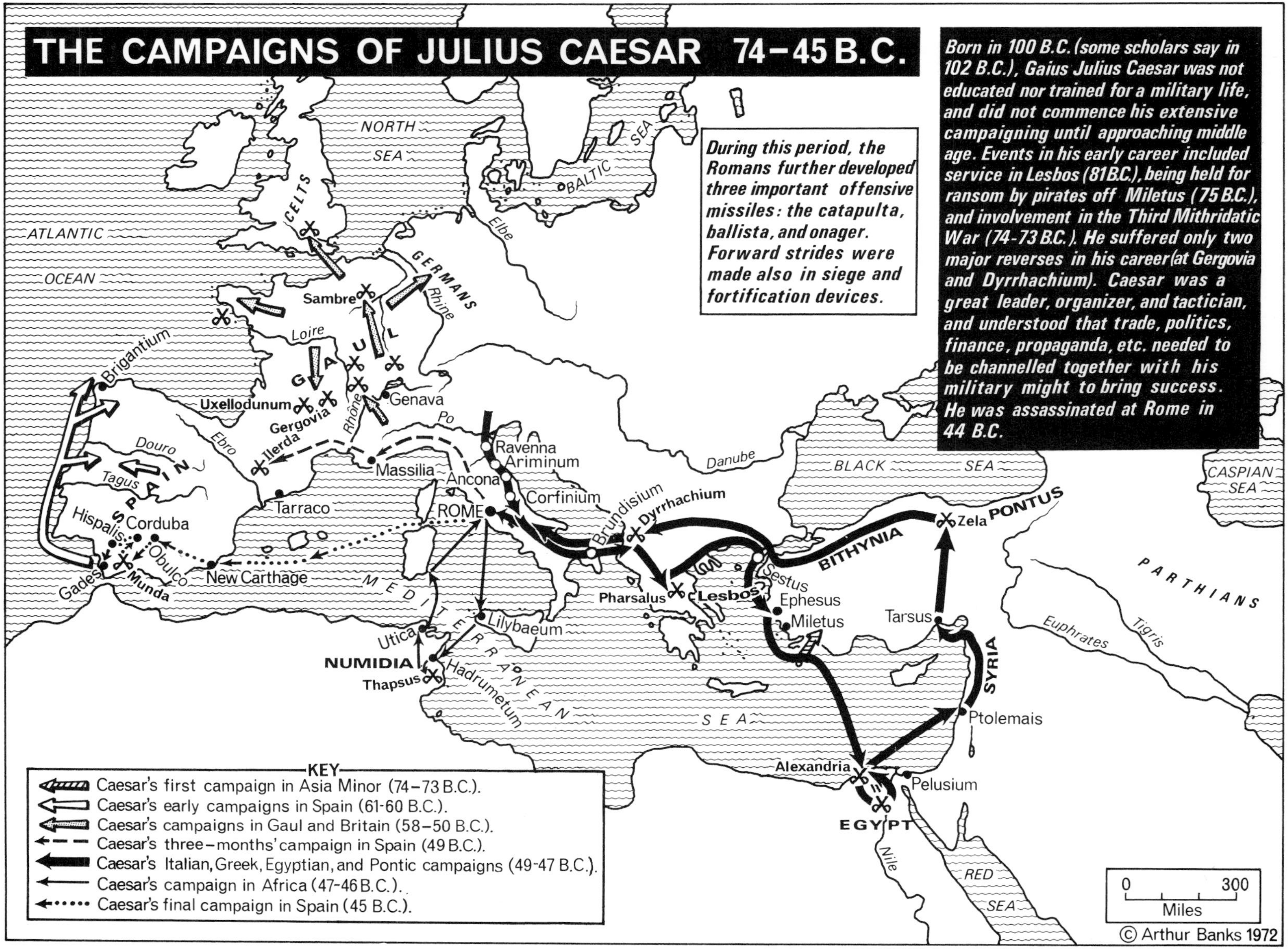

During this period, the Romans further developed three important offensive missiles: the catapulta, ballista, and onager. Forward strides were made also in siege and fortification devices.

Born in 100 B.C. (some scholars say in 102 B.C.), Gaius Julius Caesar was not educated nor trained for a military life, and did not commence his extensive campaigning until approaching middle age. Events in his early career included service in Lesbos (81 B.C.), being held for ransom by pirates off Miletus (75 B.C.), and involvement in the Third Mithridatic War (74-73 B.C.). He suffered only two major reverses in his career (at Gergovia and Dyrrhachium). Caesar was a great leader, organizer, and tactician, and understood that trade, politics, finance, propaganda, etc. needed to be channelled together with his military might to bring success. He was assassinated at Rome in 44 B.C.

CAESAR IN GAUL 58–50 B.C.

1 Gaul in Caesar's Time

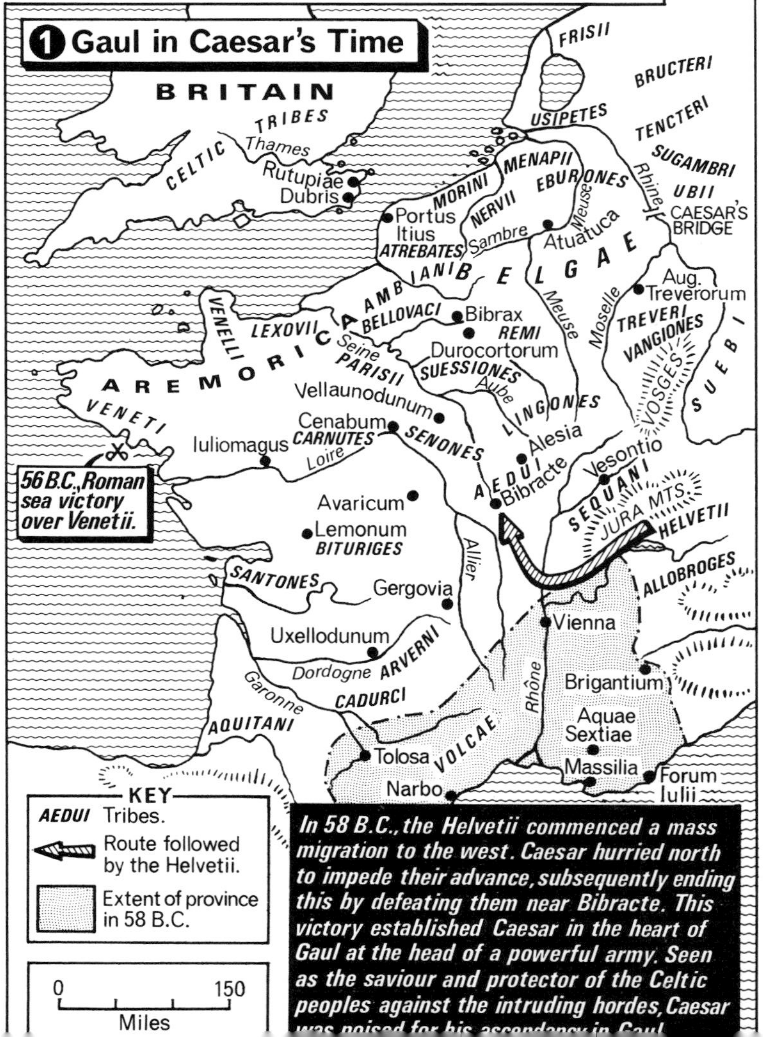

In 58 B.C., the Helvetii commenced a mass migration to the west. Caesar hurried north to impede their advance, subsequently ending this by defeating them near Bibracte. This victory established Caesar in the heart of Gaul at the head of a powerful army. Seen as the saviour and protector of the Celtic peoples against the intruding hordes, Caesar was poised for his ascendancy in Gaul

BASIC DISPOSITIONS OF CAESAR'S ARMY IN GAUL

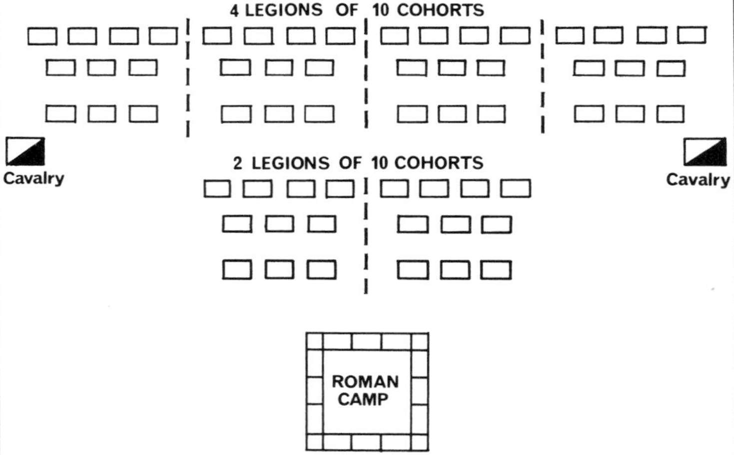

ALTERNATIVE LEGION DISPOSITIONS

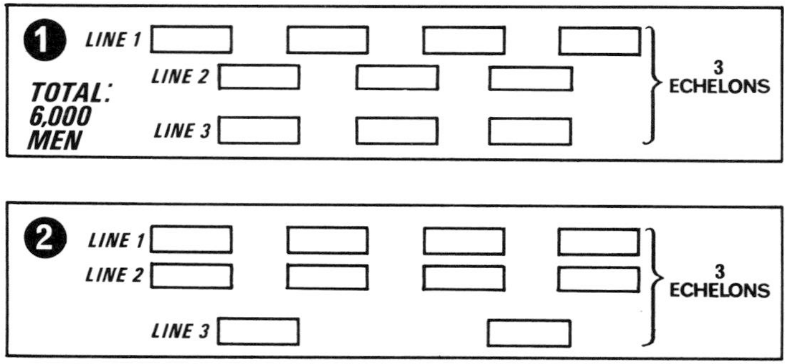

A ROMAN COHORT

2 Victory over the Helvetii 58 B.C.

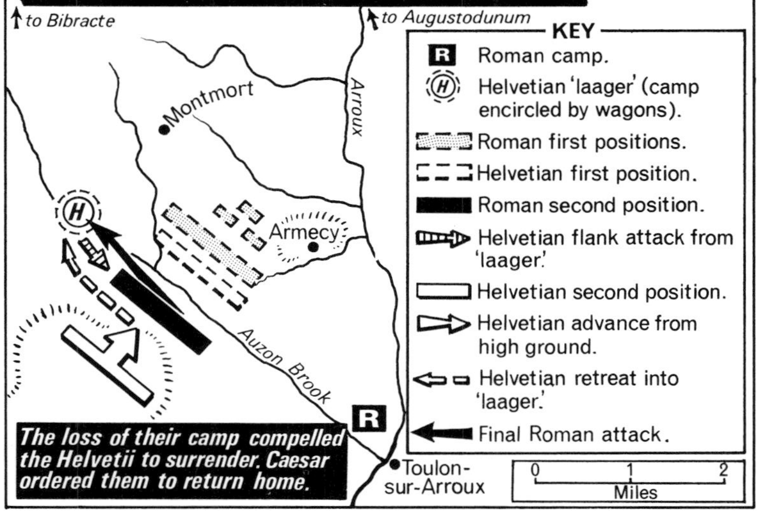
to Bibracte
to Augustodunum
Montmort
Arroux
Armecy
Auzon Brook
Toulon-sur-Arroux
The loss of their camp compelled the Helvetii to surrender. Caesar ordered them to return home.
KEY
Roman camp.
Helvetian 'laager' (camp encircled by wagons).
Roman first positions.
Helvetian first position.
Roman second position.
Helvetian flank attack from 'laager.'
Helvetian second position.
Helvetian advance from high ground.
Helvetian retreat into 'laager.'
Final Roman attack.
0 1 2
Miles

3 Victory over the Belgae 57 B.C.

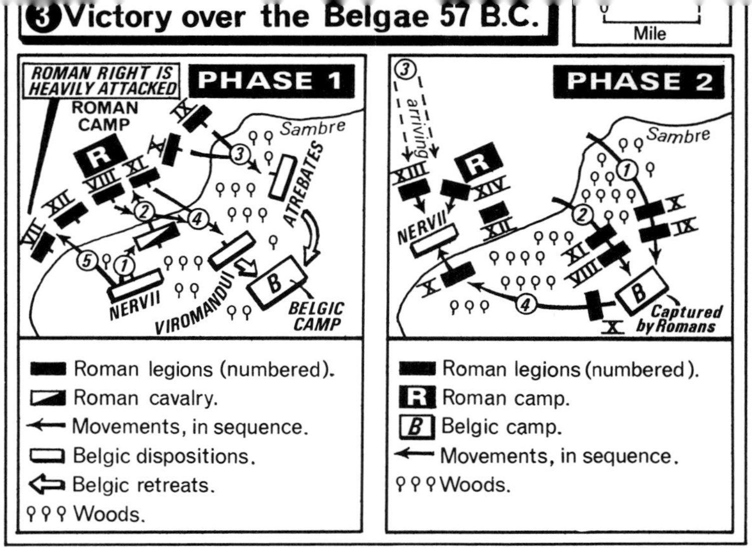
Mile
PHASE 1
ROMAN RIGHT IS HEAVILY ATTACKED
ROMAN CAMP
Sambre
ATREBATES
NERVII
VIROMANDUI
BELGIC CAMP
Roman legions (numbered).
Roman cavalry.
Movements, in sequence.
Belgic dispositions.
Belgic retreats.
Woods.
PHASE 2
arriving
Sambre
NERVII
Captured by Romans
Roman legions (numbered).
Roman camp.
Belgic camp.
Movements, in sequence.
Woods.

4 Unsuccessful Siege of Gergovia 52 B.C.

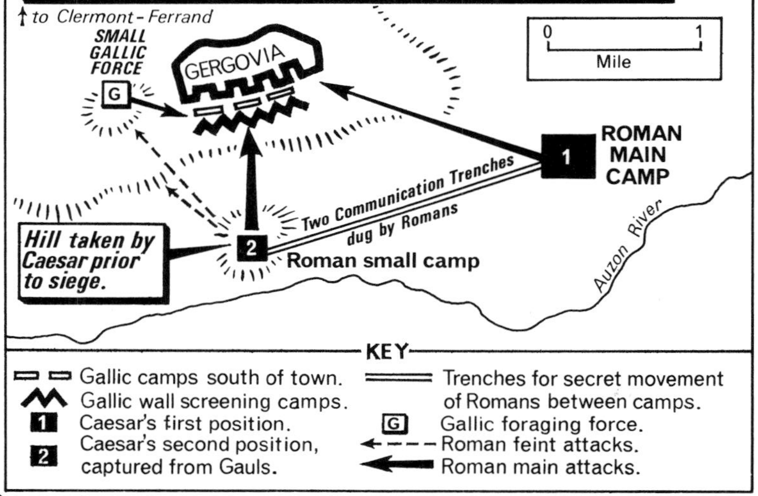
to Clermont-Ferrand
SMALL GALLIC FORCE
GERGOVIA
0 1
Mile
ROMAN MAIN CAMP
Two Communication Trenches dug by Romans
Roman small camp
Hill taken by Caesar prior to siege.
Auzon River
KEY
Gallic camps south of town.
Gallic wall screening camps.
Caesar's first position.
Caesar's second position, captured from Gauls.
Trenches for secret movement of Romans between camps.
Gallic foraging force.
Roman feint attacks.
Roman main attacks.

5 Successful Siege of Alesia 51 B.C.

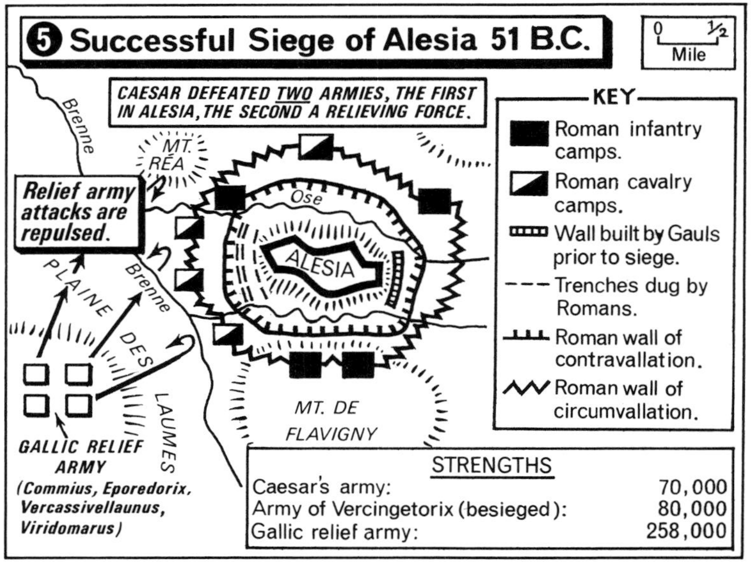
0 ½
Mile
CAESAR DEFEATED TWO ARMIES, THE FIRST IN ALESIA, THE SECOND A RELIEVING FORCE.
Brenne
MT. REA
Relief army attacks are repulsed.
Ose
ALESIA
PLAINE DES LAUMES
GALLIC RELIEF ARMY
(Commius, Eporedorix, Vercassivellaunus, Viridomarus)
MT. DE FLAVIGNY
KEY
Roman infantry camps.
Roman cavalry camps.
Wall built by Gauls prior to siege.
Trenches dug by Romans.
Roman wall of contravallation.
Roman wall of circumvallation.
STRENGTHS
Caesar's army: 70,000
Army of Vercingetorix (besieged): 80,000
Gallic relief army: 258,000

CAESAR VERSUS POMPEY

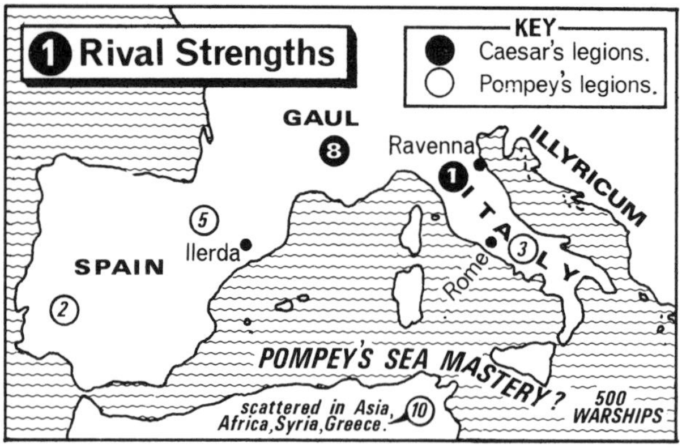

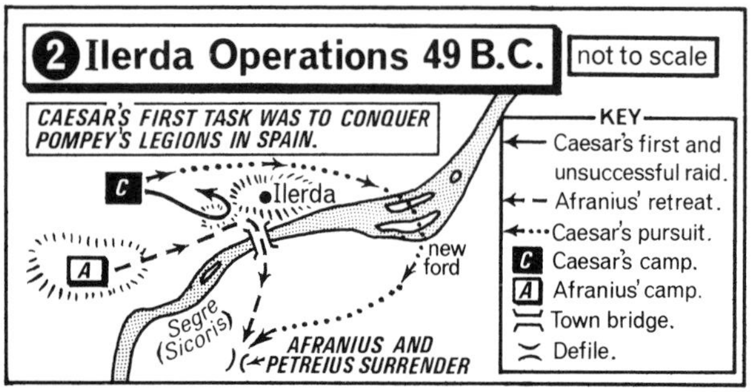

After Caesar crossed the Rubicon and moved to the south, Pompey gradually retired, eventually crossing the Adriatic to Dyrrhachium. Caesar saw that pursuit was unwise until Pompey's legions in Spain were immobilized. He accomplished this between May - July 49 B.C. near Ilerda. Returning to Italy, Caesar evaded Pompey's naval patrols and crossing to Greece, invested Dyrrhachium. Pompey broke the siege but his army was defeated at Pharsalus, 15,000 being killed and 24,000 being captured. He escaped to Egypt, only to be murdered.

4 Pharsalus: the decisive battle 48 B.C.

PHASE 1

Note: Caesar's infantry lines equalled Pompey's in length but not in density.

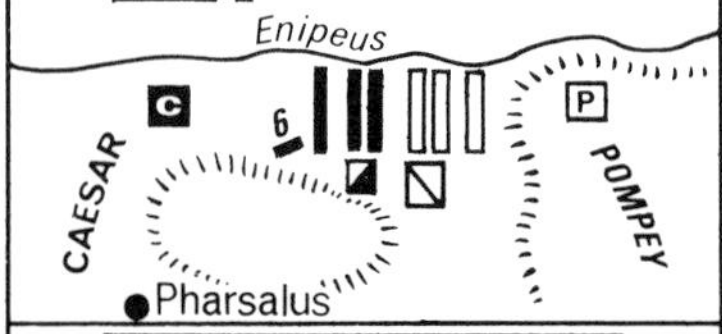

PHASE 2

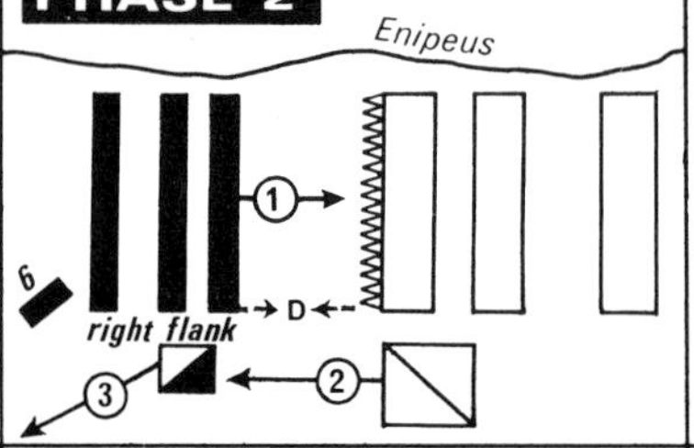

PHASE 3

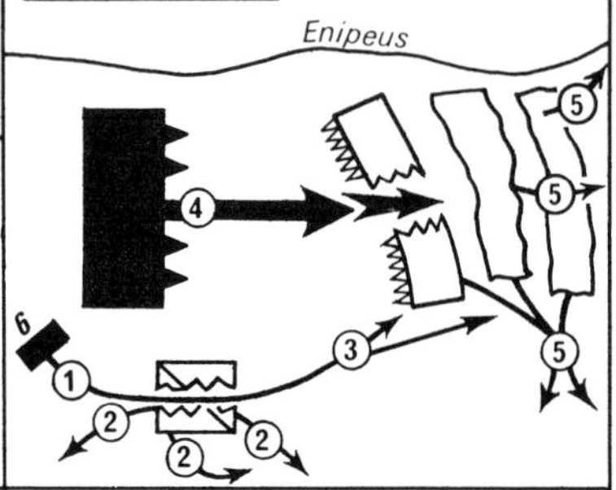

CAESAR'S DISPOSITIONS

- C Encampment.
- Cavalry (1,000).
- Infantry, in three lines (18,000).
- 6 Line of six cohorts in reserve (3,000).

POMPEY'S DISPOSITIONS

- P Encampment.
- Cavalry (6,700).
- Infantry, in three lines (38,000).

OPENING MOVES

Opening gesture: a champion from each side advances to fight a duel →D← *(object, to inspire their respective front lines).*

1. ***Caesar's infantry moves forward, hurling 'pila' (javelins) at enemy.***
2. ***Pompey's cavalry charges Caesar's cavalry (numerically inferior).***
3. ***Caesar's cavalry moves back, thus (apparently) exposing his right flank. Caesar's reserves 6 alerted.***

CAESAR'S ATTACKS

1. ***Caesar's reserve line of six cohorts engages Pompey's cavalry who panic and flee (2).***
3. ***Cohorts advance to attack left wing of Pompey's infantry, while Caesar's three lines close up to form one concerted unit.***
4. ***Caesar orders general advance.***
5. ***Attacked from two directions at same time, Pompey's army flees.***

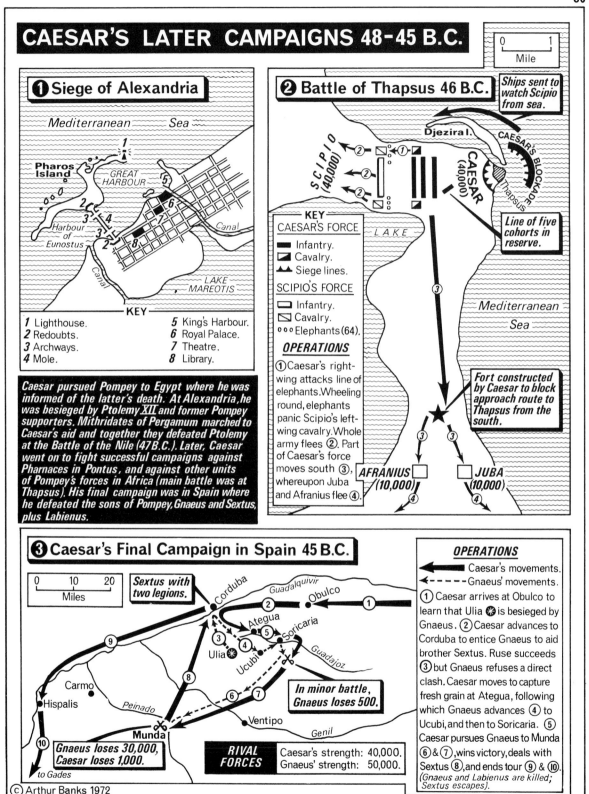

CAESAR'S LATER CAMPAIGNS 48-45 B.C.
0 1 Mile
1 Siege of Alexandria
Mediterranean Sea
Pharos Island
GREAT HARBOUR
Harbour of Eunostus
Canal
LAKE MAREOTIS
KEY
1 Lighthouse.
2 Redoubts.
3 Archways.
4 Mole.
5 King's Harbour.
6 Royal Palace.
7 Theatre.
8 Library.
Caesar pursued Pompey to Egypt where he was informed of the latter's death. At Alexandria, he was besieged by Ptolemy XII and former Pompey supporters. Mithridates of Pergamum marched to Caesar's aid and together they defeated Ptolemy at the Battle of the Nile (47 B.C.). Later, Caesar went on to fight successful campaigns against Pharnaces in Pontus, and against other units of Pompey's forces in Africa (main battle was at Thapsus). His final campaign was in Spain where he defeated the sons of Pompey, Gnaeus and Sextus, plus Labienus.
2 Battle of Thapsus 46 B.C.
Ships sent to watch Scipio from sea.
Djezira I.
CAESAR'S BLOCKADE
SCIPIO (40,000)
CAESAR (40,000)
Thapsus
Line of five cohorts in reserve.
KEY
CAESAR'S FORCE
Infantry.
Cavalry.
Siege lines.
SCIPIO'S FORCE
Infantry.
Cavalry.
Elephants (64).
LAKE
Mediterranean Sea
OPERATIONS
1 Caesar's right-wing attacks line of elephants. Wheeling round, elephants panic Scipio's left-wing cavalry. Whole army flees 2. Part of Caesar's force moves south 3, whereupon Juba and Afranius flee 4.
Fort constructed by Caesar to block approach route to Thapsus from the south.
AFRANIUS (10,000)
JUBA (10,000)
3 Caesar's Final Campaign in Spain 45 B.C.
0 10 20 Miles
Sextus with two legions.
Corduba
Guadalquivir
Obulco
Ategua
Soricaria
Ulia
Ucubi
Guadajoz
Carmo
Hispalis
Peinado
Ventipo
Genil
Munda
In minor battle, Gnaeus loses 500.
Gnaeus loses 30,000, Caesar loses 1,000.
to Gades
RIVAL FORCES
Caesar's strength: 40,000.
Gnaeus' strength: 50,000.
OPERATIONS
Caesar's movements.
Gnaeus' movements.
1 Caesar arrives at Obulco to learn that Ulia is besieged by Gnaeus. 2 Caesar advances to Corduba to entice Gnaeus to aid brother Sextus. Ruse succeeds 3 but Gnaeus refuses a direct clash. Caesar moves to capture fresh grain at Ategua, following which Gnaeus advances 4 to Ucubi, and then to Soricaria. 5 Caesar pursues Gnaeus to Munda 6 & 7, wins victory, deals with Sextus 8, and ends tour 9 & 10.
(Gnaeus and Labienus are killed; Sextus escapes).

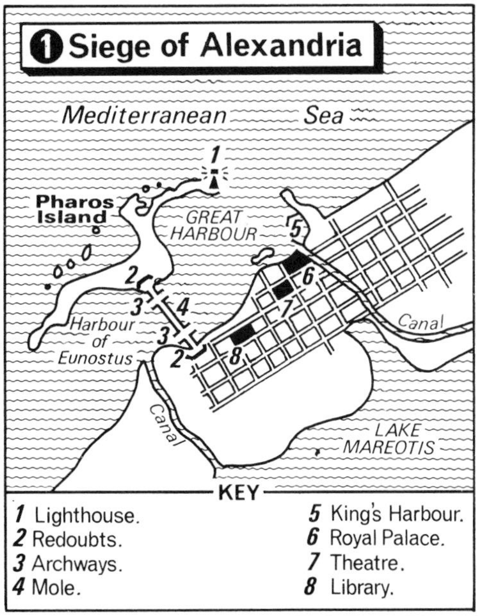

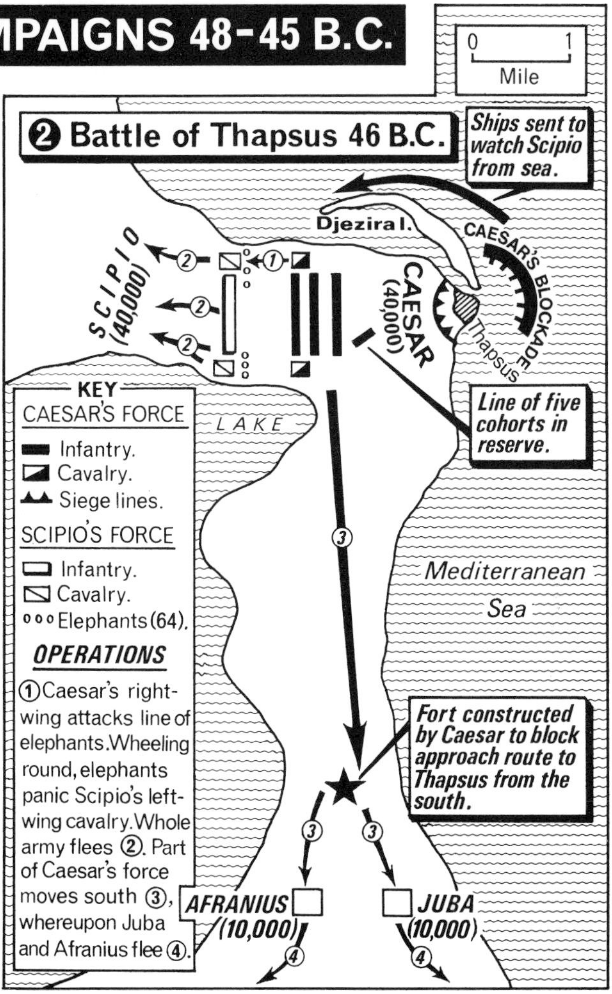

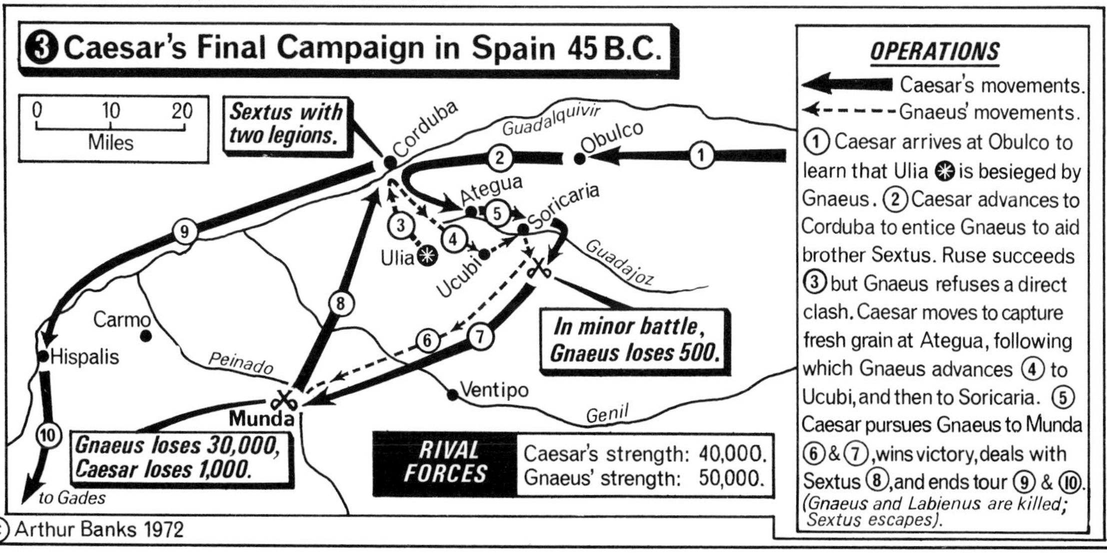

THE ROMAN MILITARY OCCUPATION OF BRITAIN c. A.D. 43 – 446

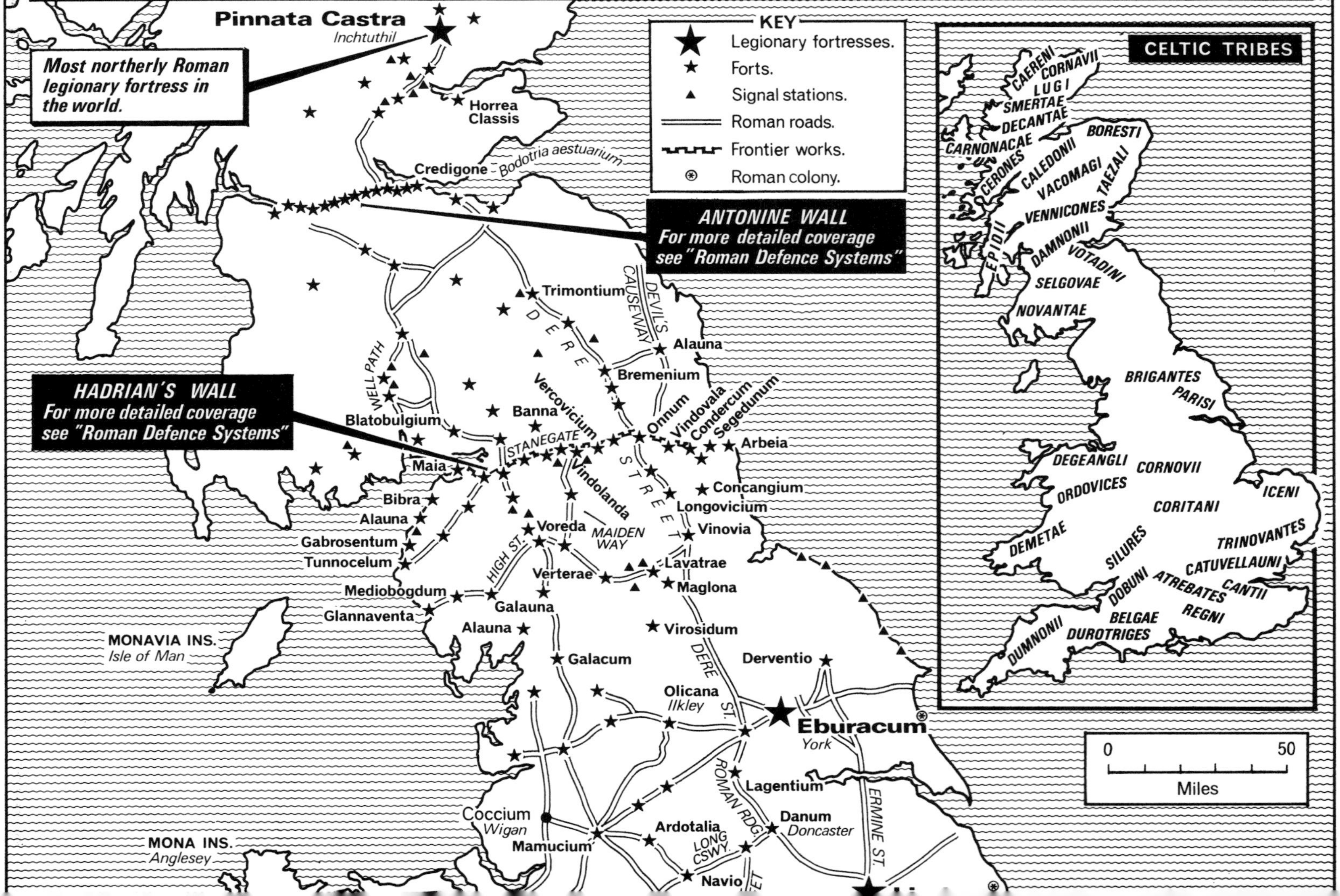
Pinnata Castra
Inchtuthil
Most northerly Roman legionary fortress in the world.
KEY
Legionary fortresses.
Forts.
Signal stations.
Roman roads.
Frontier works.
Roman colony.
CELTIC TRIBES
CAERENI
CORNAVII
LUGI
SMERTAE
DECANTAE
CARNONACAE
BORESTI
CERONES
CALEDONII
VACOMAGI
TAEZALI
VENNICONES
EPIDII
DAMNONII
VOTADINI
SELGOVAE
NOVANTAE
BRIGANTES
PARISI
DEGEANGLI
CORNOVII
ORDOVICES
ICENI
CORITANI
DEMETAE
SILURES
TRINOVANTES
CATUVELLAUNI
DOBUNI
ATREBATES
CANTII
BELGAE
REGNI
DUMNONII
DUROTRIGES
Horrea Classis
Credigone
Bodotria aestuarium
ANTONINE WALL
For more detailed coverage see "Roman Defence Systems"
HADRIAN'S WALL
For more detailed coverage see "Roman Defence Systems"
Trimontium
DEVIL'S CAUSEWAY
DERE STREET
Alauna
Bremenium
WELL PATH
Vercovicium
Banna
Blatobulgium
Onnum
Vindovala
Condercum
Segedunum
Arbeia
STANEGATE
Maia
Vindolanda
Concangium
Bibra
Longovicium
Alauna
Voreda
MAIDEN WAY
Vinovia
Gabrosentum
Tunnocelum
HIGH ST.
Lavatrae
Verterae
Maglona
Mediobogdum
Galauna
Glannaventa
Alauna
Virosidum
MONAVIA INS.
Isle of Man
Galacum
DERE ST.
Derventio
Olicana
Ilkley
Eburacum
York
0
50
Miles
Lagentium
ROMAN RDG.
ERMINE ST.
Coccium
Wigan
Danum
Doncaster
Ardotalia
LONG CSWY.
MONA INS.
Anglesey
Mamucium
Navio

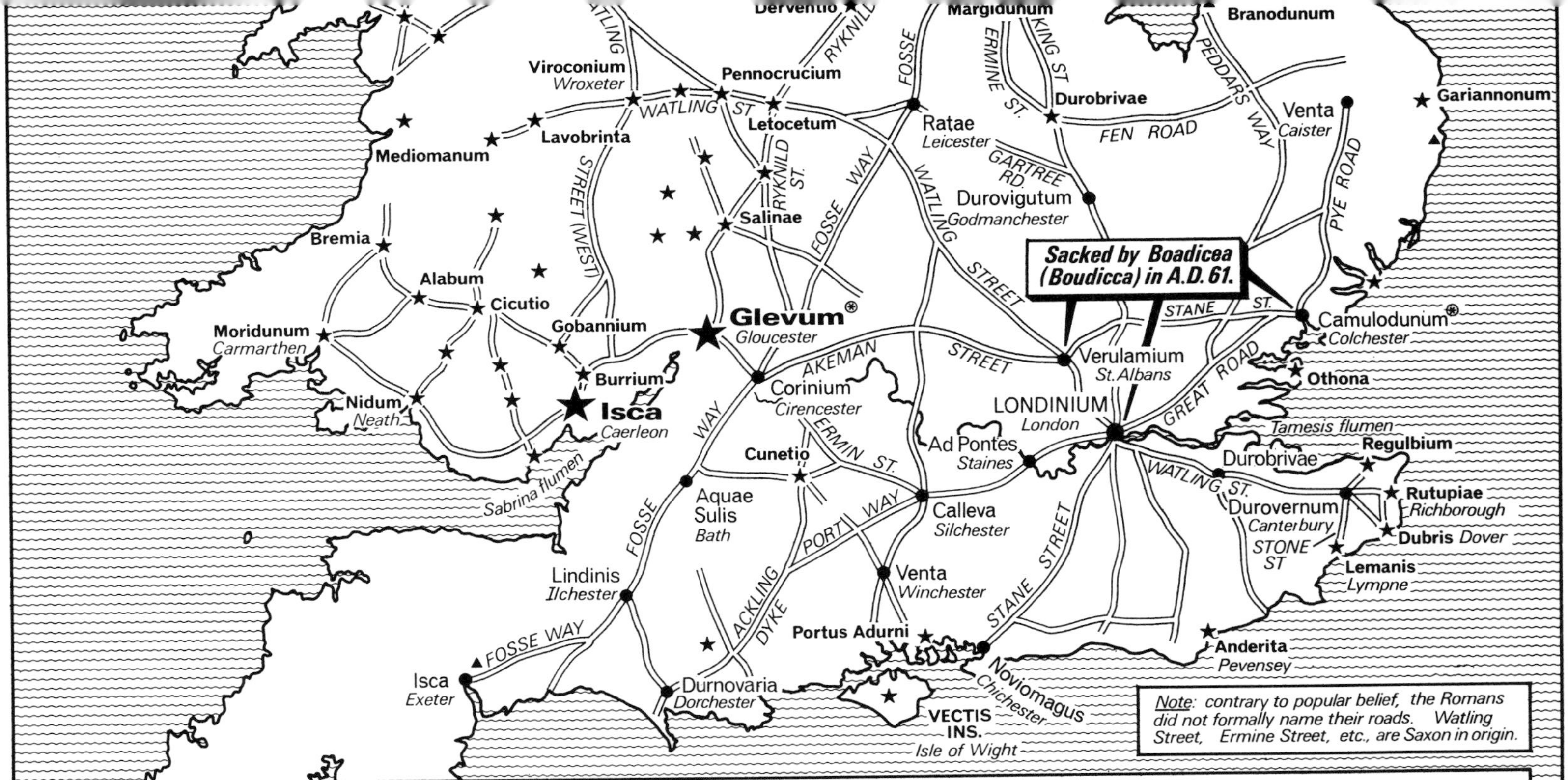

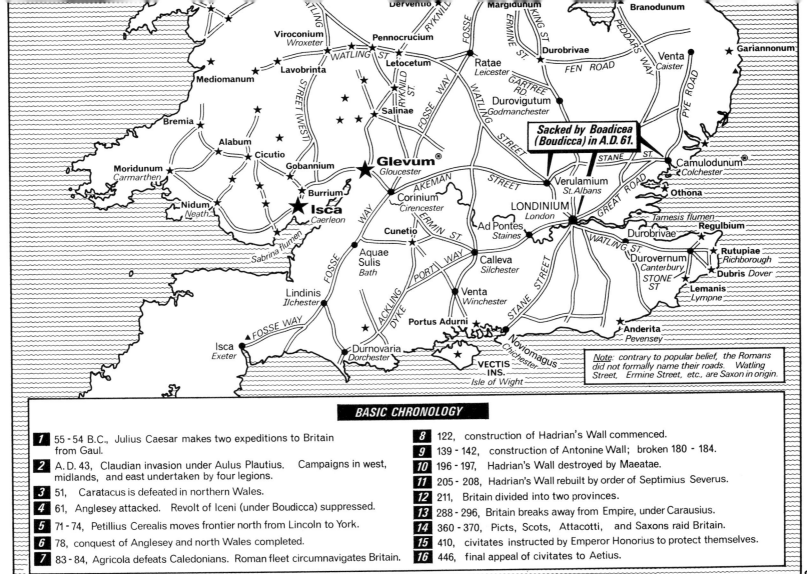

Note: contrary to popular belief, the Romans did not formally name their roads. Watling Street, Ermine Street, etc., are Saxon in origin.

BASIC CHRONOLOGY

1 55 - 54 B.C., Julius Caesar makes two expeditions to Britain from Gaul.

2 A. D. 43, Claudian invasion under Aulus Plautius. Campaigns in west, midlands, and east undertaken by four legions.

3 51, Caratacus is defeated in northern Wales.

4 61, Anglesey attacked. Revolt of Iceni (under Boudicca) suppressed.

5 71 - 74, Petillius Cerealis moves frontier north from Lincoln to York.

6 78, conquest of Anglesey and north Wales completed.

7 83 - 84, Agricola defeats Caledonians. Roman fleet circumnavigates Britain.

8 122, construction of Hadrian's Wall commenced.

9 139 - 142, construction of Antonine Wall; broken 180 - 184.

10 196 - 197, Hadrian's Wall destroyed by Maeatae.

11 205 - 208, Hadrian's Wall rebuilt by order of Septimius Severus.

12 211, Britain divided into two provinces.

13 288 - 296, Britain breaks away from Empire, under Carausius.

14 360 - 370, Picts, Scots, Attacotti, and Saxons raid Britain.

15 410, civitates instructed by Emperor Honorius to protect themselves.

16 446, final appeal of civitates to Aetius.

THE CAMPAIGN OF ACTIUM 31 B.C.

MAIN CAUSES OF THE WAR BETWEEN OCTAVIAN AND ANTONY

1. Antony's marriage to Cleopatra VII of Egypt following his divorce from Octavia, sister of Octavian. Antony's will, formally publicized by Octavian, left some Roman possessions to his children by Cleopatra. This was seen as a future threat to Rome.

2 Antony's naval and army concentrations in Greece. These were regarded in Rome as preliminaries to an invasion of Italy.

1 Strengths, Dispositions, and Early Moves

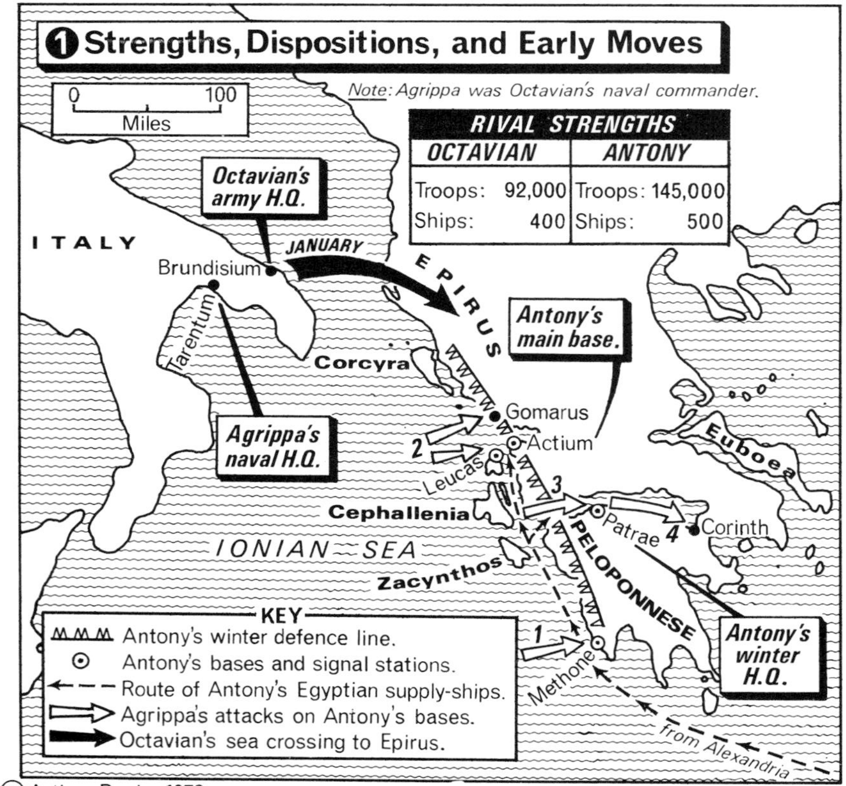

RIVAL STRENGTHS

OCTAVIAN	ANTONY
Troops: 92,000	Troops: 145,000
Ships: 400	Ships: 500

2 Antony's Raids on Octavian's Camp

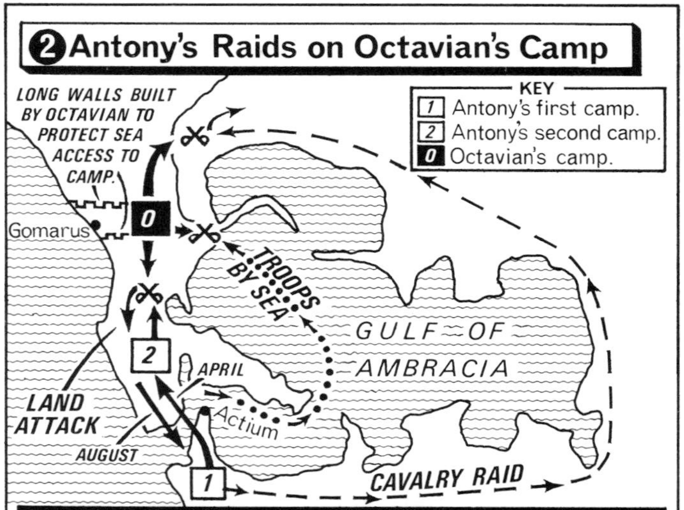

Antony's plans to defeat Octavian by combined land and sea units ended in failure. Many of his troops deserted, including leaders.

3 The Decisive Sea Fight: 2 September

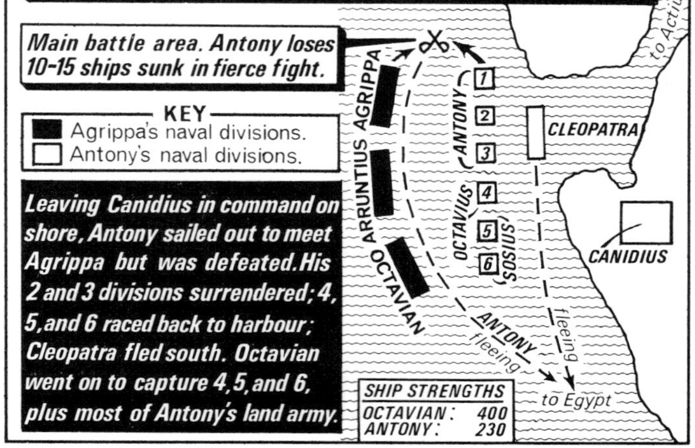

Main battle area. Antony loses 10-15 ships sunk in fierce fight.

KEY
- Agrippa's naval divisions.
- Antony's naval divisions.

Leaving Canidius in command on shore, Antony sailed out to meet Agrippa but was defeated. His 2 and 3 divisions surrendered; 4, 5, and 6 raced back to harbour; Cleopatra fled south. Octavian went on to capture 4, 5, and 6, plus most of Antony's land army.

SHIP STRENGTHS

OCTAVIAN:	400
ANTONY:	230

INDIA c.A.D.150

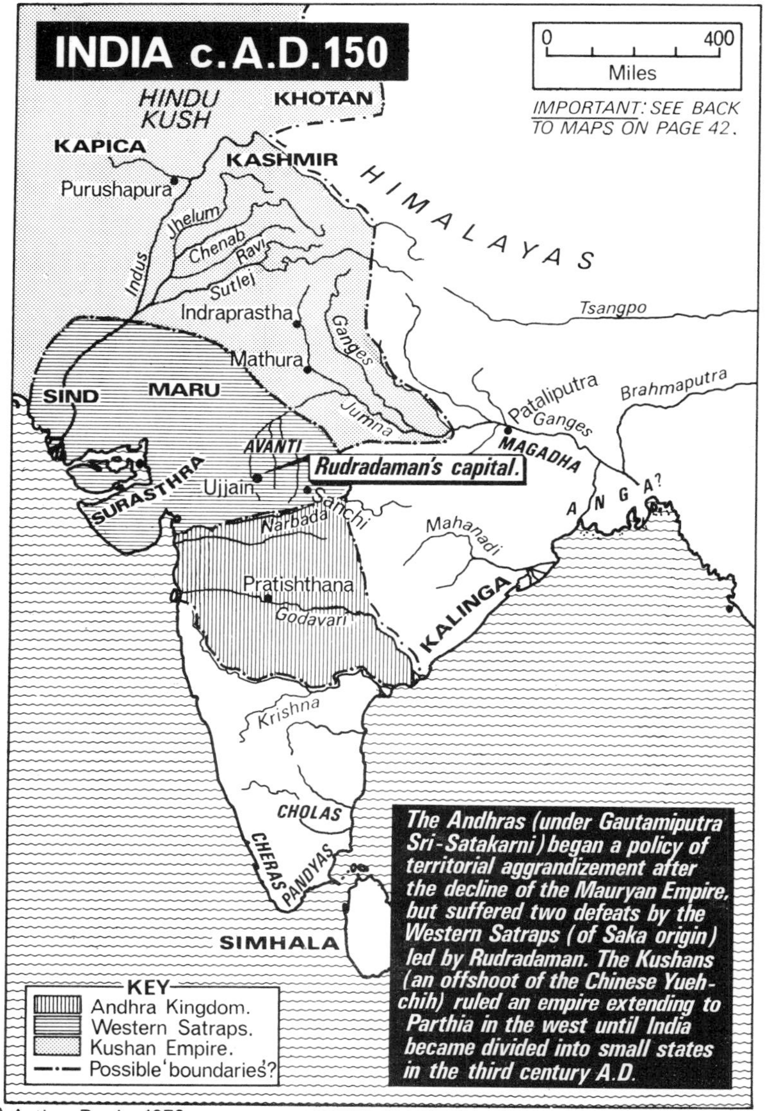

IMPORTANT: SEE BACK TO MAPS ON PAGE 42.

KEY
- Andhra Kingdom.
- Western Satraps.
- Kushan Empire.
- Possible 'boundaries'?

The Andhras (under Gautamiputra Sri-Satakarni) began a policy of territorial aggrandizement after the decline of the Mauryan Empire, but suffered two defeats by the Western Satraps (of Saka origin) led by Rudradaman. The Kushans (an offshoot of the Chinese Yueh-chih) ruled an empire extending to Parthia in the west until India became divided into small states in the third century A.D.

THE GUPTA EMPIRE c.A.D. 400

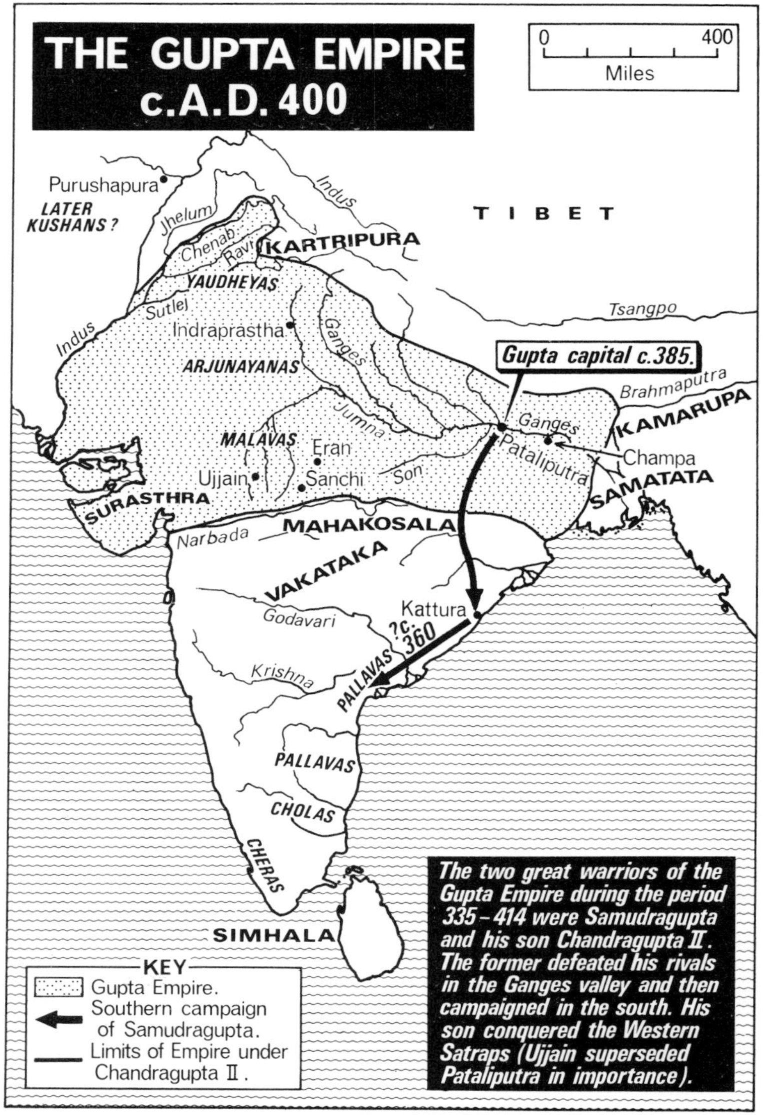

KEY
- Gupta Empire.
- Southern campaign of Samudragupta.
- Limits of Empire under Chandragupta II.

The two great warriors of the Gupta Empire during the period 335–414 were Samudragupta and his son Chandragupta II. The former defeated his rivals in the Ganges valley and then campaigned in the south. His son conquered the Western Satraps (Ujjain superseded Pataliputra in importance).

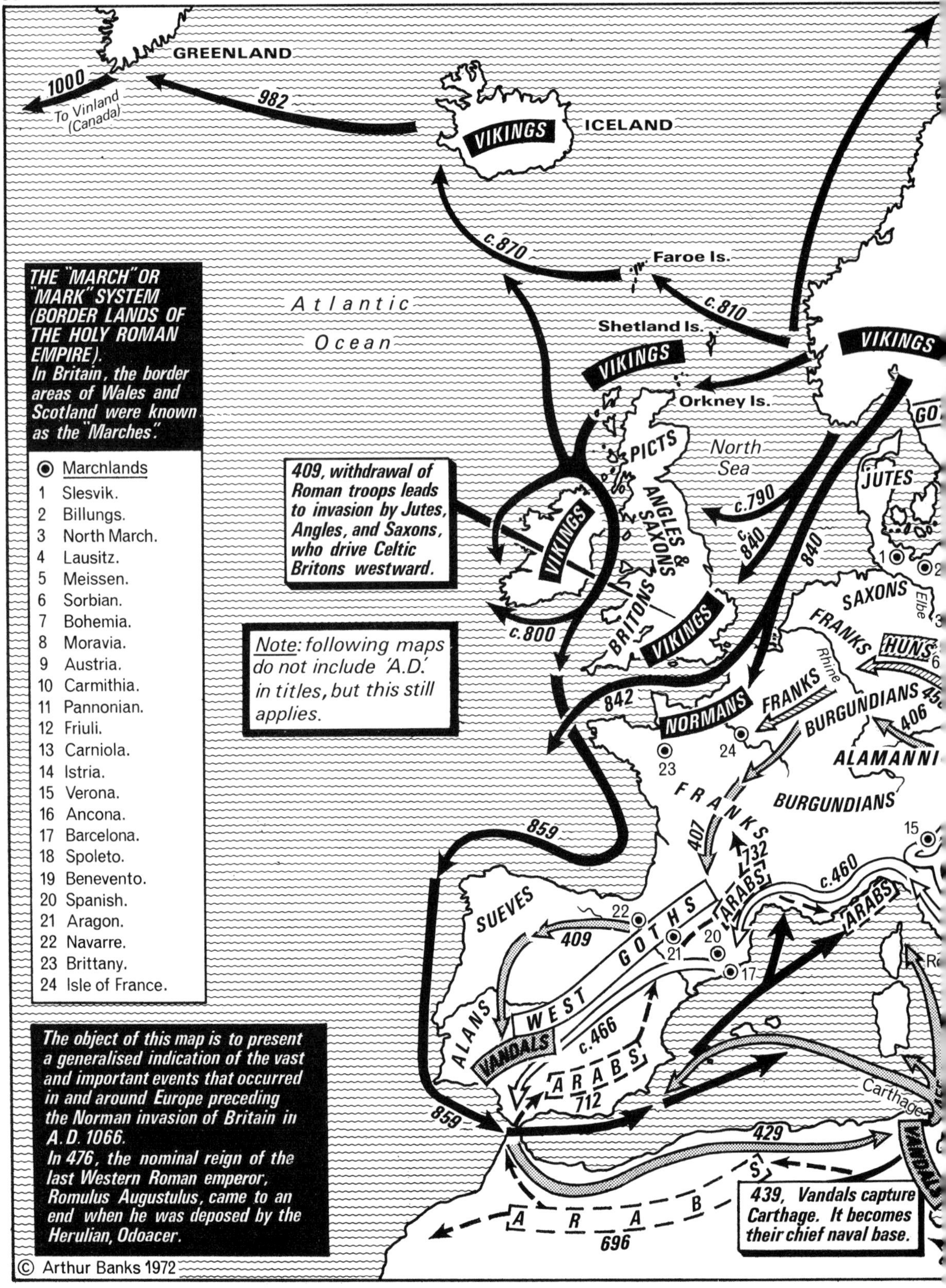
GREENLAND
1000
To Vinland (Canada)
982
ICELAND
VIKINGS
c.870
Faroe Is.
c.810
Shetland Is.
Orkney Is.
VIKINGS
VIKINGS
Atlantic Ocean
North Sea
PICTS
ANGLES & SAXONS
BRITONS
VIKINGS
VIKINGS
JUTES
c.790
c.840
840
c.800
842
859
859
NORMANS
SAXONS
Elbe
FRANKS
HUNS
Rhine
FRANKS
BURGUNDIANS
406
ALAMANNI
BURGUNDIANS
FRANKS
407
732
ARABS
c.460
ARABS
SUEVES
409
WEST GOTHS
ALANS
VANDALS
c.466
ARABS
ARABS
712
Carthage
429
ARABS
696
THE "MARCH" OR "MARK" SYSTEM (BORDER LANDS OF THE HOLY ROMAN EMPIRE). In Britain, the border areas of Wales and Scotland were known as the "Marches".
Marchlands
1 Slesvik.
2 Billungs.
3 North March.
4 Lausitz.
5 Meissen.
6 Sorbian.
7 Bohemia.
8 Moravia.
9 Austria.
10 Carmithia.
11 Pannonian.
12 Friuli.
13 Carniola.
14 Istria.
15 Verona.
16 Ancona.
17 Barcelona.
18 Spoleto.
19 Benevento.
20 Spanish.
21 Aragon.
22 Navarre.
23 Brittany.
24 Isle of France.
409, withdrawal of Roman troops leads to invasion by Jutes, Angles, and Saxons, who drive Celtic Britons westward.
Note: following maps do not include 'A.D.' in titles, but this still applies.
The object of this map is to present a generalised indication of the vast and important events that occurred in and around Europe preceding the Norman invasion of Britain in A.D. 1066. In 476, the nominal reign of the last Western Roman emperor, Romulus Augustulus, came to an end when he was deposed by the Herulian, Odoacer.
439, Vandals capture Carthage. It becomes their chief naval base.
© Arthur Banks 1972

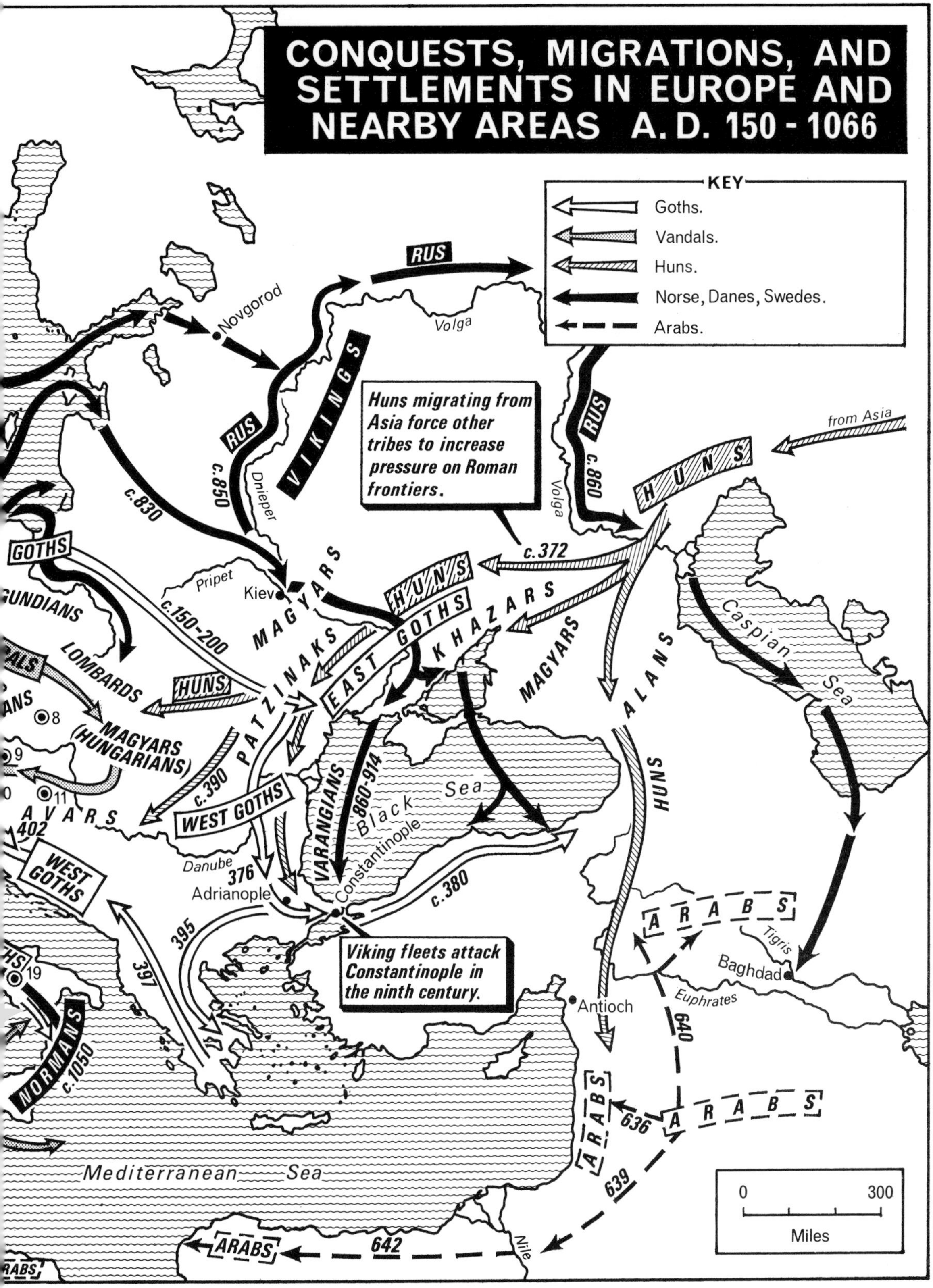

CONQUESTS, MIGRATIONS, AND SETTLEMENTS IN EUROPE AND NEARBY AREAS A. D. 150 - 1066
KEY
Goths.
Vandals.
Huns.
Norse, Danes, Swedes.
Arabs.
Huns migrating from Asia force other tribes to increase pressure on Roman frontiers.
Viking fleets attack Constantinople in the ninth century.
RUS
Novgorod
Volga
VIKINGS
RUS
c.850
c.830
Dnieper
RUS
c.860
Volga
from Asia
HUNS
c.372
GOTHS
Pripet
Kiev
c.150-200
MAGYARS
HUNS
EAST GOTHS
KHAZARS
MAGYARS
ALANS
Caspian Sea
LOMBARDS
HUNS
PATZINAKS
MAGYARS (HUNGARIANS)
8
9
11
AVARS
402
c.390
WEST GOTHS
VARANGIANS
860-914
Black Sea
Constantinople
HUNS
WEST GOTHS
Danube
376
Adrianople
c.380
395
397
ARABS
Tigris
Baghdad
Euphrates
Antioch
640
19
NORMANS
c.1050
ARABS
636
ARABS
ARABS
639
Mediterranean Sea
0
300
Miles
ARABS
642
Nile

THE PERIOD OF THE THREE KINGDOMS (SAN KUO) IN CHINA 221 – 279

Strife among the three kingdoms led to a period of anarchy in China and made possible barbarian raids on the outskirts of Chinese civilization. Wei (Tsin after 265) became the dominant power.

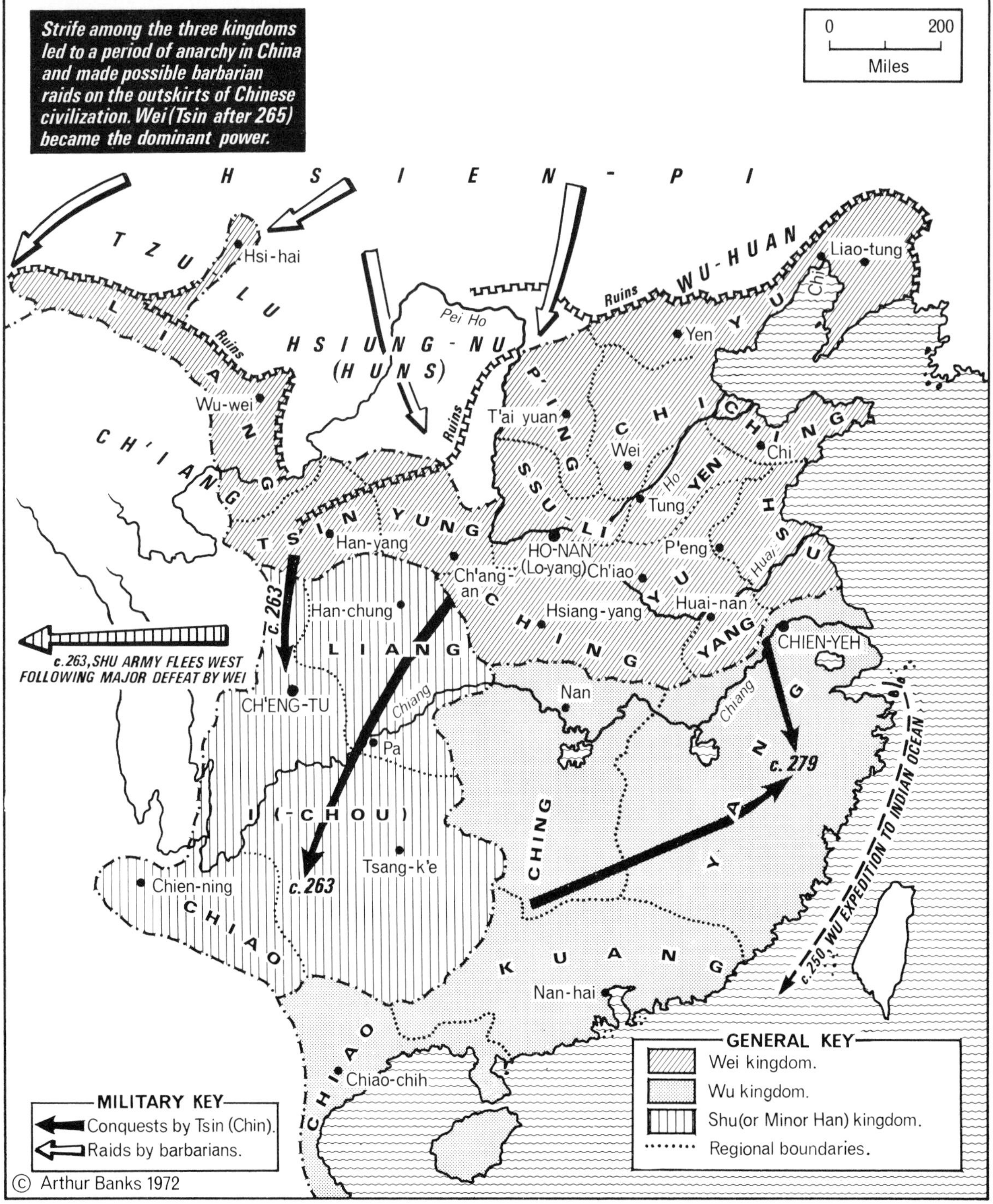

THE WESTERN TSIN (CHIN) DYNASTY IN CHINA 265 - 317

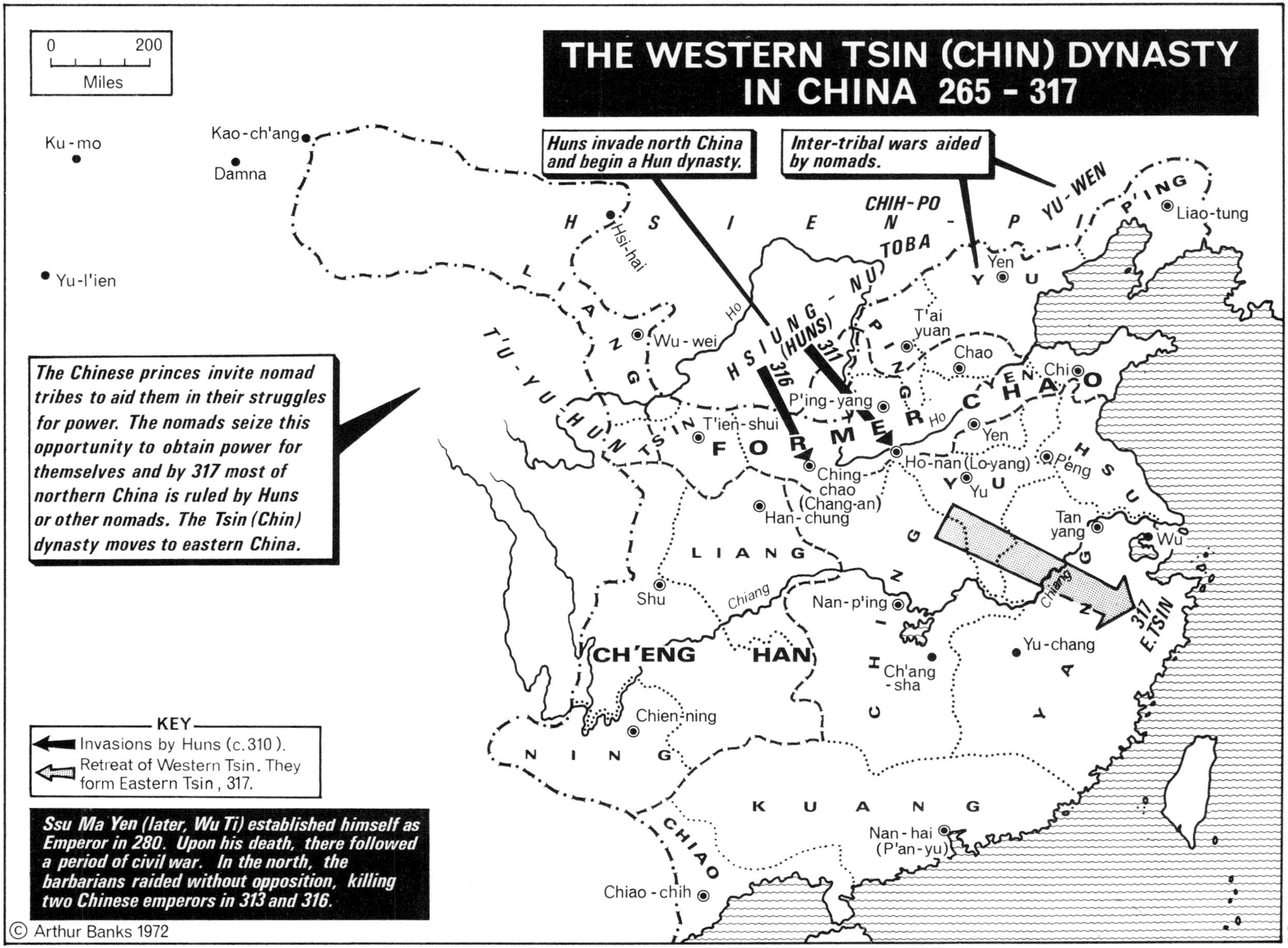

Huns invade north China and begin a Hun dynasty.

Inter-tribal wars aided by nomads.

The Chinese princes invite nomad tribes to aid them in their struggles for power. The nomads seize this opportunity to obtain power for themselves and by 317 most of northern China is ruled by Huns or other nomads. The Tsin (Chin) dynasty moves to eastern China.

Ssu Ma Yen (later, Wu Ti) established himself as Emperor in 280. Upon his death, there followed a period of civil war. In the north, the barbarians raided without opposition, killing two Chinese emperors in 313 and 316.

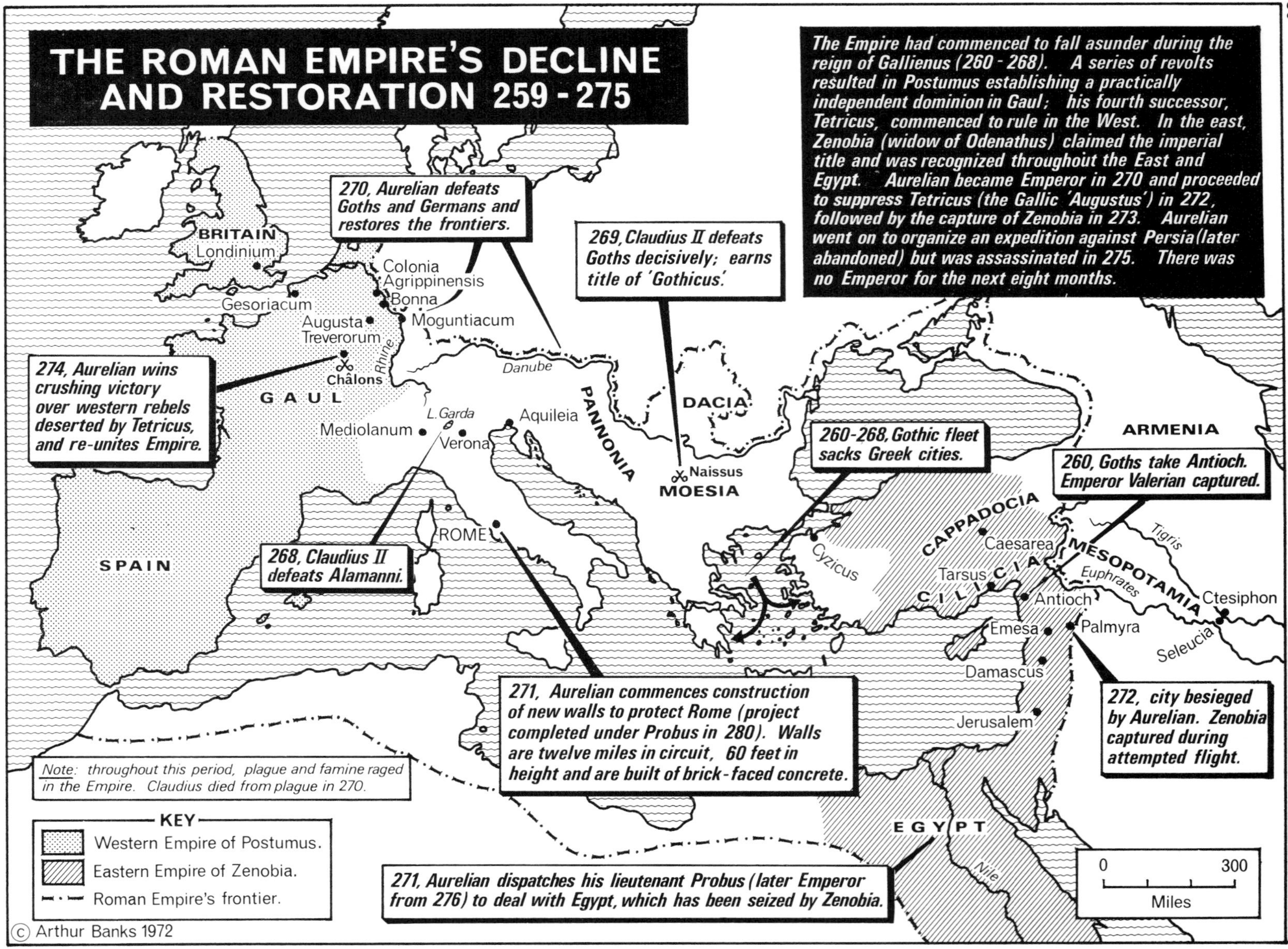

THE ROMAN EMPIRE'S DECLINE AND RESTORATION 259 - 275
The Empire had commenced to fall asunder during the reign of Gallienus (260 - 268). A series of revolts resulted in Postumus establishing a practically independent dominion in Gaul; his fourth successor, Tetricus, commenced to rule in the West. In the east, Zenobia (widow of Odenathus) claimed the imperial title and was recognized throughout the East and Egypt. Aurelian became Emperor in 270 and proceeded to suppress Tetricus (the Gallic 'Augustus') in 272, followed by the capture of Zenobia in 273. Aurelian went on to organize an expedition against Persia (later abandoned) but was assassinated in 275. There was no Emperor for the next eight months.
270, Aurelian defeats Goths and Germans and restores the frontiers.
269, Claudius II defeats Goths decisively; earns title of 'Gothicus.'
274, Aurelian wins crushing victory over western rebels deserted by Tetricus, and re-unites Empire.
260-268, Gothic fleet sacks Greek cities.
260, Goths take Antioch. Emperor Valerian captured.
268, Claudius II defeats Alamanni.
271, Aurelian commences construction of new walls to protect Rome (project completed under Probus in 280). Walls are twelve miles in circuit, 60 feet in height and are built of brick-faced concrete.
272, city besieged by Aurelian. Zenobia captured during attempted flight.
271, Aurelian dispatches his lieutenant Probus (later Emperor from 276) to deal with Egypt, which has been seized by Zenobia.
Note: throughout this period, plague and famine raged in the Empire. Claudius died from plague in 270.
KEY
Western Empire of Postumus.
Eastern Empire of Zenobia.
Roman Empire's frontier.
BRITAIN
Londinium
Gesoriacum
Colonia Agrippinensis
Bonna
Moguntiacum
Augusta Treverorum
Châlons
Rhine
GAUL
Danube
L. Garda
Mediolanum
Verona
Aquileia
PANNONIA
DACIA
Naissus
MOESIA
ARMENIA
SPAIN
ROME
Cyzicus
CAPPADOCIA
Caesarea
Tarsus
CILICIA
MESOPOTAMIA
Tigris
Euphrates
Antioch
Ctesiphon
Emesa
Palmyra
Seleucia
Damascus
Jerusalem
EGYPT
Nile
0
300
Miles

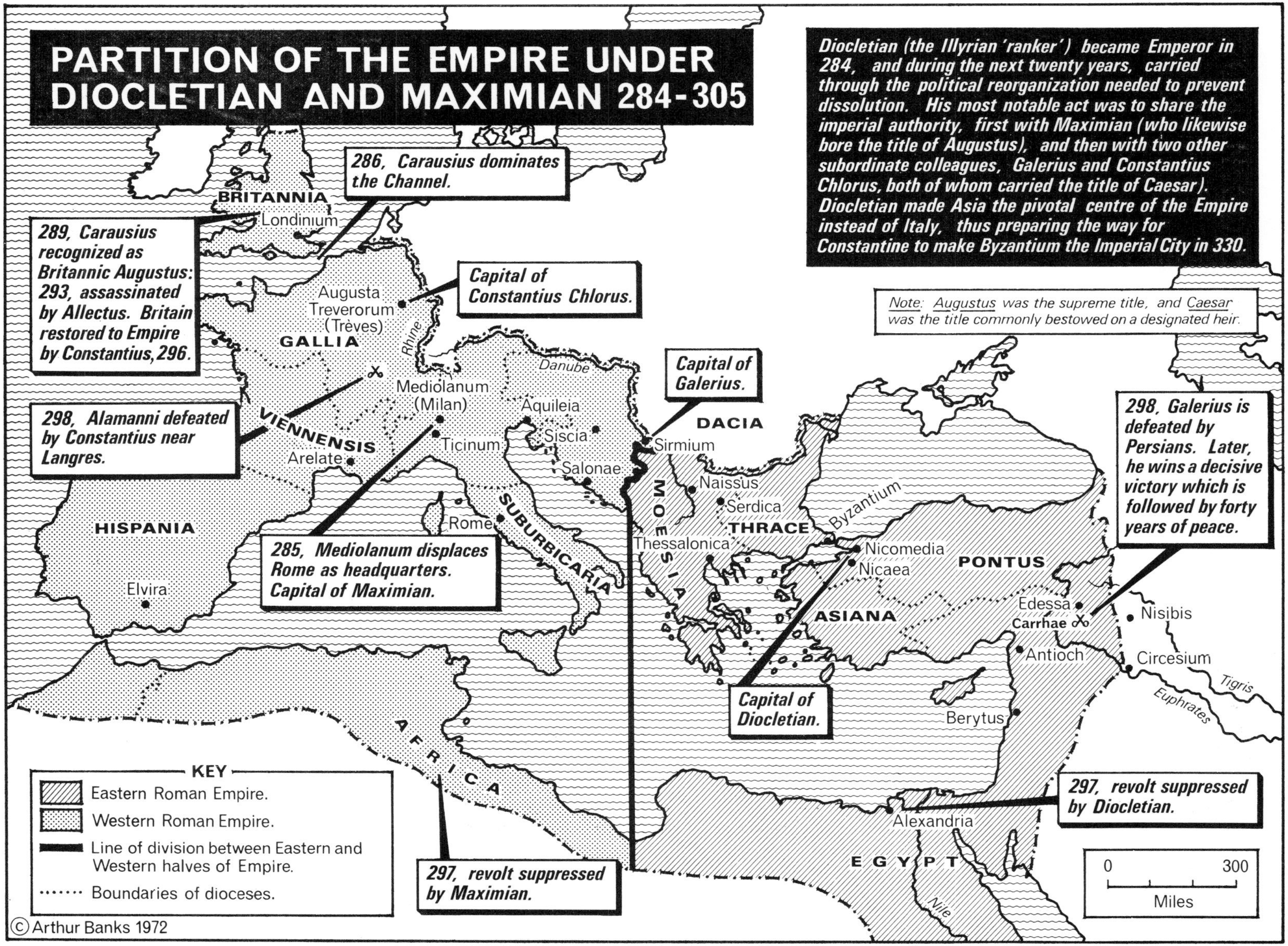
PARTITION OF THE EMPIRE UNDER DIOCLETIAN AND MAXIMIAN 284-305
Diocletian (the Illyrian 'ranker') became Emperor in 284, and during the next twenty years, carried through the political reorganization needed to prevent dissolution. His most notable act was to share the imperial authority, first with Maximian (who likewise bore the title of Augustus), and then with two other subordinate colleagues, Galerius and Constantius Chlorus, both of whom carried the title of Caesar). Diocletian made Asia the pivotal centre of the Empire instead of Italy, thus preparing the way for Constantine to make Byzantium the Imperial City in 330.
Note: Augustus was the supreme title, and Caesar was the title commonly bestowed on a designated heir.
286, Carausius dominates the Channel.
289, Carausius recognized as Britannic Augustus: 293, assassinated by Allectus. Britain restored to Empire by Constantius, 296.
Capital of Constantius Chlorus.
298, Alamanni defeated by Constantius near Langres.
285, Mediolanum displaces Rome as headquarters. Capital of Maximian.
Capital of Galerius.
Capital of Diocletian.
298, Galerius is defeated by Persians. Later, he wins a decisive victory which is followed by forty years of peace.
297, revolt suppressed by Maximian.
297, revolt suppressed by Diocletian.
BRITANNIA
Londinium
Augusta Treverorum (Treves)
GALLIA
Rhine
VIENNENSIS
Arelate
HISPANIA
Elvira
Mediolanum (Milan)
Ticinum
Aquileia
Siscia
Salonae
Danube
Rome
SUBURBICARIA
AFRICA
DACIA
Sirmium
Naissus
Serdica
MOESIA
THRACE
Thessalonica
Byzantium
Nicomedia
Nicaea
PONTUS
ASIANA
Edessa
Carrhae
Nisibis
Antioch
Circesium
Tigris
Euphrates
Berytus
Alexandria
EGYPT
Nile
0
300
Miles
KEY
Eastern Roman Empire.
Western Roman Empire.
Line of division between Eastern and Western halves of Empire.
Boundaries of dioceses.
© Arthur Banks 1972

NORTHERN CHINA IN CONFLICT 317-534

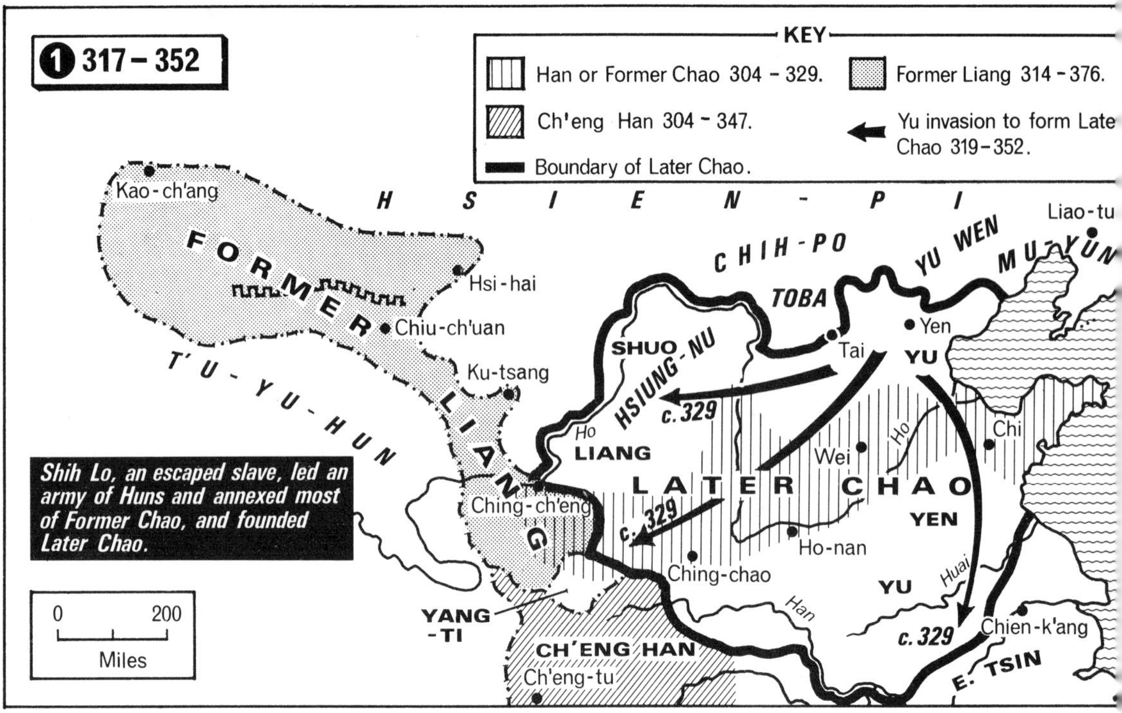
1 317 – 352
KEY
Han or Former Chao 304 - 329.
Former Liang 314 - 376.
Ch'eng Han 304 - 347.
Yu invasion to form Later Chao 319 - 352.
Boundary of Later Chao.
Kao-ch'ang
H S I E N - P I
Liao-tu
FORMER
Hsi-hai
Chiu-ch'uan
Ku-tsang
LIANG
T'U-YU-HUN
CHIH-PO
YU WEN
MU-YUN
TOBA
Yen
Tai
YU
SHUO
HSIUNG-NU
c. 329
Ho
LIANG
Wei
Chi
LATER CHAO
Ching-ch'eng
c. 329
YEN
Ho-nan
Ching-chao
YU
Huai
Han
c. 329
Chien-k'ang
E. TSIN
YANG -TI
CH'ENG HAN
Ch'eng-tu
Shih Lo, an escaped slave, led an army of Huns and annexed most of Former Chao, and founded Later Chao.
0
200
Miles

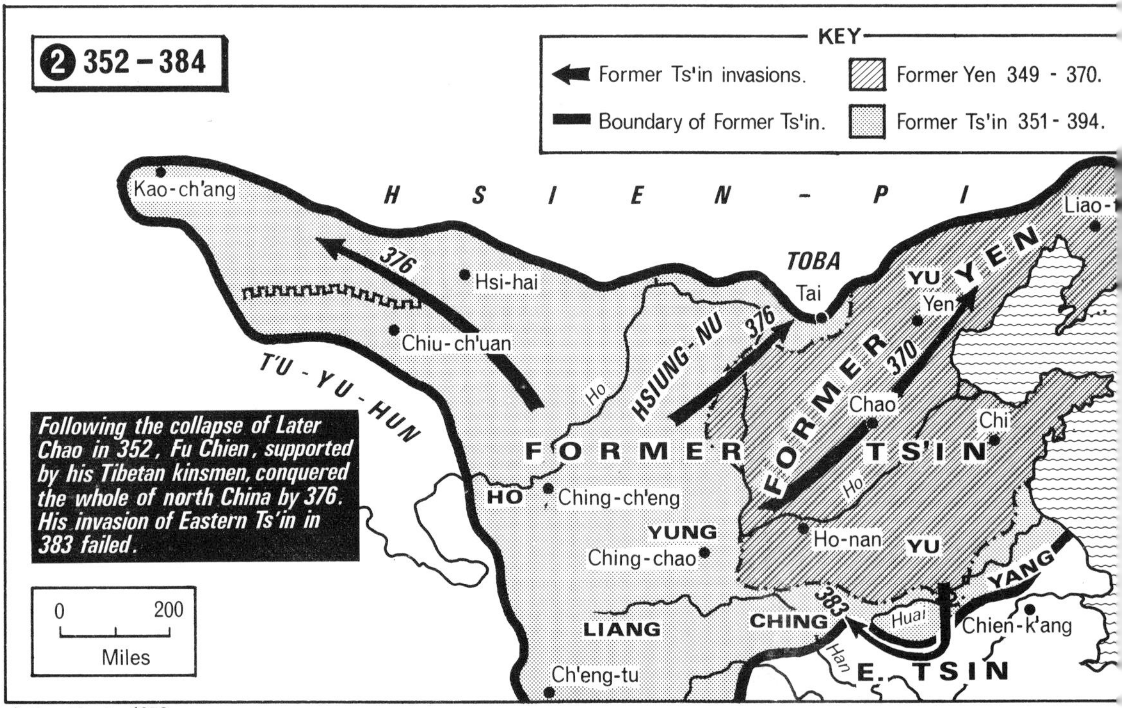
2 352 – 384
KEY
Former Ts'in invasions.
Former Yen 349 - 370.
Boundary of Former Ts'in.
Former Ts'in 351 - 394.
Kao-ch'ang
H S I E N - P I
Liao-
376
Hsi-hai
TOBA
Tai
YU
Yen
YEN
Chiu-ch'uan
HSIUNG-NU
376
FORMER
370
T'U-YU-HUN
Ho
Chao
Chi
FORMER TS'IN
HO
Ching-ch'eng
Ho
YUNG
Ho-nan
YU
Ching-chao
383
YANG
Huai
LIANG
CHING
Chien-k'ang
Han
E. TSIN
Ch'eng-tu
Following the collapse of Later Chao in 352, Fu Chien, supported by his Tibetan kinsmen, conquered the whole of north China by 376. His invasion of Eastern Ts'in in 383 failed.
0
200
Miles

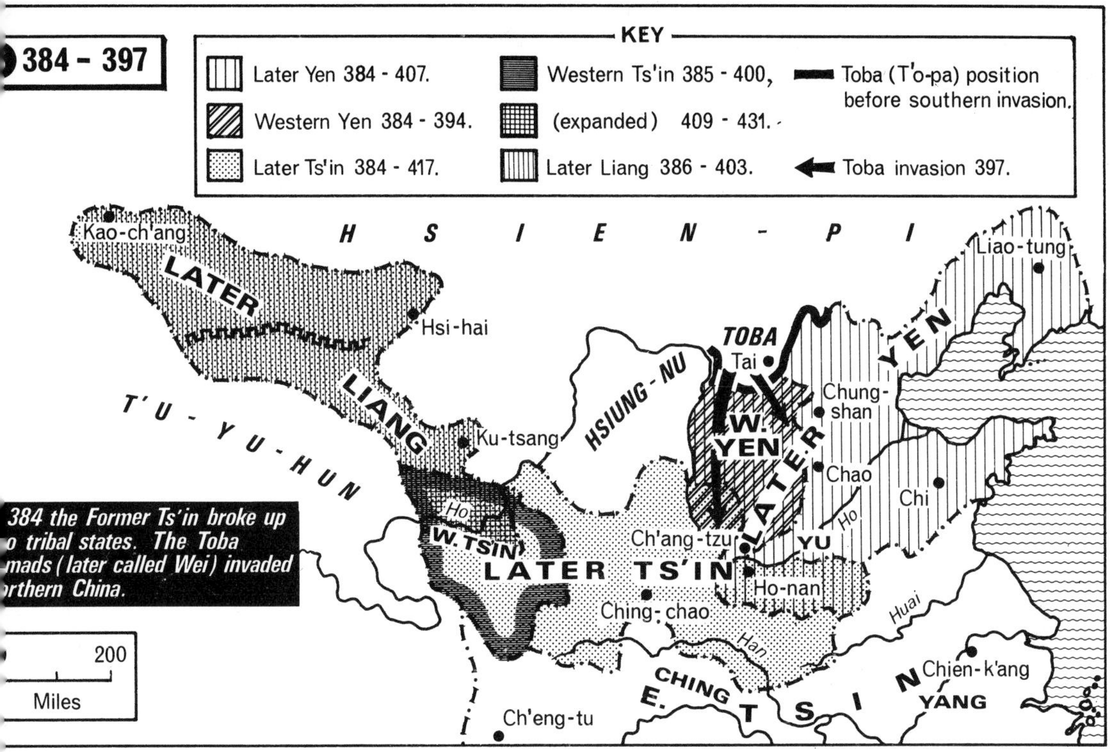
384 - 397
KEY
Later Yen 384 - 407.
Western Yen 384 - 394.
Later Ts'in 384 - 417.
Western Ts'in 385 - 400,
(expanded) 409 - 431.
Later Liang 386 - 403.
Toba (T'o-pa) position before southern invasion.
Toba invasion 397.
H S I E N - P I
Kao-ch'ang
LATER LIANG
Hsi-hai
Ku-tsang
T'U - Y U - H U N
HSIUNG - NU
TOBA
Tai
W. YEN
LATER YEN
Chung-shan
Chao
Liao-tung
Chi
Ho
W. TSIN
LATER TS'IN
Ch'ang-tzu
YU
Ho-nan
Ching-chao
Han
Huai
E. CHING
T S I N
Chien-k'ang
YANG
Ch'eng-tu
384 the Former Ts'in broke up o tribal states. The Toba mads (later called Wei) invaded rthern China.
200
Miles

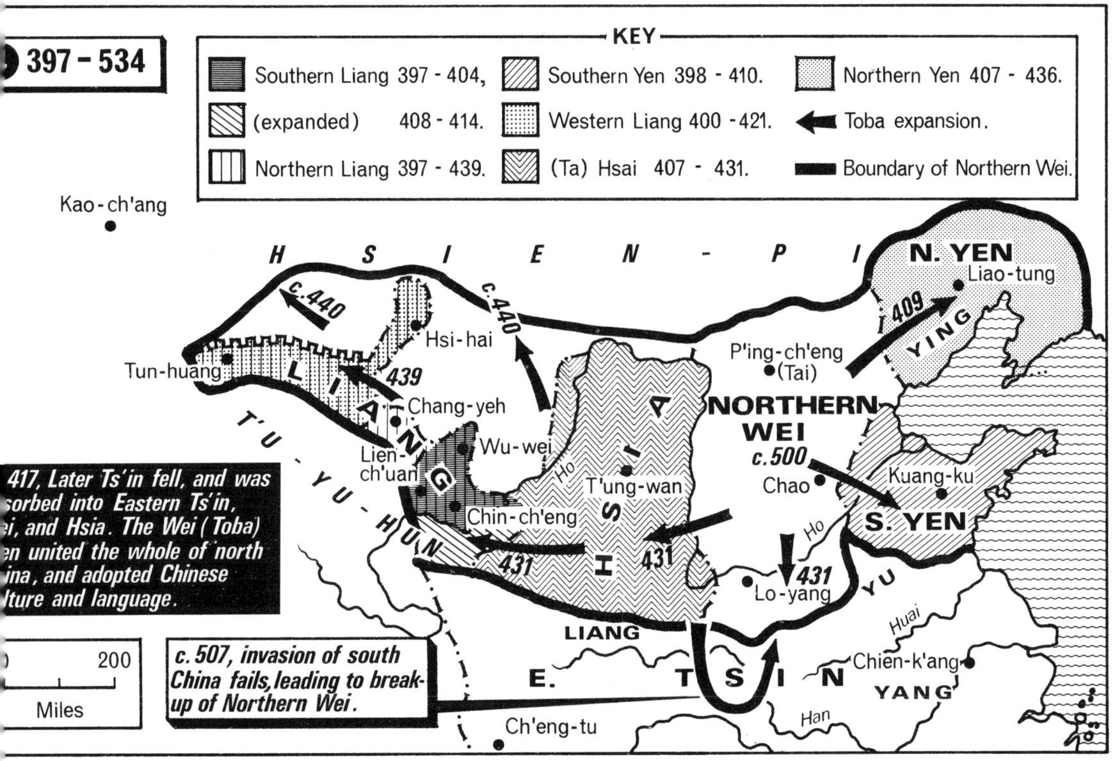
397 - 534
KEY
Southern Liang 397 - 404,
(expanded) 408 - 414.
Northern Liang 397 - 439.
Southern Yen 398 - 410.
Western Liang 400 - 421.
(Ta) Hsai 407 - 431.
Northern Yen 407 - 436.
Toba expansion.
Boundary of Northern Wei.
Kao-ch'ang
H S I E N - P I
N. YEN
Liao-tung
409
YING
c.440
c.440
Hsi-hai
Tun-huang
L I A N G
439
Chang-yeh
Wu-wei
Lien-ch'uan
P'ing-ch'eng (Tai)
NORTHERN WEI
c.500
Chao
Kuang-ku
S. YEN
HSIA
T'ung-wan
Chin-ch'eng
431
431
431
Ho
Lo-yang
YU
T'U - YU - HUN
LIANG
Huai
E. T S I N
Chien-k'ang
YANG
Han
Ch'eng-tu
417, Later Ts'in fell, and was sorbed into Eastern Ts'in, i, and Hsia. The Wei (Toba) en united the whole of north ina, and adopted Chinese lture and language.
c.507, invasion of south China fails, leading to break-up of Northern Wei.
200
Miles

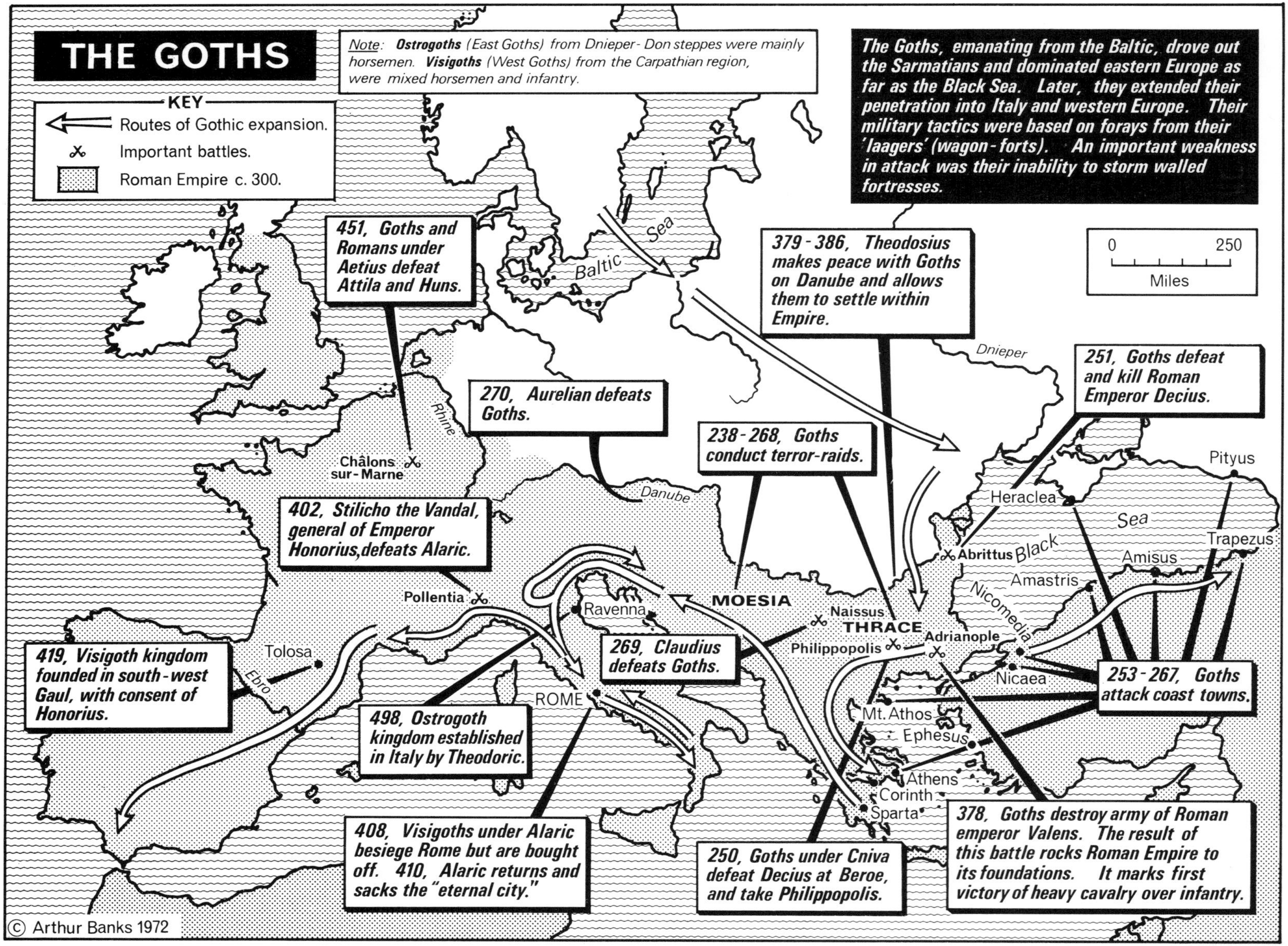
THE GOTHS
Note: Ostrogoths (East Goths) from Dnieper-Don steppes were mainly horsemen. Visigoths (West Goths) from the Carpathian region, were mixed horsemen and infantry.
The Goths, emanating from the Baltic, drove out the Sarmatians and dominated eastern Europe as far as the Black Sea. Later, they extended their penetration into Italy and western Europe. Their military tactics were based on forays from their 'laagers' (wagon-forts). An important weakness in attack was their inability to storm walled fortresses.
KEY
Routes of Gothic expansion.
Important battles.
Roman Empire c. 300.
0
250
Miles
451, Goths and Romans under Aetius defeat Attila and Huns.
379-386, Theodosius makes peace with Goths on Danube and allows them to settle within Empire.
Baltic
Sea
Dnieper
251, Goths defeat and kill Roman Emperor Decius.
270, Aurelian defeats Goths.
Rhine
Châlons sur-Marne
238-268, Goths conduct terror-raids.
Pityus
Danube
Heraclea
Sea
402, Stilicho the Vandal, general of Emperor Honorius, defeats Alaric.
Abrittus
Black
Trapezus
Amisus
Amastris
Nicomedia
Pollentia
MOESIA
Ravenna
Naissus
THRACE
Adrianople
Philippopolis
Tolosa
Ebro
419, Visigoth kingdom founded in south-west Gaul, with consent of Honorius.
269, Claudius defeats Goths.
Nicaea
253-267, Goths attack coast towns.
ROME
498, Ostrogoth kingdom established in Italy by Theodoric.
Mt. Athos
Ephesus
Athens
Corinth
Sparta
408, Visigoths under Alaric besiege Rome but are bought off. 410, Alaric returns and sacks the "eternal city."
250, Goths under Cniva defeat Decius at Beroe, and take Philippopolis.
378, Goths destroy army of Roman emperor Valens. The result of this battle rocks Roman Empire to its foundations. It marks first victory of heavy cavalry over infantry.

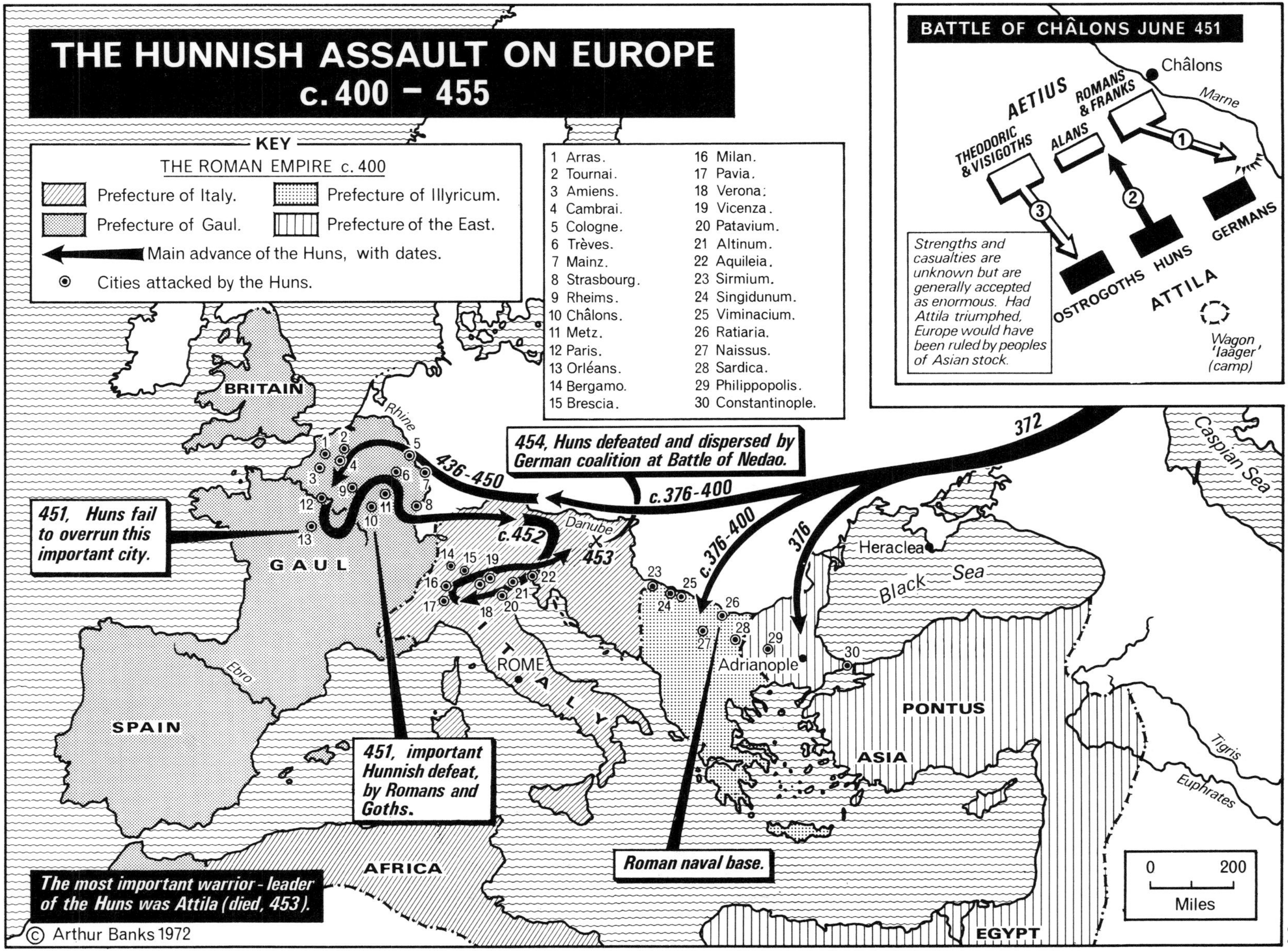
THE HUNNISH ASSAULT ON EUROPE
c. 400 – 455
KEY
THE ROMAN EMPIRE c. 400
Prefecture of Italy.
Prefecture of Illyricum.
Prefecture of Gaul.
Prefecture of the East.
Main advance of the Huns, with dates.
Cities attacked by the Huns.
1 Arras.
2 Tournai.
3 Amiens.
4 Cambrai.
5 Cologne.
6 Trèves.
7 Mainz.
8 Strasbourg.
9 Rheims.
10 Châlons.
11 Metz.
12 Paris.
13 Orléans.
14 Bergamo.
15 Brescia.
16 Milan.
17 Pavia.
18 Verona.
19 Vicenza.
20 Patavium.
21 Altinum.
22 Aquileia.
23 Sirmium.
24 Singidunum.
25 Viminacium.
26 Ratiaria.
27 Naissus.
28 Sardica.
29 Philippopolis.
30 Constantinople.
BATTLE OF CHÂLONS JUNE 451
Châlons
Marne
AETIUS
ROMANS & FRANKS
ALANS
THEODORIC & VISIGOTHS
GERMANS
HUNS
OSTROGOTHS
ATTILA
Wagon 'laager' (camp)
Strengths and casualties are unknown but are generally accepted as enormous. Had Attila triumphed, Europe would have been ruled by peoples of Asian stock.
454, Huns defeated and dispersed by German coalition at Battle of Nedao.
372
c.376-400
c.376-400
376
436-450
c.452
453
Danube
Rhine
BRITAIN
GAUL
451, Huns fail to overrun this important city.
SPAIN
Ebro
ITALY
ROME
451, important Hunnish defeat, by Romans and Goths.
Roman naval base.
Heraclea
Black Sea
Caspian Sea
Adrianople
PONTUS
ASIA
Tigris
Euphrates
EGYPT
AFRICA
0 200 Miles
The most important warrior-leader of the Huns was Attila (died, 453).
© Arthur Banks 1972

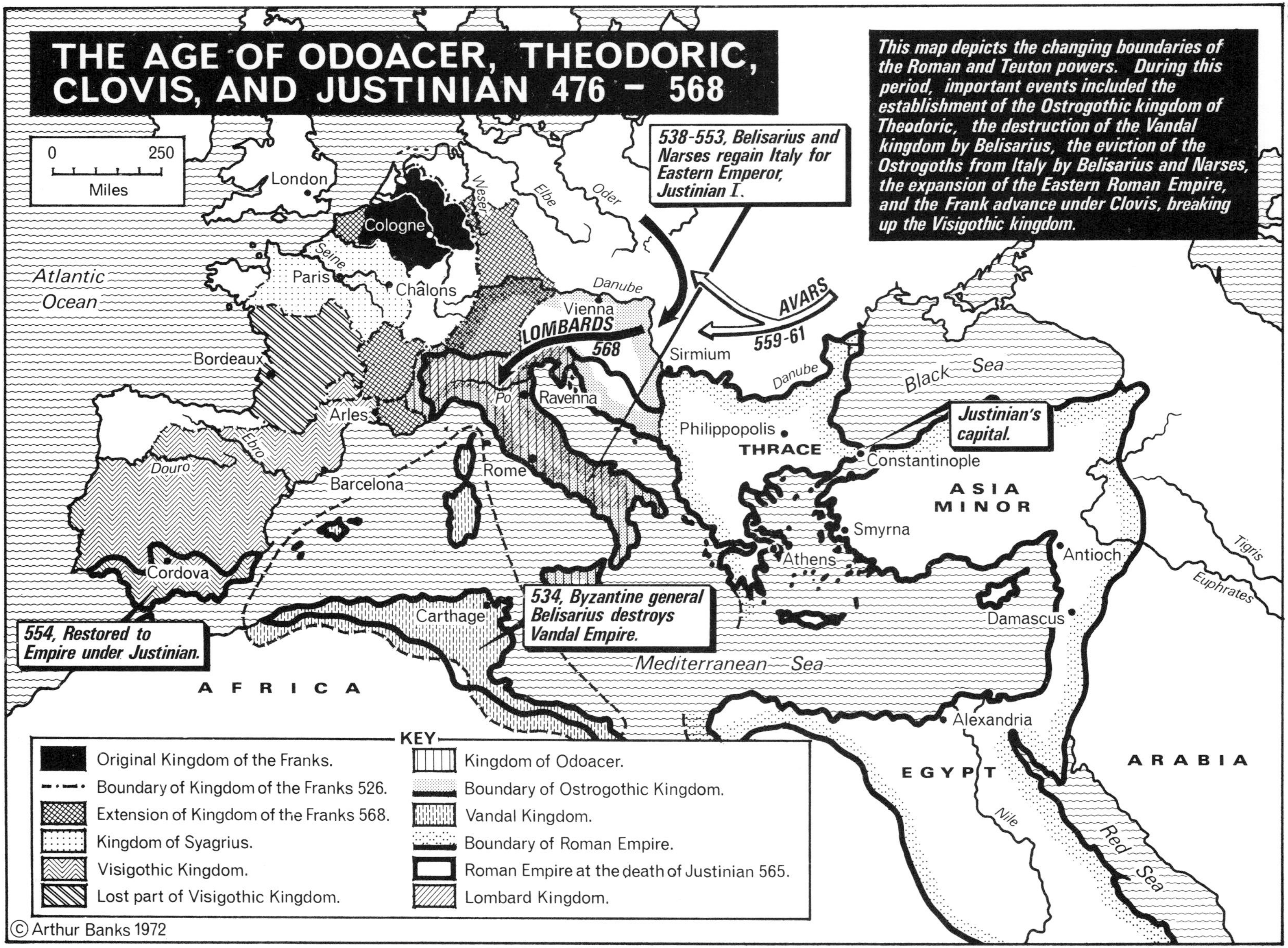
THE AGE OF ODOACER, THEODORIC, CLOVIS, AND JUSTINIAN 476 - 568
This map depicts the changing boundaries of the Roman and Teuton powers. During this period, important events included the establishment of the Ostrogothic kingdom of Theodoric, the destruction of the Vandal kingdom by Belisarius, the eviction of the Ostrogoths from Italy by Belisarius and Narses, the expansion of the Eastern Roman Empire, and the Frank advance under Clovis, breaking up the Visigothic kingdom.
0
250
Miles
London
Cologne
Weser
Elbe
Oder
Seine
Paris
Châlons
Atlantic Ocean
Danube
Vienna
LOMBARDS
568
AVARS
559-61
538-553, Belisarius and Narses regain Italy for Eastern Emperor, Justinian I.
Sirmium
Danube
Black Sea
Bordeaux
Po
Ravenna
Arles
Ebro
Philippopolis
THRACE
Justinian's capital.
Constantinople
Douro
Rome
Barcelona
ASIA MINOR
Smyrna
Athens
Antioch
Tigris
Euphrates
Cordova
Carthage
534, Byzantine general Belisarius destroys Vandal Empire.
Damascus
554, Restored to Empire under Justinian.
Mediterranean Sea
AFRICA
Alexandria
EGYPT
ARABIA
Nile
Red Sea
KEY
Original Kingdom of the Franks.
Boundary of Kingdom of the Franks 526.
Extension of Kingdom of the Franks 568.
Kingdom of Syagrius.
Visigothic Kingdom.
Lost part of Visigothic Kingdom.
Kingdom of Odoacer.
Boundary of Ostrogothic Kingdom.
Vandal Kingdom.
Boundary of Roman Empire.
Roman Empire at the death of Justinian 565.
Lombard Kingdom.
© Arthur Banks 1972

TRIBAL CONFLICT IN EASTERN EUROPE c.455 - 750

The strife was centred on three main tribes, the Slavs, the Avars, the Khazars. To a lesser extent, the Bulgars (an off-shoot of the Huns) were involved. By 455, the Hunnish invasion of Europe had ebbed, and the Slavs spread rapidly. However, a Mongol tribe known as the Avars penetrated into central Germany by c.550, and this brought them into conflict with the Slavs who eventually gained supremacy (c.650). Meanwhile, the Khazars from Asia had penetrated into the Ukraine, and by 750 had established a kingdom north of the Black and Caspian Seas. The main bulwark against further expansion of all these tribes was the Eastern Roman (or Byzantine) Empire, while, south of the Caspian and expanding westwards, Islam was rapidly becoming a major threat to the whole of southern Europe.

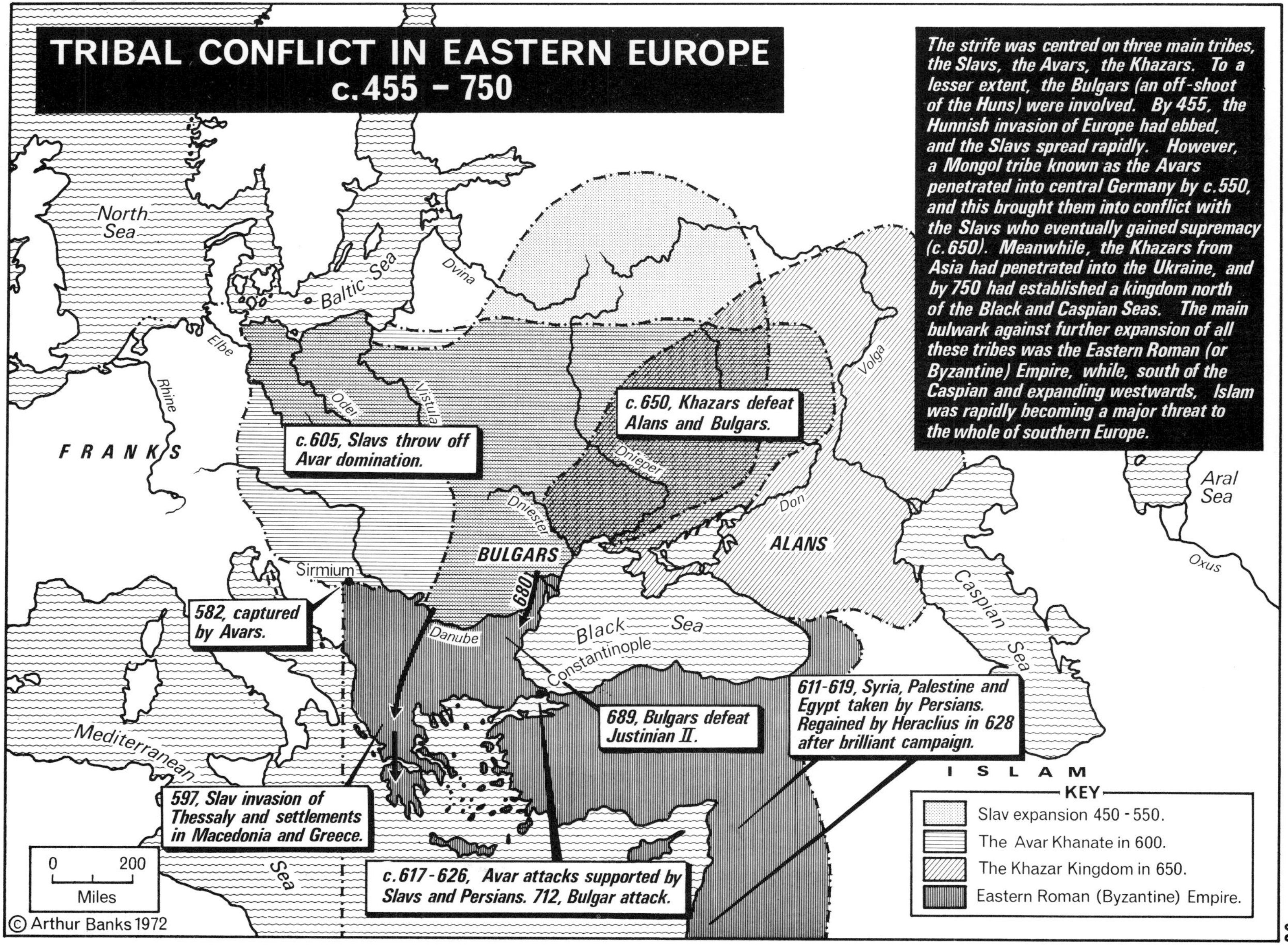

CHINA 535 - 580

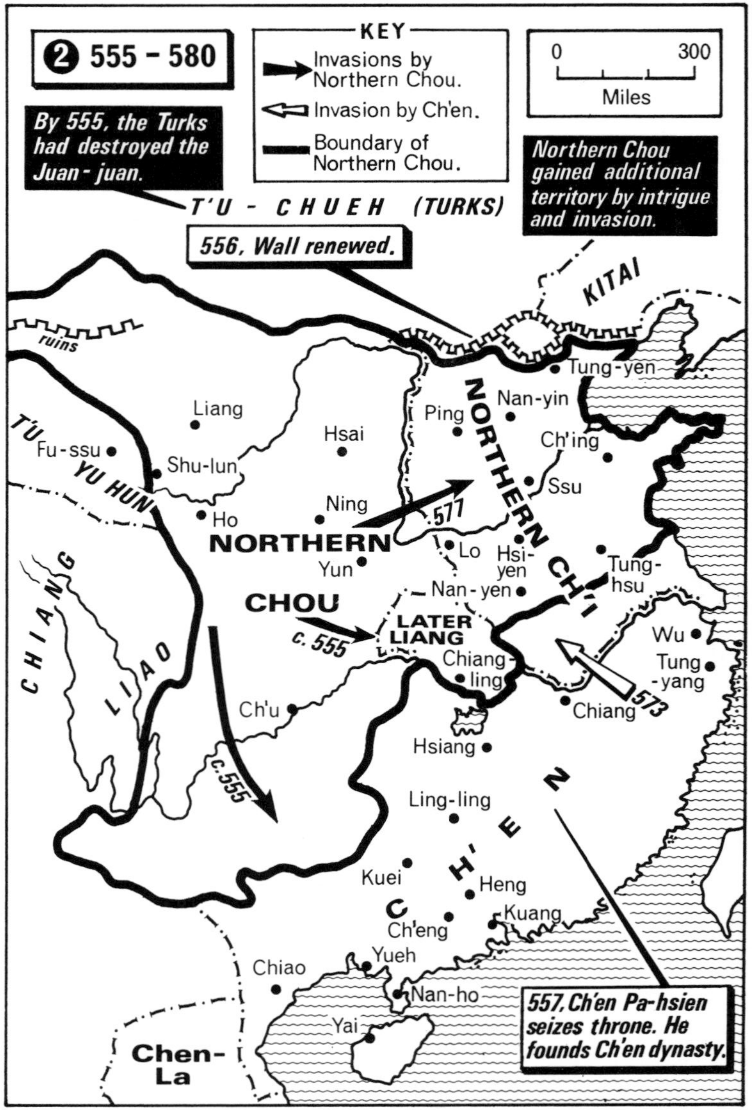

① 535 – 554

The north was locked in conflict whilst the south changed dynasties.

KEY
• Capitals of chou (provinces).

300
0 Miles

JOU-JAN OR JUAN-JUAN
(AVAR AND KHUNNI)

NOTE: THE LIANG DYNASTY WAS FOUNDED BY HSIAO YEN IN 502.

② 555 – 580

By 555, the Turks had destroyed the Juan-juan.

556, Wall renewed.

Northern Chou gained additional territory by intrigue and invasion.

KEY
Invasions by Northern Chou.
Invasion by Chen.
Boundary of Northern Chou.

300
0 Miles

557, Chen Pa-hsien seizes throne. He founds Ch'en dynasty.

© Arthur Banks 1972

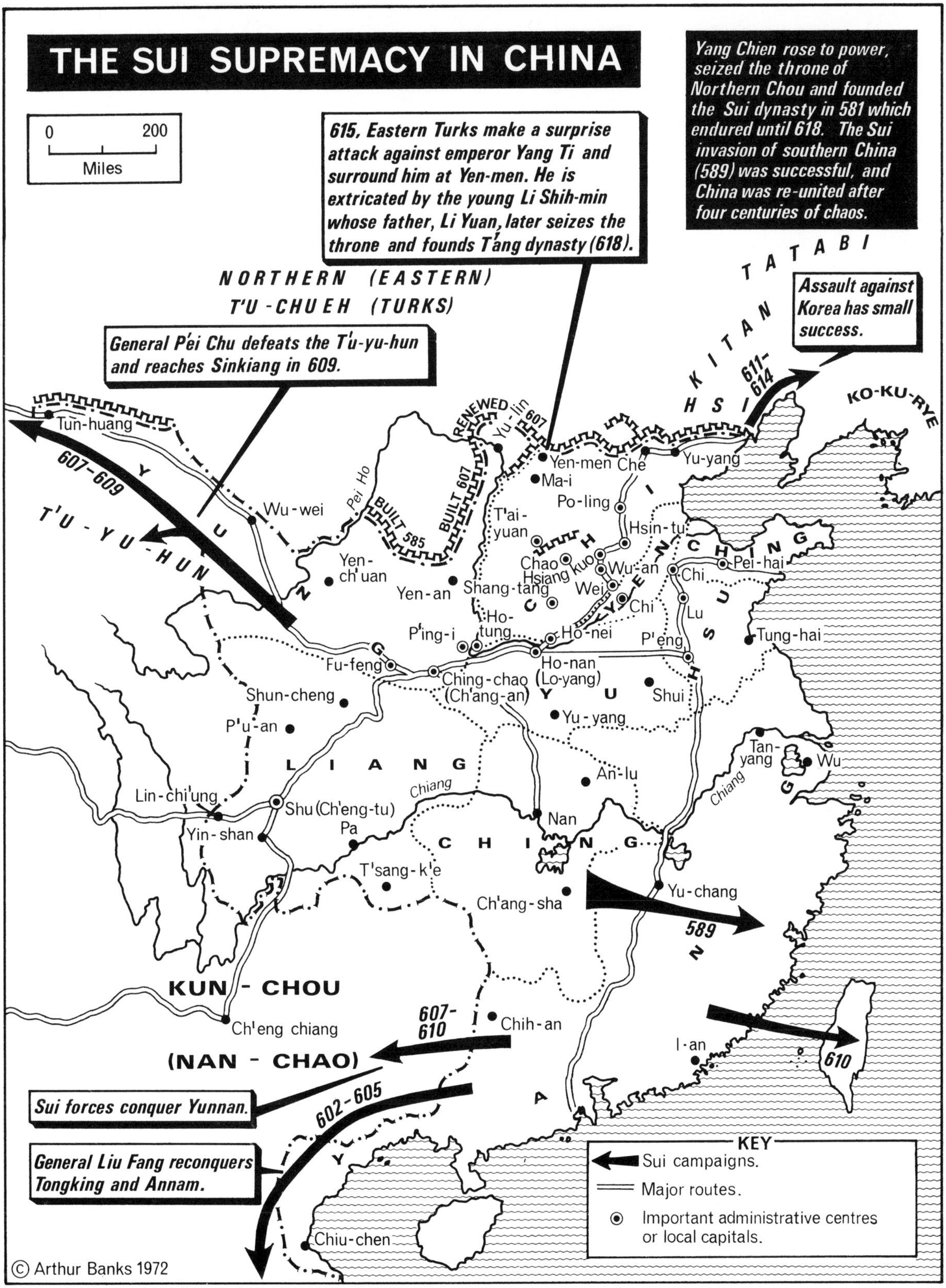
THE SUI SUPREMACY IN CHINA
Yang Chien rose to power, seized the throne of Northern Chou and founded the Sui dynasty in 581 which endured until 618. The Sui invasion of southern China (589) was successful, and China was re-united after four centuries of chaos.
0 200 Miles
615, Eastern Turks make a surprise attack against emperor Yang Ti and surround him at Yen-men. He is extricated by the young Li Shih-min whose father, Li Yuan, later seizes the throne and founds T'ang dynasty (618).
NORTHERN (EASTERN) T'U-CHUEH (TURKS)
General P'ei Chu defeats the T'u-yu-hun and reaches Sinkiang in 609.
TATABI
KITAN
HSI
Assault against Korea has small success.
611-614
KO-KU-RYE
RENEWED 607
BUILT 607
BUILT 585
Yu-lin
Tun-huang
607-609
T'U-YU-HUN
YUNG
Wu-wei
Pei Ho
Yen-ch'uan
Yen-an
Yen-men
Che
Ma-i
Po-ling
T'ai-yuan
Hsin-tu
Chao
Hsiang kuo
Wu-an
Wei
Shang-tang
Chi
Ho-tung
P'ing-i
Ho-nei
Yu-yang
CHI
YEN
HSU
CHING
Pei-hai
Chi
Lu
P'eng
Tung-hai
Fu-feng
Ching-chao (Ch'ang-an)
Ho-nan (Lo-yang)
YU
Shui
Yu-yang
Shun-cheng
P'u-an
LIANG
An-lu
Tan-yang
Wu
Chiang
Lin-chi'ung
Shu (Ch'eng-tu)
Pa
Yin-shan
Nan
CHING
T'sang-k'e
Ch'ang-sha
Yu-chang
589
YANG
KUN - CHOU
Ch'eng chiang
607-610
Chih-an
(NAN - CHAO)
Sui forces conquer Yunnan.
602-605
I-an
610
General Liu Fang reconquers Tongking and Annam.
Chiu-chen
KEY
Sui campaigns.
Major routes.
Important administrative centres or local capitals.

ISLAM'S CENTURY OF CONQUEST 632 - 732

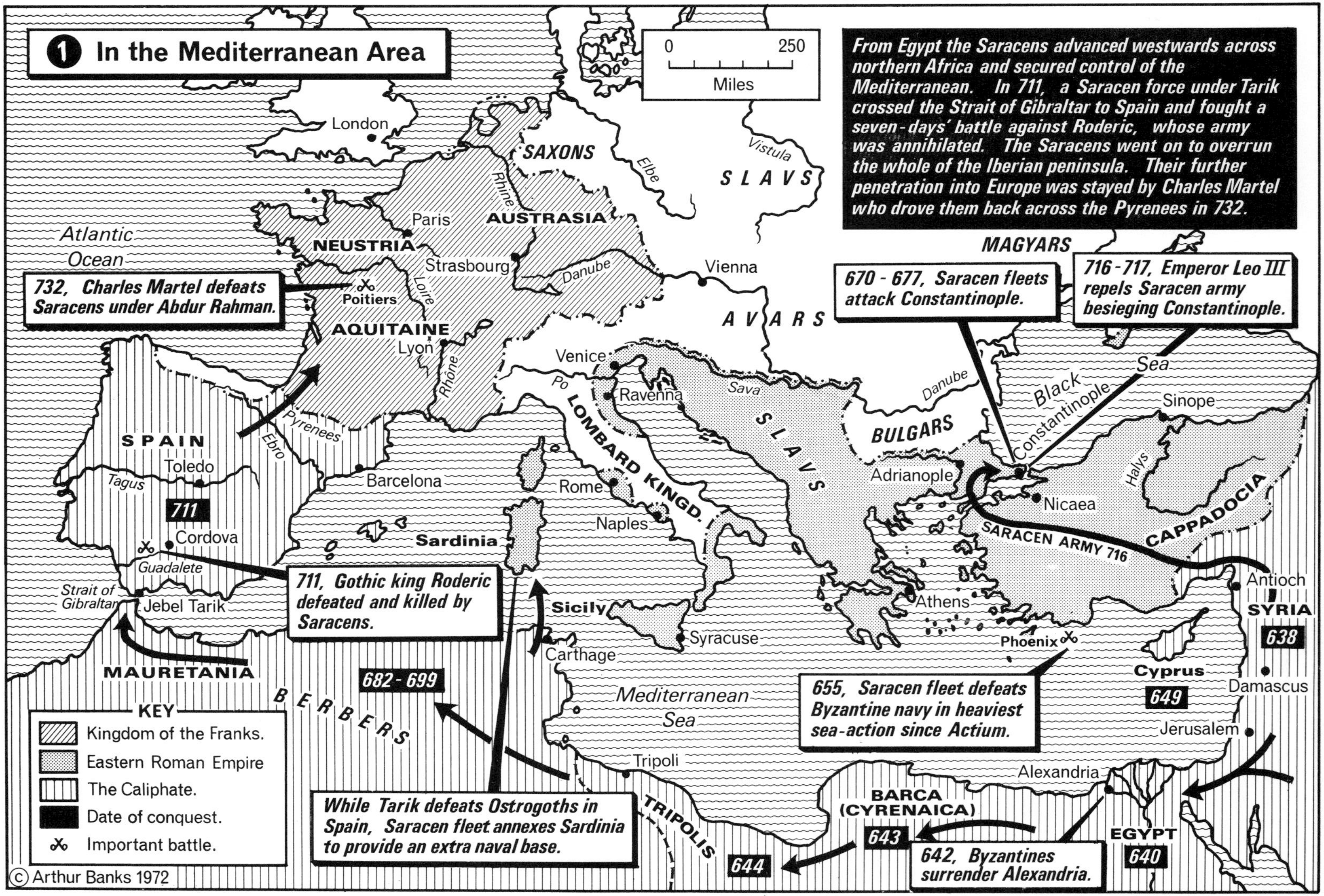
1 In the Mediterranean Area
0 250 Miles
From Egypt the Saracens advanced westwards across northern Africa and secured control of the Mediterranean. In 711, a Saracen force under Tarik crossed the Strait of Gibraltar to Spain and fought a seven-days' battle against Roderic, whose army was annihilated. The Saracens went on to overrun the whole of the Iberian peninsula. Their further penetration into Europe was stayed by Charles Martel who drove them back across the Pyrenees in 732.
London
SAXONS
Elbe
Vistula
SLAVS
Rhine
Paris
AUSTRASIA
NEUSTRIA
Strasbourg
Danube
Vienna
MAGYARS
Atlantic Ocean
732, Charles Martel defeats Saracens under Abdur Rahman.
Poitiers
Loire
AQUITAINE
Lyon
Rhône
AVARS
670 - 677, Saracen fleets attack Constantinople.
716 - 717, Emperor Leo III repels Saracen army besieging Constantinople.
Venice
Po
Ravenna
Sava
Danube
Black Sea
Constantinople
Sinope
Pyrenees
Ebro
SPAIN
Toledo
Tagus
711
Barcelona
LOMBARD KINGD.
Rome
SLAVS
BULGARS
Adrianople
Halys
Nicaea
CAPPADOCIA
SARACEN ARMY 716
Naples
Cordova
Guadalete
Sardinia
711, Gothic king Roderic defeated and killed by Saracens.
Strait of Gibraltar
Jebel Tarik
Sicily
Syracuse
Athens
Antioch
SYRIA
638
Phoenix
Carthage
MAURETANIA
BERBERS
682 - 699
Mediterranean Sea
655, Saracen fleet defeats Byzantine navy in heaviest sea-action since Actium.
Cyprus
649
Damascus
Jerusalem
Tripoli
Alexandria
BARCA (CYRENAICA)
643
TRIPOLIS
644
642, Byzantines surrender Alexandria.
EGYPT
640
While Tarik defeats Ostrogoths in Spain, Saracen fleet annexes Sardinia to provide an extra naval base.
KEY
Kingdom of the Franks.
Eastern Roman Empire
The Caliphate.
Date of conquest.
Important battle.
© Arthur Banks 1972

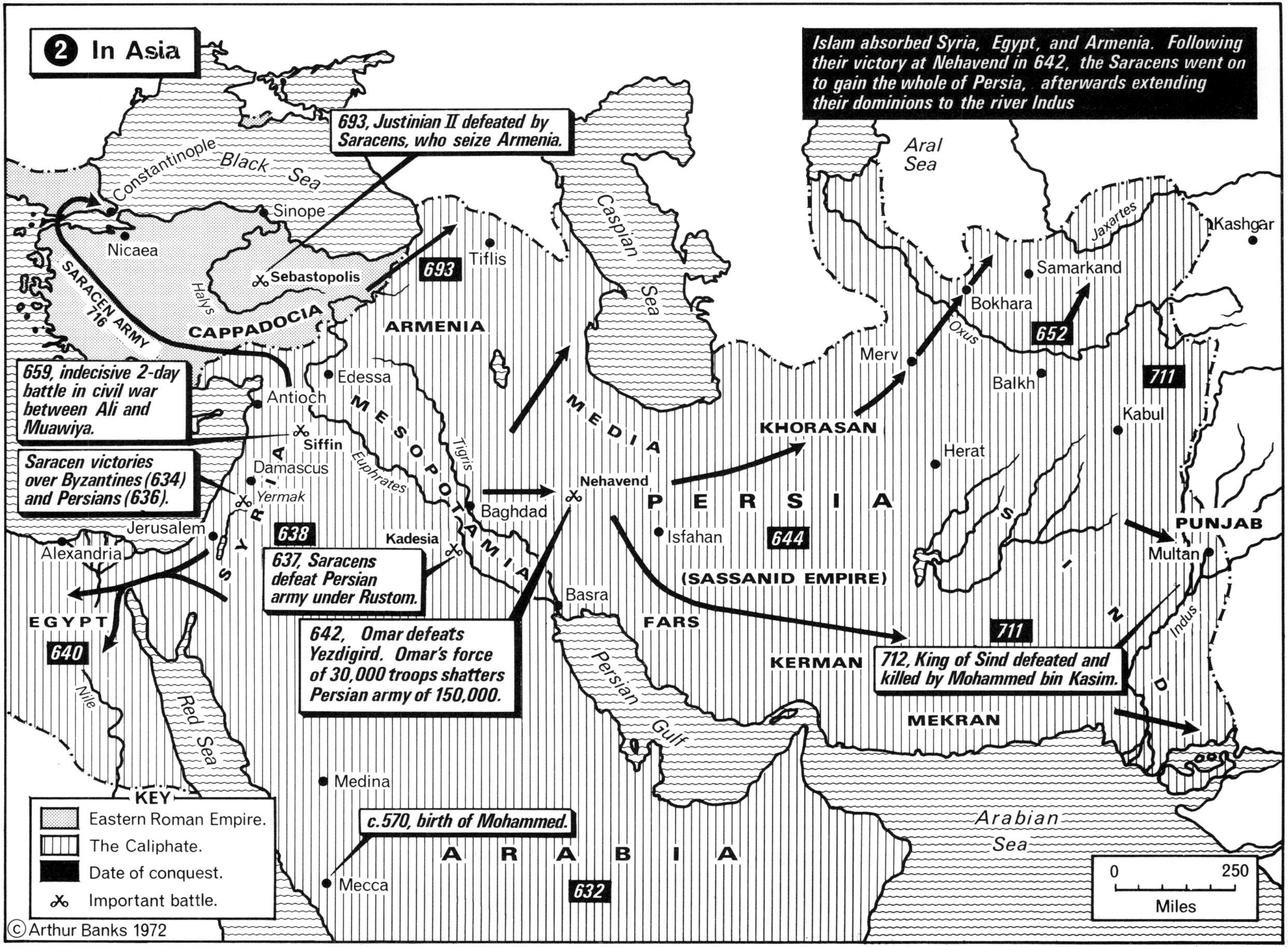

2 In Asia
Islam absorbed Syria, Egypt, and Armenia. Following their victory at Nehavend in 642, the Saracens went on to gain the whole of Persia, afterwards extending their dominions to the river Indus
693, Justinian II defeated by Saracens, who seize Armenia.
659, indecisive 2-day battle in civil war between Ali and Muawiya.
Saracen victories over Byzantines (634) and Persians (636).
637, Saracens defeat Persian army under Rustom.
642, Omar defeats Yezdigird. Omar's force of 30,000 troops shatters Persian army of 150,000.
712, King of Sind defeated and killed by Mohammed bin Kasim.
c.570, birth of Mohammed.
Constantinople
Black Sea
Sinope
Nicaea
Sebastopolis
Halys
SARACEN ARMY 716
CAPPADOCIA
ARMENIA
Tiflis
693
Caspian Sea
Aral Sea
Jaxartes
Kashgar
Samarkand
Bokhara
Oxus
652
Merv
Balkh
711
Kabul
Herat
KHORASAN
Edessa
Antioch
Siffin
Damascus
Yermak
MESOPOTAMIA
Euphrates
Tigris
MEDIA
Nehavend
Baghdad
PERSIA
(SASSANID EMPIRE)
644
Isfahan
SIND
PUNJAB
Multan
Indus
SYRIA
Jerusalem
Alexandria
638
Kadesia
Basra
FARS
KERMAN
711
MEKRAN
EGYPT
640
Nile
Red Sea
Persian Gulf
Medina
Mecca
ARABIA
632
Arabian Sea
KEY
Eastern Roman Empire.
The Caliphate.
Date of conquest.
Important battle.
0 250
Miles
© Arthur Banks 1972

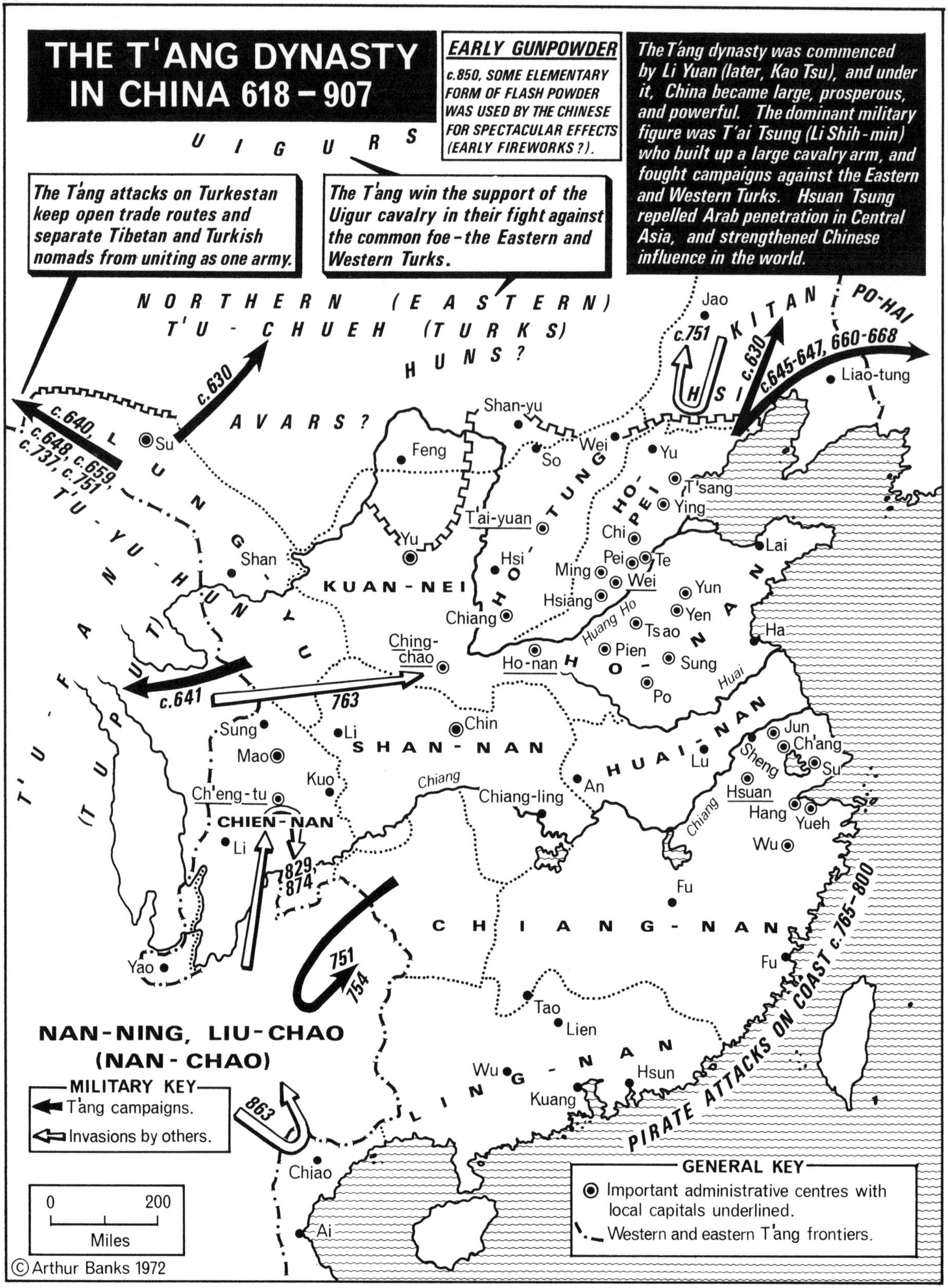
THE T'ANG DYNASTY IN CHINA 618 – 907
EARLY GUNPOWDER
c.850, SOME ELEMENTARY FORM OF FLASH POWDER WAS USED BY THE CHINESE FOR SPECTACULAR EFFECTS (EARLY FIREWORKS ?).
The T'ang dynasty was commenced by Li Yuan (later, Kao Tsu), and under it, China became large, prosperous, and powerful. The dominant military figure was T'ai Tsung (Li Shih-min) who built up a large cavalry arm, and fought campaigns against the Eastern and Western Turks. Hsuan Tsung repelled Arab penetration in Central Asia, and strengthened Chinese influence in the world.
UIGURS
The T'ang attacks on Turkestan keep open trade routes and separate Tibetan and Turkish nomads from uniting as one army.
The T'ang win the support of the Uigur cavalry in their fight against the common foe – the Eastern and Western Turks.
NORTHERN (EASTERN) T'U-CHUEH (TURKS)
HUNS ?
AVARS ?
c.630
c.640, c.648, c.659, c.737, c.751
LUNG-YU
T'U-YU-HUN
T'U-FAN (TUPUT)
c.641
763
Su
Shan
Feng
Shan-yu
So
Wei
Yu
Jao
c.751
KITAN
HSI
c.630
PO-HAI
c.645-647, 660-668
Liao-tung
HO-TUNG
HO-PEI
T'sang
Ying
T'ai-yuan
Chi
Pei
Te
Hsi
Ming
Wei
Hsiang
Chiang
KUAN-NEI
Yun
Yen
Tsao
Lai
Huang Ho
Ching-chao
Ho-nan
Pien
Sung
Po
HO-NAN
Ha
Huai
Chin
Li
SHAN-NAN
Sung
Mao
Kuo
Ch'eng-tu
CHIEN-NAN
Li
829, 874
Chiang
Chiang-ling
An
HUAI-NAN
Lu
Jun
Ch'ang
Su
Sheng
Hsuan
Hang
Yueh
Wu
Chiang
Fu
CHIANG-NAN
Fu
Yao
751
754
Tao
Lien
NAN-NING, LIU-CHAO (NAN-CHAO)
Wu
LING-NAN
Hsun
Kuang
PIRATE ATTACKS ON COAST c.765–800
863
MILITARY KEY
T'ang campaigns.
Invasions by others.
Chiao
Ai
0 200 Miles
GENERAL KEY
Important administrative centres with local capitals underlined.
Western and eastern T'ang frontiers.
© Arthur Banks 1972

HARSHA'S EMPIRE & 'THE NARBADA LINE'

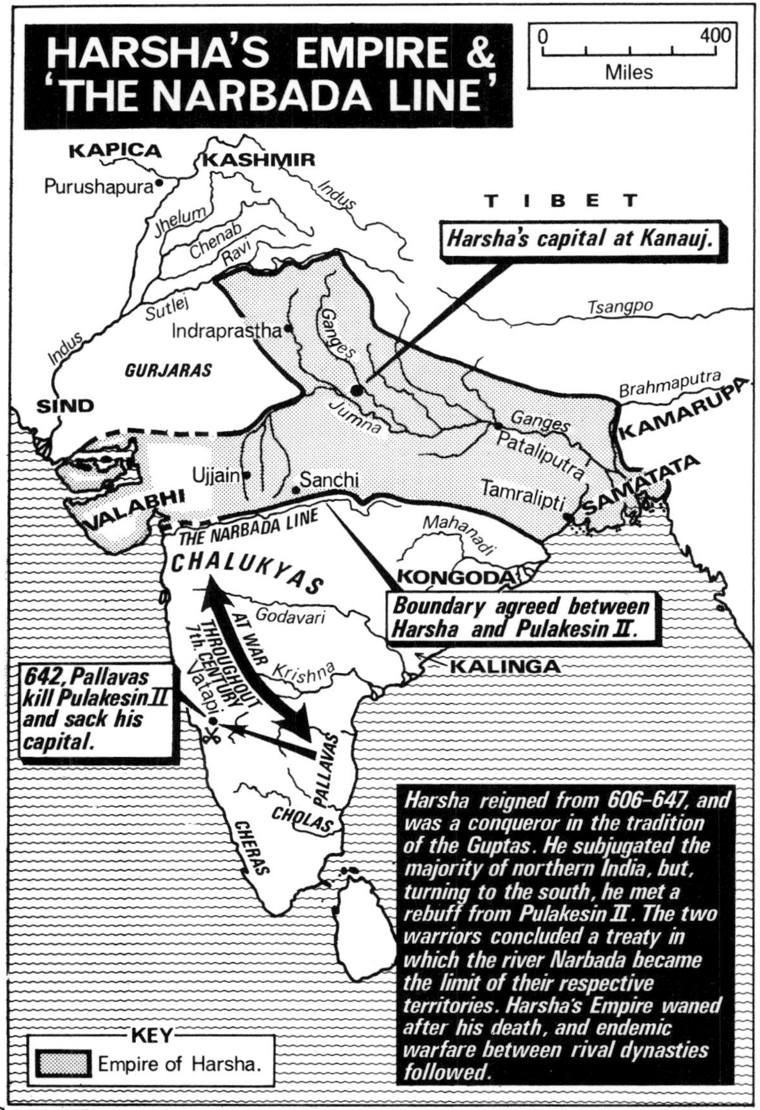

Harsha reigned from 606–647, and was a conqueror in the tradition of the Guptas. He subjugated the majority of northern India, but, turning to the south, he met a rebuff from Pulakesin II. The two warriors concluded a treaty in which the river Narbada became the limit of their respective territories. Harsha's Empire waned after his death, and endemic warfare between rival dynasties followed.

TRIPARTITE WAR

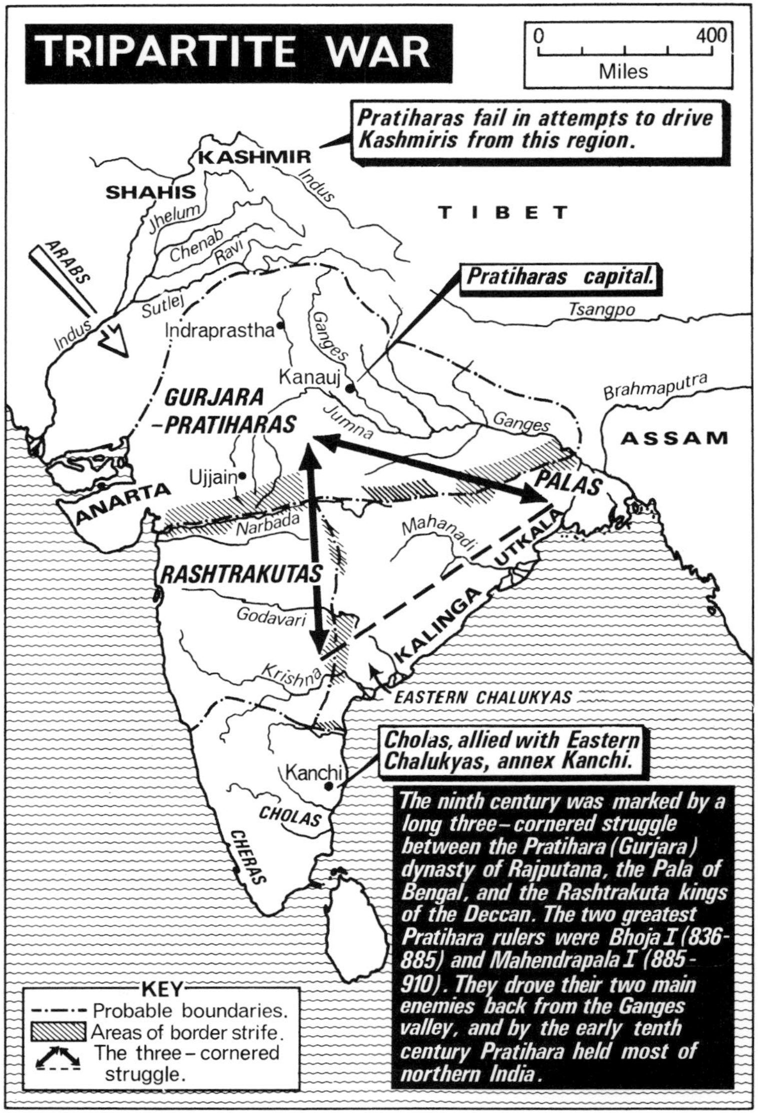

The ninth century was marked by a long three-cornered struggle between the Pratihara (Gurjara) dynasty of Rajputana, the Pala of Bengal, and the Rashtrakuta kings of the Deccan. The two greatest Pratihara rulers were Bhoja I (836-885) and Mahendrapala I (885-910). They drove their two main enemies back from the Ganges valley, and by the early tenth century Pratihara held most of northern India.

STAGES IN THE MAKING OF ENGLAND AND WALES 600 - 886

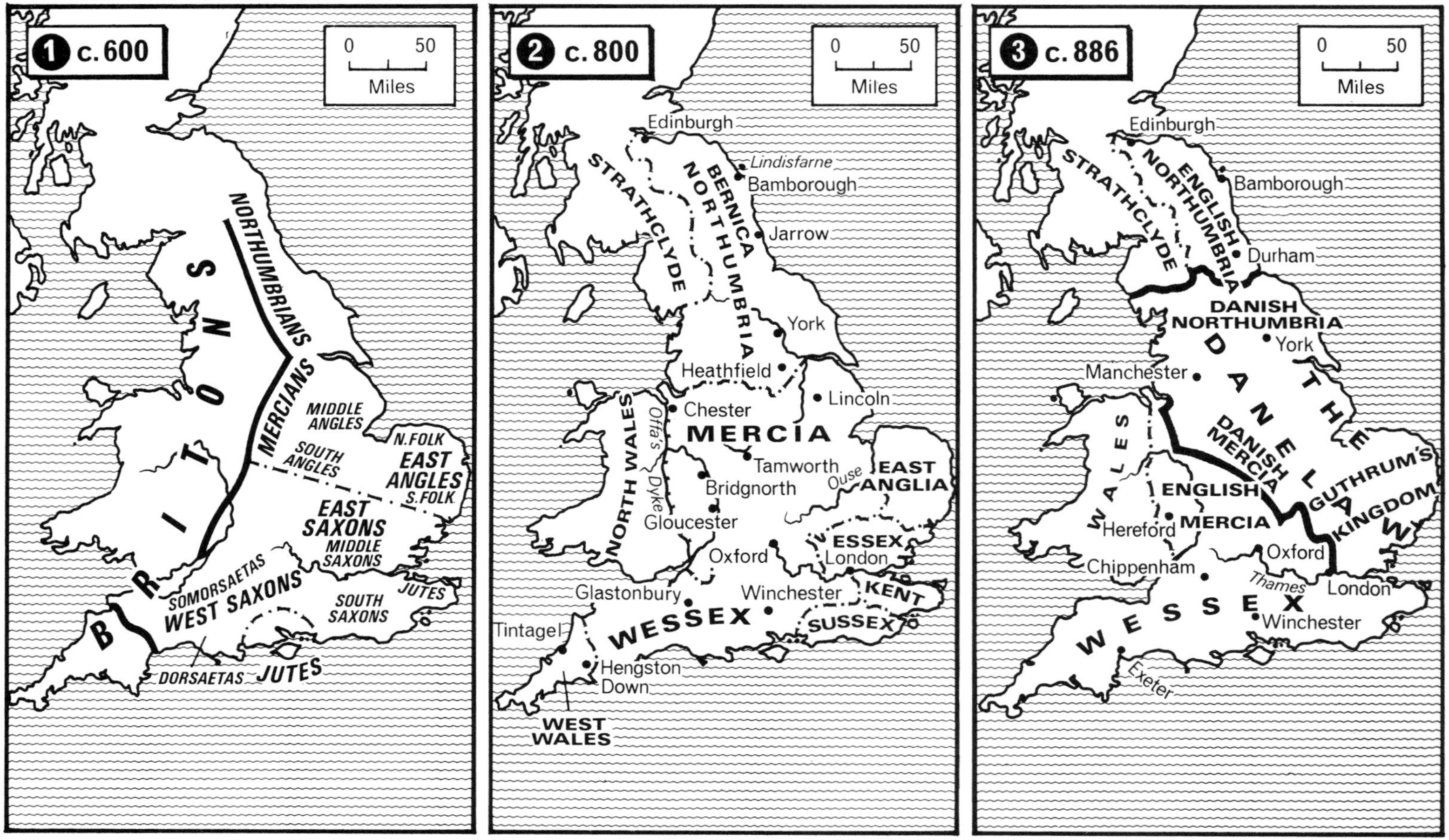

In Britain, the Britons were restricted to an ever more limited area in the west, and Northumbrian supremacy passed, first to Mercia, and thence to Wessex. Egbert's "peace" (in 800) was marred by Danish incursions culminating in the Danelaw becoming an independent region. The "Peace of Guthrum" (886), altered its boundaries in favour of Alfred the Great.

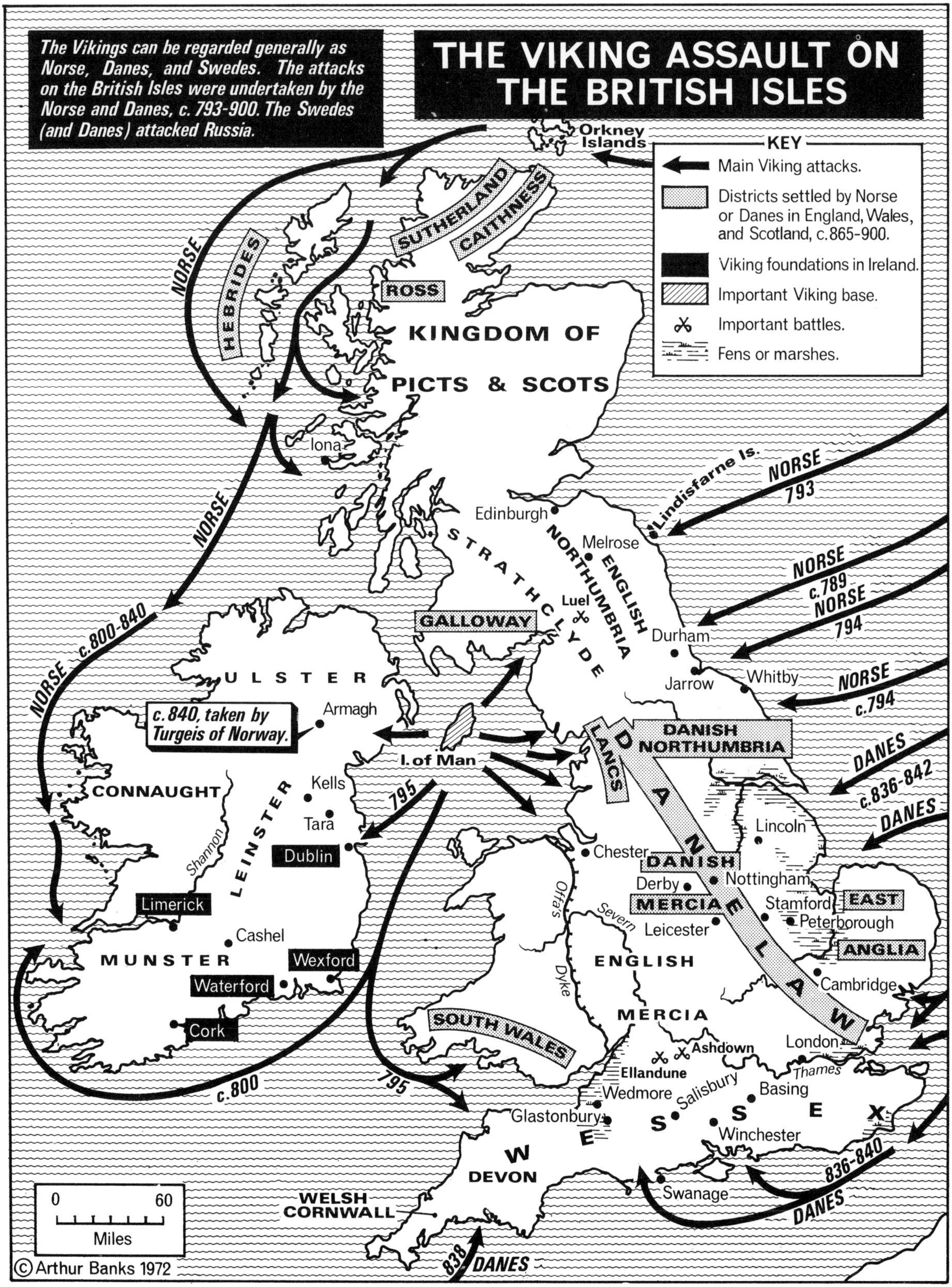
THE VIKING ASSAULT ON THE BRITISH ISLES
The Vikings can be regarded generally as Norse, Danes, and Swedes. The attacks on the British Isles were undertaken by the Norse and Danes, c. 793-900. The Swedes (and Danes) attacked Russia.
KEY
Main Viking attacks.
Districts settled by Norse or Danes in England, Wales, and Scotland, c.865-900.
Viking foundations in Ireland.
Important Viking base.
Important battles.
Fens or marshes.
Orkney Islands
SUTHERLAND
CAITHNESS
HEBRIDES
ROSS
KINGDOM OF PICTS & SCOTS
NORSE
Iona
Lindisfarne Is.
NORSE 793
Edinburgh
Melrose
STRATHCLYDE
ENGLISH NORTHUMBRIA
NORSE c.789
NORSE 794
Luel
GALLOWAY
Durham
Jarrow
Whitby
NORSE c.794
NORSE c.800-840
ULSTER
c.840, taken by Turgeis of Norway.
Armagh
DANISH NORTHUMBRIA
LANCS
I. of Man
DANES c.836-842
DANES
CONNAUGHT
Kells
Tara
795
LEINSTER
Shannon
Dublin
Lincoln
Chester
DANISH MERCIA
Nottingham
Derby
DANELAW
Stamford
EAST ANGLIA
Peterborough
Offa's Dyke
Severn
Leicester
Limerick
Cashel
MUNSTER
Wexford
Waterford
Cork
ENGLISH MERCIA
Cambridge
SOUTH WALES
Ashdown
Ellandune
London
Thames
c.800
795
Wedmore
Salisbury
Basing
Glastonbury
WESSEX
Winchester
DEVON
836-840 DANES
WELSH CORNWALL
Swanage
0 60 Miles
838 DANES
© Arthur Banks 1972

ALFRED THE GREAT 849–899

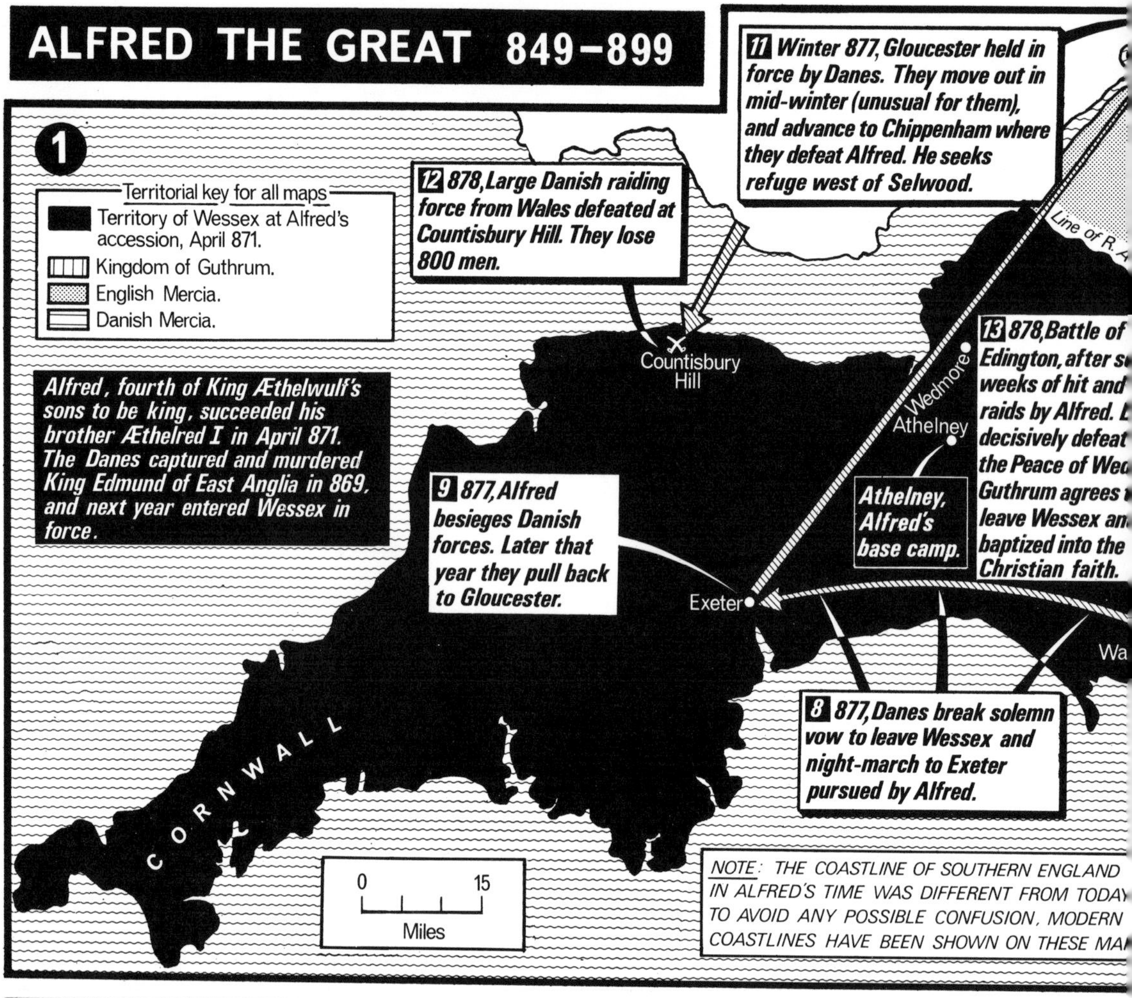

1
11 Winter 877, Gloucester held in force by Danes. They move out in mid-winter (unusual for them), and advance to Chippenham where they defeat Alfred. He seeks refuge west of Selwood.
Territorial key for all maps
Territory of Wessex at Alfred's accession, April 871.
Kingdom of Guthrum.
English Mercia.
Danish Mercia.
12 878, Large Danish raiding force from Wales defeated at Countisbury Hill. They lose 800 men.
Countisbury Hill
Alfred, fourth of King Æthelwulf's sons to be king, succeeded his brother Æthelred I in April 871. The Danes captured and murdered King Edmund of East Anglia in 869, and next year entered Wessex in force.
Wedmore
Athelney
Athelney, Alfred's base camp.
9 877, Alfred besieges Danish forces. Later that year they pull back to Gloucester.
Exeter
8 877, Danes break solemn vow to leave Wessex and night-march to Exeter pursued by Alfred.
CORNWALL
0 15
Miles
NOTE: THE COASTLINE OF SOUTHERN ENGLAND IN ALFRED'S TIME WAS DIFFERENT FROM TODAY TO AVOID ANY POSSIBLE CONFUSION, MODERN COASTLINES HAVE BEEN SHOWN ON THESE MA

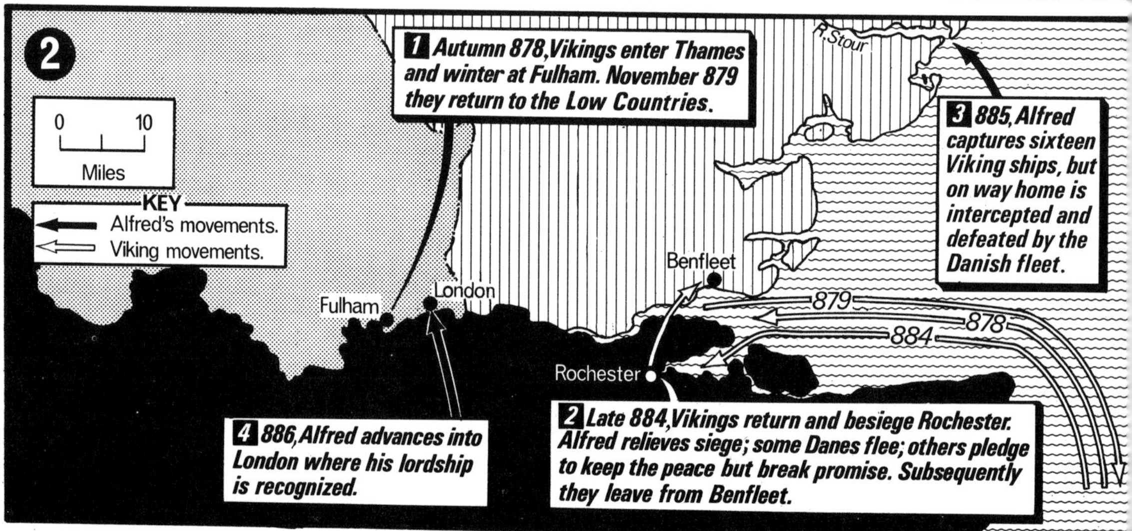

2
1 Autumn 878, Vikings enter Thames and winter at Fulham. November 879 they return to the Low Countries.
R. Stour
0 10
Miles
KEY
Alfred's movements.
Viking movements.
3 885, Alfred captures sixteen Viking ships, but on way home is intercepted and defeated by the Danish fleet.
Benfleet
London
Fulham
879
878
884
Rochester
4 886, Alfred advances into London where his lordship is recognized.
2 Late 884, Vikings return and besiege Rochester. Alfred relieves siege; some Danes flee; others pledge to keep the peace but break promise. Subsequently they leave from Benfleet.

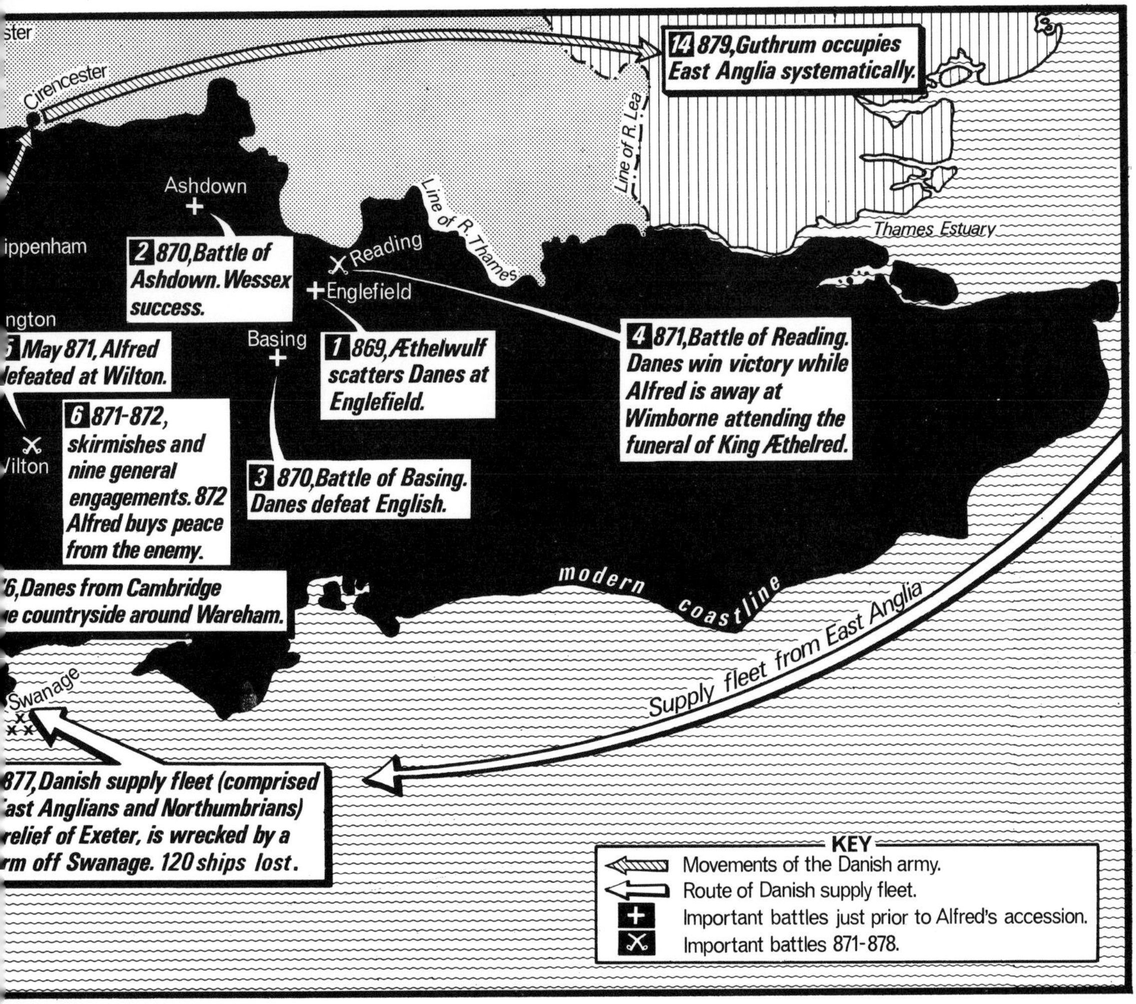

ster
Cirencester
Ashdown
ippenham
ngton
Basing
Reading
Englefield
Line of R. Thames
Line of R. Lea
Thames Estuary
14 879,Guthrum occupies East Anglia systematically.
2 870,Battle of Ashdown. Wessex success.
5 May 871, Alfred defeated at Wilton.
1 869,Æthelwulf scatters Danes at Englefield.
4 871,Battle of Reading. Danes win victory while Alfred is away at Wimborne attending the funeral of King Æthelred.
6 871-872, skirmishes and nine general engagements. 872 Alfred buys peace from the enemy.
Vilton
3 870,Battle of Basing. Danes defeat English.
76,Danes from Cambridge e countryside around Wareham.
modern coastline
Swanage
Supply fleet from East Anglia
877,Danish supply fleet (comprised East Anglians and Northumbrians) relief of Exeter, is wrecked by a rm off Swanage. 120 ships lost.
KEY
Movements of the Danish army.
Route of Danish supply fleet.
Important battles just prior to Alfred's accession.
Important battles 871-878.

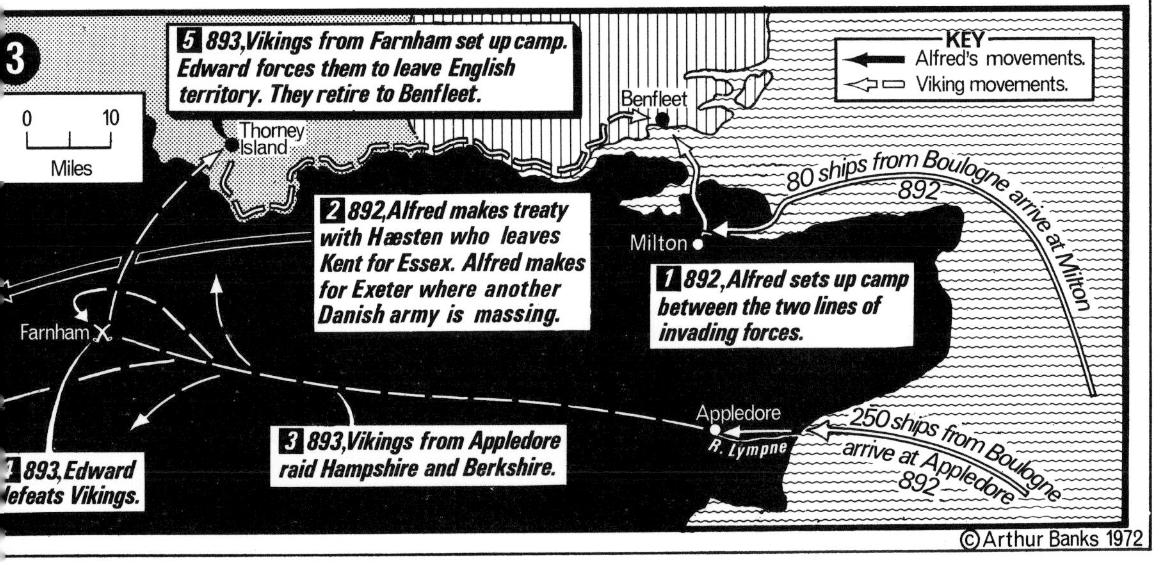

3
5 893,Vikings from Farnham set up camp. Edward forces them to leave English territory. They retire to Benfleet.
KEY
Alfred's movements.
Viking movements.
0 10
Miles
Thorney Island
Benfleet
80 ships from Boulogne arrive at Milton 892
Milton
2 892,Alfred makes treaty with Hæsten who leaves Kent for Essex. Alfred makes for Exeter where another Danish army is massing.
1 892,Alfred sets up camp between the two lines of invading forces.
Farnham
Appledore
R. Lympne
250 ships from Boulogne arrive at Appledore 892
3 893,Vikings from Appledore raid Hampshire and Berkshire.
4 893,Edward defeats Vikings.

ALFRED THE GREAT – continued

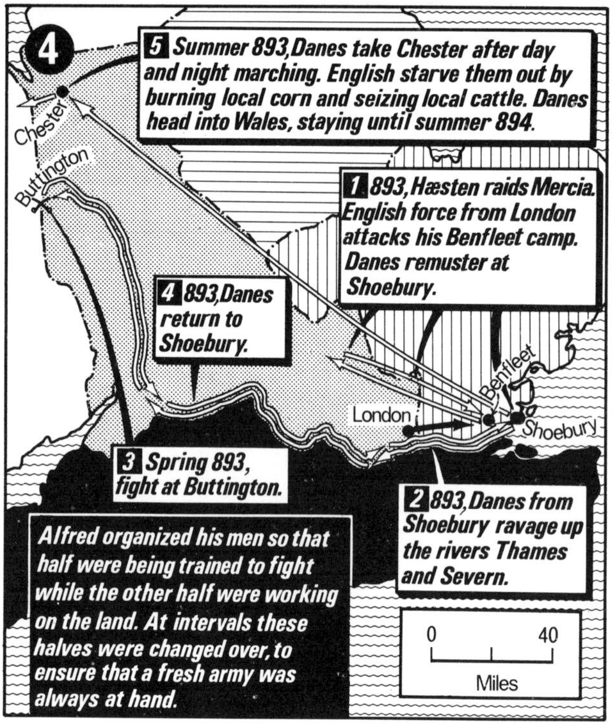
4
5 Summer 893, Danes take Chester after day and night marching. English starve them out by burning local corn and seizing local cattle. Danes head into Wales, staying until summer 894.
Chester
Buttington
1 893, Hæsten raids Mercia. English force from London attacks his Benfleet camp. Danes remuster at Shoebury.
4 893, Danes return to Shoebury.
Benfleet
London
Shoebury
3 Spring 893, fight at Buttington.
2 893, Danes from Shoebury ravage up the rivers Thames and Severn.
Alfred organized his men so that half were being trained to fight while the other half were working on the land. At intervals these halves were changed over, to ensure that a fresh army was always at hand.
0
40
Miles

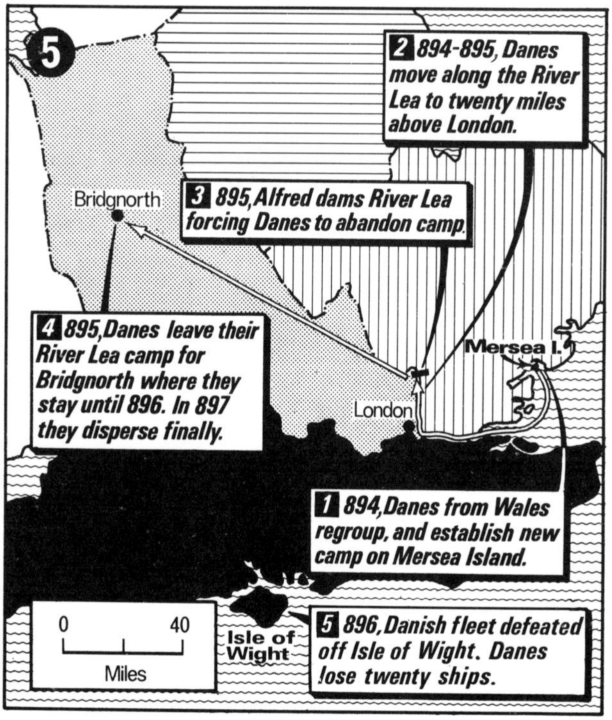
5
2 894-895, Danes move along the River Lea to twenty miles above London.
Bridgnorth
3 895, Alfred dams River Lea forcing Danes to abandon camp.
4 895, Danes leave their River Lea camp for Bridgnorth where they stay until 896. In 897 they disperse finally.
Mersea I.
London
1 894, Danes from Wales regroup, and establish new camp on Mersea Island.
0
40
Miles
Isle of Wight
5 896, Danish fleet defeated off Isle of Wight. Danes lose twenty ships.

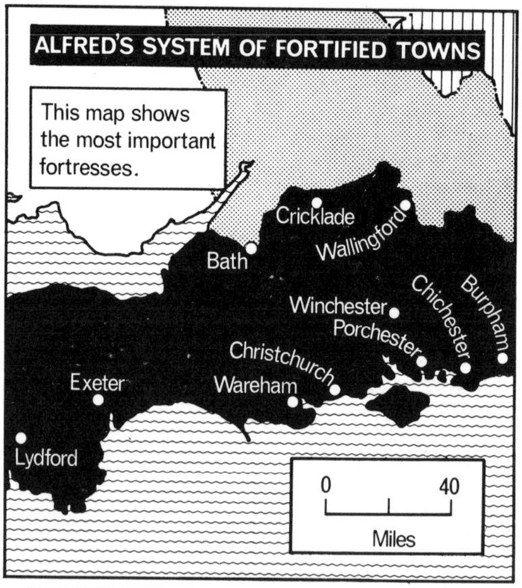
ALFRED'S SYSTEM OF FORTIFIED TOWNS
This map shows the most important fortresses.
Cricklade
Wallingford
Bath
Winchester
Chichester
Burpham
Porchester
Christchurch
Exeter
Wareham
Lydford
0
40
Miles

The story of Alfred "burning the cakes", is based on an interpolation from the annals of St. Neot in Asser's "Life of Alfred".

THE ANGLO-SAXON CHRONICLE

The Anglo-Saxon Chronicle consists collectively of 7 annalistic compilations written in Old English. (There are, too, at least 3 Latin versions.) Each begins with an outline of history from Julius Caesar until the 6th C. Until the entry for 891 the compilations are remarkably similar and until 915 much common material is used. Then the details recorded in each manuscript diverge considerably. The latest entry of all the manuscripts is for 1154 in that written at Peterborough Abbey.

The story of Alfred wandering in the Danish camp dressed as a minstrel is based on an account told in William of Malmesbury's "De Gestis Regum".

Alfred, born 849 at Wantage. Before the age of 7 he had undertaken two journeys to Rome. He was taught Latin later in life by Asser, and between 892 and 899 when he died, he produced five Latin works. (Translations of Gregory's Cura Pastoralis, Orosius's history of the ancient world, Bede's Historia Ecclesiastica, Boethius's De Consolatione Philosophiae, and St. Augustine's Soliloquies).

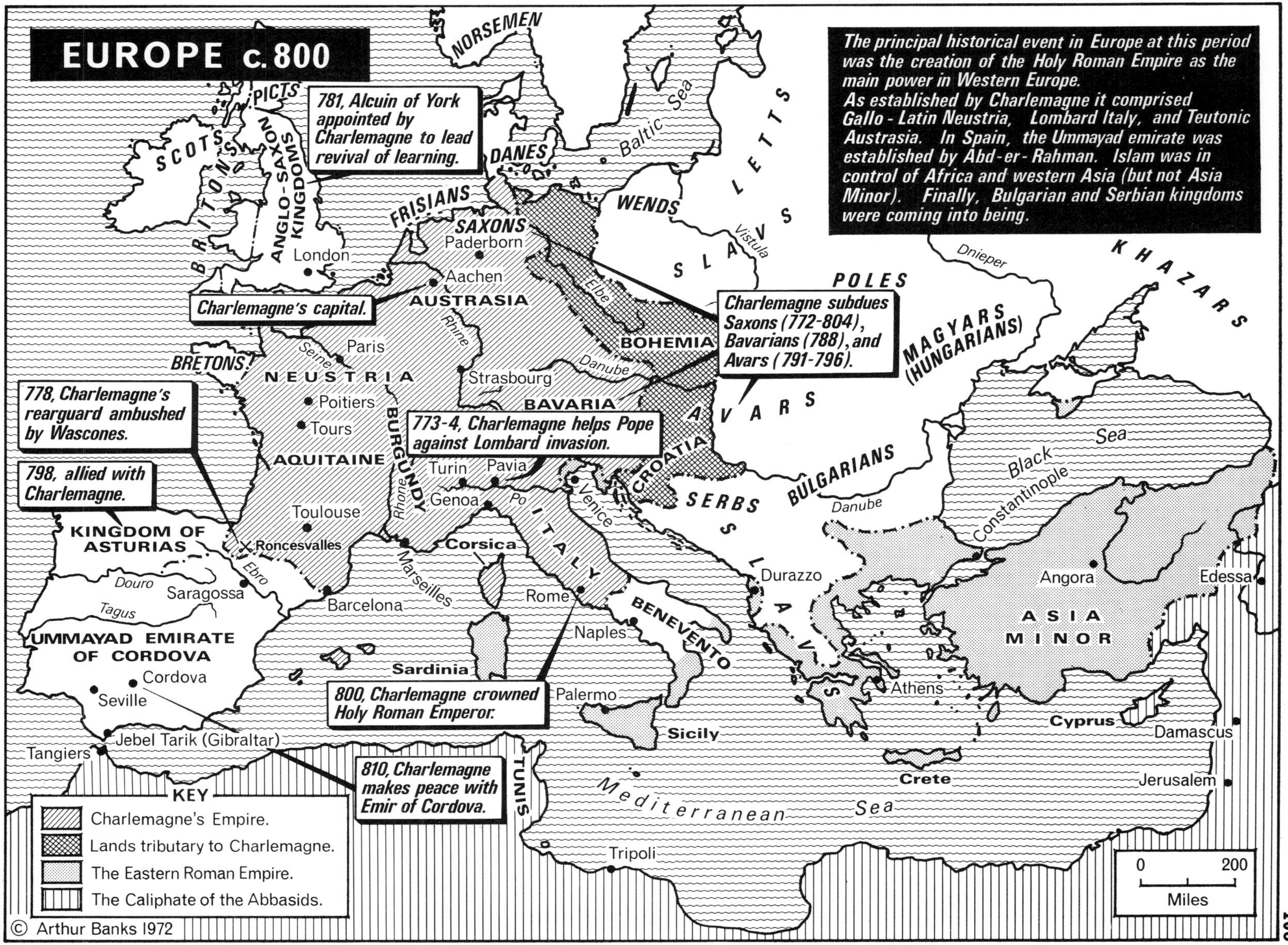
EUROPE c.800
The principal historical event in Europe at this period was the creation of the Holy Roman Empire as the main power in Western Europe.
As established by Charlemagne it comprised Gallo - Latin Neustria, Lombard Italy, and Teutonic Austrasia. In Spain, the Ummayad emirate was established by Abd-er-Rahman. Islam was in control of Africa and western Asia (but not Asia Minor). Finally, Bulgarian and Serbian kingdoms were coming into being.
781, Alcuin of York appointed by Charlemagne to lead revival of learning.
Charlemagne's capital.
778, Charlemagne's rearguard ambushed by Wascones.
798, allied with Charlemagne.
773-4, Charlemagne helps Pope against Lombard invasion.
Charlemagne subdues Saxons (772-804), Bavarians (788), and Avars (791-796).
800, Charlemagne crowned Holy Roman Emperor.
810, Charlemagne makes peace with Emir of Cordova.
NORSEMEN
PICTS
SCOTS
BRITONS
ANGLO-SAXON KINGDOMS
London
DANES
FRISIANS
SAXONS
Paderborn
Aachen
AUSTRASIA
WENDS
Baltic Sea
LETTS
SLAVS
Vistula
Dnieper
KHAZARS
POLES
MAGYARS (HUNGARIANS)
Elbe
BOHEMIA
Rhine
Danube
BRETONS
Paris
Seine
NEUSTRIA
Strasbourg
BAVARIA
Poitiers
Tours
AQUITAINE
BURGUNDY
AVARS
CROATIA
BULGARIANS
Turin
Pavia
Genoa
Po
Venice
Rhone
Toulouse
Roncesvalles
SERBS
Danube
Black Sea
Constantinople
KINGDOM OF ASTURIAS
Ebro
Marseilles
Corsica
ITALY
SLAVS
Durazzo
Angora
Edessa
Douro
Saragossa
Tagus
Barcelona
Rome
BENEVENTO
ASIA MINOR
UMMAYAD EMIRATE OF CORDOVA
Naples
Sardinia
Cordova
Seville
Palermo
Athens
Cyprus
Sicily
Damascus
Jebel Tarik (Gibraltar)
Tangiers
TUNIS
Crete
Jerusalem
Mediterranean Sea
Tripoli
KEY
Charlemagne's Empire.
Lands tributary to Charlemagne.
The Eastern Roman Empire.
The Caliphate of the Abbasids.
0 200
Miles
© Arthur Banks 1972

THE SHORT-LIVED KITAN ASCENDANCY IN CHINA

Struggles for power dominated the period 907-960 (the main moves are shown by arrows on maps). The Kitan were granted land in northern China for aid extended to the Later Tsin in their fight for supremacy. Thus, the Kitan gained a strategic foothold for their invasion.

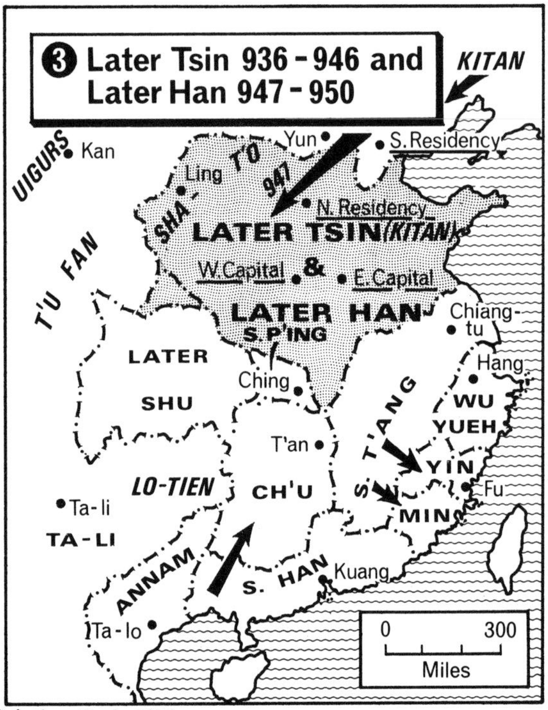

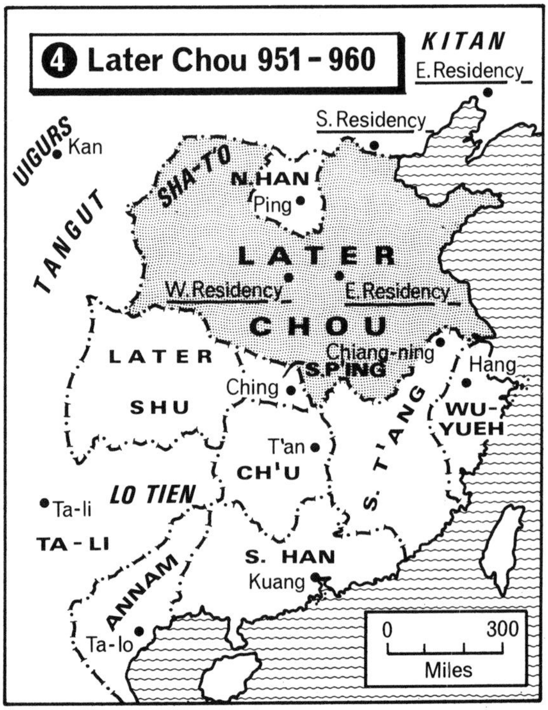

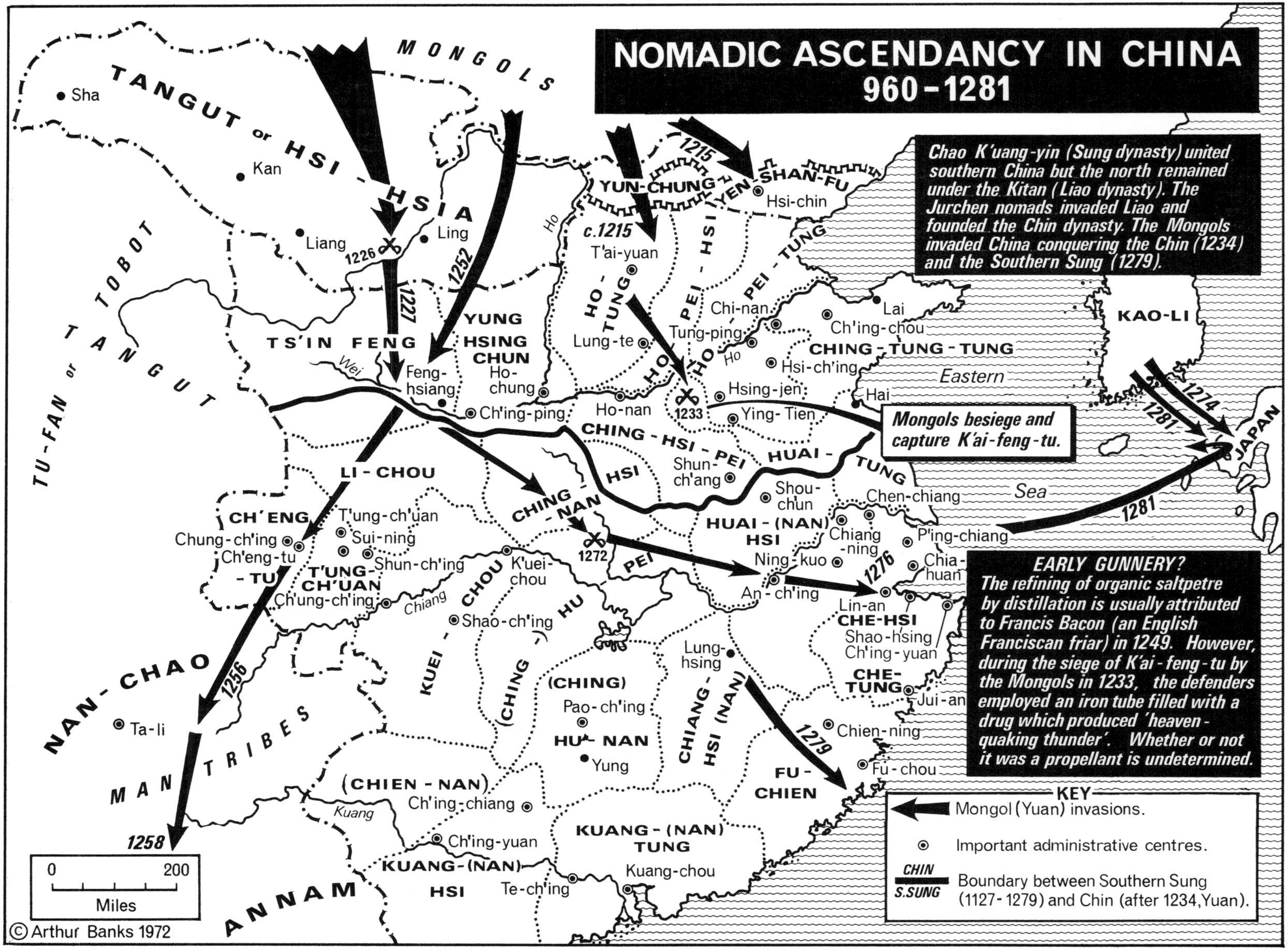
NOMADIC ASCENDANCY IN CHINA
960-1281
Chao K'uang-yin (Sung dynasty) united southern China but the north remained under the Kitan (Liao dynasty). The Jurchen nomads invaded Liao and founded the Chin dynasty. The Mongols invaded China conquering the Chin (1234) and the Southern Sung (1279).
Mongols besiege and capture K'ai-feng-tu.
EARLY GUNNERY?
The refining of organic saltpetre by distillation is usually attributed to Francis Bacon (an English Franciscan friar) in 1249. However, during the siege of K'ai-feng-tu by the Mongols in 1233, the defenders employed an iron tube filled with a drug which produced 'heaven-quaking thunder'. Whether or not it was a propellant is undetermined.
KEY
Mongol (Yuan) invasions.
Important administrative centres.
CHIN
S.SUNG
Boundary between Southern Sung (1127-1279) and Chin (after 1234, Yuan).
0
200
Miles
© Arthur Banks 1972
MONGOLS
TANGUT or HSI-HSIA
Sha
Kan
Liang
Ling
1226
1227
1252
1215
c.1215
1233
1272
1276
1279
1256
1258
1274
1281
TU-FAN or TOBOT
TANGUT
TS'IN FENG
Wei
Feng-hsiang
YUNG HSING CHUN
Ho-chung
Ch'ing-ping
Ho
YUN-CHUNG
YEN
SHAN-FU
Hsi-chin
T'ai-yuan
HO-TUNG
Lung-te
HO-PEI-HSI
HO-PEI-TUNG
Chi-nan
Tung-ping
Ho-nan
Hsing-jen
Ying-Tien
Lai
Ch'ing-chou
Hsi-ch'ing
CHING-TUNG-TUNG
Hai
Eastern Sea
KAO-LI
JAPAN
CHING-HSI-PEI
HSI
Shun-ch'ang
HUAI-TUNG
Shou-chun
Chen-chiang
HUAI-(NAN) HSI
Chiang-ning
P'ing-chiang
Ning-kuo
An-ch'ing
Chia-huan
Lin-an
CHE-HSI
Shao-hsing
Ch'ing-yuan
CHE-TUNG
Jui-an
Chien-ning
Fu-chou
FU-CHIEN
LI-CHOU
CHING-NAN
PEI
CH'ENG-TU
Chung-ch'ing
Ch'eng-tu
T'ung-ch'uan
Sui-ning
Shun-ch'ing
T'UNG-CH'UAN
Ch'ung-ch'ing
Chiang
K'uei-chou
KUEI-CHOU
Shao-ch'ing
(CHING-) HU
(CHING)
Pao-ch'ing
HU-NAN
Yung
Lung-hsing
CHIANG-HSI (NAN)
(CHIEN-NAN)
Ch'ing-chiang
Kuang
Ch'ing-yuan
KUANG-(NAN) HSI
Te-ch'ing
KUANG-(NAN) TUNG
Kuang-chou
NAN-CHAO
Ta-li
MAN TRIBES
ANNAM

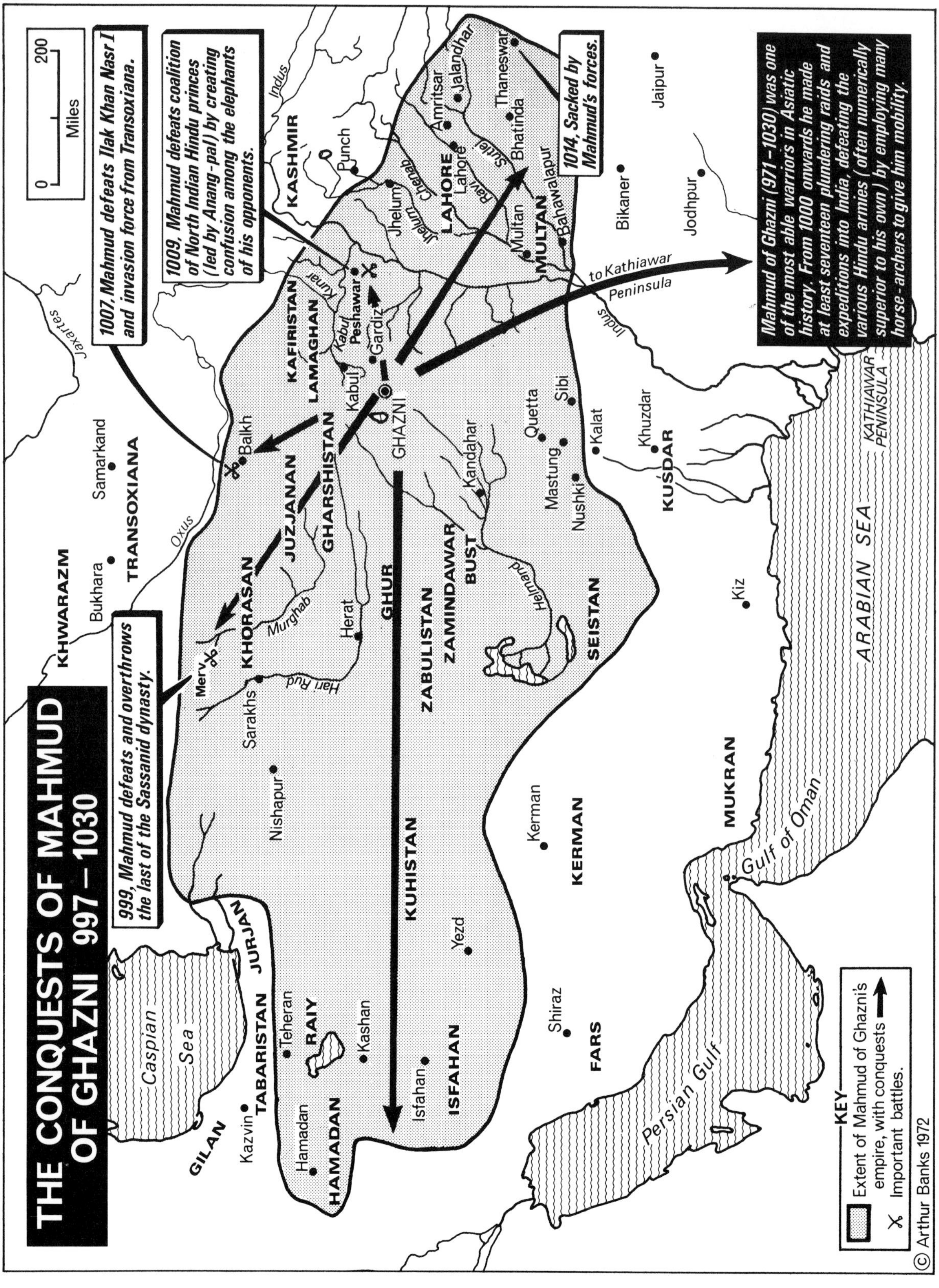
THE CONQUESTS OF MAHMUD OF GHAZNI 997 – 1030
999, Mahmud defeats and overthrows the last of the Sassanid dynasty.
1007, Mahmud defeats Ilak Khan Nasr I and invasion force from Transoxiana.
1009, Mahmud defeats coalition of North Indian Hindu princes (led by Anang-pal) by creating confusion among the elephants of his opponents.
1014, Sacked by Mahmud's forces.
Mahmud of Ghazni (971–1030) was one of the most able warriors in Asiatic history. From 1000 onwards he made at least seventeen plundering raids and expeditions into India, defeating the various Hindu armies (often numerically superior to his own) by employing many horse-archers to give him mobility.
0 200 Miles
KEY
Extent of Mahmud of Ghazni's empire, with conquests
Important battles.
© Arthur Banks 1972
Caspian Sea
GILAN
Kazvin
TABARISTAN
Teheran
RAIY
Kashan
Hamadan
HAMADAN
Isfahan
ISFAHAN
JURJAN
KHWARAZM
Bukhara
TRANSOXIANA
Samarkand
Oxus
Jaxartes
Merv
Sarakhs
Nishapur
KHORASAN
Murghab
Hari Rud
Herat
JUZJANAN
GHARSHISTAN
Balkh
GHUR
ZABULISTAN
ZAMINDAWAR
BUST
Kandahar
Helmand
SEISTAN
KUHISTAN
Yezd
Shiraz
FARS
KERMAN
Kerman
MUKRAN
Gulf of Oman
Persian Gulf
ARABIAN SEA
KATHIAWAR PENINSULA
KAFIRISTAN
LAMAGHAN
Kabul
Kabul
Gardiz
GHAZNI
Peshawar
Kunar
KASHMIR
Punch
Indus
Jhelum
Jhelum
Chenab
Ravi
Sutlej
Amritsar
Jalandhar
Lahore
LAHORE
Thaneswar
Bhatinda
Multan
MULTAN
Bahawalapur
to Kathiawar Peninsula
Bikaner
Jodhpur
Jaipur
Quetta
Sibi
Mastung
Nushki
Kalat
Khuzdar
KUSDAR
Kiz

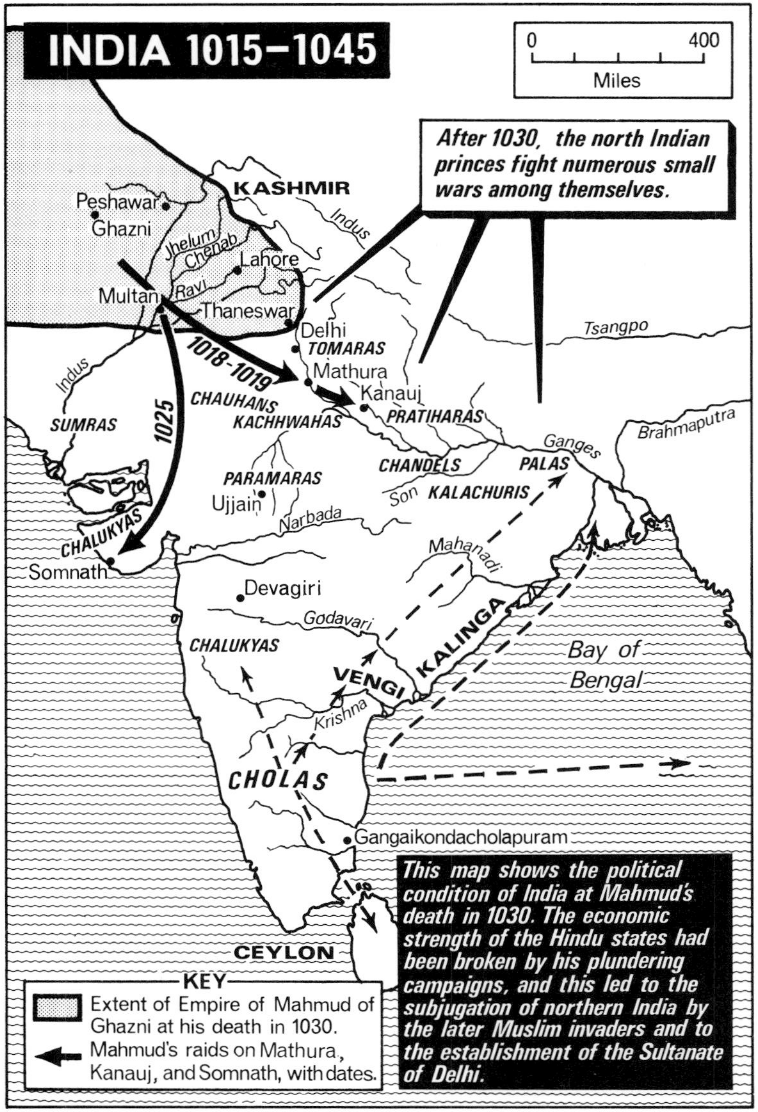
INDIA 1015–1045
0 400
Miles
After 1030, the north Indian princes fight numerous small wars among themselves.
KASHMIR
Peshawar
Ghazni
Jhelum
Chenab
Lahore
Ravi
Multan
Thaneswar
Indus
Delhi
TOMARAS
Mathura
Kanauj
1018-1019
1025
Tsangpo
SUMRAS
CHAUHANS
KACHHWAHAS
PRATIHARAS
Brahmaputra
Ganges
PALAS
CHANDELS
KALACHURIS
Son
PARAMARAS
Ujjain
Narbada
CHALUKYAS
Somnath
Mahanadi
Devagiri
Godavari
CHALUKYAS
VENGI
KALINGA
Bay of Bengal
Krishna
CHOLAS
Gangaikondacholapuram
CEYLON
This map shows the political condition of India at Mahmud's death in 1030. The economic strength of the Hindu states had been broken by his plundering campaigns, and this led to the subjugation of northern India by the later Muslim invaders and to the establishment of the Sultanate of Delhi.
KEY
Extent of Empire of Mahmud of Ghazni at his death in 1030.
Mahmud's raids on Mathura, Kanauj, and Somnath, with dates.

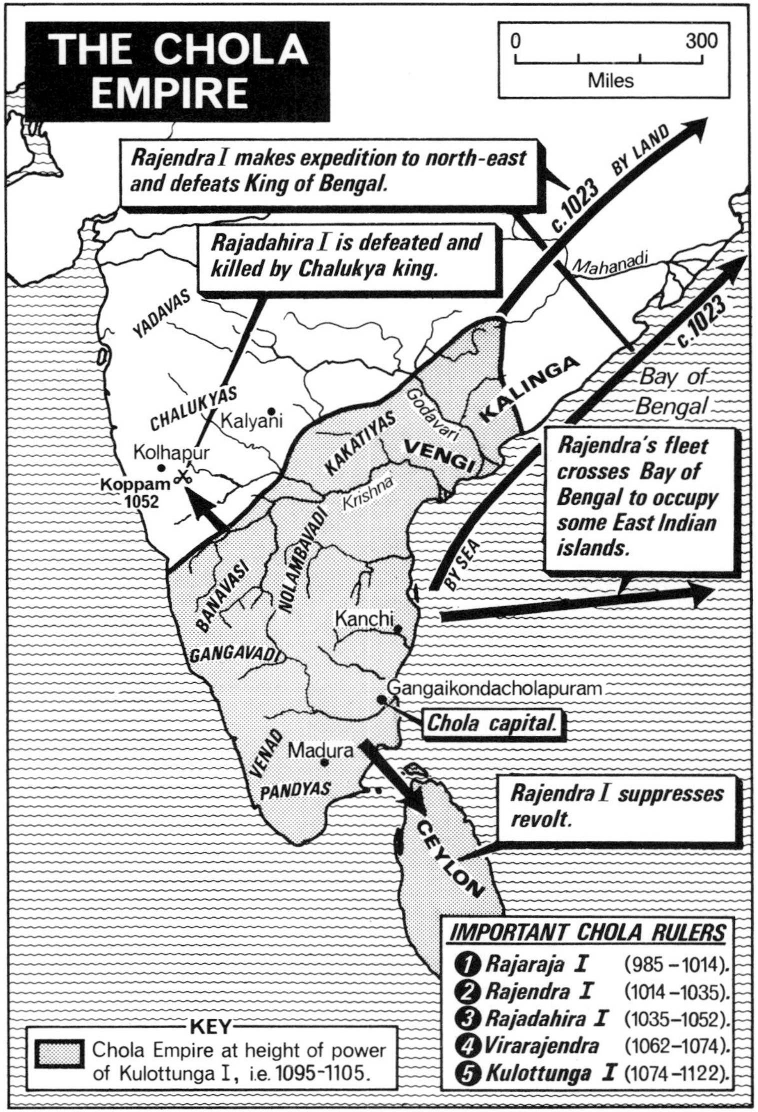
THE CHOLA EMPIRE
0 300
Miles
Rajendra I makes expedition to north-east and defeats King of Bengal.
c.1023 BY LAND
Rajadahira I is defeated and killed by Chalukya king.
Mahanadi
YADAVAS
c.1023
CHALUKYAS
Kalyani
Kolhapur
Koppam
1052
KALINGA
Bay of Bengal
KAKATIYAS
Godavari
VENGI
Krishna
Rajendra's fleet crosses Bay of Bengal to occupy some East Indian islands.
BY SEA
BANAVASI
NOLAMBAVADI
Kanchi
GANGAVADI
Gangaikondacholapuram
Chola capital.
VENAD
Madura
PANDYAS
Rajendra I suppresses revolt.
CEYLON
IMPORTANT CHOLA RULERS
1 Rajaraja I (985–1014).
2 Rajendra I (1014–1035).
3 Rajadahira I (1035–1052).
4 Virarajendra (1062–1074).
5 Kulottunga I (1074–1122).
KEY
Chola Empire at height of power of Kulottunga I, i.e. 1095-1105.

THE NORMAN INVASION OF ENGLAND 1066

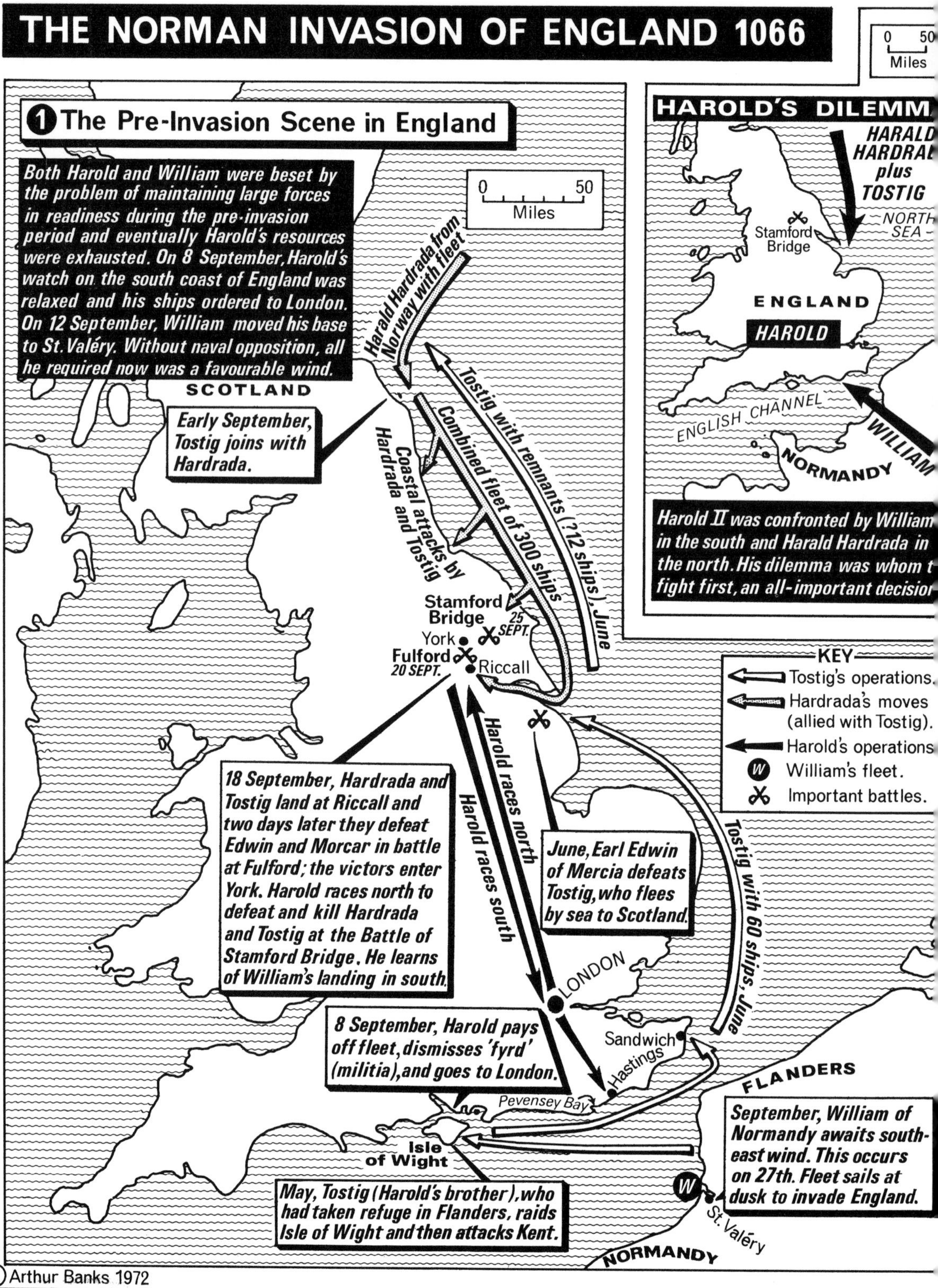

1 The Pre-Invasion Scene in England
Both Harold and William were beset by the problem of maintaining large forces in readiness during the pre-invasion period and eventually Harold's resources were exhausted. On 8 September, Harold's watch on the south coast of England was relaxed and his ships ordered to London. On 12 September, William moved his base to St. Valéry. Without naval opposition, all he required now was a favourable wind.
0 50 Miles
Harald Hardrada from Norway with fleet
SCOTLAND
Early September, Tostig joins with Hardrada.
Tostig with remnants (?12 ships), June
Combined fleet of 300 ships
Coastal attacks by Hardrada and Tostig
Stamford Bridge
25 SEPT.
York
Fulford
20 SEPT.
Riccall
Harold races north
Harold races south
18 September, Hardrada and Tostig land at Riccall and two days later they defeat Edwin and Morcar in battle at Fulford; the victors enter York. Harold races north to defeat and kill Hardrada and Tostig at the Battle of Stamford Bridge. He learns of William's landing in south.
June, Earl Edwin of Mercia defeats Tostig, who flees by sea to Scotland.
Tostig with 60 ships, June
LONDON
Sandwich
Hastings
Pevensey Bay
8 September, Harold pays off fleet, dismisses 'fyrd' (militia), and goes to London.
FLANDERS
Isle of Wight
September, William of Normandy awaits south-east wind. This occurs on 27th. Fleet sails at dusk to invade England.
W
St. Valéry
May, Tostig (Harold's brother), who had taken refuge in Flanders, raids Isle of Wight and then attacks Kent.
NORMANDY
KEY
Tostig's operations.
Hardrada's moves (allied with Tostig).
Harold's operations
William's fleet.
Important battles.
0 50
Miles
HAROLD'S DILEMM
HARALD HARDRA
plus TOSTIG
NORTH SEA
Stamford Bridge
ENGLAND
HAROLD
ENGLISH CHANNEL
WILLIAM
NORMANDY
Harold II was confronted by William in the south and Harald Hardrada in the north. His dilemma was whom t fight first, an all-important decisio

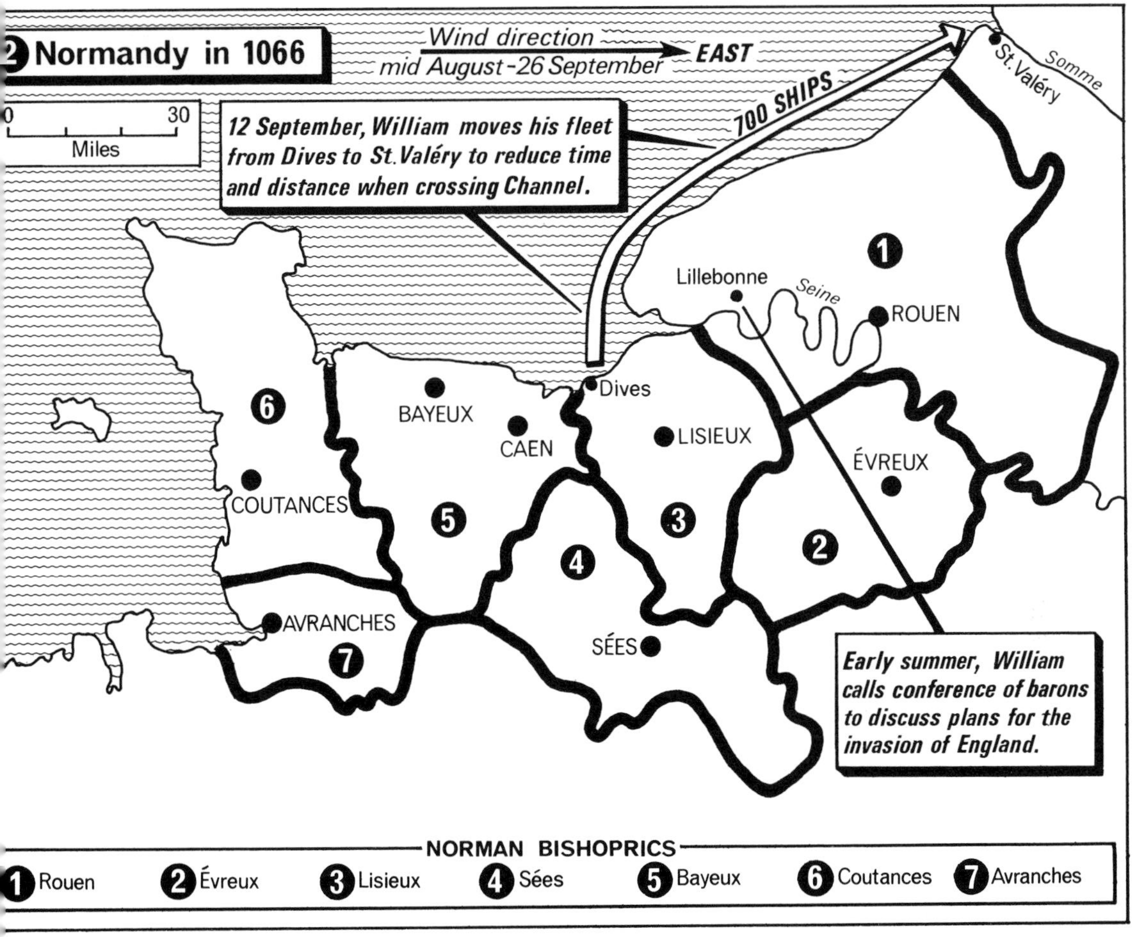

2 Normandy in 1066
Wind direction
mid August-26 September
EAST
0 30
Miles
12 September, William moves his fleet from Dives to St. Valéry to reduce time and distance when crossing Channel.
700 SHIPS
St. Valéry
Somme
Lillebonne
Seine
ROUEN
Dives
BAYEUX
CAEN
LISIEUX
ÉVREUX
COUTANCES
AVRANCHES
SÉES
1
2
3
4
5
6
7
Early summer, William calls conference of barons to discuss plans for the invasion of England.
NORMAN BISHOPRICS
1 Rouen
2 Évreux
3 Lisieux
4 Sées
5 Bayeux
6 Coutances
7 Avranches

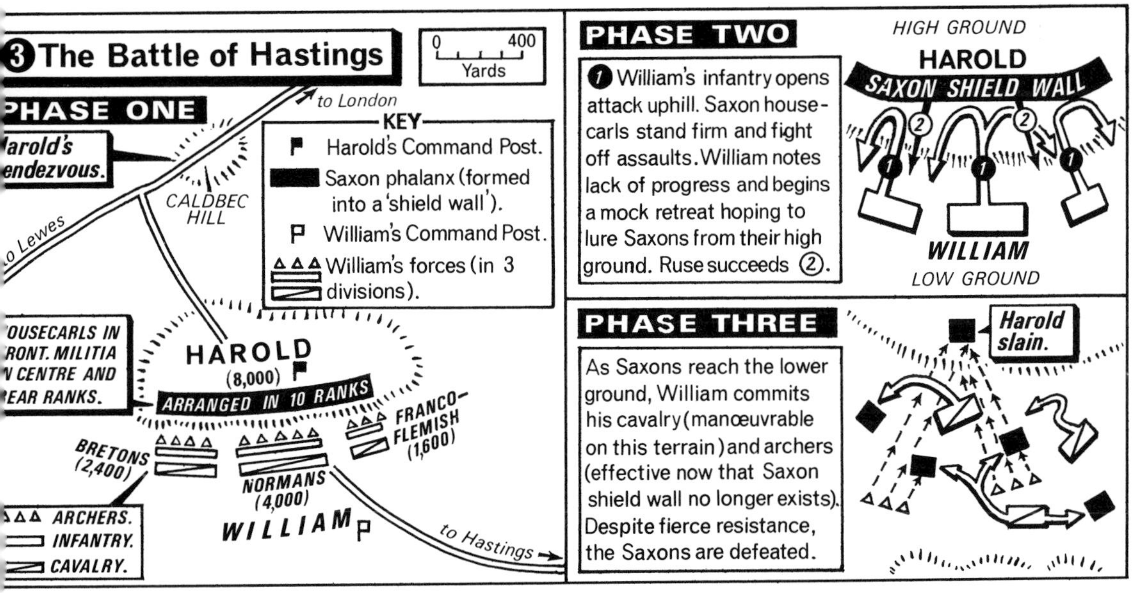

3 The Battle of Hastings
0 400
Yards
PHASE ONE
arold's endezvous.
to London
KEY
Harold's Command Post.
Saxon phalanx (formed into a 'shield wall').
William's Command Post.
William's forces (in 3 divisions).
CALDBEC HILL
o Lewes
OUSECARLS IN RONT. MILITIA N CENTRE AND EAR RANKS.
HAROLD
(8,000)
ARRANGED IN 10 RANKS
BRETONS (2,400)
NORMANS (4,000)
FRANCO-FLEMISH (1,600)
WILLIAM
ARCHERS.
INFANTRY.
CAVALRY.
to Hastings
PHASE TWO
1 William's infantry opens attack uphill. Saxon house-carls stand firm and fight off assaults. William notes lack of progress and begins a mock retreat hoping to lure Saxons from their high ground. Ruse succeeds 2.
HIGH GROUND
HAROLD
SAXON SHIELD WALL
WILLIAM
LOW GROUND
PHASE THREE
As Saxons reach the lower ground, William commits his cavalry (manœuvrable on this terrain) and archers (effective now that Saxon shield wall no longer exists). Despite fierce resistance, the Saxons are defeated.
Harold slain.

THE IMPORTANCE OF THE ENGLISH CHANNEL IN WAR

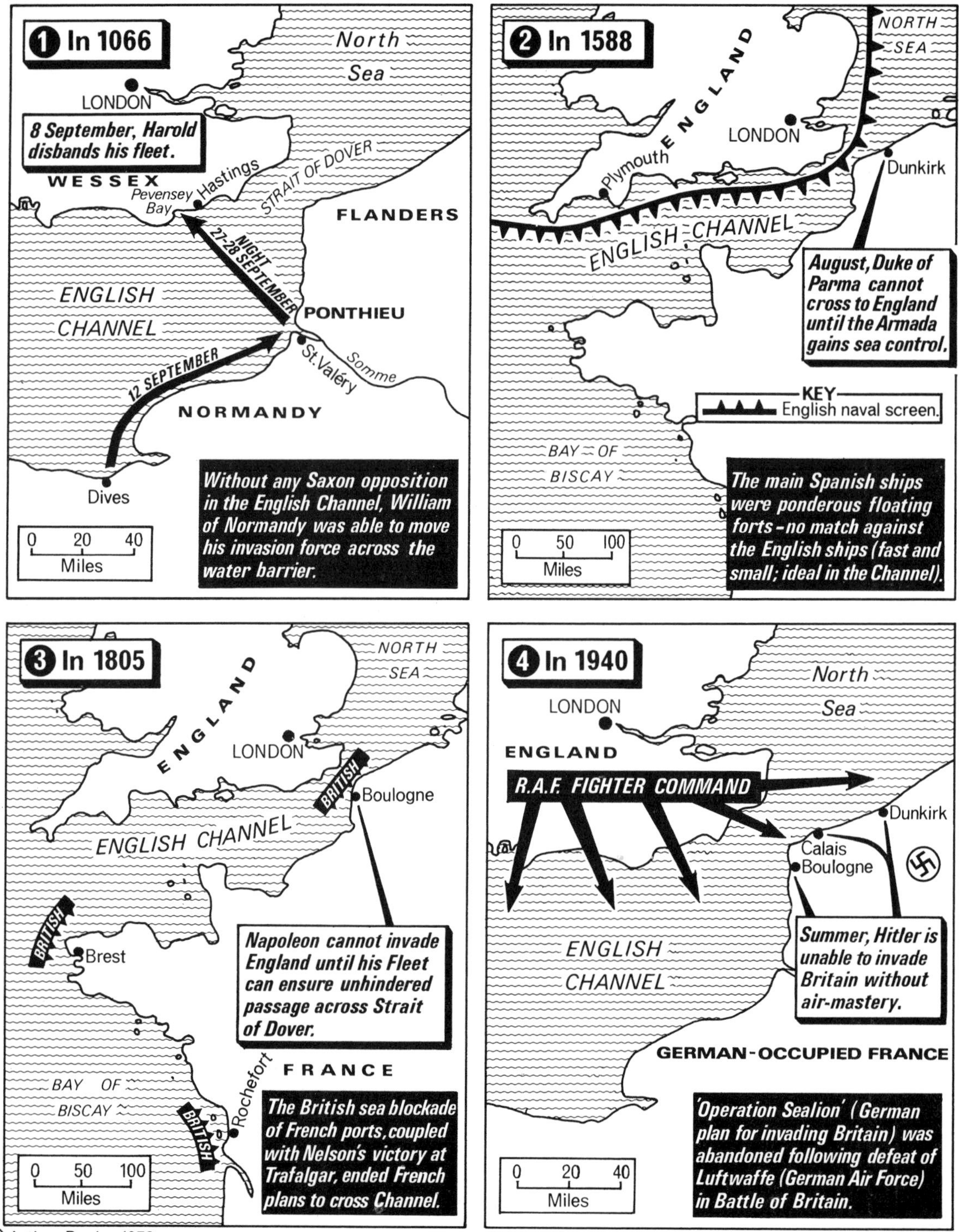
1 In 1066
North Sea
LONDON
8 September, Harold disbands his fleet.
WESSEX
Pevensey Bay
Hastings
STRAIT OF DOVER
FLANDERS
NIGHT 27-28 SEPTEMBER
ENGLISH CHANNEL
PONTHIEU
St. Valéry
Somme
12 SEPTEMBER
NORMANDY
Dives
0 20 40 Miles
Without any Saxon opposition in the English Channel, William of Normandy was able to move his invasion force across the water barrier.
2 In 1588
NORTH SEA
ENGLAND
LONDON
Plymouth
Dunkirk
ENGLISH CHANNEL
August, Duke of Parma cannot cross to England until the Armada gains sea control.
KEY
English naval screen.
BAY OF BISCAY
The main Spanish ships were ponderous floating forts - no match against the English ships (fast and small; ideal in the Channel).
0 50 100 Miles
3 In 1805
NORTH SEA
ENGLAND
LONDON
BRITISH
Boulogne
ENGLISH CHANNEL
BRITISH
Brest
Napoleon cannot invade England until his Fleet can ensure unhindered passage across Strait of Dover.
FRANCE
Rochefort
BAY OF BISCAY
BRITISH
0 50 100 Miles
The British sea blockade of French ports, coupled with Nelson's victory at Trafalgar, ended French plans to cross Channel.
4 In 1940
North Sea
LONDON
ENGLAND
R.A.F. FIGHTER COMMAND
Dunkirk
Calais
Boulogne
ENGLISH CHANNEL
Summer, Hitler is unable to invade Britain without air-mastery.
GERMAN-OCCUPIED FRANCE
0 20 40 Miles
'Operation Sealion' (German plan for invading Britain) was abandoned following defeat of Luftwaffe (German Air Force) in Battle of Britain.

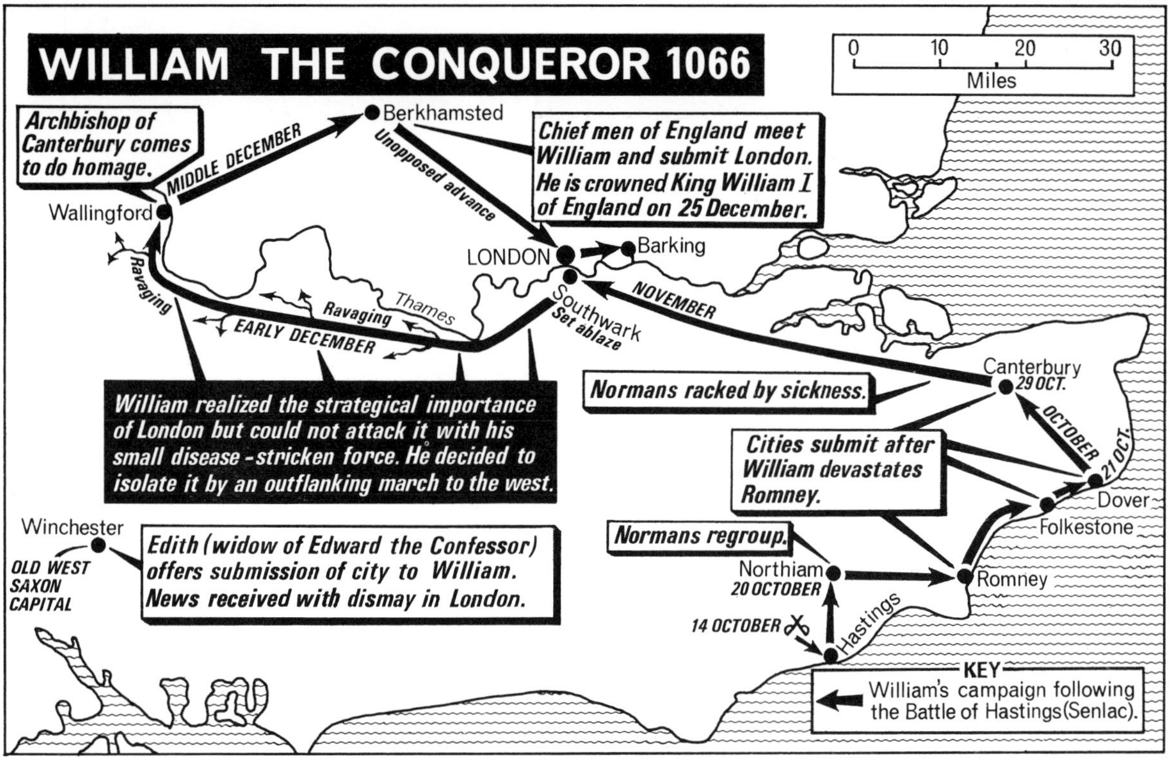
WILLIAM THE CONQUEROR 1066
0 10 20 30
Miles
Archbishop of Canterbury comes to do homage.
MIDDLE DECEMBER
Berkhamsted
Unopposed advance
Chief men of England meet William and submit London. He is crowned King William I of England on 25 December.
Wallingford
LONDON
Barking
Ravaging
Ravaging
Thames
EARLY DECEMBER
Southwark
Set ablaze
NOVEMBER
William realized the strategical importance of London but could not attack it with his small disease-stricken force. He decided to isolate it by an outflanking march to the west.
Normans racked by sickness.
Canterbury
29 OCT.
OCTOBER
21 OCT.
Cities submit after William devastates Romney.
Dover
Folkestone
Normans regroup.
Winchester
OLD WEST SAXON CAPITAL
Edith (widow of Edward the Confessor) offers submission of city to William. News received with dismay in London.
Northiam
20 OCTOBER
Romney
14 OCTOBER
Hastings
KEY
William's campaign following the Battle of Hastings (Senlac).

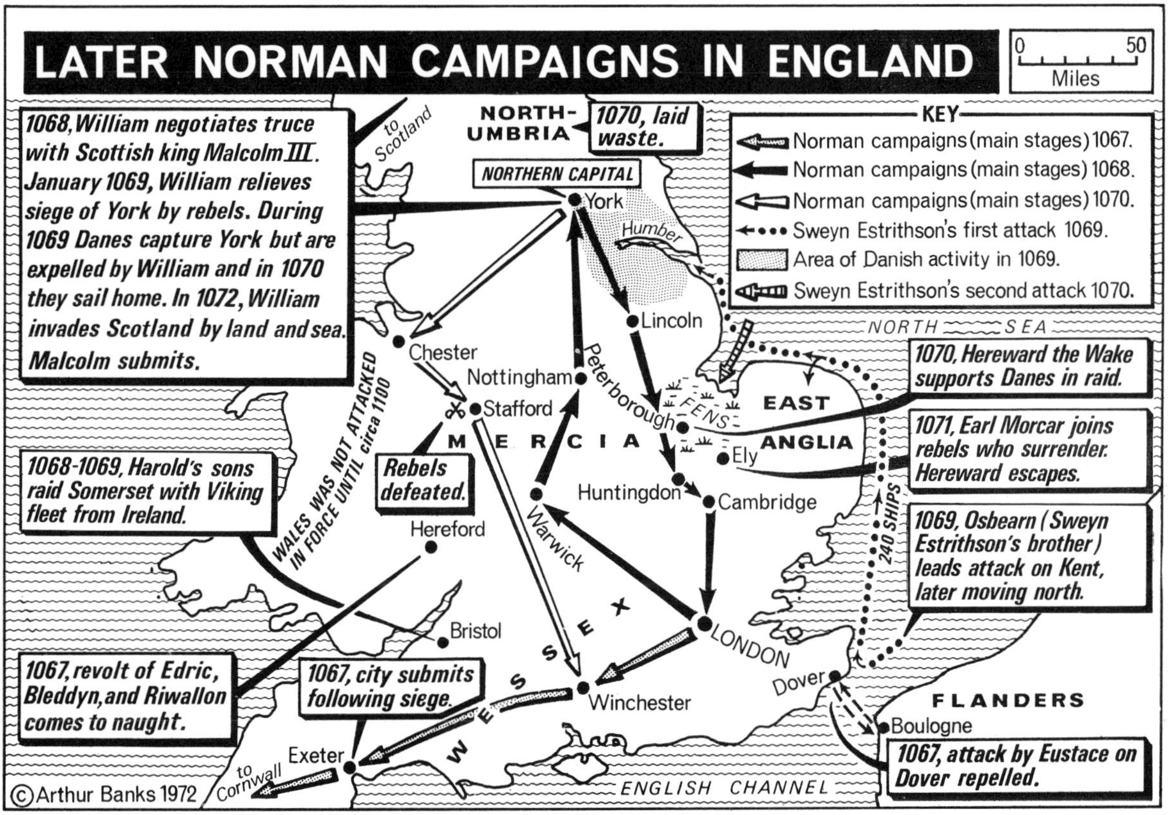
LATER NORMAN CAMPAIGNS IN ENGLAND
0 50
Miles
1068, William negotiates truce with Scottish king Malcolm III. January 1069, William relieves siege of York by rebels. During 1069 Danes capture York but are expelled by William and in 1070 they sail home. In 1072, William invades Scotland by land and sea. Malcolm submits.
to Scotland
NORTH-UMBRIA
1070, laid waste.
NORTHERN CAPITAL
York
Humber
KEY
Norman campaigns (main stages) 1067.
Norman campaigns (main stages) 1068.
Norman campaigns (main stages) 1070.
Sweyn Estrithson's first attack 1069.
Area of Danish activity in 1069.
Sweyn Estrithson's second attack 1070.
Lincoln
NORTH SEA
Chester
Nottingham
Peterborough
FENS
1070, Hereward the Wake supports Danes in raid.
EAST ANGLIA
Stafford
WALES WAS NOT ATTACKED IN FORCE UNTIL circa 1100
M E R C I A
Ely
1071, Earl Morcar joins rebels who surrender. Hereward escapes.
1068-1069, Harold's sons raid Somerset with Viking fleet from Ireland.
Rebels defeated.
Huntingdon
Cambridge
240 SHIPS
Hereford
Warwick
1069, Osbearn (Sweyn Estrithson's brother) leads attack on Kent, later moving north.
Bristol
W E S S E X
LONDON
1067, revolt of Edric, Bleddyn, and Riwallon comes to naught.
1067, city submits following siege.
Winchester
Dover
FLANDERS
Boulogne
Exeter
to Cornwall
1067, attack by Eustace on Dover repelled.
ENGLISH CHANNEL

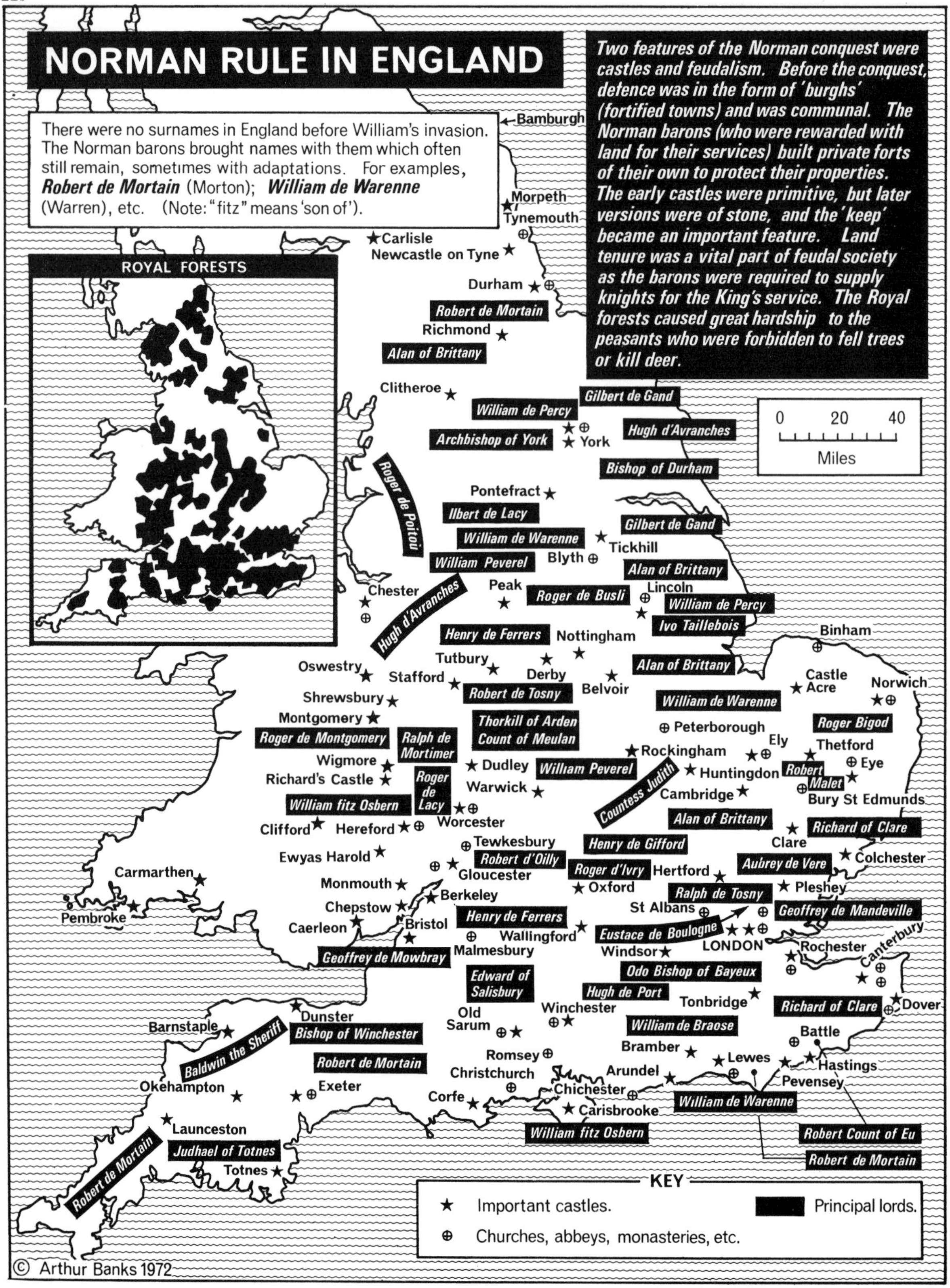
NORMAN RULE IN ENGLAND
There were no surnames in England before William's invasion. The Norman barons brought names with them which often still remain, sometimes with adaptations. For examples, *Robert de Mortain* (Morton); *William de Warenne* (Warren), etc. (Note: "fitz" means 'son of').
Two features of the Norman conquest were castles and feudalism. Before the conquest, defence was in the form of 'burghs' (fortified towns) and was communal. The Norman barons (who were rewarded with land for their services) built private forts of their own to protect their properties. The early castles were primitive, but later versions were of stone, and the 'keep' became an important feature. Land tenure was a vital part of feudal society as the barons were required to supply knights for the King's service. The Royal forests caused great hardship to the peasants who were forbidden to fell trees or kill deer.
ROYAL FORESTS
0 20 40
Miles
Bamburgh
Morpeth
Tynemouth
Carlisle
Newcastle on Tyne
Durham
Robert de Mortain
Richmond
Alan of Brittany
Clitheroe
Gilbert de Gand
William de Percy
Hugh d'Avranches
Archbishop of York
York
Bishop of Durham
Roger de Poitou
Pontefract
Ilbert de Lacy
Gilbert de Gand
William de Warenne
Tickhill
William Peverel
Blyth
Alan of Brittany
Chester
Hugh d'Avranches
Peak
Roger de Busli
Lincoln
William de Percy
Ivo Taillebois
Henry de Ferrers
Nottingham
Binham
Tutbury
Oswestry
Stafford
Derby
Belvoir
Alan of Brittany
Castle Acre
Norwich
Shrewsbury
Robert de Tosny
William de Warenne
Montgomery
Thorkill of Arden
Count of Meulan
Roger Bigod
Peterborough
Roger de Montgomery
Ralph de Mortimer
Ely
Thetford
Rockingham
Eye
Wigmore
Dudley
William Peverel
Huntingdon
Robert Malet
Richard's Castle
Roger de Lacy
Warwick
Countess Judith
Cambridge
Bury St Edmunds
William fitz Osbern
Worcester
Alan of Brittany
Clifford
Hereford
Richard of Clare
Tewkesbury
Henry de Gifford
Clare
Ewyas Harold
Robert d'Oilly
Aubrey de Vere
Colchester
Carmarthen
Gloucester
Roger d'Ivry
Hertford
Monmouth
Oxford
Ralph de Tosny
Pleshey
Pembroke
Berkeley
St Albans
Chepstow
Geoffrey de Mandeville
Henry de Ferrers
Caerleon
Bristol
Wallingford
Eustace de Boulogne
Malmesbury
LONDON
Windsor
Rochester
Geoffrey de Mowbray
Canterbury
Odo Bishop of Bayeux
Edward of Salisbury
Hugh de Port
Tonbridge
Richard of Clare
Dover
Old Sarum
Winchester
Dunster
Barnstaple
Bishop of Winchester
William de Braose
Battle
Baldwin the Sheriff
Bramber
Romsey
Lewes
Hastings
Robert de Mortain
Arundel
Christchurch
Pevensey
Okehampton
Exeter
Chichester
Corfe
William de Warenne
Carisbrooke
Launceston
William fitz Osbern
Robert Count of Eu
Judhael of Totnes
Robert de Mortain
Robert de Mortain
Totnes
KEY
★ Important castles.
⊕ Churches, abbeys, monasteries, etc.
Principal lords.
© Arthur Banks 1972

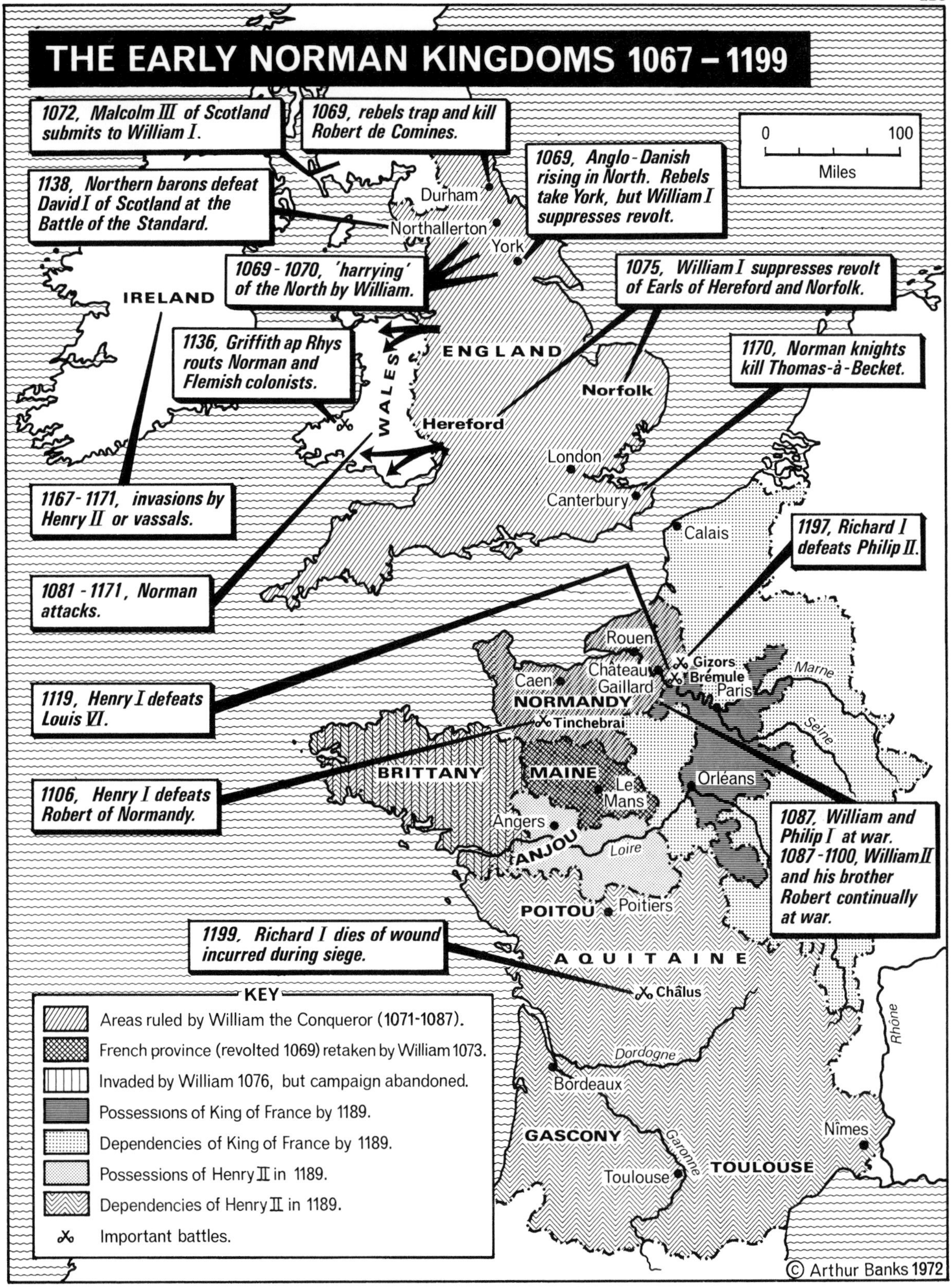
THE EARLY NORMAN KINGDOMS 1067 – 1199
1072, Malcolm III of Scotland submits to William I.
1069, rebels trap and kill Robert de Comines.
0 100 Miles
1138, Northern barons defeat David I of Scotland at the Battle of the Standard.
1069, Anglo-Danish rising in North. Rebels take York, but William I suppresses revolt.
Durham
Northallerton
York
1069 - 1070, 'harrying' of the North by William.
1075, William I suppresses revolt of Earls of Hereford and Norfolk.
IRELAND
1136, Griffith ap Rhys routs Norman and Flemish colonists.
ENGLAND
WALES
1170, Norman knights kill Thomas-à-Becket.
Norfolk
Hereford
London
Canterbury
1167 - 1171, invasions by Henry II or vassals.
Calais
1197, Richard I defeats Philip II.
1081 - 1171, Norman attacks.
Rouen
Gizors
Château Gaillard
Brémule
Caen
Paris
Marne
NORMANDY
1119, Henry I defeats Louis VI.
Tinchebrai
Seine
BRITTANY
MAINE
Le Mans
Orléans
1106, Henry I defeats Robert of Normandy.
Angers
ANJOU
Loire
1087, William and Philip I at war. 1087-1100, William II and his brother Robert continually at war.
POITOU
Poitiers
1199, Richard I dies of wound incurred during siege.
AQUITAINE
Châlus
KEY
Areas ruled by William the Conqueror (1071-1087).
French province (revolted 1069) retaken by William 1073.
Invaded by William 1076, but campaign abandoned.
Possessions of King of France by 1189.
Dependencies of King of France by 1189.
Possessions of Henry II in 1189.
Dependencies of Henry II in 1189.
Important battles.
Rhône
Dordogne
Bordeaux
GASCONY
Garonne
Nîmes
TOULOUSE
Toulouse
© Arthur Banks 1972

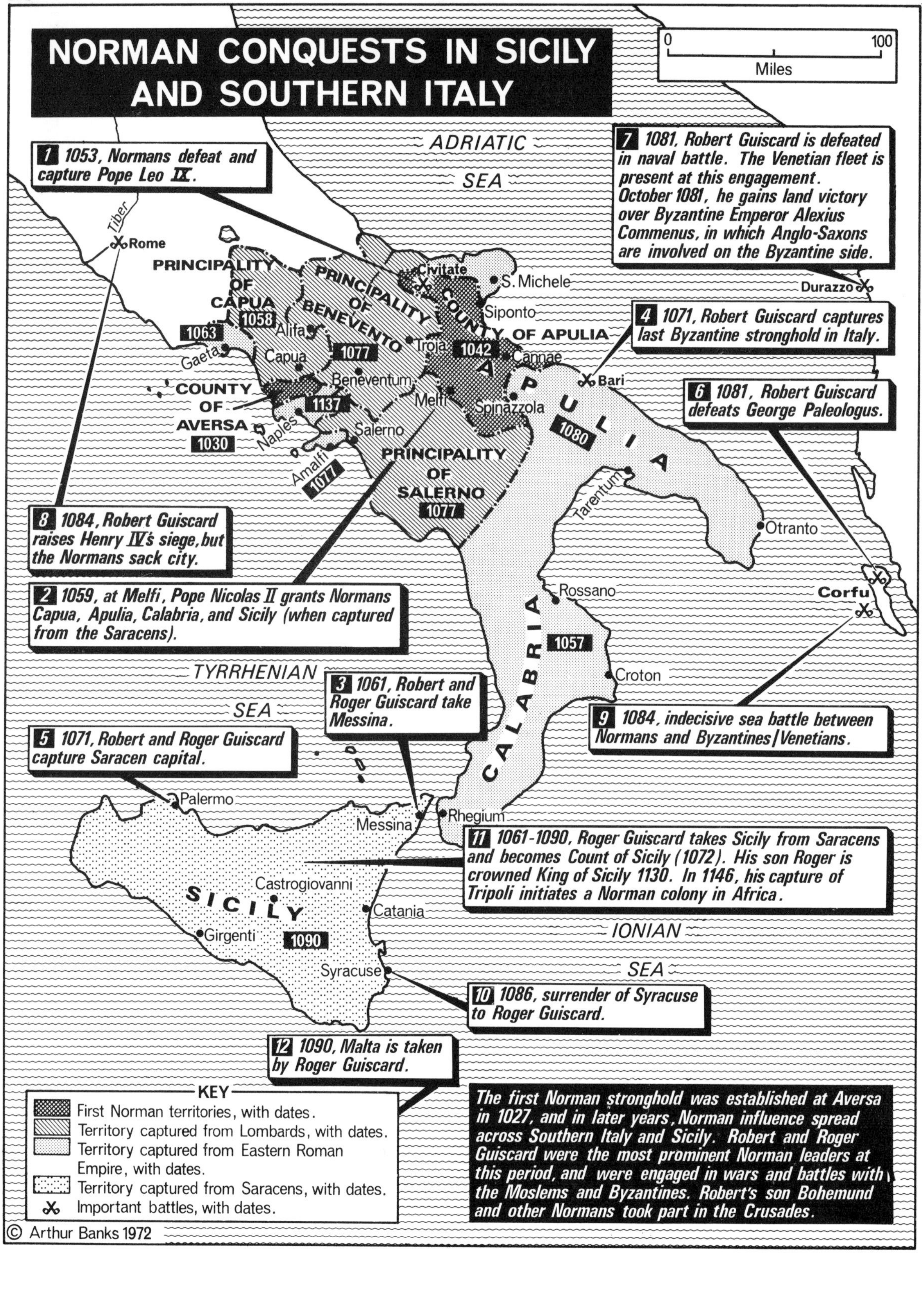
NORMAN CONQUESTS IN SICILY AND SOUTHERN ITALY
0
100
Miles
ADRIATIC
SEA
1 1053, Normans defeat and capture Pope Leo IX.
7 1081, Robert Guiscard is defeated in naval battle. The Venetian fleet is present at this engagement. October 1081, he gains land victory over Byzantine Emperor Alexius Commenus, in which Anglo-Saxons are involved on the Byzantine side.
Tiber
Rome
PRINCIPALITY OF CAPUA
1058
1063
PRINCIPALITY OF BENEVENTO
PRINCIPALITY
Civitate
S. Michele
Siponto
COUNTY OF APULIA
Durazzo
4 1071, Robert Guiscard captures last Byzantine stronghold in Italy.
Alifa
Gaeta
Capua
1077
Troja
1042
Cannae
Bari
Beneventum
COUNTY OF AVERSA
1030
1137
Melfi
Spinazzola
6 1081, Robert Guiscard defeats George Paleologus.
Naples
Salerno
APULIA
1080
Amalfi
1077
PRINCIPALITY OF SALERNO
1077
Tarentum
Otranto
8 1084, Robert Guiscard raises Henry IV's siege, but the Normans sack city.
Rossano
Corfu
2 1059, at Melfi, Pope Nicolas II grants Normans Capua, Apulia, Calabria, and Sicily (when captured from the Saracens).
1057
TYRRHENIAN
SEA
Croton
3 1061, Robert and Roger Guiscard take Messina.
9 1084, indecisive sea battle between Normans and Byzantines/Venetians.
5 1071, Robert and Roger Guiscard capture Saracen capital.
CALABRIA
Palermo
Messina
Rhegium
11 1061-1090, Roger Guiscard takes Sicily from Saracens and becomes Count of Sicily (1072). His son Roger is crowned King of Sicily 1130. In 1146, his capture of Tripoli initiates a Norman colony in Africa.
Castrogiovanni
SICILY
Catania
Girgenti
1090
IONIAN
SEA
Syracuse
10 1086, surrender of Syracuse to Roger Guiscard.
12 1090, Malta is taken by Roger Guiscard.
KEY
First Norman territories, with dates.
Territory captured from Lombards, with dates.
Territory captured from Eastern Roman Empire, with dates.
Territory captured from Saracens, with dates.
Important battles, with dates.
The first Norman stronghold was established at Aversa in 1027, and in later years, Norman influence spread across Southern Italy and Sicily. Robert and Roger Guiscard were the most prominent Norman leaders at this period, and were engaged in wars and battles with the Moslems and Byzantines. Robert's son Bohemund and other Normans took part in the Crusades.
© Arthur Banks 1972

THE GROWTH OF THE FRENCH MONARCHY 987–1328

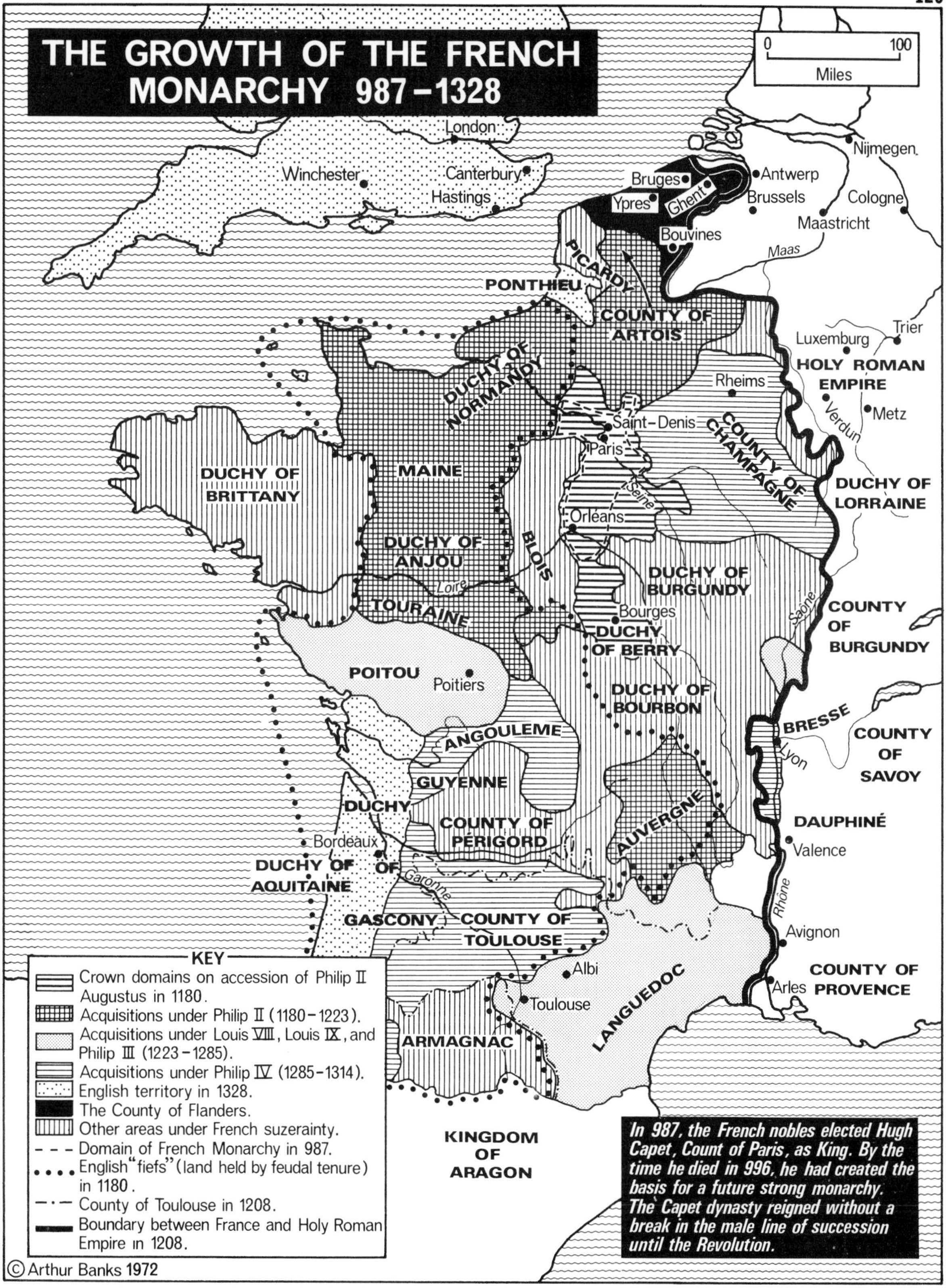

In 987, the French nobles elected Hugh Capet, Count of Paris, as King. By the time he died in 996, he had created the basis for a future strong monarchy. The Capet dynasty reigned without a break in the male line of succession until the Revolution.

THE EARLY CRUSADES 1096 - 1192

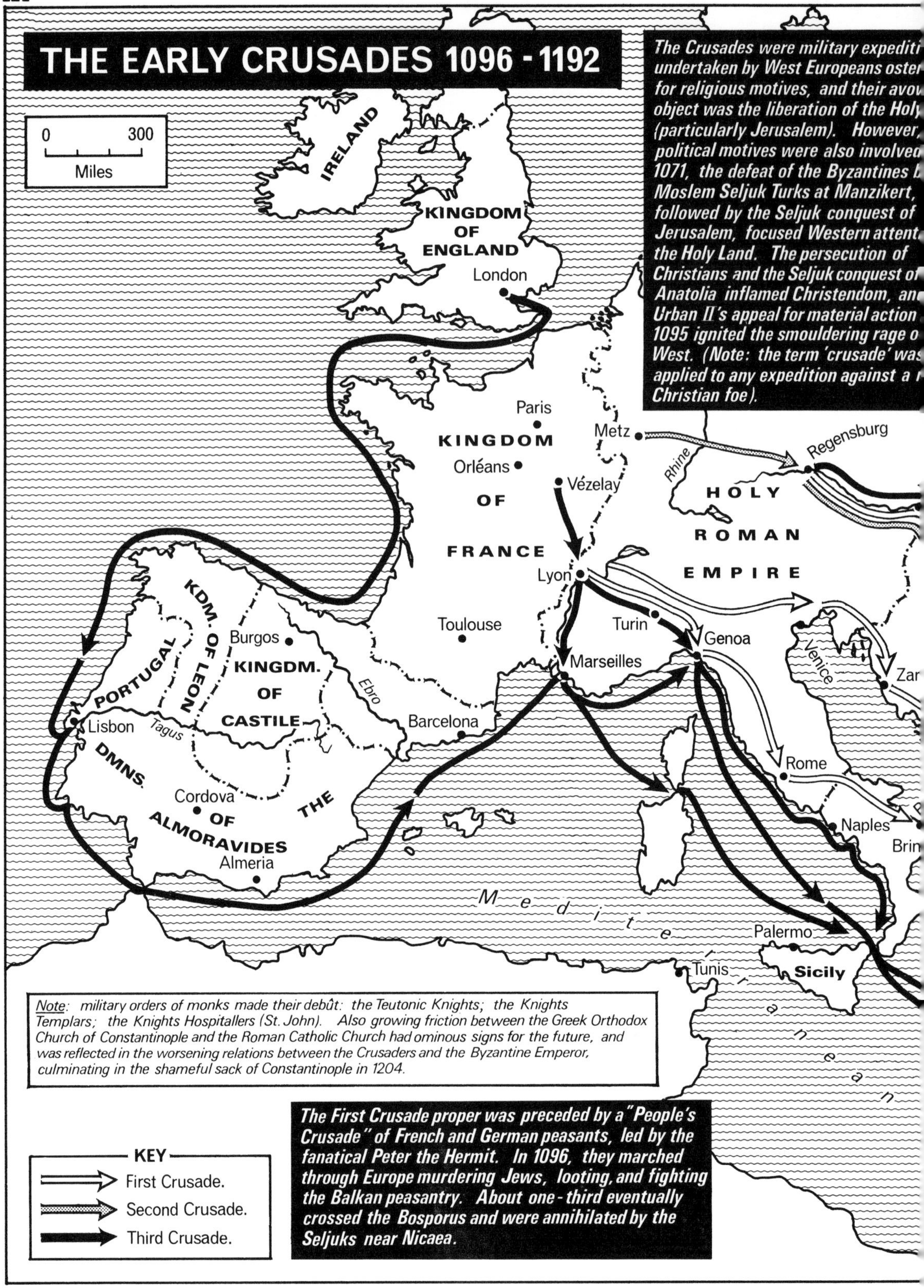

The Crusades were military expediti
undertaken by West Europeans oste
for religious motives, and their avo
object was the liberation of the Hol
(particularly Jerusalem). However,
political motives were also involve
1071, the defeat of the Byzantines b
Moslem Seljuk Turks at Manzikert,
followed by the Seljuk conquest of
Jerusalem, focused Western attent
the Holy Land. The persecution of
Christians and the Seljuk conquest o
Anatolia inflamed Christendom, an
Urban II's appeal for material action
1095 ignited the smouldering rage o
West. (Note: the term 'crusade' was
applied to any expedition against a r
Christian foe).

Note: military orders of monks made their debût: the Teutonic Knights; the Knights Templars; the Knights Hospitallers (St. John). Also growing friction between the Greek Orthodox Church of Constantinople and the Roman Catholic Church had ominous signs for the future, and was reflected in the worsening relations between the Crusaders and the Byzantine Emperor, culminating in the shameful sack of Constantinople in 1204.

The First Crusade proper was preceded by a "People's Crusade" of French and German peasants, led by the fanatical Peter the Hermit. In 1096, they marched through Europe murdering Jews, looting, and fighting the Balkan peasantry. About one-third eventually crossed the Bosporus and were annihilated by the Seljuks near Nicaea.

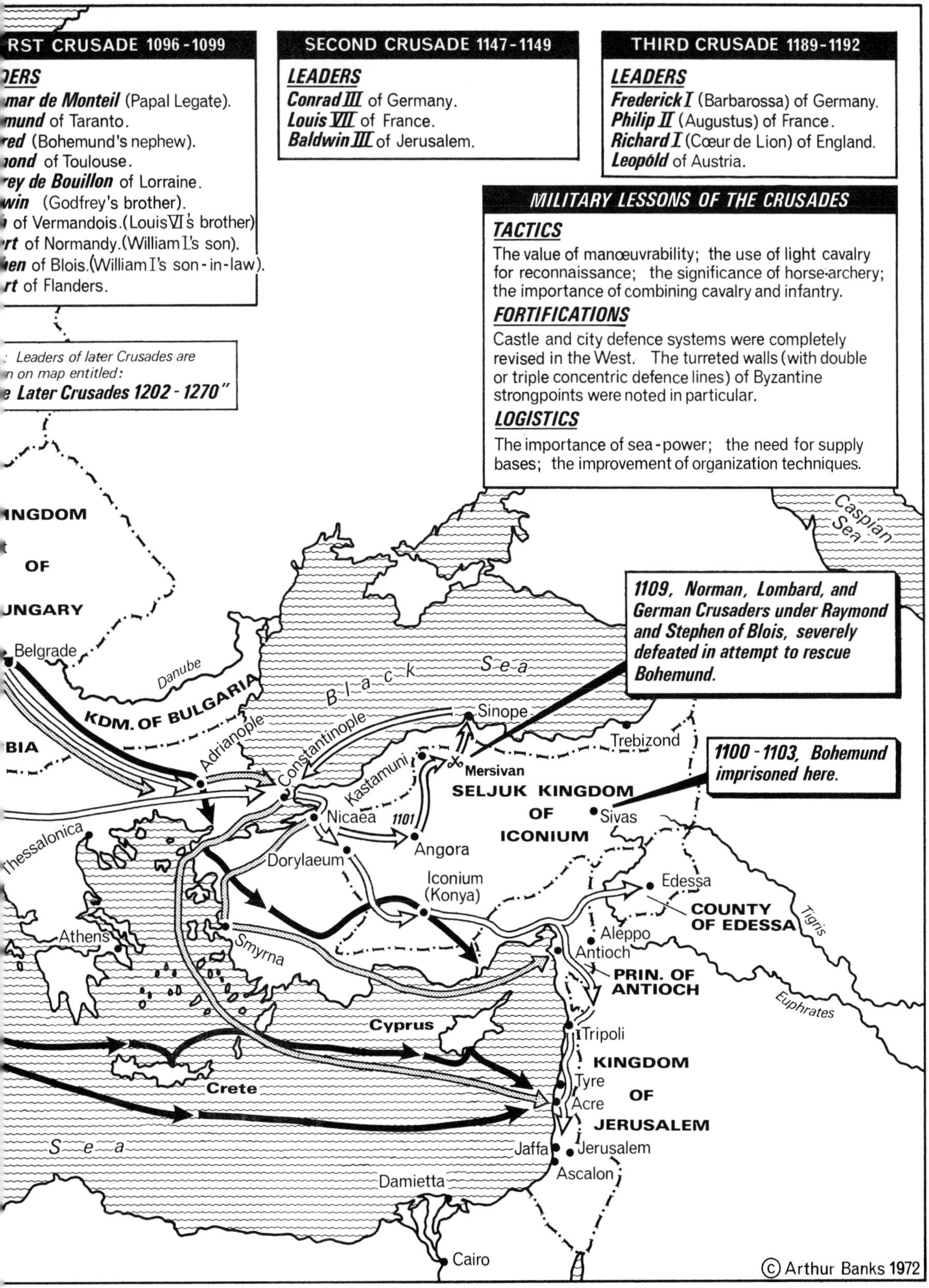
RST CRUSADE 1096-1099
)ERS
mar de Monteil (Papal Legate).
mund of Taranto.
red (Bohemund's nephew).
nond of Toulouse.
rey de Bouillon of Lorraine.
win (Godfrey's brother).
of Vermandois. (Louis VI's brother)
rt of Normandy. (William I's son).
en of Blois. (William I's son-in-law).
rt of Flanders.
SECOND CRUSADE 1147-1149
LEADERS
Conrad III of Germany.
Louis VII of France.
Baldwin III of Jerusalem.
THIRD CRUSADE 1189-1192
LEADERS
Frederick I (Barbarossa) of Germany.
Philip II (Augustus) of France.
Richard I (Cœur de Lion) of England.
Leopóld of Austria.
MILITARY LESSONS OF THE CRUSADES
TACTICS
The value of manœuvrability; the use of light cavalry for reconnaissance; the significance of horse-archery; the importance of combining cavalry and infantry.
FORTIFICATIONS
Castle and city defence systems were completely revised in the West. The turreted walls (with double or triple concentric defence lines) of Byzantine strongpoints were noted in particular.
LOGISTICS
The importance of sea-power; the need for supply bases; the improvement of organization techniques.
: Leaders of later Crusades are
n on map entitled:
e Later Crusades 1202 - 1270"
INGDOM
OF
JNGARY
Belgrade
Danube
KDM. OF BULGARIA
BIA
Black Sea
Caspian Sea
1109, Norman, Lombard, and German Crusaders under Raymond and Stephen of Blois, severely defeated in attempt to rescue Bohemund.
1100 - 1103, Bohemund imprisoned here.
Sinope
Trebizond
Mersivan
Adrianople
Constantinople
Kastamuni
SELJUK KINGDOM OF ICONIUM
Sivas
Thessalonica
Nicaea
1101
Angora
Dorylaeum
Iconium (Konya)
Edessa
COUNTY OF EDESSA
Tigris
Athens
Smyrna
Aleppo
Antioch
PRIN. OF ANTIOCH
Euphrates
Cyprus
Tripoli
KINGDOM OF JERUSALEM
Tyre
Acre
Crete
Sea
Jaffa
Jerusalem
Ascalon
Damietta
Cairo
© Arthur Banks 1972

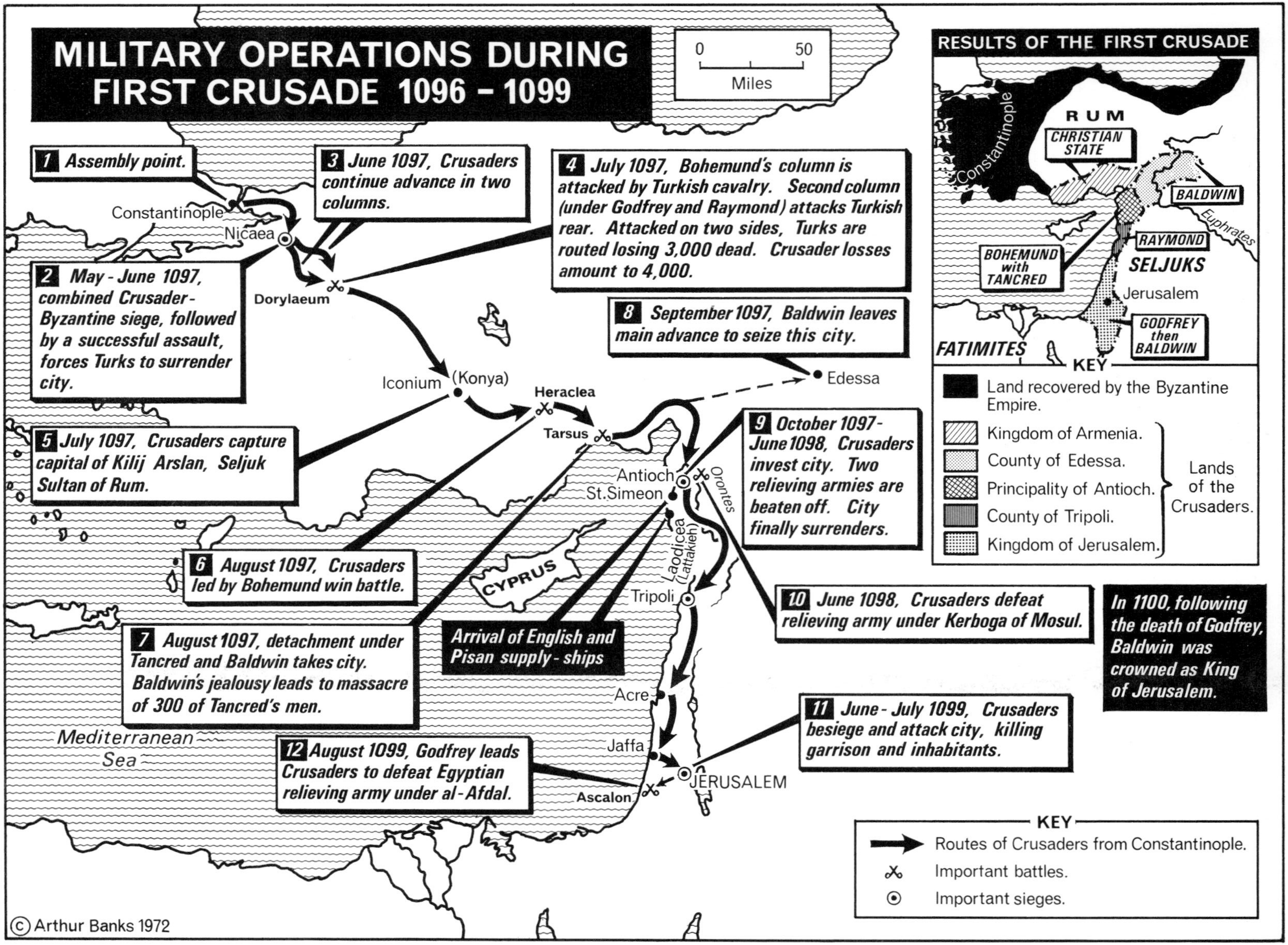
MILITARY OPERATIONS DURING FIRST CRUSADE 1096 – 1099
0 50
Miles
1 Assembly point.
Constantinople
Nicaea
2 May - June 1097, combined Crusader-Byzantine siege, followed by a successful assault, forces Turks to surrender city.
3 June 1097, Crusaders continue advance in two columns.
Dorylaeum
4 July 1097, Bohemund's column is attacked by Turkish cavalry. Second column (under Godfrey and Raymond) attacks Turkish rear. Attacked on two sides, Turks are routed losing 3,000 dead. Crusader losses amount to 4,000.
8 September 1097, Baldwin leaves main advance to seize this city.
Edessa
Iconium
(Konya)
Heraclea
Tarsus
5 July 1097, Crusaders capture capital of Kilij Arslan, Seljuk Sultan of Rum.
Antioch
St.Simeon
Orontes
9 October 1097-June 1098, Crusaders invest city. Two relieving armies are beaten off. City finally surrenders.
Laodicea
(Lattakieh)
CYPRUS
6 August 1097, Crusaders led by Bohemund win battle.
Tripoli
10 June 1098, Crusaders defeat relieving army under Kerboga of Mosul.
In 1100, following the death of Godfrey, Baldwin was crowned as King of Jerusalem.
7 August 1097, detachment under Tancred and Baldwin takes city. Baldwin's jealousy leads to massacre of 300 of Tancred's men.
Arrival of English and Pisan supply-ships
Acre
11 June - July 1099, Crusaders besiege and attack city, killing garrison and inhabitants.
Mediterranean Sea
12 August 1099, Godfrey leads Crusaders to defeat Egyptian relieving army under al-Afdal.
Jaffa
JERUSALEM
Ascalon
KEY
Routes of Crusaders from Constantinople.
Important battles.
Important sieges.
© Arthur Banks 1972
RESULTS OF THE FIRST CRUSADE
Constantinople
RUM
CHRISTIAN STATE
BALDWIN
Euphrates
RAYMOND
BOHEMUND with TANCRED
SELJUKS
Jerusalem
GODFREY then BALDWIN
FATIMITES
KEY
Land recovered by the Byzantine Empire.
Kingdom of Armenia.
County of Edessa.
Principality of Antioch.
County of Tripoli.
Kingdom of Jerusalem.
Lands of the Crusaders.

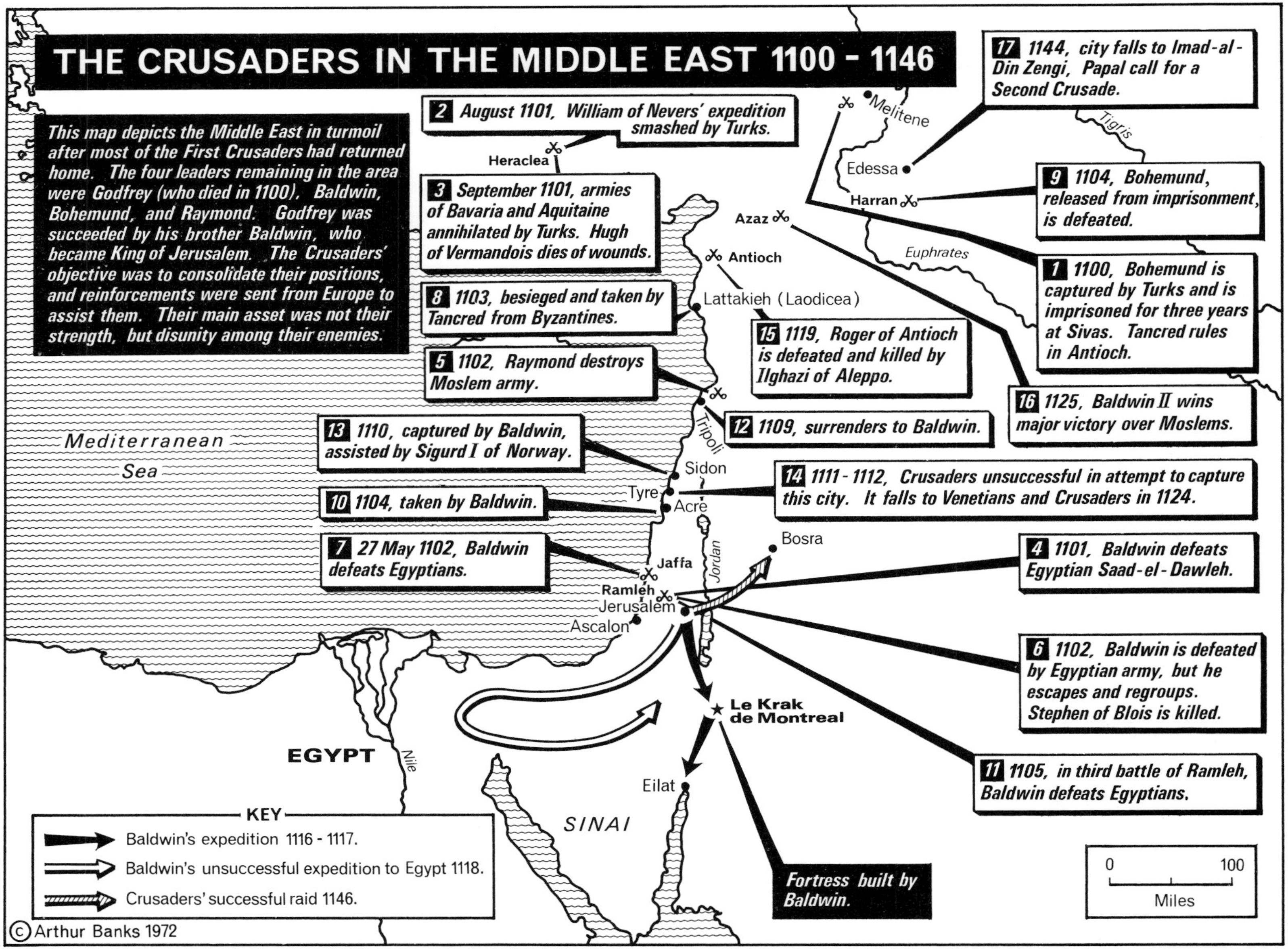
THE CRUSADERS IN THE MIDDLE EAST 1100 - 1146
This map depicts the Middle East in turmoil after most of the First Crusaders had returned home. The four leaders remaining in the area were Godfrey (who died in 1100), Baldwin, Bohemund, and Raymond. Godfrey was succeeded by his brother Baldwin, who became King of Jerusalem. The Crusaders' objective was to consolidate their positions, and reinforcements were sent from Europe to assist them. Their main asset was not their strength, but disunity among their enemies.
2 August 1101, William of Nevers' expedition smashed by Turks.
3 September 1101, armies of Bavaria and Aquitaine annihilated by Turks. Hugh of Vermandois dies of wounds.
8 1103, besieged and taken by Tancred from Byzantines.
5 1102, Raymond destroys Moslem army.
13 1110, captured by Baldwin, assisted by Sigurd I of Norway.
10 1104, taken by Baldwin.
7 27 May 1102, Baldwin defeats Egyptians.
17 1144, city falls to Imad-al-Din Zengi, Papal call for a Second Crusade.
9 1104, Bohemund, released from imprisonment, is defeated.
1 1100, Bohemund is captured by Turks and is imprisoned for three years at Sivas. Tancred rules in Antioch.
15 1119, Roger of Antioch is defeated and killed by Ilghazi of Aleppo.
16 1125, Baldwin II wins major victory over Moslems.
12 1109, surrenders to Baldwin.
14 1111 - 1112, Crusaders unsuccessful in attempt to capture this city. It falls to Venetians and Crusaders in 1124.
4 1101, Baldwin defeats Egyptian Saad-el-Dawleh.
6 1102, Baldwin is defeated by Egyptian army, but he escapes and regroups. Stephen of Blois is killed.
11 1105, in third battle of Ramleh, Baldwin defeats Egyptians.
Fortress built by Baldwin.
Heraclea
Melitene
Edessa
Harran
Tigris
Euphrates
Azaz
Antioch
Lattakieh (Laodicea)
Tripoli
Sidon
Tyre
Acre
Jordan
Bosra
Jaffa
Ramleh
Jerusalem
Ascalon
Le Krak de Montreal
Eilat
Mediterranean Sea
EGYPT
Nile
SINAI
KEY
Baldwin's expedition 1116 - 1117.
Baldwin's unsuccessful expedition to Egypt 1118.
Crusaders' successful raid 1146.
0 100 Miles
© Arthur Banks 1972

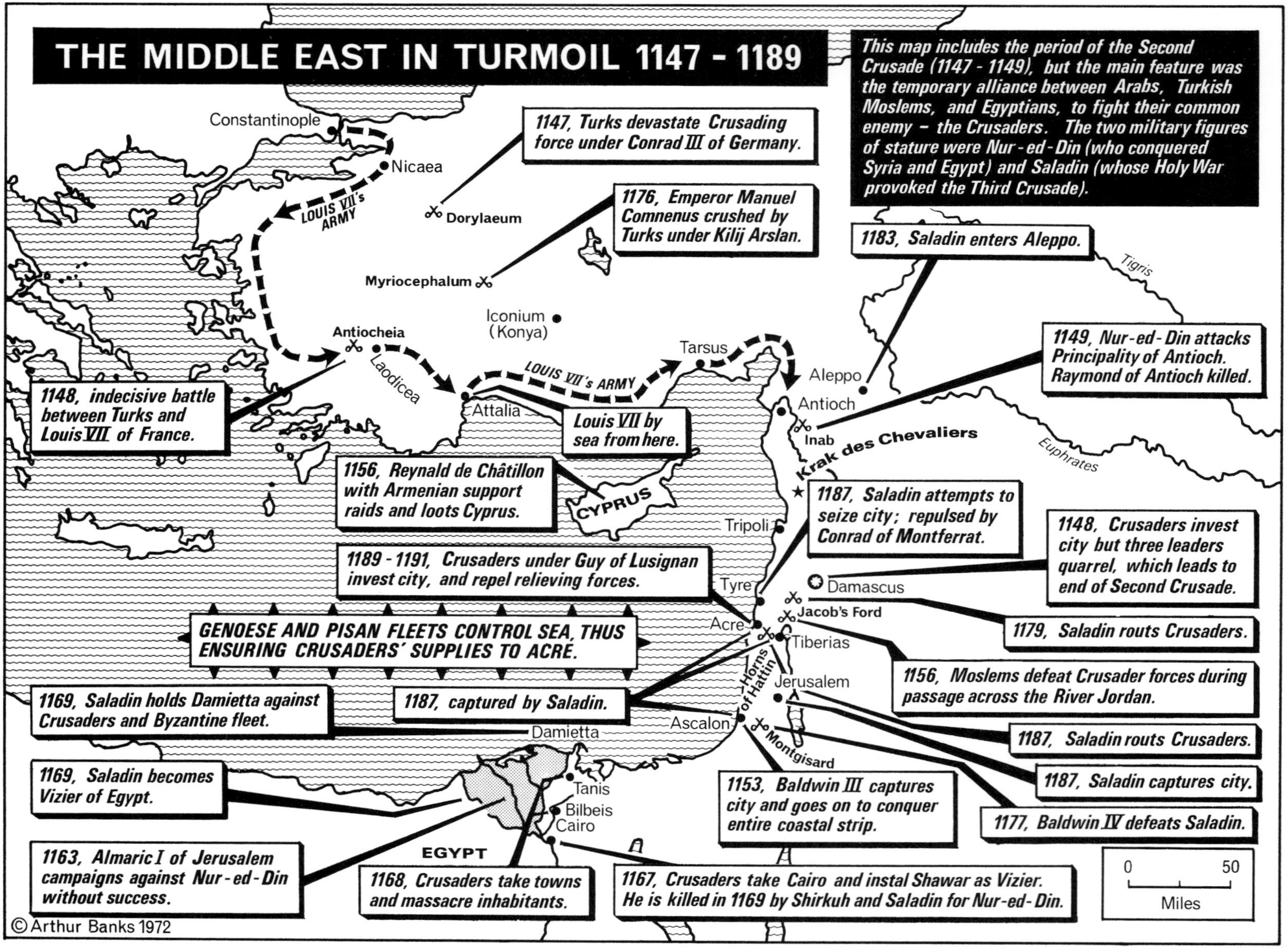
THE MIDDLE EAST IN TURMOIL 1147 - 1189
This map includes the period of the Second Crusade (1147 - 1149), but the main feature was the temporary alliance between Arabs, Turkish Moslems, and Egyptians, to fight their common enemy – the Crusaders. The two military figures of stature were Nur-ed-Din (who conquered Syria and Egypt) and Saladin (whose Holy War provoked the Third Crusade).
Constantinople
Nicaea
LOUIS VII's ARMY
1147, Turks devastate Crusading force under Conrad III of Germany.
Dorylaeum
1176, Emperor Manuel Comnenus crushed by Turks under Kilij Arslan.
Myriocephalum
Iconium (Konya)
Antiocheia
Laodicea
Attalia
LOUIS VII's ARMY
Tarsus
Louis VII by sea from here.
1183, Saladin enters Aleppo.
Tigris
Aleppo
Antioch
Inab
1149, Nur-ed-Din attacks Principality of Antioch. Raymond of Antioch killed.
Krak des Chevaliers
Euphrates
1148, indecisive battle between Turks and Louis VII of France.
1156, Reynald de Châtillon with Armenian support raids and loots Cyprus.
CYPRUS
1187, Saladin attempts to seize city; repulsed by Conrad of Montferrat.
Tripoli
1148, Crusaders invest city but three leaders quarrel, which leads to end of Second Crusade.
1189 - 1191, Crusaders under Guy of Lusignan invest city, and repel relieving forces.
Tyre
Damascus
Jacob's Ford
Acre
Tiberias
GENOESE AND PISAN FLEETS CONTROL SEA, THUS ENSURING CRUSADERS' SUPPLIES TO ACRE.
1179, Saladin routs Crusaders.
1156, Moslems defeat Crusader forces during passage across the River Jordan.
Horns of Hattin
Jerusalem
1169, Saladin holds Damietta against Crusaders and Byzantine fleet.
1187, captured by Saladin.
Damietta
Ascalon
Montgisard
1187, Saladin routs Crusaders.
1169, Saladin becomes Vizier of Egypt.
Tanis
Bilbeis
Cairo
1153, Baldwin III captures city and goes on to conquer entire coastal strip.
1187, Saladin captures city.
1177, Baldwin IV defeats Saladin.
EGYPT
1163, Almaric I of Jerusalem campaigns against Nur-ed-Din without success.
1168, Crusaders take towns and massacre inhabitants.
1167, Crusaders take Cairo and instal Shawar as Vizier. He is killed in 1169 by Shirkuh and Saladin for Nur-ed-Din.
0 50
Miles
© Arthur Banks 1972

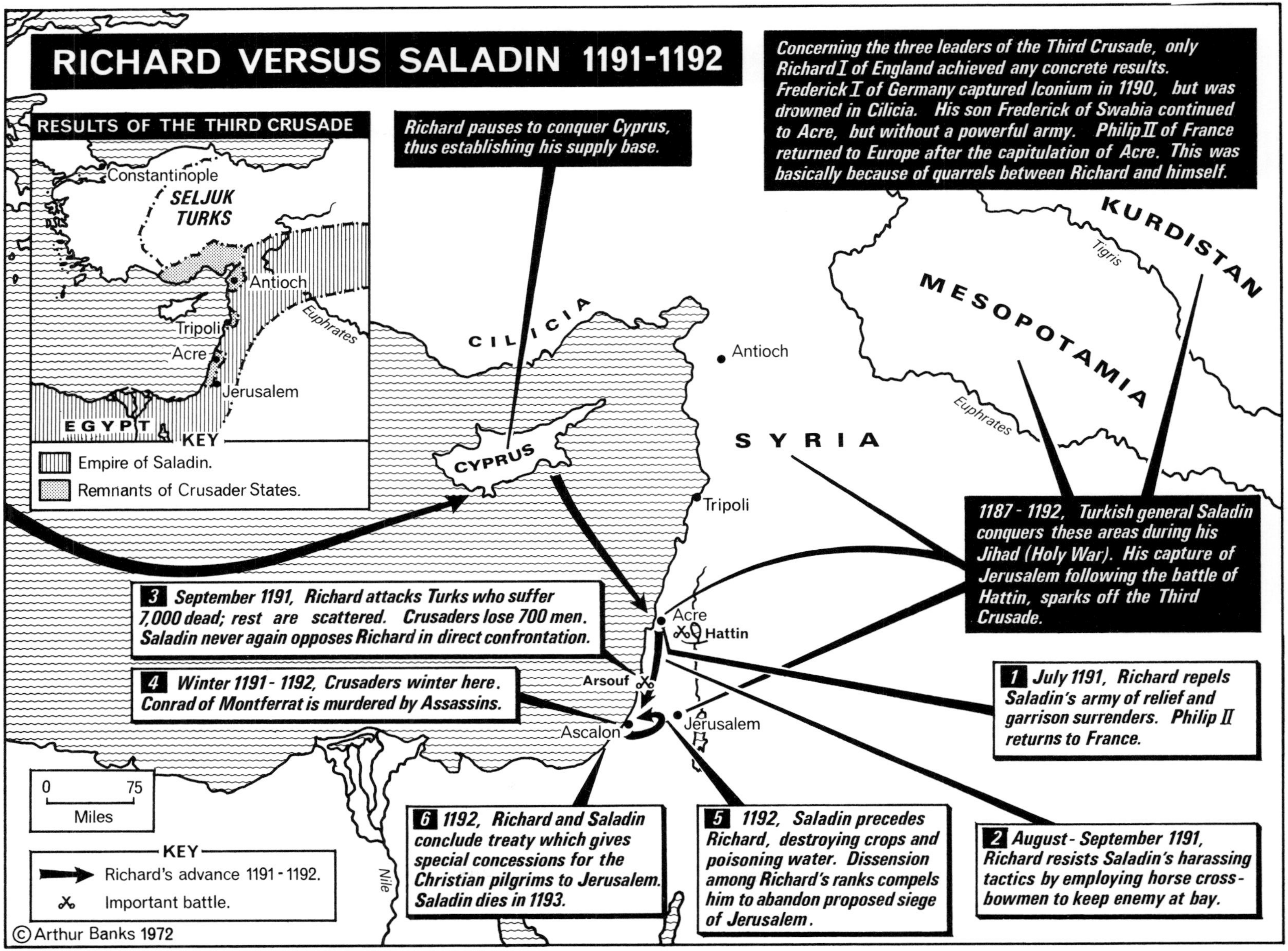

RICHARD VERSUS SALADIN 1191-1192
RESULTS OF THE THIRD CRUSADE
Constantinople
SELJUK TURKS
Antioch
Tripoli
Acre
Jerusalem
Euphrates
EGYPT
KEY
Empire of Saladin.
Remnants of Crusader States.
Richard pauses to conquer Cyprus, thus establishing his supply base.
Concerning the three leaders of the Third Crusade, only Richard I of England achieved any concrete results. Frederick I of Germany captured Iconium in 1190, but was drowned in Cilicia. His son Frederick of Swabia continued to Acre, but without a powerful army. Philip II of France returned to Europe after the capitulation of Acre. This was basically because of quarrels between Richard and himself.
KURDISTAN
Tigris
MESOPOTAMIA
Euphrates
CILICIA
Antioch
SYRIA
CYPRUS
Tripoli
1187 - 1192, Turkish general Saladin conquers these areas during his Jihad (Holy War). His capture of Jerusalem following the battle of Hattin, sparks off the Third Crusade.
3 September 1191, Richard attacks Turks who suffer 7,000 dead; rest are scattered. Crusaders lose 700 men. Saladin never again opposes Richard in direct confrontation.
Acre
Hattin
Arsouf
4 Winter 1191 - 1192, Crusaders winter here. Conrad of Montferrat is murdered by Assassins.
Ascalon
Jerusalem
1 July 1191, Richard repels Saladin's army of relief and garrison surrenders. Philip II returns to France.
0 75
Miles
KEY
Richard's advance 1191 - 1192.
Important battle.
Nile
6 1192, Richard and Saladin conclude treaty which gives special concessions for the Christian pilgrims to Jerusalem. Saladin dies in 1193.
5 1192, Saladin precedes Richard, destroying crops and poisoning water. Dissension among Richard's ranks compels him to abandon proposed siege of Jerusalem.
2 August - September 1191, Richard resists Saladin's harassing tactics by employing horse cross-bowmen to keep enemy at bay.
©Arthur Banks 1972

FOURTH CRUSADE 1202-1204

LEADERS
Boniface of Montferrat.
Louis of Blois.
Baldwin of Flanders.
Henry (brother of Baldwin).
Henry Dandolo, Doge of Venice.
Simon de Montfort.

FIFTH CRUSADE 1218-1221

LEADERS
Frederick II of Germany. *(who never participated)*
John of Brienne, King of Jerusalem.
Hugh of Cyprus.
Cardinal Pelagius.
Hermann von Salza.
Louis of Bavaria.
Andrew of Hungary.
Leopold of Austria.

CHILDREN'S CRUSADES 1212

There were two crusades by children. The first was led by a French shepherd boy named Stephen; the second by a German boy named Nicholas. Both crusades were marked by intense suffering.

SIXTH CRUSADE 1228 - 1229

LEADERS
Frederick II of Germany.
Hermann von Salza.

SEVENTH CRUSADE 1248 - 1254

LEADERS
Louis IX of France.
Robert of Artois } brothers of Louis IX
Charles of Anjou }
William, Earl of Salisbury.

EIGHTH CRUSADE 1270

LEADERS
Louis IX of France, (died at Tunis).
Charles of Anjou.

Note: Prince Edward of England arrived in the Holy Land (1271) to find that the Crusade had ended. After a year in Acre he made a truce and returned to England.

THE LATER CRUSADES 1202 - 1270

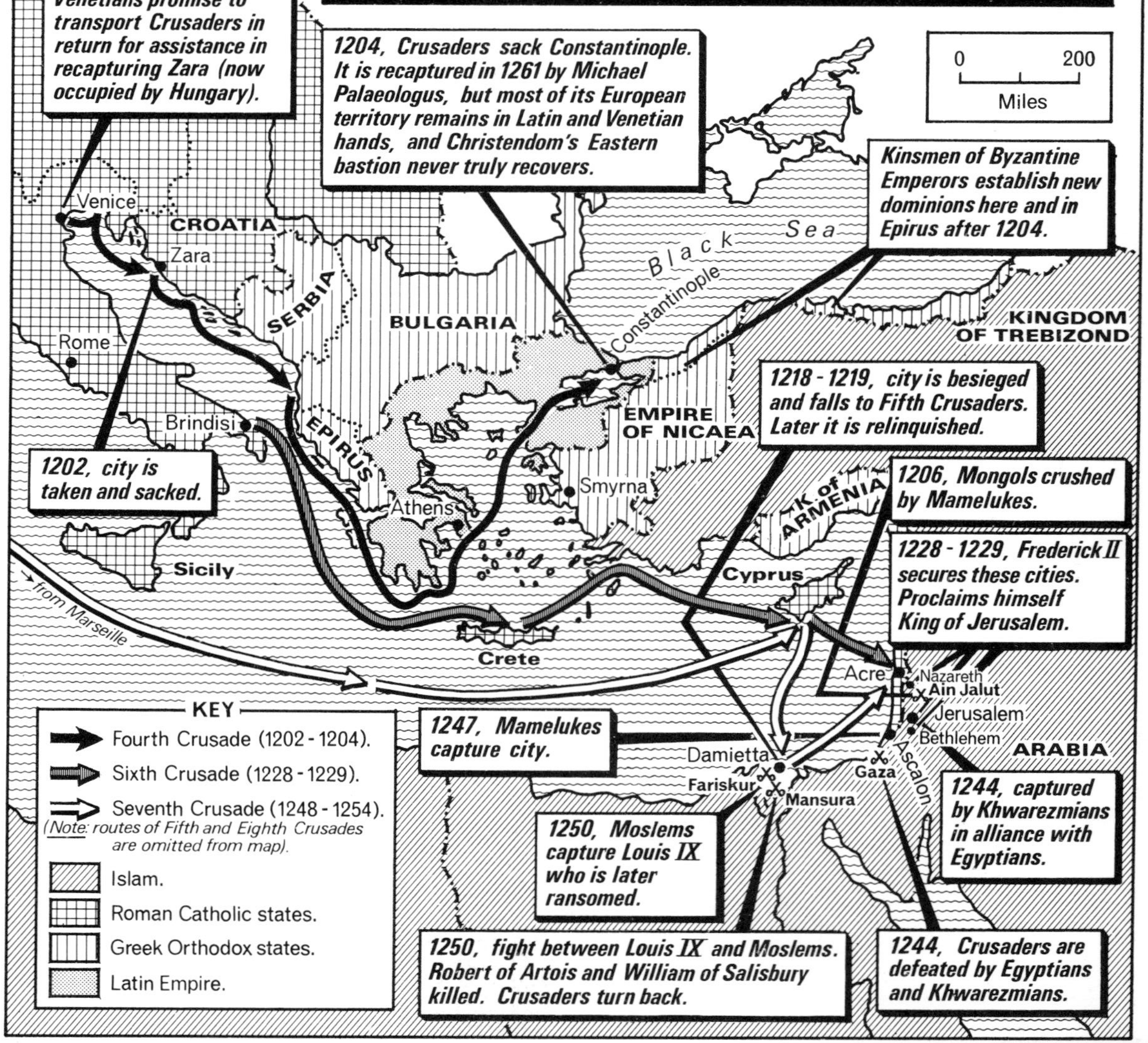
0 200 Miles
1202, assembly point for Fourth Crusade. Venetians promise to transport Crusaders in return for assistance in recapturing Zara (now occupied by Hungary).
1204, Crusaders sack Constantinople. It is recaptured in 1261 by Michael Palaeologus, but most of its European territory remains in Latin and Venetian hands, and Christendom's Eastern bastion never truly recovers.
Kinsmen of Byzantine Emperors establish new dominions here and in Epirus after 1204.
1218 - 1219, city is besieged and falls to Fifth Crusaders. Later it is relinquished.
1206, Mongols crushed by Mamelukes.
1228 - 1229, Frederick II secures these cities. Proclaims himself King of Jerusalem.
1244, captured by Khwarezmians in alliance with Egyptians.
1244, Crusaders are defeated by Egyptians and Khwarezmians.
1250, fight between Louis IX and Moslems. Robert of Artois and William of Salisbury killed. Crusaders turn back.
1250, Moslems capture Louis IX who is later ransomed.
1247, Mamelukes capture city.
1202, city is taken and sacked.
Venice
Zara
CROATIA
SERBIA
BULGARIA
Rome
Brindisi
EPIRUS
Athens
Sicily
Crete
Smyrna
Constantinople
Black Sea
EMPIRE OF NICAEA
KINGDOM OF TREBIZOND
K. of ARMENIA
Cyprus
Acre
Nazareth
Ain Jalut
Jerusalem
Bethlehem
Ascalon
Gaza
ARABIA
Damietta
Fariskur
Mansura
from Marseille
KEY
Fourth Crusade (1202 - 1204).
Sixth Crusade (1228 - 1229).
Seventh Crusade (1248 - 1254).
(Note: routes of Fifth and Eighth Crusades are omitted from map).
Islam.
Roman Catholic states.
Greek Orthodox states.
Latin Empire.

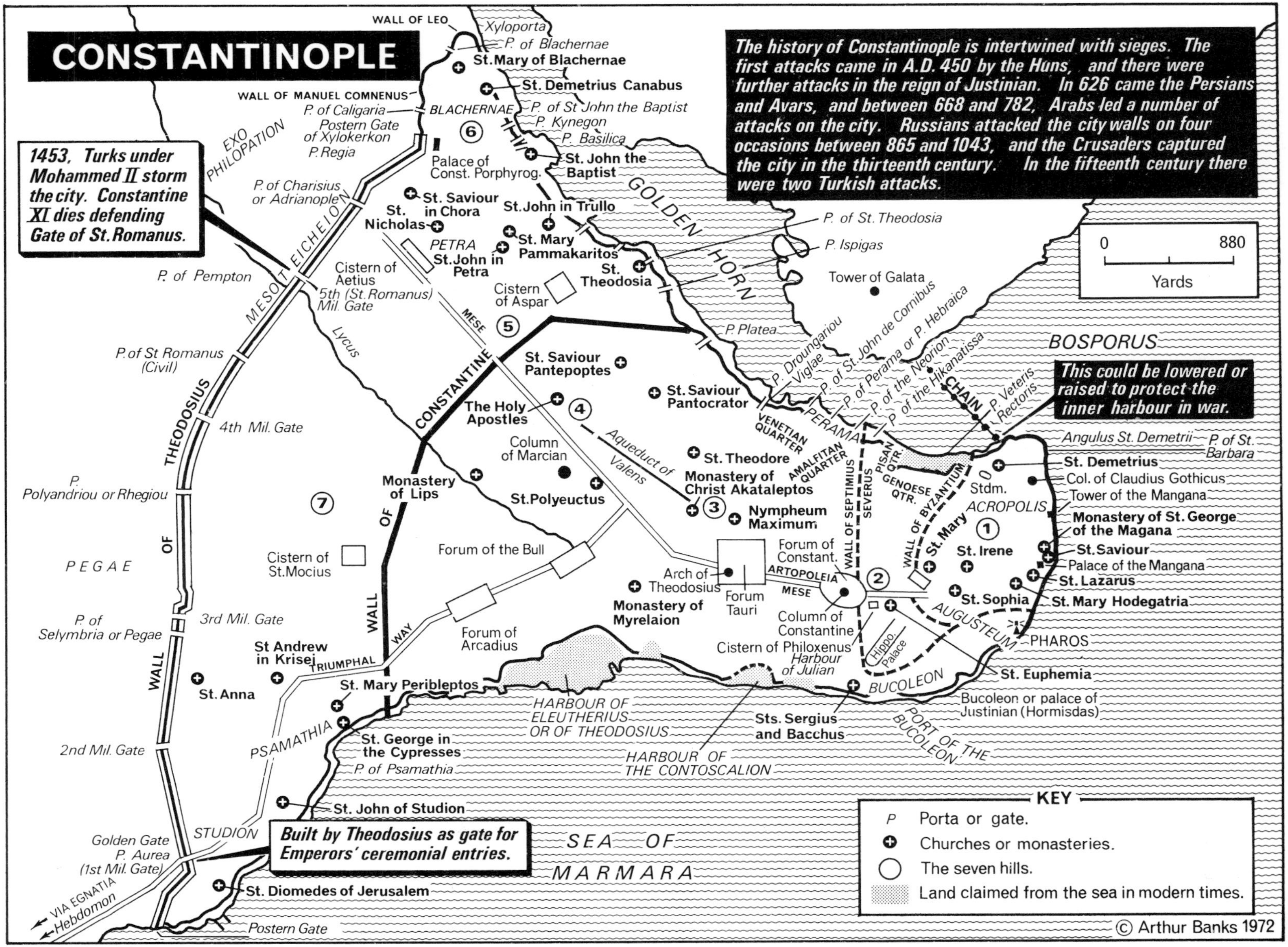
CONSTANTINOPLE
The history of Constantinople is intertwined with sieges. The first attacks came in A.D. 450 by the Huns, and there were further attacks in the reign of Justinian. In 626 came the Persians and Avars, and between 668 and 782, Arabs led a number of attacks on the city. Russians attacked the city walls on four occasions between 865 and 1043, and the Crusaders captured the city in the thirteenth century. In the fifteenth century there were two Turkish attacks.
1453, Turks under Mohammed II storm the city. Constantine XI dies defending Gate of St. Romanus.
This could be lowered or raised to protect the inner harbour in war.
Built by Theodosius as gate for Emperors' ceremonial entries.
0
880
Yards
WALL OF LEO
Xyloporta
P. of Blachernae
St. Mary of Blachernae
St. Demetrius Canabus
WALL OF MANUEL COMNENUS
P. of Caligaria
BLACHERNAE
P. of St John the Baptist
P. Kynegon
P. Basilica
Postern Gate of Xylokerkon
P. Regia
EXO PHILOPATION
Palace of Const. Porphyrog.
St. John the Baptist
GOLDEN HORN
P. of Charisius or Adrianople
St. Saviour in Chora
St. Nicholas
St. John in Trullo
PETRA
St. John in Petra
St. Mary Pammakaritos
St. Theodosia
P. of St. Theodosia
P. Ispigas
Tower of Galata
P. of Pempton
MESOTEICHEION
Cistern of Aetius
5th (St. Romanus) Mil. Gate
Cistern of Aspar
MESE
Lycus
P. Platea
BOSPORUS
P. of St Romanus (Civil)
THEODOSIUS
St. Saviour Pantepoptes
St. Saviour Pantocrator
P. Droungariou
Viglae
P. of St. John de Cornibus
P. of Perama or P. Hebraica
P. of the Neorion
P. of the Hikanatissa
CHAIN
P. Veteris Rectoris
4th Mil. Gate
CONSTANTINE
The Holy Apostles
VENETIAN QUARTER
PERAMA
Angulus St. Demetrii
P. of St. Barbara
Column of Marcian
Aqueduct of Valens
St. Theodore
AMALFITAN QUARTER
PISAN QTR.
St. Demetrius
Col. of Claudius Gothicus
P. Polyandriou or Rhegiou
Monastery of Lips
St. Polyeuctus
Monastery of Christ Akataleptos
WALL OF SEPTIMIUS SEVERUS
GENOESE QTR.
WALL OF BYZANTIUM
Stdm.
Tower of the Mangana
ACROPOLIS
Monastery of St. George of the Magana
Nympheum Maximum
St. Mary
St. Irene
St. Saviour
Palace of the Mangana
PEGAE
Cistern of St. Mocius
Forum of the Bull
Forum of Constant.
ARTOPOLEIA
MESE
Arch of Theodosius
Forum Tauri
St. Lazarus
St. Sophia
St. Mary Hodegatria
Monastery of Myrelaion
Column of Constantine
AUGUSTEUM
P. of Selymbria or Pegae
3rd Mil. Gate
WALL
WAY
Forum of Arcadius
Cistern of Philoxenus
Harbour of Julian
Hippo. Palace
PHAROS
St Andrew in Krisei
TRIUMPHAL
St. Euphemia
St. Anna
St. Mary Peribleptos
BUCOLEON
Bucoleon or palace of Justinian (Hormisdas)
HARBOUR OF ELEUTHERIUS OR OF THEODOSIUS
Sts. Sergius and Bacchus
PORT OF THE BUCOLEON
PSAMATHIA
St. George in the Cypresses
2nd Mil. Gate
P. of Psamathia
HARBOUR OF THE CONTOSCALION
St. John of Studion
STUDION
Golden Gate
P. Aurea
(1st Mil. Gate)
SEA OF MARMARA
VIA EGNATIA
Hebdomon
St. Diomedes of Jerusalem
Postern Gate
KEY
P Porta or gate.
Churches or monasteries.
The seven hills.
Land claimed from the sea in modern times.
© Arthur Banks 1972

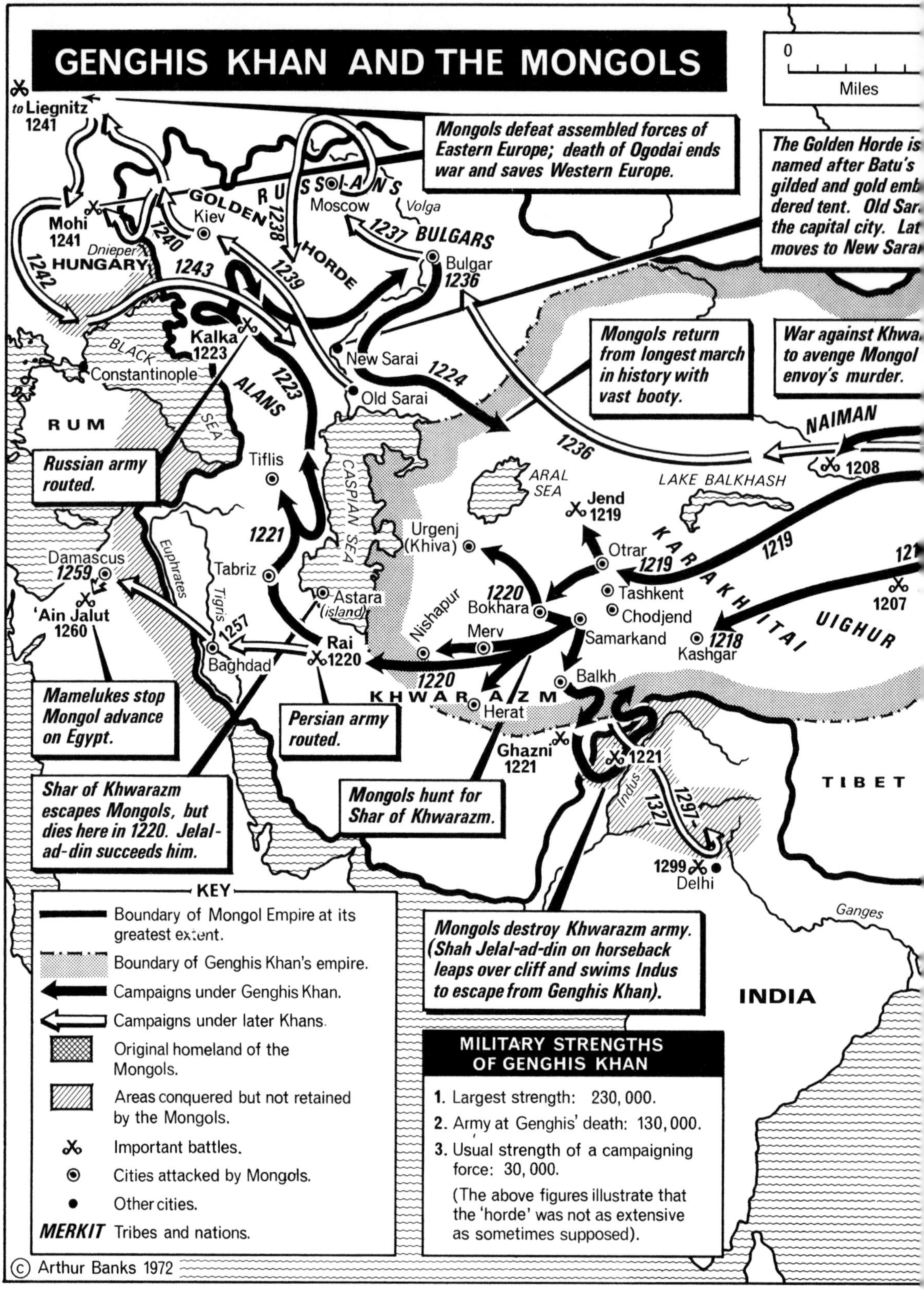
GENGHIS KHAN AND THE MONGOLS
0
Miles
to Liegnitz
1241
Mongols defeat assembled forces of Eastern Europe; death of Ogodai ends war and saves Western Europe.
The Golden Horde is named after Batu's gilded and gold emb dered tent. Old Sar the capital city. Lat moves to New Sara
RUSSIANS
GOLDEN HORDE
Moscow
Volga
1237
BULGARS
Bulgar
1236
Kiev
1238
1239
1240
1243
Mohi
1241
Dnieper
HUNGARY
1242
Kalka
1223
BLACK SEA
Constantinople
New Sarai
Old Sarai
1224
ALANS
1223
RUM
Mongols return from longest march in history with vast booty.
War against Khwa to avenge Mongol envoy's murder.
NAIMAN
1208
1236
LAKE BALKHASH
ARAL SEA
Russian army routed.
Tiflis
CASPIAN SEA
Jend
1219
KARA KHITAI
1219
Otrar
1219
Urgenj (Khiva)
1221
Tabriz
Astara (island)
Damascus
1259
'Ain Jalut
1260
Euphrates
Tigris
1257
Baghdad
Rai
1220
1220
Bokhara
Nishapur
Merv
Samarkand
Tashkent
Chodjend
Kashgar
1218
UIGHUR
1207
1220
Balkh
KHWARAZM
Herat
Ghazni
1221
1221
Mamelukes stop Mongol advance on Egypt.
Persian army routed.
Shar of Khwarazm escapes Mongols, but dies here in 1220. Jelal-ad-din succeeds him.
Mongols hunt for Shar of Khwarazm.
TIBET
Indus
1297-1327
1299
Delhi
Ganges
INDIA
KEY
Boundary of Mongol Empire at its greatest extent.
Boundary of Genghis Khan's empire.
Campaigns under Genghis Khan.
Campaigns under later Khans.
Original homeland of the Mongols.
Areas conquered but not retained by the Mongols.
Important battles.
Cities attacked by Mongols.
Other cities.
MERKIT Tribes and nations.
Mongols destroy Khwarazm army. (Shah Jelal-ad-din on horseback leaps over cliff and swims Indus to escape from Genghis Khan).
MILITARY STRENGTHS OF GENGHIS KHAN
1. Largest strength: 230,000.
2. Army at Genghis' death: 130,000.
3. Usual strength of a campaigning force: 30,000.
(The above figures illustrate that the 'horde' was not as extensive as sometimes supposed).
© Arthur Banks 1972

ghis Khan (1162 - 1227), one of the greatest captains in military history, was the son of a Mongol chieftain whose ily lived in the area south-east of Lake Baikal. As a boy he was known as Temujin, and succeeded his father hief at the age of thirteen. After a number of early struggles to maintain his position, he proclaimed himself ghis Khan in 1206. He went on to conquer a huge area of Asia and Europe, and by the time of his death, an pire had been established from China to the River Dnieper in Russia. Its making, however, cost 18,000,000 lives, the Mongols were savage horse-warriors who massacred and destroyed wherever they rode. The Mongols settled ntually in the area to the north of the Caspian and Black Seas, their domain being the Empire of the Golden Horde.

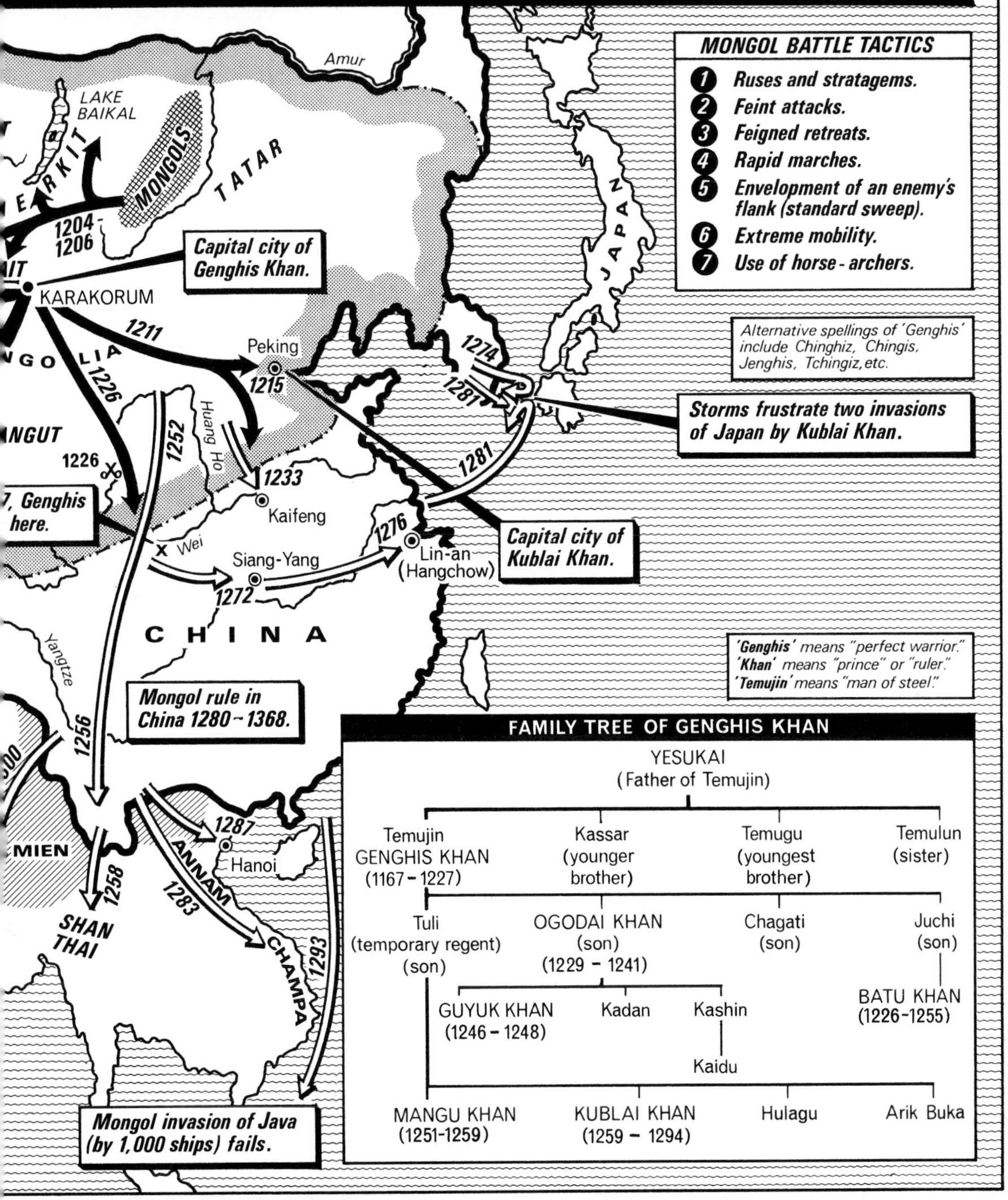
Amur
LAKE BAIKAL
MONGOLS
TATAR
ERKIT
1204-1206
IT
Capital city of Genghis Khan.
KARAKORUM
1211
Peking
1215
NGOLIA
1226
NGUT
1226
1252
Huang Ho
1233
7, Genghis here.
Kaifeng
Wei
Siang-Yang
1272
1276
Lin-an (Hangchow)
Capital city of Kublai Khan.
CHINA
Yangtze
Mongol rule in China 1280-1368.
1256
MIEN
1258
SHAN THAI
1287
Hanoi
ANNAM
1283
CHAMPA
1293
Mongol invasion of Java (by 1,000 ships) fails.
1274
1281
1281
JAPAN
Storms frustrate two invasions of Japan by Kublai Khan.
MONGOL BATTLE TACTICS
1 Ruses and stratagems.
2 Feint attacks.
3 Feigned retreats.
4 Rapid marches.
5 Envelopment of an enemy's flank (standard sweep).
6 Extreme mobility.
7 Use of horse-archers.
Alternative spellings of 'Genghis' include Chinghiz, Chingis, Jenghis, Tchingiz, etc.
'Genghis' means "perfect warrior."
'Khan' means "prince" or "ruler."
'Temujin' means "man of steel."

FAMILY TREE OF GENGHIS KHAN

YESUKAI (Father of Temujin)

- Temujin GENGHIS KHAN (1167 – 1227)
  - Tuli (temporary regent) (son)
    - MANGU KHAN (1251-1259)
    - KUBLAI KHAN (1259 – 1294)
    - Hulagu
    - Arik Buka
  - OGODAI KHAN (son) (1229 – 1241)
    - GUYUK KHAN (1246 – 1248)
    - Kadan
    - Kashin
      - Kaidu
  - Chagati (son)
  - Juchi (son)
    - BATU KHAN (1226-1255)
- Kassar (younger brother)
- Temugu (youngest brother)
- Temulun (sister)

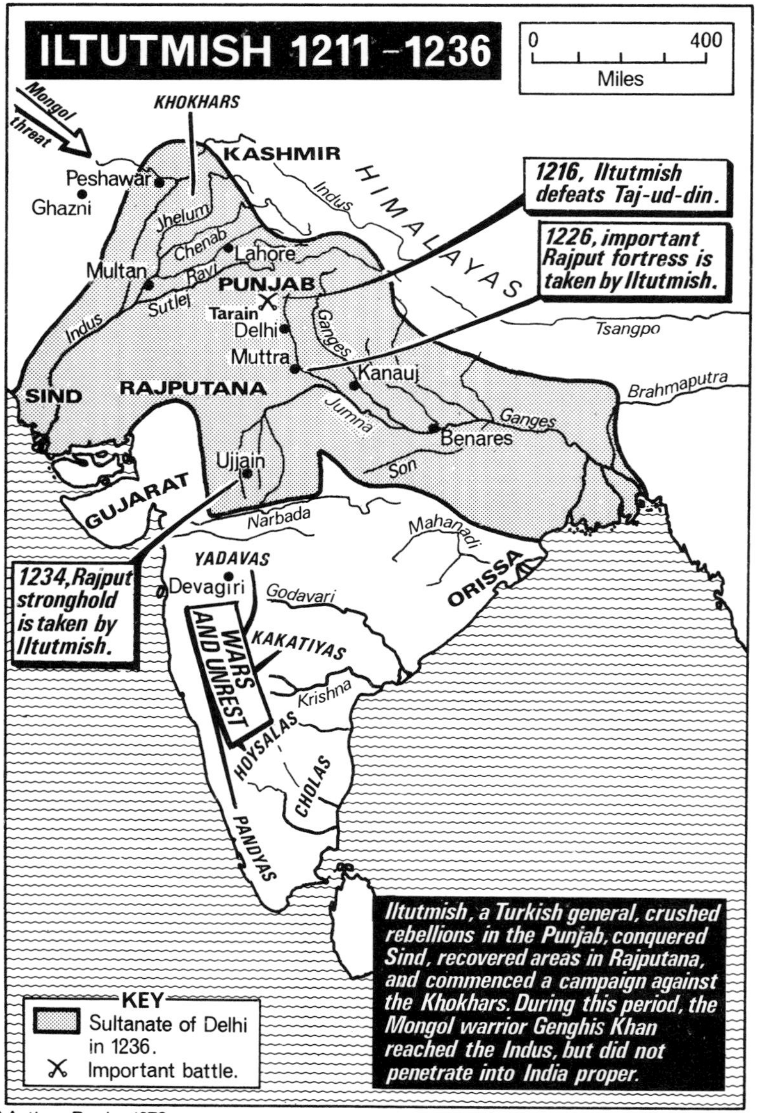
ILTUTMISH 1211–1236
0 400 Miles
Mongol threat
KHOKHARS
KASHMIR
Peshawar
Ghazni
Jhelum
Chenab
Lahore
Multan
Ravi
PUNJAB
Sutlej
Tarain
Delhi
Indus
Muttra
Ganges
Kanauj
SIND
RAJPUTANA
Jumna
Benares
Ganges
Son
Ujjain
GUJARAT
Narbada
Mahanadi
HIMALAYAS
Tsangpo
Brahmaputra
YADAVAS
Devagiri
Godavari
ORISSA
KAKATIYAS
WARS AND UNREST
Krishna
HOYSALAS
CHOLAS
PANDYAS
1216, Iltutmish defeats Taj-ud-din.
1226, important Rajput fortress is taken by Iltutmish.
1234, Rajput stronghold is taken by Iltutmish.
KEY
Sultanate of Delhi in 1236.
Important battle.
Iltutmish, a Turkish general, crushed rebellions in the Punjab, conquered Sind, recovered areas in Rajputana, and commenced a campaign against the Khokhars. During this period, the Mongol warrior Genghis Khan reached the Indus, but did not penetrate into India proper.

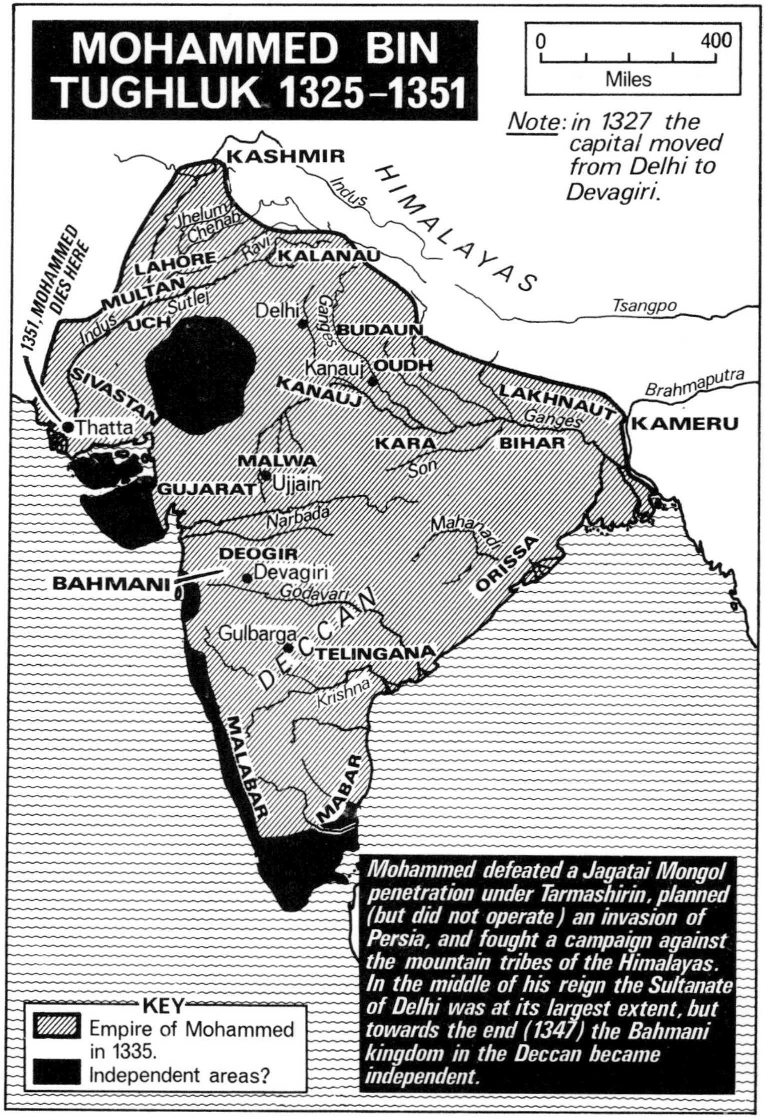
MOHAMMED BIN TUGHLUK 1325–1351
0 400 Miles
Note: in 1327 the capital moved from Delhi to Devagiri.
KASHMIR
HIMALAYAS
Indus
Jhelum
Chenab
Ravi
KALANAU
LAHORE
MULTAN
Sutlej
UCH
Delhi
Ganges
BUDAUN
Tsangpo
1351, MOHAMMED DIES HERE
SIVASTAN
Thatta
Kanauj
OUDH
KANAUJ
LAKHNAUT
Ganges
KAMERU
Brahmaputra
KARA
BIHAR
MALWA
Son
GUJARAT
Ujjain
Narbada
Mahanadi
DEOGIR
Devagiri
BAHMANI
Godavari
ORISSA
DECCAN
Gulbarga
TELINGANA
Krishna
MALABAR
MABAR
KEY
Empire of Mohammed in 1335.
Independent areas?
Mohammed defeated a Jagatai Mongol penetration under Tarmashirin, planned (but did not operate) an invasion of Persia, and fought a campaign against the mountain tribes of the Himalayas. In the middle of his reign the Sultanate of Delhi was at its largest extent, but towards the end (1347) the Bahmani kingdom in the Deccan became independent.

THE IMPORTANCE OF GEOGRAPHY IN THE MILITARY HISTORY OF NORTHERN INDIA

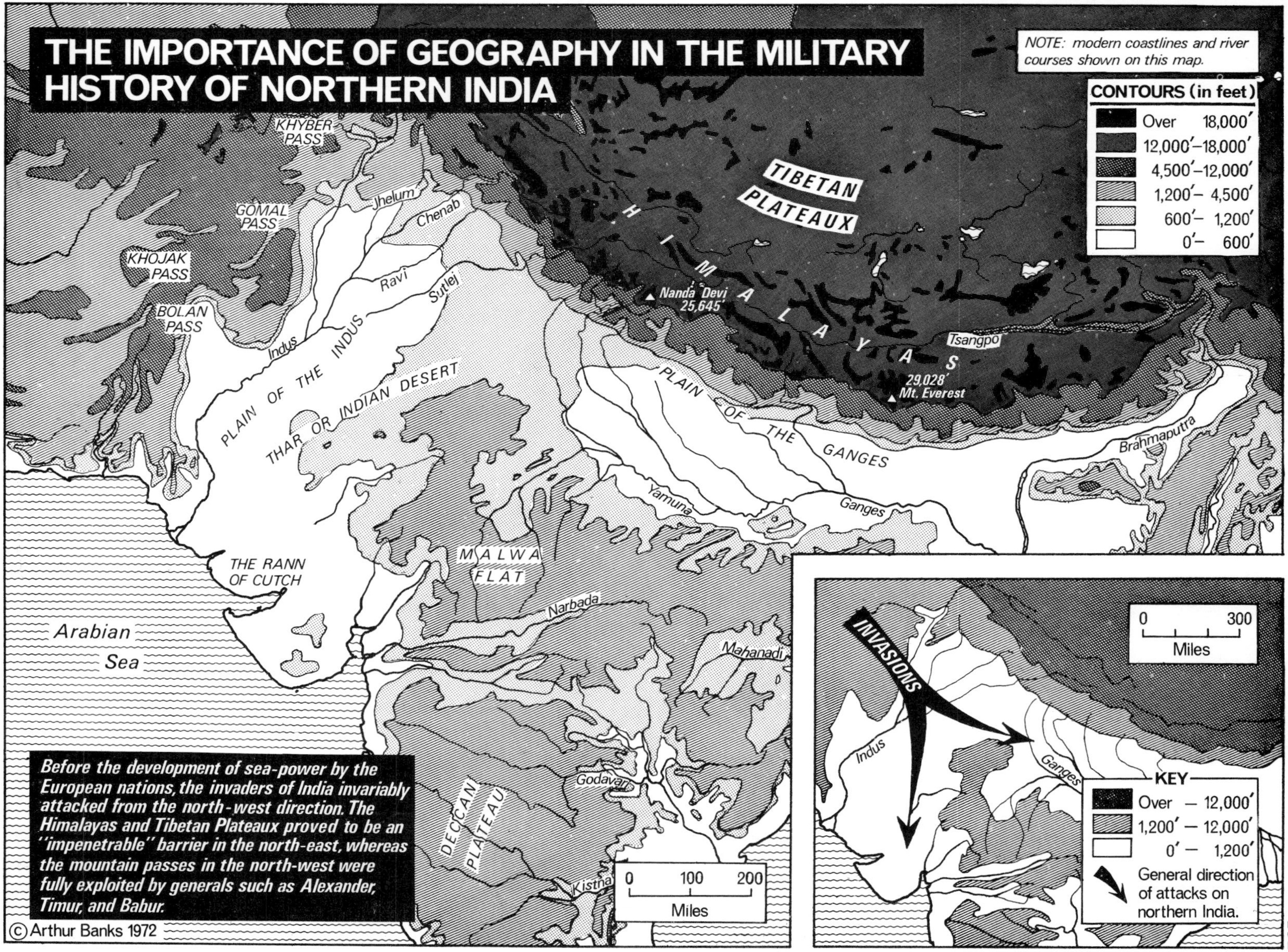

Before the development of sea-power by the European nations, the invaders of India invariably attacked from the north-west direction. The Himalayas and Tibetan Plateaux proved to be an "impenetrable" barrier in the north-east, whereas the mountain passes in the north-west were fully exploited by generals such as Alexander, Timur, and Babur.

THE CAMPAIGNS OF TIMUR (TAMERLANE) 1369 – 1405

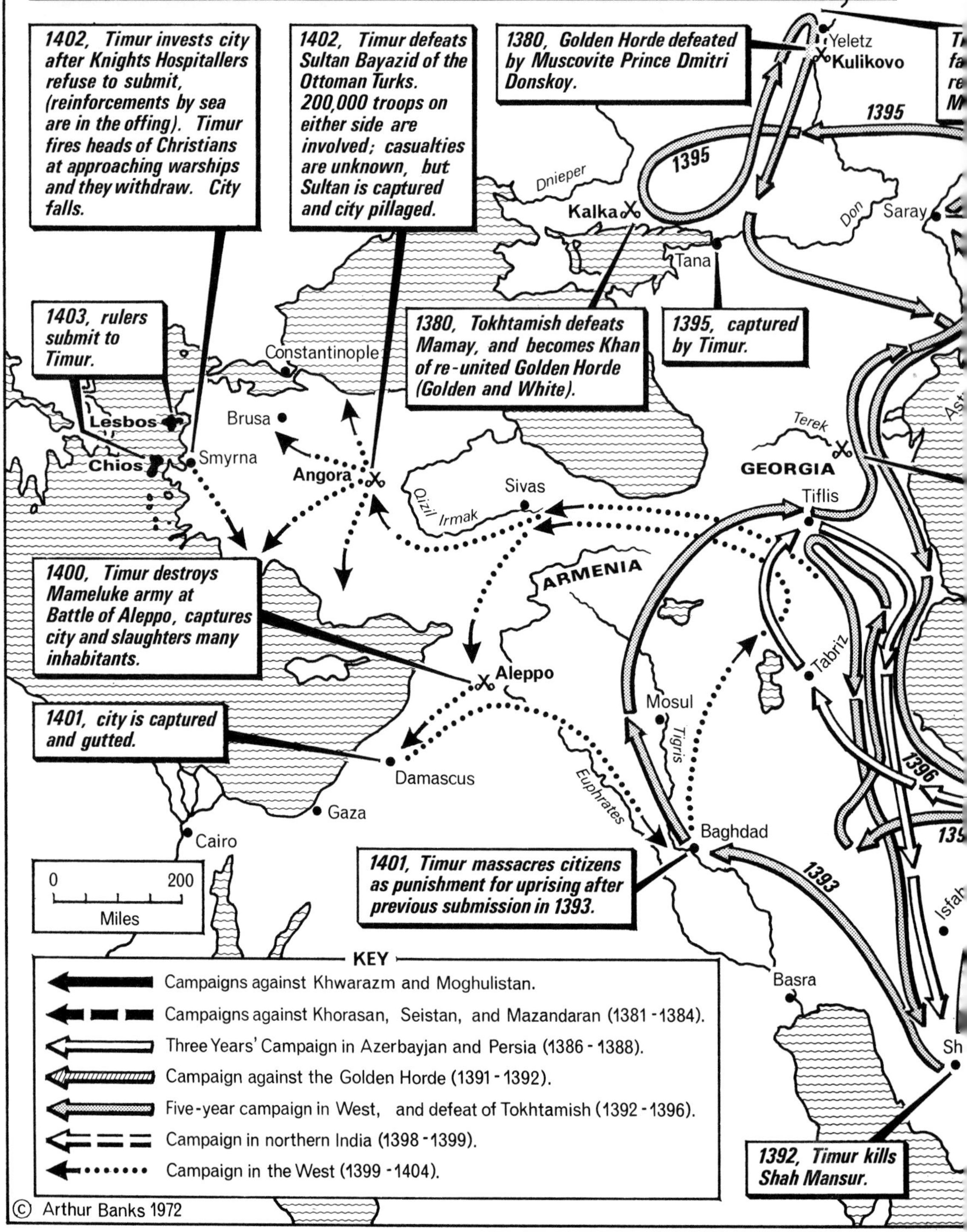
1402, Timur invests city after Knights Hospitallers refuse to submit, (reinforcements by sea are in the offing). Timur fires heads of Christians at approaching warships and they withdraw. City falls.
1402, Timur defeats Sultan Bayazid of the Ottoman Turks. 200,000 troops on either side are involved; casualties are unknown, but Sultan is captured and city pillaged.
1380, Golden Horde defeated by Muscovite Prince Dmitri Donskoy.
Yeletz
Kulikovo
1395
1395
Dnieper
Kalka
Don
Saray
Tana
1403, rulers submit to Timur.
Constantinople
1380, Tokhtamish defeats Mamay, and becomes Khan of re-united Golden Horde (Golden and White).
1395, captured by Timur.
Lesbos
Brusa
Chios
Smyrna
Angora
Terek
GEORGIA
Sivas
Qizil Irmak
Tiflis
ARMENIA
1400, Timur destroys Mameluke army at Battle of Aleppo, captures city and slaughters many inhabitants.
Aleppo
Tabriz
Mosul
Tigris
1401, city is captured and gutted.
Damascus
Euphrates
1396
Gaza
Baghdad
Cairo
1401, Timur massacres citizens as punishment for uprising after previous submission in 1393.
1393
0 200 Miles
KEY
Campaigns against Khwarazm and Moghulistan.
Campaigns against Khorasan, Seistan, and Mazandaran (1381 - 1384).
Three Years' Campaign in Azerbayjan and Persia (1386 - 1388).
Campaign against the Golden Horde (1391 - 1392).
Five-year campaign in West, and defeat of Tokhtamish (1392 - 1396).
Campaign in northern India (1398 - 1399).
Campaign in the West (1399 - 1404).
Basra
1392, Timur kills Shah Mansur.
© Arthur Banks 1972

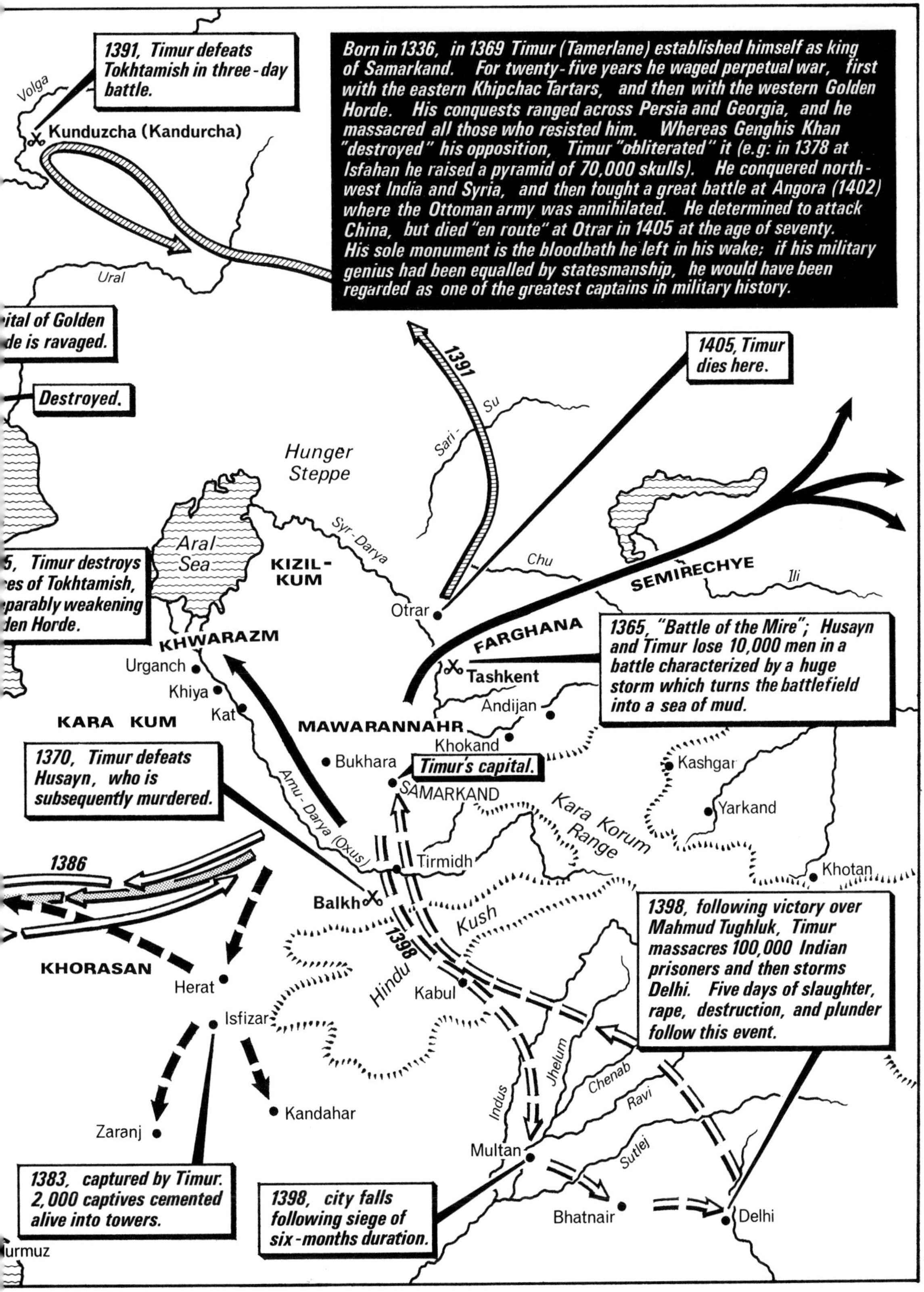

Born in 1336, in 1369 Timur (Tamerlane) established himself as king of Samarkand. For twenty-five years he waged perpetual war, first with the eastern Khipchac Tartars, and then with the western Golden Horde. His conquests ranged across Persia and Georgia, and he massacred all those who resisted him. Whereas Genghis Khan "destroyed" his opposition, Timur "obliterated" it (e.g: in 1378 at Isfahan he raised a pyramid of 70,000 skulls). He conquered north-west India and Syria, and then fought a great battle at Angora (1402) where the Ottoman army was annihilated. He determined to attack China, but died "en route" at Otrar in 1405 at the age of seventy. His sole monument is the bloodbath he left in his wake; if his military genius had been equalled by statesmanship, he would have been regarded as one of the greatest captains in military history.
1391, Timur defeats Tokhtamish in three-day battle.
Volga
Kunduzcha (Kandurcha)
Ural
ital of Golden de is ravaged.
Destroyed.
1391
Sari-Su
1405, Timur dies here.
Hunger Steppe
Aral Sea
Syr-Darya
5, Timur destroys es of Tokhtamish, parably weakening den Horde.
KIZIL-KUM
Chu
SEMIRECHYE
Ili
Otrar
KHWARAZM
FARGHANA
1365, "Battle of the Mire"; Husayn and Timur lose 10,000 men in a battle characterized by a huge storm which turns the battlefield into a sea of mud.
Urganch
Tashkent
Khiya
Andijan
Kat
KARA KUM
MAWARANNAHR
Khokand
1370, Timur defeats Husayn, who is subsequently murdered.
Bukhara
Timur's capital.
Kashgar
SAMARKAND
Amu-Darya (Oxus)
Kara Korum Range
Yarkand
1386
Tirmidh
Khotan
Balkh
Hindu Kush
1398
1398, following victory over Mahmud Tughluk, Timur massacres 100,000 Indian prisoners and then storms Delhi. Five days of slaughter, rape, destruction, and plunder follow this event.
KHORASAN
Herat
Kabul
Isfizar
Jhelum
Chenab
Indus
Ravi
Kandahar
Zaranj
Multan
Sutlej
1383, captured by Timur. 2,000 captives cemented alive into towers.
1398, city falls following siege of six-months duration.
Bhatnair
Delhi
lurmuz

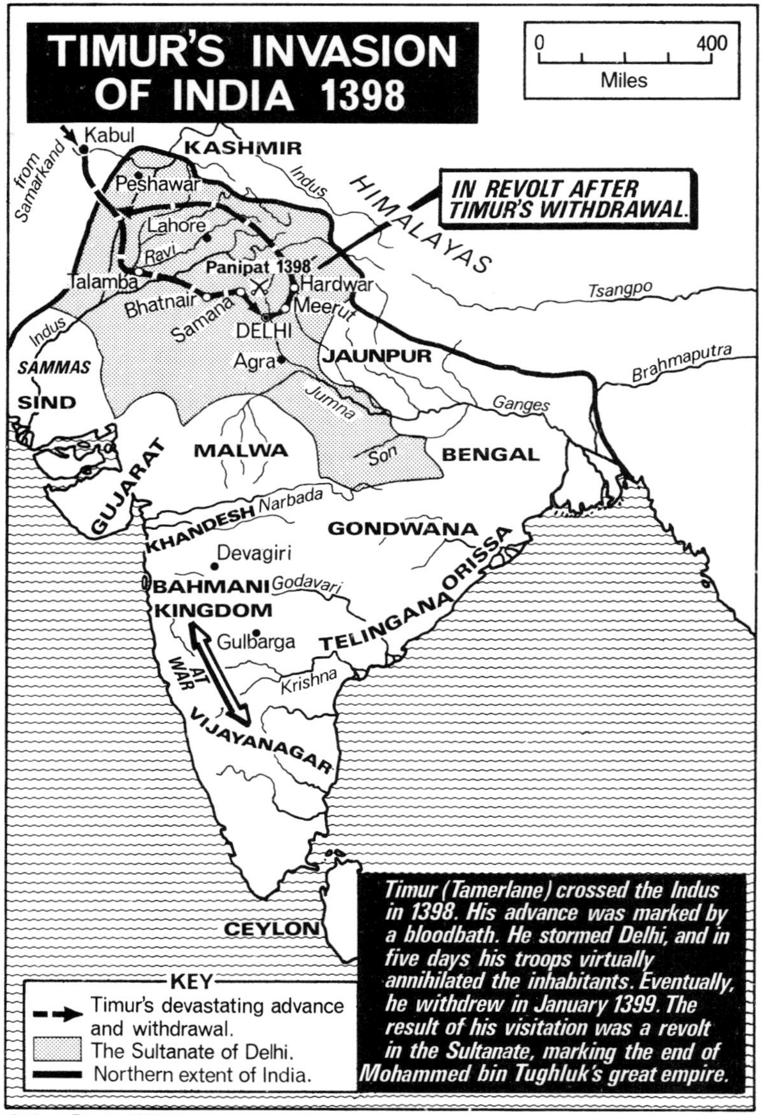

Timur (Tamerlane) crossed the Indus in 1398. His advance was marked by a bloodbath. He stormed Delhi, and in five days his troops virtually annihilated the inhabitants. Eventually, he withdrew in January 1399. The result of his visitation was a revolt in the Sultanate, marking the end of Mohammed bin Tughluk's great empire.

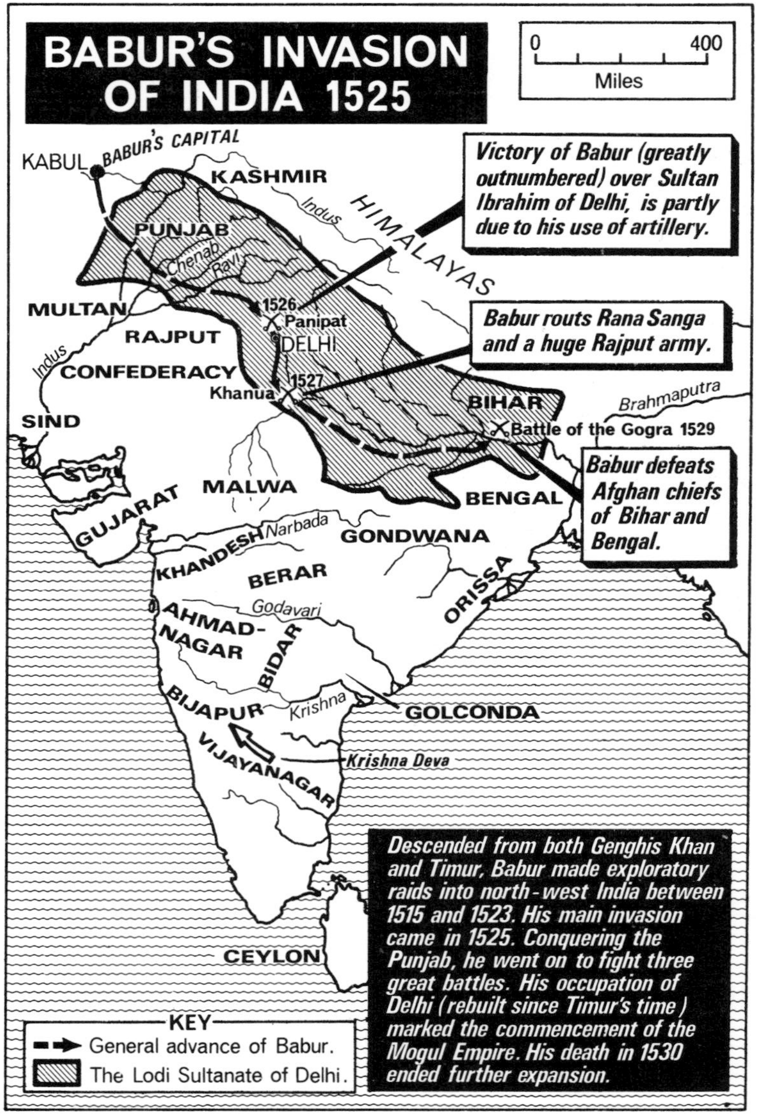

Descended from both Genghis Khan and Timur, Babur made exploratory raids into north-west India between 1515 and 1523. His main invasion came in 1525. Conquering the Punjab, he went on to fight three great battles. His occupation of Delhi (rebuilt since Timur's time) marked the commencement of the Mogul Empire. His death in 1530 ended further expansion.

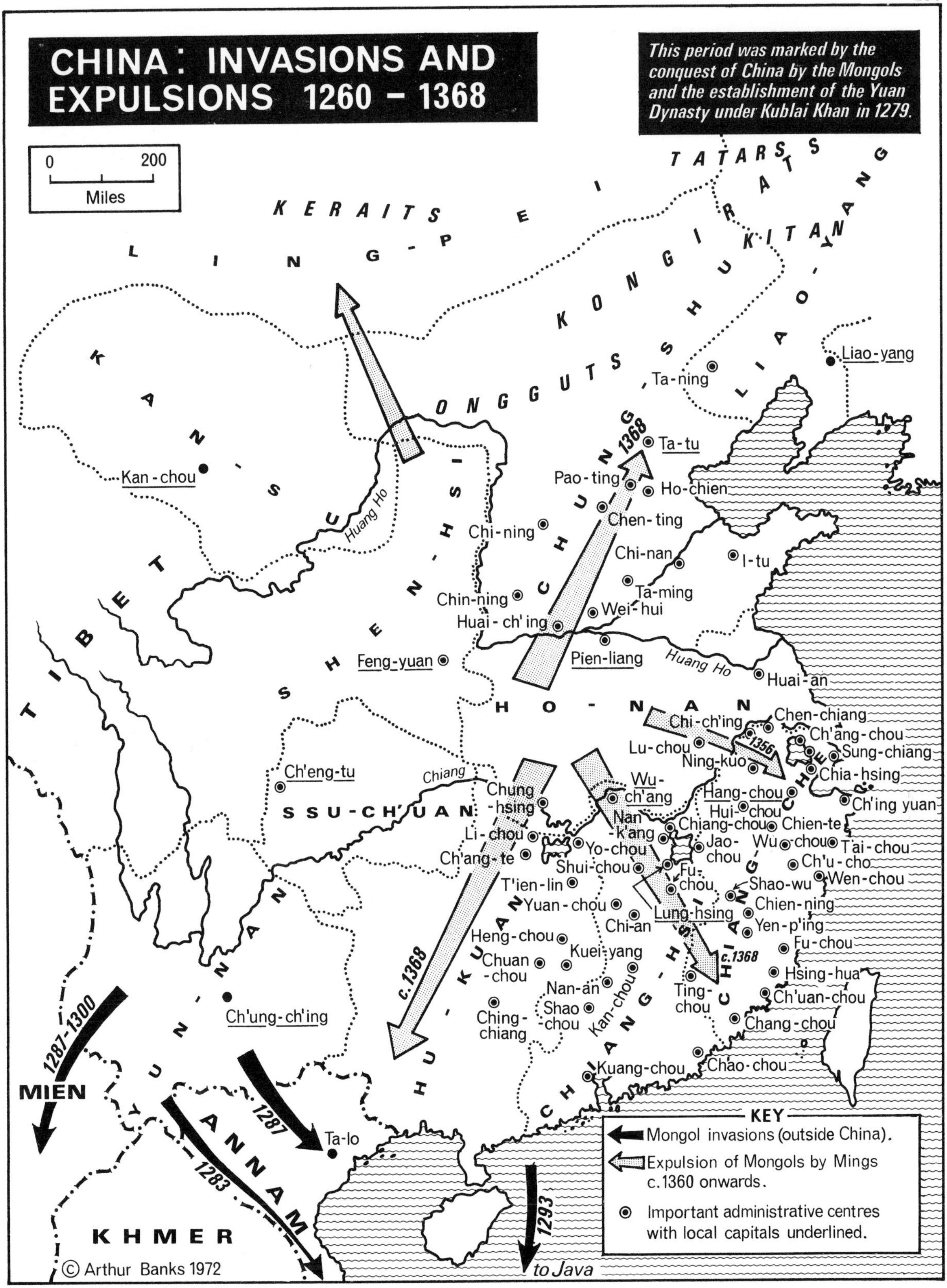
CHINA : INVASIONS AND EXPULSIONS 1260 – 1368
This period was marked by the conquest of China by the Mongols and the establishment of the Yuan Dynasty under Kublai Khan in 1279.
0 200 Miles
KERAITS
TATARS
LING-PEI
KONGIRATS
KITANS
LIAO-YANG
SHUI
KAN-SU
ONGGUTS
SHEN-HSI
CHUNG-SHU
TIBET
HO-NAN
SSU-CH'UAN
YUN-NAN
HU-KUANG
CHIANG-HSI
CHIANG-CHE
MIEN
ANNAM
KHMER
Liao-yang
Ta-ning
Ta-tu
Pao-ting
Ho-chien
Chen-ting
Chi-ning
Chi-nan
I-tu
Ta-ming
Chin-ning
Wei-hui
Huai-ch'ing
Kan-chou
Huang Ho
Feng-yuan
Pien-liang
Huai-an
Chi-ch'ing
Chen-chiang
Ch'ang-chou
Sung-chiang
Lu-chou
Ning-kuo
Chia-hsing
Ch'eng-tu
Chiang
Chung-hsing
Wu-ch'ang
Hang-chou
Ch'ing yuan
Hui-chou
Nan-k'ang
Chiang-chou
Chien-te
Li-chou
Jao-chou
Wu-chou
T'ai-chou
Yo-chou
Ch'ang-te
Shui-chou
Fu-chou
Ch'u-cho
T'ien-lin
Shao-wu
Wen-chou
Yuan-chou
Lung-hsing
Chien-ning
Chi-an
Yen-p'ing
Heng-chou
Fu-chou
Chuan-chou
Kuei-yang
Hsing-hua
Nan-an
Ting-chou
Ch'uan-chou
Shao-chou
Kan-chou
Ching-chiang
Ch'ung-ch'ing
Chang-chou
Chao-chou
Kuang-chou
Ta-lo
1368
1356
c.1368
c.1368
1287-1300
1287
1283
1293
to Java
KEY
Mongol invasions (outside China).
Expulsion of Mongols by Mings c.1360 onwards.
Important administrative centres with local capitals underlined.
© Arthur Banks 1972

TWO IMPORTANT SIEGES OF CONSTANTINOPLE

❶ The Unsuccessful Siege of 717 - 718

ARMED STRENGTHS	
THE ATTACKERS (under Maslama)	THE DEFENDERS (under Leo III)
In 717. 80,000 troops, plus 80,000 troops aboard 1,800 ships under Suleiman. In 718. 400 ships under Sofiam. 360 ships under Yezid. 40,000 troops under Merdasan.	Troop strengths unknown. Population of city: approx 600,000. Naval strength unknown, but much inferior to the Moslem force.

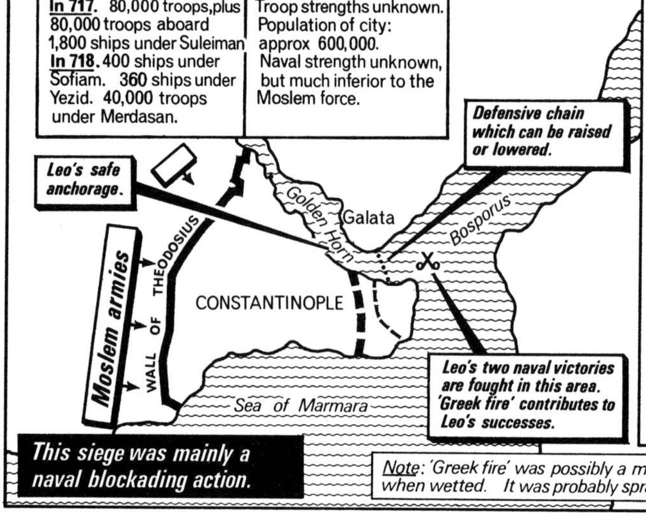

This siege was mainly a naval blockading action.

MAIN EVENTS

August 717. Leo prepares for siege by stockpiling granaries and arsenals, repairing walls, and mounting defensive weapons.

September 717. Suleiman (Maslama's general) leads blockading squadron to sever sea communications between Constantinople and cities of Cherson and Trebizond. Leo's fleet advances from Golden Horn and destroys 20 Moslem ships.

Winter 717-718. Three months of bitterly cold weather decimates besiegers.

Spring 718. Reserve army and ships arrive to strengthen Moslems.

June 718. Leo's fleet sallies from Golden Horn and routs Moslem fleet, following which Leo attacks and defeats Merdasan on land.

August 718. Maslama raises siege.

Note: 'Greek fire' was possibly a mixture of sulphur, naphtha, and quicklime, which ignited when wetted. It was probably sprayed by a hose operating from a siphon system.

❷ The Successful Siege of 1453

ARMED STRENGTHS	
THE ATTACKERS (led by Mohammed II)	THE DEFENDERS (led by Constantine XI)
80,000 troops. 100 heavy cannon. 250 ships.	7,000 troops. 26 ships.

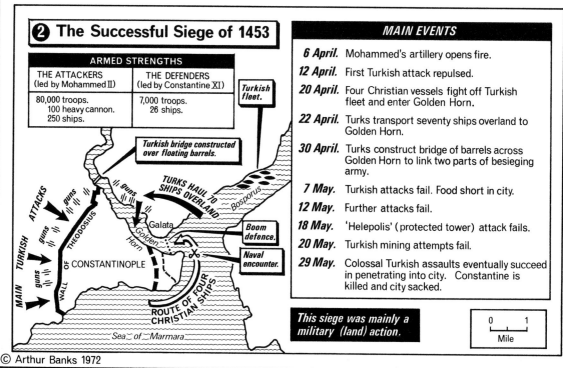

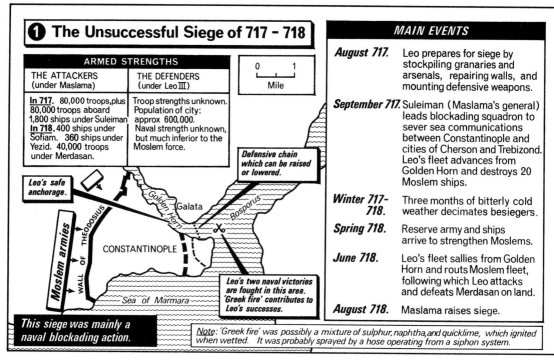

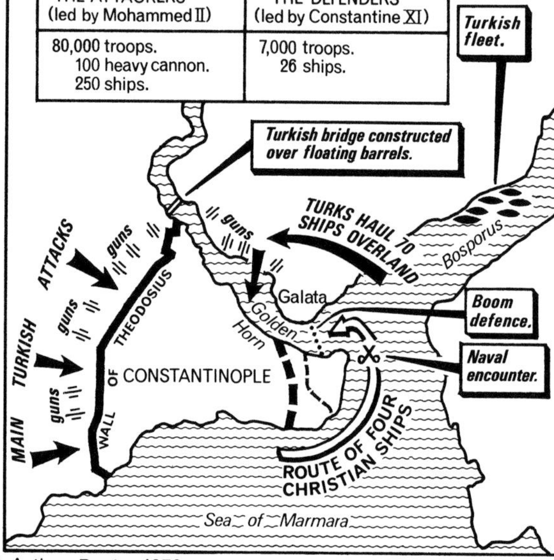

MAIN EVENTS

6 April. Mohammed's artillery opens fire.

12 April. First Turkish attack repulsed.

20 April. Four Christian vessels fight off Turkish fleet and enter Golden Horn.

22 April. Turks transport seventy ships overland to Golden Horn.

30 April. Turks construct bridge of barrels across Golden Horn to link two parts of besieging army.

7 May. Turkish attacks fail. Food short in city.

12 May. Further attacks fail.

18 May. 'Helepolis' (protected tower) attack fails.

20 May. Turkish mining attempts fail.

29 May. Colossal Turkish assaults eventually succeed in penetrating into city. Constantine is killed and city sacked.

This siege was mainly a military (land) action.

0 1
Mile

TWO IMPORTANT SIEGES OF RHODES

1 The Unsuccessful Siege of 1480

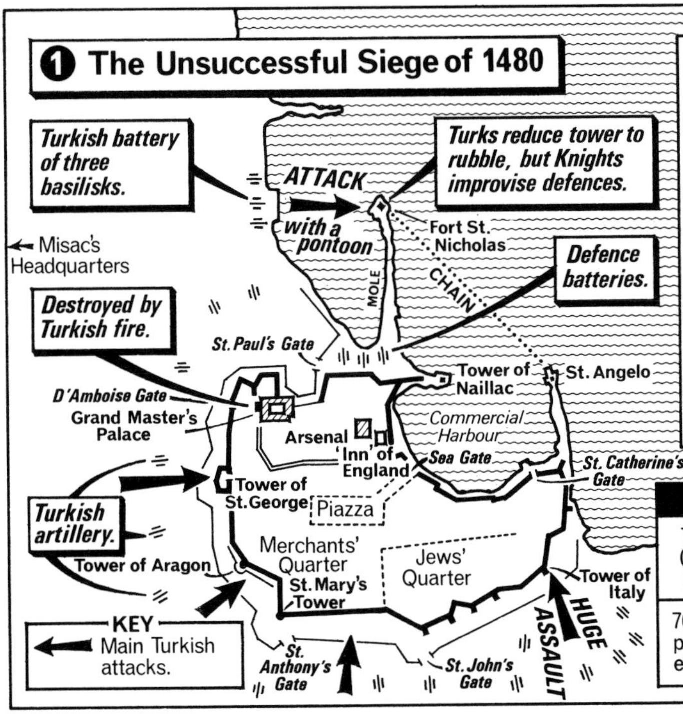

MAIN EVENTS

April.	d'Aubusson prepares for siege.
May.	Turkish barrage opens, directed particularly against Fort St. Nicholas and mole.
June.	Turkish attempts to storm Fort St. Nicholas end in failure.
July.	Turks capture Tower of Italy but are repulsed (3,000 slain).
August.	Turks call off siege. Their losses amount to 9,000 dead and 15,000 wounded. Christian losses (from sickness in addition to fighting) are 1,000.

ARMED STRENGTHS

THE ATTACKERS (led by Misac Palaeologos Pasha).	THE DEFENDERS (led by d'Aubusson and A. de Monteil).
70,000 troops, plus cannons, towers, etc., 109 ships.	600 Knights, 1,500 mercenaries, plus de Monteil's retinue.

2 The Successful Siege of 1522

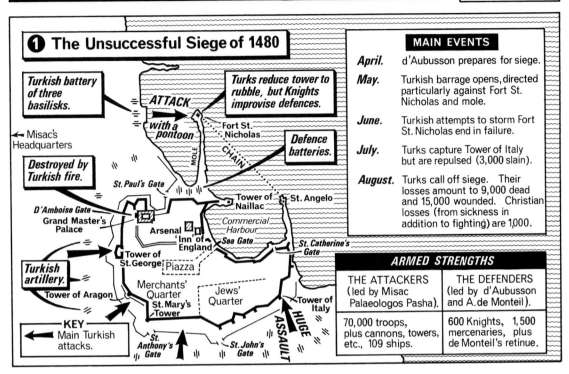

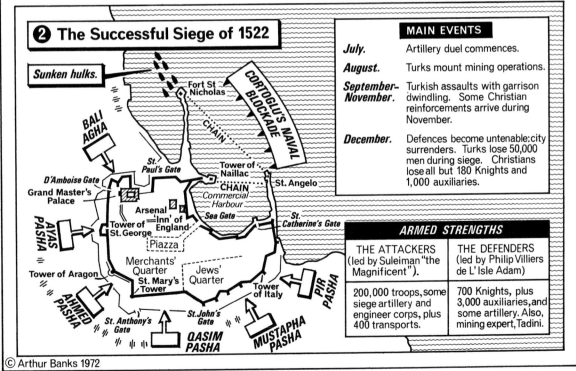

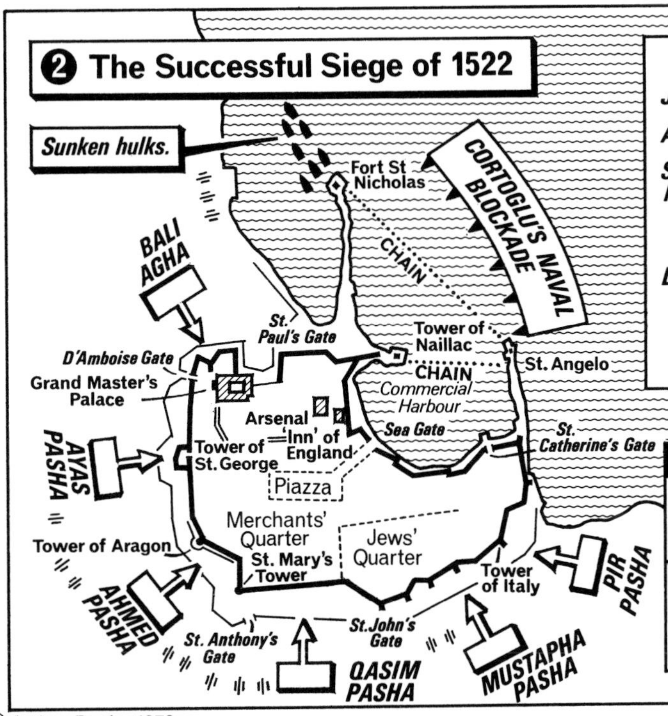

MAIN EVENTS

July.	Artillery duel commences.
August.	Turks mount mining operations.
September-November.	Turkish assaults with garrison dwindling. Some Christian reinforcements arrive during November.
December.	Defences become untenable: city surrenders. Turks lose 50,000 men during siege. Christians lose all but 180 Knights and 1,000 auxiliaries.

ARMED STRENGTHS

THE ATTACKERS (led by Suleiman "the Magnificent").	THE DEFENDERS (led by Philip Villiers de L'Isle Adam)
200,000 troops, some siege artillery and engineer corps, plus 400 transports.	700 Knights, plus 3,000 auxiliaries, and some artillery. Also, mining expert, Tadini.

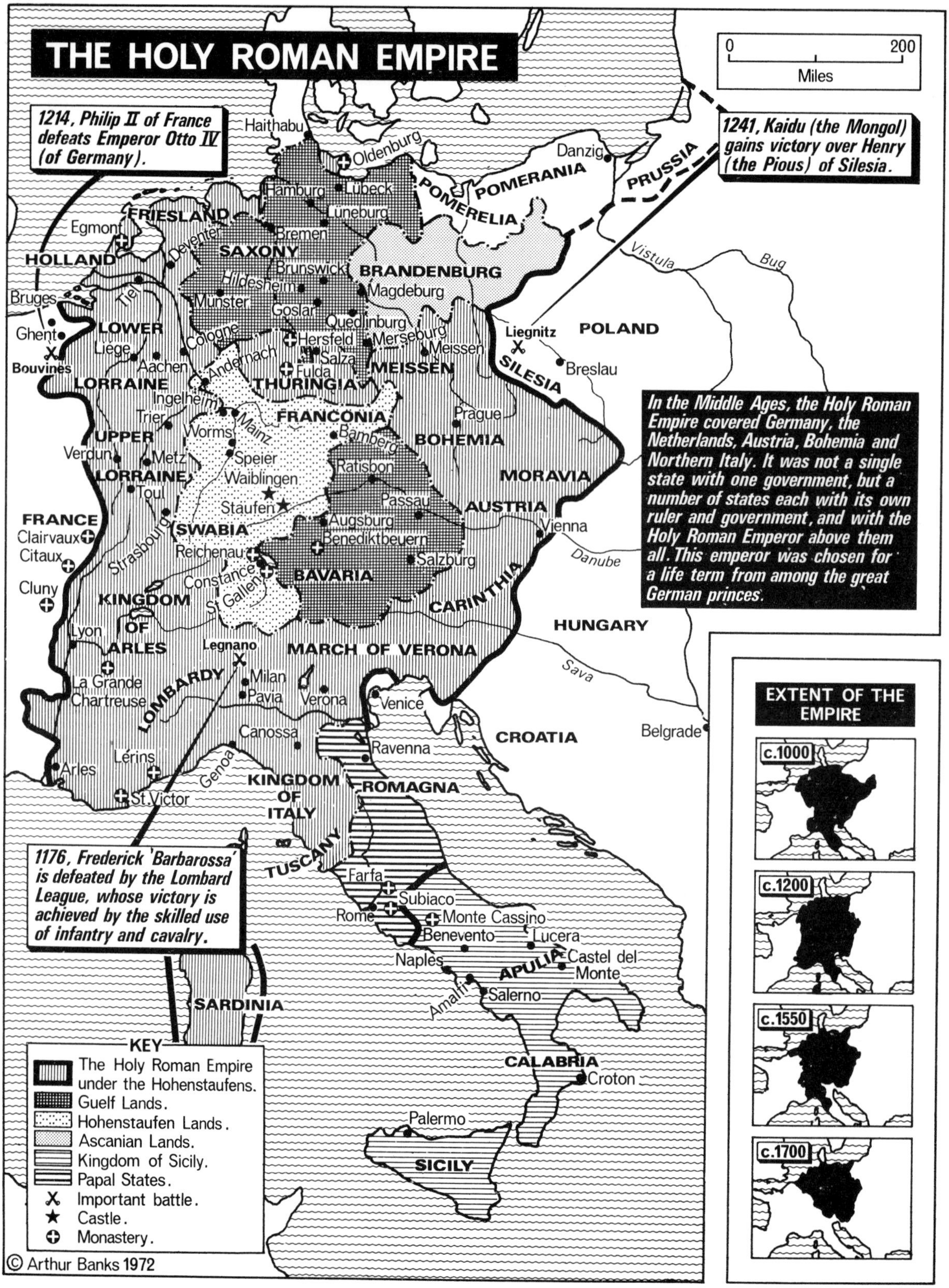
THE HOLY ROMAN EMPIRE
0 200
Miles
1214, Philip II of France defeats Emperor Otto IV (of Germany).
1241, Kaidu (the Mongol) gains victory over Henry (the Pious) of Silesia.
In the Middle Ages, the Holy Roman Empire covered Germany, the Netherlands, Austria, Bohemia and Northern Italy. It was not a single state with one government, but a number of states each with its own ruler and government, and with the Holy Roman Emperor above them all. This emperor was chosen for a life term from among the great German princes.
1176, Frederick 'Barbarossa' is defeated by the Lombard League, whose victory is achieved by the skilled use of infantry and cavalry.
Haithabu
Oldenburg
Danzig
POMERANIA
PRUSSIA
POMERELIA
Hamburg
Lübeck
Lüneburg
Bremen
FRIESLAND
Egmont
HOLLAND
Deventer
SAXONY
Brunswick
BRANDENBURG
Hildesheim
Magdeburg
Bruges
Tiel
Munster
Goslar
Quedlinburg
Ghent
LOWER
Cologne
Hersfeld
Merseburg
Meissen
Liegnitz
POLAND
Bouvines
Liege
Aachen
Andernach
Salza
Fulda
MEISSEN
SILESIA
Breslau
LORRAINE
Ingelheim
THURINGIA
Trier
FRANCONIA
Prague
Worms
Mainz
Bamberg
BOHEMIA
UPPER
Verdun
Metz
Speier
Ratisbon
LORRAINE
Waiblingen
MORAVIA
Toul
Passau
Staufen
AUSTRIA
FRANCE
Augsburg
Clairvaux
SWABIA
Benediktbeuern
Vienna
Citaux
Strasbourg
Reichenau
Salzburg
Danube
Constance
Cluny
St Gallen
BAVARIA
KINGDOM
CARINTHIA
OF
HUNGARY
Lyon
ARLES
Legnano
MARCH OF VERONA
La Grande Chartreuse
LOMBARDY
Milan
Pavia
Verona
Sava
Venice
Canossa
CROATIA
Belgrade
Ravenna
Lérins
Arles
Genoa
KINGDOM OF ITALY
ROMAGNA
St.Victor
TUSCANY
Farfa
Subiaco
Rome
Monte Cassino
Benevento
Lucera
Naples
APULIA
Castel del Monte
Amalfi
Salerno
SARDINIA
CALABRIA
Croton
Palermo
SICILY
Vistula
Bug
KEY
The Holy Roman Empire under the Hohenstaufens.
Guelf Lands.
Hohenstaufen Lands.
Ascanian Lands.
Kingdom of Sicily.
Papal States.
Important battle.
Castle.
Monastery.
EXTENT OF THE EMPIRE
c.1000
c.1200
c.1550
c.1700

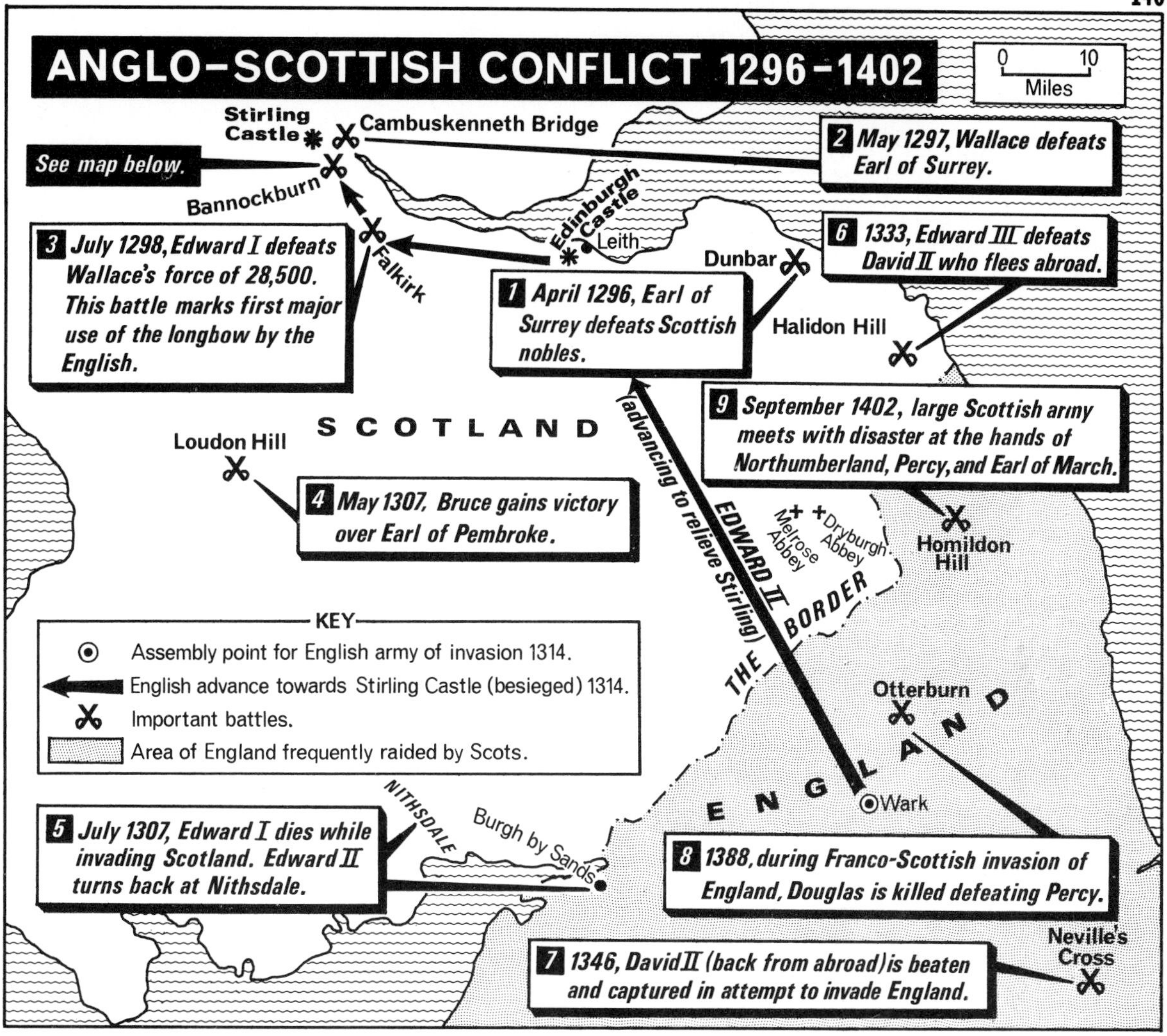
ANGLO-SCOTTISH CONFLICT 1296-1402
0 10 Miles
Stirling Castle
Cambuskenneth Bridge
See map below.
Bannockburn
Falkirk
Edinburgh Castle
Leith
Dunbar
Halidon Hill
2 May 1297, Wallace defeats Earl of Surrey.
3 July 1298, Edward I defeats Wallace's force of 28,500. This battle marks first major use of the longbow by the English.
6 1333, Edward III defeats David II who flees abroad.
1 April 1296, Earl of Surrey defeats Scottish nobles.
9 September 1402, large Scottish army meets with disaster at the hands of Northumberland, Percy, and Earl of March.
SCOTLAND
Loudon Hill
4 May 1307, Bruce gains victory over Earl of Pembroke.
(advancing to relieve Stirling)
EDWARD II
Melrose Abbey
Dryburgh Abbey
Homildon Hill
THE BORDER
KEY
Assembly point for English army of invasion 1314.
English advance towards Stirling Castle (besieged) 1314.
Important battles.
Area of England frequently raided by Scots.
Otterburn
ENGLAND
Wark
NITHSDALE
Burgh by Sands
5 July 1307, Edward I dies while invading Scotland. Edward II turns back at Nithsdale.
8 1388, during Franco-Scottish invasion of England, Douglas is killed defeating Percy.
Neville's Cross
7 1346, David II (back from abroad) is beaten and captured in attempt to invade England.

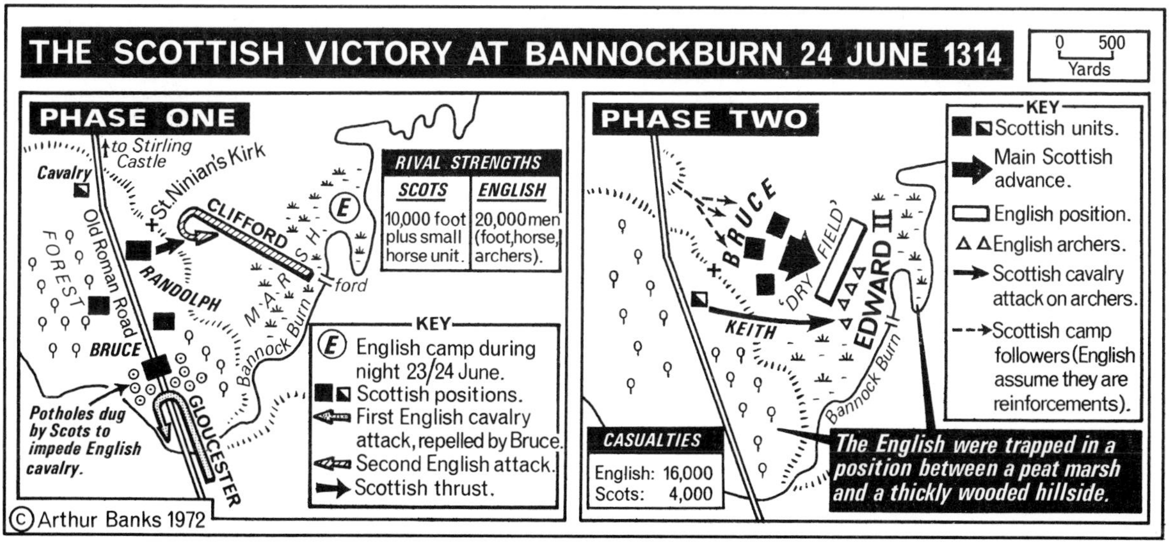
THE SCOTTISH VICTORY AT BANNOCKBURN 24 JUNE 1314
0 500 Yards
PHASE ONE
to Stirling Castle
Cavalry
St. Ninian's Kirk
CLIFFORD
E
MARSH
Old Roman Road
FOREST
RANDOLPH
ford
Bannock Burn
BRUCE
GLOUCESTER
Potholes dug by Scots to impede English cavalry.
RIVAL STRENGTHS
SCOTS: 10,000 foot plus small horse unit.
ENGLISH: 20,000 men (foot, horse, archers).
KEY
English camp during night 23/24 June.
Scottish positions.
First English cavalry attack, repelled by Bruce.
Second English attack.
Scottish thrust.
© Arthur Banks 1972
PHASE TWO
BRUCE
'DRY FIELD'
EDWARD II
KEITH
Bannock Burn
KEY
Scottish units.
Main Scottish advance.
English position.
English archers.
Scottish cavalry attack on archers.
Scottish camp followers (English assume they are reinforcements).
CASUALTIES
English: 16,000
Scots: 4,000
The English were trapped in a position between a peat marsh and a thickly wooded hillside.

THE HUNDRED YEARS' WAR 1337-1453

Note: the war actually spanned 120 years as French raids across the English Channel went on until 1457.

❶ The Sluys-Crécy Period 1337-1347

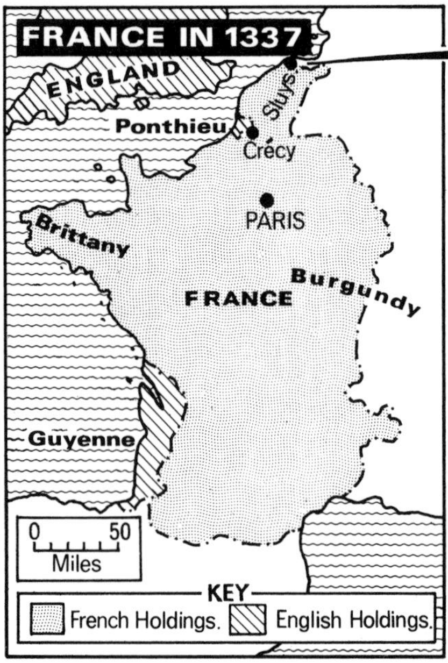

THE ENGLISH NAVAL VICTORY AT SLUYS 24 JUNE 1340

A French fleet of 190 ships, anchored in the Zwin river, is attacked by an English fleet of 150 ships. The English steer straight in to the French, and their archers lay down a hail of arrows. Blinded by the onslaught, the French are also cramped for movement because of their moorings. The English men-at-arms complete the carnage. 166 French ships are sunk or captured, and this victory gives England command of the English Channel.

MAIN CAUSES OF THE HUNDRED YEARS' WAR

1. English rage over French support for the Scots in their wars with England.
2. French suspicions concerning English commercial interests in Flanders.
3. The feudal relationship between French and English kings in France.

TEN BASIC STAGES OF THE HUNDRED YEARS' WAR

1. 1337–1347, Sluys/Crecy period.
2. 1347–1354, Period of truce.
3. 1355–1360, Poitiers period.
4. 1360–1367, Period of uneasy peace.
5. 1368–1396, Du Guesclin and after.
6. 1396–1413, Period of uneasy truce.
7. 1413–1428, Period of Henry V.
8. 1429–1444, Joan of Arc's influence.
9. 1444–1449, Truce of Tours.
10. 1449–1453, The French resurgence.

EDWARD III's CAMPAIGN IN NORTHERN FRANCE 1346-1347

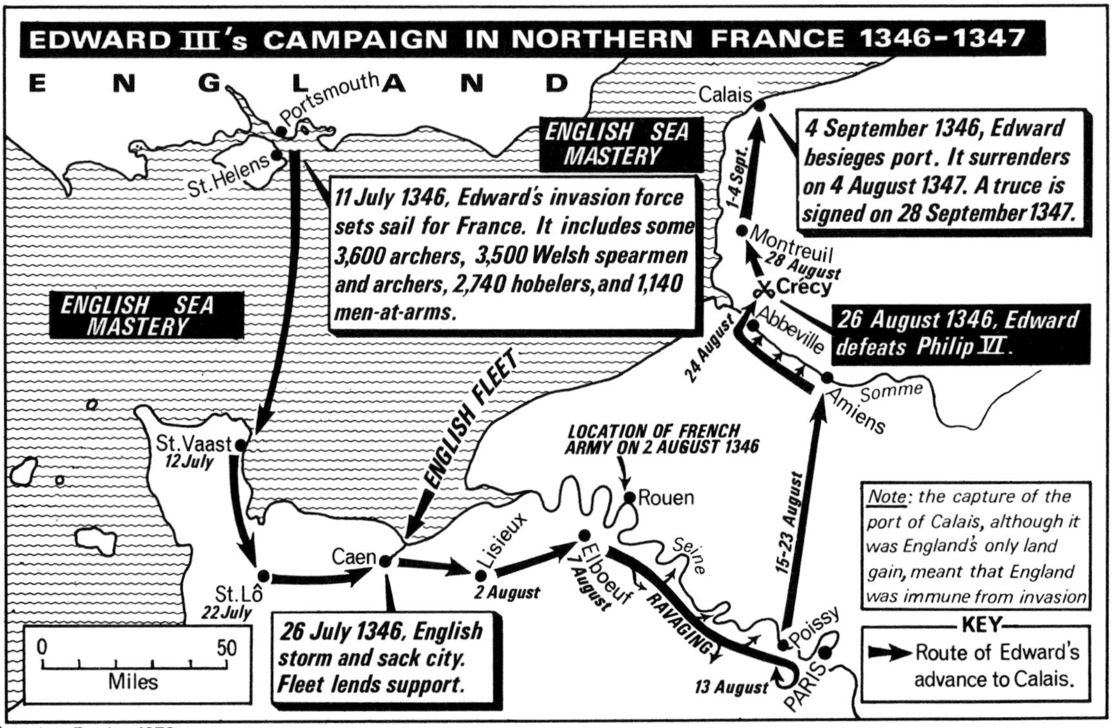

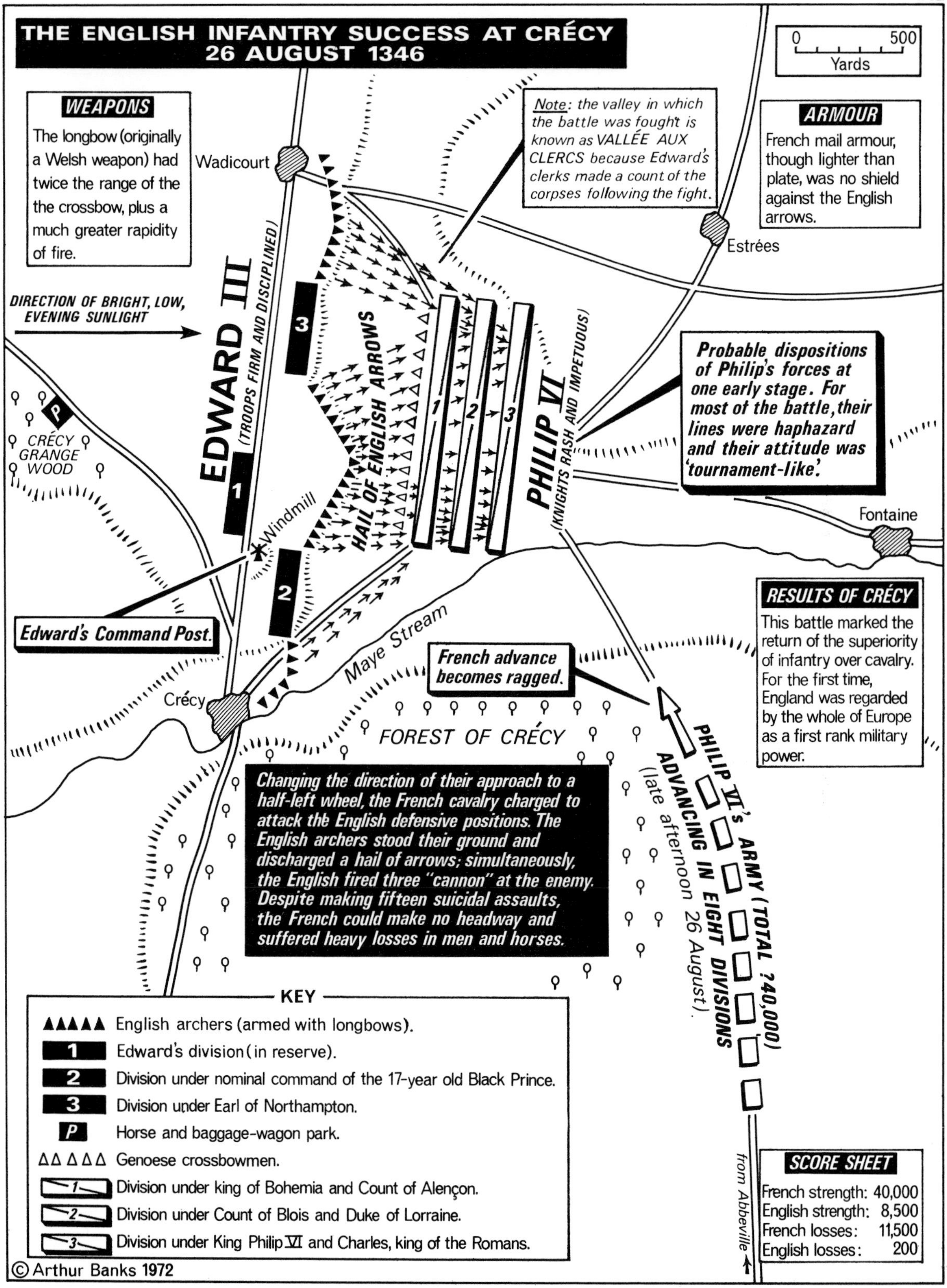
THE ENGLISH INFANTRY SUCCESS AT CRÉCY
26 AUGUST 1346
0 500
Yards
WEAPONS
The longbow (originally a Welsh weapon) had twice the range of the the crossbow, plus a much greater rapidity of fire.
Note: the valley in which the battle was fought is known as VALLÉE AUX CLERCS because Edward's clerks made a count of the corpses following the fight.
ARMOUR
French mail armour, though lighter than plate, was no shield against the English arrows.
Wadicourt
Estrées
DIRECTION OF BRIGHT, LOW, EVENING SUNLIGHT
EDWARD III
(TROOPS FIRM AND DISCIPLINED)
HAIL OF ENGLISH ARROWS
PHILIP VI
(KNIGHTS RASH AND IMPETUOUS)
Probable dispositions of Philip's forces at one early stage. For most of the battle, their lines were haphazard and their attitude was 'tournament-like'.
CRÉCY GRANGE WOOD
Windmill
Fontaine
Edward's Command Post.
Maye Stream
French advance becomes ragged.
RESULTS OF CRÉCY
This battle marked the return of the superiority of infantry over cavalry. For the first time, England was regarded by the whole of Europe as a first rank military power.
Crécy
FOREST OF CRÉCY
Changing the direction of their approach to a half-left wheel, the French cavalry charged to attack the English defensive positions. The English archers stood their ground and discharged a hail of arrows; simultaneously, the English fired three "cannon" at the enemy. Despite making fifteen suicidal assaults, the French could make no headway and suffered heavy losses in men and horses.
PHILIP VI's ARMY (TOTAL ?40,000) ADVANCING IN EIGHT DIVISIONS
(late afternoon 26 August).
KEY
English archers (armed with longbows).
1 Edward's division (in reserve).
2 Division under nominal command of the 17-year old Black Prince.
3 Division under Earl of Northampton.
P Horse and baggage-wagon park.
Genoese crossbowmen.
1 Division under king of Bohemia and Count of Alençon.
2 Division under Count of Blois and Duke of Lorraine.
3 Division under King Philip VI and Charles, king of the Romans.
from Abbeville
SCORE SHEET
French strength: 40,000
English strength: 8,500
French losses: 11,500
English losses: 200
© Arthur Banks 1972

THE HUNDRED YEARS' WAR -continued

2 Spread of the Black Death to Europe

The Black Death, a form of bubonic plague, apparently commenced in China and was carried west by traders. In 1348 it devastated France and England alike, and one third of the population of each country died. During this period, the two states were in a state of truce, but no major campaigns could be undertaken while the pestilence raged. There were later visitations of the disease, but the first one was the most deadly in terms of numbers.

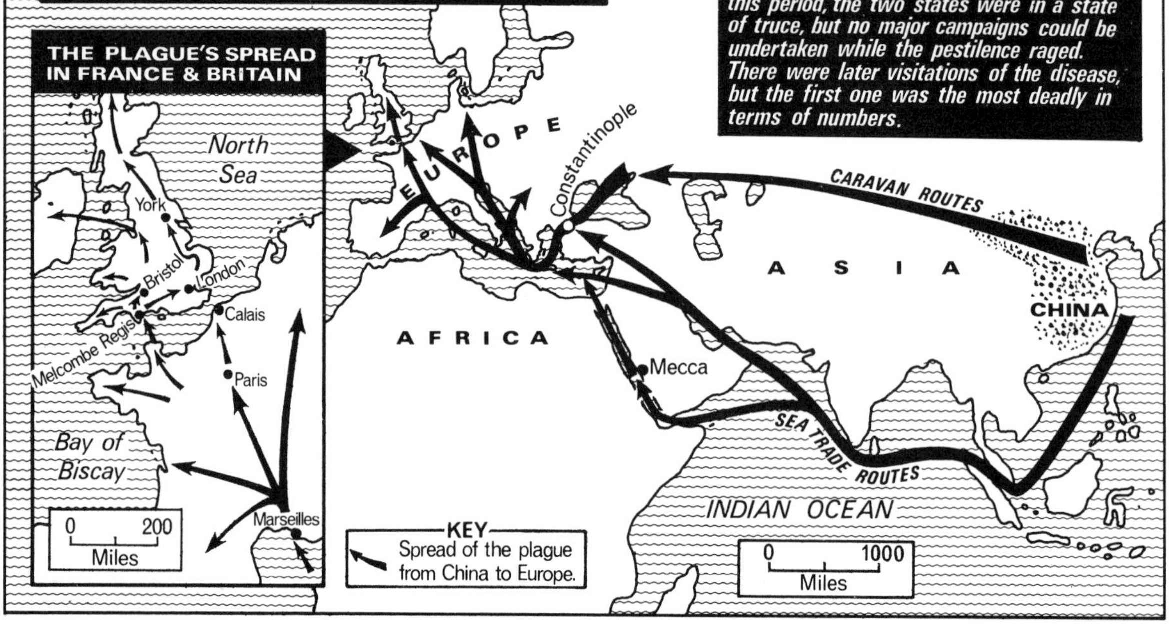

3 The Black Prince's Campaigns

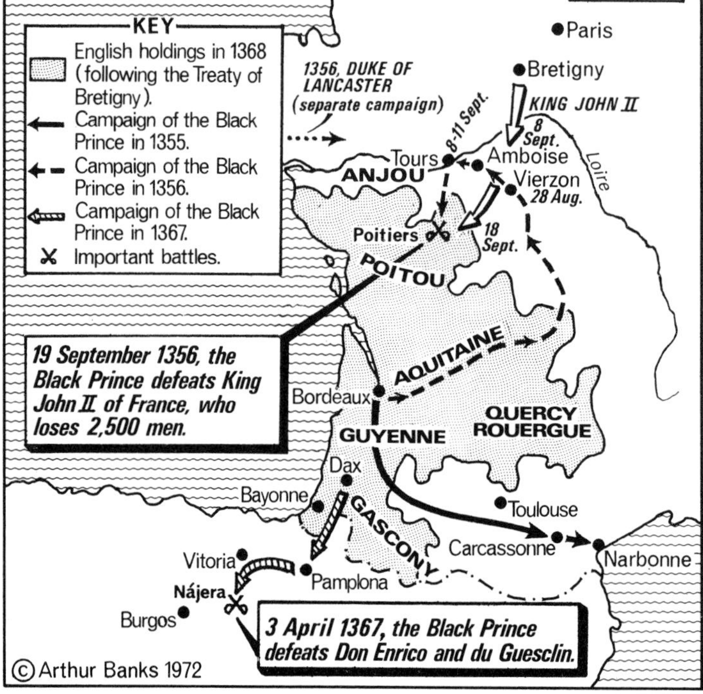

THE BATTLE OF POITIERS 19 SEPTEMBER 1356

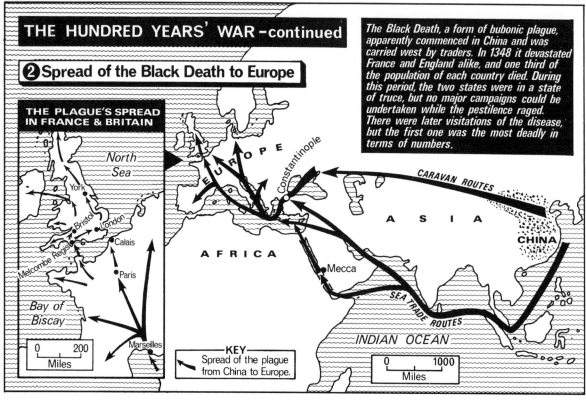

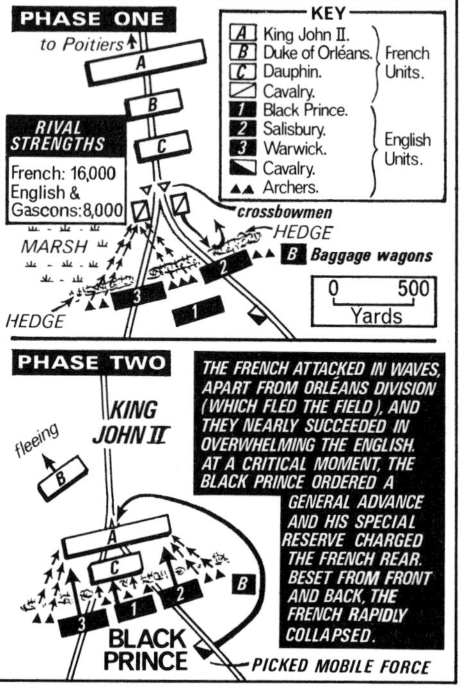

THE FRENCH ATTACKED IN WAVES, APART FROM ORLÉANS DIVISION (WHICH FLED THE FIELD), AND THEY NEARLY SUCCEEDED IN OVERWHELMING THE ENGLISH. AT A CRITICAL MOMENT, THE BLACK PRINCE ORDERED A GENERAL ADVANCE AND HIS SPECIAL RESERVE CHARGED THE FRENCH REAR. BESET FROM FRONT AND BACK, THE FRENCH RAPIDLY COLLAPSED.

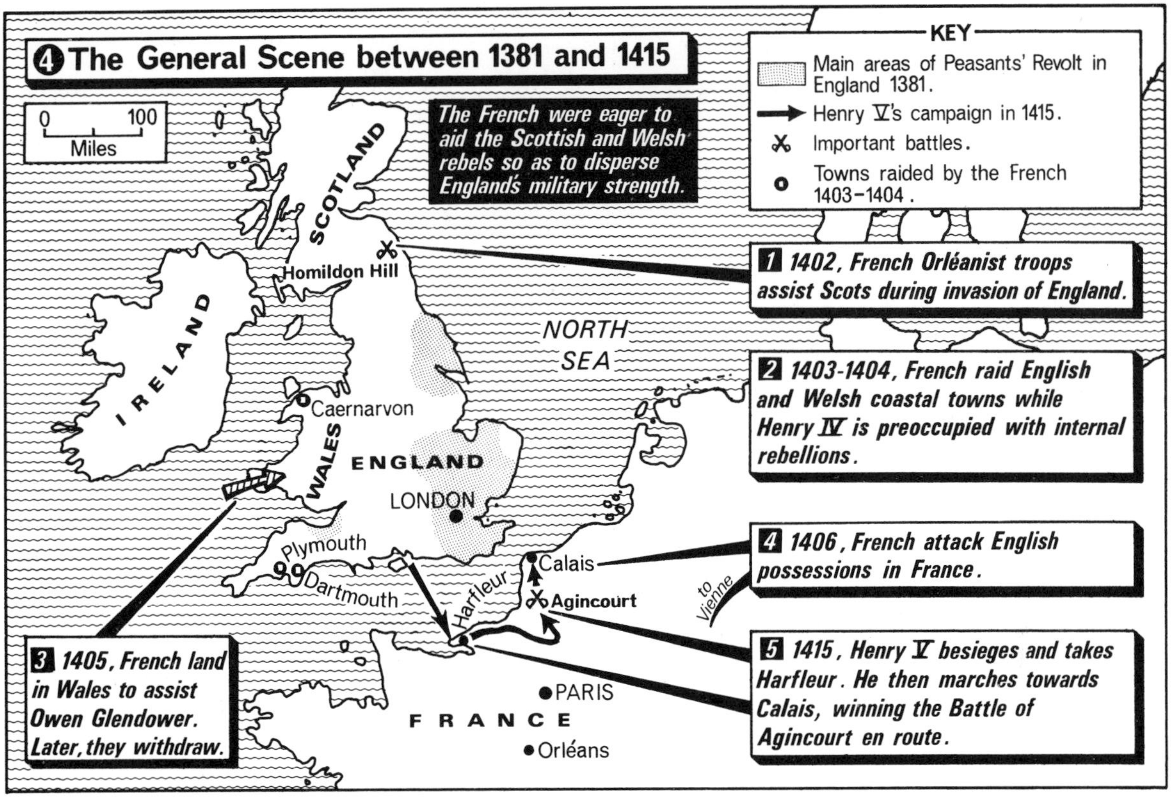

4 The General Scene between 1381 and 1415
0 100 Miles
The French were eager to aid the Scottish and Welsh rebels so as to disperse England's military strength.
KEY
Main areas of Peasants' Revolt in England 1381.
Henry V's campaign in 1415.
Important battles.
Towns raided by the French 1403–1404.
SCOTLAND
Homildon Hill
IRELAND
NORTH SEA
Caernarvon
WALES
ENGLAND
LONDON
Plymouth
Dartmouth
Harfleur
Calais
Agincourt
to Vienne
PARIS
FRANCE
Orléans
1 1402, French Orléanist troops assist Scots during invasion of England.
2 1403-1404, French raid English and Welsh coastal towns while Henry IV is preoccupied with internal rebellions.
3 1405, French land in Wales to assist Owen Glendower. Later, they withdraw.
4 1406, French attack English possessions in France.
5 1415, Henry V besieges and takes Harfleur. He then marches towards Calais, winning the Battle of Agincourt en route.

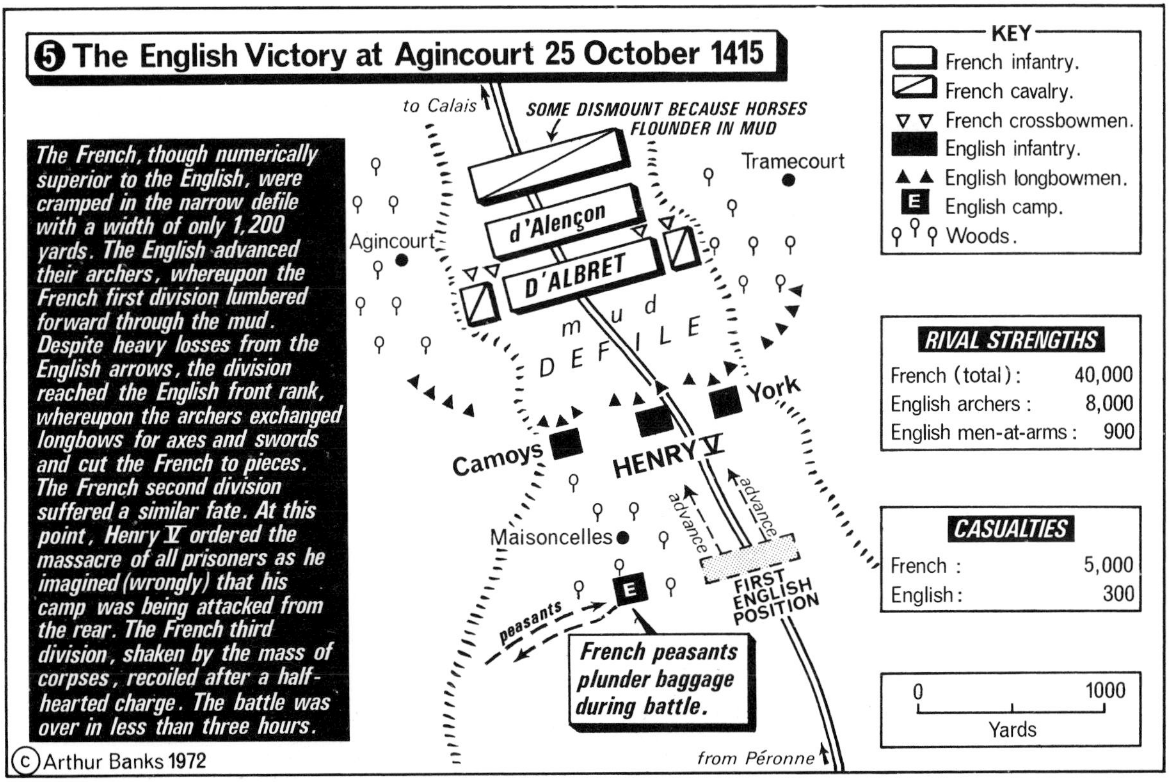

5 The English Victory at Agincourt 25 October 1415
The French, though numerically superior to the English, were cramped in the narrow defile with a width of only 1,200 yards. The English advanced their archers, whereupon the French first division lumbered forward through the mud. Despite heavy losses from the English arrows, the division reached the English front rank, whereupon the archers exchanged longbows for axes and swords and cut the French to pieces. The French second division suffered a similar fate. At this point, Henry V ordered the massacre of all prisoners as he imagined (wrongly) that his camp was being attacked from the rear. The French third division, shaken by the mass of corpses, recoiled after a half-hearted charge. The battle was over in less than three hours.
to Calais
SOME DISMOUNT BECAUSE HORSES FLOUNDER IN MUD
Tramecourt
Agincourt
d'Alençon
D'ALBRET
mud
DEFILE
York
Camoys
HENRY V
advance
advance
Maisoncelles
FIRST ENGLISH POSITION
peasants
French peasants plunder baggage during battle.
from Péronne
KEY
French infantry.
French cavalry.
French crossbowmen.
English infantry.
English longbowmen.
E English camp.
Woods.
RIVAL STRENGTHS
French (total): 40,000
English archers: 8,000
English men-at-arms: 900
CASUALTIES
French: 5,000
English: 300
0 1000 Yards

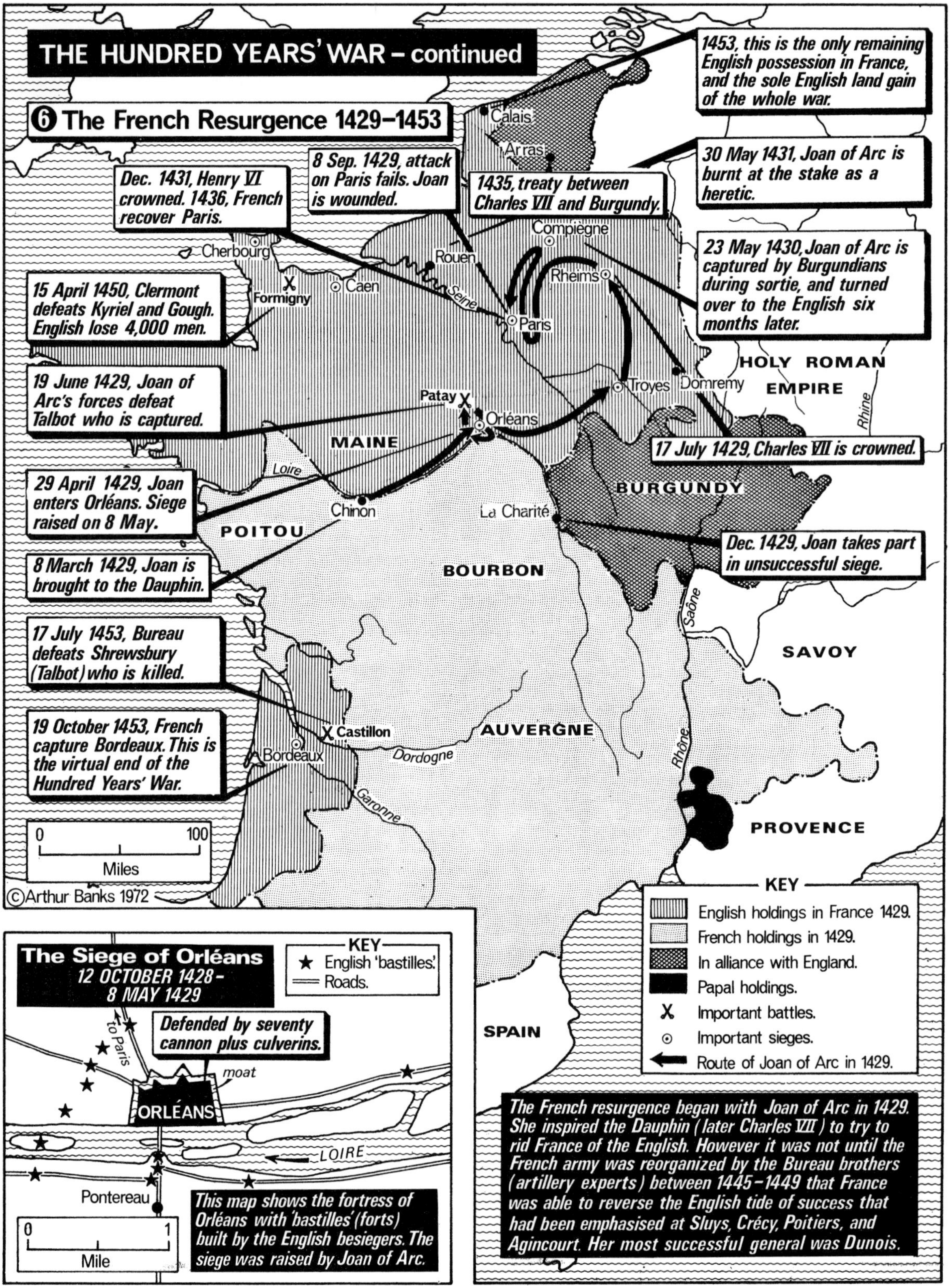
THE HUNDRED YEARS' WAR – continued
6 The French Resurgence 1429–1453
1453, this is the only remaining English possession in France, and the sole English land gain of the whole war.
Dec. 1431, Henry VI crowned. 1436, French recover Paris.
8 Sep. 1429, attack on Paris fails. Joan is wounded.
1435, treaty between Charles VII and Burgundy.
30 May 1431, Joan of Arc is burnt at the stake as a heretic.
23 May 1430, Joan of Arc is captured by Burgundians during sortie, and turned over to the English six months later.
15 April 1450, Clermont defeats Kyriel and Gough. English lose 4,000 men.
19 June 1429, Joan of Arc's forces defeat Talbot who is captured.
29 April 1429, Joan enters Orléans. Siege raised on 8 May.
8 March 1429, Joan is brought to the Dauphin.
17 July 1453, Bureau defeats Shrewsbury (Talbot) who is killed.
19 October 1453, French capture Bordeaux. This is the virtual end of the Hundred Years' War.
17 July 1429, Charles VII is crowned.
Dec. 1429, Joan takes part in unsuccessful siege.
Calais
Arras
Compiègne
Cherbourg
Rouen
Rheims
Formigny
Caen
Seine
Paris
HOLY ROMAN EMPIRE
Patay
Troyes
Domremy
Rhine
Orléans
MAINE
Loire
BURGUNDY
Chinon
La Charité
POITOU
BOURBON
Saône
SAVOY
Castillon
AUVERGNE
Bordeaux
Dordogne
Rhône
Garonne
PROVENCE
0 100 Miles
©Arthur Banks 1972
KEY
English holdings in France 1429.
French holdings in 1429.
In alliance with England.
Papal holdings.
Important battles.
Important sieges.
Route of Joan of Arc in 1429.
SPAIN
The Siege of Orléans 12 OCTOBER 1428 – 8 MAY 1429
KEY
English 'bastilles'.
Roads.
Defended by seventy cannon plus culverins.
to Paris
moat
ORLÉANS
LOIRE
Pontereau
0 1 Mile
This map shows the fortress of Orléans with 'bastilles' (forts) built by the English besiegers. The siege was raised by Joan of Arc.

The French resurgence began with Joan of Arc in 1429. She inspired the Dauphin (later Charles VII) to try to rid France of the English. However it was not until the French army was reorganized by the Bureau brothers (artillery experts) between 1445–1449 that France was able to reverse the English tide of success that had been emphasised at Sluys, Crécy, Poitiers, and Agincourt. Her most successful general was Dunois.

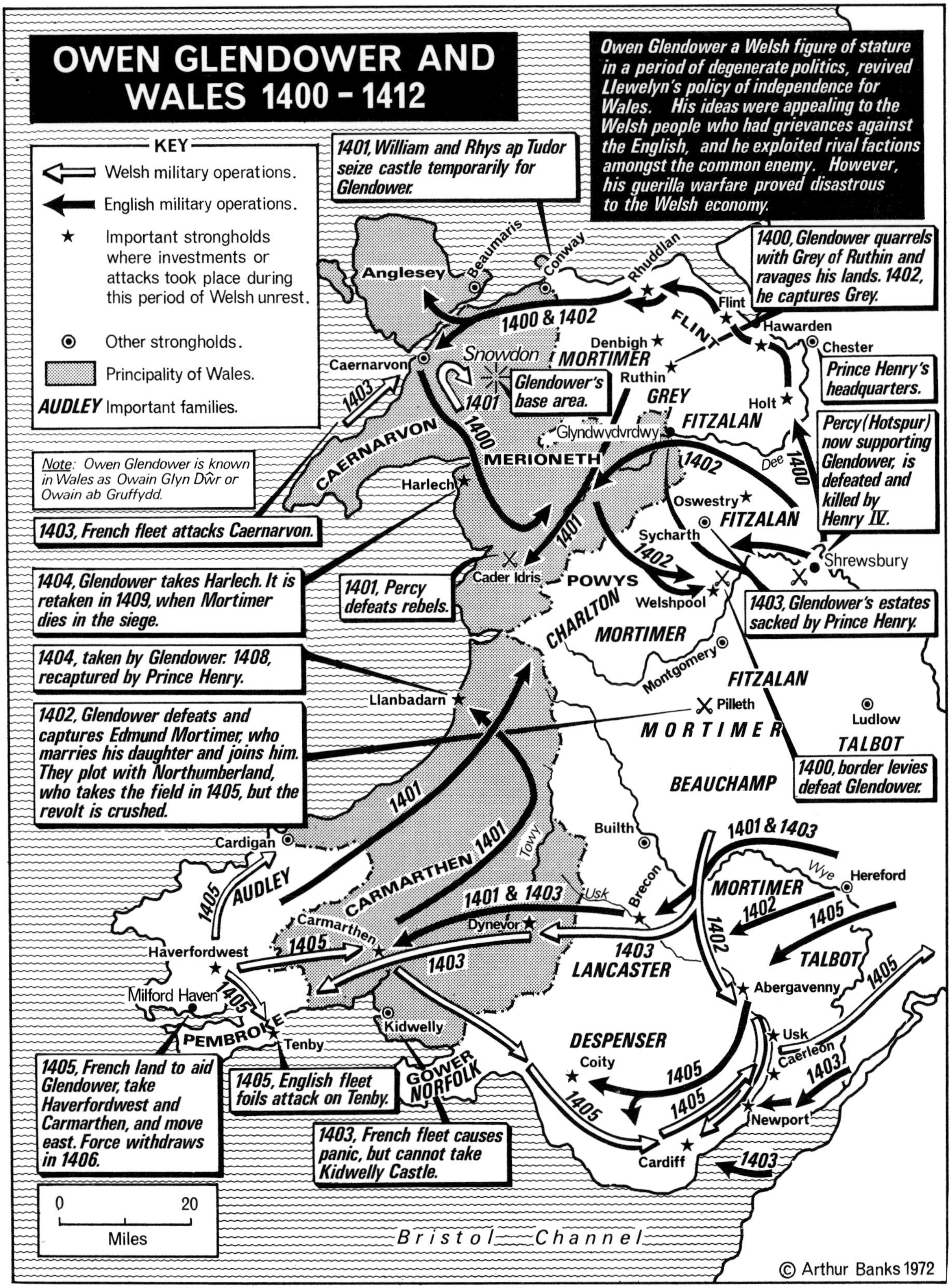
OWEN GLENDOWER AND WALES 1400 - 1412
Owen Glendower a Welsh figure of stature in a period of degenerate politics, revived Llewelyn's policy of independence for Wales. His ideas were appealing to the Welsh people who had grievances against the English, and he exploited rival factions amongst the common enemy. However, his guerilla warfare proved disastrous to the Welsh economy.
KEY
Welsh military operations.
English military operations.
Important strongholds where investments or attacks took place during this period of Welsh unrest.
Other strongholds.
Principality of Wales.
AUDLEY Important families.
Note: Owen Glendower is known in Wales as Owain Glyn Dŵr or Owain ab Gruffydd.
1401, William and Rhys ap Tudor seize castle temporarily for Glendower.
1400, Glendower quarrels with Grey of Ruthin and ravages his lands. 1402, he captures Grey.
Prince Henry's headquarters.
Percy (Hotspur) now supporting Glendower, is defeated and killed by Henry IV.
Glendower's base area.
1403, French fleet attacks Caernarvon.
1404, Glendower takes Harlech. It is retaken in 1409, when Mortimer dies in the siege.
1401, Percy defeats rebels.
1403, Glendower's estates sacked by Prince Henry.
1404, taken by Glendower. 1408, recaptured by Prince Henry.
1402, Glendower defeats and captures Edmund Mortimer, who marries his daughter and joins him. They plot with Northumberland, who takes the field in 1405, but the revolt is crushed.
1400, border levies defeat Glendower.
1405, French land to aid Glendower, take Haverfordwest and Carmarthen, and move east. Force withdraws in 1406.
1405, English fleet foils attack on Tenby.
1403, French fleet causes panic, but cannot take Kidwelly Castle.
Anglesey
Beaumaris
Conway
Rhuddlan
Flint
Haverfordwest
Hawarden
Chester
Denbigh
Ruthin
Holt
Caernarvon
Snowdon
MORTIMER
GREY
FITZALAN
CAERNARVON
Glyndwydvrdwy
MERIONETH
Dee
Harlech
Oswestry
Sycharth
Shrewsbury
Cader Idris
POWYS
Welshpool
CHARLTON
MORTIMER
Montgomery
FITZALAN
Llanbadarn
Pilleth
Ludlow
MORTIMER
TALBOT
BEAUCHAMP
Builth
Cardigan
Towy
Wye
Hereford
AUDLEY
CARMARTHEN
Usk
Brecon
MORTIMER
Carmarthen
Dynevor
LANCASTER
TALBOT
Haverfordwest
Milford Haven
Abergavenny
PEMBROKE
Tenby
Kidwelly
DESPENSER
Coity
Usk
Caerleon
GOWER
NORFOLK
Newport
Cardiff
1400 & 1402
1401
1400
1402
1403
1401 & 1403
1405
0 20 Miles
Bristol Channel

THE WARS OF THE ROSES 1455 - 1485

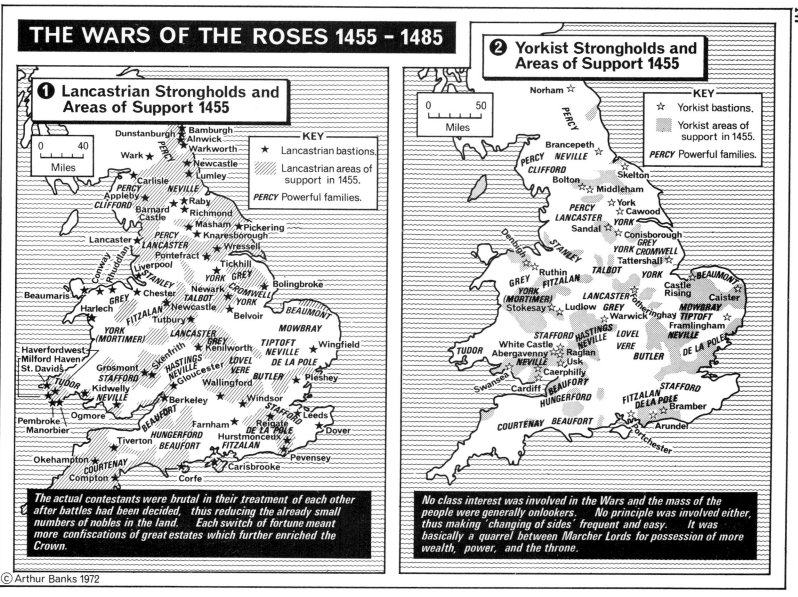

❶ Lancastrian Strongholds and Areas of Support 1455

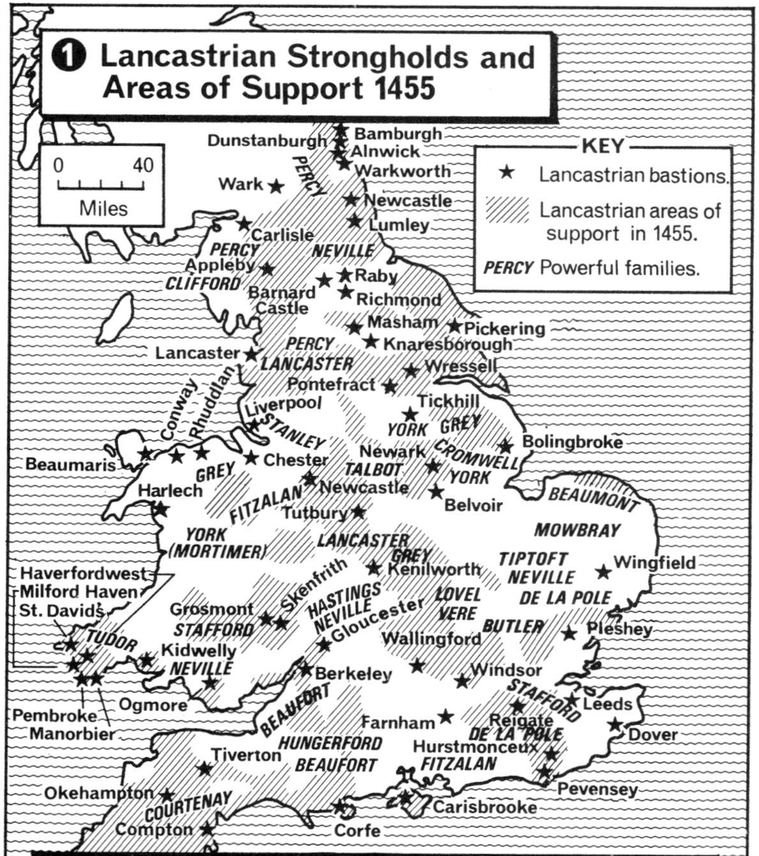

The actual contestants were brutal in their treatment of each other after battles had been decided, thus reducing the already small numbers of nobles in the land. Each switch of fortune meant more confiscations of great estates which further enriched the Crown.

❷ Yorkist Strongholds and Areas of Support 1455

No class interest was involved in the Wars and the mass of the people were generally onlookers. No principle was involved either, thus making 'changing of sides' frequent and easy. It was basically a quarrel between Marcher Lords for possession of more wealth, power, and the throne.

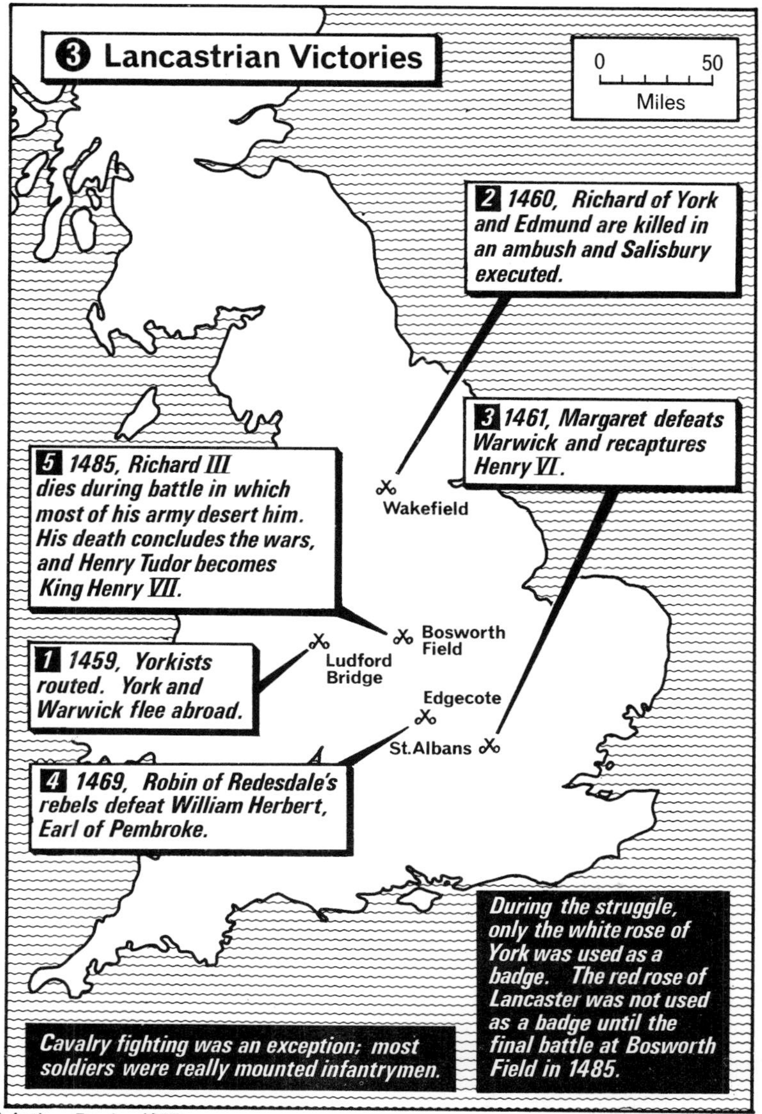
3 Lancastrian Victories
0 50 Miles
2 1460, Richard of York and Edmund are killed in an ambush and Salisbury executed.
3 1461, Margaret defeats Warwick and recaptures Henry VI.
5 1485, Richard III dies during battle in which most of his army desert him. His death concludes the wars, and Henry Tudor becomes King Henry VII.
Wakefield
Bosworth Field
Ludford Bridge
1 1459, Yorkists routed. York and Warwick flee abroad.
Edgecote
St.Albans
4 1469, Robin of Redesdale's rebels defeat William Herbert, Earl of Pembroke.
During the struggle, only the white rose of York was used as a badge. The red rose of Lancaster was not used as a badge until the final battle at Bosworth Field in 1485.
Cavalry fighting was an exception; most soldiers were really mounted infantrymen.

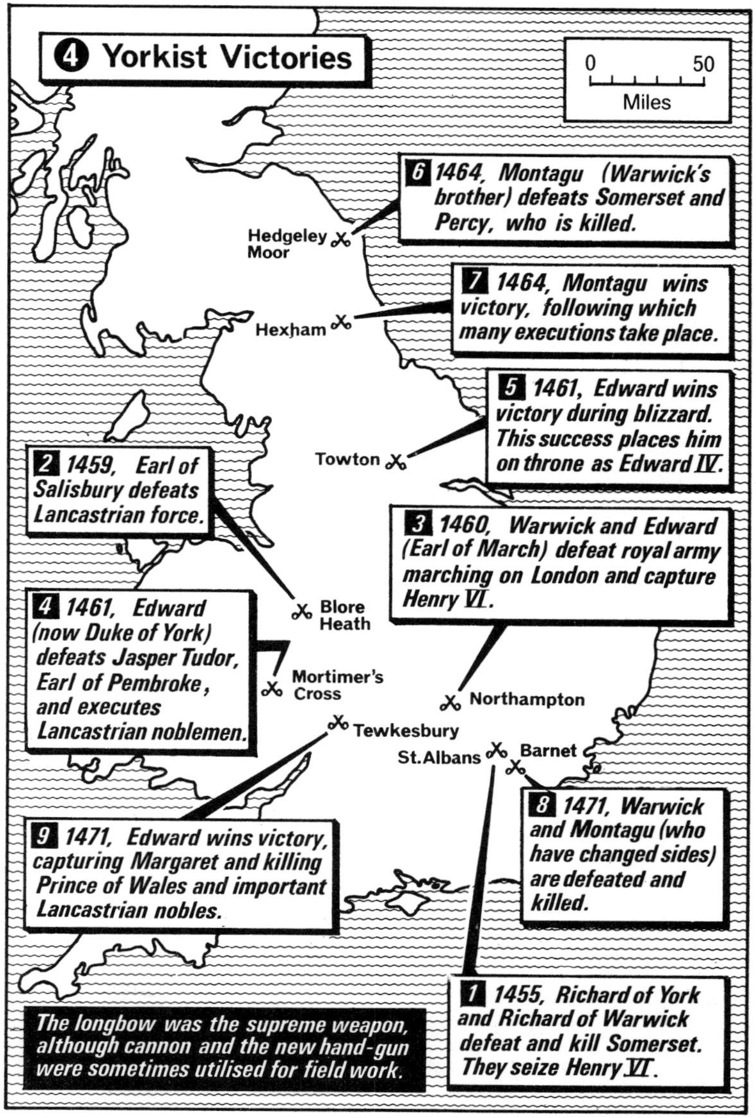
4 Yorkist Victories
0 50 Miles
6 1464, Montagu (Warwick's brother) defeats Somerset and Percy, who is killed.
Hedgeley Moor
7 1464, Montagu wins victory, following which many executions take place.
Hexham
5 1461, Edward wins victory during blizzard. This success places him on throne as Edward IV.
Towton
2 1459, Earl of Salisbury defeats Lancastrian force.
3 1460, Warwick and Edward (Earl of March) defeat royal army marching on London and capture Henry VI.
Blore Heath
4 1461, Edward (now Duke of York) defeats Jasper Tudor, Earl of Pembroke, and executes Lancastrian noblemen.
Mortimer's Cross
Northampton
Tewkesbury
St.Albans
Barnet
8 1471, Warwick and Montagu (who have changed sides) are defeated and killed.
9 1471, Edward wins victory, capturing Margaret and killing Prince of Wales and important Lancastrian nobles.
1 1455, Richard of York and Richard of Warwick defeat and kill Somerset. They seize Henry VI.
The longbow was the supreme weapon, although cannon and the new hand-gun were sometimes utilised for field work.

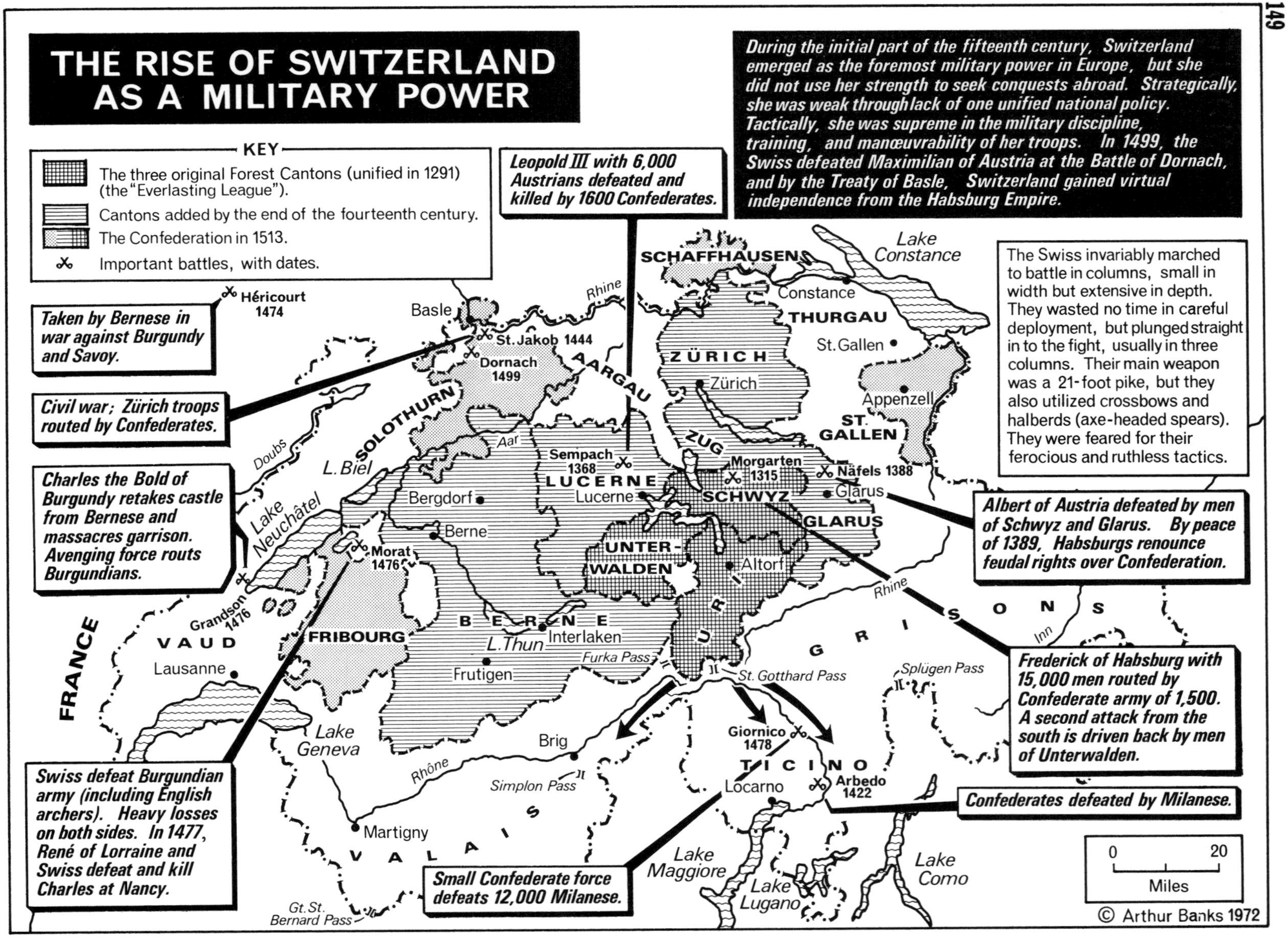
THE RISE OF SWITZERLAND AS A MILITARY POWER
KEY
The three original Forest Cantons (unified in 1291) (the "Everlasting League").
Cantons added by the end of the fourteenth century.
The Confederation in 1513.
Important battles, with dates.
During the initial part of the fifteenth century, Switzerland emerged as the foremost military power in Europe, but she did not use her strength to seek conquests abroad. Strategically, she was weak through lack of one unified national policy. Tactically, she was supreme in the military discipline, training, and manœuvrability of her troops. In 1499, the Swiss defeated Maximilian of Austria at the Battle of Dornach, and by the Treaty of Basle, Switzerland gained virtual independence from the Habsburg Empire.
Leopold III with 6,000 Austrians defeated and killed by 1600 Confederates.
The Swiss invariably marched to battle in columns, small in width but extensive in depth. They wasted no time in careful deployment, but plunged straight in to the fight, usually in three columns. Their main weapon was a 21-foot pike, but they also utilized crossbows and halberds (axe-headed spears). They were feared for their ferocious and ruthless tactics.
Taken by Bernese in war against Burgundy and Savoy.
Civil war; Zürich troops routed by Confederates.
Charles the Bold of Burgundy retakes castle from Bernese and massacres garrison. Avenging force routs Burgundians.
Albert of Austria defeated by men of Schwyz and Glarus. By peace of 1389, Habsburgs renounce feudal rights over Confederation.
Frederick of Habsburg with 15,000 men routed by Confederate army of 1,500. A second attack from the south is driven back by men of Unterwalden.
Confederates defeated by Milanese.
Swiss defeat Burgundian army (including English archers). Heavy losses on both sides. In 1477, René of Lorraine and Swiss defeat and kill Charles at Nancy.
Small Confederate force defeats 12,000 Milanese.
Héricourt 1474
Basle
St. Jakob 1444
Dornach 1499
Rhine
SCHAFFHAUSEN
Lake Constance
Constance
THURGAU
St. Gallen
ZÜRICH
Zürich
Appenzell
ST. GALLEN
AARGAU
SOLOTHURN
Aar
Doubs
L. Biel
Lake Neuchâtel
Sempach 1368
LUCERNE
Lucerne
ZUG
Morgarten 1315
Näfels 1388
Glarus
SCHWYZ
GLARUS
Bergdorf
Berne
UNTER-WALDEN
Altorf
Morat 1476
Grandson 1476
VAUD
FRANCE
Lausanne
FRIBOURG
BERNE
L. Thun
Interlaken
Furka Pass
Frutigen
URI
Rhine
GRISONS
Inn
St. Gotthard Pass
Splügen Pass
Lake Geneva
Brig
Giornico 1478
TICINO
Arbedo 1422
Locarno
Rhône
Simplon Pass
Martigny
VALAIS
Lake Maggiore
Lake Lugano
Lake Como
Gt. St. Bernard Pass
0 20 Miles

EXPANSION OF THE OTTOMAN EMPIRE TO 1566

The Osmanli (Ottoman) branch of the Turkish peoples was responsible for creating an empire which grew from a small area in north-west Asia Minor (in the thirteenth and fourteenth centuries) to cover a huge area of south-west Europe and the Middle East by the time of Suleiman the Magnificent. In 1453, Sultan Mohammed the Conqueror captured Constantinople and this became the capital of the Ottoman Empire until its final collapse after the First World War.

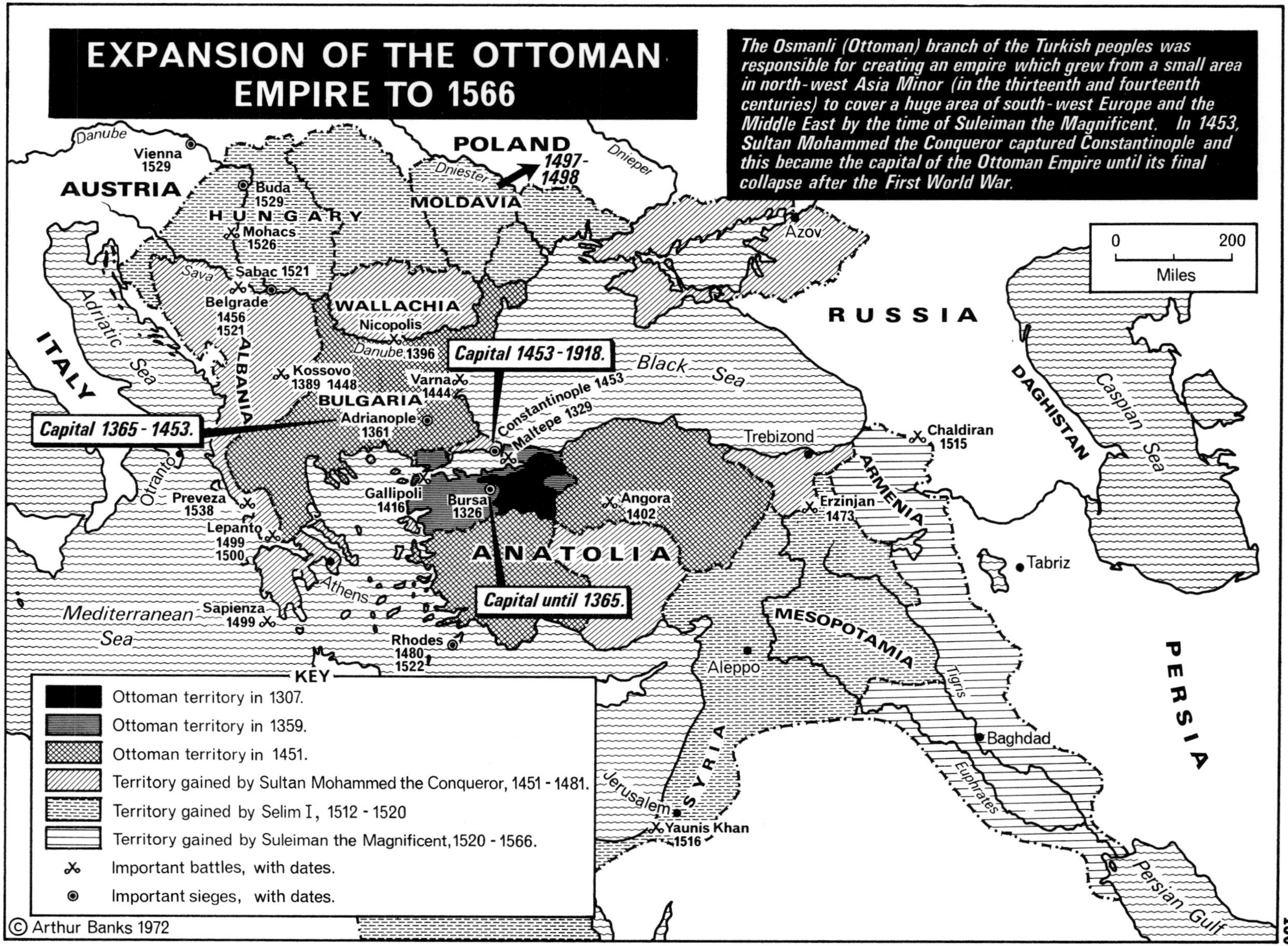

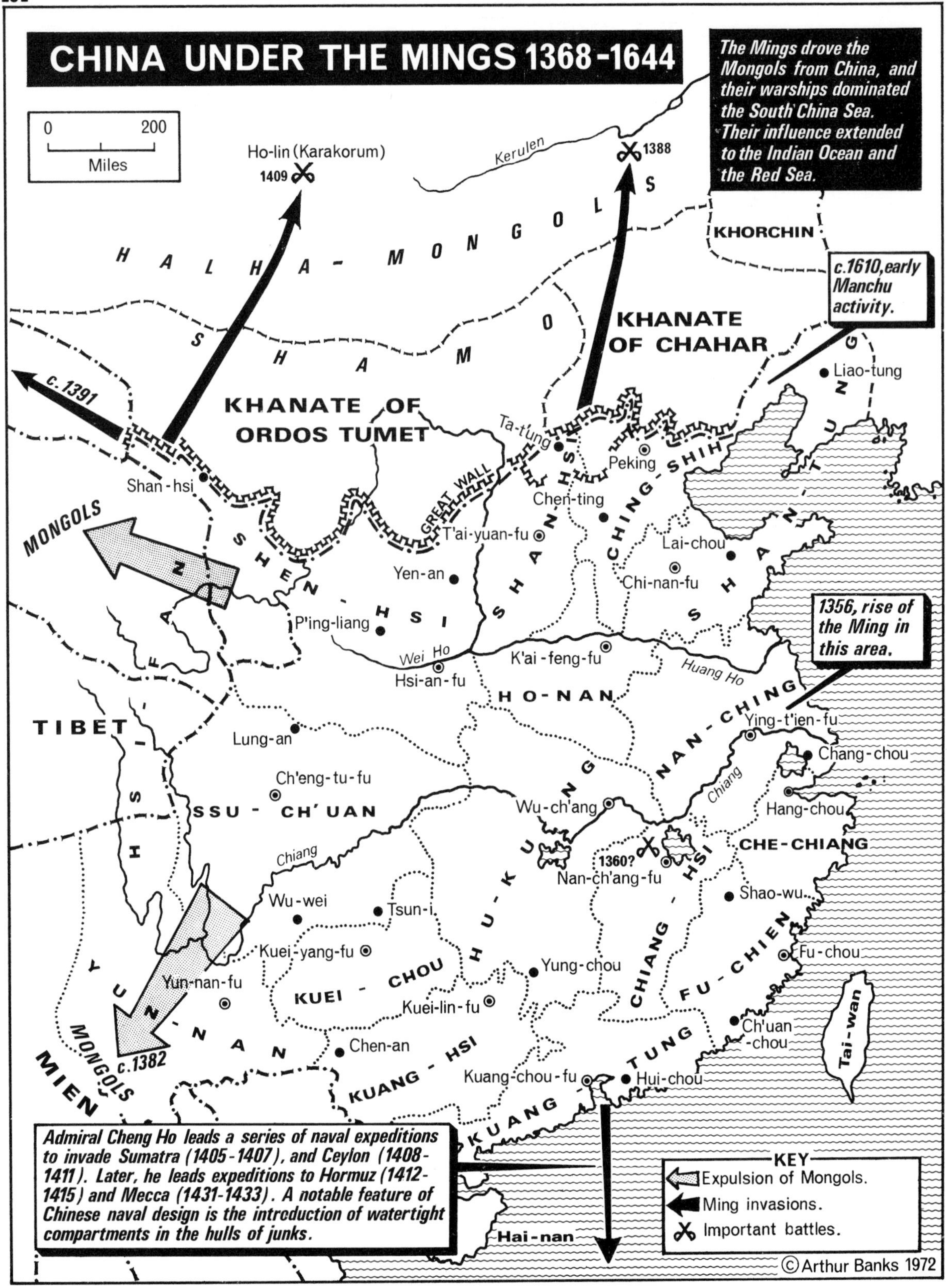
CHINA UNDER THE MINGS 1368-1644
The Mings drove the Mongols from China, and their warships dominated the South China Sea. Their influence extended to the Indian Ocean and the Red Sea.
0 200 Miles
Ho-lin (Karakorum)
1409
Kerulen
1388
HALHA - MONGOLS
KHORCHIN
c.1610, early Manchu activity.
SHAMO
KHANATE OF CHAHAR
Liao-tung
c.1391
KHANATE OF ORDOS TUMET
Ta-t'ung
Peking
GREAT WALL
Shan-hsi
MONGOLS
Chen-ting
T'ai-yuan-fu
Lai-chou
Yen-an
Chi-nan-fu
SHEN-HSI
SHAN-HSI
CHING-SHIH
SHAN-TUNG
P'ing-liang
1356, rise of the Ming in this area.
Wei Ho
K'ai-feng-fu
Hsi-an-fu
Huang Ho
HO-NAN
TIBET
Lung-an
Ying-t'ien-fu
NAN-CHING
Chang-chou
Ch'eng-tu-fu
SSU-CH'UAN
Wu-ch'ang
Chiang
Hang-chou
CHE-CHIANG
1360?
Nan-ch'ang-fu
Chiang
Wu-wei
Tsun-i
Shao-wu
HU-KUANG
CHIANG-HSI
Kuei-yang-fu
Fu-chou
Yung-chou
Yun-nan-fu
KUEI-CHOU
FU-CHIEN
Kuei-lin-fu
YUN-NAN
Ch'uan-chou
Tai-wan
MONGOLS
c.1382
Chen-an
MIEN
KUANG-HSI
Kuang-chou-fu
Hui-chou
KUANG-TUNG
Admiral Cheng Ho leads a series of naval expeditions to invade Sumatra (1405-1407), and Ceylon (1408-1411). Later, he leads expeditions to Hormuz (1412-1415) and Mecca (1431-1433). A notable feature of Chinese naval design is the introduction of watertight compartments in the hulls of junks.
Hai-nan
KEY
Expulsion of Mongols.
Ming invasions.
Important battles.
©Arthur Banks 1972

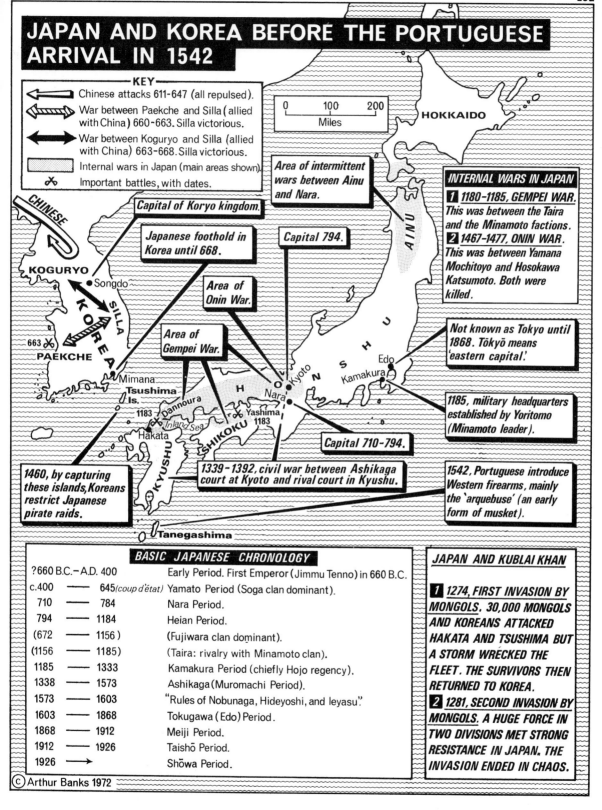

JAPAN AND KOREA BEFORE THE PORTUGUESE ARRIVAL IN 1542

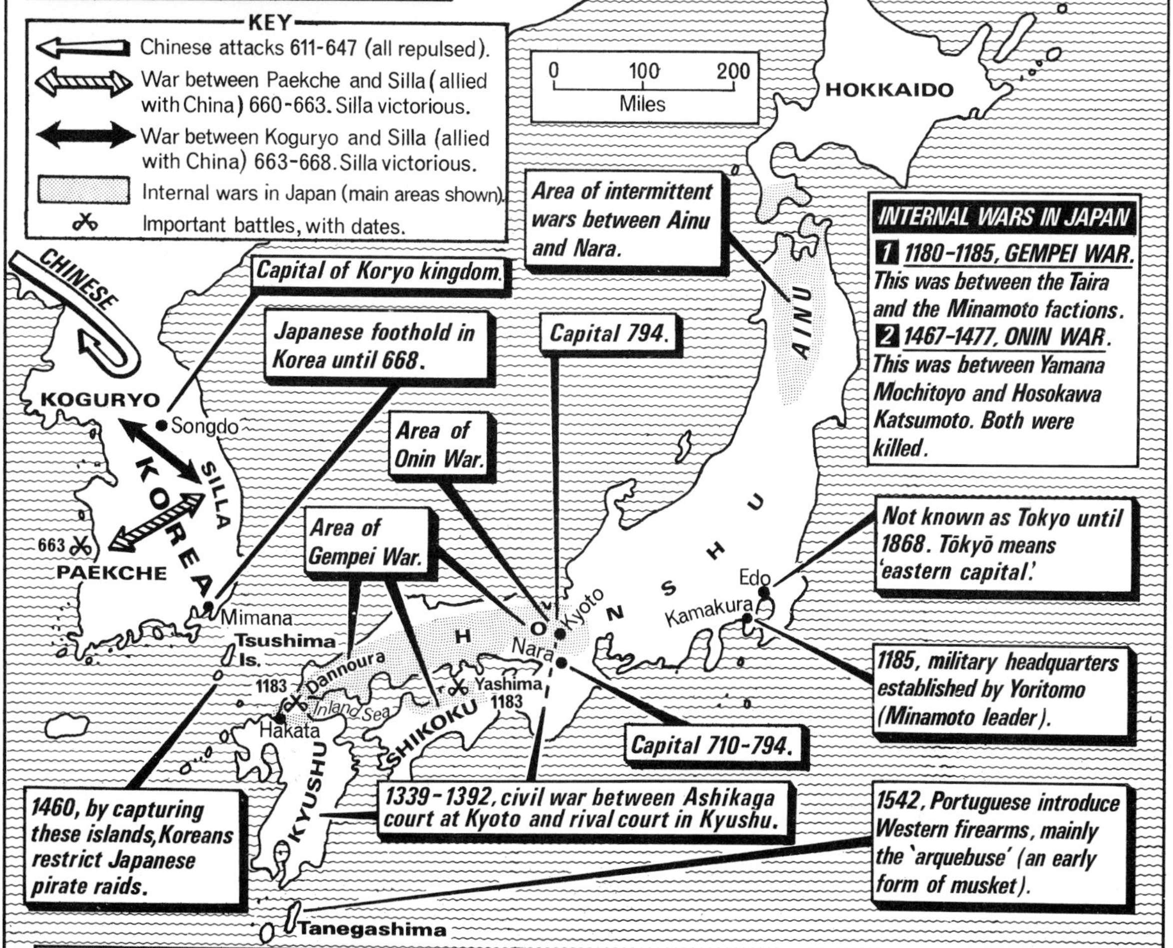
KEY
Chinese attacks 611-647 (all repulsed).
War between Paekche and Silla (allied with China) 660-663. Silla victorious.
War between Koguryo and Silla (allied with China) 663-668. Silla victorious.
Internal wars in Japan (main areas shown).
Important battles, with dates.
0 100 200
Miles
HOKKAIDO
Area of intermittent wars between Ainu and Nara.
AINU
INTERNAL WARS IN JAPAN
1 1180-1185, GEMPEI WAR. This was between the Taira and the Minamoto factions.
2 1467-1477, ONIN WAR. This was between Yamana Mochitoyo and Hosokawa Katsumoto. Both were killed.
CHINESE
Capital of Koryo kingdom.
Japanese foothold in Korea until 668.
Capital 794.
KOGURYO
Songdo
Area of Onin War.
SILLA
KOREA
Area of Gempei War.
663
PAEKCHE
Mimana
Tsushima Is.
HONSHU
Not known as Tokyo until 1868. Tōkyō means 'eastern capital.'
Edo
Kamakura
Kyoto
Nara
1183 Dannoura
Inland Sea
Yashima 1183
Hakata
SHIKOKU
KYUSHU
1185, military headquarters established by Yoritomo (Minamoto leader).
Capital 710-794.
1339-1392, civil war between Ashikaga court at Kyoto and rival court in Kyushu.
1460, by capturing these islands, Koreans restrict Japanese pirate raids.
1542, Portuguese introduce Western firearms, mainly the 'arquebuse' (an early form of musket).
Tanegashima

BASIC JAPANESE CHRONOLOGY

?660 B.C.–A.D. 400		Early Period. First Emperor (Jimmu Tenno) in 660 B.C.
c.400	— 645 (coup d'état)	Yamato Period (Soga clan dominant).
710	— 784	Nara Period.
794	— 1184	Heian Period.
(672	— 1156)	(Fujiwara clan dominant).
(1156	— 1185)	(Taira: rivalry with Minamoto clan).
1185	— 1333	Kamakura Period (chiefly Hojo regency).
1338	— 1573	Ashikaga (Muromachi Period).
1573	— 1603	"Rules of Nobunaga, Hideyoshi, and Ieyasu".
1603	— 1868	Tokugawa (Edo) Period.
1868	— 1912	Meiji Period.
1912	— 1926	Taishō Period.
1926	→	Shōwa Period.

JAPAN AND KUBLAI KHAN

1 1274, FIRST INVASION BY MONGOLS. 30,000 MONGOLS AND KOREANS ATTACKED HAKATA AND TSUSHIMA BUT A STORM WRECKED THE FLEET. THE SURVIVORS THEN RETURNED TO KOREA.

2 1281, SECOND INVASION BY MONGOLS. A HUGE FORCE IN TWO DIVISIONS MET STRONG RESISTANCE IN JAPAN. THE INVASION ENDED IN CHAOS.

FOUR LATER VIEWS OF THE WORLD

❶ According to Idrisi 1154

Mohammed al Idrisi, Arab geographer and scientist, was born at Ceuta in 1099. In 11 he completed his "Kitāb Rūjār (The Book of Roger) for the ki of Sicily, Roger II. Prior to th he had travelled extensively.

❷ According to Fra Mauro 1450

Fra Mauro, a Venetian mon and cartographer, produced a world map from detail accumulated during the previ two centuries. His work w notable for details on Afric and Asia in particular.

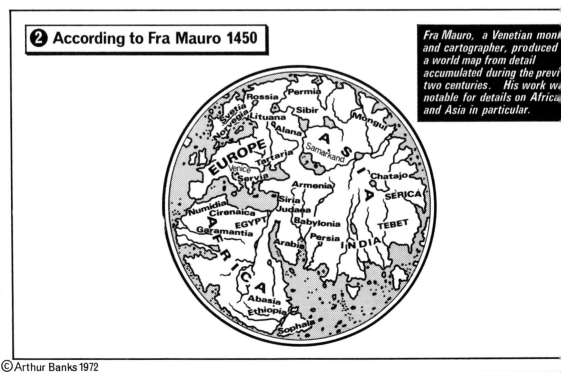

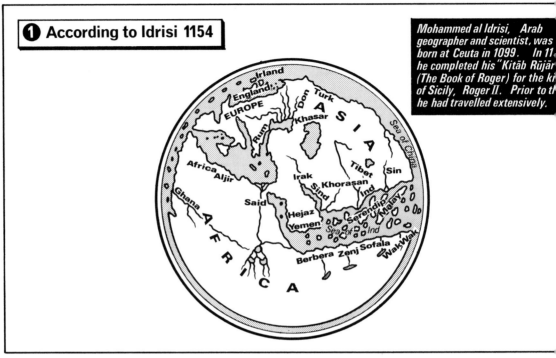

3 According to Schöner 1523

Johannes Schöner (1477 - 1547) was a German mathematician and cosmographer at Nüremberg. He produced maps of the world in the form of wooden globes covered with paper "gores".

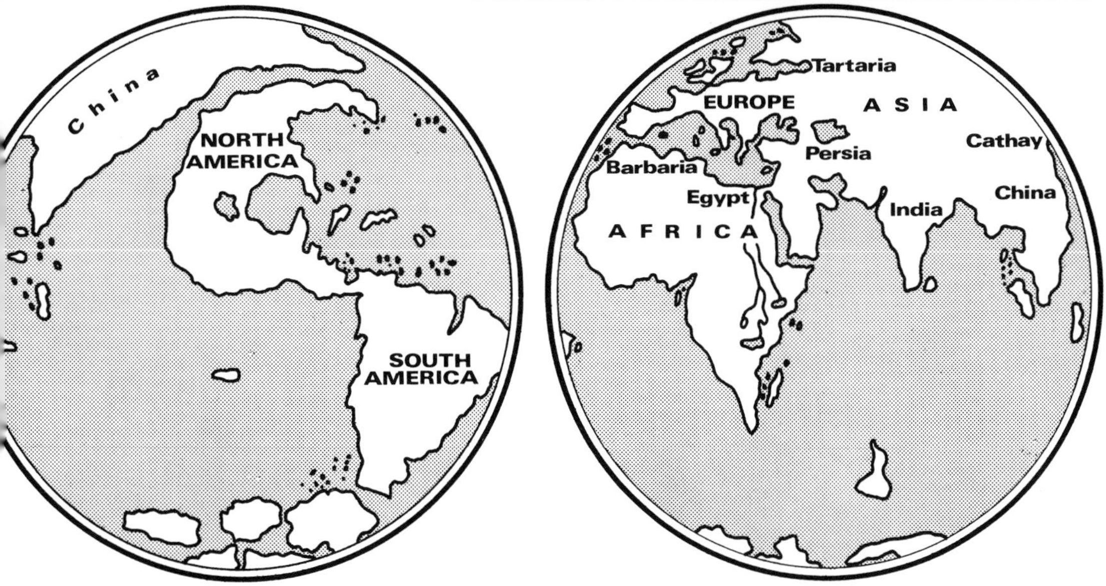

4 According to Ortelius 1570

Abraham Ortelius, a Dutch cartographer (1527 - 1598), was a friend of Mercator. He produced an atlas of the world entitled "Theatrum Orbis Terrarum" containing seventy maps.

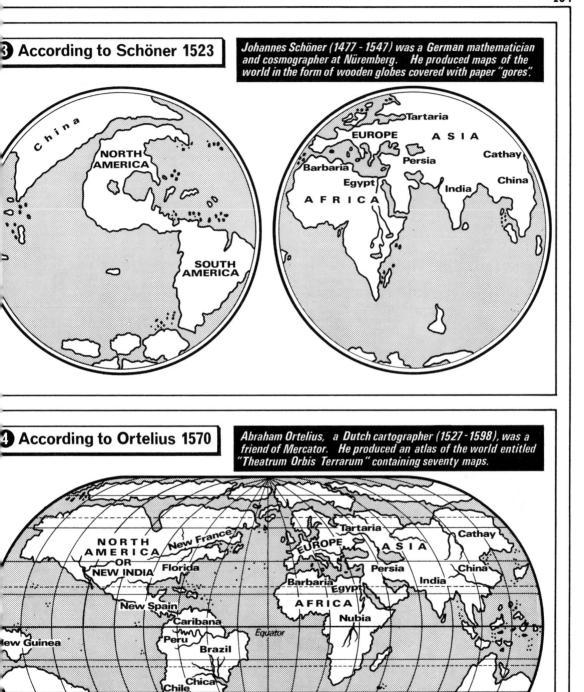

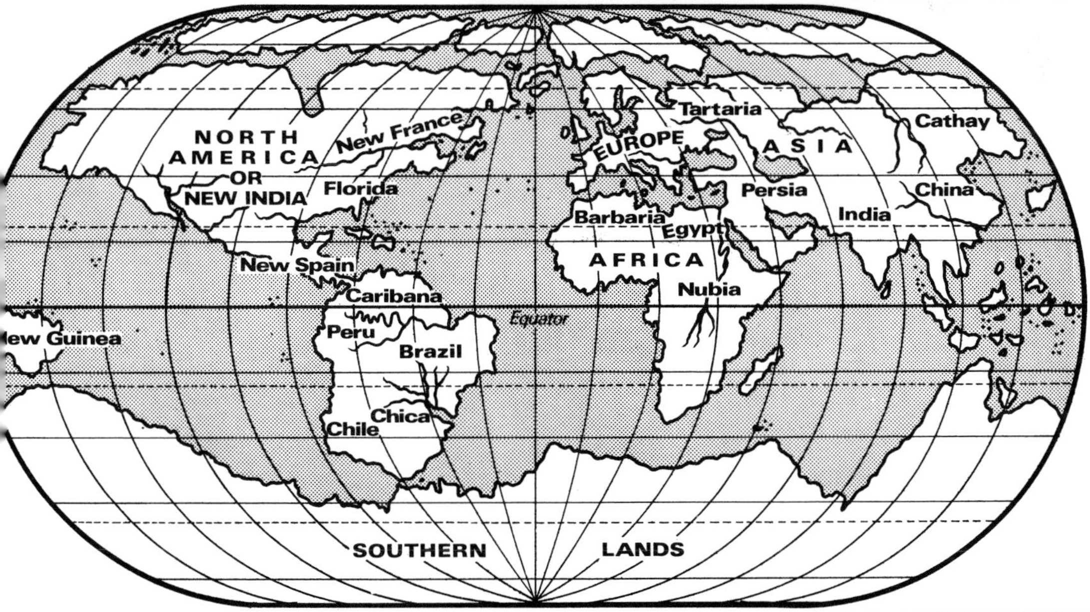

INDEX OF BATTLES, SIEGES, WARS, CAMPAIGNS, ETC

In the case of battles, only the place name is given. Dates are given only when necessary to distinguish between battles at the same site.

INDEX OF INDIVIDUALS

INDEX OF RACES, TRIBES, AND ALL NAMED GROUPS OF PEOPLE

GEOGRAPHICAL INDEX